AN HISTORIAN IN PEACE AND WAR

Ashgate Studies in First World War History

Series Editor

John Bourne
The University of Birmingham, UK

The First World War is a subject of perennial interest to historians and is often regarded as a watershed event, marking the end of the nineteenth century and the beginning of the 'modern' industrial world. The sheer scale of the conflict and massive loss of life means that it is constantly being assessed and reassessed to examine its lasting military, political, sociological, industrial, cultural and economic impact. Reflecting the latest international scholarly research, the Ashgate Studies in First World War History series provides a unique platform for the publication of monographs on all aspects of the Great War. Whilst the main thrust of the series is on the military aspects of the conflict, other related areas (including cultural, political and social) are also addressed. Books published are aimed primarily at a post-graduate academic audience, furthering exciting recent interpretations of the war, whilst still being accessible enough to appeal to a wider audience of educated lay readers.

Also in this series

'A Student in Arms'
Donald Hankey and Edwardian Society at War
Ross Davies

The Ordeal of Peace: Demobilization and the Urban Experience
in Britain and Germany, 1917–1921
Adam R. Seipp

Britain, Russia and the Road to the First World War
The Fateful Embassy of Count Aleksandr Benckendorff (1903–16)
Marina Soroka

Conservative Politics in National and Imperial Crisis
Letters from Britain to the Viceroy of India 1926–31
Edited by Stuart Ball

An Historian in Peace and War

The Diaries of Harold Temperley

Edited by

T.G. OTTE
University of East Anglia, UK

ASHGATE

© T.G. Otte 2014

All rights reserved. No part of this publication may be reproduced, stored in a retrieval system or transmitted in any form or by any means, electronic, mechanical, photocopying, recording or otherwise without the prior permission of the publisher.

T.G. Otte has asserted his right under the Copyright, Designs and Patents Act, 1988, to be identified as the editor of this work.

Published by
Ashgate Publishing Limited
Wey Court East
Union Road
Farnham
Surrey, GU9 7PT
England

Ashgate Publishing Company
110 Cherry Street
Suite 3-1
Burlington, VT 05401-3818
USA

www.ashgate.com

British Library Cataloguing in Publication Data
A catalogue record for this book is available from the British Library

The Library of Congress has cataloged the printed edition as follows:
Temperley, Harold William Vazeille, 1879-1939.
  An historian in peace and war: the diaries of Harold Temperley / edited by T.G. Otte.
    pages cm. -- (Ashgate studies in First World War history)
  Includes bibliographical references and index.
    ISBN 978-0-7546-6393-5 (hardcover : alk. paper) -- ISBN 978-1-4724-3449-4 (ebook) -- ISBN 978-1-4724-3450-0 (epub) 1. Temperley, Harold William Vazeille, 1879-1939--Diaries. 2. Historians--Great Britain--Diaries. 3. Scholars--Great Britain--Diaries. 4. Soldiers--Great Britain--Diaries. 5. World War, 1914-1918--Personal narratives, British. 6. Paris Peace Conference (1919-1920) I. Otte, Thomas G., 1967- editor. II. Title.
  D15.T45A3 2014
  907.2'02--dc23
  [B]
                                                                            2013043321

ISBN 978-0-7546-6393-5 (hbk)
ISBN 978-1-4724-3449-4 (ebk – PDF)
ISBN 978-1-4724-3450-0 (ebk _ ePUB)

Printed in the United Kingdom by Henry Ling Limited,
at the Dorset Press, Dorchester, DT1 1HD

For Neville Temperley

Contents

Series Editor's Preface   *ix*
Preface and Acknowledgements   *xi*

Introduction: An Historian in Peace and War   1

The Diaries, 1916–1939

1916   39

1917   81

1918   229

1919   365

1920   463

1921–1939   495

Index   575

Series Editor's Preface

Harold Temperley was one of Britain's foremost diplomatic historians of the twentieth century, renowned for his work on the foreign policy of Canning, for his writing on the politics and diplomacy of Eastern Europe and the Balkans and for his editing (with G.P. Gooch) of *British Documents on the Origins of the War*. Now, perhaps long overdue, he adds diarist to his list of accomplishments. Temperley was 35 when the Great War began and only recently married, but he volunteered for military service, which was prematurely ended by dysentery and other diseases before his regiment, the Fife and Forfar Yeomanry, landed on the Gallipoli peninsula. Although Temperley's health was permanently impaired by his experiences, his illness happily saw him transferred to other duties, as a general staff officer at the War Office, initially posted to Section 2(a) of Military Intelligence. The First World War was really the first time that the British state had exploited the expertise of academics. Temperley was among a number of other historians, including Lewis Namier, G.W. Prothero and R.W. Seton-Watson, who became Whitehall warriors and who were to play important parts in the formulation of British peace planning, especially in relation to the former Austro-Hungarian Empire. Although Temperley's influence on policy was real, he was, perhaps, not at the very heart of decision-making. This was fortuitous. The most illuminating diarists tend to be, in Professor Otte's felicitous phrase, the ones with 'ringside seats' rather than the contestants. Temperley began his diaries in the autumn of 1916 and continued them until his premature death in July 1939, since when they have remained in the possession of his family. It is to their credit and to that of Temperley's expert editor and sympathetic interpreter, Professor T.G. Otte, that the diaries now take their place alongside those of J.W. Headlam-Morley and Harold Nicolson as essential sources for anyone wishing to understand the development of British foreign policy and diplomacy between 1916 and 1919.

John Bourne
Centre for War Studies
The University of Birmingham
July 2013

Preface and Acknowledgements

The First World War and the subsequent peace settlement shaped the short twentieth century that followed. The profound significance of the events of 1914–19 was also appreciated by Harold Temperley, whose diaries are presented here. An established scholar at the outbreak of the war, and later one of Britain's foremost modern and more especially diplomatic historians, the conflict also shaped Temperley's own life and career. He enlisted in the army in August 1914. Invalided during the Dardanelles campaign in 1915, he spent the remainder of the war and its immediate aftermath as a general staff officer in military intelligence. In this function he played a significant role in preparing British strategy for the eventual peace conference and in finalizing several of the post-war boundaries in Eastern Europe. Later, in the 1920s and 1930s, Temperley was to co-edit the British diplomatic documents on the origins of the war; and the vicissitudes of modern Great Power politics were to be his principal preoccupation, both in his scholarly pursuits and as a current political concern.

The reasons for keeping diaries may be as varied as their authors' characters and lives. In Temperley's case, a natural literary ease and fluency may, in part, explain his motivations. He was certainly in the habit of writing up impressions in diary form since 1900. Until the war, however, he did not keep a daily diary, but rather a form of travel journal, which he kept during his summer visits to continental destinations, and in which he recorded historical reflections on the countries visited or impressions of local historical monuments, museums and art galleries. It seems that Temperley did not keep a diary during the first two years of the war; at least, none survives. This changed from the autumn of 1916 onwards. Firmly installed at the War Office as an intelligence officer, he now made a more or less daily record of his activities and observations. As a professional historian he naturally appreciated the significance of eyewitness accounts, and it seems clear from the nature of the source that he meant eventually to publish at least parts of his diary. His premature death, in 1939, prevented this. Later attempts in this direction by his widow led nowhere.

Indeed, it is remarkable that the diaries should have lain slumbering for so long since in a tin trunk in Temperley's Somerset home. As a historical source, their value is immense. If Temperley was not at the very heart of British or Allied decision-making during those years, he had at any rate a ringside seat. And trained to observe accurately, he recorded the concerns and confusions of wartime, conscious always of the historical significance of what he observed. There are few sources that match Temperley's diary. That by the diplomat

Harold Nicolson and the posthumously published memoir by J.W. Headlam-Morley, the Foreign Office's first historical adviser, capture some of the events and preoccupations at the Paris peace conference. But Temperley's diary offers a vivid impression of the preparatory work for this event as well as, and, uniquely, the focus of his observations is on the events in Eastern and South Eastern Europe, an area largely ignored by historians of the period.

Temperley was not entirely free from personal bias, as his diary entries show. His staunchly pro-Serb or pro-Yugoslav sentiments are, perhaps, scarcely surprising in the historian of Serbia. Inevitably, their flipside were his equally strong anti-Austrian inclinations. Like many of his generation, he fell under the spell of Lloyd George as the dynamic war-leader, at least for some of the time. His attitude towards Viscount Grey of Fallodon, the Foreign Secretary until December 1916, was dismissive; that towards Winston Churchill, whose fertile brain had led to the Dardanelles disaster, bordered on fierce personal hatred. For all his scepticism, as befits a professional historian, Temperley was not entirely immune to some of the wartime *canards*. Thus, for instance, he fell for John Charteris's propaganda hoax of a German '*Kadaververwertungsanstalt*' ('corpse rendering plant'), one of the most striking propaganda coups of the war. There are shades of that kind of social anti-Semitism that was the worm in the bud of liberal Edwardian England. But in all of this, too, the diary offers a revealing light on the concerns of those years; and in Temperley's case, whatever his social prejudices, he came to view the aspirations of the nascent Zionist movement with sympathy.

Given the wider significance of Temperley's diaries during his time in military intelligence, I decided to present this material here in its entirety. Merely to select from it would have compromised the vital essence of the material. Some later entries after 1921 are included here, in so far as they refer to his activities during the war and the subsequent peace-making conferences. Some of the pre-war entries, relevant to the proper understanding of Temperley the man and historian, feature in the introduction to the diaries.

A few words need to be said on the editing process. In line with current practice, I sought to interfere as little as possible.[1] Some interference, however, was necessary. The diary bears undeniable traces of the pressures on a wartime intelligence officer in Whitehall. Some of the entries were dashed off at great speed. Abbreviations abound; punctuation appears perfunctory; sentences may sometimes be incomplete; and the spelling of some names is often haphazard. For the sake of preserving the authenticity of the source I have refrained from modernizing the text. But where the original text is abbreviated, I used [ ] to extend the abbreviations. Occasionally, Temperley returned to earlier entries and added further observations. These are marked thus: < >. Random jottings pepper

---

[1] See P.D.A. Harvey, *Editing Historical Records* (London, 2001), *passim*.

the diary – usually notes on geographical information or railway timetables, sometimes calculations of personal expenditure. They are not reproduced here. Very rarely, Temperley later struck out entries. Some of these are included here, largely because I judged them to be of sufficient importance and interest; and they are clearly marked ~~thus~~.

In the course of editing Harold Temperley's diaries I have incurred a number of debts of gratitude, and it is a great personal pleasure to acknowledge them here. Tom Gray at Ashgate has been a very patient editor, and for that I am most grateful. Keith Neilson offered invariably constructive advice on various aspects of the project. I am indebted to Zara Steiner for her comments on my attempt to make sense of Temperley as a scholar, and to Karl W. Schweizer for sharing with me his thoughts on Sir Herbert Butterfield and his fraught relations with his *quondam* supervisor Temperley. Jim Beach generously offered advice on certain aspects of military intelligence during the First World War, and so did David French. Andrew Lambert and Nick Black provided information on naval intelligence personnel. I am also happy to acknowledge my debt to Alan Sharp and Erik Goldstein for their help with matters pertaining to the Political Intelligence Department. John Maurer and David Nickles made it possible to identify various members of the US foreign and armed services, and without John Fisher's assistance some of the British intelligence agents, gentlemen or not, would have remained even more shadowy. Christopher Wilkinson provided the vital clue to one of Ibsen's lesser known plays, and for that, too, I am most grateful. Two of my colleagues at the University of East Anglia, Jan Vermeiren and Nicholas Vincent, helped me to understand Josef Redlich, the Austrian legal and constitutional historian, and the Magyar *bulla aurea* of 1222. I am also greatly indebted to Eleftheria Daleziou and Natalia Vogeikoff-Brogan of the American School of Classical Studies, Athens, for their generous and prompt help.

My wife and daughter showed their usual, unruffled patience with me, while I spent long hours deciphering Temperley's usually less than legible jottings, and for that, too, I am most grateful.

My greatest debt, however, is to Harold Temperley's son, Professor H.N.V. Temperley, and his family, who kindly gave me access to the diaries and other papers, and offered pertinent advice on them. I rather fear that I have kept him waiting for longer than both he and I had originally thought possible, and I can only hope that the finished product will make amends for the long wait. It is to him that I dedicate this volume.

North Norfolk, TGO
May 2013

Introduction:
An Historian in Peace and War

> A tale is more warmly coloured if it takes shape among the scenes which it describes.
>
> Harold Temperley.[1]

All too frequently, studies of past historians and their work re-affirm the ancient distinction between the *vita contemplativa* and the *vita activa*. The cloistered nature of academia, focused on the 'life of the mind' and seemingly shielded from the practical side of the human condition, may well lend itself to such treatment. And yet it means to ignore an important aspect of the life and work of some twentieth-century scholars. True, until the second half of that century few, if any, academics played any significant part in framing government policy in Great Britain. In this respect, as in so many others, the period of the two global conflicts acted as catalyst, and brought university dons into the orbit of officialdom.[2]

During the First World War some scholars became involved in government propaganda, though not necessarily in an official capacity. John Holland Rose, the distinguished Cambridge historian of the Napoleonic era, for instance, suggested 'some semi-official means' to counter enemy press campaigns in the neutral countries.[3] Others, small in number and mostly, but not exclusively, historians, were co-opted into the official hierarchy in the course of the war. The most notable of them was, perhaps, H.A.L. Fisher, another historian of Napoleonic Europe and then vice-chancellor of Sheffield University, who became President of the Board of Education in the Lloyd George coalition and was the prime minister's only, somewhat tenuous, link with the Edwardian Liberal intelligentsia.[4] Fisher's was an appointment in which the author of the diaries presented here, Harold Temperley, took a quasi-paternal pride: 'It was I

---

[1] *England and the Near East: The Crimea* (London, 1936), xi.

[2] T.W. Heyck, *The Transformation of Intellectual Life in Victorian England* (London and New York, 1982), 22–38. In America, too, the war transformed the role of some academic professions, see R.L. Church, 'Economists as Experts: The Rise of an Academic Profession, 1870–1917', in L. Stone (ed.), *The University of Society*, ii, *Europe, Scotland, and the United States from the 16th to the 20th Century* (London, 1975), here 599–600.

[3] Rose to Balfour, 28 Jan. 1915, Balfour MSS, British Library, Add. MSS 49863.

[4] K.O. Morgan, 'Lloyd George's Stage Army', in A.J.P. Taylor (ed.), *Lloyd George: Twelve Essays* (London, 1971), 299–300; for Fisher's tenure of the Board see D. Dean, 'The Dilemmas of

that introduced him to L[loyd] G[eorge] and spoke of him in high terms as a splendid man, so even I can claim my share in cabinet-making. A very little one it is. Still it is something, and that is always better than nothing.'[5]

Some scepticism may well be justified here.[6] But if Temperley exaggerated his influence in the matter, his reflections are nevertheless suggestive. Influence in high places was something desirable for the trained political historian, and Temperley delighted in having it. And to that extent it also reflected the creative tension between the scholar pursuing the *vita contemplativa* in the grooves of academia and the student of the past who had sipped from the tonic of the *vita activa* of high politics.

Harold Temperley was one of a number of dons whose role during the First World War and in the subsequent peace conferences has now been recognized by historians. Some of them were already well-established scholars when they moved to Whitehall. G.W. Prothero, for instance, the long-serving editor of the organ of the educated classes of Victorian and Edwardian Britain, the *Quarterly Review*, who had written an 'admirable volume on the causes which have led up to the present war',[7] headed the Historical Section, first under Admiralty auspices and eventually under the Foreign Office. Its remit was to elucidate current affairs from a historical perspective. Ill-health prevented Prothero from taking up the position of Historical Adviser to the British delegation at the Paris peace conference, offered to him in November 1918.[8] That role fell to J.W. Headlam-Morley, another historian who had already found a niche for himself well before the war as a senior civil servant at the Board of Education and during the war at the Department of Information's Intelligence Bureau, and who would later become the Foreign Office's first Historical Adviser.[9]

---

an Academic Liberal Historian in Lloyd George's Government: H.A.L. Fisher at the Board of Education, 1916–1922', *History* lxxix, 255 (1994), 57–81.

[5] Temperley diary, 9 Dec. 1916.

[6] Fisher and Lloyd George were acquainted since around 1900, see D. Ogg, *Herbert Fisher, 1865–1940: A Biography* (London, 1947), 45; instrumental in Fisher's appointment were Lloyd George's advisers Thomas Jones and Christopher Addison, see Dean, 'The Dilemmas', 59–61.

[7] Balfour to Prothero (private), 7 Apr. 1916, Balfour MSS, Add. MSS. 49864. The work in question was *German Policy before the War* (London, 1916); for some of the propaganda work see S. Wallace, *War and the Image of Germany: British Academics, 1914–1918* (Edinburgh, 1988), 167–90.

[8] For detailed discussions see C.W. Crawley, 'Sir George Prothero and His Circle of Friends', *Transactions of the Royal Historical Society* (5) xx (1970), 101–27; and E. Goldstein, 'Historians Outside the Academy: The Experience of the Foreign Office Historical Section, 1917–1920', *Historical Research* lxiii, 2 (1990), 195–211.

[9] A. Headlam-Morley, 'Introduction', in A. Headlam-Morley, R. Bryant and A. Cienciala (eds), *Sir James Headlam-Morley: A Memoir of the Paris Peace Conference* (London, 1972), ix–xl; E. Goldstein, '"A Prominent Place Would Have To Be Taken by History": The Origins of a Foreign Office Historical

But below such established figures as Prothero and Headlam-Morley a whole phalanx of younger historians cut their teeth in policy advice and intelligence work as Whitehall backroom boys, many of whom would rise to academic and public prominence in the 1920s and 1930s. Among others at the Foreign Office's Political Intelligence Department, the historian Lewis Namier, the classicist Alfred Zimmern and the Balkans specialist R.W. Seton-Watson honed their skills as intelligence analysts.[10] In the economic sphere, the partly German-trained economic historian and statistician, W.J. Ashley, advised on food control and rationing.[11] The various branches of military intelligence, meanwhile, found use for the expertise and skills of younger dons, such as the Edinburgh geographer Alan Grant Ogilvie, the diplomatic historian C.K. Webster, the student of nineteenth-century Russia B.H. Sumner, and Harold Temperley.[12]

Temperley's route into officialdom had not been straightforward, but in that respect his career was rather typical of many of the academics in wartime Whitehall. Born on 20 April 1879 into a clerico-academic family – his father was a gifted mathematician at Queen's College, Cambridge, who died young, and his maternal grandfather had been an Episcopalian minister – Harold William Vazeille Temperley was educated at Sherborne. In 1898, he entered King's College, Cambridge, to study history,[13] which subject was then in its first bloom after the introduction of the Historical Tripos nearly a quarter of a century earlier and following the spadework done by Oscar Browning and Prothero.[14] By all accounts, Temperley flourished, too. His work was said to have contained 'a good deal of cloudiness and pomposity of expression', but

---

Section', in T.G. Otte (ed.), *Diplomacy and Power: Studies in Diplomatic Practice. Essays in Honour of Keith Hamilton* (Leiden, 2012), esp. 89–102.

[10] For discussions of this see K.J. Calder, *Britain and the Origins of the New Europe, 1914–1918* (Cambridge, 1976); H. and C. Seton-Watson, *The Making of a New Europe: R.W. Seton-Watson and the Last Years of Austria-Hungary* (London, 1981), 203–334; E. Goldstein, *Winning the Peace: British Diplomatic Strategy, Peace Planning, and the Paris Peace Conference, 1916–1920* (Oxford, 1991), 57–89.

[11] A. Ashley, *William James Ashley: A Life* (London, 1932).

[12] For Webster see P.A. Reynolds and E.J. Hughes (eds), *The Historian as Diplomat: Charles Kingsley Webster and the United Nations, 1939–1946* (London, 1976), 1–2.

[13] For Temperley's life see the valuable biography by J.D. Fair, *Harold Temperley: A Scholar and Romantic in the Public Realm* (London and Toronto, 1992), and J.D. Fair, 'The Peacemaking Exploits of Harold Temperley in the Balkans, 1918–1921', *Slavonic and East European Review* lxvii, 1 (1989), 68–93; see also obituary, *The Times*, 12 July 1939; G.P. Gooch, *Harold Temperley, 1879–1939* (London, 1940); L.M. Penson, 'Harold Temperley, 1879–1939', *History* xxiv, 94 (1939), 121–4.

[14] See the reflections by one of Temperley's later pupils, J.O. McLachlan, 'The Cambridge Historical Tripos', *Cambridge Historical Journal* ix, 1 (1947), 78–104; also D. Cannadine, 'What is History Now?', in J. Morrill (ed.), *The Promotion of Knowledge: Lectures to Mark the Centenary of the British Academy, 1902–2002* (Oxford, 2004), 33–6.

from it 'there emerged an expression of power, a hint of genuine creativeness'.[15] In his final year, he was awarded the Gladstone Memorial Prize for his work in Part II of the Historical Tripos, and he won the Prince Consort Prize for a dissertation on the growth of the office of prime minister in the eighteenth century. He nevertheless failed to get elected to a fellowship at King's in 1903. After a short spell at the University of Leeds, he returned to Cambridge in the autumn of 1905 to take up a fellowship at Peterhouse. Thus began an association that would last until his death in July 1939.[16]

The focus of much of Temperley's research during those early Petrian years was very much on British history during the long eighteenth century. He contributed several chapters on it to the *Cambridge Modern History*, Acton's *grand projet* now led towards completion by Sir Adolphus Ward, the Master of Peterhouse and to some extent Temperley's mentor.[17] Recognizing his protégé's organizational skills and his sheer capacity for work, Ward made him part of the editorial team, and left much of the hard graft of the work involved to him.[18]

Temperley's own contributions to the series were characterized by strongly Whiggish inclinations,[19] which he shared with Ward. Whether in dealing with the stupidities of the Stuarts and the virtues of the stolid *stadholder*, or the trimmings and intrigues that attended the manoeuvres of Halifax, Walpole and the Pelhams, or the politics of parliamentary reform before 1832, his sympathies tended towards the side of progress and reform. They were checked, however, by a Rankeian restraint, and Temperley always strove for balance in his assessments.

---

[15] H. Butterfield, draft MS of Temperley biography, Butterfield MSS, Cambridge University Library, BUTT/9, fo. 13. Butterfield, Temperley's perhaps most illustrious student, was asked by the Temperley family to write a biographical sketch of Temperley but never made much progress with it. To his great discredit he pretended to the end of his life to be working on it, see Butterfield to Neville Temperley, 4 May 1968, Butterfield MSS, Cambridge University Library, BUTT/531/T38; see also M. Bentley, *The Life and Thought of Herbert Butterfield: History, Science and God* (Cambridge, 2011), 244–5.

[16] Fair, *Temperley*, 44–57; L.P. Wilkinson, *Kingsmen of a Century, 1873–1972* (Cambridge, 1980), 205–6.

[17] Temperley dedicated his 1917 *History of Serbia* to Ward; see also his contribution to the memorial volume for Ward, 'Two Legends Connected with Thomas Gray', in P. Giles (ed.), *In Memoriam Adolphus William Ward, Master of Peterhouse (1900–1924)* (Cambridge, 1924), 103–23. For the *CMH* see R.T. Wright, *The Cambridge Modern History: An Account of Its Origins, Authorship and Production* (Cambridge, 1907).

[18] See e.g. Temperley to Satow, 22 Jan. 1907, Satow MSS, The National Archives (Public Record Office), PRO 30/33/12/3, discussing various corrections to Satow's chapter in volume xi of the *CMH*; see also S. Leathes, 'The Editorial Methods of Sir Adolphus Ward', *Cambridge Historical Journal* i, 2 (1924), 219–21.

[19] Temperley was involved in the university's Liberal Club, see C.E. Goodrich et al. (Liberal Club) to Temperley, 12 July 1913, Temperley MSS, congratulating him on his forthcoming wedding.

The revolution of 1688, he noted for instance, 'only moved along the path already marked out for it by the political developments of the generation immediately preceding'.[20] The 1832 Reform Bill, meanwhile, 'did little to destroy some of the evils which it attacked'. And yet, he concluded that '[t]he Revolution of 1688 was completed by the Revolution of 1832', the latter being the 'culminating point of a period of steady progress'.[21] The eighteenth century, by contrast, was something of a fallow period, 'one of peace, uneventful, almost undisturbed'. It was characterized by stock-jobbing, commercial disputes and currency manipulations, 'its type, if not its hero, a businessman'. Its two redeeming aspects were 'the development of England's parliamentary system' and 'the gradual rise to power of the most extraordinary genius of the age', William Pitt the Elder.[22]

The focus on heroic statesmanship is characteristic of much of Temperley's contributions to the *CMH*. Thus he praised William III, though not an ideal British monarch, for having 'assured the triumph of constitutional England' and having 'laboriously and triumphantly toiled, amid infinite difficulties, for the general interests of the continent'.[23] Canning's brief premiership 'seemed ... an age of gold succeeding one of iron', and Canning himself the sort of heroic statesman who dominated the scene, even if, '[p]rogressive in everything else, he was utterly hostile to Reform'.[24]

Much of Temperley's work at that time and later revolved around the twin concerns with constitutional principles and political leadership. Nor was this surprising. Temperley, as Maurice Cowling noted, was 'like so many other Liberals of his generation ... left high-and-dry by the death of the Liberal party in the 1920s'.[25] It was a characteristically unkind observation, but, for once, not entirely without merit. Already in his first book, a biographical study of George Canning, Temperley had nailed his colours firmly to the mast of reform. This was no weighty work of profound research, but it revealed something of its

---

[20] H.W.V. Temperley, 'The Revolution and the Revolutionary Settlement in Great Britain: (I) England (1687–1702)', in A.W. Ward, G.W. Prothero and S. Leathes (eds), *The Cambridge Modern History*, v, *The Age of Louis XIV* (Cambridge, 1907), 251.

[21] H.W.V. Temperley, 'Great Britain (1815–1832)', in A.W. Ward, G.W. Prothero and S. Leathes (eds), *The Cambridge Modern History*, x, *Restoration* (Cambridge, 1907), 616, 617 and 619.

[22] H.W.V. Temperley, 'The Age of Walpole and the Pelhams', in A.W. Ward, G.W. Prothero and S. Leathes (eds), *The Cambridge Modern History*, vi, *The Eighteenth Century* (Cambridge, 1909), 40, 69, and 73.

[23] Temperley, 'Revolutionary Settlement', 277.

[24] Temperley, 'Great Britain (1815–32)', 592.

[25] M. Cowling, *Religion and Public Doctrine in Modern England* (Cambridge, 1980), 219; C. Parker, *The English Historical Tradition since 1850* (Edinburgh, 1990), 113. What Cowling did not know was that Temperley 'regularly voted Labour' in the 1920s, H.N.V. Temperley, 'Recollections of my father', unpubl. TS, Temperley MSS, fo. 15.

author's innate Whiggism. The Canning who emerged from Temperley's pen was a capable man who rose by dint of his talents and hard work, at a time when aristocractic connections were a surer route to success. This was 'a statesman so high-souled and great-hearted' that even his Toryism retained a Whiggish core. Indeed, Canning's chief domestic legacy lay in 'his education of the Tory party' to embrace change pragmatically; and in this Temperley found 'a service of the greatest magnitude not only to them but to the nation'. Where his own sympathies lay was never in any doubt: 'Yet perhaps the most genuine and unaffected of all tributes to his memory came ... from a boy who undertook a pilgrimage from Eton to Westminster Abbey, there to mourn and pray at the tomb of his hero. That boy was William Ewart Gladstone, who, musing over that great name ... drew from it perhaps something of the loftiness and inspiration of his own high ideals'.[26]

Subsequently, Temperley moderated his enthusiasm, and stressed 'the fact that he was unprogressive on the vital question of the next few years'. For all Canning's progressive achievements abroad 'it can hardly be pronounced that, on the side of domestic policy, the death of this extraordinary man was inopportune either to his country or his fame'.[27]

Temperley's own reformism is best described as cautious in the tradition of Whiggish constitutionalism. It was also very much in evidence in his *Senates and Upper Chambers*, which owed its genesis to the party-political warfare triggered by Lloyd George's 'People's Budget' in 1909. Britain's constitution, he averred, 'alone preserved sufficient vitality for the future'. Yet he urged caution when seeking sensible and practicable reforms. Britain's unwritten constitutional arrangements were not 'reared on scientific principles' but rather resembled '"a living mystic tree", the processes of whose "secret growth" defy the analysis of the intellect'.[28] If anything, he sought not to associate himself with certain parts of the Radical platform, and insisted on the need for a proper historical perspective: 'The appeal to history must not be like the appeal to the Bible, and the text ought never to be torn from its surroundings to hurl at the head of a political opponent. So long as history is a mere quarry for missiles, no valuable results can be obtained'. Temperley's own ideal was that of a Senate with suspensory powers, sufficient to defend minorities, but not strong enough to foist its will on the second chamber.[29]

[26] H.W.V. Temperley, *Life of Canning* (London, 1905), 69, 108 and 238–9.
[27] Temperley, 'Great Britain (1815–32)', 592.
[28] H.W.V. Temperley, *Senates and Upper Chambers: Their Use and Function in the Modern State, With a Chapter on the Reform of the House of Lords* (London, 1910), 1 and 25. The poetic allusion – here D.G. Rosetti's 'Blessed Damozel' – is typical: 'We two will lie i' the shadow of/ That mystic tree/ Within whose secret growth the Dove/ Is sometimes felt to be'.
[29] Temperley, *Senates*, 11. For Temperley's own scheme of reforms see *Senates*, 201–7. Its modest nature rather flies in the face of Fair's assertion of Temperley's 'radical faith', Fair, *Temperley*, 75.

Temperley's published work in these years was primarily concerned with British history. Constitutional developments, more especially, attracted his attention, such as in his 1912 article on the practice of holding cabinets in the eighteenth century, which Sir William Anson, Warden of All Souls and doyen of constitutional scholars, praised as 'of real value to students who want to ascertain the lines on which [political] practice moved'.[30] At the same time, Temperley began to extend his research to areas with which his name would later become associated, the history of Eastern Europe and of Great Power diplomacy. His work on Canning had already marked a first excursion into the latter field. But here, too, Temperley's judgment was coloured by his liberal outlook. He praised Canning's political gospel, 'cosmopolitan in one respect [and] ... patriotic in another', that every nation had a right to conduct its own affairs. Canning was the first to foresee and to promote 'the growth of national liberty on the Continent of Europe'.[31] He 'admitted the United States to be the leading power in America'; and he was 'prepared to introduce America into Europe and Europe into America, to deny the exclusive pretensions of the Holy Alliance to intervene in Spanish America, and check the exclusive pretensions of [John Quincy] Adams to place his continent in a water-tight compartment and reserve America for the Americans'.[32]

To Temperley's mind, Canning's legacy remained pertinent to contemporary Britain. His views on the affairs of the East, on relations between Europe and America, 'on the commercial supremacy and political influence of England may have lost neither their truth nor their interest'. Indeed, he concluded his paean on the heroic statesman with the exhortation that '[i]f England does not enshrine and hallow the name of Canning it will be a sign that it is not well with her. For all her foreign ministers none have loved her more passionately, and

---

Temperley interviewed the former Canadian prime minister, Sir Charles Tupper, and the Austrian constitutional scholar Josef Redlich on the workings of second chambers, see memo. Temperley, 30 Apr. 1910 [on conversation with Tupper], and diary, ? Aug. 1909, and Redlich to Temperley, 31 Aug. 1910, Temperley MSS. Temperley had first met Redlich in 1909, see Redlich diary, 2 Sept. 1909, F. Fellner and D.A. Corradini (eds), *Schicksalsjahre Österreichs: Die Erinnerungen und Tagebücher Josef Redlichs, 1869–1936* (2 vols, Vienna, 2011), i, 248.

[30] Anson to Temperley, 4 Dec. 1912, Temperley MSS; see H.W.V. Temperley, 'Inner and Outer Cabinet and Privy Council, 1679–1783', *English Historical Review* xxvii, 108 (1912), 682–99 and 'Documents Illustrative of the Powers of the Privy Council in the Seventeenth Century', *English Historical Review* xxviii, 109 (1914), 127–31; 'Inner and Outer Cabinets: Their Development in the Eighteenth Century', *English Historical Review* xxxi, 122 (1916), 291–6; 'Debates on the Declaration Act and the Repeal of the Stamp Act, 1766', *American Historical Review* xvii, 3 (1912), 563–86.

[31] Temperley, *Canning*, 276, and 9–10.

[32] H.W.V. Temperley, 'The Later American Policy of George Canning', *American Historical Review* xi, 4 (1906), 779 and 780.

none have left a name more instinct with the memories of freedom or of light, or more justly entitled to the gratitude not only of England but of mankind'.[33]

The development of British political liberties, the emergence of Britain as a global empire, and the superiority of Britain's political institutions were at the core of Temperley's publications in those last years before 1914. As with Canning, so he elevated the elder Pitt to the status of a heroic statesman. He praised 'that intense and burning ardour for liberty, which possessed the very soul of Chatham ... [and] that ardour explains his defence of the Irish Parliament, of the oppressed but ignoble Wilkes, and his love for "the long injured, long neglected country of America"'.[34] Only Chatham had 'a real coherent plan which would have reconciled empire and liberty'. Unlike any of his contemporaries, he 'possessed instinctive understanding and sympathy with the turbulent colonial assemblies. He asserted that ... they had developed a more practical liberty in the freer air of the New World'.[35] Temperley's writings at this stage revealed an intellectual preoccupation with the twin problems of liberty and empire. They were, as his biographer observed, 'a profession of political faith with strong moral overtones and a conviction of right'.[36]

If Temperley's instincts were Whiggish, they were leavened with a good dose of Rankean or Actonian realism and critical judgment based on the close study of original source material. In a paper on the origins of the Anglo-Spanish War of 1739, the so-called 'War of Jenkins' Ear', he wove together commercial, domestic, parliamentary and strategic factors into a coherent and sustained analysis of Walpole's and Newcastle's decision-making. In so doing, he laid open the paramountcy of the interests of the London merchant oligarchy and the power of the London mob. The combination of the two furnished the moral basis for unity in the war with Spain, but it also showed up future divisions between the metropolitan elites and those of the North American colonies. At the same time, the breach with Spain cemented the Bourbon *pacte de famille* that was to bedevil British imperial policy throughout the eighteenth century. It was the 'first act of an eighty years' struggle' in the Western hemisphere, which ended with Canning's support for Spain's former American colonies and the proclamation of the Monroe Doctrine: 'Bourbonism in its two branches was at length met in the New World by Anglo-Saxondom in its two branches, and the result was the entire defeat of the two Latin Powers and the dissolution of

---

[33] Temperley, *Canning*, 280.

[34] H.W.V. Temperley, 'The Latest Monument to Chatham', *Contemporary Review* cv, 3 (Jan. 1914), 364; for his early interest in the elder Pitt, H.W.V. Temperley, 'Pitt's Retirement from Office, 5 Oct. 1761', *English Historical Review* xxi, 82 (1906), 327–30.

[35] H.W.V. Temperley, 'Chatham, North, and America', *Quarterly Review* 4 (Oct. 1914), 301 and 308; see also H.W.V. Temperley, 'Chatham and His Latest Biographer', *Contemporary Review* xcix (Jan. 1911), 148–54.

[36] Fair, *Temperley*, 87.

that once formidable union, which had first seriously threatened the English dominions in 1739'.[37] Various publications in those years testify to Temperley's growing interest in the United States and in diplomatic history. He was now teaching a paper on British foreign policy, 1739–1815, and he planned a monograph on the subject, a 'preliminary sketch' to a series of studies planned by Temperley and Webster that was to 'indicate the underlying motives of our policy in the XVIIIth century, in order that the XIXth might be more clearly understood'.[38]

His interest in America, meanwhile, was strengthened by two visits to the United States and Canada in 1911 and 1912; they also reinforced his Atlanticism. He accepted with alacrity an invitation to deliver lectures on British history from 1688 to 1832 at Harvard during the Michaelmas term of 1911. He 'specially want[ed] to impress Harvard with the idea that young Cambridge is producing good researchers', not at all self-evident in those days.[39] Temperley enthusiastically immersed himself in American life, and also made the acquaintance of Theodore Roosevelt, whom he had first met at the Travellers' Club in December of that year, and who had made a strong impression on him: 'He looks more like a wild man of the woods, strangely daubed with culture, or a man of the Pleistocene – brought up in modern ideas – than anything I have ever seen'.[40] No doubt, Roosevelt, well-versed in the arts of the modern politician, knew how to charm the visiting scholars, extolling for instance the virtues of Cambridge over those of its older sibling on the banks of the Isis, before praising Temperley's recent foray into comparative constitutional studies. Even so, the Rooseveltian blend of the cerebral man of action conformed to Temperley's own ideal of the heroic statesman. At their second meeting in New York, in early 1912, the visitor steered the former president onto European affairs. In Germany, Roosevelt asserted, materialism was 'rampant'; Prussia, the largest state of the new empire, was all-demanding and all-devouring: '[E]verything's got to be sacrificed to Prussia, and Prussia has been the same all the time. From the Great Elector to Frederic and downwards Carlyle's history was aimed at justifying what was wrong. It is the justification of modern Germany, and also

---

[37] H.W.V. Temperley, 'The Causes of the War of Jenkins' Ear', *Transactions of the Royal Historical Society* (1) iii (1909), 197–236 (quotes from 235–6).

[38] Temperley to Webster, 7 Aug. 1911, Webster MSS, London School of Economics Archives, Webster 1/1/76; cf. draft by Webster of project of a *History of British Foreign Policy, 1815–1848*, encl. in Temperley to Webster, 28 Feb. 1912, Webster MSS, London School of Economics Archives, Webster 1/2/20. Temperley's interest in diplomatic history thus took root well before the war; for a different interpretation see R.J. Evans, *Cosmopolitan Islanders: British Historians and the European Continent* (Cambridge, 2009), 111.

[39] Temperley to Webster, 7 Aug. 1911, Webster MSS, Webster 1/1/76; also Fair, *Temperley*, 82.

[40] Temperley diary, 12 Dec. 1911. He later reflected that Roosevelt's 'statesmanlike instinct often leads him aright', 20 Dec. 1911.

makes it intelligible. Carlyle seems to think that what is immoral may become moral for great ends. But Frederic, Frederic, what did he do?'[41]

Roosevelt's discourse on Frederick the Great was instructive, for it reflected also Temperley's growing interest in European diplomatic history. An indefatigable traveller, he had embarked on a walking holiday of Germany in the summer of 1903, accompanied by W.F. Reddaway, an historian of Scandinavia and Eastern Europe who was to become one of Temperley's closest friends.[42] The tour was significant in two respects. It was his first direct encounter with German life and culture, and it sowed the seeds for his third book, a study of Austro-Prussian relations in the late 1770s.

Temperley was by no means anti-German, and was deeply appreciative of German culture and scholarship. When visiting Martin Luther's study at Wartburg castle, he reflected on the greatness of that disputatious little monk's achievements. He was moved by the swords of King Gustavus Adolphus of Sweden and Bernard of Saxe-Weimar, 'the two bravest champions of Lutheranism' displayed 'close by the place where Luther had thundered forth those burning words, which a century afterwards were to restore their hearts and strengthen their arms. [...] This is where German as a language had its birth and popularity, and where individualism in religion had its great incentive'.[43]

And yet, on their travels, the English ramblers encountered 'an immense self-consciousness, a straining after effect, however empty and worthless, a vainglorious boastfulness which cannot be called patriotism, a subservience to the glorious past which augurs ill for the future'. In their domestic politics, by contrast, the German people were meek and submissive: 'The Prussian eagle portrayed [everywhere] ... with the invariable statue of Wilhelm [I] der Grosse, are symbols of servility and centralization'.[44]

With Reddaway as his *cicerone*, Temperley traversed the battlefields of Mollwitz, where Frederick II had raised Prussia to the rank of a Great Power, of Rossbach and Leuthen, where he confirmed her rise in Europe, and of Zorndorf, where he defended it with blood and iron. Certainly, the Frederician historical legacy left a strong impression on him. At Leuthen, the King 'had for once proved

---

[41] Temperley diary, 16 Jan. 1912. For TR's praise for *Senates and Upper Chambers*, see diary, 12 Dec. 1911.

[42] William Fiddian Reddaway (1872–1949) had taught Temperley as an undergraduate; he is best known for his *CMH* contributions on Poland and Scandinavian kingdoms, *Documents of Catherine the Great: The Correspondence with Voltaire and the "Instructions" of 1767* (Cambridge, 1931) and (ed.), *The Cambridge History of Poland* (Cambridge, 1941).

[43] Temperley diary, 12 Aug. 1903.

[44] Temperley diary, 11 Aug. 1903. The tour of the battlefields also confirmed his conviction that Carlyle was an 'unsafe guide to facts', Temperley to Satow, 6 Mar. 1916, Satow MSS, PRO 30/33/13/2; also diary, 15 Aug. 1903, on the visit to the battlefield of Rossbach.

rashness the height of prudence ... [I]t made him immortal'.[45] The Potsdam parade ground was 'where[,] as Reddaway said, the Prussian state was made'. Nevertheless, ready as he was to acknowledge Frederick's historical greatness, he found the posthumous cult of his personality oppressive, and with it 'the faded garments so carefully preserved [at Berlin and Potsdam] for the flunkey-souls of the Prussian sightseer'.[46] Indeed, he speculated that contemporary Germans were 'surfeited with glory and their fall in the future may not be far off. The collapse of Frederic's army on his death should warn the Prussians not to mistake newly won glory for progressive reform and increasing strength. Fame is to a nation what the rider is to the winged horse in Tennyson's Vision of Sin'.[47] Here again are reflected his concerns with liberty and progress, just as his scholarly writings on eighteenth-century Britain had done.

If Temperley's impressions of Wilhelmine Germany were critical, they were rooted in Edwardian preconceptions, a form of British exceptionalism, common to the period. They are also to be found in his views of France. For all his Whiggish instincts, Temperley was suspicious of the country and its political traditions. The French revolution, he noted during a visit to Paris in 1910, 'has sacrificed as many thousand souls to its ambitions on guillotine and on barricades, as ever the Grand Monarque [Louis XIV] sent to death in Flanders and Germany'. Indeed, French political traditions were somewhat unwholesome: 'It does not seem to me conceivable that a monarchy – Orleanist, Bourbonist, legitimist or constitutionalist – can ever be restored; but a Napoleonic monarchy – despotic or liberal – this is not impossible'. The history of the country, he observed, was 'always dominated and directed by personalities, by vast conceptions of men, whose ideas and policies continue to affect French history long after the men themselves have perished'.[48]

In those years Temperley also immersed himself in East European history and literature, often in conjunction. Slavic and Hungarian authors, such as Hendryk Sienkiewicz and Mór Jokai, more especially, attracted him. He held both in high esteem, and their work furnished him with constant points of reference for his reflections on Eastern European history. On visiting, in October 1905, Vychod, the Czech castle where Vladislav II Jagellonský was crowned King of Bohemia in 1471, he reflected that the frescoes in the great hall of the castle were 'designed exactly like Sienkiewicz's the Kreuz Ritter, to give the Germans

---

[45] Temperley diary, 31 Aug. 1903.
[46] Temperley diary, 12 Sept. 1903.
[47] Temperley diary, 12 Sept. 1903; see Tennyon's 'The Vision of Sin': 'I had a vision when the night was late./ A youth came riding toward a palace gate./ He rode a horse with wings, that would have flown,/ But that his heavy rider kept him down', J.C. Collins (ed.), *The Early Poems of Alfred Lord Tennyson* (London, s.a.), 283.
[48] Temperley diary, 'France 1910', n.d. His wartime and immediate post-war experiences led to an 'almost pathological hatred of France', H.N.V. Temperley, 'Recollection', fo. 18.

an impression they cannot forget. Sienkiewicz begins by enforcing the evils and cruelties of the Germans upon the reader and ends up by describing in an epic strain the glorious victory in which Poland overcame them and brought about their complete defeat'.[49]

But it was the Magyar novelist, one of the revolutionaries of 1848, who appealed to Temperley's sense of the dramatic as much as to his liberal instincts. To Temperley's mind, Jokai's literary output was on a par with that of Sir Walter Scott. There was a crucial difference, however: 'Bygone ages chiefly interest him [Jokai] in so far as they present not a picture, but a message to the men of to-day. [...] But for Scott the preservation of a tradition or a memory was enough; Jokai demanded from the past both inspiration and hope'. And in his use of the past as the raw material for his novels 'he succeeded in transfiguring not only the past but the present'. In so doing, he also captured some of the true essence of the past.[50] Historians should not look 'for details or for facts' in Jokai or Sienkiewicz, he observed years later, 'but their superb enthusiasm and their profound imaginative sympathies supply the best key to the profound and tragic histories of [Poland and Hungary]'.[51]

Temperley's enthusiasm for Jokai never waned. In the years after 1903, it reflected a newly found interest in Eastern European history; and for now it expressed itself in broadly Magyar-friendly observations. Later the Magyars would be replaced in his affections by the Serbs. But the reverse of both these elective affinities was a deep and profound antipathy to everything Habsburg. It was scarcely surprising that this should have been so. Austria, after all, occupied a place of special opprobrium in the liberal pantheon as the 'prison of the nationalities'.[52]

Temperley had visited Eastern Central and South Eastern Europe for the first time in the summer of 1905; 16 further visits to the region were to follow over the years. During a tour of Slovakia and Austrian Poland, in August 1907, he was moved to contemplate the past glories and present grievances of the diverse nationalities under Habsburg rule. On visiting Kraków and the tomb of Jan Sobieski III, the Polish king whose winged hussars had helped to relieve Vienna

---

[49] Temperley diary, 23 Oct. 1905; Sienkiewicz's *Krzyżacy* (Danzig, 1900) appeared in English translation as *The Knights of the Cross*.

[50] H.W.V. Temperley, 'Maurus Jokai and the Historical Novel', *Contemporary Review* lxxxvi (July 1904), 108–9 and 110; see also H.W.V. Temperley, 'Introductory Essay', in H. Marczali, *Hungary in the Eighteenth Century* (Cambridge, 1910), lxiii. Temperley returned to the subject a quarter of a century later, H.W.V. Temperley, *Foreign Historical Novels* (London, 1929), 5–6.

[51] H.W.V. Temperley, *Research and Modern History: Inaugural Lecture delivered at Cambridge, November 19th, 1930* (London, 1930), 19.

[52] Seton-Watson, *Making of a New Europe*, 21–102; see also the pertinent reflections by A. Sked, 'Historians, the Nationality Question, and the Downfall of the Habsburg Empire', *Transactions of the Royal Historical Society* (5) xxxi (1980), 175–93.

in 1683, he noted: 'What a mockery, what a Mephistophelean sneer of fate, that the man who saved Austria from destruction should find as his reward a tomb in territory which the grateful Habsburgs filched from his native land'. During his stay in Slovakia he was also confronted for the first time with the effects of the Budapest government's vigorous Magyarization policy.[53]

Temperley recorded some of his impressions in an article in the *Westminster Review*. Though remarkable more for its reserve, the article nevertheless reflected some of Temperley's favourite themes, most notably liberty and empire. Britain, he asserted, was 'the classic land of liberty, the defender of the oppressed, the arbiter of justice'. Her moral suasion brought hope to beleaguered minorities abroad, such as the Slovaks in the Hungarian half of the Habsburg monarchy. If their grievances were real, their voices would be heard. Public opinion, he averred, 'however immaterial and illusive in appearance', had great potential power, 'and in no country is this more the case than our own. Just lately an eminent Slovak writer and political leader has written to me as follows:– "English help is of more value to us than that of the whole Slavonic world". A notable confession for a Slav'.[54] In a similar vein, he had earlier commented, with a view to Britain's own imperial problems, that '[t]he Empire's unity must be based ... on the foundations of justice as well as of interest ... and the greatest material advantage of England is that of justice, her greatest interest that of honour'.[55]

Temperley returned to Hungary in the spring of 1909, and found his Magyar friends and interlocutors little receptive to the needs of the minorities in the Transleithanian half of the Dual Monarchy. Count Albert Apponyi, a seasoned veteran of Magyar politics and then Minister of Education, dismissed British press reports on the oppression of minorities in Hungary as 'distinctly superficial and inaccurate in their views'.[56] On his return home, Temperley reflected 'that it is quite useless to even [*sic*] talk about the Nat[ionalit]ies question with a Magyar or Magyarphil. On that they dare not speak out'. The best course of action, he thought, was for political commentators, such as Seton-Watson, to continue their campaigns on behalf of the ethnic minorities currently living in

---

[53] Temperley diary 1907.
[54] H.W.V. Temperley, 'Racial Strife in Hungary', *Westminster Review* (Jan. 1908), 1–12. Later, he came to a more differentiated view and noted that continental professors and Balkan diplomats regarded public opinion as a diplomatic weapon of the British government, to Satow, 5 Mar. 1916, Satow MSS, PRO 30/33/13/2; see also his criticism of the Duke of Newcastle for 'turn[ing] with every popular breath', 'War of Jenkins' Ear', 228.
[55] H.W.V. Temperley, 'The Imperial Control of Native Races', *Contemporary Review* lxxxix (Jan. 1906), 813.
[56] Temperley diary, 26 Mar. 1909.

the shadows of the Habsburgs' double-headed eagle: 'The douche of cold facts must eventually tell'.[57]

Privately, he was sceptical of Budapest's nationalizing policy. The Magyars, he thought, were 'a race of very considerable political ability and distinctly superior to the other races in Hungary. Even so their success has been very partial, has been dearly bought at the price of utter alienation of the subject races, greatly intensified national feeling, and the destruction of a healthy system of local government'. In a similar manner, in Prussian Poland, 'where a race, immensely superior in political ability and energy, has sought to denationalize the Poles[;] the result seems as far off as ever, unless the inhuman plans of wholesale depopulation of the Polish settlers and their replacement by Germans is carried out'.[58]

If Temperley's faith in the moral force of British public opinion remained strong, he had also lost none of his admiration for Hungary's culture and history or for his many Magyar contacts. One of these was Henrik Marczali, the distinguished Budapest historian, through whom he gained an entrée to some of the surviving revolutionaries of 1848, such as Artur Görgey, who had led the Honved militia against the Austrians but had ultimately been forced to surrender at Világos (now Şiria) to the advancing Russian relief army on 13 August 1849, thus terminating the revolution. The encounter appealed to Temperley's sense of the dramatic and his veneration for the great men of history: 'On the whole, a man true as steel, upright in every sense of the world [*sic*], simple, frank and manly. A true hero, who never valued ought but truth, who fought for country and fame – in the great sense only. He has not been much praised, indeed, nor has he found the fame, which will one day be his. [...] History will do him justice, and statues will rise to him, when the grave has closed over him'.[59]

The Marczali connection was also important in terms of Temperley's own scholarly development. At the invitation of the Hungarian Academy of Sciences, in 1878, Marczali had written a history of the Magyar lands under the Habsburg emperors Joseph II and Leopold II at the end of the eighteenth century, which Temperley persuaded Cambridge University Press to publish in an English translation. To it Temperley contributed an introductory essay, in which he sketched the broad sweep of Hungarian history before 1780. It was Temperley's first attempt to write the history of a country other than his own. Marczali's study opened with a sociological probe into the conditions of late eighteenth-century Hungary as penetrating as Toqueville's dissection of the *ancien régime*.

---

[57] Temperley to Seton-Watson, 25 Apr. 1909, Butterfield MSS, BUTT/311; for Seton-Watson's campaign on behalf of the Slovaks see Seton-Watson, *Making of a New Europe*, 43–56.
[58] Temperley diary, 8 Sept. 1910.
[59] Temperley diary, 23 Mar. 1909. Temperley's prediction was at least partially correct: an equestrian statue to Artur Görgey (1818–1916) was erected at Buda castle in 1935.

Temperley praised his friend's attempt 'to emancipate' the student of the past 'from the influence of history that is merely political'. If the historian was to establish 'an organic evolution from the past [to the present]', it was necessary to extend the scope of historical enquiry beyond the study of political parties and institutions to 'that of society, of beliefs, of the culture and the thought of the past'.[60]

Two aspects of Temperley's treatment of the subject are worthy of note. The first was his focus on the issue of liberty and his anti-Habsburg inclinations as its corollary; the second was his growing interest in geopolitics. Central to his introduction to Marczali's study was the assertion that the liberties of 1848 were pre-modern in essence. As evidence he instanced the *Bulla Aurea*, which 'the weak, extravagant, and militarily incompetent Andreas II' had been forced to sign in 1222, a sort of Magyar *Magna Carta*, 'the first in a long line of statutes and customs which form an unwritten constitution'. Its effect was to restrict royal power through an assembly of estates, a mechanism 'which has become the root of every modern constitution through the agency of Locke'.[61]

Hungary's history, however, was primarily a military one, and the country's ancient liberties crumbled as foreign empires encroached upon its territory. The Magyar defeat at Mohács at the hands of the advancing Ottomans in 1526 thus brought two-thirds of Hungary, including eventually Buda, under Turkish rule. This, however, was only one part of the fall-out of Mohács, indeed 'the least evil: in order to resist the Turk Hungary had to accept a German ruler in the Habsburgs', whom Temperley described as 'absolutising alien King[s]'. Mohács thus inaugurated a period of friction that was to last until the disintegration of the Habsburg empire in 1918. The Hungarians, many of them Calvinists, loved their 'bigoted ... and brutal' Habsburg rulers in the seventeenth century no more than the Ottomans. Mohács, then, also set the scene for Joseph II's attempts to reform the Magyar lands 'according to the hard reason and doctrinaire theories of an eighteenth-century philosophy', the subject of Marczali's book.[62]

But his foray into Hungarian history was significant also in that it foreshadowed Temperley's growing interest in the 'influence of geography on historical and racial development'. The heart of Hungary was the fertile but flat great and little Alföld or lowlands, a region which would occupy Temperley's

---

[60] Temperley, 'Introductory Essay', lxiv; see also H.W.V. Temperley, 'How the Hungarian Frontiers Were Drawn', *Foreign Affairs* vi, 1 (1927–8), 432–47.

[61] Temperley, 'Introductory Essay', xxviii, xxix, xxxix; for some of the background see H. Marczali, *Ungarische Verfassungsgeschichte* (Tübingen, 1910), 22–3. E. Hantos, *The Magna Carta of the English and of the Hungarian Constitution: A Comparative View of the Law and the Institutions of the Early Middle Ages* (London, 1904) and W.S. McKechnie, 'Magna Carta (1215–1915): An Address Delivered on its Seventh Centenary', in H.E. Malden (ed.), *Magna Carta Commemorative Essays* (London, 1917), esp. 16–25, give a flavour of contemporary thinking.

[62] Temperley, 'Introductory Essay', lvi and xviii.

attention in his role as a technical expert at the Paris peace conference in 1919. The Alföld, he observed in 1910, 'invited invasion, for its fertility suggests wealth and its situation weakness; mounted invaders could pour up the valleys of the Danube and the Tisza, and sweep over its wide plains with ease. Like Sparta such a land has no walls, and its strength could only lie in stout hearts and strong hands'. The mountaineers in the Tatra, the Carpathian and Dalmatian Alps could exploit nature to repel invading hordes; not so the lowlanders: 'Therefore the race, which dominates the two Alfölds ... will either be at once overcome or else will become fierce and strong, steeled and disciplined by hard necessity. Such are the probabilities of the natural situation, and the historic evolution has tended to conform to them'.[63] During the war, Temperley's instinctive anti-Habsburgism was to shape his intelligence analyses and policy submissions, and he would have to grapple with the forces of geopolitics. The roots of both, however, reached backwards to his intellectual interests in the first decade after 1900.

Into this decade also fell his next project, a study of Austro-Prussian relations during the War of the Bavarian Succession of 1778–9, the so-called 'Potato War'. The book was substantially completed in 1911, and Temperley anticipated its publication in October of the following year.[64] Various delays were compounded by the outbreak of the First World War, and the work did not appear in print until 1915. It marked a confluence of his two recent scholarly pursuits, the first being 'his interest in the Prussian King, which came to me as we [Temperley and Reddaway] tramped his Silesian battlefields'. The other had been his friend Marczali's work on Joseph II.[65] In Temperley's hands the Austrian emperor emerged as a curious and fascinating mixture of divergent character traits and impulses, warm-hearted and yet harsh towards subordinates; full of 'vigour and reforming zeal', yet given to 'fickleness and confusion of thought'; 'but none can deny him as warm a zeal for his people ... a heart as tender as ever beat in the breast of a sovereign'. The portrait of Frederick, by contrast, is much less sympathetically drawn, a harsh cynic and well past his prime as a soldier.[66]

Frederic the Great and Kaiser Joseph had caused Temperley 'a great deal of pain to bring it to birth'. Based on a careful study of unpublished dispatches from British envoys and a variety of published German and Russian documents, he treated the Bavarian succession struggle as 'an illustration of Eighteenth century diplomacy & diplomats', their mechanistic pursuit of the *raison d'état* and disregard for any notion of universal morality.[67] Even so, he delineated

---

[63] Temperley, 'Introductory Essay', xix and xxi.
[64] Temperley to Webster, 7 Aug. 1911, Webster MSS, Webster 1/1/76; Gooch, *Temperley*, 10.
[65] H. Temperley, *Frederic the Great and Kaiser Joseph: An Episode of War and Diplomacy in the Eighteenth Century* (London, 1915), x–xi.
[66] Temperley, *Frederic*, 31, 19–23; see also S.B. Fay's review in *American Historical Review* xx, 4 (1915), 846–8.
[67] Temperley to Webster, 1 Apr. 1915, Webster MSS, Webster 1/2/113.

Frederick's attempts, in his struggle with the Habsburgs, 'to turn the moral opinion of the Empire and of Europe against Kaiser Joseph'. The war itself was long on manoeuvres and short on military engagements; it was 'a classic war of positions'. Its real significance lay in the Peace of Teschen that concluded it in 1779, as Temperley demonstrated by placing it in a broader European context. With France and Britain at war in the Americas, 'Russia was for the first time introduced into German affairs, and behind her negotiators stood the vast mass of the Russian army'. After Teschen, Prussia and Austria 'supported the tottering fabric of the Empire like two pillars against danger from within; it was defended from without by two buttresses in the shape of Russia and of France'. As for Frederick, he had taken up arms ostensibly to preserve the status quo within the Empire against Austrian aggrandisement: 'He had not gained his way by arms – his soldiers had done nothing but steal plums; but his diplomacy had prevented stealing provinces'.[68] Temperley drew broader lessons still. The striking feature of the Teschen treaty was its moral force. There was no partition of Germany, as had been feared; and, although it 'did not deal absolute justice ... it stopped the more marked display of force. It protested with effect against unbridled aggression'. The 'Potato War' and the diplomatic manoeuvrings that produced the Peace of Teschen reflected the many facets of the *ancien régime*:

> The personal force of rulers, dominating their peoples ... the shameless claim, backed by forgeries and supported by arms ... the war which ruined the peasants of Bohemia for objects of which they knew or cared nothing, the peace which made half-Oriental Russia a guardian of the sanctity of Germanic treaties; last of all the piteous spectacle of Bavaria herself, ruled by one ready to betray her, hurled this way and that in the eddies of diplomacy ... It was such incidents and such rulers that caused the shame and the splendour, the glory and the misery, of the old regime.[69]

In his final assessment, Temperley underscored both the continuities with more recent events and the momentous change that was to come to Europe after Teschen. For Germany, the war had revealed for the first time 'that terrible unknown power [of Russia] which has remained a standing menace to Teutonism ever since'. And yet a new force was about to emerge in European politics, and 'the armies which Frederic and Joseph had trained were to go down in utter ruin before the *Marseillaise* and the ragged volunteers of France'. As the envoys of the old regime were haggling over the details of Teschen, Temperley concluded with a flourish, 'there was playing among the Corsican rocks a boy who was to teach the world that it was not only despots who dreamt of war, and that the armed

---

[68] Temperley, *Frederic*, 8, 100, 148, 191 and 204.
[69] Temperley, *Frederic*, 208, 210 and 211.

champion of the rights of the people could plan partitions more shameless than those of Poland and conquests more extensive than those of Bavaria'.[70]

Frederic the Great and Kaiser Joseph marked the maturing of Temperley as a scholar. 'I remember that I once thought your style the weakest thing about you', commented Oscar Browning, his *quondam* mentor at King's, 'but you have greatly improved'.[71] As Herbert Butterfield later reflected, Temperley had

> caught a piece of a story that made a rounded whole, and saw here what a novelist might call an artistic opportunity ... Its combination of diplomacy and war (without too much fighting) was exactly to his taste ... But with all this, the history could be told as a tale – it is more the sheer story than anything else that Temperley ever produced.[72]

Temperley's concluding reflection on this unwarlike war of long ago indicated his own growing interest in the rising force of nationalism in modern Europe; and this increasingly concentrated his attention on Serbia. He had first visited the country in 1905, and this was followed almost every year by a tour of South Eastern Europe. Temperley was no pleasure-seeking Edwardian tourist. There was little comfort to be found during his trip to Albania in the early autumn of 1910 in the aftermath of the failed rebellion against Turkish overlordship there. Nor was it very safe. He himself was fired upon by brigands in the mountains around Elbasan; and on one occasion he had to pull his own revolver to rescue his Turkish guide from being shot by an Albanian peasant.[73]

The young don travelled for a purpose, however. He sought to immerse himself in the culture and history of the region in its original setting; and he sought to understand its current politics: 'My chief mission here', he recorded, 'is not artistic but political, and I seek everywhere information from all sources'. He was moved by the plight of the Albanians. Austria-Hungary, self-proclaimed protector of the Catholic tribes in the North, had 'proved useless'. The native 'Beys were in flight, the Turks in possession. The rule was that of bayonet and bastinado'. Temperley's humanitarian concerns were real enough: 'That the general treatment of the Albanians has been inhuman I do not doubt – Greeks and Vlachs ... testify to it as freely as the Albanians themselves'.[74] But his impressions were also infused with a sense of the impending end of Turkish rule in Europe:

---

[70] Temperley, *Frederic*, 210 and 212.

[71] Browning to Temperley, 19 Feb. 1915, Temperley MSS. Temperley had presented him with an inscribed copy of the book on the previous day, presentation copy in author's possession; for the argument of Temperley as a scholar at the peak of his powers, see also Fair, *Temperley*, 100–101.

[72] H. Butterfield, 'New Introduction', in H. Temperley, *Frederic the Great and Kaiser Joseph* (London, repr. 1968), as quoted in Fair, *Temperley*, 96.

[73] Temperley diary, 28 and 30 Sept. 1910.

[74] Temperley diary, 29 Sept. 1910.

[T]he Young Turks are emulating the exploits of Abdul Hamid [II], but have applied them to a country which he always wisely left alone ... The old policy of *divide et impera* was to sow dissensions between Ghegs and Tosks, so as to play off one against the other, and to turn their divisions to the advantage of the Turk. The new policy is to unite them against the Turk by a common policy of oppression and degradation. [...] The attempt is a senseless folly, as the Beys return, as the Turkish soldiers evacuate the country, the smouldering embers will burst into flame, and the Albanians, so often the Praetorians of the Turkish Empire, may end by overthrowing it. All this may be far off, though I think not so very far, but one thing at least I know. The Turks cannot permanently subdue a race that is partly Christian, that has schools and a language of its own, as well as a fierce spirit of liberty. As my old teacher in history, Lord Acton, used to say "a nation derives its rights and its power from the memory of a former independence". My friends in Hungary will know the truth of this ... One day the Young Turks will know it too.

The rugged landscape of Albania and the simple dignity of its inhabitants made a lasting impression on Temperley: 'Their wild virtues, their pride, their simplicity and their courage, will soon perhaps be exchanged for the smooth politeness, the meanness and materialism of a modern state and society. May the day be a distant one! I think it was Goethe who said "a man who has been among the palm trees is never the same again". I at least can say that this saying is true of one who has been among the Albanian oaks'.[75] Indeed, Temperley's travel diaries of those years give the impression of a man relieved of all that was mean and restraining in contemporary European civilization. Passing through Munich *en route* to the Adriatic and Montenegro in 1913, he noted, that the Bavarian capital's famous Hof Bräu was 'a sort of Stock-Exchange of beer – apotheosis of bourgeois pleasure – a beautiful court full of filthy smells & people'.[76] Beyond lay the wild and majestic Balkans: 'I am going off to the Sanjak of Novibazar where I expect to forget civilization for a time', he confided to Webster in the 1920s.[77]

Whatever the attractions of Balkans for Temperley, he was a shrewd observer of Near Eastern politics. His 1910 visit to the region had also taken him to Constantinople where he witnessed the Sultan's appearance at the last *Selamlik*: 'the solemn tribute of the Commander of the Faithful to the religious fanaticism of his subjects'. The ceremony struck Temperley as appealing 'to the two most powerful instincts of the Mussulman – religion and war'. The now dominant Young Turk movement, he reflected while at Salonika, 'were pursuing a purely

---

[75] Temperley diary, 1 Oct. 1910. Appropriately, the Goethe quote is from the *Elective Affinities*: 'Es wandelt niemand unter Palmen, und die Gesinnungen ändern sich gewiss in einem Lande, wo Elefanten and Tiger zu Hause sind', J.W. von Goethe, *Die Wahlverwandschaften*, part II, book 7, *Sämtliche Werke* (40 vols, Stuttgart and Berlin, s.a.) xxi, 212.
[76] Temperley diary, 2 Sept. 1913.
[77] Temperley to Webster, 20 July 1927, Webster MSS, Webster 1/9/43.

Hamidian line of policy [of playing off minorities against each other]'. As its more liberal members were gradually discredited, so 'the Committee becomes increasingly aggressive in reaction'.[78]

The movement, he wrote to Seton-Watson, 'though militarist, was also intensely national, while the liberal tone was ... a veneer'. Its main idea was 'to get a strong army and navy, so as to be independent of any European power'. The greatest danger facing Turkey was the Young Turks' attempted 'Osmanisation of European Turkey', which was likely to produce the opposite effect there.[79] Under the impression of what he had witnessed at Constantinople, Temperley was by no means certain of the outcome of such a policy. He acknowledged that there was 'a real desire among the Turks to improve their condition by borrowing Western and civilized ideas in a larger measure than that which they have ever consented to before'. And yet the Young Turk leadership's newly found sense of strength seemed to rest primarily on military force: 'Now these things are ominous – in a few years from now, if the present regime continues, the Turks will be incomparably stronger than at any time during the last century and a half. [...] [T]heir grip on the Bosporus and European Turkey will be firmer than ever'. To Temperley's mind this raised the wider international question of whether 'this newly acquired power [will] be used with the genuine intention of promoting progress and making the reconciliation of East and West possible, or will it be employed merely as a means of reestablishing the old conditions, by illusory concessions to Western opinions?' He was particularly perturbed by attempts to instrumentalize the past for propaganda purposes. 'Dubious heroes are reclaimed from the past with the idea of glorifying the present', he noted with a view to the erection of a monument over the grave of Mustapha Bairakdar: 'This worthy was conspicuous in 1807 for overthrowing the reforming Sultan Selim III, for bringing up the new Sultan Mustapha [IV] in the ways of reaction and for speedily undoing the Selimite reforms. [...] For these services to the Ottoman State the present "constitutional" government propose to honour him as one of its heroes'.[80]

Turkey's swift and sudden collapse during the First Balkan War two years later confirmed Temperley's gloomy prognostications. The consequences of the demise of an empire that had dominated the Balkans and the Eastern Mediterranean for nearly half-a-millennium were to be a major concern for Temperley during his time as a military intelligence officer after 1916.

---

[78] Temperley diary, 15 and 18 Sept. 1910.
[79] Temperley to Seton-Watson, 11 Sept. 1910, as quoted in Butterfield, Temperley MS biography, Butterfield MSS, BUTT/9, fo. 53a.
[80] Temperley diary, 11? Sept. 1910; see S.J. Shaw, *Between Old and New: The Ottoman Empire under Sultan Selim III, 1789–1807* (Cambridge, MA, 1971), 378–95.

Of all the countries of South Eastern Europe it was Serbia that attracted him the most, though he never failed to take her people 'with the necessary grain of salt'.[81] That affinity was rooted in the contrast between the country's past, its current backwardness, and its potential future. Travelling through Serbia in the spring of 1909, just after the Bosnian annexation crisis, he reflected on Serbia's past: 'And yet, and yet, there was culture here in the time of the Romans ... and Servia was a centre of civilization even so late of [*sic*] the fifteenth century ... Truly the Serb is one who seems to have learnt nothing & forgotten everything'.[82] Modern Serbia, he thought, was 'still a country of peasants and swineherds – a country of the earth indeed'. Economically, the land-locked country was dependent on neighbouring Austria-Hungary, and would remain so unless it gained access to the Adriatic. But Temperley took a more optimistic view of its potential:

> The best chance of their advance is through imbibing French civilization & ideas, which are more suitable to their passionate directness and Oriental fire than any German or English ideas can be. The greatest element of their strength is in the people themselves, who, for all their defects, have a certain dogged Slavonic obstinacy ... which won them their independence of Turkey in the past & will (or may) win them their independence of Austria in the future. Pan-Slavism is a dream. Pan-Serbism may become a reality. With Serb agitation within Austria-Hungary, & Russian pressure from without, Servia may one day extend its boundaries & the union of the Serbs be realized by the aid of a great power, just as was the union of the Italians.[83]

Clearly, Temperley himself had drunk a deep draught of pan-Serbism or Yugoslavism. He learnt the Serbian language and was steeped in the country's folklore and mythology. He also wrote a history of Serbia which was nearly finished when war began, but was not published until 1917. As it belongs in the main to the pre-war years, and gives context to Temperley's wartime activities, it is touched upon here. The book is enlivened by Temperley's own intimate knowledge of Balkan history and scenery. As G.P. Gooch noted, it 'breathes a warm admiration for the Serbian race'.[84] Indeed, in his treatment of the Karadjordjević regime, restored in 1903 after the violent overthrow of the rival Obrenović dynasty, Temperley sanitized some of the new regime's excesses. He did not pretend that the Serbs were particularly well governed, but emphasized that

---

[81] Seton-Watson draft Temperley obituary, n.d. [1939], Seton-Watson MSS, School of Slavonic and East European Studies, London, SEW/17/28/4, fo. 2.
[82] Temperley diary, 27 Mar. 1909.
[83] Temperley diary, 30 Mar. 1909.
[84] Gooch, *Temperley*, 11.

they were nearly ungovernable, their hatred of alien bureaucracy and resistance to land taxation making them truculent, indeed warlike. Yet, underneath it all, he detected a fundamentally democratic attitude, if primitive. The Serb nation, he concluded, had 'a spirit which has something of true nobility in it'. Once the strength and ardour of the peasantry has been aroused, Temperley averred, and 'is directed in the right channels by the intellectual leaders of Serbia there is no doubt as to the result. If the Serbian puts half the energy into the works of peace that he has expended on those of war, there is no fear as to the future of his race'.[85]

Temperley's interest in Serbia and later Yugoslavia never failed. Indeed, according to Seton-Watson, he more than once spoke of his wish to be buried in Serb soil.[86] No doubt, Temperley's elective affinity with Serbia sprang from a strong streak of romantic imagination, an appreciation of the drama of the past and the wild landscape that provided its setting, as is illustrated by an entry in his diary nearly a dozen years after the war: 'I am sorry to have to leave D[orothy, his second wife] but I don't see how I can do this tour except by myself. The stony crags of Herzegovina are not for anyone but me. I hope to penetrate into the real fastnesses, where heroism burned, and where the Turks were defeated'.[87]

In light of such statements, it would be tempting to view Temperley principally as an idealist romantic of a peculiarly English variety. Some scholars, indeed, have done so. In Maurice Cowling's acerbic critique Temperley was 'a romantic supporter of the nationalities'.[88] And in the assessment of his most famous former student, Herbert Butterfield, Temperley did not study the past as a 'means for the better understanding of the present'. On the contrary, he was a 'romantic in the sense that he loved the past because it was past – loved the very pastness of it – a thing which is always necessary in the last resort if the story of bygone centuries is not to be distorted'.[89]

Superficially persuasive though they are, such comments require to be taken with a good degree of scepticism. Cowling's studied rudeness is more suggestive of his perversely provocative paleo-conservative crusade against what he took to be the malaise of secular, post-war Britain than of any true insight into the

---

[85] H.W.V. Temperley, *History of Serbia* (London, 1917), 68–70, 282 and 285. Cowling rightly described Temperley's treatment of the Karadjordjović years as a whitewash, Cowling, *Public Doctrine*, 217.

[86] Seton-Watson draft Temperley obituary, n.d. [1939], Seton-Watson MSS, SEW/17/28/4, fo. 7; an interesting parallel with the Swiss doctor, Rodolphe Reiss, see diary, 20 Oct. 1918.

[87] Temperley diary, 21 July 1930.

[88] Cowling, *Public Doctrine*, 218.

[89] Butterfield, 'New Introduction', as quoted in Fair, *Temperley*, 97. Oddly, that was precisely the charge Butterfield levied against Whig history: 'The study of the past with one eye ... upon the present is the source of all sins and sophistries in history', H. Butterfield, *The Whig Interpretation of History* (London, repr. 1950), 31; see also Bentley's speculation that that work was 'a mild joke against Temperley', Bentley, *Butterfield*, 160.

historian Temperley.[90] A penchant for Swinburnian overtones does not make a romantic mind. Butterfield's reflections, meanwhile, are rooted more in his own life-long attempt to emancipate himself from his former tutor's influence and from his own profound sense of inadequacy. Whether or not Butterfield's Delphic definition of romanticism captured the real essence of the phenomenon,[91] he certainly failed to understand Temperley's idea of history, as will be discussed below. Seton-Watson was nearer the mark, when he noted that 'his eager enthusiasm for many causes ... was balanced by a highly developed strain of criticism and scepticism, [and] great skill in sifting, weighing and selecting facts'.[92]

The introduction to Temperley's wartime diaries is not the place for an in-depth discussion of his intellectual and scholarly development beyond what is necessary for an appreciation of his role in the First World War. It will suffice here to emphasize the distorting effect of viewing Temperley through the prism of his most famous pupil – what might be called the Butterfield legend.[93] Indeed, it would be an interesting counterfactual to speculate what Temperley's later reputation might have been, if arguably his most talented research student, C.R. Sproxton, had not been killed on active service in 1916, and, presumably, then been elected to the fellowship that went to Butterfield. Sproxton, whose Prince Consort prize essay on Palmerston and the Hungarian revolution was published posthumously in 1919, was very much in Temperley's mould. Temperley, indeed, referred to him as 'my man'.[94]

Whatever might have been had it not been for the war, August 1914 irrevocably changed the trajectory of Temperley's own career. The outbreak of war found him on a walking tour of Dartmoor. While some members of the Cambridge faculty had publicly urged the government to remain aloof from the unfolding continental conflict, Temperley accepted the need for intervention.

---

[90] The fact that Temperley 'did not believe' (H.N.V. Temperley, 'Recollections', fo. 4 and 10) made him a natural target for Cowling's ire. For instructive comments see R. Brent, 'Butterfield's Tories: "High Politics" and the Writing of Modern British Political History', *Historical Journal* xxx, 4 (1987), 943–54; N. Annan, *Our Age: The Generation that Made Post-War Britain* (London, 1991 (pb.)), 365–6.

[91] H.G. Schenck, *The Mind of the European Romantics: An Essay in Cultural History* (Oxford, 1979), 3–8; S. Bann, *Romanticism and the Rise of History* (New York, 1995), 3–16.

[92] Seton-Watson draft Temperley obituary, n.d. [1939], Seton-Watson MSS, SEW/17/28/4, fo. 7.

[93] John Fair's biography perpetuates the notion of a Butterfield connection, Fair, *Temperley*, 167–89. Tellingly, Butterfield's biographer has inverted the relationship and asserted an intellectual vacuum at the core of Temperley's scholarship, Bentley, *Butterfield*, 41.

[94] Temperley to Seton-Watson, 29 Aug. 1912, Butterfield MSS, BUTT/311; Sproxton to Temperley, 26 Jan. 1914, Temperley MSS, thanking him for his help in preparing the essay; cf. H.W.V. Temperley, 'Charles Sproxton', in C.R. Sproxton, *Palmerston and the Hungarian Revolution* (Cambridge, 1919), vii.

In a strongly worded letter he attacked 'the circular which has gone forth, as it were in Cambridge's name, advocating English neutrality'. Britain's treaty obligations towards Belgium aside, he observed that, 'in every century since the fourteenth, England has managed her policy on the assumption that the Low Countries must always be in the hands of a friendly power or of one too weak to endanger our sea power'.[95]

Temperley, married since the previous summer, volunteered for active duty and enlisted as a First Lieutenant, later Captain, in the Fife and Forfar Yeomanry.[96] He went out to the Eastern Mediterranean in 1915 for the planned assault on the Dardanelles, though fortunately never reached the Turkish Straits. He was soon invalided out after contracting dysentery and other diseases. Indeed, he was never fully to recover from them, and his previously iron constitution was left fragile and prone to bouts of fever and exhaustion.[97] It also left him with an abiding hatred of the author of the Gallipoli campaign: 'Winston's stuff is all lies'.[98] Temperley's war was by no means over after Gallipoli. Having nearly lost his services altogether, the War Office belatedly came to realize that his expertise in the affairs of South Eastern Europe could be put to better use than by despatching him as canon fodder in the East. In the spring of 1916 he was assigned to the War Office as a General Staff Officer, eventually working for Section 2(a) of Military Intelligence. The scholar-diplomat Sir Ernest Satow commented in his diary:

> Harold W.V. Temperley came ... to lunch, and we had much interesting conversation. He has been in the Yeomanry almost since the war broke out, and contracted dysentery at Gallipoli, from which he has fairly well recovered. A big man, clean-shaven, wearing spectacles, 37 years of age, a fellow of Peterhouse, history his Fach [i.e. subject].[99]

---

[95] Draft letter by Temperley, 4 Aug. 1914 (copy), Butterfield MSS, BUTT/8; for the letter of 1 Aug. 1914 see S. Wallace, *War and the Image of Germany: British Academics, 1914–1918* (Edinburgh, 1988), 24–7.

[96] T.E.B. Howarth, *Cambridge Between Two Wars* (London, 1978), 26. Temperley's first wife (Dorothy Mary) Gladys Bradford (1885–1923), of Newnham College, was an historian herself, see G. Temperley, *Henry VII* (Boston, MA, 1914). Her death, on 23 Feb. 1923, left Temperley a 'fundamentally insecure person', something his remarriage six years later did not remedy and something that may explain his many explosive quarrels with all and sundry, see H.N.V. Temperley, 'Recollections', fo. 4.

[97] Temperley to Webster, 24 Sept. 1919, Webster MSS, Webster 1/3/49; Fair, *Temperley*, 107–9, for the details.

[98] Temperley to Pickthorn, 24 Oct. 1923 (copy), Temperley MSS; see also Temperley diary, 11 Mar. 1917. (Sir) Kenneth Pickthorn (1892–1975) of Corpus Christi College was a well-known Conservative-supporting historian and later MP.

[99] Satow diary, 9 Mar. 1916, Satow MSS, PRO 30/33/17/3.

At MI2(a) his brief was to draw up background memoranda on Balkan developments. Here his knowledge of the region and his understanding of its history stood him in good stead. In the spring of 1918, now promoted to the rank of Major, he was appointed head of MI2E, later MI6b, which 'was specially instructed to deal with the political side of problems of the settlement in which the General Staff were interested'.[100] Temperley himself was now widely recognized as Whitehall's foremost authority on the Balkans.[101]

And, *pace* Butterfield, Temperley was not shy to use his scholarship to inform current policy-making. Nor should it be surprising that this was so. The main thrust of the Cambridge School that so scandalized Butterfield in later years was to emphasize the connection between the past and the present. In his undergraduate days, Temperley had been secretary to Oscar Browning's Political Society at King's, which had been established precisely for the purpose of elucidating current problems through history.[102] And both Prothero, who had supported Temperley's failed attempt to win a fellowship at King's in 1903, and Ward, his later mentor at Peterhouse, saw history as a useful adjunct to politics. As Ward had asserted in his 1873 inaugural at Owens College, Manchester: 'The cultivated mind ... is and must be on the side of progress and peace ... When the education, and more especially the higher education of a country is fostered, there lies the best promise of progress and of peace'.[103] For his part, Prothero had insisted that 'history is the mother, in more senses than one, of politics', and that no other than historical training 'is so proper for the citizen of a self-governing State'.[104]

Temperley was a more rigorous scholar than either Prothero or Ward, more aware of the complexities of the past. Yet his views on the uses of history did not differ substantially from theirs. While recuperating from his Dardanelles exertions in 1915–16, he reflected on the subject. Strategy, he noted, straddled military matters and diplomatic questions:

> But between these two broad aspects of the question ... there is a department of specialised political knowledge which is essential to the full understanding of the significance and trend of military events. [...] The political side of strategy requires a knowledge which cannot be improvised and is based on the study of

---

[100] 'Sketch of the History of the Military Section, British Delegation, Congress of Paris, December 1918 – July 1919', Sept. 1919, Temperley MSS, fo. 1.
[101] Fair, 'Peacemaking Exploits', 72–3.
[102] I. Anstruther, *Oscar Browning: A Biography* (London, 1983), 85.
[103] A.W. Ward, 'The Peace of Europe', in A.W. Ward, *Collected Papers: Historical, Literary, Travel and Miscellaneous* (5 vols, London, 1920), i, 53.
[104] G.W. Prothero, 'Presidential Address', *Transactions of the Royal Historical Society*, n.s. xvi (1902), viii.

history and a considerable acquaintance with contemporary politics, economics and diplomacy.[105]

As a student of the Near East, Temperley could not but acknowledge the significance of military factors. Eastern Europe, he reflected, 'is the one unappropriated part of Europe, so that neighbouring or aggressive nations have always regarded it as their prize'. In a lengthy and never published essay, he contemplated, à la Creasy, the decisive battles in the history of the region. Emperor Otto I's defeat of the Magyar invaders at the Lechfeld in 933 had secured Germany in the South East, and started her eastward expansion. It was not halted until the battle of Tannenberg (Grunwald) in 1410, which in turn secured Poland till the end of the eighteenth century. In the North East, the battle of Poltava in 1709 destroyed Swedish military power in the Baltic and made Russo-Prussian competition for power and influence the dominant feature of the politics of that region. The battle of Mollwitz, in 1741, at the beginning of the First Silesian War, established Prussia's superiority over Austria, even if it still required two further wars to confirm it. Thus begun the extrusion of the Habsburgs from the affairs of Germany. In the South East, the battles of Kosovo (1389) and Mohács (1526) destroyed the Serb and Magyar empires, and handed mastery of the Balkans to the Osmanli.

Even here, Temperley's earlier concern with liberty and reform asserted itself. The Turks' failure to capture Vienna in 1683 was the outward sign of the Ottoman Empire's impending decline. It was 'a signpost, not an agent of decay', Temperley argued: 'The internal disorders of Turkey and the alteration of her military system and her unprogressive policy had already fixed the period of her decline'. In turn, Turkish weakness drew Austria further into South Eastern Europe and led to the conquest of much of Hungary and the Banat. When the Habsburg advance was checked in 1738–9, and Belgrade and Serbia returned to Turkish rule, it signalled Austria's vulnerability, as Frederick the Great was not slow to realize: 'Belgrad [*sic*] begat Mollwitz [1741] as Mollwitz begat Königgrätz [1866]'.[106] The loss of Belgrade was the last decisive battle in the Balkans, Temperley observed. Its strategic importance, however, had not changed: 'Belgrade *was* and Serbia is the cork to the Balkan bottle, and he who held it could prevent anyone else from drinking Byzantine wine. I say *was* because owing to modern guns and monitors, Belgrade is no longer a defensible fortress. The cork is now the Morava valley as a whole from Belgrade to Nish.' As for the current conflict, Temperley suggested that, 'since the decisive battles in the Balkans have always been sieges, a new leaguer of Byzantium may be the

---

[105] Temperley, 'War notes: Montenegro – Strategy', c. 1915–16, Temperley MSS.
[106] H.W.V. Temperley, 'Army Book 152 (Decisive Battles)', Temperley MSS, fos. 2, 27–8 and 31.

final determining event of its history'.[107] If, at one level, Temperley's prediction was wide of the mark, at another it was not, given that for Britain the war in the Near East ended in the Turkish Straits in 1922.

Significantly, in terms of Temperley's career, a series of bureaucratic reorganizations now gave him greater scope to influence policy. As an internal history of the General Staff military intelligence section noted, prior to 1917, '[n]o department of Government made adequate preparations for the Peace Congress. The men who could be entrusted with the responsibility for such work were overwhelmed with other and more pressing duties; the situation was liable to such great fluctuations that it was difficult if not impossible to draw up schemes far in advance'.[108] For his part, Temperley did not shy away from urging his political masters to address such shortcomings: 'Temperley came in with a suggestion that we should have a small historical staff to look into the past history of some of the debatable questions, more particularly in the Balkans and Poland, which will come up at the Peace Conference'.[109] Temperley's direct influence on policy-making ought not to be exaggerated, though he quite clearly helped to shape some of Lloyd George's speeches.[110] Even so, his acquaintance Satow glimpsed what drove Temperley when wrote to him that he was 'sure that you must find the diplomatic side of your work immensely interesting. To have a finger in the pie is a great happiness'.[111]

As Temperley's wartime diaries show, he revelled in having 'a finger in the pie'. This is not the place to discuss at length Temperley's work at the War Office. His diaries testify to that, as they do to his return to the Balkans as acting military attaché, then as a technical expert at the Paris peace conference, and as a delegate at the subsequent conference at Paris to determine the boundaries of Albania.[112] It will suffice here underscore the extent to which his sympathies for Greece and Serbia shaped his policy submissions. He rejoiced, for instance, at seeing Kavalla restored to Greece: 'I well remember visiting that spot in 1911 and sitting on the hill above it, and wondering whether it would ever belong to Greece again. We little dreamed in those days of the changes we now see'.[113]

---

[107] Temperley, 'Army Book 152 (Decisive Battles)', Temperley MSS, fos. 33 and 38.

[108] 'Sketch of the History of the Military Section, British Delegation, Congress of Paris, December 1918 – July 1919', Sept. 1919, Temperley MSS, fo. 2; Goldstein, *Winning the Peace*, 51–2.

[109] Amery diary, 3 Feb. 1917, in J. Barnes and D. Nicholson (eds), *The Leopold Amery Diaries, 1896–1929* (London, 1980), 141; see also Temperley diary, 2 Mar. 1918. For a detailed discussion of preparations for the peace conference see Goldstein, *Winning the Peace, passim*.

[110] See Temperley diary, 8 Aug. 1917.

[111] Satow to Temperley, 8 Apr. 1917, Temperley MSS.

[112] See also Fair, 'Peacemaking Exploits', 68–93; and Fair, *Temperley*, 105–46.

[113] Temperley to Gennadius, 11 Oct. 1918, Gennadius MSS, American School of Classical Studies, Athens, folder 6/5. Temperley was mistaken: he had visited Kavalla in 1910, see diary 12 Sept. 1910, Temperley MSS.

The events of the war and its end made a lasting impression on Temperley, the diplomatic historian who had earlier, in his work on the Peace of Teschen, grappled with the problems of peace-making as a purely intellectual exercise. By a stroke of good fortune, Temperley was present in the *salle des glaces* when the German delegates signed the peace treaty on 28 June 1919, exactly five years after the Sarajevo assassination that had triggered the chain reaction that led to war:

> In the park the water was playing in the fountains for the first time since the war. Wilson, Clemenceau, Lloyd George and Sonnino walked down the tapis vert, were uproariously cheered and with difficulty protected from the crowd. Immediately after ... the cuirassiers all suddenly sheathed their swords – I suppose a symbolic and conscious act. In a word a great moment but I fear a peace without victory just as we had a victory without peace.[114]

The experiences of 1919 also shaped Temperley's political outlook. Like many of his generation, he came to look upon the League of Nations as the best means of organizing international politics. On his return to Cambridge in the Michaelmas term of 1919, now promoted to a readership, he sought to infuse the teaching of history with the internationalism of the new era: 'We are seriously endeavouring to turn the serious attention of our young men in the direction of International Politics and the League of Nations'.[115] He was conscious of the broader historical import of the Paris conference, as he explained in a lecture on the subject in the mid-1920s. There had been other major peace congresses: 'But this Conference was ... and will prove more important than these. It attempted more, it covered wider areas, it has legislated for every corner of the earth – not only for Europe, half of which it has remodeled on a system which is practically the opposite of what has previously prevailed – but for the world'.[116]

The previous system was that of the 'balance of power', now 'somewhat antiquated' and largely discredited, as Temperley acknowledged. Even so, he mounted a robust defence of Britain's historical record in this respect. The rise of powers with hegemonic ambitions, he argued,

> grad[uall]y forces all powers, or the majority of them, to combine ag[ain]st her from a sense of common danger. Now this happened in the case of Louis XIV, Napoleon and William II. But the weak point of the idea is that the powers,

---

[114] Temperley diary, 28 June 1919.
[115] Temperley to Gennadius, 8 Nov. 1919, Gennadius MSS, folder 6/5.
[116] H.W.V. Temperley, 'Peace Conference Lecture', MS notes, Temperley MSS, part I, fo. 1; for a modern assessment see W.R. Keylor, 'Versailles and International Diplomacy', in M. Boemeke, G.D. Feldman and E. Glaser (eds.), *The Treaty of Versailles: A Reassessment after 75 Years* (Cambridge, 1995), 469–505.

which thus combine, may only do so slowly, and in accordance with their own special interests. Each power is the judge in its own cause, and no one knows how & when it will decide. Hence no concerted plan. [...] What you want is [that] all nations should combine at once ag[ain]st the domination nation. How can you do this best? Clearly not by the Bal[an]ce of Power but by the League. For the League implies definite texts – limitation of armaments, territorial guarantees, prohibition of war.[117]

The 1919 settlement 'did rep[resen]t an attempt to resettle Europe on the basis of nat[iona]l self-det[erminatio]n'. Temperley was by no means blind to its shortcomings and failures. The continent's ethnographic complexities, more especially, confounded the peace-makers: 'The destinies of certain peoples were decided by about 30 or 40 men, many of whom knew very little about the ethnic questions at issue'. For his own part, Temperley admitted to partial defeat on this point: 'Ethnography is the beginning of all study of boundaries. I wish it were the end of it'.[118]

For all its lofty ambitions, in at least one respect the 1919 settlement fell well short of the achievements of previous peace treaties: 'The moral is that statesmen like Cast[lerea]gh, if narrow and hard, were more prudent than the men of our day. We c[oul]d not give [a] more lasting peace than they did, it is already apparent that we have not'.[119] Nevertheless, the League provided the only viable mechanism now for resolving international disputes: 'One thing is certain ... there is no remedy for the ills of the world if the League does not succeed'. In that event, 'war will come again & a more terrible & devastating war than we can imagine. It can only be averted by a res[olu]te resort to the ways of peace, and for that the only instrument is the League'.[120]

Towards the end of the conference, Temperley was appointed editor to supervise the production of a semi-official history under the newly founded Royal Institute for International Affairs.[121] While some of the participants of the peace conference looked askance at this multivolume compilation,[122] the

[117] Temperley, 'Peace Conference Lecture', part II, fos. 14–15.
[118] Temperley, 'Peace Conference Lecture', part II, fos. 9–10.
[119] Temperley, 'Peace Conference Lecture', part II, fo. 89.
[120] Temperley, 'Peace Conference Lecture', part II, fo. 91.
[121] 'Report of the Provisional Committee appointed to prepare a Constitution, and select the original members of the British Branch of the Institute of International Affairs', n.d. [1919], Headlam-Morley MSS, Churchill College Archive Centre, Cambridge, HDLM/Acc. 727/43; Temperley to Webster, 24 Sept. 1919, Webster MSS, Webster 1/3/49.
[122] Sir Robert Borden, the Canadian prime minister, complained that he had not been given due prominence: 'There is not the slightest reference to me in the index of either volume although the Prime Ministers of each of the other Dominions are specifically mentioned in relation to the work of the Conference. The only reference to myself [*sic*] ... is at page 503, vol. I, where in a

work nevertheless offers a glimpse into Temperley's views on international affairs. In his editorial guidance, he urged the various contributors to 'aim at the international point of view, [and] to adopt a Geneva perspective'. The 1919 settlement was 'a great constructive experiment', 'a definite attempt to establish the reign of law above that of force'.[123]

The war of 1914–18, he observed in 1920, had been 'a conflict between the principles of freedom and of autocracy, between the principles of moral influence and of material force, of government by consent and of government by compulsion', a conflict in which Temperley explicitly associated 'Anglo-Saxondom [with] ... democracy itself'. The Paris peace settlement had 'deliberately sought to change the centre of gravity and thus bring Europe and America into harmony and thus create an international organization'. With the League a new body had been created 'to enforce peace and repair wrong or injustice'. In future, he prognosticated, the 'welfare of the world depends upon its democracies understanding the new principles on which they are to be governed, and on their combining together to make the noblest of them a reality'.[124]

The mature scholar of international repute Temperley was vociferous in his condemnation of all attempts to turn history into the handmaiden of religious, philosophical or political dogma: 'History should be studied for herself alone. The appeal history makes is both intellectual and emotional but it is limited and objective in its scope, and becoming more so'.[125] For all that, he projected the old Liberal programme of progress and reform onto a larger canvass, 'with moral progress measured by the international advance of the principles of Wilson and the League of Nations'.[126] Temperley understood that, as any political entity, the League would be 'incessantly developing and changing its colours and shape'. Its continued validity, indeed necessity, was never in doubt, however.[127]

The war years and his involvement in the peace conference and its aftermath also sharpened Temperley's focus on the historical problem of the 'balance of

---

list of Commissioners my name is mentioned as Vice-President of the Commission on Greek and Albanian Affairs', Borden to Christie (confidential), 20 Nov. 1920, Perley MSS, Library and Archives of Canada, Ottawa, MG II D12, vol. 12, file 3.

[123] H.W.V. Temperley, 'Suggestions to Contributors', n.d. [1919], Webster MSS, Webster 1/3/30.

[124] H.W.V. Temperley, 'Introduction', in H.W.V. Temperley (ed.), *A History of the Peace Conference of Paris* (6 vols, London, 1920–4), i, xxiii xxx and xxxi.

[125] Temperley, *Research and Modern History*, 18; Howarth, *Cambridge*, 199; for a Butterfield-inspired critique of Temperley's 'technical history', see M. Bentley, *Modernising England's Past: English Historiography in the Age of Modernism, 1870–1970* (Cambridge, 2005), 108.

[126] See the pertinent observations by V. Feske, *From Belloc to Churchill: Private Scholars, Public Culture, and the Crisis of British Liberalism, 1900–1939* (Chapel Hill, NC, 1996), 168–9.

[127] H. Temperley, *The Second Year of the League: A Study of the Assembly of the League of Nations* (London, 1923), v and *passim*.

power'. If in the eighteenth century it meant 'equalization of Power or "rationing" of power', by the end of the nineteenth century, equilibrist ideas had created 'an extremely perilous situation when increases of armaments was added to the narrowing down of competing groups'. After the world war, he concluded that '[t]here is no more room for national individualism & loose unions of free states than there is for neutrals. So I am led to think that the League of Nations ... is the true solution, for the Balance of Power, in the sense of organized allied groups, means ultimately war, and war will not be possible if existing governments are to remain'.[128]

For all the significance Temperley attached to the League, he was nevertheless sceptical about the utility of international law. It was akin, he thought, to what 'people meant in the 18th century by the law of nations. That is, something nobody exactly understands but which they find very convenient to use in argument against an opponent who is considered very wicked'.[129] Nor, indeed, was he blind to the inherent fragility of the League as 'an experiment of great novelty and daring'. Its very *raison d'être* was 'opposed to instincts and traditions that are stronger than is usually recognized, because they are instincts and traditions – not reasons and clearly expressed aims'. To succeed it required 'the support of all those who see beyond the limits of the nation state'. The League as an attempt to organize peace was thus 'at once necessary, reasonable, and possible'.[130]

To the end, Temperley continued to regard the League as necessary and reasonable. In 1934, he became the first president of the internationalist New Commonwealth Institute, and in that role did much to preserve 'the research character of the Institute' against attempts to manipulate its work for political ends.[131] And as president of the International Congress for Historical Sciences in the 1930s he emphasized scholarly cooperation as the 'way of peace'.[132] But by the late 1930s, he, too, began to doubt whether the League was possible any longer.[133] British foreign policy, meanwhile, seemed to have settled into a neo-Canningite groove, as he noted with a touch of complacency in 1938: 'England

---

[128] Temperley to Satow, 21 July 1920, Satow MSS, PRO 30/33/13/10. The letter also foreshadowed Temperley's return to the subject of Canning's foreign policy.

[129] Temperley to Satow, 18 Apr. 1923 (TS copy), Temperley MSS; see also 'War of Jenkins' Ear', 219–20: 'that last refuge of bankrupt diplomatists of that age, "the Law of Nations"'.

[130] A.J. Grant and H.W.V. Temperley, *Europe in the Nineteenth and Twentieth Centuries (1789–1932)* (London, 4th edn repr. 1935), 691; see also his letter to *The Times*, 17 Sept. 1923, commenting on Italy's attempts to subvert the League structures.

[131] Schwarzenberger to Butterfield, 3 May 1949, Butterfield MSS, BUTT/8. Georg Schwarzenberger (1908–91), a German-Jewish refugee, Professor of International Law, University College London, 1962–75.

[132] 'Historians in Congress', *The Times*, 30 Aug. 1938. Temperley was president of the congress, 1933–38.

[133] Temperley to Seton-Watson, 25 June 1938, Butterfield MSS, BUTT/311.

will never guarantee Czecho-Slovakia, because, except in Shakespeare, it is not on the sea. But I am not very despondent on the situation. Hitler knows well enough that the Czechs will fight, and that it is a very different pair of shoes from Austria'.[134]

Temperley, in fact, derived no small degree of satisfaction from the re-emergence of the Canning tradition. In a letter to *The Times* he emphasized that Neville Chamberlain's speech in parliament on the Runciman mission to Prague was 'a conscious (or unconscious) echo of Canning's very words'.[135] In response, the prime minister opted for the 'unconscious echo' and suggested that his words were 'simply the continuity of English thought in somewhat similar circumstances'.[136] Indeed, Chamberlain subsequently read Temperley's 1925 study of Canning's foreign policy, which he 'found ... so fascinating that I preferred it to any novel or detective story even after a day on the moors'. He had not been 'brought up not as a politician but as a business man [*sic*], and until quite recently I had no notion that I should ever have any special responsibility for foreign affairs. My history has therefore been somewhat neglected and ... I did not realize that Canning had such a definite foreign policy'. Temperley's monograph, he concluded, had given him 'great encouragement & fortification to find how closely the views & principles at which I had empirically arrived resembled those enunciated by Canning. The parallels in the problems continually recur and it is an added strength to feel that I am walking in the footsteps of that great man'.[137] For his part, Temperley encouraged the premier to emulate Canning. Convalescing in a nursing home, he confessed that

> I was thrilled to hear of your going to meet Hitler and of your intentions to return. Your position seems to me exactly like Canning's over Portugal [in 1823] when he sent troops to uphold her territorial integrity in accordance with our old treaties and thereby upheld not only Portugal but the sanctity of treaties. This was the occasion of his famous Speech about calling the New World into existence. You are now in the same position. The support of the whole country is with you. May you have the same dazzling success! God be with you in these days![138]

---

[134] Temperley to Seton-Watson, 23 Mar. 1938, Seton-Watson MSS, SEW/17/28/4; Temperley, 'Hungarian Frontiers', 438; see also his letter to *The Times*, 4 May 1938, in which he emphasized the role of Czechoslovakia as an element of stability. Temperley became a founder-member of the London-based Czechoslovak Committee, see letter to *The Times*, 21 May 1938.
[135] Temperley to *The Times*, 28 July 1938.
[136] Chamberlain to *The Times*, 29 July 1938.
[137] Chamberlain to Temperley, 11 Sept. 1938, Temperley MSS.
[138] Temperley to Chamberlain, 20 Sept. 1938, Chamberlain MSS, Birmingham University Library, NC 7/11/31/268; also in Fair, *Temperley*, 285.

Temperley was not to live to witness how 'dazzling success' at Munich turned to ashes within less than a year. 'Peace proclaimed – I hope a lasting one', he had recorded in his diary at the time.[139] It was the last flickering of his internationalism.

By 1938, Temperley had long ceased to be involved behind the scenes of international diplomacy. He had returned to Cambridge and academic work in 1921, where Canning, his old hero, attracted his attention once more. There was little of the youthful exuberance of 1905, however, in his altogether more restrained and vastly more scholarly chapter in A.W. Ward's *Cambridge History of British Foreign Policy* and then in his masterly monograph on Canning, which established him as one of the foremost diplomatic historians of his generation and which gave Neville Chamberlain so much food for thought over a dozen years later.[140] Further work on diplomatic history was to follow over the years, though the planned three-volume study of Britain in the Near East up to 1878 never materialized beyond the first instalment which examined the period until the end of the Crimean War.[141] Between 1924 and 1938, in conjunction with G.P. Gooch, he edited the British official documents on the origins of the war.[142] From 1923 he was the founder editor of the *Cambridge Historical Journal*, until he stepped down in 1937.[143] In 1925, the university awarded him the degree of D.Litt. in recognition of his scholarly work. Temperley, as one of the assessors commented, was 'one of the chief living authorities on the history of British diplomacy', and his work would 'remain for many years the chief authority on the subject'. He also praised the compilation on the 1919 peace conference and his own contributions to it 'connected with the dissolution and liquidation of the Austrian Monarchy. In fact he ranks among the few writers who have applied

---

[139] Temperley diary, 30 Sept. 1938, Temperley MSS.

[140] H.W.V. Temperley, 'The Foreign Policy of Canning, 1820–1827', in A.W. Ward and G.P. Gooch (eds), *Cambridge History of British Foreign Policy, 1783–1919* (3 vols, Cambridge, 1921–3), ii, 51–118; H.W.V. Temperley, *The Foreign Policy of Canning, 1822–1827* (London, 1925); see also Howarth, *Cambridge*, 112–13.

[141] Temperley to Hymans, 14 May 1923, Temperley MSS; Temperley, *England and the Near East: The Crimea* (London, 1936). Arrangements had been made with Longmans, Temperley to Webster, 20 June 1935, Webster MSS, 1/14/30. The project led to the famous rift with Webster, not healed until the autumn of 1938, see Webster to Temperley, 29 Sept. 1938, Temperley MSS; and vice versa, 4 Oct. [1938], Webster MSS, 1/16/73.

[142] G.P. Gooch and H.W.V. Temperley (eds), *British Documents on the Origins of the War, 1898–1914* (11 vols, London, 1926–38); 'Origins of the War', *The Times*, 10 Oct. 1927; for the background see F. Eyck, *G.P. Gooch: A Study in History and Politics* (London, 1982), 359–405; and K.A. Hamilton, 'The Pursuit of "Enlightened Patriotism": The British Foreign Office and Historical Researchers during the Great War and Its Aftermath', *Historical Research* lxi, 3 (1988), 316–44.

[143] Reddaway to Temperley, 28 Nov. 1937, Temperley MSS.

themselves with real knowledge and historical training to the very difficult task of writing contemporary history'.[144]

There were the inevitable disappointments of academia. Temperley, it seems, may well have entertained secret hopes for the Regius chair when it fell vacant in 1927. Whatever his own ambitions, the appointment of G.M. Trevelyan meant 'goodbye to the day dreams of enthroning Modern and Diplomatic History on the Regius Chair'.[145] Nevertheless, in 1930, the university made him professor of modern history. His inaugural lecture, delivered in November of that year, revealed something of his personal scholarly *credo*. Immersion in the past through studying the sources and through imbibing something of the culture of foreign countries was central to his mind:

> I do not think that any historian, however gifted, is within the range of understanding the situation [Sarajevo, 28 June 1914] unless he has known Serbian or Bosnian students or *Comitadjis* at first hand. They are not all like either the students or even the burglars [!] with whom we are ... familiar in more Western lands. Similarly the Turk, as he was in the old days in Macedonia before the Balkan Wars, is a personage who had to be seen to be believed.[146]

Temperley's ability to draw on his own personal experience, noted G.M. Trevelyan, made his pronouncements all the more authoritative.[147] His academic progress continued at a steady pace. Publications kept pouring forth from his pen: 'I am doing what I hope never to do again – that is preparing for press five books at one time'.[148] In May 1938 his 'great enterprise [the *British Documents*] ha[d] now come to a successful conclusion'.[149] Two months later

---

[144] Headlam-Morley, 'Report on the Application of Mr. Harold Temperley, for the Degree of Doctor of Letters', 18 Apr. 1925, Headlam-Morley MSS, HDLM/Acc. 727/39; also Clapham to Headlam-Morley, 3 and 6 Mar. 1925 and replies 5 and 7 Mar. 1925, Headlam-Morley MSS, HDLM/Acc. 727/39. The reason for Temperley's application was rooted in University politics. He was alone among those dons opposed to automatic doctorates of Divinity to bishops in not having a doctorate himself, H.N.V. Temperley, 'Recollections', fo. 20.

[145] Temperley to Webster, 20 July 1927, Webster MSS, Webster 1/9/43; see D. Cannadine, *G.M. Trevelyan: A Life in History* (London, 1993 (pb)), 16. Temperley had also tried to get Headlam-Morley interested, Temperley to Headlam-Morley, 11 June 1927, Headlam-Morley MSS, HDLM/Acc. 727/40.

[146] Temperley, *Research and Modern History*, 10–11; also 'Professor Temperley on Research', *The Times*, 20 Nov. 1930.

[147] Trevelyan to Temperley, 19 Nov. 1930, Temperley MSS.

[148] Temperley to Betty Behrens, 1 Apr. 1938, Behrens MSS, CCAC, BEHR/Add/14.

[149] Gaselee to Temperley, 14 May 1938, Temperley MSS.

he succeeded Field Marshal Lord Birdwood as Master of Peterhouse.[150] He was not to occupy the Master's Lodge on the Trumpington Road for long. On 11 July 1939, he died after a protracted illness, to some extent the after-effect of his old wartime infirmities.[151]

---

[150] He was proposed by W. Emery Barnes, Roy Lubbock, Herbert Butterfield, Bertrand L. Hallwood, Ernest Barker, Charles Burkill, H.S. Sams, W.K.C. Guthrie, R.G. Heard and Munia Postan, to Temperley, 6 Dec. 1937, Temperley MSS.
[151] He had suffered a coronary thrombosis on 24 Apr. 1939, see H.N.V. Temperley, 'Recollections', fo. 22.

The Diaries, 1916–1939

1916

19th June 1916[1]

The crisis in Greece is rapidly approaching a head. The elements are three men: Venizelos[2], Constantine,[3] Sarrail[4] – statesman, King, general. The crisis dates from September last year when Venizelos asked us to Salonika. Looking back it seems to me very doubtful if he did. <The F[oreign] O[ffice] could find no direct evidence that he asked us.> He has threatened an unqualified denial, and appealed to the honour and moral character of Sir Edward Grey[5] to prevent that assertion being made. He has formally protested when the troops arrived – the wish he originally expressed was general not specific, and qualified by the King's accompanying request not to send 150,000 troops.

None the less we came, to find ourselves surrounded by spies, agents, provocateurs and pro-German intrigues of all sorts, emanating from Consuls & wireless. The King's game was deep and crafty. He proclaimed himself not a pro-German but a Greek – he kept his army mobilised, he resisted steadily every attempt to benefit or assist the Allies, and resisted it in the name of Greek patriotism. He proclaimed the wrongs of Greece to the world in indignant tones to cosmopolitan or neutral or German journalists. He kept in office a ministry of patriarchal place-hunters in which Skoloudis[6] was suspected of being in German

---

[1] Inserted at end of volume Jan.–June 1917.

[2] Eleftherios Kyriakou Venizelos (1864–1936), Greek politician of Cretan extraction; Cretan Minister of Justice, 1899–1901 and 1908–10; Cretan Prime Minister, 1910; Greek Prime Minister, 1910–15, 1915, 1917–20, 1924, 1928–32, 1932 and 1933; Foreign Minister, 1915; Minister of Military Affairs, 1917–20.

[3] King Constantine I of Greece (née of Schleswig-Holstein-Sonderburg-Glücksburg) (1868–1923), King of the Hellenes, 1913–17 and 1920–22; in exile June 1917–Dec. 1920 and since Sept. 1922.

[4] General Maurice-Paul-Emmanuel Sarrail (1856–1929), French army officer with openly Socialist views; commanded 3rd Army, 1914; 'Army of the Orient' at Salonika, 1915–17; interfered in Greek politics; French high commissioner in Syria, 1924–25.

[5] Sir Edward Grey (1862–1933), 1st Viscount Grey of Fallodon, cr. 1916, politician; MP (Lib.) Berwick-upon-Tweed, 1885–1916; Parliamentary Under-secretary for Foreign Affairs, 1892–95; Foreign Secretary, 1905–16; ambassador at Washington, 1919–20.

[6] Stephanos Skouloudis (1838–1928), Greek diplomat and Liberal politician; Foreign Minister, 1897; Prime Minister, 1915–16.

paper [*recte* pay]. He called together a mock parliament and piled up a deficit of millions. For what? He showed his hand at the end of May. Long before he had refused the Serbians a land-passage from Corfu to Salonika, and set his sister to write a letter to reveal that he would blow up the Canal of Corinth rather than admit the Serbians through it. The Serbians, who were his allies whom he had abandoned, and whose treaty with him committed him to allowing the passage of troops. But it was all in vain – by the end of May over 110,000 Serbians had reached Salonika. At the same time, by a singular coincidence, 25,000 Bulgars advanced down the valley of the Struma, seized Fort Rupel, the key of the defile within Greek territory. The Greeks exchanged shots with their hereditary enemies. Apparently the rifles went off by themselves for orders from Athens forbade all resistance. One gleam of spirit Greece showed. When Bulgaria remonstrated over the bloodshed, Skoloudis declined indignantly to discuss the matter. No wonder! Greek women were being violated, Greek peasant shot, Greek cattle driven off in the districts which 'Ὁ Ναπολέων τῆς Ἑλλαδός'[7] had won for a happier Hellas in the days when he agreed with Venizelos. The thousands of pounds spent of Fort Rupel,[8] the key to Macedonia, weighed little beside the private designs of the King. Submarines appeared mysteriously off Salamis, secret meetings took place between the Greek Chief of Staff and the German Minister and Constantine at last appeared mysterious no longer. The secret Legations. The Allies at last were awakened and naval restrictions (the euphemism for a blockade) began on 6th May June.

Venizelos left office in the first week of October 1915, after having climbed the heights and been hauled down to the depths, Without office, a mere tongue and a mere name, he remained the greatest man in Greece, perhaps in the World. His huge parliamentary majority was destroyed by a dissolution and a new and packed parliament of pensioners assembled. Venizelos never hesitated. He denounced the sham assembly and forbade his followers to sit in it, a stroke as daring as unprecedented. Political abstention meant political annihilation to the Tories under Bolingbroke[9] and the Whigs under Fox.[10] It increased the influence of Venizelos in the ultimate events. Political practices he eschewed, the political

---

[7] The Napoleon of the Hellenes.

[8] Fort Rupel protected the Rupel pass into Bulgaria and the Struma Valley, the main invasion route south to Salonika. Its occupation on 26 May 1916 led to the *Noemvriana* ('November events') in 1916, the confrontation between King Constantine and Prime Minister Venizelos.

[9] Henry St. John (1678–1751), 1st Viscount Bolingbroke, cr. 1712, politician and diplomat; MP (Tory) Wootton Bassett, 1701–12; Secretary for War, 1704–1708; Secretary of State for Northern Department, 1710–13; for Southern Department, 1710–14; plotted Jacobite restoration in 1715; in French exile, 1715–23 and 1735–42; best known as the author of *A Dissertation on Parties* (1733–34) and *Idea of a Patriot King* (1738).

[10] Charles James Fox (1749–1806), politician; MP (Whig) Midhurst, 1768–84, Westminster, 1780–1806; Foreign Secretary, 1782, 1783 and 1806; Whig leader, 1783–1806.

education <of the peope>, through the Press and by lectures, he planned and achieved. While the debts mounted, and the Greek army remained mobilised, he poured forth his indignant tale of wrongs in the Keryx.[11] Sarrail consolidated his hold on Salonika, expelled Germans, and, after the Bulgarian advance on Rupel, proclaimed martial law. Venizelos steadily worried at the Government – a constitutional Halifax of discretion.[12] Seats fell vacant – a follower offered himself at Chios and found none to oppose him, he stood for Mitylene and triumphed – a follower stood for Drama, the town where it was remembered Venizelos had been willing to surrender Cavalla, a town with a fez vote of Turkish inhabitants who saw in Venizelos their greatest foe. Drama elected the Venizelist by thousands, despite the intrigues of the Court. Triumphant in three election, the Venizelists still refused to sit in a parliament they had taught everyone to dispise. Even the machinations of the Government could not withstand his influence. A mob, urged on by the police, broke the windows of his newspaper offices, but popular influences remained on his side. The King declared that On the Fete day of the Independence of Greece, the crowd had praised Venizelos to his face and gathered round him in thousands whilst the King passed comparatively unnoticed and sent the police to disperse the admirers of his rival. A curious parallel was here to the Mansion House Feast when <the young> George III was disregarded by the mob, drew horses out of Pitt's carriage & long embraced his footmen and kissed his horses. Later, after the Rupel incident, the King on <the King's birthday the King told> a diplomatist of the Entente that the crowd was with difficulty prevented from taking the horses from the carriage of the German Minister. (One hardly understands the difficulty as he rode in a motor!) All the other popular émentes, by which the King's instruments set such store, were equally ludicrous and hollow. The Venizelos was mighty yet. His newspapers came out in black, when they announced the fall of Rupel and asked if was <it> for this that the <Greek> Army remained mobilised? He himself felt this danger. "Men watching to kill you", said one warning to him. He burnt his boats in the Keryx and attacked the King and Ministry openly, trusting to Greece and to his star. He planned to go to Salonika, with regiments that were faithful to him, and there to proclaim a Provisional Government, not throwing off allegiance to the King, but governing in his name and without him. England looked coldly on this project, but offered to send a gunboat to the Piraeus to protect him. It is believed that his arrest and that his chief supporters was planned. But the Entente front was firm and the plan failed.

---

[11] *Ethnikos Keryx* (*National Herald*), New York-based Greek-language newspaper, founded in 1915.

[12] George Savile (1633–1695), Viscount Halifax, cr. 1668, 1st Marquess of Halifax, cr. 1682, politician; Lord Privy Seal, 1682–85 and 1688–90; Lord President of the Council, 1685; supported the Stuart Restoration in 1660, but transferred his allegiance to William of Orange in 1688, see his *The Character of a Trimmer* (1690).

1916 Ll[oyd] G[eorge] Interview

21/8/16

Views of Lloyd George[13] at breakfast.

Grey hair, a little pursed up mouth, no sign of – curious, rather shifty eyes – 1 different from the other – fleshy as the underjaw.

1st about the Eisteddfod – wonderful Aberystwyth, scenery grand all around – we want space – a plan – it's quite Athenian. A sycophant we have to thank. There is the finest air, straight from the Atlantic.

I felt it like a consecration, in the midst of war. I did really – and these rolling organs of voice, deepmouthed [*sic*]. This man was a talent – he stitched notes together – all from Wagner, one from Li[s]zt[,] one from Beethoven, a tailor by profession & by trade, a poor musician but he understood the Welsh – he had an idea that mountaineers can sing – a mountaineer, if consumptive, has to go to the plains, if he goes into the hills he must have (an expansive gesture) a bellows. That's what the tailor understood.

<u>Moi</u> 'A tailor sh[oul]d understand chest measurements'.

He (laughing): 'A point'.

Parry[14] on the other hand is a genius. *Dies irae* D – D – D ... singing tune.

The best Eisteddfod I was ever at – the seriousness, the war. <Before going to another Eisted[dfod]> I sh[oul]d like to go to a hotel & get away for a few days from this dirty bloody business, I should really.

Now about high politics. What are the main points?

Eng[lan]d – I don't want the war to end too soon. Why? Our position next year will be much greater – we shall be the finest armed fleet & army. We shall be giving Russia then the crumbs, just the crumbs! In 1915 we had only 75,000 shells on the L[ines] of C[ommunication]. How we did it, I don't know. We shall have a greater prod[uctio]n than France: we went for guns, they for shells in 1915.

---

[13] David Lloyd George (1863–1945), 1st Earl Lloyd George of Dwyfor, cr. 1945, politician; MP (Lib), Carnarvon Boroughs, 1890–1945; President of the Board of Trade, 1905–1908; Chancellor of the Exchequer, 1908–15; Minister of Munitions, 1915–16; Secretary of State for War, 1916; Prime Minister, 1916–22.

[14] Sir (Charles) Hubert (Hastings) Parry, 1st Bart. (1848–1918), English composer; Director of the Royal College of Music, 1895–1918; Professor of Music, Oxford, 1900–1908. The reference is to Parry's *Thanksgiving Te Deum*, first performed at the Three Choirs Festival in September 1900, see J. Dibble, *C. Hubert H. Parry: His Life and Music* (Oxford, 1998 (pb)), 371–73.

Our young officers – very plucky fellows but fine – some we know big game shooters, athletes, philistines (with a look at D[avid] D[avies][15]) – very plucky but they didn't know their business. Then they will, better than the Germans. They didn't know about this trench warfare – they believed in manoeuvres, great charges over wide spaces, storming with a rush – not digging (expanding his hands).

Russia is a danger – there are no men, at least no great men – the country, the people are good, the Government is horrible – the Czar is a very weak man. They get rid of all their good men, or men with liberal ideas – Sazonoff,[16] Polivanoff.[17] I heard a story from Wolfe Murray[18] who was over in Russia at a reception in the field by the Czar. He passed round bowing & speaking a word here & there, and he cut Polivanoff dead, the war min[iste]r who had come all the way from Petrograd to see him.

Oh terrible – reactionaries and bureaucrats put up their heads directly victory begins to show.

Now it is better for us that we should be in Germany than they. On the Western front the defences are so strong, the slaughter so great. They have twice as many men there & nearly three times – prob[abl]y the same number of guns. In the West we have 2 divisions every 2 miles – in the East it is 22. We do really. On a thousand mile front they will break through.

What w[oul]d suit us is that we sh[oul]d be in Cologne, and they more or less where they are, at any rate not beyond the Vistula.

Our guns will be tremendous because we made guns, while France made shells. We shall have far greater output than France and give Russia the crumbs, just the crumbs.

Autonomy for Poland, of the Slavs. We have done our best for [them]. We are bound by Treaties, with Russia over Turkey, with R[omani]a which I don't like. We have done our best for the Slavs and backed Russia.

But mind you, we cannot say no to Russia too much because in the military sense they have played the game – oh, yes, absolutely – backed up up everywhere, gallantly & recklessly. Chivalry – look at East. Russia in the beginning of the war & look at Galicia in response to Italy.

---

[15] David Davies (1880–1944), 1st Baron Davies, cr. 1932, politician and philanthropist; MP (Lib.), Montgomeryshire, 1906–29.

[16] Sergei Dimitrievich Sazonov (1860–1927), Russian diplomat; minister at Holy See, 1906–1909; Assistant Foreign Minister, 1909–10; Foreign Minister, 1910–16; represented White Russians at Paris peace conference, 1919.

[17] General Alexei Andre'evich Polivanov (1855–1920), Russian army officer; Chief of General Staff, 1906; Vice-minister of War, 1906–12; Minister of War, 1915–16; joined Red Army in 1920.

[18] General Sir James (Wolfe) Murray (1853–1919), British army officer; Army representative on British parliamentary delegation to Russia, 1912; Chief of the Imperial General Staff, 1914–15; General Officer Commanding, Eastern Command, 1915–17.

France cannot help us much – she is an ally, and the enemy is on her soil. Therefore she sympathizes with Russia.

But we wish to keep our heads – we wish to do something for civilization with France. We cannot say too much of morals because of those horrible black countries.

If we could have come without them, and said to Russia 'you cannot take Poland & too much of Galicia'. We are a swollen boa constrictor, with our little cobras. Botha[19] wants [German] S[outh] W[est] Africa & E[ast] Africa – hundreds of thousands of miles of territory. New Zealand wants Samoa & Australia all little colon[ie]s – no we can't protest, when we are gorged with Mesopotamia'.

23/11/16

<u>An anecdote</u> at first hand about Sir J[ohn] Cowans[20] – a letter was written by one who was a subordinate. The case with regard to this man is that he has been found wanting of severe criticism. To whom does the country look, high or low, for justice without fear of favour? Whom does it trust? Can you not fulfil this trust? If you do fulfil it, it will carry the nation with you and so on in an exciting strain, and one very remarkable to a high person. The high person came in, glared hard at the trembling subordinate, glared long – then, sharply, 'I am making this man a [Knight of the] G[rand] C[ross of the] B[ath], decorating him, you know'. Then suddenly roared with laughter 'Your letter was quite right – he *is* going. And now he has gone'. <But he didn't go – he was too indispensable. He was retained, and informed of His Majesty's displeasure.>

Gov[ernmen]t Fr[ench] views on <u>Mil[itar]y Conv[entio]n</u> 9th Aug[ust 1916]

1. Max[imu]m of 10 days betw[een] Allied offensive at Sal[oni]ca & R[omania]n [offensive] on A[ustria-]H[ungary].
2. Decl[aratio]n of war by R[omani]a on A[ustria-]H[ungary] & defensive attitude of R[omania]ns on Bulg[aria]n frontier.
3. Adm[issio]n of R[omani]a to peace neg[otiatio]ns on footing of equality.
4. Promise of Powers not to treat before assuring to R[omani]a promised terr[itor]ies with reserve of their own aspirations.
5. Sugg[estio]n that Allied army sh[oul]d begin at Sal[oni]ca 3 days after agreement, & R[omani]a 13 days at the latest. (10 acc[ord]ing to 18/8/16)

---

[19] General Louis Botha (1862–1919), Boer leader and South African politician; Prime Minister, Transvaal, 1907–10; Prime Minister of the Union of South Africa, 1910–19.

[20] General Sir John Stephen Cowans (1862–1921), army commander; entered army, 1881; Director-General of the Territorial Forces, 1910–12; Quartermaster-General, 1912–19.

Russian Amb[assado]r on Pol[itical] Convention 9/8/16
P
in R[omani]a to 1/14
Off[ensi]ve from Sal[oni]ca depends on F[ran]ce & Eng[lan]d
Project

1. G[reat] B[ritain], F[rance], I[taly] & R[ussia] guarantee present terr[itoria]l integ[rit]y of R[omani]a.
2. R[omani]a to declare war on A[ustria-]H[ungary] & to break dip[lomati]c, ec[onomic] & commercial relations with enemies of Allies.
3. G[reat] B[ritain], F[rance], I[taly] & R[ussia] recognize to R[omani]a r[igh]t of annexing terr[itor]ies of A[ustria-]H[ungary] as
4. n[ea]r Novoselitza, up Pruth to frontier of Galicia at confluence of Pruth & Czeremos – follows frontier of Gal[ici]a & Buk[ovina] & Gal[ici]a & H[ungar]y to p[oin]t Stag hill 1655 – line of sep[aratio]n betw[een] waters of Tisza & Visso to touch the Tisza near where it unites with the Visso (Between confl[uen]ce of Visso & Tisza & Stag – frontier ult[imat]ely est[ablish]ed by a mixed R[usso-]R[omanian] delimit[atio]n comm[issio]n.) descends the Tisza from confl[uen]ce of Tisza & Szamos, passing 4 km N[orth] of the said confl[uen]ce the village of VASAROS – NAMENY - S[outh] S[outh-]W[est] to a point 6 km to N[orth] of DEBRECZEN. From this it will follow the same direction & pass 3 km W[est] of the confluence of the Criseko (Körös) & S[outh], making a bend, a km W[est] of village BEKES-SAMSONIN to rejoin Tisza at height of village ALGYO – N[orth] of SZEGEDIN[21] descend Tisza & follow Danube to R[omania]n frontier. (R[omani]a will not erect fortifications n[ea]r Belgrade in a zone to be det[ermine]d subsequ[entl]y & will only keep police forces in this zone. R[omania]n Gov[ernmen]t will indemnify Serbs of Banat who emigrate.

   1. to settle the 100 disputes over bound[arie]s etc. that will arise
   2. to put into effect internat[iona]l[i]sed control where deemed desirable – Macedonia, Albania, Luxemburg etc.

None of these things can be done – they will change the face of the world – if they are only partially done, they will [incomplete]

4 General Principles

(1) Balance of Power

---

[21] Szeged in the Great Plain of southern Hungary.

(2) Naval Supremnacy
(3) Nat[iona]l[it]y – r[igh]t of ea[ch] nation to exist
~~(4) Moral Principles~~
Internationality – est[ablishme]nt of a moral tribunal.

'The most fatal & in their sequel the most gigantic errors of men are also frequently the most excusable & the least gratuitous. They are committed when a strong impetus of right carries them up to a certain point, and a residue of that impetus, drawn from the contact with human [passion and] infirmity, pushes them beyond it. They vault into the saddle; they fall on the other side'.[22]

The only way to square up with France first, & neg[otia]te with Italy & Russia later.

We shall have to deal with all sorts of complicated questions. How are to meet them? Without forethought we shall be done in the deals. By thinking out our policies beforehand with regard to ea[ch] c[oun]try & disput[ed] terr[itor]ies. Having a policy on everything – map – boundaries – nat[ionali]ty questions – strategical etc.

What is that policy

(1) Bal[an]ce of Power
                        operations of power not entirely satisfying
(2) Naval Supremacy
                        both old & fairly obvious
(3) Nat[ionali]ty – new & not sufficiently tried, but use it so far as you can, e.g. Alsace Lorraine, Poland etc. Work it out carefully.
(4) Internat[ionali]ty – est[ablishme]nt of an international tribunal – most essential.

'Whence came you Venizelos o'er the dark Aegean wave?
I came from fettered Athens where a man must be a slave.
I go to the free islands, not to conquer but to save
Freedom breaking, freedom waking o'er the sea-girt anchored fleet.
Vessels wrought of Gods call making Chios, Mytilene, Crete
Lesbos, Samos, Lemnos waking Eleutherios to greet.
How far is Venizelos from the sovereign Constantine?
Far as old Olympus towers o'er Salonica's sealine.
Far as tyranny the hatred is from Liberty divine.
Bound in Athens lies my Hellas, weary limbs distraught
Snowy breast all bruised and wounded by a tyrant's heavy chain.
Heart and spirit free for ever in the Isles of Greece again'.

---

[22] William Gladstone, in Apr. 1871, commenting on the Franco-German War, see J. Morley, *The Life of William Ewart Gladstone* (3 vols, London, 1903), ii, 358.

17 Oct. [1916]

Things in Roumania going better, those in Greece worse. Russian diplomats are angry with Sarrail suggesting that his activity as a politician is only equalled by his tardiness as a general. They especially complain of his going down to the quay to greet Venizelos, saying that it is impossible to distinguish between an official and an unofficial handshake. Russia seems to fear the republicanism of France. Roumania doing better. Av[erescu][23] thinks he has the situation in hand with the 2nd or Northern Armies. Russian assistance beginning to tell. 3 Army Corps are a considerable force. A new plan for the winter attack on P's routes worked out & I wrote tod[a]y in summary that Venizelos' men, Gen[eral] Danglis,[24] Zambourakis, Joannae Christodolous, his prefect of Salonica, M. Adossides expected at Samos. Politis[25] his foreign minister late secretary general to Foreign Dep[artmen]t. [H]is Cretan administrators [and] the widely admired and universally liked Admiral Kunduriotis[26] [*sic*] were administrators of a type – far superior to the corrupt and self-seeking politicians and the pathetic professors (Lambris[27] [*sic*] etc.) who formed King Constantine's kaleidoscopic ministries!

18 Oct[obe]r [1916]

Since Tino's [i.e. Constantine's] display yesterday it seems to be clear that he still has considerable backing in Athens. As many Greeks are corrupt and self-seeking and German gold and threats are both abundant this is not surprising. Russia continues to hold herself resolutely pro-dynastic and to hold us to our

---

[23] Marshal Alexandru Averescu (1859–1938), Romanian military commander and politician; Chief of General Staff, 1911–13; commanded 2nd army, 1916; 3rd army from Sept. 1916; Foreign Minister, 1918; Prime Minister, 1918, 1920–21, 1926–27.

[24] General Panagiotis Danglis (1853–1924), Greek artillery officer and politician; chief of staff to Crown Prince Constantine's Army of Thessaly, 1912; a member of the Greek delegation at the London Peace Conference, 1912–13; MP (Lib.) for Epirus, 1915; Minister for War, 1916–18; president of the Liberal party, 1921–24.

[25] Nikolaos Politis (1872–1942), Greek diplomat; professor of law at Paris before 1914; Greek Foreign Minister, 1916–20, and 1922; Greek representative to the League of Nations; minister at Paris, 1935.

[26] Admiral Pavlos Kountouriotis (1855–1935), Greek naval officer and politician; aide-de-camp to King George I of Greece, 1908–11; commanded Greek fleet at battles of Elli (Dec. 1912) and Limnos (Jan. 1913); Navy Minister, 1917–20; Regent, 1920; President of Second Hellenic Republic, 1924–26 and 1929.

[27] That is, Professor Spyridon Lampros (1851–1919), Greek historian and politician; Provost of University of Athens, 1893–94 and 1912–13; Prime Minister, Oct. 1916–Feb. 1917.

promises. I wonder if the French will find some means to force the situation. I think probably.

The plan has changed from an attack via Xanthi or Drama[28] against Philippopolis to one via the Vardar line – Üsküb – Stip[29] with flank protection.

Old Barclay[30] at Bucharest said that as he had received warning on the 14th that the enemy might be there in a few hours he had destroyed all the archives and ciphers except 1915 and 1916, i.e. all the materials which mattered nothing, and left the compromising documents which would be exposed to the world as the diplomacy of *perfide Albion*, like our negotiations with Belgium found <by the Germans> in the archives of Brussels.[31]

19 October [1916]

Tino is drinking whiskey hard. His interview with the Russian Minister on 16th Sept[embe]r in which he spoke of 14 German divisions ag[ain]st R[ussi]a, the concentration of men & munitions at Larissa, the retention of Metaxas,[32] though he speaks poorly of Dusmanis,[33] the organized new design of Reservists, all <tend to> give the case against him. When we add to this his anger about the blowing up of the bridge at Demirhissar[34] (which prevented the railway connection with Seres), the information conveyed to us that the second Greek Army Corps was to go to the Struma (just about the time the occupation of Fort Rupel[35] by Bulgar-Germans was being arranged behind our backs, the construction of a road northwest from VODENA[36] to connect up with the Bulgarian one across the CRNA[37] and thus facilitate a Bulgarian advance from the West, the refusal to transport his allies the Serbs across Greece at the moment the surrender

---

[28] Greek towns in Thrace.
[29] Now Štip (Macedonia).
[30] Sir George Head Barclay (1862–1921), British diplomat; entered diplomatic service, 1886; minister at Tehran, 1908–12; at Bucharest, 1912–19; he left Bucharest on 25 Nov. 1916, and returned with the Romanian forces, 30 Nov. 1918; retired, 1919.
[31] See Auswärtiges Amt (ed.), *Das Erste Belgische Graubuch* (Berlin, 1915), *Das Zweite Belgische Graubuch* (Berlin, 1914) and *Belgische Aktenstücke, 1905–1914* (Berlin, 1915).
[32] General Ioannis Metaxas (1871–1941), Greek general and politician; Chief of General Staff, 1913–17; Prime Minister (with dictatorial emergency powers), 1936–41.
[33] Admiral Sofoklis Dousmanis (1868–1952), Greek naval officer and Royalist supporter; Chief of Naval General Staff, 1915–17, and 1921–22; Navy Minister, 1935.
[34] *Recte* Demirhisar, now Sidirokastro (Greece) in the Serres region of northern Greece on the Krousovitis river; in 1915 it fell under the control of the Central Powers.
[35] See entry 19 June 1916.
[36] Now Edessa (Greece).
[37] Also Crna Reka, a river in Macedonia; tributary of the Vardar river.

of Rupel was being arranged <with his hereditary enemies> and the advance against Vodena being planned, the fierce anger against Venizelos who would have frustrated these schemes, the German submarine near Salamis, the secret meetings with the German Minister and attaché, the secret messages which necessitated the control of the wires and the Government cipher by the French, the spies in Salonica, the intercepted correspondence, the telephoned speech of the Kaiser[38] overheard at Verdun – that Greece is our (Germany's) ally –, the kidnapping <by Bulgaria> of the IV Greek Army Corps at Kavalla[39] with the collusion of Pro-German officers, the evidence is overwhelming. For a moment, after the entry of Roumania [into the war], he seems genuinely to have hesitated, when he dismissed Dousmanis & Metaxas for Moschopoulos,[40] but the old German fear or love reasserted itself.

It is very like James II[41] & France: 'Come what may I never will declare war against France'. For James read Tino and for France Germany and you have the present situation.

20th [October 1916]

Sir F[rancis] Elliot[42] replied to the Gr[ee]k C[our]t Marshal as follows. The latter came from the K[ing] to complain of an incident in which the Athens crowd hissed the French marine patrols, caused a bayonet charge, and finally were only dispersed by being reminded by M. Mercouris,[43] an ex-mayor, that the King disapproved. The King's name could not be used for ever. Sir F[rancis] answered that it had so often been invoked by the party of disorder that its use against them could hardly be condemned and that M. Mercouris, like others who had raised the devil, found a difficulty in allaying it.

---

[38] Wilhelm II of Hohenzollern (1859–1941), King of Prussia and German Emperor, 1888–1918; abdicated 9 Nov. 1918.
[39] Now Kavala in southern Thrace (Greece).
[40] Lieutenant-General Konstantinos Moschopoulos (1854–1942), Greek army officer; Chief of General Staff, 1916–17; military governor of Epirus and Corfu, 1917–20.
[41] James II (and VII) Stuart (1633–1701), King of England, 1685–88; exiled in France since 1688.
[42] Sir Francis Edmund Hugh Elliot (1851–1940), British diplomat; entered diplomatic service, 1874; agent and consul-general at Sofia, 1895–1903; minister at Athens, 1903–17; Deputy Controller, Foreign Trade Department of Foreign Office, 1917–19.
[43] Georgios S. Mercouris (1886–1943), Greek politician; Minister for Food and Supply, 1921; Minister for the National Economy, 1926; Greek delegate to League of Nations, 1927; founded Greek National Socialist Party, 1934; Governor of the Bank of Greece, 1934.

21st [October 1916]

Letter from Strutt,[44] A[ide] D[e] C[amp] to Sarrail – Sal[oni]ca Sarrail v[er]y strained towards Cordonier[45] [sic] (who has since been degarnéréd). French v[er]y good men – hopeless transport – bad div[isiona]l c[ommande]rs & staff. S[arrai]l fully conscious of these defects – thought well of him, in spite of crit[ici]sms as a man who made up his mind and went straight to his end. Amery[46] says of him – 'a Lord Murray of Elibank,[47] but cast in a more heroic mould'.

Russians truly magnificent in every way.

S[er]b[ia]ns rather sick of doing all the fighting with no help from Fr[ance]. Voivode Mishitch[48] 'rotter of worst'.

Brit[i]s[h] tremendous sickness. B[riga]des masquerading as Div[isio]ns & B[attalio]ns as B[riga]des – all good exc[ept] X – got slaughtered at Nevoljen,[49] 9,000 cas[ualt]ies – dead everywhere, I sat on one by mistake. At least we, if on W[est], sh[oul]d have been in Mon[asti]r[50] by now.

Bulgars 'strategy'? tactics pitiable – do not like prolonged shellfire and incapable of standing up to heavy punishment for long.

R[omania]n Conv[entio]n p[oin]ts[51]

---

[44] Lieutenant-Colonel Edward Lisle Strutt (1874–1948), officer and mountaineer; served Boer War, 1900–1902, and Great War, 1914–19; helped the Emperor Charles into exile in Switzerland and then Madeira, 1919; High Commissioner of Danzig, 1920; second-in-command of British expedition to Mount Everest, 1922; President of the Alpine Club, 1935–38.

[45] General Victor Louis Émilien Cordonnier (1858–1936), French military commander; commanded left wing of Allied army during autumn offensive 1916; resigned over differences with Sarrail and retired on health grounds.

[46] Leopold Charles Maurice Stennett Amery (1873–1955), politician; MP (Cons.), Birmingham South (Sparkbrook), 1911–45; intelligence officer at Salonika, 1915; Assistant Secretary to the War Cabinet, 1917–19; Parliamentary Under-secretary for the Colonies, 1919–21; Financial Secretary to the Admiralty, 1921–22; First Lord of the Admiralty, 1922–24; Colonial Secretary, 1925–29; Secretary of State for India, 1940–45.

[47] Alexander William Charles Oliphant Murray (1870–1920), 1st Baron Murray of Elibank, cr. 1912, Liberal politician; MP (Lib.) Midlothian, 1900–1906 and 1910–12; Peebles and Selkirk, 1906–10; Comptroller of the Household, 1905–1909; Under-secretary of State for India, 1909–10; Parliamentary Secretary to the Treasury (that is, Chief Whip), 1910–12; resigned over Marconi shares scandal.

[48] *Vojvoda* (Field Marshal) Živojin Mišić (1855–1921), Serbian military commander; commanded First Serbian Army on the Salonika Front, 1916–18; Chief of Staff, Serbian Army High Command, 1918–20; Chief of General Staff, 1920–21.

[49] The Bulgarians repulsed French forces near the villages of Evikeni, Nevoljen and Topalovi on the Struma, southwest of Lake Doiran, 22–25 Oct. 1916.

[50] Now Bitola (Macedonia).

[51] The Treaty of Bucharest of 17 Aug. 1916 was signed following a separate Anglo-Romanian military convention of 13 Aug., negotiated and signed by Lt.-Col. C.B. Thomson (see entry

17/8/16 Pol[itical] to Theiss⁵² & Czernovitz⁵³
Equal[it]y at peace [conference]
Guarantee of terri[itoria]l integr[it]y by end of war by It[aly], F[ance], Russ[ia] Engl[an]d – equality of vote at peace conf[eren]ce – secret till end of war.

22 [October 1916]

Tino's effort great – he assents to demands for dismissal of his troops in Thessaly all except 3rd & 4th Corps (⅔ of whole) – 10,000 & 16th Brig[a]de on a war footing, about 10,000 men. Also at the same time as he wishes to demobilize he distributes 500 rifles & 10,000 r[oun]ds to the inhab[itan]ts of Volo. Poor innocent Tino!

24th [October 1916]

King of Sp<ain>⁵⁴ says he has inform[atio]n from Dobrudsha [*sic*] that Bulgaria was instructed by Germany to offer a secret treaty to R[omani]a & declare war immediately after. Thus was R[omani]a deceived – very likely say I.

25th [October 1916]

R[omania]n news bad.

Sal[oni]ca dec[isio]n again altered – after deciding ag[ain]st any offensive from Sal[oni]ca in May we decided for one in July, and after deciding not to reinforce at all, in October we decided to reinforce with 4 heavy batteries and 19,000 men, & <u>now</u> going further with a div[isio]n provided the Fr[ench] give one.

A description by a journalist today of an incident at Predeal Pass⁵⁵ in Roumania. Staff waiting. German officers impassive, erect, grimly professional,

---

17 Apr. 1917). Under article IV of the treaty, Romania was promised the Habsburg territories of Transylvania, the Banat and the Bukovina. Romania entered the war against the Central Powers on 27 Aug. 1916.

⁵²   Now Tisza or Tisa, river flowing from the Eastern Carpathenians to the Danube east of Novisad.

⁵³   Now Chernivtsi (Ukraine).

⁵⁴   Alfonso (León Fernando María Jaime Isidro Pascual Antonio de Borbón y Austria-Lorena) XIII (1886–1941), King of Spain, 1886/1902–1931.

⁵⁵   Pass in the Carpathian Mountains between Braşov and Bucharest.

Hungarian staff jovial, genial, expansive – sit on the ground, unpack their mule panniers, take out their lunch and take their Tokay. Then the news arrives, the pass is being forced, our troops <have> advanced. 'Eljen' cry the Magyars, waving their glasses and their flasks, 'here's to our gallant soldiers!' Nothing say the German officers – professional, unelated [sic], impassive & grimly erect. Strange this is almost word for word like Jokai's[56] scene of Germans and Magyars in Transsylvania in the mid-seventeenth century. Prince Kemeny[57] and his Magyar magnates sit cheerily over their dinner and their wine. A messenger comes in 'The Turks are approaching'. 'They will not disturb my dinner', says the Prince and he and his mercenaries sit. 'I should like to see those Turks', says the German captain of mercenaries arising. 'Better sit on', says the Kemeny, waving his glass. The German passes out, professional, impassive. Later on Kemeny himself sallies out, well-flushed with wine, interferes with the German's orders, loses the battle and his life – all for a glass of wine and a dinner. The parallel is almost exact. I hope that the Hungarians may lose the pas and that the shade of Jokai, that divine master of romance, may forgive me.

28th [October 1916]

Greek demobilization ordered. Tinos sh[oul]d knuckle under. He has 15,000 men in Thessaly which he now promises to disband. He has apparently become reconciled to the Venizelists, though he hopes Venizelos will not come to Athens, and has apparently satisfied the Central Powers. In all a marvellous man. He is said to drink whisky heavily of late.

The K[in]g of Roumania displays same character – sacks Gen[eral] Culcer[58] of the 1st Army, warns Averesco [sic] of the 2nd of the fate of Culcer and points out that in the north they have succeeded because they counterattacked. <The counter-attacks in the north – the R[omania]n general who of all has done the best is General Presan[59] [sic] – appointed because his sister was the 'bonne amie'

---

[56] Mór (also Maurus) Jókai (nee Móric Jókay de Ásva) (1825–1904), Hungarian Romantic dramatist, poet and politician; see H.W.V. Temperley, 'Maurus Jokai and the Historical Novel', *Contemporary Review* lxxxvi (July 1904), 107–14.

[57] János Kemény (1607–62), Hungarian aristocrat; Prince of Transylvania, 1661–62; defeated by the Ottomans and killed in battle of Nagyszőllős, Jan. 1662.

[58] General Ioan Culcer (1853–1928), Romanian military commander; Secretary-general of War Ministry, 1904–1907; commanded 5th Army Corps, 1913–16; 1st Army, Aug.–Oct. 1916; Minister for Public Works, 1918.

[59] General Constantin Prezan (1861–1943), Romanian military commander; commanded 4th Army Corps, 1915–16, Fourth Army, 1916–17; Chief of General, 1917–20; Marshal of Romania, 1930.

of the King, an updated version of Arabella Churchill,[60] Charles II[61] & James and the Duke of Marlborough.[62]>

Dobrudja very bad. Mackensen[63] and Falkenhayn[64] are the refutation of Tolstoy's view that the soldiers and not the generals decide campaigns.[65]

29th [October 1916]

No news but R[omani]a doing better – bridge at Crna Voda[66] not entirely smashed, enough to pass on foot.

1st [November 1916]

R[omania]n cereals £19 mil[lion] total necessary or desired. Oil £7 mil[lion].

Doing slightly better – the Russian bear is slow but his hug is terrible.

Intrigues in Greece continue and as Venizelos and Kounduriotis [*sic*] said, the German submarine which torpedoed the Venizelist volunteer steamer could not have done so without the knowledge or aid of the official Greek Government. The French official report confirms this.

Queer things happen in Parliament. Lord R[obert] Cecil[67] says he doesn't know whether M. Venizelos has been communicated with – as to being recognized as a de facto government. We know in the office well enough. Court

---

[60] Arabella Churchill (1648–1730), the mistress of King James II, and the mother of four of his children (FitzJames Stuart).

[61] Charles II Stuart (1630–85), King of England, 1660–85.

[62] John Churchill (1650–1722), 1st Duke of Marlborough, soldier; Commander-in-Chief of Forces, 1690–91, 1702–1708; Captain-General, 1702–11; Master-General of the Ordnance, 1702–12 and 1714–22.

[63] Field Marshal (Anton Ludwig) August von Mackensen (1849–1945), German soldier; commanded XVII Army Corps, 1908–14; commanded Ninth Army, 1914–15; Eleventh Army and Army Group Kiev, 1915; led *Heeresgruppe Mackensen* on campaigns against Serbia and Romania, 1915–18; military governor Romania, 1917–18; prisoner-of-war, 1918–19; retired from army, 1920; Prussian state councillor, 1933–45.

[64] General Erich von Falkenhayn (1861–1922), German soldier; Prussian war minister, 1913–14; Chief of the General Staff, 1914–16; commanded Ninth Army in Transylvania, 1916–17; military commander in Palestine, 1917–18; commanded Tenth Army in Byeloarussia, 1918; retired from army, 1919.

[65] See Leo N. Tolstoy, *Notes for Officers, Notes for Soldiers* (London, 1901).

[66] Now Cernavodă.

[67] Lord (Edgar Algernon) Robert Gascoyne-Cecil (1864–1958), 1st Viscount Cecil of Chelwood, cr. 1923, politician; MP (Cons.) Marylebone East, 1906–10, Hitchin, 1911–23; Parliamentary Under-secretary of State for Foreign

intrigues abound, and are suspected in high places. It is said that a letter from the Queen of Greece[68] to the Kaiser with a plan of Suez has been intercepted and Sir E[dward] G[rey][69] said he would not interfere with [an] accusation of the King. Venizelists and Greeks (official) fired on one another the day before yesterday. The existing situation cannot last when 'Greek meets Greek'.

2nd Nov[embe]r [1916]

They say (2 good auth[orit]ies[)] that Lord Northcliffe[70] presented an ultimatum about 1 week ago to L[loyd] G[eorge] and that it has been rejected. Cause in doubt – no press facilities to exclusion of other papers – first signs of storm in attack on L[loyd] G[eorge] in Dail M[ail] over raising the military age to 41. If this succeeds no doubt they will take up the matter in the 'Times'. Just as with poor old K[itchener] <- confirmed on 17th when the Times suggested L[loyd] G[eorge] for Food-Dictator.>[71]

3rd Nov[embe]r [1916]

Lord R[obert] C[ecil] on Venizelos inexplicable. He said V[enizelos] & the Greek Gov[ernmen]t invited us to Sal[oni]ca whereas V[enizelos] has denied it – and we knew his it denial to be true. <The F[oreign] O[ffice] 4 months ago c[oul]d find no evidence of his invitation.> He also says appar This was quite gratuitous and most undiplomatic.

He also says that he does not know whether the de facto recognition has been communicated to V[enizelos] but it is a [fact]. I know that it has verbally. Each of these facts is in the advisory F[oreign] O[ffice] telegrams. How can a minister or his secretaries get up his case for him so badly?

Affairs, 1916–19 (Minister of Blockade, 1916–18); Lord Privy Seal, 1923–24; Chancellor of the Duchy of Lancaster, 1924–29; Nobel Peace laureate, 1937.

68 Princess Sophie (Dorothea Ulrike Alice) of Prussia (1870–1932), Queen of the Hellenes as consort of King Constantine, 1913–17 and 1920–22; sister of Kaiser Wilhelm II.

69 See entry 19 June 1916.

70 Alfred Charles William Harmsworth (1865–1922), Baron Northcliffe, cr. 1905 (1st Viscount, cr. 1918), newspaper and publishing magnate (Amalgamated Press Ltd.); owner of *The Times* and *Daily Mail*; campaigned for establishment of Ministry of Munitions, 1915.

71 'Political Notes: The "Food Dictator". Some Suggestions', *The Times*, 17 Nov. 1916.

<7th November [1916]

As a pendant to this, we have L[or]d R[obert] C[ecil]'s explanation in the H[ouse] of C[ommons] today.[72] He says that the British Government will prevent Tino from persecuting any officers or officials who leave for Salonika and will take immediate action, if any case is brought to their notice (by M. Venizelos, whom they have not officially recognized). So that in order to recognize the needs of the dynasty, and the desires of Russia, we do not permit a King to punish his own subjects for deserting. Oh wonder F[oreign] O[ffice] or strange Holy Mother Russia. How much both of you have to account for.>

5 Nov[embe]r [1916]

Russia, Italy, England demand recall of General Sarrail.

6 Nov[embe]r [1916]

K[ing] of Montenegro[73] surpasses himself in his visit to the front, breaks off programme to go to a ruined church & pray for the Allies <– prayed aloud in French most beautifully for about a quarter of an hour>, and suspects a discouragement, showers decorations, giving Sir D[ouglas] Haig[74] the gold medal of Obilitch,[75] the highest distinction in Montenegro and, ironically enough, the commemoration of a successful assassination.

---

[72] *Hansard* lxxxvii (7 Nov. 1916), cols. 148–62.

[73] Nikola I Mirkov Petrović-Njegoš (1841–1921), Prince of Montenegro, 1860–1910; King of Montenegro, 1910–18; composed the music to the patriotic song '*Onamo, 'namo*' ('There, over there').

[74] Field Marshal Sir Douglas Haig (1861–1928), 1st Earl Haig, cr. 1919, military commander; entered army, 1884; service in Sudan, 1898, and Boer War, 1900–1902; Chief of General Staff (India), 1909–12; General Officer Commanding-in-Chief, Aldershot, 1912–14; Commander First Army, 1914–15; Commander-in-Chief, British Expeditionary Force, 1915–18.

[75] Bravery medal, instituted by Petar II Petrović-Njegoš (1813–51), Serb Orthodox Prince-Bishop of Montenegro (r. 1830–51), and named after Miloš Obilić (died 1389), Serbian knight in the service of Prince Lazar of Serbia and legendary assassination of Sultan Murad I in the battle of Kosovo in 1389.

7 Nov[embe]r [1916]

Saw Lloyd George – he has a battle-face and a habit of command, which I did not realize until now. One thinks now of his achievements. The result of that unsavoury scandal – in which Mrs G[eorge] C[ornwallis]-West[76] amée played the part of Potiphar's wife[77] to a young Canadian soldier, and indeed Sir John Cowans,[78] the Q[uarter] M[aster] G[eneral] to order him to France, when he was unfit to go, and the Q[uarter] M[aster] G[eneral] unfit to order him – is perhaps to the good. The Q[uarter] M[aster] G[eneral] is severely reprimanded by a committee of inquiry. Hence, under the new chief, he becomes a tame rabbit. His departments are revised – Sir Eric Geddes,[79] a deputy manager of a railway, becomes head of the railway department, Lord Rothermere,[80] Northcliffe's brother, of the Army Clothing Dep[artmen]t. The last was due to a sad scandal, which came up over clothing in the courts. 'Is it advance or contracts?' asks L[loyd] G[eorge] of his secretary when the malversations of certain clothing contractors and officials were denounced by Judge Low.[81] 'Contracts I think, Sir', said the secretary. 'You'd better make certain the head of the department goes to me now', said L[loyd] G[eorge]. And he did. C'est la guerre. The result of all this mess is that 2 highly specialised civilians have got their feet well into departments they well understand how to manage, and that the Q[uarter] M[aster] G[eneral], the military head of the whole affair, has been cowed and rendered obedient. Sir J[ohn] Cowans is a sort of military Fouquet, beloved of women, loose in accounts and life, but of supreme ability at need. Now cowed, escaped with difficulty from ruin, he is in the hands of a master, who will use his talents to keep him up to the mark. Thus chance gave

---

[76] Lady Randolph Churchill (née Jeanette 'Jennie' Jerome) (1854–1921), married, 1900, Capt. George Frederick Myddleton Cornwallis-West (1874–1951), Scots Guards; divorced, 1914.

[77] *Genesis* 40.

[78] See entry 23 Nov. 1916.

[79] Sir Eric Campbell-Geddes (1875–1937), businessman and politician; Deputy General Manager North-Eastern Railway, 1911–15; Deputy Director-General of Munitions Supply, 1915–16; Director-General of Military Railways and Inspector-General of Transportation with the British Expeditionary Force (with the rank of Honorary Major-General), 1916–17; MP (Cons.) Cambridge, 1917–22; First Lord of the Admiralty, 1917–19; Minister without Portfolio, 1919; Minister of Transport, 1919–21; chairman National Expenditure committee ('Geddes Axe'), 1921.

[80] Harold Sidney Harmsworth (1868–1940), Baron Rothermere, cr. 1914 (1st Viscount, 1919), newspaper proprietor; owner of Associated Newspapers Ltd. (*Daily Mirror*); President of the Air Council, 1917–18; advocated revision of Trianon treaty and appeasement of Hitler in 1930s.

[81] Sir Frederick Low (1856–1917), lawyer and politician; called to the bar, 1890; KC, 1902; MP (Lib.), Norwich, 1910–15; judge King's Bench Division of the High Court, 1915–17.

the opportunity – ability has used it, and the nation will profit both by the vices and the abilities of our military Fouquet,[82] and the genius of our civil war-chief.

8 Nov[embe]r [1916]

The pubished revelations of Admiral Kou[n]duriotis are of high value. He says that he jumped to his feet in the Cabinet when the surrender at Rupel was known, shouting at the top of his voice 'I will not be a party to the parting with any part of Greek soil which her sons won with their blood or smuggling away a parcel of land'. Sko[u]loudis[83] rumbled and grumbled and produced a document signed by the German Minister three days before the surrender promising to restore Rupel later. Thus every word uttered by Sko[u]loudis in the Chamber and to the Entente on this subject was a deliberate lie, i.e. if we believe Konduriotis, who is the best-beloved of all Greek sailor and the most honest man in Greece after Venizelos. Konduriotis warned Tino in the second week of September of the consequences of his policy and 15 days later on the 24 Sept[embe]r left with Venizelos for Crete and freedom.

Small things have the greatest importance in war – because a commercial submarine gets to America, it becomes possible for Germany to sell vast stocks of securities (it was not possible hitherto because England censored the markets). Because Sweden along can manufacture or produced the world's share of ball-bearings and certain other products essential to munitions therefore Sweden's neutrality or hostility is of the most serious moment to the vast and mighty Entente. These instances are like those of the hair which stops the most complicated and vast machine, or the rat which nibbles at a dyke and floods a province with the Zuyder Zee.

I think the feeling against Tino is rising and even – blest miracle! – being perceived by the F[oreign] O[ffice]. M. Politis, who has recently joined M. Venizelos, had been under-secretary (permanent) to the Greek F[oreign] O[ffice] till a few weeks ago. He must know most of the secrets and will continue to produce them until the atmosphere is that of a Turkish bath, and Tino is reduced by the vapour to one quarter of his natural size.

---

[82] Nicolas Fouquet (1615–1680), Vicomte de Melun et de Vaux, Marquis de Belle-Isle, French politician; *procureur-général*, 1650–53; Superintendent of Finance, 1653–61; fell out of Royal favour and incarcerated in the fortress of Pignerol, where he died

[83] See entry 19 June 1916.

9th Nov[embe]r [1916]

Asquith[84] addresses the blunders of Lord R[obert] C[ecil]. According to him we went to Salonica with the assent of the Greek Government (in spite of a protest) a good instance of the mot juste. Subsequently Sko[u]loudis achieved the record number of 63 protests against us but these last were of the nature of a manifesto.

The Serbs continue to fight heroically everywhere. In the Dobrudsha outnumbered and surrounded they fought till only 800 were left – more now seem to be coming in. They neither take nor give prisoners – earlier they bayoneted 3,000. Espionage at Athens has its humours – of the cocottes all but two, who are subsidized by us, are German, and next to them the priestly class are most pro-Hun, so that love and religion unite.

One Muse now taken by the Huns, previously used for contraband of love, is now used for contraband of war – and Baron Schenck's[85] guineas clunked most for the Hellenes in a Hydropathic at Kephissia[86] whither the Athenians went for weekends and for pleasures.

10th Nov[embe]r [1916]

13 Nov[embe]r [1916]

The Greek plot thickens but Politis has a Fortunatus[87] purse of secret documents, which will shame Tino before the world. He has now characteristically agreed to punish Venizelist officers for leaving Salonica, but says nothing of the rank & file, a characteristic subterfuge. The situation is impossible & must shortly be cleared. It is, however, interesting that Politis thinks the entente made a blunder in not recognizing the Kalageropoulos[88] Ministry but that of Venizelos.

---

[84] Herbert Henry Asquith (1852–1928), 1st Earl of Oxford and Asquith, cr. 1925, politician; MP (Lib), Fife, 1885–1918, Paisley, 1920–24; Home Secretary, 1892–95; Chancellor of the Exchequer, 1905–1908; Prime Minister, 1908–16; Secretary of State for War, 1914; leader of the Liberal party, 1908–26.

[85] Baron von Schenck, director of German propaganda at Athens, was expelled from Greece in Oct. 1916.

[86] Now Kifisia, an affluent northern suburb of Athens; in the late nineteenth century, it became a popular summer resort for Greece's political and commercial elites.

[87] The hero of an early sixteenth-century German proto-novel (1509).

[88] Nikolaos Kalogeropoulos (1851–1927), conservative Greek politician; Prime Minister, Sept.–Oct. 1916, and Feb.–Apr. 1921.

Venizelos now says that the royalists have moved north of Ekaterini[89] and thus violated the neutral zone occupied by the French. Meanwhile the Greek Government has protested against the seizure of the Greek light flotilla by the French on the ground that Greece has uniformly observed a 'benevolent neutrality' towards the Entente, Ll[oyd] G[eorge] saw me once more today in D[avies]'s room and, to my surprise, recognized me and spoke a friendly word.

14 Nov[embe]r [1916]

R[omania]n affairs look bad – passes may be forced as reserves are lacking. No use to cry over the past, but when a nation cannot make plans, and has only 3 telephones per corps, and when supplied with 100, cannot use them or the lines –

About Poland I understand from Fitzgibbon Young[90] that Austria worked hard for a Poland including Russian Poland and Posen under a Habsburg prince. The Germans declined this, but concessions, white eagle etc., were sent by Francis Joseph[91] to the officers of the Polish Legion, just at the moment when the Germans turned them out, dissolved the Legion and deposed of them.

15 Nov[embe]r [1916]

Tino again encroaching on Venizelist terr[itor]y. Venizelos acting with great moderation and statesmanship.

Roumania's reserves are small immediate, not more than 130,000 against 200,000 casualties.

The Serbians \<at Monastir> have excelled all previous performances by taking 600 Germans in their last bag of 1,000. This is a great effort and will, I hope, bring its reward – the fall of Monastir.

---

[89] Now Kateriri on coast of the Gulf of Thessaloniki.

[90] Robert Fitzgibbon Young (1879–1960), civil servant and historian of Bohemia; a cousin of James, Viscount Bryce; history master, Manchester Grammar School, 1905–1906; Lecturer in History and Politics, Leeds University, 1906–1907; Inspector (since 1909, Examiner), Board of Education, 1907–14; seconded for war service under the Foreign Office; Lieutenant, Royal Navy Volunteer Reserves; temporary secretary to British diplomatic mission to Prague, Dec. 1918–June 1919; Secretary to Consultative Committee of the Board of Education, 1920–39; external examiner to London University, Diploma in Slavonic Studies, 1924–27; cf. his 'The Teschen Question', in H.W.V. Temperley (ed.), *A History of the Peace Conference of Paris* (London, 1921), vol. iv.

[91] Francis Joseph I of Habsburg-Lorraine (1830–1916), Emperor of Austria, 1848–1916, Apostolic King of Hungary etc., 1867–1916.

16 Nov[embe]r [1916]

Serbs again to the fore, both in north and south. Two of their <companies> cut off by the fall of a bridge from their comrades in the Dobrudja,[92] lapt into the river 'like Horatius and swam',[93] half-a-mile or so across the freezing Danube to the opposite shore. By heaven it is Homeric and reminds me of exploits related of the Cossacks in Gogol's 'Taras Bulba'.[94] In [the] Monastir fighting they have equally excelled, and have broken through the inner line, from Bukri[95] to Chegel & Bukri, capturing both Germans and Bulgars. Meanwhile, owing to this, the French have advanced from Kenali, which they have taken and go to Viro.[96] Monastir should fall in a day or two. Sarrail ought to retain his command. He has not kept all his previous troops on the frontier but attracted 2 extra Bulgar regiments and 1 German division.

The news from Roumania is very gloomy. The last reserves are thrown into the fighting line, and the Germans at some points are 20 miles within the frontier, and emerging from the hills. I fear that there may be disaster, unless there is some strong rally or a Russian offensive. It is partly Roumanian morale – the R<oumanians> of Bessarabia are reckoned the worst troops in the Russian army, I am told. Generals Janin[97] and Ferrier may save them at the last, but Western R[omani]a to the Alt[98] would be abandoned.

17th Nov[embe]r [1916]

Today Venizelos has given specific instances – of a priest who was imprisoned & flogged by the Royalists for having celebrated the national movement by a

---

[92] Region between the lower Danube and the Black Sea, including the Danube delta.

[93] See (LXIII) 'Never, I ween, did swimmer/ In such an evil case/ Struggle through such a raging flood/ Safe to the landing place', T.B. Macaulay, 'Lays of Ancient Rome: Horatius', *Lord Macaulays Essays and Lays of Ancient Rome* (London, 1892), 840.

[94] *Taras Bulba* (1835/1842), a romanticized historical novel by Nikolai Gogol about the enonymous Zaporozhian Cossack and his two sons Anrdriy and Ostap.

[95] Village near Bitola (Monastir), on the right bank of the river in the Kenali salient.

[96] River Viro, south of Bitola.

[97] General Pierre-Thiébaut-Charles-Maurice Janin (1862–1946), French soldier; educated Military Academy, St. Cyr; member of military mission to Russia, 1893; seconded to Imperial Military Academy St. Nicholas, Moscow, 1912–14; brigade commander at the Marne, 1914; chief of French military mission to Russia, 1916–18; commander of French forces in Siberia, and of Czechoslovak Legion, 1918–20; see his *Ma mission en Sibérie 1918–1920* (Paris, 1933).

[98] River Olt in Romania, which rises in the Eastern Carpathians and joins the Danube at Turnu Măgurele.

Te Deum and the mayor of a commune, who was imprisoned, and had his left arm broken for his patriotism.

Even now the R[omani]an G[eneral] S[taff] do not consider the situation serious, which is all to the good. But they have never yet been right in their appreciation of the situation.

I saw a series of photographs, all unpublished, today from an officer who came from Corfu, all unpublishable. I should like to get them printed and set round the walls of the F[oreign] O[ffice] to haunt the inmates with the ghastly misery they brought about by their muddling and indecision. They say 15–20,000 Serbs and 60,000 out of 70,000 Austrian prisoners died.

Pictures of men, so thin that the backbone stood out and the ribs made a pattern like wood-carving, pictures of men dying in agony, of men slowly sinking with unalterable pain on their faces, heaps of dead bodies being flung into the sea – one picture was particularly grim – a tangled heap of dead bodies, one set face, <beautiful in its repose and regular in its outlines> staring upwards, the light striking it and turning it white as marble, as it catches the central figure in a picture of Rembrandt. Pictures of horror, etched in with the acid of pain – indescribable, indescribable.

18th Nov[embe]r [1916]

Today I came across a quotation, reflecting on the value of R[omania]ns as soldiers in Sienkiewicz.[99] With Fire & Sword c.III Skshetuski[100] read 'Why is Wallachian cavalry called light? Answer because it is lightfooted in flight. Amen. How this is true'.

'The people are of weaker temper than with us' (in Poland).

'That they are traitors is undoubted & that is proven by the adventures of Prince Michael[101]. I have heard as a fact that their soldiers are nothing to boast of by nature. But the prince has an excellent Wallachian regiment, but to tell the truth I don't think it contains even two hundred Wallachians!'

---

[99] Henryk (Adam Aleksander Pius) Sienkiewicz (1846–1916), Polish journalist and novelist; Nobel Prize in Literature, 1905.

[100] Jan Skrzetuski, a fictional Polish nobleman in Sienkiewicz's 1884 novel *Ogniem i mieczem* (*With Fire and Sword*), the first of trilogy set in the seventeenth-century Polish-Lithuanian Commonwealth.

[101] Michał Wołodyjowski, fictional Polish warrior-hero in Sienkiewicz's trilogy.

19 Nov[embe]r [1916]

Fall of Monastir,[102] due entirely to the Serbian encircling movement, from the bend of the Crna. The French advanced straight on Monastir after the Serbs had compelled the Bulgars to retire by their threat to the flank. Strange anniversary, the day on which the Serbs stormed Monastir four years ago. What ages of suffering since then for the Serbians and the whole human race. Humour or humours – Sarrail whose dismissal three Allies demanded, is now on top – Venizelos is also a rising star, Tino I hope a finally setting one. On a flagrant case of espionage of Allies with Greeks through the Turkish Legation the Brit[ish] Min[ister, Sir Francis Elliot] has at last protested and the French Admiral has acted. The German, Austrian, Bulgarian and Turkish Legations are to leave by Wednesday. The Admirals' broom sweeps clean.

20th Nov[embe]r [1916]

Situation in Roumania necessitates the abandonment of Western Wallachia to the Alt. This has always been contemplated by the Roumanian General Staff, who view the situation with equanimity, strengthened by Berthelot.[103] The situation is such that only an offensive can save them – you cannot defend to sides of a square against an enemy except by attacking him on one side of it. Old General Grigorescu[104] talked about atrocities of Austrians were worse than Germans and Magyars who were worse than Austrians – shocking! Then we talked of destroying the corn. 'Oh', said he, 'very easy but very naasty [*sic*]' – pih, pih (blowing) – typhus germs on the stocks of the corn. And they (the Germans) know it – 'Ah! Even the poisoned sweets and the dynamite of the German Legation in Bucharest were no more shocking than this'.

---

[102] During the first battle of Monastir, 3. Oct.–27. Nov. 1916, the Central Powers withdrew from Bitola (Monastir) on 18 November.

[103] General Henri Mathias Berthelot (1861–1931), French officer; appointed to General Staff, 1907; chief-of-staff under Joffre during Battle of the Marne, 1914; chief of French military mission in Romania, 1916–18; commanded Fifth Army, 1918; military governor of Metz, 1919–22, of Strasburg, 1923–26.

[104] General Eremia Grigorescu (1863–1919), Romanian soldier; entered artillery; commanded 1st Army at the battle of Mărășești, Aug.–Sept. 1917; Minister of War, Oct.–Nov. 1918.

Heard privately of some distressful incidents about Kitchener[105] & FitzGerald. Poor FitzG[erald]'s[106] body when brought back had no money on it (an absurdity for an A[ide] D[e] C[amp]) – all his medals & orders have been stolen, except 1 found in a cardboard box in the basement of York House. Apparently a foreign man-servant there was under suspicion and was to be relieved, but, before the relief, went out most unwillingly with K[itchener]'s party and was drowned. Fitz[Gerald] has no will, no mufti clothes, no jewellery left behind. Is it really possible without collusion of this foreign servant who must have stripped the place bare before going [?][107]

21 Nov[embe]r [1916]

Admiral du Fournet's[108] billet-doux presented to the four Legations at Athens, telling them that, if they do not present themselves at the Piraeus tomorrow morning <for a sea voyage> he will send and fetch them. The German and Austrian [ministers] have declined to come, so there may be a pretty scene. The S[team] S[hip] is termed the "Marienbad" so they will be taking the waters in more ways than one. For du Fournet it should be the Frenchman's greatest day since Sedan.

The Serbs achieve feats like Marko Kraljevitch[109] of Old – the 10th cavalry swam the CRNA and appeared from the east, while the French entered it from the South. Gallant peasant-knights, the bravest of the brave.

In R[omani]a things go from bad to worse, the officers' one idea seems to be to dance every night in Bucharest while the men lie in snow and ice repelling night attacks. The Roumanian technique seems deplorable – no idea of trenches or of scientific soldiery, of reconnaissance. The C[hief of the]

---

[105] Field Marshal Sir Herbert Horatio Kitchener (1850–1916), 1st Earl Kitchener of Khartoum, cr., commander and politician; commissioned into Royal Engineers, 1871; *Sirdar* of Anglo-Egyptian army, 1890–99; Governor-General, Sudan, 1899; commander British forces, Boer War, 1900–1902; Commander-in-Chief, India, 1902–1909; consul-general and agent at Cairo, 1911–14; Secretary of State for War, 1914–16.

[106] Captain Oswald Fitzgerald (1875–1916), soldier; officer in 18th Bengal Lancers; Kitchener's aide-de-camp and companion, 1907–16.

[107] Fitzgerald was rumoured to have been Kitchener's lover, which might explain the absence of papers.

[108] Vice-admiral Louis Dartige du Fournet (1856–1949), French naval commander; Vice-Admiral, 1913; commander of 3rd Squadron stationed in Syria; evacuated some 4,000 Armenian refugees from Musa Dagh, near Antioch, Sept. 1915.

[109] Prince Marko Mrnjavčević (c. 1335–95), Serbian king, 1371–95; referred to as Kraljević (Prince) Marko in southern Slav epic poetry; also used as a surname: Marko Kraljević.

I[mperial] G[eneral] S[taff][110] predicted defeat in details on the submission of their first plan –subsequently he pointed out that all war should proceed on a definite plan 'I have been unable up to the present to <u>trace any such plan</u>'. This was some 4 weeks ago, and advised the immediate adoption of a definite one <, above all cooperate with Russia>. That's Wully.

One begins to understand that simple squarefaced straightness like this, not tricky intriguing, is the soul of warfare. So also recently he sent a wire to the Belgians in East Africa that we would not now consider staking out claims, but must adopt a military policy alone. That's Wully.

22 Nov[embe]r [1916]

Light on the Italians today. In the first palce a communiqué on their services at Monastir <twice as long as the French & Serbian communiqué>, proving that their forces (1 brigade!) made its capture possible. In the second place a mem[orandu]m or rather 2 mem[orand]a applying for terr[itor]y in Asia Minor, to us <u>separately</u>, i.e. without knowledge of France or Russia. F[oreign] O[ffice] wisely said they would only negotiate à quatre. The mem[orand]a began with saying that Italy was to be praised and favoured by the Allies because without being forced or menaced, she came into the war. It ended by saying that her designs, if realized, would promote the reign of justice and tranquillity on earth. The centre part of the discourse was occupied with suggested deals <deals & ideals>. It complained of the Treaty of 30 Ap[ril 19]15,[111] which allotted apparently Con[stantino]ple & Armenia to Russia – Smyrna and a long tongue inland to Greece – east and west & inland of Alexandretta to France, internationalised Palestine and gave Mesopotamia to England. These arrangements neglected the view that Italy was a Mediterranean power. She must have the south of the Bursa vilayet, perhaps Smyrna, the part of the Baghdad railway at AIDALIN and KONIEH – & access to the sea at AIDIN[112] – modest Italy.

---

[110] Field Marshal Sir William Robertson (1860–1933), military commander; entered army as a private in the 16th Lancers, 1877; Commandant, Staff College, Camberley, 1910–13; Chief of the Imperial General Staff, 1915–18; General Officer Commanding-in-Chief, Eastern Command, 1918; Commander-in-Chief, British Army on the Rhine, 1919–20.

[111] Under the Treaty of London (sometimes Pact of London), of 26 Apr. 1915, between the Entente Powers and neutral Italy, the latter committed herself to join the war against the Central Powers, and in return was promised territories in the Tyrol, along the Adriatic coast, central Albania and in Asia Minor. Italy declared war on Austria-Hungary in May 1915, and on Germany in 1916.

[112] Now Aidin, Konya, Adana (Turkey).

Story of Winston today, told by Lord C[harles] Beresford[113] – word of honour a friend of mine. Winston got hold of a colonel and an admiral to make a plan for Gallipoli, requiring 300,000 men. When he saw it Winston tore it up and concealed it, knowing that 300,000 could not be got.

Amid all the Roumanian pother there is one ray. The Russian G[eneral] S[taff] holds that the German plan against Roumania has completely failed. The pincers were to meet – Falkenhayn and Mackensen, at Predeal and Rustchuk,[114] and gradually squeeze in to Bucharest. But the nut has proved too tough and Sakharoff[115] is driving Mackensen back in the Dobrudja, while Falkenhayn failed at the Predeal [and] can only overrun Wallachia.

23 Oct[obe]r [*recte* November 1916]

Anecdote of Sir W[illiam] Robertson. I cleared up espionage matter on his house today, servants being sacked. At the last conf[eren]ce in Paris Sir W[illiam] R[obertson] received an opinion from a former general as follows 'I came here not to receive advice but to give an opinion'.

Some heavy duty work via M[I]1[116] re Seton W[atson].[117] I hope it will be stopped by ref[eren]ce direct to S[ecretary] of S[tate, viz. David Lloyd George]. It has been stopped once, viz. the game of conscripting him. Now it has been revived, but will, I hope, be stopped by the great man, as he has stopped other jobs.

---

[113] Admiral Charles William de la Poer Beresford (1846–1919), 1st Baron Beresford, cr. 1916, naval commander and politician; Junior Naval Lord of the Admiralty, 1886–88; Commander-in-Chief, Channel Fleet, 1903–1905 and 1907–1909, Mediterranean Fleet, 1905–1907; MP (Cons.), County Wexford, 1874–78, Maryleborn East, 1885–89, City of York, 1898–1900, Woolwich, 1902–1903, Plymouth, 1910–16.

[114] Now Ruse (Bulgaria).

[115] General Vladimir Viktorovich Sakharov (1853–1920), Russian military commander; entered army, 1871; active service, Russo-Japanese War, 1904–1905; commander 11th Army Corps, 1914 and 1915–16; Governor of Orenburg, 1914–15; commander, Danube Army, 1916–17; executed by the Green Army, 1920.

[116] Military Intelligence, Section 1, a department of the Directorate of Military Intelligence, responsible for code-breaking.

[117] Robert William Seton-Watson (1879–1951), historian and writer ('Scotus Viator'); honorary secretary, Serbian Relief Fund, 1914–18; founder-editor, *New Europe*, 1916; served Royal Ambulance Corps, 1917; War Cabinet Intelligence Bureau, Enemy Propaganda Department, 1917–18; attended Paris Peace Conference as adviser to Czech and Yugoslav delegations, 1919; Masaryk Professor of Central European History, 1922–45; Professor of Czechoslovak Studies at Oxford, 1945–49; President of Royal Historical Society, 1946–49.

24th Nov[embe]r [1916]

FitzM[aurice][118] talk. After the death of the Archduke F[ranz] F[erdinand][119] he came up to the F[oreign] O[ffice] & said 'that's the sequel. Armageddon's on'. <Fitzmaurice said John Bull[120] 'To Hell with Serbia', July 7 [19]14, was got at by Austrian propaganda and even Leo Maxse[121] of the National Review.> It was, and the F[oreign] O[ffice] did not believe it. In May 1915 Bax-Ironside[122] fumbled & flopped at Sofia. He rose at 11, dallied till 5, played bridge till 12 or 1 pm. A master worthy of the F[oreign] O[ffice].

Serbia broke the treaty – Buc[h]arest was a treaty which could not but be broken.

Recently Russia got up via Stürmer[123] a new idea for the independence of Poland. Why? It depended on Constantinople. The Russian people would depend on Constantinople. If it was published they sh[oul]d have Con[stantino]ple it c[oul]d be published that Poland sh[oul]d be indep[enden]t. France agreed but we shuffled & held back.

25 Nov[embe]r [1916]

At last Tino is to be brought to book. If he does not yield his superfluous armament, then it will be taken & he will be thrown down. Our min[iste]rs as

---

[118] Gerald Henry Fitzmaurice (1865–1939), consular official; entered consular service, 1885; Vice-consul at Smyrna, 1895–97; Second Dragoman at Constantinople, 1897–1907; British Commissioner, Aden Frontier Delimitation, 1902–1905; Chief Dragoman at Constantinople, 1907–14; attached to Sofia legation, 1914–15; employed in Admiralty, 1915–19; in Foreign Office, 1919–21; retired, 1921.

[119] Franz Ferdinand von Habsburg, Archduke of Austria-Este (1863–1914), heir presumptive to Austro-Hungarian throne, 1889–1914; Inspector-General of Habsburg armed forces, 1913–14; assassinated at Sarajevo, 28 June 1914.

[120] *John Bull*, an ultra-patriotic journal edited by Horatio Bottomley, MP (1866–1933), since 1906; it was originally anti-Serbian, but Bottomley swiftly changed course, see J. Symons, *Horatio Bottomley* (London, 1955), 162–3.

[121] Leopold James Maxse (1864–1932), journalist; editor of the Conservative-leaning *National Review*, 1893–1932; persistently warned against 'German menace' before 1914.

[122] Sir Henry George Outram Bax-Ironside (1859–1929), diplomat; entered diplomatic service, 1883; minister-resident at Caracas, 1902–1907; minister at Santiago de Chile, 1907–1909; at Berne, 1909–11; at Sofia, 1911–15; retired, 1918. Bax-Ironside was one of the original bridge players.

[123] Baron Boris Vladimirovich Stürmer (1848–1917), Russian politician; member of the State Council since 1904; Prime Minister and Foreign Minister, Jan.–Nov. 1916; arrested in Feb. 1917, and died at Peter-and-Paul Fortress, Sept. 1917.

usu[al] have explained that it is not they but the Admiral who has acted. Thank God for such an Admiral, even tho[ugh] he be a Frenchman.

The situation is very grave.

26th Nov[embe]r [1916]

Owing to dip[lomati]c remonstrances the dethronement of Tino was omitted from the programme.

27th [November 1916]

Lord R[obert] Cecil told a strange lie in the House tonight – said dynastic considerations did not count in the least.[124] In heaven's name what does count then? Russia has been the sole argument hitherto as to the 'hands off Tino' attitude. I begin to think it is only a pretext for the favourite F[oreign] O[ffice] game of doing nothing. In 1915, as I was warned long ago, Russian approval and acquiescence were quoted for our hopeless blunders in Serbia – prob[abl]y as wrongly as today in Greece. Apparently with regard to the Venizelos muddle, the papers can announce that Venizelos can declare war. We refuse to recognize it, and also because it destroys the argument for Venizelists being volunteer in Sarrail's Salonika army. We do not, however, contest that Venizelos can declare war. He has announced that 'he is in conflict with the throne' and we think that nothing can be better or simpler than recognition of two Kings of Brentford[125] in Greece. Oh! marvellous F[oreign] O[ffice] – the chord of harmony in a world turned upside down.

Nov[embe]r 28th [1916]

R[omani]a going downhill, Buc[hares]t being a second time evacuated and papers and MSS burnt by our man of iron (Sir G[eorge] B[arclay]). Even now, if the R[omanian]s were not tailors or women, they are almost 4 to 1 and could turn the Huns.

---

[124] *Hansard* vol. 88 (15 Nov. 1916), cols. 103–20.
[125] Two characters who appear hand-in-hand in *The Rehearsal*, a satirical Restoration play attributed to George Villiers, 2nd Duke of Buckingham.

29th Nov[embe]r

Today the Russian offensive, fixed for the 9th then for the 14th, then for the 23rd and then for the 28th, began!

Nov[ember] 30th

Am trying to get a mem[orandu]m into G[eneral] H[ead] Q[uarters] & D[irector of] M[ilitary] O[perations],[126] being a new plans for an offensive. Thought to be interesting re universal sup[port] & offensive policy.

Dec[ember] 1st [1916]

<L[loyd] G[eorge] intended to resign in April over Kut,[127] but deferred out of deference to the premier.> Hear that L[loyd] G[eorge] is very dissatisfied with the Premier. Expects either to resign or to go on a Midlothian campaign which will force the P[remier] to [resign?]. The situation is very critical on all sides. Roumania is giving way, but may stand near Bucharest. Tino is still foxing, and seems to have deluded the French Admiral on Thursday [30 November]. Du Fournet issued a strong communiqué as to Allied intentions, but afterwards withdrew it, owing to the King's promise that in no case would force be authorized by him. This was probably bluff and blarney of the worst type. French transports with troops have arrived at the Piraeus. There are no reserves whatever at Salonika. The French are very weak there and Hun-Bulgar attacks have begun again, no doubt in collusion with Tino.

Dec[embe]r 2nd [1916]

The worst has happened. During the occupation of the Piraeus firing began. The Legation was attacked, and 200 Allied seaman cut off at one point. Heavy losses feared. This will bring things to a definite head. Tino deluded the Admiral as he has so often deluded us before, and the latter is now blamed for weakness.

---

[126] Major-General Sir Frederick Barton Maurice (1871–1951), military officer; joined army, 1892; Director of Military Operations, 1915–18; sacked after publicly criticizing Lloyd George for misleading the public over the strength of British forces in France, May 1918; resigned; co-founder of Royal British Legion, 1921; Professor of Military Studies, University of London, 1926–51.

[127] Surrender of 8,000 British troops at Al-Kut in Mespotamia, on 29 Apr. 1916, after four months' siege.

The statue of Byron[128] was found blind-folded during the fighting at Athens, doubtless the act of one who had a fine eye for dramatic effect.

A concerted attack from nearly all sides on Asquith (& Grey and Balfour[129] in some cases) began today. Northcliffe has boxed the compass once more, and come out for L[loyd] G[eorge] whom he assailed a week ago. I gather that he now supports him.

Dec[ember] 3

News throws all blame on the King's deceit and the Admiral's [i.e. Kountouriotis] vanity, on the French Admiral first for believing Tino's assurances that there would be no disorder, second for indicating to him beforehand the position at the Zappeion heights north of Piraeus etc., which we intended to occupy. These places also were apparently chosen without the slightest regard for military considerations and were subject to artillery fire from previously prepared bastions & surrounded by men who were hastily mobilised reservists. Not only has Tino broken his word, but his premier promises proved illusory or fallacious, as every other promise has done. Venizelists are being hunted through the streets and shot at by men with or without uniform but all wearing the King's portrait, a Greek St. Bartholomew.[130] The Venizelist houses are sacked and looted, including that of Venizelos himself, and also some of British intelligence officers, and our Legation was fired on. In return our Battleships fired on the Stadium, and one shell struck the palace, and a fragment was brought in while the King was interviewing [Sir Francis] Elliot <which seems to have affected the negotiations>. In the provinces events are more varied and at Volo[131] a naval threat by the French caused the surrender of 3 batteries

---

[128] George Gordon, 6th Baron Byron of Rochdale (1788–1824), poet and Hellenophile; died at Missolonghi.

[129] Arthur James Balfour (1848–1930), 1st Earl Balfour, cr. 1922, politician; MP (Cons), Hertford, 1874–85, Manchester East, 1885–1906, City of London, 1906–1922; President of the Local Government Board, 1885–86; Secretary of State for Scotland, 1886–87; Chief Secretary for Ireland, 1887–92; First Lord of the Treasury, 1891–92 and 1895–1905; Lord Privy Seal, 1902–1903; Prime Minister, 1902–1905; First Lord of the Admiralty, 1915–16; Foreign Secretary, 1916–19; Lord President of the Council, 1919–22 and 1925–29; leader of the Conservative Party, 1902–1911.

[130] Massacre of Hugenots in Paris and surrounding areas, commencing on 23 Aug. 1572 (St. Bartholomew Day) and lasting several weeks, killing between 5,000 and 30,000 French Protestants.

[131] Now Volos, coastal city in Thessaly.

minus the breech blocks. At Larissa[132] the regulars are carrying off materiel into the interior in requisitioned country-carts.

The blow to our prestige will be great, the loss in our dead considerable, while we have the shame of being unable to protect our friends.

Dec[embe]r 4th [1916]

The atrocities will be awful at Athens. I hear of 2 Greek nurses wearing the Red Cross <& tending a wounded porter at our Leg[ation]>, whom the ruffians seized and tried to rape in the latrines; they saw Venizelists battered to death with eyes gouged out, the late Chief of Police chained to a wall and beaten on the head with a club by a priest, and we are helpless. Reinforcements must go to Salonika – we cannot land several divisions, and the Venizelists will be maltreated. An American witness saw the entirely unprovoked attack on Venizelos' house, led by a General wearing the Greek order of the Redeemer.

Dec[ember] 5th [1916]

Day of omen. L[loyd] G[eorge] has resigned.[133] Asquith after accepting more than L[loyd] G[eorge] demanded on Sunday, ends by jibbing and going back altogether on Monday. May the old past master fall. Grey is out too I hear & hope. <I saw L[loyd] G[eorge] today in earnest converse with Max Aitken[134] (as I have seen him several times recently). He looked worried and waved his hand to me distractedly.>

View of Beatty[135] – from a friend. He says the Admiralty are a pack of old women and that he was more exhausted arguing with them than with the Battle of Jutland. He also thinks Jellicoe[136] was too slow to cut them off. They will be a

---

[132] Now Larisa, capital of Thessaly.

[133] Lloyd George tendered his resignation on 4 Dec.; this led to the fall of Asquith and Lloyd George's accession to the premiership on 7 Dec.

[134] William Maxwell 'Max' Aitken (1879–1964), 1st Baron Beaverbrook, cr. 1917, newspaper tycoon and politician; proprietor of *London Evening Standard* and *Daily Express*; MP (Cons.) Ashton-under-Lyne, 1910–16; Minister of Information, 1918; Chancellor of the Duchy of Lancaster, 1918; Minister of Aircraft Production, 1940–41; Minister of Supply, 1941–42; Minister of War Production, 1942–43; Lord Privy Seal, 1943–45.

[135] Admiral David Richard Beatty (1871–1936), 1st Earl Beatty, cr. 1919, naval commander; Private Naval Secretary to First Lord of the Admiralty, 1912–13; Commander-in-Chief, Grand Fleet, 1916–19; First Sea Lord, 1919–27.

[136] Admiral Sir John Rushworth Jellicoe (1859–1935), Viscount, cr. 1918, 1st Earl Jellicoe, cr. 1925, British naval commander; Director of Naval Ordnance, 1905–1907; aide-de-camp to

good combination – Jellicoe cool & intellectual, Beatty daring and dauntless – & will end the submarines if anyone will or can.

The Serbs are marvellous as ever and have surpassed even themselves, capturing amid the icy weather on Macedonian mountains a height north of GRUNISHTE and the town of STARAVINA.[137]

Dec[ember] 7 [1916]

Still the maze of intrigue – L[loyd] G[eorge] will triumph, I think, now. Asquith's chance lay in the refusal of Lord Robert Cecil & Austen [Chamberlain][138] to cooperate with L[loyd] G[eorge]. That removed, and Labour conciliated, L[loyd] G[eorge], the strongman of the moment, will triumph. I see the whole thing working up from L[loyd] G[eorge]'s mem[orandu]m on Serbia in April 1915 to the conscription fight, when Amery supplied him with the figures <I know because I was in the room and they spoke on the telephone> on which he stood his stand & threatened to resign, to the Roumanian memorandum when he moved a big offensive at Salonika to support Roumania and, finally, the demand for the small War Council and the exclusion <from it> of the Premier. It has all been on the 'win-the-war' line & L[loyd] G[eorge] has behaved with discretion when we remember his ardent nature, and the intolerable delays of the Parliamentarian.[139] Good luck to his efforts.

The F[oreign] O[ffice], in what I hope is its final effort under V[iscoun]t Grey, has fairly excelled itself today. It informed Burrows[140] of London University that we sh[oul]d require 10 Divisions to deal with Greece, and that the W[ar] O[ffice] had told them so. Subsequently Burrows brought this news to the W[ar] O[ffice] and the whole thing was denied. It turned out

---

King Edward VII, 1906–1907; Second-in-Command, Atlantic Fleet, 1907–1908; Third Sea Lord and Controller of the Navy, 1908–11; Commander-in-Chief, Grand Fleet, 1914–16; First Sea Lord, 1916–17; Governor-General of New Zealand, 1920–24.

[137] Gruništa and Staravina, a village and town northeast of Monastir (Bitola), on the east bank of the Crna river.

[138] Sir (Joseph) Austen Chamberlain (1863–1937), politician; MP (Lib. Un.), East Worcestershire, 1892–1914, Birmingham West, 1914–37; Civil Lord of the Admiralty, 1895–1900; Financial Secretary of the Treasury, 1900–1902; Postmaster-General, 1902–1903; Chancellor of the Exchequer, 1903–1905 and 1919–21; Secretary of State for India, 1915–17; Minister without Portfolio, 1918–19; Lord Privy Seal, 1921–22; Foreign Secretary, 1924–29; First Lord of the Admiralty, 1931.

[139] That is, Asquith.

[140] (Ronald) Montagu Burrows (1867–1920), historian and archeologist; Professor of Greek at University College, Cardiff, 1898–1908; at the University of Manchester, 1908–13; Principal of King's College London, 1913–20.

ultimately that the F[oreign] O[ffice] had misread a telegram and that the telegram merely embodied Tino's view on the subject so that, according to the F[oreign] O[ffice] the military views of Tino may be accepted as those from the W[ar] O[ffice]! I see that The Times attacks our Intelligence for saying the estimate was that the Greek Army was not worth getting to cooperate against the Bulgars. Now says The Times, it appears to be extremely favourable!

The paradox is true – they can equip perhaps 70,000 men. If 250,000 came in, we should have had to equip 180,000. But they will be unable to do more than raid the lines at EKSCSU,[141] SOROVITCH[142] and VERRIA,[143] roads and transports are too great a difficulty.

Dec[ember] 8 [1916]

L[loyd] G[eorge] was up till a quarter to 4 today, and well be up at a quarter to 8 tomorrow. The King is amazed at his capacity for work, and thinks he does more in a day than was expected in a month. I suppose this is after experience of Squithie. Hard work will win, I think. I hear Asquith at the Reform Club[144] today spoke as if between the lines he had evidence of an intrigue behind the scenes for a year and would, if necessary, produce it. The Liberal opposition will thus support the Gov[ernmen]t until they have a chance to overthrow it. According to this witness, Mond,[145] who raised a voice for L[loyd] G[eorge], was howled down. At the doors Haldane[146] was received with shouts of 'traitor'.

Visc[oun]t Grey still maintains his reputation in the last hours of his office. He has tried to stop the formal proclamation of blockade on the ground that this is an act of war. <In this he was prevented by the French.> He has also tried, and unfortunately succeeded, in prevening British ships from interrupting the passage between Negropont and the mainland at Chalcis. Owing to this influence troops have been ferried over to the mainland to the extent of a regiment, to strengthen Tino's forces and to persecute the Venizelists. His ground for doing this was that

---

[141] Presumably Ersekë in southeastern Albania.
[142] Now Amyntaio in northern Greece.
[143] Now Veria, west of Thessaloniki.
[144] Temperley was a member of the Reform Club.
[145] Sir Alfred Moritz Mond (1868–1930), 1st Lord Melchett, cr. 1928, industrialist, financier and politician; MP (L) Chester, 1906–10; Swansea, 1910–18; Swansea West, 1918–23; (C since 1926) Carmarthen, 1924–28; First Commissioner of Works, 1916–21; Minister of Health, 1921–22.
[146] Richard Burdon Haldane (1856–1928), 1st Viscount Haldane of Cloan, cr. 1911, lawyer and politician; MP (Lib.) Haddingtonshire, 1885–1911; Secretary of State for War, 1905–12; Lord Chancellor, 1912–15 and 1924; Leader of the House of Lords, 1924; leader of the Labour Party in the House of Lords, 1924–28.

we were not at war! Du Fournet is sacked for LeBon – this at present secret.[147] Meanwhile troops have been conveyed from the Morea to Athens, though the Corinth bridge is commanded by our guns. Even Grey has not often got as far as this. He reinforces the enemy at the same time as he accepts the enemy's reports in preference to our own as to our intentions and capacities.

A Roumanian effort has just come to my ear. General Presan [sic] with 5 div[ision]s decided to cover Bucharest with 1 cavalry div[ision] and strike N[orth] W[est] of Bucharest for the German communications. The result was the Germans captured Bucharest, and caught him on the left flank before his infantry had reached their objective. The primitive clumsiness punished by the master nonetheless – many Germans have been killed, and the Russians will now take up the ball.

They say Joffre[148] is out, and Nivelle[149] the new Generalissimo. Joffre is made a Maréchal de France, an office revived specially for him. It reminds one of Louis XIV who created 8 marshals on the death of Turenne[150] to mark his sense of loss.

Dec[embe]r 9th [1916]

L[loyd] G[eorge] again winning, so D[avies] tells me, though the Liberals will not join him. Strange about Fisher[151] <being President of the Board of Education>. It was I that introduced him to L[loyd] G[eorge], and spoke of him in high terms as a splendid man, so even I can claim my share in

---

[147] Temperley was mistaken. The command went to Vice-Admiral Dominique-Marie Gauchet (1853–1931), French sailor; entered navy, 1876; active service Indochina and Senegal; commander 1st Squadron, 1911–14; Director of Naval Operations, 1914–15; Dardanelles, 1915; Commander, Allied Forces in the Mediterranean, 1916–18.

[148] Marshal Joseph Jacques Césaire Joffre (1852–1931), French military commander; entered army, 1870; active service, Franco-Prussian War, 1870, Sino-French War, 1884–85; Commander-in-Chief, French Army, 1911–16; head of French Military Mission to Romania, 1917; to USA, 1917; Leader of Allied Supreme War Council, 1918.

[149] General Robert Georges Nivelle (1856–1924), French artillery officer; commanded French Third Army at Verdun, 1916; Commander-in-Chief of French forces on Western Front, Dec. 1916–May 1917; responsible for Nivelle Offensive, Apr. 1917; served in Africa, 1917–18; retired, 1921.

[150] Henri de la Tour d'Auvergne, Vicomte de Turenne (1611–75), French military commander; served in Netherlands army before entering French service, 1630; active service in Thirty Years' War, Franco-Spanish War, Dutch War of 1672; took part in Fronde, 1648–53; Marshal of France, 1643, Marshal General of France, 1661.

[151] Herbert Albert Laurens Fisher (1865–1940), historian and Liberal politician; Fellow New College, 1888–1913; Vice-chancellor, University of Sheffield, 1913–16; MP (Lib.) Sheffield Hallam, 1916–18, (Coal. Lib) Combined English Universities, 1918–26; President of the Board of Education, 1916–22; Warden of New College, Oxford, 1926–40.

cabinet-making.[152] A very little one it is. Still it is something, and that is always better than nothing. L[loyd] G[eorge] worked 9 hours at the W[ar] O[ffice], living on tea and cigars, and not leaving the precincts, a fact Northcliffe only records. Northcliffe is rather anti-Asquith than pro-L[loyd] G[eorge], I think, and, except that L[loyd] G[eorge] is unusually approachable by the Press, may not have much in it. I see Northcliffe is attacking him again about the appointment of Balfour to the F[oreign] O[ffice]. Vis[coun]t Grey of Fallodon, I understand, spent his last day at the F[oreign] O[ffice] today, an eleven years' regime fraught with every blunder. The one that will live longest is the published utterance to Lichnowsky[153] in the Papers as the origin of the war: 'British Interests in Serbia are *nil*'[154] <made by Buchanan[155]>. In other words he did not know that the Belgrade-Nish railway was part of the Berlin to Baghdad through-line. This was in July 1914 so that, in June or May, when he came to an agreement about Bagdad with Germany he was signing away concessions of which he had not the faintest conception of the value or purport.[156] That utterance and the offer of Cyprus to Greece will remain immortal.

Dec[ember] 12th [1916]

Peace – in the words of the German Emperor – scraps of paper to be binding and swords to beaten into spades. A peace-offer by wireless <openly> by 4 <of the most> despotic monarchs in the world, while we <democrats> still fumble on the backstairs of secret diplomacy.[157] Now I understand why several days ago L[loyd] G[eorge]'s private secretary [Philip Kerr[158]] wanted me to write

---

[152] In fact, Fisher first met Lloyd George through his father-in-law, Sir Courtney Ilbert, around 1900, see D. Ogg, *Herbert Fisher, 1865–1940: A Biography* (London, 1947), 45.

[153] Karl Max, Prince von Lichnowsky (1860–1928), German diplomat; entered diplomatic service, 1885; ambassador at Vienna, 1902–1904; at London, 1912–14.

[154] Tel. Buchanan to Grey (no. 166, urgent), 24 July 1914, G.P. Gooch and H.W.V. Temperley (eds), *British Documents on the Origins of the War, 1898–1914* (11 vols, London, 1928–38), xi, no. 101; also J.W. Headlam-Morley, *The History of the Twelve Days, July 24th to August 4th, 1914: Being an Account of the Negotiations Preceding the Outbreak of War Based on the Official Publications* (London, 1915), 304.

[155] Sir George William Buchanan (1854–1924), diplomat; entered diplomatic service, 1876; agent and consul-general at Sofia, 1903–1908; minister at The Hague, 1908–10; ambassador at St. Petersburg, 1910–18; at Rome, 1918–21.

[156] See 'German-British Convention', 15 June 1914, in *BD* x/2, no. 249 encl.

[157] Following the fall of Romania, the Central Powers issued a peace offer on 12 Dec. 1916. The offer was rejected by the Entente Powers on 30 Dec.

[158] Philip Henry Kerr (1882–1940), 11th Marquess of Lothian, succ. 1930, politician and diplomat; served in South African government, 1905–1910; founder-editor of the *Round*

an article on 'What Peace Means'. That, according to L[loyd] G[eorge], is the greatest danger.

Dec[ember] 14th [1916]

Tino is desperately manoeuvring to gain time – among other things he offered to telegraph to Sarrail as one solider to another, an offer which was contemptuously ignored. Meanwhile the blockade tightens, though it may take 3 months to starve them out. It won't take more than 3 weeks for them to feel the effects. The <ultimatum> proposed on the 9th is still hanging fire, going the rounds of the diplomatic circumlocution office. I gather demands will be for 2 divisions [in] Thessaly, 3 divisions [in] Athens and 10 divisions in the Morea. Commerce of course will also be controlled. The Russians are fighting under great difficulties against the Huns in the Dobrudja and Wallachia, but they do not run like the Roumanians. They will hardly hold the Buzeu line, but should be alright on the Sereth.[159] L[loyd] G[eorge] is still ill. I gather from D[avid] D[avies] that he hoped to include a good many more Liberals than he actually secured. Also apparently D[avid] D[avies] for 3 weeks before the crash had written him some very hot letters telling him to resign, the opinion philosopher. So it was not all ambition. I went into Miss Stephenson's[160] [sic] room, and saw there a very large cigar-case, handsomely initialled in silver. 'That', said D[avid] D[avies], 'is what L[loyd] G[eorge] says is the only positive result of my conference on Irish affairs'.[161] I am not sure his premiership was not another.

Dec[ember] 15th [1916]

The F[oreign] O[ffice] excelled itself. V[iscoun]t Grey in his last ultimatum, the night he left, demanded the withdrawal of troops from Thessaly. Subsequently he had to substitute Northern Greece as Thessaly as a term does not exist <except

---

Table Journal, 1910; private secretary to Lloyd George, 1916–22; Chancellor of the Duchy of Lancaster, 1931; Parliamentary Under-secretary of State for India, 1931–32; ambassador at Washington, 1939–40

[159] Buzeu fell on that same day; on 8 Jan. 1917, the Romanian and Russian forces were pushed back beyond the Sereth (now Siret, a river that rises from the Carpathians and flows southward joining the Danube near Galați.

[160] Frances Stevenson (1888–1972), Countess Lloyd-George of Dwyfor, cr. 1943, personal secretary, confidante and mistress of Lloyd George; married Lloyd George, 1943, following death of his first wife.

[161] Lloyd George held a conference with various Irish Nationalist representatives on 23 June 1916.

as an administrative district> and the withdrawal from it, unless strictly defined, would therefore be useless. In fact V[iscoun]t Grey meant from all Greece north of the Morea.[162] I think the explanation is that the F[oreign] O[ffice] either does not have maps or does not look at them. The ultimatum was presented by Elliot on the 14th, and after revision, included withdrawal of specified troops and materiel from north Greece and the immediate suspension of movements of troops elsewhere. It was in the name of the 4 powers, though the Italians have secretly sought to moderate the demands and intrigued with Tino. Elliot thinks Tino will accept, but makes clear that reparation is to come.

The peace kite appears to have originally flown from Hungary, which indicates their danger.

Dec[embe]r 16 [1916]

The F[oreign] O[ffice] is immortal.

An attack by King,[163] MP, on Sir W[illiam] Robertson is not altogether unjustified.[164] I rather doubt if the C[hief of the] I[mperial] G[eneral] S[taff] should make speeches, still less sneer at politicians as he did in a recent speech at the Union Jack Club. Moreover his rostra are insignificant – a village in Lincolnshire, a public school, a soldier's home. His speeches have created a lively excitement with L[loyd] G[eorge], as touching on political matters, e.g. we have not 'only to win the war but to win the peace'. Did that mean that soldiers were to dictate the peace to civilians, or that conscription must continue, so as to render peace secure [?]. In the first case it was a danger to civil liberty little less serious than that of Germany.

Dec[ember] 18th [1916]

Last night enjoyed the unwonted luxury of being undisturbed in bed as orderly officer except by the promptings of Beecham.[165] Tino has begun to move <his troops to the Morea> and reparation has yet to be demanded. The Roumanian situation is still anxious and the Russians are still by no means certain of holding the Sereth. The whole Roumanian army is now recruiting [*recte* retreating] behind that line. It has not always fought badly – the Orsova division

---

[162] That is, north of the Peleponnese.

[163] Joseph King (1860–1943), financier, politician and patron of Haslemere Peasant Arts movement; MP (Lib.) North Somerset, 1906–18.

[164] King asserted widespread dissatisfaction with Roberts, see *Hansard* lxxxviii (15 Dec. 1916), cols. 1058–9, and *The Times*, 16 Dec. 1916.

[165] That is, Beecham's Pills.

fought magnificently, so did the 11th [division], but the collapse of certain units at critical points always involved the break-down of the line of defence.

Was glad that someone in [the] F[oreign] O[ffice] succeeded in stopping the appointment of Heaton Armstrong[166] as assistant M[ilitary] A[ttaché] to Roumania. I was sorry for the fellow as he got his kit. But the principle that the son of a foreign mother should not go to Buc[h]arest was sound, more especially as he talked a lot outside of what he was going to do, and was private secretary to William the Weed[167] in Albania in 1914. Then he was imprisoned in Germany and exchanged. I wonder greatly why – since he was under 40 and not ill. I should suspect him of being a German agent.

I heard of another man recently who took the title of Captain and got himself self-appointed by a telegram agent to the Venizelist Government <seemingly a pure adventurer>.

Dec[ember] 19th [1916]

D[irector of] M[ilitary] I[ntelligence][168] came in and said that L[loyd] G[eorge] made a fine speech, with little padding, and thumping the table magnificently in favour of the Army.[169] That was old Robertson's account, who went to hear it.

The Russo-Roumanian business continues to be serious, and the congestion on the Russian lines is so great that they can receive no more goods at present. R[omani]a is fast becoming a Russian dependency, as the Roumanian army is now so reduced. Inspired an article, which appeared in the 'Times' today representing the very great services of Russia to the Roumanian cause in sending more troops than she contracted for, defending the flanks, and immobilizing 12 Austrian divisions in Moldavia.[170] Destruction of corn and oil is reported as

---

[166] Captain Duncan Heaton-Armstrong (1886–1969), British officer; private secretary and comptroller of the private purse to Prince Wilhelm zu Wied, Jan.–Aug. 1914; see D. Heaton-Armstrong, *The Six Month Kingdom: Albania 1914*, G. Belfield (ed.) (London, 2005).

[167] Prince Wilhelm Friedrich Heinrich zu Wied (1876–1945), German aristocrat; selected by the Great Powers to assume the throne of Albania; reigned as *mbret*, Mar.–Sept. 1914.

[168] Lieutenant-General Sir George Mark Watson Macdonogh (1865–1942), military intelligence officer; commissioned into Royal Engineers, 1884; General Staff Officer, 1906; Head of Section 5, Director of Military Intelligence, 1912–14; Senior Officer in charge of intelligence, British Expeditionary Force, 1914–16; Head of MI7, 1916; Director of Military Intelligence, 1916–18; Adjutant-General to the Forces, 1918–22; Colonel Commandant, Royal Engineers, 1924.

[169] During the Second Reading of the Consolidated Funds (Appropriation) Bill on 19 December, 'House of Commons', *The Times*, 20 Dec. 1916.

[170] Leader 'The Hunger March Across Rumania', *The Times*, 19 Dec. 1916.

very complete, a result almost wholly due to Colonel Norton-Griffiths,[171] who was sent out on this mission and has done splendidly <overcoming at last the interested opposition of Bratianu[172]>. He is now burning corn at Braila. There seems to be friction between Russians and French, owing perhaps to the latter's mission under Berthelot.

Dec[ember] 22 [1916]

According to good information Milner[173] sent for Amery from Salonica. Latter is now on the C[ommittee of] I[mperial] D[efence]. His views are, in brief, that a great attack was planned on the Krusha[174] Balkan by the Bulgars against the Italians early in October, but this was avoided by the successes of the Serbs at Monastir and the English push on the Struma.[175] The English push he thought not a clever plan but an accident. The Bulgars came down into the plain in antiquated mass attacks, within the range of British guns, to the great amazement of the gunners. Result – death in holocausts.

The almost complete destruction of <Roumanian> oil is confirmed.

Dec[ember] 27th [1916]

Apparently President Wilson[176] USA has tried to force peace on us by the threat of embargo or war, because Germany has threatened him with submarines.[177] Truly

---

[171] Lieutenant-Colonel Sir John 'Empire Jack' Norton-Griffiths (1871–1930), 1st Bart., cr. 1922, army engineer; served Boer War; carried out railway construction projects in Southern Africa, 1903–1908; established Royal Engineers Tunnelling Company on Western Front, 1915; in charge of sabotage operations against Romanian oil fields, 1916; MP (Cons.) Wednesbury, 1910–18, Wandsworth Central, 1918–24.

[172] Ion I.C. Brătianu (1864–1927), Romanian politician; Foreign Minister, 1902–1904, 1908–1909, 1916–18, 1918–19; Prime Minister, 1909–11, 1914–18, 1918–19, 1922–26, 1927.

[173] Sir Alfred Milner (1854–1925), 1st Viscount Milner, cr. 1902, colonial administrator and politician; Minister without Portfolio (in War Cabinet), 1916–18; Secretary of State for War, 1918–19; for the Colonies, 1919–21.

[174] Now Kroussa.

[175] (Greek Strimonas), a river that rises in the Vitosha mountains south of Sofia and runs southwards to the Strymonian Gulf in the Aegean.

[176] (Thomas) Woodrow Wilson (1856–1924), US academic and politician; Professor of Jurisprudence and Political Economy, Princeton, 1890–1910; President of Princeton University, 1902–1910; Governor of New Jersey, 1911–13; 28th US President, 1913–21.

[177] President Wilson's peace note to the European belligerents and neutrals of 18 Dec. 1916, see J.B. Scott (ed.), *President Wilson's Foreign Policy: Messages, Addresses, Papers*

we live in a strange world, where a neutral tries to force us into peace because Germany wishes to force him into war. No more news of German doings in Macedonia. There is an intercepted telegram from the Kaiser to Queen Sophie [of Greece], in which he declares Tino must go to war with us, and then may be assured of German support. This telegram the Italians do not think conclusive of Tino's guilt. Will they ever that anything is? They are pro-Tino because they are anti-Venizelos, i.e. against the man who gave his word to them about Epirus and kept it. A thing no other modern Greek statesman ever did.

Dec[ember] 28 [1916]

French insist on liking and dying for Sarrail who wants to attack Tino.

Dec[ember] 29 [1916]

Saw Mrs. St. Clair Stobart,[178] remarkable for Stobart Hospital in Serbia and the 'Flaming Sword', an account of her retreat. A wonderful woman-feminist and energiser.

She had a great hatred of Phillips,[179] M[ilitary] A[ttaché] in Serbia who, she says, was anti-Serb and entirely misconceived the situation. She told Sir Edward Grey this.

Dec[ember] 30th [1916]

The great German idea now is for a big Eastern offensive next year. We shall therefore have a big Western one. L[loyd] G[eorge], as an off-set to Roumania, wishes to go to Jerusalem. Some say this is the act of a demagogue – perhaps it is that of a crusader or a Christian.

The Dobrudja campaign of which I saw an ac[count] today is painful reading. The R[omania]ns did not dig trenches – it was useless labour, had no field-telephones, had observation ladders, and had no idea of hiding artillery.

(New York, 1918), 235–44.

[178] Mabel Anne St Clair Stobart (1862–1954), suffragette; founder of Women's Convoy Corps and Women's National Service League (1912); commanded a mobile field hospital for the Serbian Army Medical Services at Scutari, 1915–16.

[179] Brigadier-General George Fraser Phillips (1863–1921), soldier; entered army, 1885; commander, International Force and Governor of Scutari (Shkodër), 1913–14; active service, France, 1914–15; Military Attaché to Serbia and Montenegro, 1915–16; Head of British Military Mission to Greece, 1916–17; Commandant, Paris region, 1917–18; Albania, 1918–20.

Zaiontchovsky[180] was not greatly to blame and had a bad chief of staff. The demoralized Rumans on his right gave way and uncovered his right flank, where the two Serbian divisons were surrounded and fought till only 2,000 were left, neither asking nor giving quarter. They, ever they seem seem to show some distaste for war – and the 3rd reserve division may not be used. What a history – 2 divisions out of 3 annihilated on the Dobrudja – 15–20,000 at Corfu, 60–80,000 in the great retreat – 17,000, perhaps ~~25,000~~ 30,000 in the attack on Monastir. What a holocaust – of what heroes. O freedom, in they name! I saw some 30 or 40 of these poor fellows, now dead in the Dobrudja on their way out, rough, ruddy and coffee-coloured. They bayoneted 3,000 prisoners and gave their lives like heroes for an idea.

31 Dec[embe]r [1916]

The Greek situation is getting worse. I think there will be war as a New Year's gift. The arrangements to which the Gr[ee]k Gov[ernmen]t consented as to the transfer of troops do not appear to have been carried out in honest fashion. 65 represent one regiment, 115 another and so on. The tone of the Greek state papers has become hostile and they have not answered one of our communications for six days. Well they have brought it on themselves. Tino is false, fickle and cunning – comme un Grèc du Bas-Empire.

It was Gallieni,[181] I hear, who saved Paris, France, perhaps the world. When the Germans came near Paris, Gallieni as Governor, on his own authority and at his own risk, organised an army and sent it to take the Germans in [the] flank on the Ourcq.[182] There it appeared, very greatly to their astonishment, and Joffre, who had not conceived the plan, commended the author. The French had expected an advance via Luxemburg and the Ardennes and down the right bank of the Meuse. Even when informed by our airmen, they regarded movements on the left bank as simply those of a flank guard.

---

[180] General Andrei Medardovich Zayonchkovski or Zaionchkovski (1862–1926), Russian soldier; entered army, 1888; commanded 85th Vyborg Infantry Regiment and 2nd brigade, 3rd Siberian Infantry Division, 1904–1905; commander, 30th Army Corps, 1914–16; commander, Russian-Romanian army in Dobruja, 1916–17; retired, Apr. 1917; joined Red Army, 1918; professor, Red Army Military Academy; author of *Podgotovka Rossii k mir: Voyne. Plan Voyni* (Moscow, 1926).

[181] General Joseph Simon Galliéni (1849–1916), French military commander and colonial governor; retired Apr. 1914; recalled Aug. 1914; organized 'taxi army' during Battle of the Marne, Sept. 1914; Minister of War, 1915–16.

[182] A tributary of the Marne.

1917

2nd January [1917]

Lloyd George feels he has burnt his boats and that there is no course for him but success. He wants it, a big, or at least a brilliant one immediately and then he will be safe. Meanwhile England suffers in his personal reaction after his triumph.

The Russo-Roumanian imbroglio thickens. No one would have thought that a nation would come so low as Roumania. Yet, in the spring, she will have 500,000 men and now has perhaps 300,000. Russia meanwhile seems to seek a pretext for escaping from her old obligations under the convention. In some ways a separate peace of Roumania would be an advantage as we should not be embarrassed by their claims at the final Round-Table. Meanwhile the Russians will probably eventually hang on to the Dobrudja because it will be the pathway to Constantinople.

I hear on good authority that Nivelle, with the bull-dog jaw, is a supremely confident man, confident above all of breaking through this year. I fancy the French offensive will begin very early. Lyautey[1] also appears to be a man of iron firmness, possibly a dictator in the future. Sarrail also a candidate for that post – dreams perhaps in his imperial exile of returning to France like Napoleon of old, with laurels of the Great Hun upon him. My source was my old friend Major Escoffier[2] – I do not think we can break the front.

---

[1] General (Louis) Hubert (Gonzalve) Lyautey (1854–1934), French military commander; Resident-general at Fez, 1912–25; Minister of War, Dec. 1916–Mar. 1917; associated with *Croix de feu* in 1930s.

[2] Maurice Alexandre Escoffier (1879–1959), French historian; lecturer in contemporary history, École Libre des Sciences Politiques, 1906–10; professor there, 1910–45; tutor to Prince of Wales during stay in France, 1912; active service, 1914–18; assistant military attaché at London, 1916–18; attached to secretariat of Paris peace conferece, 1919; Secretary-General, French Section, League of Nations, 1919–21; editor, *Revue des sciences politiques*, 1919–39; Escoffier and Temperley met at Cambridge, see entry 20 Jan. 1917; not to be confused with Auguste Escoffier (1846–1935), head chef at London's Carlton Hotel, 1899–1920.

3rd January [1917]

A long refutation by Mr. Rendel,[3] 3rd Sec[retar]y of Athens Legation, of the idea that there was a Venizelist plot there. This accusation is, in itself, disposed by the fact that when first charged with the murder of Venizelists the Professor-Premier[4] made no accusation of their plots. That was first uttered several days later. Our refutator is at pains to show that the hatching of a plot was all the other way, that the doors of Venizelists were splashed with red paint, and that Royalists and Reservists organised themselves wearing the King's portrait and white brassards, like St. Bartholomew conspirators. The Venizelists had no weapons except those which every Greek has against housebreakers and a few rockets in Venizelos' house which were distorted into bombs. The forget letter attributed to Venizelos apparently had great popular effect, though transparently a fabrication. The American Minister's evidence, and some other eyewitnesses prove conclusively that no firing, so as far as known, was begun or was provoked by Venizelists. Our refutator concluded his erudite disourse by a comparison of the whole affair to the Athenian conduct at Cercyra[5] in 332 [sic] BC.[6]

4th January [1917]

A British military eyewitness, who happened to be sight-seeing below the Parthenon, on the 1st December, saw Greek riflemen hidden behind the Parthenon walls open fire on the French were well on the skyline. He considered <under> the circumstances that the act was little short of murder. No doubt they fired from the Parthenon because they knew we would not shell it. No wonder the statue of Byron was blindfolded![7]

---

[3] Sir George William Rendel (1889–1979), diplomat; entered diplomatic service, 1913; 3rd secretary at Athens, 1915–17; transferred to Foreign Office, 1919; senior clerk, Eastern Department, 1930–38; minister at Belgrade, 1941–43 (ambassador since 1942); UK representative on United Nations Relief and Rehabilitation Administration, 1944–45; ambassador at Brussels, 1947–50.

[4] That is, Professor Spyridon Lampros (1851–1919), see entry 17 Oct. 1916.

[5] Kerkyra, main city on Corfu.

[6] Presumably a reference to Pericles' alliance with Korkyra in 432 BC, which was the cause of the Peleponnesian War, 431–404 BC. Thucydides, *Istorion*, book I, cc. 43–4.

[7] See entry 2 Dec. 1916.

5th January [1917]

First call 10 Downing Street, through the little gardengate [*sic*] at the back of the House Guards, into a deep well-like room where D[avid] D[avies] is. I heard two interesting things, one how L[loyd] G[eorge] got round the C[hief of the] I[mperial] G[eneral] S[taff, Robertson]. Sir Henry Wilson is going to Russia. L[loyd] G[eorge] now in Italy thought he sh[oul]d go there too.[8] The C[hief of the] I[mperial] G[eneral] S[taff] was not so favourable. So L[loyd] G[eorge] said nothing for 4 or 5 days. Then, at the last meeting of the Cabinet, just before starting, he turned round to the C[hief of the] I[mperial] G[eneral] S[taff :] 'I think it would be rather good for Wilson to go with us and learn what we discussed there'. Presses a bell, as the servants appears – 'Tell Sir H[enry] W[ilson] to pack up his things at once'. C[hief of the] I[mperial] G[eneral] S[taff] still unable to get a word out, finds himself outmanoeuvred.

6th January [1917]

Interview with Jovanovich,[9] Serbian Minister. He speaks very clearly, plenty of good sense, no gesture or excitement, excellent abilities, possibly not very great driving force. A black head[,] rather untidy hair and ragged moustache.

He th[in]ks the Croatian danger is considerable – the plan of Franz Ferdinand, what was it [but] an Austrian Jugoslavia [?].[10] Also the Hungarian plan to have Bosnia Herzegovina and Montenegro. This might be done, but there would be intrigues, conspiracies, never-ending after the war again. Not but what we would not consent to much. We are a small nation. We must accept not our own conditions but those of others, if it is necessary for the larger interest. Thus we should expect a strong Austro-Hungarian demand for an embouchure on the Adriatic coast. Let them take Fiume, if they wish. If it is neutralized or free port, it is alright.

As for Italy, another question, another danger for us. But here again, what can a small nation of from 10 to 12,000,000 do against 40 millions? What have they not got, or will they not have? What have they got to fear? Trieste, Valona,[11]

---

[8] At the Allied conference at Rome conference, 4–7 Jan. 1917.

[9] Jovan M. Jovanović-Pižon (1869–1939), Serb diplomat, politician and historian; entered Foreign Ministry, 1900; Secretary-General, Foreign Ministry, 1908–12; Foreign Minister, June–Aug. 1912; minister at Vienna, 1912–14; Deputy Foreign Minister, 1914–16; minister at London, 1916–19; at Washington, 1920; leader of the Agrarian Party, 1923–39.

[10] The archduke advocated a reform of the Dual Monarchy along 'trialist' lines to give the Slav population a greater share in its affairs.

[11] Now Vlorë (Albania).

something in Dalmatia. They can neutralize our ports. Even for forty years we shall not be dangerous.

Roumania – he did not think any worse of her than others but appeared to consider her as worthless from a military point of view. He relied on the Entente, i.e. France and England but most on England. Thought old King Nicholas of any side where he found his account, and told the story of the 10,000 troops he wished to sell to Austria.

8th January [1917]

Giving to the [*sic*] Sarrail 'a free hand' has ended in the French asserting a blunder and confessing to a ~~blunder~~ manoeuvre. The Rome conference has ended by a 48 hours ultimatum to Tino.

10th January [1917]

L[loyd] G[eorge] is fairly satisfied with [the] Italian results – there has been a general resolution as to more cooperation and a special means to improving communications between Santa Quaranta[12] and Monastir. This will, however, involved considerable difficulties of supply and ditto duties of protection. The ultimatum <to Tino> expires today. Milne[13] thinks that an attack on Tino would be a thing for which we have neither troops nor opportunity, involving a separate command and separate army, while decisive results could hardly be obtained even if we got to Larissa.

Sarrail and the Venizelists are of course in favour of it, though for different reasons.

The Prime Minister's Council of Intelligence is announced today. I met them once again – old W.G.S. Adams,[14] greyheaded now and dogged as ever, David Davies, my tried friend, and Philip Kerr.[15] The one is general, the second

---

[12] Sarandë on the Southern Albanian coast opposite Corfu.

[13] Field Marshal Sir George Francis Milne (1866–1948), 1st Baron Milne, cr. 1933, British military commander; commissioned into Royal Artillery, 1885; served India, Second Boer War, Western Front, 1914–15; Commander-in-Chief Salonika Army, 1915–18; head of military administration Black Sea area, 1918; occupied Constantinople, 1920; Chief of the Imperial General Staff, 1926–33.

[14] William George Stewart Adams (1874–1966), academic and civil servant; superintendent of statistics, Irish Department of Agriculture, 1905–10; Gladstone Professor of Political Science, Oxford, 1912–33; founding-editor *Political Quarterly*, 1915–16; Ministry of Munitions, 1915–16; Private Secretary to Lloyd George, 1916–18; Warden of All Souls, 1933–45.

[15] See entry 5 Dec. 1916.

Parl[iamentar]y & military, the 3rd foreign and imperial. The third has too much of Oxford and the groves of Academe, the desire for Leagues of Peace and internationalized states to suit our modern deserts of reality, I am afraid. I hammered into him the careful working out of the Eastern frontier, historically, geographically, strategically, and made some progress, I think.

12th [January 1917]

Nothing much. My interview with Jovanovitch was considerably longer than that of the Foreign Secretary on the 1st Jan[uar]y and disclosed more important details. I hope it may prove to be of service.

The calling of the new Greece 'into existence to redress the balance of the old'[16] goes not as smoothly as might be. Our attitude in the past seems to have been one of simple and feeble acquiescence in adoring French policy which, under Grey, we were not men enough either to support or to disclaim. The result was that we did just enough to discredit Venizelos and to encourage Tino to resist the French. The new ultimatum to Tino was theatrically accepted by the Greek Governments but their reservations were so many that the acceptance mattered little. What can we do now? With an uncertain reply after the ultimatum, in which we have promised to restrain Venizelos by force of arms.

15th [January 1917]

The Roumanian danger grows more real. With the fall of Braila and Reni the lateral connecting line with Odessa goes – the railway communications with Kishineff and Jassy[17] are few and bad. Russia is at the end of her transport resources and, if the Germans have enough men and resources, I see no reason why they should not reach Odessa. If they had tried for it in August 1914 they must have got there, have roped in Roumania, Bulgaria, Turkey, perhaps Greece, and certainly the Empire of the World. We were saved only by the mercy of God.

This brings me to the responsibility of bringing in Roumania, surely the greatest blunder and greatest responsibility of the Alliance. Looking up the files again what strikes us? I hear they were looked up recently to fix the blame and can ~~conjecture~~ sum [up] the result. So far as I can gather, the Russians were

---

[16] A reference to George Canning's boast to have called the new world into existence to redress the balance of the old, see H.W.V. Temperley, *Life of Canning* (London, 1905), 191.

[17] Now Chişinău (Moldova) and Iaşi (Romania).

not responsible. Alexeieff[18] just said he didn't care whether they did or not and then fixed a time-limit by which they must come in. We feebly followed the French lead, I think. The French drove furiously and promised an offensive from Salonica. We had declined that in June and May, and restricted our terms to a containing attack. Then, at the last moment, we (i.e. the F[oreign] O[ffice]) caved in, and instructed the ~~Amb[assado]r~~ Min[iste]r [Sir George Barclay] to 'withdraw any qualifying clause'. Briand[19] claimed the credit, but why should he bear all the blame? Why not Viscount Grey of Fallodon? One thing in our favour – the Roumanian military plan was Roumanian, i.e. damnably bad and at the time was criticized by our C[hief of the] I[mperial] G[eneral] S[taff] and defeat in detail predicted. That proves that the military plan was not framed by us. It was an ambitious bubble fanned by the puffed-up breath of a vain people.

18th [January 1917]

Apparently the destruction of grain is fairly complete and Norton-Griffiths,[20] the pocket whirlwind of destruction, will return home full of glory. The Russians helped to destroy corn at the beginning but afterwards held their hands partly under desire to save some for themselves.

The Roumanian influence was steadily ag[ain]st destruction all the time, and peasants and soldiers threatened the intrepid whirlwind. Even when the King consented the Roumanian Min[iste]r of Foreign Affairs withheld his official consent in order to evade <personal> responsibility. He who avoids responsibility avoids credit.

Went to see D[avid] D[avies], starting for Russia – Milner also going, I gather with letter recommending Liberalism as an antidote.

Men say the Czar[21] is still uxorious and that, if the lady could be in a convent for a year, a counter-distraction might set him on a right course in politics.

Sat in Elizabeth Asquith's[22] boudoir, now a busy secretary's room.

---

[18] General Mikhail Vasili'evich Alekse'ev (1857–1918), Russian military commander; Chief of Staff, South Western front, 1914–15; Chief of Staff to Nicholas II, 1915–17; Commander-in-Chief, Feb.–July 1917; led anti-Bolshevik Volunteer Army, 1917–18; killed in action, Sept. 1918.

[19] Aristide Briand (1862–1932), French politician; Prime Minister, 1909–11, 1912, 1915–17, 1921–2, 1925–6, 1929; Foreign Minister, 1915–17, 1921–2, 1925–6, 1926–32.

[20] See entry 19 Dec. 1916.

[21] Nicholas II Romanov (1868–1918), Tsar of all the Russias, 1894–1917; assassinated, 17 July 1918.

[22] Elizabeth Charlotte Lucy, Princess Bibesco (née Asquith) (1897–1945), socialite and writer; daughter of H.H. Asquith and his second wife, Margot Tennant; organized and performed in matinées for servicemen during the First World War; married, 1919, the Romanian diplomat Prince Antoine Bibescu (1878–1951).

Tino has theatrically accepted our demands – in practice he has send about 8,000 men to Morea instead of 15,000. Venizelos is however on the whole optimistic, moderate as usual, and thinks conscription has been very successful.

Had to deal severely with a prepared Foreign Office proclamation, which stated that the Allies had recognized the government of Salonica as a 'sovereign state' – wrong in two ways. Russia probably and Italy almost certainly has not recognized the Gov[ernmen]t and, as Tino is still de iure lord and master of Venizelist Greece, the latter cannot be a sovereign state. I suggested a proclamation declaring the Salonica gov[ernmen]t a sovereign state.

20th [January 1917]

Lunched with Capt[ain] Escoffier[23] yesterday. Strange that I should have met him years ago at Cambridge as a French historian with a strong anti-English bias and a profound belief in the French army. Now he has been governor of the Prince of Wales during his stay in Paris, wounded at Verdun, in attendance on General Nivelle,[24] and is now <assistant> attaché to Colonel Panouse.[25] He was very frank on all his experiences. He thought the Prince of Wales[26] intelligent – gave as his private opinion that the French could not break the Western front, but believed Nivelle thought they could. He said that at the first day of the Conference Nivelle was very dissatisfied, at the second satisfied because because he thought that the views he advocated had been adopted. Nivelle was a Colonel of artillery when the war began, what a country and what a man. He said Joffre as technical adviser to the French Government demanded 70 officers on his staff, Lyautey gave up the job and became a Marshal of France. He will be the great man of the war as the victor of the Marne and the Yser, though Gallieni saved France.

23rd [January 1917]

Once more on Roumania – working out the responsibility. Roughly Alexeieff[27] took the sound view at first, he didn't care if Roumania came in, if she did or

---

[23] See entry 2 Jan. 1917.
[24] See entry 8 Dec. 1916.
[25] Major-General (Artus Henri) Louis Vicomte de La Panouse (1863–1944), French soldier; entered army, 1883; Military Attaché at London, 1915–22.
[26] (Edward Albert Christian George Andrew Patrick) David Windsor (1894–1972), Prince of Wales, 1910–35; King Edward VIII of the United Kingdom and the Dominions of the British Commonwealth, Emperor of India, Jan.–Dec. 1936; thereafter Duke of Windsor.
[27] See entry 15 Jan. 1917.

did not, and preferred a guarantee of neutrality. Subsequently, under political pressure he modified this but apparently always insisted that she should come in at a definite time. Ultimately also he acquiesced in the initial ultimatum of Russia. As Roumania refused to declare war on Bulgaria he also approved the ambitious plan of campaign ag[ain]st Transylvania. France was very active at the end – Joffre's telegram of propaganda impressed Bratiano [*sic*], and they promised both munitions and an offensive affirmée from Salonica, neither of which were wholly fulfilled. England seems to have been very keen on bringing in R[omani]a but the C[hief of the] I[mperial] G[eneral] S[taff] opposed the Transylvanian attack. His efforts were somewhat frustrated by the F[oreign] O[ffice], which withdrew 'qualifying clauses' about the offensive from Salonica and gave in on all points at the last. The C[hief of the] I[mperial] G[eneral] S[taff] however prevented a really elaborate offensive in June or July from Salonica, and thus incurred considerable responsibility. Our efforts in regard to Salonica will not probably impress historians. In June we declined even a limited offensive – in August we declined to send reinforcements and explained to the Serbs, who demanded them, that they could not be fed. In the saem month we gave way both to the Serbs and the French on the same point.

25th Jan[uar]y [1917]

As a somewhat grim pendant to the above reflections on Roumania. I saw an account by a neutral today. Of course we know one cause already. Iliesco[28] [*sic*], the court favourite, wished to do Averescu, the ranker, out of the command as Chief of Staff. To do this he could not put forward himself, he was too junior, but he put forward the then-expired cipher General Zottu,[29] who became Chief of Staff. Then Iliesco, already Secretary-General, got himself appointed in attendance on the King. The royal name covered his plans and enabled him to foil Averescu and Georgescu who wished a big offensive in the Dobrudja. This I already knew. The new information was to the effect that Zoltu, who was deeply committed to Germany both by intention and interest, remained a mere cipher except in so far as he sold information to the enemy. Then when, just before the fall of Bucharest, the Bulgar-Germans crossed at Zimnicea,[30] Zottu with 60,000

---

[28] Brigadier-General Dumitru Iliescu (1865–1940), Romanian officer and politician; commissioned into artillery, 1886; Secretary-General, Ministry of War, 1914–18; Deputy Chief of the General Staff, Aug.–Oct. 1916; Chief of the General Staff, Oct.–Dec. 1916; resigned, 1918.

[29] General Vasile Zottu (1853–1916), Romanian military commander; Chief of General Staff, Mar.–Nov. 1911, and 1914–16; commander, fortress Bucharest, 1911–14; committed suicide, 12 Nov. 1916.

[30] The southernmost town of Romania, situated on the left bank of the Danube. German troops crossed here and so brought down the Romanian front in Greater Wallachia.

did nothing except wait. Then the King summoned a council at Bucharest, Averescu, Zottu, the French General Berthelot. Averescu boldly taxed Zottu, with faint-heartedness, German intrigues and treachery. After some discussion, Zottu confessed. He was allowed to commit suicide. Whether this improvement on Jacob's ladder[31] really took place or not I am not certain, but it may have done. <A less poetical account says he went mad and killed himself in the process.> At the Crown Council, Carp[32] said 'Though I have 3 sons fighting in the army, I hope Roumania will be entirely destroyed'. Officers ran away very often I fear. At the moment the Roumanians have rallied. But who knows?

27th January [1917]

Recent information direct from Venizelos is that that great man has expressed himself as on the whole optimistic. He has now all new Greece, except Epirus, and all the Cyclades, except Milos, with Chios, Lemnos, Lesbos, Samos, Samothrace, Mytilene and Crete. Moderate and honourable as ever, he has cleared out of Corfu, because he occupied it a few hours after the ultimatum of Jan[uar]y 8th was accepted by Tino. He has also refused the adhesion of SKOPELOS, one of the northern Sporades, because it came on the 21st January. He has likewise declined to stir up Epirus because he does not wish to interfere with Italy, which refuses to recognize his agents, to press for the release of Venizelists at Athens, <which blockades vessels from Salonica to Dodecanese, and which forgets his sympathy towards Italy. I cannot but think that the truest friend the Entente has in Europe will one day reap his reward, and that the volatile citizens of old Greece will one day turn round completely once more and burn incense before the idol they are now spitting upon.

Venizelos has his trouble – he had to suppress outrages by his own followers in Chalcidia[33] and had to suppress a rebellion there provoked by the application of conscription to a population too primitive and ignorant to appreciate this necessity of modern civilization (*sic*). Then at Naxos, an enemy workers' village was attacked by Venizelists – 20 killed & 50 wounded, to the sorrow of the great chief.

Russians and French have improved the occasion by occupying M[oun]t Athos. There are 17 Greek monasteries there, 1 Russian, 1 Bulgar and 1 Serb <with about ½ total monk population>, and submarine intrigues are suspected. The Holy Synod governs but the main influence is Russian, and the status

---

[31] *Genesis* 28, 10–19.
[32] Petre P. Carp (1837–1919), Romanian politician; Prime Minister, 1900–1901, 1910–12; favoured Central Powers during the war.
[33] Chalkida, main town on Euboea.

[is] that defined in 1430, on surrendering to the Turk, i.e. quasi-independence, qualified by a Turkish resident governor and tribute. In 1913 there was much talk of internationalisation, but at the personal request of Venizelos this broke down. Russia retained a predominant influence, but no Greek resident governor or tribute have materialised as yet. The F[oreign] O[ffice], from whom I requested information, put their Athos expert on to me. He expertness was surprising. He said the monks on Athos were all Russia and did not know there had ever been a governor there or tribute paid.

28 Jan[uar]y [1917]

Balfour submitted a memo[randum] to the War Cabinet [on] the 23rd, entirely characteristic but based on imperfect knowledge. Epigrams abounded as 'the French minister (at Athens, Guillemin[34]), after long being mistrusted by the world, is at length being distrusted by his own government'[;] 'Constantine had earned universal contempt both from friend and foe'[;] 'Sarrail showed more interest in politics than in soldiering'[;] 'London Conference was one of those which decided nothing'. In short everything was absurd, and no true remedies were apparent. A characteristic Balfourian effort. Two questions at the end. Has 'Philosophic Doubt', 'Economic Notes on Insular Free Trade', 'Decadence'; & any other of his works ever concluded with anything but questions?[35] (1) On whom is to fall the general military responsibility for checking the transfer of Greek troops to the Morea? (2) Is there any advantage if we are convinced of Greek treachery, in attacking Greece previous to any overt act on her part?

29th Jan[uar]y [1917]

I heard a story about him [Balfour] at lunch with a friend of mine and his niece[36] and other just after his smart note to Wilson[:] 'Have you read the papers today?', said one[:] 'They are full of praise of you'. 'Oh', said A[rthur] J[ames] B[alfour] diffidently, 'I haven't had time to read them yet and I don't <u>always</u> read them'. 'Oh, but you should today, uncle', says the niece, 'it's

---

[34] Jean Marie Auguste René Guillemin (1862–1938), French diplomat; counsellor at Vienna, 1902–10; minister at Lima, 1910–12; minister at Athens, 1915–17; minister at Christiana, 1918–19; first placed on retired list, 1915.

[35] *A Defence of Philosophic Doubt* (London, 1879); *Economic Notes on Insular Free Trade* (London, 1903), and *Decadence: First Henry Sidgwick Memorial Lecture* (Cambridge, 1908).

[36] Blanche Elizabeth Campbell Dugdale (née Balfour) (1890–1948); employed in Naval intelligence during the First World War; one of the most committed of British 'gentile Zionists'.

the first time in six months that they've not had another article against you'. A.J. B[alfour]'s laugh was the loudest of any.

The Deutsche Bank has defaulted with respect to the Salonica Railway. Sir Adam Block[37] thinks that it is not any Machiavellian designs but simply a sign of financial weakness. <u>Oh utriam!</u>

The Greek barometer is slowly setting & away from 'stormy' but is still fine cloudy weather. A considerable number of guns have at last come down, and Sarrail is now unchallenged military controller.

31st [January 1917]

Saw Diomedes,[38] direct from Venizelos, as agent. He had several topics, one the wickedness of not letting the Greeks run their own light flotilla. Greek mariners knew every creek and bay in the islands whilst Englishmen & Frenchmen could not know them in the same way. The prevention of Greeks being allowed to use their naval strength was very serious from every point of view – moral & material – and discouraging to the Venizelist movement. On the Venizelist troops he stressed the point that they were very keen and also immune from malaria, therefore their place was the Struma in the campaign of this year. He said they could be brought up to 60,000 men, and that it depended solely on our supply of the means to produce this result.

He bade us not to believe in Tino & regarded the breach as irrevocable <as, I think, all Venizelists do>.

Personally I rather sympathize with the Venizelists in both respects, and I believe, via a naval officer, that the chief reason the French do not employ the Venizelist light squadron is that Tino flattered Admiral Dartige de Fournet. I understand at the naval conference the French accepted our policy of dealing with the Adriatic.

Jovanovich, whom I also saw, rather deprecated the view that the Russian internal situation was bad.

---

[37] Sir Adam Samuel James Block (1856–1941), diplomat; joined Levant consular service, 1877; consul at Constantinople, 1890–94; chief dragoman, 1894–1903; resigned, 1903; on Council of Ottoman Public Debt, 1903–1907; President of British Chamber of Commerce Constantinople, 1907–18; Controller of Finance Section, War Trade Department, 1915–16; dto., Ministry of Blockade, 1916–18; Commissioner on Financial Commission, Constantinople, 1920–21.

[38] Alexandros Diomedes (1875–1950), Greek academic and politician; Professor of Law and Economics, National University of Athens, 1905–10; MP (Lib.), 1910–23; Finance Minister, 1912–15, and 1922; Governor of the Bank of Greece, 1928; Prime Minister, 1949–50.

1st February [1917]

The firmness of Sarrail in refusing all concessions in the military sense seems to have united with the strictness <of the blockade> to convince Tino that we are really in earnest. There are now piteous appeals to raise the blockade, and there has been, for the last ten days or so, a reasonably fair attempt to carry out the military transfer. There is also a noticeable change in Greek press utterances and in public opinion though no one dares yet to speak of Venizelos in Athens except as 'the Man of Crete' and though the Venizelist press does not exist in Old Greece. If the F[oreign] O[ffice] had the smallest chance they would at once insist upon officiallyinspired Entente newspapers being set up. The Italians are quieter and, according to Milner, have moderated their pretensions on Smyrna.

2nd February [1917]

Went to dine with Aubrey Herbert,[39] who has had a remarkable time in this war, wounded in retreat from Mons, at Gallipolli, at surrender of Kut, and at Salonica. His latest stage is here, to work for Albania and a Balkan policy. He consulted me because Lord Robert Cecil, after 2 ½ years muddle, has at last confessed that the F[oreign] O[ffice] has no Balkan policy and has asked for suggestions about constructing one. Aubrey has written a memo[randum], mad & brilliant like the author, hoping Italy may be brought out of Valona by Corfu and pointing out that his interview with the Crown Prince of Serbia[40] suggested a great moderation on the Serbia side, and that therefore the Albanians of Ipek and Prisrend – of Albania proper – and the Southeast part of Macedonia were in the market for negotiation. He regards all Albanian leaders as discredited and confesses Albania cannot stand alone.

3rd February [1917]

One explanation of German peace proposals occurs to me today, when I learnt from a d m op. <(i.e. D[irector of] M[ilitary] O[perations] Sir Frederic

---

[39] Hon. Aubrey Nigel Henry Molyneux Herbert (1880–1923), traveller, intelligence officer and politician; MP (Cons.) Somerset South, 1911–18, Yeovil, 1918–23; affiliated with Foreign Office Arab Bureau, 1915–18; was twice offered the crown of Albania.

[40] Alexander I (Aleksandar I Karadjordjević) (1888–1934), Prince of Serbia; Regent of the State of the Serbs, Croats and Slovenes, 1918–21; King of the Serbs, Croats and Slovenes, 1921–29; King of Yugoslavia, 1929–34; assassinated at Marseilles, 1934.

Maurice[41])> source that this year we shall take the field with seven times the munition power of last year. On the Somme the Germans said it was hell, so this year will be the seventh hell.

Even now though I think the best opinion is that the Germans are near exhaustion point, doubts still supervene occasionally. The last batch of secret evidence direct from Germany contained about 12 statements of distress and 2 of tolerable conditions. The latter may, of course, be inspired as propaganda, but I doubt it.

I heard a forecast from a good source of what are supposed to be Germany's real needs, i.e. that they must have 2 months absolutely free of blockade after the end of May, in order to get in the materials for their new harvest. (This agrees with other statements to the effect that nitrates etc. are absolutely necessary to them.) Therefore they must have peace actually operative before the end of May. This would agree with their frantic haste to conclude peace, and their equally frantic threat to the USA, which has now been answered by breaking all diplomatic relations.

If the forecast of terms they would accept (from a good source) were accurate, these were thus:

1. Evacuation of Belgium.
2. Part of Alsace Lorraine to France.
3. Control of Balkan states.
4. Freedom of channels (neutralization) Dardanelles, Panama, Suez, Gibraltar.
5. Freedom of the seas.
6. Trade and free access on basis of most favoured nation to all British colonies, i.e. means they will give up their own.

(4) destroys the advantage of the Berlin to Bagdad route.

(6) would give them the opportunity to Germanise British colonies and seize key industries.

But the terms offered show that they are beaten, for how would these look to Germany?

---

[41] Major-General Sir Frederick Barton Maurice (1871–1951), 1st Bart., soldier; entered army, 1892; instructor at Staff College, 1913–14; Director of Military Operations, 1915–18; forced to resign after publicly criticizing Lloyd George, see below entry 7 May 1918 et seq.; founder of the British Legion, 1920.

6th February [1917]

[Sir Francis] Elliot, after having invited the Gov[ernmen]t to raise the blockade, has reconsidered it and only asks for supplies of coal and corn. Coal is a desideratum at present as there is acute distress, both in Italy and France because 'the black diamonds' and 'the bread of industry' are scanty. Greece (Royalist) sent in an urgent appeal for raising the blockade on the 30th Jan[uar]y.

The Italian attitude causes anxiety they have sent <5 Feb[ruar]y> 300 men to Corfu, which has just been evacuated by Greeks, and the French have nominated a German-named gentleman, Gen[eral] Baumann,[42] as Governor of the Island. I am afraid it all looks like Italian designs on the island of which we have heard rumours before. No wonder the Italians hate Venizelos, who might prevent this. Today the Foreign Minister in Italy pleaded ignorance of the whole matter when taxed with the occupation of Corfu.

7th Feb[ruar]y [1917]

In spite of 18 ships down yesterday and 23 today, I believe the Admiralty is pretty confident of keeping down the submarine menace. At the worst there remains escorting, a slow and difficult process but still a possibility. It is now a hunger war by us on Greece & Germany, by Germany on the world.

I undertstand from Diomede [*sic*], via Panouse French M[ilitary] A[ttaché], that he wishes if possible an English prince for Greece, as the whole Greek gang, except possibly the children of Prince George of Greece, are thoroughly Prussianised. It is evident that both the French and Venizelos have determined in good time and season to have Tino out. It believe it is right. Greece is behaving better and at last really trying hard to transport the right number of men, now that the blockade is hitting her belly. The situation is still serious – two Frenchmen are still missing and Venizelists in outlying parts of the provinces are still in chains, whilst the King's Government shows signs of wishing to requisition Greek ships for their own use, a demand we shall not grant. Provisioning Venizelist Greece is a serious matter as the Venizelist government has not shown exceptional efficiency in that direction, and we shall have to intervene now to do it and to save their prestige. It is difficult for we are hard hit for ships. Greece (Royalist) will be harder hit still for, even if the blockade is relaxed, no ships can reach her before the end of February.

---

[42] Brigadier-General Albert Baumann (1869–1945), French soldier; Baumann was of German-Jewish extraction.

Feb[ruar]y 8th [1917]

Sent by Burrows[43] a long letter from Venizelos of which the following is the substance. It has a double interest as having been written before the tragic émeute of Dec[ember] 1st, and having been finished afterwards. From Sal[oni]ca Nove[mber] 17/30 'The responsibility for all the wretchedness of Greece rests, not on the Greek people, who were from the beginning wholeheartedly on the side of the Entente, but on the Powers of the Entente which after repeated blunders have made easy the work of unbridled German propaganda and of the King, who, after all, is not a Greek!'

'The Greek people ... as soon as it saw that even after the Bulgarian occupation of Kavalla and after the Roumanian declaration of war the King persisted in the same criminal policy did at last rise, but instead of meeting with wholehearted encouragement from the Powers of the Entente, it immediately received a severed <u>avertissement</u> that this movement must not assume an anti-dynastic character ... we wish neither to change our family nor to replace our ruling family by another'.

' ... it is impossible to imagine why this strenuous attempt should be made (by the Powers) to save him <u>personally</u> from the national consequence of his treachery'.

'This attempt which in effect excuses such a terrible political crime is not only opposed to the elementary dictates of political morality; but it is also opposed to the political interests of the Entente Powers and to the vital interests of Greece'.

'Greek existence as an independent state and Greek progress are only possible if Greece remains in close contact with the Western Powers'.

' ... if King Constantine after all his treachery remains on the throne it would be idle to hope that an honest observance of the Constitution might be secured by means of a Constituent Assembly. Since there could exist no sanction for such sincere observance of the Constitution, what would be the object of inscribing new advances on the charter?'

'Moreover King Constantine was not content only to impose his personal foreign policy against the will of the nation; but he joined hands with the old party spirit which the people has graphically named 'the regime of rot' (φαυλοκρατιά),[44] which was dissolved by the Revolution of 1909 and by my own five years of administration, which the people called 'The Reformation'.[']

'The preservation of the dynasty. The Crown-Prince, in respect of Germanophile feelings is not different from his father; but he has not the prestige and consequently the power which Constantine acquired by his victories in the Balkan Wars, and with the explicit safeguards which will be introduced by the

---

[43] See entry 7 Dec. 1916.
[44] Literally 'rule of corruption'.

Constituent Assembly and with the example of his father's punishment before him, the Crown-Prince, when he became King, would necessarily keep to the role of constitutional monarch'.

Suggests that they should recognize Prov[isiona]l Gov[ernmen]t and leave only Ad[mira]l Fournet at Athens and forbid import of petrol & export of currants. 'If this course were followed and we were provided with the necessary means of organising our forces the King's authority would in six months extend not much beyond the Royal Estate of Tatoi (Deceleia).[']⁴⁵ Recommends development of Greek (Venizelist) marine and army.

Complains of neutral zone, which cuts him off from Thessaly 'which would give us an admirable source of reservists and which is by a large majority on our side'.

'I was amazed to read the last announcement of Under-Secretary Lord Robert Cecil in the H[ouse] of C[ommons] according to which I am exercising authority in the name of King Constantine. This is a material error. The authority of the Provisional Government is exercised in the name of Nation, from which it also received its mandate; but the fact that in the districts where the authority of the Provisional Government of Athens has been brought to an end is sufficient to prove that we do not act in the name of King Constantine: if the heading of our public documents bears the title of the Kingdom of Greece, this is only because we wish to show clearly that we look for no permanent division of the state, nor for the destruction of the monarchy as such; but if we are content to accept the principle of royal authority it does not by any means follow that we exercise our authority in the name of King Constantine, whom we conscientiously believe to have betrayed the <the interests of the> nation'.

'All that I write to you about the King you can make use of, but not as coming officially from me for that would reflect on the Powers which naturally I have every wish to avoid'.

P.S. December 3 [1916]

'Before finding an opportunity to forward to you this letter, the bloody events of the last two days have taken place in Athens, which are enough to reveal even to the most blind all the frightfulness of King Constantine's true disposition. We will see if, even after these events the protecting hand of the Powers will continue to be extended over the head of such a tyrant'.

I fear the F[oreign] O[ffice] is playing a bad part – there seems to be evidence that it has given the tip to the Press not to attack Tino and not to praise Venizelos. At least Diomedes, his min[iste]r, has attracted almost no attention in the Press and a communiqué of confidential information about Venizelos which I issued

---

⁴⁵ Tatoi Palace, the summer residence of the Kings of the Hellenes, in northern Attica, on the site of Dekeleia, an ancient Spartan fort, see Thucydides, *Istorion*, Book VII, c. 19.

to the Press a fortnight ago has not inspired a single journalist to praise him. <(It also produced a protest from the Foreign Office to the War Office.)> I hope it is not true. Mark Sykes[46] knows nothing of a Balkan policy being considered by the F[oreign] O[ffice] so that Aubrey Herbert's theme of a repentant Lord Robert Cecil on the look out for a Balkan policy seems but a dream.

I heard other things of Gennadius[47] who related his interview with the King (King George V). He referred to the views of the Czar of Russia in favour of Tino. 'We know better than that, don't we Hardinge?'[48] said the King. An interesting conversation, if it is true that George strongly objected to our treatment of Tino sometime in 1915. The Italians have insulted Venizelos worse than ever (a.) by suppressing an important interview in which he showed his sympathy for Italy, (b.) by definitely refusing to recognize his representatives.

Feb[ruary] 9th [1917]

Following is an authentic tale of what the Duke of Connaught[49] recently said to a friend of mine about that dismissed, ex-minister of war in Canada, Sir Sam Hughes,[50] whom our journalistic comedians described as the 'Kitchener of Canada': 'Wherever', said the Duke, 'I sought to build up, he sought to pull down'. A dark intriguing coarse-hewn, coarse-handed man, I fear.

---

[46] Colonel Sir (Tatton Benvenuto) Mark Sykes (1879–1919), 6th Baronet, succ. 1913, officer and politician; MP (Cons.) Hull Central, 1912–19; helped to establish the Arab Bureau; negotiated Anglo-French (Sykes-Picot) Agreement, 1916; died at Paris Peace Conference, Apr. 1919.

[47] Ioannis Gennadius (1844–1932), Greek scholar and diplomat; entered diplomatic service, 1870; minister-resident at London, 1886–8; minister at Washington, 1888–92; resigned, 1892, and lived as private scholar; minister at London and at The Hague, 1910–18; Greek representative at the Washington Conference, 1922.

[48] Sir Charles Hardinge (1858–1944), 1st Baron Hardinge of Penshurst, cr. 1910, diplomat and colonial administrator; entered diplomatic service, 1880; Assistant Under-secretary for Foreign Affairs, 1903–4; ambassador at St. Petersburg, 1904–6; Permanent Under-secretary for Foreign Affairs, 1906–10, and 1916–20; Viceroy of India, 1910–16; superintending ambassador, Paris Peace Conference, 1919; ambassador at Paris, 1920–2.

[49] Prince Arthur (William Patrick Albert) of Saxe-Coburg-Gotha (1850–1942), Duke of Connaught and Strathearn, cr. 1874, third son of Queen Victoria and Prince Albert; commissioned into Royal Engineers, 1868; General Officer Commanding-in-Chief, Aldershot, 1893–98; Commander-in-Chief, Ireland, 1900–4; Governor-General of Canada, 1911–16.

[50] Sir Samuel Hughes (1853–1921), Canadian politician; MP (Lib.-Cons.) Victoria North Riding, 1892–1904, Victoria, 1904–21; Minister of Militia and Defence, 1911–16.

Feb[ruary] 11 [1917]

Iliescu, that once damné <General> of Roumania, who has now returned from France, which he visited almost immediately, carried with him on the way, much to our astonishment, 3 ladies, with 3 different entries as to their complexions – in their passports thus (1.) highly coloured (2.) artificial (3.) painted. (3) also was described as by profession <u>artiste lyrique</u>!

Incidentally, in some way or other our secret service obtained from No. 3's corsage a letter to Iliescu, in which a certain colonel wrote evidently in farewell 'some speak of you only as a great minister, but I think of you as a great general'. Most of those who have seen him here, think him a little intriguing man with no great character or abilities. General Georgescu, a sound and clever soldier, will not speak to him. There was a low intrigue of Iliescu's by which Georgescu was turned out, because he supported an offensive in the Dobrudja, along with Averescu, England, France, & common sense. In the same way, in order to prevent Averescu from being what he was in 1913, C[hief] of S[taff], Iliescu, conscious that he could not himself, aspired to the post in name, continued to do so in reality. By recalling Zottu, an amiable time-expired cipher, to be chief of staff, Iliescu as Secretary-General of War, continued to have the ear of the King. Thus he controlled the situation, imposed the crazy plan of invading Transylvania in 18 columns. He as a soldier is far more than Bratianu responsible for Roumania's downfall. May it hand round his neck as closely as it did round the Ancient Mariner's.

Incidentally Roumania is not to have representation save on Roumanian affairs at the Petrograd Conference. In discussion of peace, according to the Convention, she was to have equality. This may be technically defended as a step of war, but it does not resemble equality. Direct news states that the condition of Roumania is still deplorable. Russian troops have to march everywhere – their ambulances are far superior to the Roumanian – the latter can neither organise feed nor control their armies. Roumanian officers run away – or go on leave, powdered and painted and perfumed in the streets of Jassy. The railway lines are foul with dung, for there are no latrine trenches dug for soldiers – even an amputated leg was thrown out at a station. The control officers at important stations are often Germans or Pro-Germans. There is still a big Pro-German party among the wealthier classes and the Russians, who have saved them, are hated and thwarted. No good can come with a joint control of railways, or with hatred between Allies.

I am inclined to think Take Ionescu,[51] with a bad record in the past, may be good in the future. He at least is a visionary, but a man with a vision. He did not

---

[51] Take Ionescu (1858–1922), Anglophile Romanian lawyer, politician and diplomat; Minister of Religious Affairs, 1891–95, 1899–1900; Finance Minister, 1900, 1904–1907;

finally take office until Dec[ember] 22 because he had stipulated Iliescu should be expelled, and he is now acting minister for foreign affairs, with a wider range and a keener sight than any other Roumanian, keen enough to see that it is folly to crab Russia or quarrel with the Entente.

Feb[ruary] 12th [1917]

Mirko[52] and Nikita[53] v K[ing] of M[ontenegro]
<V[ide] Feb[ruary] 22nd>

Feb[ruary] 15 [1917]

Acc[ordin]g to testimony of a British officer there is a good deal of desertion among the Serbs to the Bulgars. The latter treated the villagers well, and both sides seem to have made up their minds that the odds are even, each has had his revenge of the other.

General Dmitri [*sic*] Popovich,[54] a regicide, and Governor of Macedonia in 1915 has been arrested by Sarrail possibly for very good reasons.

Anent Roumania Iliescu's sins multiply. Apparently he talked of nothing but the greatness of Germany to Panouse and stated that 2 million tons of wheat (instead of Norton-Griffith's 1¼ million) had fallen into German hands. If true, as 1¼ million would feed 120 million people for 83 days, the rest would do it for 150, i.e. nearly 5 months.

The submarine game goes merrily on, but I hear on the Somme we hold an easy mastery to date and take few prisoners only because the men run too quick [*sic*].

A thread or two of Bulgarian humour from letters to British [soldiers?] on the Struma[:] 'You think we have not enough food but we have – enough even to feed the commandant of Ellsham[55] [*sic*](a notoriously fat British officer). You dear stupid old British Tommy Atkins!'

Minister of the Interior, 1911–13; advocated pro-Entente policy; Vice-Premier, 1917–18; Foreign Minister, 1920–22; Prime Minister, 1921–22.

   52   Prince Mirko Dmitri Petrović-Njegoš of Montenegro (1879–1918), second son of King Nikola I of Montenegro; died in exile in Vienna.

   53   King Nicholas' nickname, see entry 6 Jan. 1917.

   54   General Damjan Popović (1857–1928), Serb soldier; implicated in 1903 assassination of the Obrenović king.

   55   RFC Elsham Wolds airfield in North Lincolnshire, which operated from Dec. 1916 until June 1919.

Another side of the shield came in when a British airman dropped a pair of old boots in the Bulgar lines with the message that they came off a Bulgar prisoner but were so old that we had to provide a new pair for him. Pictures of fat Bulgarian prisoners in British camps have many times induced desertion when dropped from aeroplanes.

Incidentally the relations of Germans and Bulgars are bad as the latter break the eighth commandment, and the former never ask them to have a drink in consequence.

Incidentally there is a sidewind down the field from the Bulgarian camp, a whisper of a separate peace.

Feb[ruary] 14th [1917]

There is a sequel not unhumorous to the Naxos incident, where 20 villagers of Apeiranthos[56] were killed and 50 wounded on January 15th by Venizelists supported by a British machinegun and sailors. Venizelos was troubled by the heavy casualties. The explanation, according to a traveller of 1910 who cannot be accused of arrière pensée, lies in the local conditions. Naxos stands aloof from the rest of the islands by reason of the boorishness of its population and Apeiranthos from the rest of Naxos for the same reason. According to local legend Apeiranthos was founded by Barabbas[57] and his descendants inherit his proclivities. The Apeiranthites say that Barabbas was a Cretan. Anyway this indicates a local cause of hostilities which has ended bloodily. Up till now there has not been a whisper in the press but this cannot last for ever. Mailbags have been delivered in Continental Greece so that the secret will soon be out. It is rather important because emery is worked there.

Feb[ruary] 15th [1917]

From an important source, the peace terms of Germany was ready to accept a week ago –

1. Evacuation of Belgium provided industrial guarantees given that Germany will retain industrial control.

---

[56] Apeiranthos, a mountainous village on the island of Naxos, some 17 miles northeast of the capital of the island.
[57] Biblical figure; insurrectionary sentenced to death, but freed by Pontius Pilate during Passover.

2. Evacuation of Northern France but retention of a slice on pretence of rectifying the frontier.
3. Erection of Russian Poland as an independent kingdom but retention of a slice for Germany.
4. Rehabilitation of Serbia provided Bulgaria keeps what she wishes.
5. Return of all colonies & indemnity from Entente.

The main idea of Germany is to detach Russia and thus with Japan to control the world.

Distress in Germany great even among the rich but not enough to compel surrender before next harvest. German hatred of <u>USA</u> more suitable because of passage of munitions. The four great men of Germany do not seem very great. Hindenburg[58] is a cipher and merely a mask for Ludendorf[f][59] <who is really dictator>. The Kaiser is kept in the background on military grounds for fear of defeat. The chancellor[60] seems chiefly anxious to retain his post. The submarine campaign is a last effort to avert defeat.

Feb[ruary] 16th [1917]

It is said, on the authority of Emil Klaes[s]ig[61] to Wolff's Bureau,[62] that Wilson, even if war begins with Germany, does not intend to confiscate interned German ships or to sequester private German property. In the former case, apart from the loan, there would be little advantage in the USA.

---

[58] Field Marshal General Paul Ludwig Hans Anton von Beneckendorff und von Hindenburg (1847–1934), German military commander and politician; entered Prussian army, 1866; active service Austro-Prussian War, 1866, Franco-German War, 1870–1; retired, 1911; recalled, Aug. 1914; commander 8th Army, 1914; 9th Army, 1914; Supreme Commander East, 1914–16; Chief of the General Staff, 1916–19; President of Germany, 1925–34.

[59] General Erich Friedrich Wilhelm Ludendorff (1865–1937), German military commander; commissioned into army, 1885; General Staff officer, 1894–1905; Deputy Chief of Staff, 2nd Army, Aug. 1914; Chief of Staff, 8th Army, 1914–16; Quarter Master-General, 1916–18.

[60] Theobald von Bethmann Hollweg (1856–1921), German politician; entered Prussian civil service, 1882; Provinvial President of Brandenburg, 1899–1905; Prussian Minister of the Interior, 1905–7; Imperial Minister of the Interior, 1907–9; Prussian Minister-President and German Chancellor, 1909–17.

[61] Emil Klaessig Jr., US journalist of German extraction; editor of Continental Telegraph Company, New York; New York correspondent for Wolff's news agency since 1903.

[62] *Wolffs Telegraphisches Bureau* (1849–1934), news-agency, one of the three European telegraph monopolies of the period, founded by Bernhard Wolff (1811–79).

There has been a new counterblast <confidentially> issued to the Press as a set-off to Haig's extraordinary rhodomontade of yesterday.[63] <An interview in which Haig talked about breaking the front. He never meant it to be published.> This suggests that Germany has increased her divisions to 205 and probably to 250, by calling up the manpower of Belgium, Poland etc. Thus she has banked everything on success this year. Unfortunately for her, even being held this year, is ruin for her next. So that, far from Haig's confident dictum about 'breaking the front', it may be our game simply to hold on in the West, i.e. if we can stay the pace. This is no doubt very wise but what can the Press think of the two military voices. They usually trust 'the man on the spot' and think the War Office fools. In this case the exception will prove the rule, I fear.

Feb[ruary] 17th [1917]

Apparently Charteris[64] was responsible for Haig's indiscretion. Haig talked, as the D[irector of] M[ilitary] O[perations, Maurice] does here, to journalists in private, & Charteris, always the âme damnée of Haig, sanctioned its publication without consulting the Field Marshal. Incidentally it has done good as well as harm. He missed out any reference to Nivelle by gross error of judgment, but this boastful attitude much reassured the French, whose reserves are exhausted, and whose annual class is only 180,000 as against 400,000 in Austria-Hungary and 500,000 in Germany.

Feb[ruary] 18th [1917]

The Italian campaign ag[ain]st Venizelos grows more & more discreditable. They represent him now as a spent force, and the Reservists as the living heart of Greece. This opinion is not shared by [Sir Francis] Elliot or by Sarrail, but Venizelos is moderate, and has shown that he intends to win back Greece by constitutional methods after the war. He could easily foment revolution in

---

[63] Haig's interview with a correspondent of Havas, see 'Sir D. Haig on the War. This Year's Task. Decision In The West', *The Times*, 16 Feb. 1917.

[64] Brigadier-General John Charteris (1877–1946), officer and politician; commissioned into Royal Engineers, 1896; Assistant Military Secretary to General Officer Commanding-in-Chief, Aldershot, 1912–14; Chief of Army Intelligence, British Expeditionary Force HQ, 1915–18; dismissed Jan. 1918; Deputy Director of Transportation, General HQ, France, 1918; Director of Movements and Quartering, India, 1920–21; Col, 1921; Deputy Adjutant and Quartermaster General, Eastern Command, India, 1921–22; retired, 1922; MP (Cons.), Dumfriesshire, 1924–29. Charteris was behind the story of the German *Kadaververwertungsanstalten* ('corpse utilization factories'), one of the most notorious propaganda hoaxes of the war, see below entry 29 Apr. 1917.

Epirus or in Thessaly, but has promised to pursue only a peaceful propaganda in these parts. Italy has seized Corfu, its thought to have sent the mails to Greece to enlighten here, refuses absolutely to help in provisioning Venizelos, and seems to make fair weather with the advocate raising the blockade and ingratiating ourselves [*sic*] with the Reservists.

The French, as usual, take a decided line. Jonnart, the new minister, says Italy is playing servant. Admiral Gauchet[65] says he will bombard Athens if the signs of a revived émeute go on. He said this to M. Zalocostas[66] (the Foreign Minister of Greece), a man on whom Elliot thinks it useless to waste breath. When addressed in private by Elliot, however, he moderated his tone, and said that he meant only that, in the case of renewed bombardment, the shots would really go off. There were a good many 'duds' in the bombardment of the 1st December.

A thoroughly mischievous design was recently discovered by the French. The sides of the Corinth Canal has been tunnelled and mined with an obvious attempt to block the Canal. On an explanation being requested, Lambros[67] said it was the foundations of an emergency bridge, subsequently an officially issued communiqué has said something quite different. It says that it was done when a Venizelist plot was feared.

Elliot and [the] Russian and French ministers communicated a strongly worded representation to the Press today showing the bad faith of the Greek Government in fairly unambiguous terms.

Feb[ruary] 19th [1917]

The provisioning of Greece will become a serious question as the submarine campaign has laid up 5 Greek ships in America, due in the middle of March for Greece – so that, even if the blockade is raise, there may be serious starvation. Venizelist Greece may suffer.

German wireless states that Iliescu is very unpopular in Roumania and that his ears were boxed in Jassy as he walked down the street <by a woman>. There is no doubt that pro-German traitors exist and are a serious danger. The O[fficer] C[ommanding] 18th Div[isio]n, Alexandru Sturdza,[68] went out in a

---

[65] Admiral Dominique-Marie Gauchet (1853–1931), French naval commander; commissioned into navy, 1879; head of Department of Administration and Supply, 1914–15; commander French Squadron in Dardanelles, 1915–16; 2nd Squadron in Mediterranean, 1916; Commander-in-Chief, French forces Mediterranean, 1916–19; retired, 1919.

[66] Evgenios Zalokostas (1855–1919), Greek diplomat and politician; minister at Sofia, 1899–1910; Foreign Minister, Oct. 1916–Apr. 1917.

[67] See entry 16 Oct. 1916.

[68] Colonel Alexandru Dimitrie Sturdza (1869–1939), Romanian solider; son of Dimitrie Sturdza (1833–1914), four-times Prime Minister of Romania; educated at Potsdam War Academy;

motor-car – his chauffeur was found murdered and he himself went over to the German lines. Officers get into plain clothes as the Germans enter a town, go on unlimited leave, & still strut about Jassy with pencilled eyebrows in the face of the grim contemptuous Russians.

Feb[ruary] 20th [1917]

Considerable danger of a pro-Austrian party at the F[oreign] O[ffice] headed by Drummond,[69] Theo Russell,[70] and, in a whisper, Milner not essentially averse. The idea is to leave Austria shorn of Bosnia-Herzegovina, Spalato,[71] Trieste & Trentino & poss[ibl]y Galicia but to restore Transylvania. If this is done it will at once and for ever bring Roumania back into the Central Europa orbit and thus permanently enclose her, as the Central Powers need [the] Danube Delta &c.

That is bad, but, of course, the military question is another story. Without Austria Germany must be irretrievably smashed & smashing of Germany may be impossible, except by some such means as this. God help us if it is so.

Feb[ruary] 21st [1917]

According to [General George Fraser] Phillips[72] the rifles that still remain for Greece to pass are bear 100,000 whereas we say it is only 60,000, so that they still have the power for the guerrilla offensive. Opportunity Tino's gang may get, ill-will they never lack. The blockade question will become serious, for famine is said to begin in earnest on the 15th March, and relief will not appear until early April and then will, in the first instance, go to Venizelist Greece, which is already better rationed than Royalist [Greece]. Parcels of barley from Cyprus and rice and maize from Egypt may eke out a pittance, but Tino's friends, like Allan

---

commanded 8th Romanian Division (not 18th), deserted en route to inspecting 10th Division.

[69] Sir (James) Eric Drummond (1876–1951), 16th Earl of Perth, succ. 1937, civil servant and diplomat; entered Foreign Office, 1900; private secretary to Sir Edward Grey, 1908–10 and 1911 and 1915, to Asquith, 1912–15; to A.J. Balfour, 1916–19; Secretary-General to League of Nations, 1919–33; ambassador to Italy, 1933–39.

[70] Sir (Odo William) Theo(philus Villiers) Russell (1870–1951), diplomat; entered diplomatic service, 1892, assistant private secretary to Sir Edward Grey, 1905–1908; embassy counsellor, 1909–14; diplomatic secretary to Foreign Secretary, 1915–19; minister at Berne, 1919–22; at the Vatican, 1922–28; at The Hague, 1928–33.

[71] Now Split (Croatia).

[72] See entry 29 Dec. 1916.

Breck and David Balfour in the heather, 'maun brook many an empty belly'[73] ere they see the ships bringing in enough bread. It will be a lesson, for the Greeks will be hit heavily in the belly, a not insensitive point.

Feb[ruary] 22nd [1917]

Having no separate diary of Montenegro I hear mite the detail of the Cabinet intrigues of Mirko & Montenegro – a little developed since the 12th February. Nicholas appears to have imitated the famous Simon Lord Lovat[74] <in the Jacobite forty-five>, whom incidentally, except that he is a poet, he greatly resembles in shrewd peasant cunning & intrigue. Lovat sent one son to serve King George, another to serve Prince Charlie & himself mediated between the two, determined to jump on the right side when victory declared itself. Ultimately, Simon Lovat ended on the scaffold after being immortalised by Hogarth.[75]

What will Nikita's end be?

It is probable that he feared assassination when he left Montenegro in 1916. He will certainly receive it if he returns in 1917 or 1918. In the early part of the last year he was hard pressed by Radovic,[76] <his premier> a strong JugoSlav and consented to a plan by which Montenegro was to be absorbed ultimately in Serbia (incidentally a plan already acceded to by him in 1914 and since discredited by his suspected treachery). After his visit to the Italian front however he refused to sign Radovic's plan and disavowed the whole project <and dismissed Radovic>. The inference is that Italian influence, so bitterly hostile to the JugoSlavs, dissuaded Nicholas from a plan which would benefit them.

Meanwhile, after Mirko, Nicholas' second son, remained behind, first to organise resistance, it was said, then to obtain the benefit of the doctors of Vienna, whither he repaired. This light-headed, high-blowing prince, a musical composer, a roué, and the original of Danilo[77] in 'the Merry Widow',[78] may not

---

[73] 'Ye maun lie bare and hard, and brook mauny an empty belly', R.L. Stevenson, *Kidnapped* (1886), ch. 18.

[74] Simon Fraser (c. 1667–1747), 11th Lord Lovat, Scottish Jacobite leader and Chief of Clan Fraser; executed at Newgate Prison, Mar. 1747.

[75] William Hogarth (1697–1764), English painter and engraver, chiefly known for his satirical works.

[76] Andrija Radović (1872–1947), Montenegrin politician; Finance Minister, 1905–1906 and 1916; Foreign Minister, 1907; Prime Minister, 1907 and May 1916–Jan. 1917.

[77] Danilo Aleksandar Petrović-Njegoš (1871–1939), Crown Prince of Montenegro; eldest son of King Nikola I; titular king and head of government-in-exile, 1–7 Mar. 1921.

[78] Captain Danilo Danilovitch, embassy attaché, is the principal male part in *Die lustige Witwe* ('The Merry Widow') (1905) by Franz Lehár. In 1934, Prince Danilo of Montenegro

be as bad as he is painted, though his wife does not share this opinion.[79] It is said that he was at one time pro-Entente and refused to resign his right to the throne, which his elder brother Danilo had been persuaded to do. He was threatened with death by Xenia[80] and Nikita, fled to the British Minister for protection which he did not receive, and turned in despair to make terms with Austria-Hungary. That Austria has learnt to use him as a tool is shown by the fact that he is publicly announced as praying at the tomb of Francis-Joseph. A later design still is to make him a king, with a piece of Herzegovina, Montenegro and Southern Serbia to rule over. Bulgaria will take Macedonia and the right bank of the Morava.[81] Serbia proper will be bounded by the Morava, <the Danube, the Drina[82] and> a line drawn north of Uskub, and thus be emasculated and surrounded. Croatia will receive home-rule and thus the Jugo-Slavs will be split into three. Mirko would then enjoy a power and a kingdom greater than King Nicholas would ever have aspired to. So the latter seemed to think for Czech evidence from Rome states that there is no sort or kind of doubt that <u>Nicholas</u> has been intriguing with Austria via Switzerland, doubtless with the view of substituting himself for his son in the new arrangement. The fact appears certain, and Caillaux[83] and Jacob Schiff[84] and the Viennese bankers play unhallowed parts in the game. I fancy Nikita's letter is short, perfidy to the Entente, perfidy to Serbia, perfidy to Jugo-Slavia, perfidy to Italy, perfidy even to Austria – it is a pretty story. What confirms the truth of the above is that the Montenegrin Government has issued a solemn statement denying all rumours of negotiation with Austria. In the great

---

successfully sued Metro-Goldwyn-Meyer for libel and false depiction of himself in the film version of 'The Merry Widow'.

[79] Queen Militza of Montenegro (née Duchess Jutta Auguste Charlotte Jutta Alexandra Georgina Adophine of Mecklenburg-Strelitz) (1880–1946), consort of Prince Danilo; m. Danilo, 1899.

[80] Xenia Petrovic-Njegoš (1881–1960), Princess of Montenegro; second youngest daughter of King Nikola I of Montenegro; she acted as an influential (anti-Austrian) counsellor to the king in later years; in French exile since 1918.

[81] Presumably the Zapadna (Western) Morava in central Serbia, a tributary of the Velika (Great) Morava, which latter traverses Serbia in north–south direction.

[82] A tributary of the Sava river, forming the border with Bosnia-Herzegivina.

[83] Josephe Marie Auguste Caillaux (1863–1944), French politician; Finance Minister, 1899–1902, 1906–1909, 1911, 1925, 1926; Prime Minister, 1911–12; Paymaster-General, 1914; arrested, convicted and imprisoned, 1918, for plotting with the enemy; rehabilitated, 1924.

[84] Jacob Henry (née Jakob Heinrich) Schiff (1847–1920), German-born American banker and philanthropist; head of Kuhn, Loeb & Co. banking firm since 1885; extended loans to Japan during Russo-Japanese War, 1904–1905; favoured US peace mediation after 1914; target of anti-Semitic campaigns.

days of Brussiloff's offensive[85] Nikita 'as a Slav Prince and Russian field marshal was holding out to Petrograd[,] his feeble arms weakened by age and disaster'. These arms seem to have since turned, <and> not always feebly, to Rome and <to> Vienna.

Feb[ruar]y 23rd [1917]

Roumania is one vast intrigue and hotbed of German propaganda. Iliescu now wishes to go to Switzerland, an almost certain proof that he is a traitor. Alexander Sturdza, O[ffier] C[ommanding] of the 10th Division, deserted openly to the Germans, leaving a murdered chauffeur to tell the tale. Zottu was of course openly pro-German. Three Roumanian ministers, at Athens, Cairo and Constantinople, remained in Bucharest and have been degraded. General Sosek [sic][86] has been sentenced to hard labour for cowardice at the battle of Argesul.[87] Ganiceanu, the Military Attaché at Athens, was arrested as a traitor by the secret Entente police at Athens, and subsequently allowed to visit England. The arms factories at Craiova and Bucharest were handed over almost intact to the Germans. Prince Bibescu has incurred the odium for assisting Norton-Griffiths to destroy the oil [wells]. Four or five railway station masters are openly pro-German and the only solution is Russian railway control.

---

[85] General Aleksei Alekse'evich Brusilov (1853–1926), Russian military commander, noted for his offensive tactics; commanded offensives in Mar. 1916 and June 1917; sacked after failure of second offensive and on account of his support for capital punishment; Inspector of Cavalry, 1921–24.

[86] General Alexandru Socec (1859–1928), Romanian soldier and courtier; son of refugee from Austrian Transylvania; entered army, 1880; Cavalry School, Vienna, 1884–85; aide-de-camp to Crown Prince Ferdinand, 1889–93; Brigadier, 1913; Ploeisti Command, 1916; commanded 13th Infantry Division, 1916; commanded reserves during the battle of Argeș; courtmartialled but absolved after his files disappeared from war ministry; see his *Episod de pe Argeș* (Bucharest, 1922).

[87] The battle along the Argeș river, 1–5 Dec. 1916, broke Romanian resistance.

Feb[ruary] 24th [1917]

Recently in Sweden Rizoff,[88] the Bulgarian Minister at Berlin, sought out the Russian Minister,[89] who refused to see him without his Entente colleagues, and offered him a separate peace. He did not descend to details but said the terms were more favourable than could be offered to Russia in 3 or 4 months hence. The Russian minister declined saying the Alliance was <u>solidaire</u>. Rizoff is a wild Macedonian but he probably spoke the mind of Germany tamely enough upon this occasion. I wonder if the F[oreign] O[ffice] is in a position to appreciate Bulgarian or Balkan matters. Lamb,[90] late Consul-General of Salonica and B[ulgarian] A[dministered] M[acedonia] and Albanian boundary commissioner, is used by them on coal. Heard,[91] Consul-General at Sofia, was used to deal with prisoners <and ultimately shoved off on to us [War Office]>. Du Vallon[92] and Geary,[93] both political consuls at one time in the Balkans,

---

[88] Dimitar Hristov Rizov (1862–1918), Bulgarian journalist, politician and diplomat; MP, 1886–7; entered diplomatic service, 1897; agent at Skopje, 1897–9; at Cetinje, 1903–1905; at Belgrade, 1905–1907; minister at Rome, 1908–15; at Berlin, 1915–18.

[89] Anatoly Vasil'evich Neklyudov (1856–1934), Russian diplomat; embassy counsellor at Paris, 1905–11; minister at Sofia, 1911–13; at Stockholm, 1913–17; appointed ambassador at Madrid, Apr. 1917; retired, Sept. 1917; see his *Diplomatic Reminiscences before and during the World War, 1911–1917* (New York, 1920).

[90] Sir Harry Harling Lamb (1857–1948), consular official; entered consular service, 1879; chief dragoman at Constantinople, 1903–7; consul-general at Salonika, 1907–13; British commissioner on the International Commission of Control in Albania, 1913–14; head of Foreign Office contraband department, 1914–15; in charge of British Adriatic mission, 1915–16; employed at Foreign Office, 1916–18; attached to Salonika military mission, 1918; chief political officer, British High Commission at Constantinople, 1920–21; consul-general at Smyrna, 1921–23.

[91] Captain William Beauchamp Heard (1877–1923), consular official and intelligence officer; entered consular service, 1900; acting vice-consul at Sofia, 1902–1903; vice-consul at Smyrna, 1904; at Adis Ababa, 1904–6; at Diabakir, 1906; special service, Sudan, 1906; vice-consul at Beirut, 1908–9; at Sofia, 1909–15; acting consul at Phililppopolis, 1915; intelligence officer, 29th Brigade, 1915; consul at Serres, 1916; employed at Foreign Office, 1916–17; employed in Enemy Propaganda Department, Apr.–Sept. 1918; Commercial Commissioner at Sofia, 1919–23.

[92] Hubert Caliste de Jacobi Du Vallon (1877–1951), consular official; joined consular service, 1900; vice-consul at Salonika, 1905–6; resigned, 1906; Captain 11th Btn., West Yorkshire Regiment; relinquished commission on account of war wounds, Feb. 1919.

[93] Arthur Bernard Geary (b. 1878), consular official; entered consular service, 1901; acting vice-consul at Bitlis, 1905–1906; vice-consul at the Dardanelles, 1907–8; acting consul at Basra, 1908–1909; Monastir, 1909–12; at Alexandria, 1912–13; Registrar Alexandria Prize Court, 1914–16; attached to General Headquarters, Indian Expeditionary Force (with rank of

were not employed by them at all, nor I think was Heathcote.[94] Greatest of all, Fitzmaurice,[95] the true voice of England in the East for ten years, is left to assist the Admiralty. The near East is thus managed by George Clerk[96] who was once in Constantinople for a few years, and other ignoramuses who committed us in the famous state paper of 1914 to the monumental statement 'British interests in Serbia are nil',[97] in other words Belgrade is not on the way between Bagdad and Berlin.

Feb[ruar]y 26th [1917]

There has been a snap at Slatina southwest of Ersek where 150–200 Greek comitajis wiped out a French patrol of 12 Senegalese and then bolted north. As the affair took place north of the neutral zone the Greeks have no defence. It is an interesting comment on Sarrail that Milne wires that he <S[arrail]> attaches no political importance to the incident, and Granville wires that S<arrail> considers it confirms the French fears of risings etc. in that area. Thessaly must rise soon, I think. Anyhow Venizelos says that ¾ of its people are for him; Diomedes regards a rising as certain – the Greek garrison is reduced to 2,000 in that area, and the French demand permission to occupy Volo and Larissa, to which Italy and Russia have already consented. There has also been a Venizelist & famine riot at Volo. Then I think Venizelist Greece will be extended. Incidentally, Corfu, to which we promised that the Royalist administration should return as Venizelists only seized it on Jan[uar]y 8th (after the acceptance of our ultimatum by the Royalists), Corfu, I say, declares it is all Venizelist and will resist Royalists by force. Altogether there are the makings of a pretty muddle.

General Staff Officer), 1916–17; attached to Cairo agency, 1917–18; consul at Piraeus, 1918; acting consul-general at Alexandria, 1918–19; consul at Cairo, 1919–22; retired, 1922.

[94] Walter John Heathcote (1870–1936), consular official; entered consular service, 1894; consul at Monastir, 1907–9; resigned, 1909.

[95] See entry 24 Nov. 1916.

[96] Sir George Russell Clerk (1874–1951), diplomat; entered Foreign Office, 1899; senior clerk, Eastern Department, 1913–19; accompanied Lord Milner on mission to Russia, 1917; private secretary to Marquess of Curzon, 1919; minister at Prague, 1919–26; ambassador at Ankara, 1926–29; at Brussels, 1929–34; at Paris, 1934–37.

[97] Temperley was mistaken; the statement was made by Sir George Buchanan, see entry 9 Dec. 1916.

February 27th [1917]

The repeated questions in the Commons touch the Magyar forgeries for the purposes of propaganda passed off on the 'Morning Post' as genuine by a Magyar in this country. The editor of the 'Morning Post'[98] in trying to defend his forger & showed his good faith by making the most grotesque blunders. He was apparently ignorant that all publications of speeches in Hungary are protected by law, that no special editions are ever published in Budapest, that the Journal des Debats[99] in Paris and the Pester Lloyd[100] in Budapest have both laughed at the dupery of the 'Morning Post'.[101]

Yet in spite of the evident proofs of forgeries for propaganda purposes neither the Foreign Office nor Home Office are able to prosecute or do anything but suggest that the charges are strenuously denied, as if charges of a forgery are not usually denied or as if the denial in this instance does not in itself prove the truth.

Lunched with Adams yesterday, head of the P[rime] M[inister]'s department. He said L[loyd] G[eorge] could do nothing for 2 days before his great speech on reductions in pocket belly, wine and luxury of last Friday, but that he was fairly satisfied with the results. Irish negotiations are going on but pessimism is evident. The Cabinet is having minutes and agenda, and special ministers called in ad hoc – much time is thus saved. He thought the P[rime] M[inister]'s appearance in Parliament <frequent enough> sufficient to ensure the link between executive and legislative. That at any rate was the idea and intention of the P[rime] M[inister], as devoted a Parliamentarian as well could be. Bonar Law's[102] triumph was great and deserved for he stuck to patriotism and 5 % against City calculations and 5½ % to 6 %. It is also true (this from another source) that the Treasury expected £600,000,000 to be a successful loan and no one expected £1,000,000,000. German newspapers, after the £600,000,000 was announced, said that was an obvious failure, but £1,000,000,000 might be called

---

[98] Howell Arthur Keir Gwynne (1865–1950), author and journalist; editor of the conservative-leaning *Morning Post*, 1911–37.

[99] *Journal des débats*, a conservative French daily newspaper, published from 1789 to 1944.

[100] *Pester Lloyd*, a liberal German-language daily newspaper in Hungary, published from 1854 to 1945.

[101] The paper's Budapest correspondent, Josef Szebenyei, was writing his articles from London, and was interned following repeated questions in the Commons, see H. Hanak, 'The New Europe, 1916–1920', *Slavonic and East European Review* xxxix, 4 (1960–1), 381.

[102] Andrew Bonar Law (1858–1923), Canadian-born businessman and politician; MP (Cons.), Glasgow Blackfriars, 1900–6, Camberwell, 1906–10, Lancashire (Bootle), 1911–18, and Glasgow Central, 1918–23; Parliamentary Secretary to the Board of Trade, 1902–5; Colonial Secretary, 1915–16; Chancellor of the Exchequer, 1916–19; Lord Privy Seal, 1919–21; Prime Minister, 1922–23; leader of the Conservative Party, 1911–21 and 1922–23.

a success. So that even according to Hun statistics it is a brilliant success. It will give, I think, L[loyd] G[eorge] the success he desires to assure his government.

Feb[ruary] 28th [1917]

Nothing seems to be clearer than that the submarine campaign may cause grave difficulties. Some precautions are being taken to make things better for Venizelist Greece but even there there may be a famine, partly owing to maladministration. The attitude of Italy is deplorable – she has declined to send <a> vessel to provision Greece, except under guarantee that it will not be remonstrated with because 4 <Greek> ships lie idle in <her> ports. France & Italy seem to be drifting apart and both trying to seize as much territory in Epirus <& Albania> – France by Ochrida[103] to Ersek,[104] Italy south of Ersek well into Epirus and below the neutral zone at Koritza.[105] The French reply to this will be the occupation of Larissa and Volo, I suppose. Italy may then bid for Janina.[106]

1st March [1917]

Some signs abound that Germany is once more working up again for peace. So at least say the pressgang who lay claim to an 'illative sense' in examining propaganda. Some of the claims the Germans make in public are absurd ¾ million <tons> shipping [sunk] in a month when it is more like 330,000 tons. As they wisely say, there is no means of finding out. If the secret report of the session of the Reichstag was right, England has still 5 months to go and Germany but one. That would explain much.

2nd March [1917]

The great Venizelos is still serene, still insistent on pacific propaganda in Thessaly against the wilder schemes of his followers, and the designs of the French. Some credit him with discouragement but of this there is no sign. He is moderate as ever. Events have not aided him altogether of late. The French prefer to work through the National Bank of Greece, which is accessible to Royalist influences and reject the Ionian Bank, which is favourable to Salonica. We endorse this

---

[103] Now Ohrid (Macedonia).
[104] Now Ersekë in southeastern Albania.
[105] Now Korçë (Albania).
[106] Now Ioannina (Greece).

view with reluctance. We refuse, after much discussion and going back on our previous F[oreign] O[ffice] view, to put Venizelist consuls on the same level as Royalist ones in Egypt. The ground urged is that the Venizelist state is not fully sovereign, a matter pointed out to the F[oreign] O[ffice] over the proposed proclamation, so that even the F[oreign] O[ffice] is capable of learning something. (v[ide] Jan[uary] 18th) Venizelists can either submit to Royalist courts or put themselves under protection of the British military authorities. This again is a moral blow. Lastly the Italians refused to deal with or to recognize Venizelos officially. All in all enough to have daunted Caesar. Yet the great man still thinks that moderation should be the rule and that the Entente will prevail and that the King should not be dealt with till after the war, and even ready to accept the Crown Prince whatever his wild followers may say. 'If Germany wins, then for me and my followers there will remain emigration <to America>', says he. One thinks of Hampden[107] and Cromwell,[108] or of the Dutch who contemplated returning to Java if Louis Quatorze[109] got to Amsterdam.

3rd March [1917]

An encouraging letter from [H.A.L.] Fisher, stressing the value of history – 'the more history, the better in this war'. Though now transfigured by Cabinet-rank, and lifted inconceivably beyond any other academic mortal, he remains as kindly as ever. Whether at Oxford or Sheffield he was always the mild Olympian, as he no doubt now is at the Cabinet. Strange that I first got hold of him for L[loyd] G[eorge].[110] He is a big man – with the biggest educational opportunity anybody in England ever had.

5th March 1917

The other day I noticed a reference from China – to an 'incredible story', viz. that the German Minister in China[111] has asserted to the Chinese Foreign

---

[107] John Hampden (c. 1595–1643), Parliamentarian leader; MP Grampound, 1621–2, Wendover, 1624–9, Buckinghamshire, 1640–3; mortally wounded in battle of Chalgrove Field, June 1643.
[108] Oliver Cromwell (1599–1658), Military and Parliamentarian leader; MP Huntingdon, 1628–9, Cambridge, 1640–9; Lord Protector, 1653–8.
[109] Louis XIV de Bourbon (1638–1715), King of France and Navarre, 1643–1715; at the beginning of the Franco-Dutch War (1672–8) French troops reached as far north as Utrecht.
[110] See entry 9 Dec. 1916.
[111] Admiral Paul von Hintze (1864–1941), German soldier, diplomat, and politician; entered navy, 1882; Naval Attaché at St. Petersburg, 1903–8; Military Plenipotentiary

Minister[112] that Germany could supply all from her own resources <and could make glycerine from dead bodies>.[113] I drew the attention of the pressgang. They have already material to go on – an alleged diary of a man, highly skilled in science, who was put on to turn out human honey and oil by these fiends of science. If it can be substantiated, this ghoulish nightmare ought to discredit even the Hun. Even here I can see nothing worse than the logical following out of scientific materialism to a restless current of conclusion. If you kill the souls of men, you may easily make use of their bodies.

6th March [1917]

The Italians go full tilt on their selfish career. After weeks of negotiation we have to give up in despair and allow them to go on supplying lemons to Germany and Austria – trading with the enemy. They refuse to send more than 2,000 tons of sulphur to Greece when at least 7 times that amount is necessary. They have sent crack divisions to Salonika, one was beaten back from the Bistritza[114] on to the Krusha Balkan[115] by the Bulgars <early in October>, the other was turned off Hill 1050 Pasalova by the Germans on the 12th – 14th February, a hill the Serbs had won with blood and labour, which is good as an observation post and affords opportunity to turn the flank and creep up to Prilep. What is the In addition they decline to recognize Venizelos, and have dissociated themselves from protests to Tino, at the same time refusing to provision Greece. Whom are they benefiting but themselves?

7th March [1917]

The incident of Corfu is interesting. On the 10th Jan[uary] we occupied it in collusion with Venizelists. As this was a few hours after the Royalist acceptance of the ultimatum we decided to reinstate the Royalist officials and remove the Venizelist troops. It was then found that the islanders were resolved to resist. Venizelos, being consulted, wisely refused to give an opinion. Finally, we have

---

at St. Petersburg, 1908–11; minister at Mexico City, 1911–14; at Peking, 1914–17; at Christiania, 1917–18; State Secretary, June–Sept. 1918.

[112] Wu Tingfang (Ng Choy) (1842–1922), Chinese diplomat and politician; minister at Washington, 1896–1902; Foreign Minister, Nov. 1916–July 1917; Prime Minister, 23–25 May 1917.

[113] See entry 17 Feb. 1917; this was a propaganda hoax.

[114] Now the Haliakmon; it rises in the Grámmos mountains in northern Greece, near the Albanian border and joins the Thermaic Gulf west of the delta of the Axios (Vardar).

[115] Now Kroúsia mountains, west of Lake Dojran, on the Greek–Macedonian border.

withdrawn the Venizelist troops and left the islanders to administer themselves with a few British troops to aid them. Thessaly will go the same way if the French occupy Larissa and Volo, as they obviously intend to do. We after feeble protests will no doubt accept.

March 8th [1917]

The measures of Bulgaria are curious. Nish is to be called Ferdinandville,[116] a hamlet Radoslavoff,[117] and all Serbia, east of the Morava, a complex of Serbs, Rumans & Bulgars, is to be annexed to Bulgaria. Macedonia south of Uskub appears annexed already and Bulgar schools are appearing in Prishtina and Prisrend,[118] so the whole is a denationalisation design. I think of Acton[119] – 'A State which is incompetent to satisfy different races condemns itself; a state which labours to neutralise, to absorb or to expel them destroys its own vitality. … The theory of nationality therefore is a retrograde step in history … it announces the approach of the end of the revolutionary period … it has an important mission in the world and marks the final conflict and therefore the end of two forces which are the worst enemies of civil freedom – the absolute monarchy and the revolution'. 1862 – Nationality in History of Freedom, pp. 298–300.[120] Over 50 years ago, abstract but pregnant. It take it that nationality overcomes the King's absolutism and the people's democracy because neither can defy it. What nationality itself cannot defy is another nationality, and the schools at Prisrend, the Bulgarisation of Transylvanian Serbia are useless because exhausting. Similar energy shown in munitions or trench-digging would be more profitable.

I think, too, Ferdinand and Kaiser Wilhelm will be punished in the end by the force they exploited, i.e. nationality. Neither one nor the other can reconcile or include diverse nationalities, for the federal principle is impossible for Bulgaria and impracticable for non-German nationalities under German rule. Russia, if she frees Poland, Finland and the Ukraine, will gain strength. We rest our chief strength today on free and real and coexistent nationalities in our colonies.

---

[116] After Ferdinand (Maximilian Karl Leopold Maria) I of Saxe-Coburg-Gotha (1861–1948), Prince of Bulgaria, 1887–1908; King of Bulgaria, 1908–Oct. 1918.

[117] After Vasil Radoslovov (1854–1929), Bulgarian politician; Prime Minister, 1886–7 and 1913–18.

[118] Now Prizren (Kosovo).

[119] Sir John Emerich Dalberg Acton (1834–1902), 1st Baron Acton, cr. 1869, historian and politician; MP (Lib.) Carlow Borough, 1859–65, Bridgnorth, 1865–66; Regius Professor of Modern History, Cambridge, 1895–1902.

[120] J.E.D. Lord Acton, 'Nationality' [1862], id., *The History of Freedom and Other Essays*, ed. J.N. Figgis and R.V. Laurence (London, 1907), 298–300.

Serbia, if she is to live, in an enlarged Jugo-Slavia, can only live by Federation. So we are for national right and federal duties.

March 9th [1917]

I heard today that Diomedes specifically proposed to a friend of mine that the {Allies} <Royalists> should withdrawn from Thessaly (i.e. the 2,000 left) and the revolution would then come of itself. Perhaps that is what he meant by regarding revolt as inevitable. Venizelos does not and seems to discourage it. Venizelos' followers wish doubtless to outrun the constable. There are 3 policies to the fore among the Powers – Russia wishes us to combine them into one <Our news states them as follows> (1.) Italy – a divided and weak Greece, therefore support of Constantine ag[ain]st Venizelos. (2.) France – originally support of Venizelos, then under influence of unofficial agent M. Benazet[121] support of Tino, finally asserting the security of the Army of the East as an excuse for anything. (3.) Our policy – as asserted by us, is a strong Greece, and therefore ultimate conciliation between Venizelos and the King. (The latter seems to me impossible.) Kalegeropoulos[122] and our D[eputy] A[djutant and Quartermaster-General][123] at Salonica think the same.

March 11th [1917]

Sir Mark Sykes, <a Catholic,> an anti-Home Ruler and Tory, <talked to me> on the new government. The little man <(Lloyd George)> is an instrument – he does not lead the House, he runs away from it. Bonar Law does not lead it – he is respectable. Squith does lead it, and it hangs on him whenever he rises to speak. As for ministers, that I see, there is no character in any of them. George

---

[121] Paul Louis Théodore Bénazet (1876–1948), French politician; deputy (Parti républicain-socialiste), 1906–32; Senator, 1933–40; concluded an agreement with King Constantine (23 Oct. 1916) that provided for the withdrawal of the Greek army from Thessaly; pan-European activist after 1919.
[122] See entry 13 Nov. 1916.
[123] Major-General Sir William Henry Rycroft (1861–1925), soldier; entered army, 1879; active service, Nile Expedition, 1884–85; North West Frontier, 1897–98; on staff South African War, 1899–1900; Somaliland, 1902–1905; commander, 11th Hussars, 1904–1908; Assistant Quartermaster-General, Southern Command, 1913–14; active service, Western Front, 1914–16; Salonika, 1916–18; Deputy Assistant and Quartermaster-General Salonika forces, Feb.–Aug. 1918; Quartermaster-General, 1918; on Irish Command, 1919–21; retired, 1921; Governor, British North Borneo, 1922–25; resigned, 1925.

Nathaniel [Curzon][124] is an ego-maniac with the corners not rubbed off. Milner has sat too long in the outer darkness to see again the light. The garden suburb secretaries cannot redeem the situation. One type, one character I see in what he writes – the King.

Winston[125] did a good thing the other day, the last day of the Dardanelles report[126] <where he was so attacked> – marched into the United Services Club, conspicuously lunched, stood afterwards for an hour, as conspicuously, with his back to the fire. Impudence will not save you today, Master Winston!

The Dardanelles report was meant to kill the Kitchener legend. This it cannot do. England knows a man if she does not know a genius.

March 12th [1917]

Epirus and Thessaly. My views on this subject are that we must gain over these 2 districts to our side by one means or another. They comprised 80,000 voters (approximately, giving an average for Koritza not then enfranchised) at the Greek election of 1915. Apart from them Royalist Greece has about 300,000 voters Venizelist Greece 296,000 (less a possible reduction of voters east of [the] Struma. They were 65,000 – they may now be less). Consequently, Epirus and Thessaly will either be occupied by France or actively propagandised by her in the next few weeks. But Thessaly alone may not give victory to Venizelos in that great national assembly which will decide the fate of Greece and of Constantine after the war. Epirus alone can make victory certain; Epirus, which includes large numbers of Venizelists, and which is undergoing terrible sufferings on its coast from the blockade. As France and England have just protested against the system of terrorization practised there by the Royalists the situation is thus. An Epirot,

---

[124] George Nathaniel Curzon (1859–1925), Baron Curzon of Kedleston, cr. 1898, 1st Earl Curzon, cr. 1911, 1st Marquess Curzon of Kedleston, cr. 1921, politician and colonial administrator; MP (Cons.) Southport, 1886–98; Parliamentary Under-secretary for India, 1891–92; for Foreign Affairs, 1895–98; Viceroy of India, 1898–1905; Lord Privy Seal, 1915–16; President of the Air Board, 1916–17; Lord President of the Council, 1916–19 and 1924–25; Foreign Secretary, 1924–25.

[125] Sir Winston Leonard Spencer Churchill (1874–1964), politician; MP (Cons.; Lib., since 1904) Oldham, 1900–1906; Manchester North West, 1906–8; Dundee, 1908–22; (Cons.) Epping, 1922–45; Woodford, 1945–64; Parliamentary Under-secretary for the Colonies, 1906–1908; President of the Board of Trade, 1908–10; Home Secretary, 1910–11; First Lord of the Admiralty, 1911–15 and 1939–40; Chancellor of the Duchy of Lancaster, 1915; Minister of Munitions, 1917–19; Secretary of State for War and Air, 1919–21; Colonial Secretary, 1921–22; Chancellor of the Exchequer, 1924–29; Prime Minister, 1940–45 and 1951–55; Minister of Defence, 1940–5 and 1951–52.

[126] *The First Report of the Dardanelles Commission (Cd. 8490)* (1917).

who trusts us and supports Venizelos, is starved by the one and persecuted for doing the other. Result[:] a certain inclination towards Royalism. The remedies for this one (1.) relaxation of blockade specially for Epirus, known to be done by France. [(2.)] British or advance of French patrols to keep Royalists and Italians in order in Epirus, or appearance of French & British cruiser off the coast, or distribution of papers and propaganda in the Venizelist or Entente sense for propaganda purposes.

March 13th [1917]

<True> anecdote of how we are governed. Last night Lloyd George, Curzon, Hardinge & Austen [Chamberlain] discussed whether Mesopotamia should be under India or a separate control. L[loyd] G[eorge] had nearly carried the day but happened to quote a gentleman who had lived 30 years in Bagdad. This so ruffled the temper and stiffened the backs of these Oriental experts, Curzon and Hardinge, that they at once outvoted L[loyd] G[eorge]. Had he not put them on their mettle by quoting Orient experience superior to their own, they would doubtless have yielded.

March 14th [1917]

The general Bagdad situation is that a bold push and cooperation with Russians may ultimately lead us far as Mosul. In Armenia the Russians have exactly numerical superiority equivalent to the Turkish reserves (say 100,000) when they strike there they should reach Sivas,[127] and Sivas should prove the back-door of Constantinople.

March 15th [1917]

The Roumanian situation was painted in the darkest colours by N[orton-] G[riffiths]. R[omania]n soldiers dying of starvation, crawling with lice – medical trains resting for 3 days in stations, the soldiers with gangrened wounds and no food – espionage everywhere – ministers impotent or treacherous – the result the same in either case. Immediate action was necessary and an Allied Court to try cases of treachery. Averescu and Presan were good men but hampered by great difficulties and impossible subordinates.

---

[127] In eastern central Turkey.

Now the news is a bit more cheering. The trains are again beginning to run – it is impossible to evacuate either R[omania]ns the Roumanian civil population or <the> army. With care and a decent system of rationing and railway improvement, the situation may still be saved. Grave news elsewhere, but I don't put this on paper even yet (March 16th). I do now[:] the abdication of the Czar and the almost bloodless Russian Revolution. In days gone by, when the tale comes to be told, there will be a grim history. I learn on good authority in the first days of the war that the Munitions Ministry could not get the Russian Government to give an orders – why not?

Yesterday, though I forgot to put it in, I learnt from unimpeachable authority (Prof[essor] O[man][128]) that, when the F[oreign] O[ffice] had put in the note about the Czecho-Slovaks, they were confounded because Balfour asked them who they were. Balfour has been trying to find out since from Prof[esso]r O[man] and a number of maps etc. are being prepared, none of them authoritative, conflicting seriously with other maps elsewhere, and without any serious mobilisation of historical men or munitions. Oh F[oreign] O[ffice]! Oh F[oreign] O[ffice]!

March 16 [1917]

Emperor Charles[129] and Germany said to be specially annoyed and hostile and coldness between him and the Kaiser very evident. Said to be annoyed with Tisza[130] for mislaying his coronation-speech and to be determined to have him out, though to be cautious about it.

All from a reliable source via Switzerland. Russia – Stürmer and Galitzin[131] were torn in pieces by the mob, but one appears officially as having died of fright and the other committing suicide.[132]

---

[128] Sir Charles William Chadwick Oman (1860–1946), military historian and politician; Fellow of All Souls, 1881–1946; Chichele Professor of Modern History, 1905–46; MP (Cons.) Oxford University, 1919–35.

[129] Karl (Franz Joseph Ludwig Hubert Georg Otto Marie) I of Habsburg-Lorraine (1887–1922), last Habsburg emperor; Emperor Charles (Karl) I of Austria and King Charles (Károly) IV of Hungary, 1916–18.

[130] Count István Tisza de Borosjenő et Szeged (1861–1918), Hungarian politician; Prime Minister, 1903–1905 and 1913–17; Minister of the Interior, 1903–1905; Minister *ad laterem*, 1903–1904 and 1915; assassinated, 31 Oct. 1918.

[131] Prince Nikolai Dmitri'evich Galitsyn (1850–1925), Russian politician; member of the State Council, 1915; last Imperial Russian Prime Minister, Jan.–Mar. 1917; executed July 1925.

[132] Stürmer was executed in September 1917, Galitsyn in 1925.

March 17th [1917]

Elliot has said 3 or 4 times that he will return to Athens from the transport with the first cargo-boat. Now the cargo-boat has arrived but the French will not allow it to be unloaded. Elliot complains of gross breach of faith, but, after saying he will land, say he now will not. At the same time we represent from England to Paris that he must. France represents that we must remove him and L[loyd] G[eorge] has already suggested a change all round. So that for [*sic*] the cross-currents are as conflicting as those of love. Tom Cunningham[133] [*sic*], the late M[ilitary] A[ttaché at] Athens, came to me today and said the guns taken at Cavalla were old Turkish ones (90 of which 48 were field!) it would have been an unneutral [*sic*] act to destroy them, though apparently quite right to resist us taking the guns which Tino had offered to give us.

March 19th [1917]

The Epirus-Ithaca terrorization has been taken up and cruiser will no doubt appear off the coast in due course. Meanwhile Sarrail is making a good push N[orth] W[est] of Monastir, has captured hill 1248 and 1300 prisoners – a present doubtless for the lady he soon takes to [be his] wife <I don't [know] which of the very many.> They say his offensive plan was not expected, a sure way to make him execute one. A push everywhere – Presba, Monastir, Doiran,[134] Struma – might succeed, as the Turkish Divisions begin to slink away Bagdad-wards.

March 20th [1917]

The excisions from the Dardanelles Report now published are extraordinary. One is a telegram from Venizelos, promising us 3 divisions saying the King has been sounded and is likely to consent. A telegram which he never could have despatched unless he trusted in our honour not to reveal it. Why we should seek to betray him now because he trusted us, and did something, in his great zeal for us, which was strictly unconstitutional, I cannot conceive. Is it a bêtise, a betrayal or a mixture of the two?

---

[133] Brigadier-General Sir Thomas Andrew Alexander Montgomery Cuninghame (1877–1945), officer; entered Rifle Brigade, 1897; active service Boer War, 1899–1902; Military Attaché at Vienna and Cetinje, 1912–14; General Staff Officer, French Headquarters, 1914–15; Military Attaché at Athens, 1915–16; General Staff Officer, 34th Brigade, 1917–18; British Military Representative at Vienna, 1919–20; Military Attaché at Vienna and Prague, 1920–23.

[134] Lake Dojran on the Graeco-Macedonian frontier, the site of three battles (Feb. and Apr. 1917, and Sept. 1918).

Zaimis[135] has suggested that the effect in Greece would be magical if we took up a new policy and forced it on the French. He regards Sarrail and Venizelos as equally dangerous – strange for one of his moderate temper.

March 21 [1917]

Lunch with D[avid] Davies. According to him (first time I've seen him since his return from Russia) a palace revolution was thought imminent not a popular one. Milner apparently was wooden and a failure and, on one occasion, when he broached a railway project to the Czar the latter turned his back and the conversation [ended]. Norton-Griffiths apparently got the Russians' back up. Empire Jack[136] blustered too much. A Russian general has been shot on the Northern front.

The P[rime] M[inister] is very unbusinesslike. Just now he spends all his time at the War Cabinet and does not see his secretaries for ten minutes in the day.

The Cabinet has been over a month shilly-shallying about the Taranto-French route to Salonica without deciding anything. D[avid] D[avies] putting in a strong minute on the subject.

March 22 [1917]

While J.R.M. Butler[137] was talking to L[loyd] G[eorge] today, a burly blustering man burst into the room and addressed the Premier. "You know this National Service Scheme is a complete failure. It'll never be right until there is a decent plan, or indeed any plan at all would be better than the present mess.["] L[loyd] G[eorge] took it very quietly and headed him off gently.

March 23 [1917]

Emperor Carl's peace terms said to be – severance from Germany, commercial facilities, partial restoration of Serbia & Montenegro, a con[stitutiona]l

---

[135] Alexandros Zaimis (1855–1936), Greek politician; High Commissioner on Crete, 1906–8; Prime Minister, 1897–99, 1901–1902, Oct.–Nov. 1915, June–Sept. 1916, Feb.–June 1917, 1926–28; President of the Hellenic Republic, 1929–35.

[136] Norton-Griffiths, see entry 19 Dec. 1916.

[137] James Ramsay Montagu Butler (1889–1975), historian; military service, 1914–18; member of British delegation at Paris peace conference, 1919; MP (Ind.), Cambridge University, 1922–23; Army Intelligence Corps, 1939–45; Regius Professor of Modern History, 1947–54; vice-master of Trinity College, Cambridge, 1955–60.

federation of Austria-Hungary spoilt by assertion that the Czechs reconciled etc. <via C[oun]t Hoyos.[138]>

[March] 24 [1917]

Gypsy told fortune – I had had hardships <& came across the water> – things would be lucky to me henceforth. I had to go across the water again. I would get a surprise in 3 months & my work & things would be lucky. After the war I would be in a bigger place than I am now.[139]

Elliot landed at Athens from a ship, followed by the other Legations.

[March] 25th [1917]

French: Thessaly, Milos, Naxos – that is their aggressive programme at present. The people of Thessaly, terrified by armed gangs, have declared that, whatever happens, they will not again hand their crops over to Old Greece, but will exist by force. As the Provisional Government is helpless to assist them, they have appealed to Sarrail. He will no doubt be pleased to listen, and incidentally secure Volo and the Larissa-Plati railway line for France. Milos, where Venus was found, has already been occupied by the French. They aimed at Naxos also but, finding the British there, politely explained that they only wished to secure the enemy mines against the Royalists. The significance of the move is that Milos is Venizelist, and the action of the French is on the face of it, anti-Venizelist. Where will they stop? I think at Athens when Tino is comfortably on board a steamboat.

[March] 26th [1917]

Russia: Affairs seem to be settling down a little. The Grand-Ducal element has to become patriotic or disappeared, but there is a danger of division between

---

[138] (Ludwig) Alexander (Georg) Count von Hoyos, Baron zu Stichsenstein (1876–1937), Austro-Hungarian diplomat; entered diplomatic service, 1900; *chef de cabinet* to Foreign Minister, 1912–17; Minister at Christiania, 1917–18; retired, 1918.

[139] The fortune-teller's prognostication was premature; Temperley did not cross any water until the autumn of 1918.

Milyukoff[140] and his Cadets and the International Socialists of the Kerensky[141] type. <I should probably have said Lenin[142] type.>

Bratiano has been protesting against the fact that Take Ionescu must be intriguing against him, because he has given two men introductions to L[loyd] G[eorge]. For Bratiano to complain of intrigue is like the Kaiser complaining of 'frightfulness'. Barclay bravely adds that he had no previous thought of an intrigue ag[ain]st Bratiano. Poor Bratiano – still poorer Barclay! Innocent lambs be they.

[March] 27th

Albania: Apparently on the 16th December Albania, or rather the Koritza area, south of Barmasi[143] and west of the Koritza-Ersek road, was proclaimed autonomous by the French. The good effect of this was somewhat marred by the Roumanian disaster but a local gendarmerie, partly paid locally, has been organized, recruits come in, and the autonomists of Koritza conduct a local propaganda not without its effects on border tribes.

The Austrian reply was to proclaim autonomy of Albania (curious that, as in Poland, when a country is proclaimed autonomous or independent, the proclaimed promptly introduces compulsory military service). Gendarmerie and bands are being raised, the chief organizer being Zitkowsky,[144] formerly Austrian Consul at Monastir, whom I remember well <with whom I have played tennis> and to whom I gave a silver matchbox on his wedding day.

[March] 28th [1917]

Bulgaria – after a close examination of Bulgarian statistics of manpower, with all the aids of Somerset House we still come to a missing 70,000. The class of 1918 (and possibly even of 1919) being largely drawn upon, and all evidences

---

[140] Pavel Nikolayevich Milyukov (1859–1943), Russian politician; founder and leader of the Constitutional Democrat Party (Kadets); in French exile since 1917.

[141] Alexander Fyodorovich Kerensky (1881–1970), Russian politician; Prime Minister of the Russian Provision Government, Feb.–Nov. 1917

[142] Vladimir Ilyich Lenin (née Ulyanov) (1870–1924), Bolshevik leader; Chairman of the Council of People's Commissars of the Russian Soviet Federative Socialist Republic, 1917–22; of the Soviet Union, 1922–4.

[143] Now Barmash, near Korçë (Albania).

[144] Heinrich Zitkovszky von Szemeszova and Szohorad (b. 1883), Austro-Hungarian consul; entered consular service, 1907; vice-consul at Monastir, 1909–14; consul-general at Odessa, 1918.

of exhaustion of men being found, there still remain 80,000 unaccounted for. What is the explanation? I don't know – nobody knows – possibly they are not there. I am inclined to think that if you take 945,000 men from an almost wholly agricultural country it is not surprising that to make a ball, 70,000 have to remain behind.

[March] 29th [1917]

Roumania. Politics have been mixed, the army much disgusted with the Bratianus and Iliescu[145] their tool have quite seriously contemplated a military dictatorship but failed because they could not choose between Avarescu and Presan. The Queen has favoured a non-party ministry with Presan or Misu[146] (min[iste]r in Eng[lan]d) at the head. Take Ionescu while declining to be dictated to by his own party, is probably intriguing ag[ain]st Bratiano.

There has been a sharp stop to all these intrigues put by the Russian Revolution. This has brought the King on Bratiano's side and made all realize the perils of war and revolution.

Avarescu recently dined with the King and was decorated by him.

[March] 30th [1917]

Wonders will never cease. A few days ago the island <of Zante>, by a spontaneous movement, declared for adhesion to Venizelos. This movement we declined to suppress, but it was suppressed and by whom? the French Admiral of all people. Either a bêtise or a deliberate blow at Venizelism. Meanwhile, the Italians advance in Epirus and even are said to establish schools there. They are exciting the suspicions of the Royalists though, characteristically enough, the protest against their encroachments comes from Venizelos. The French interfere with his chartering sailing vessels and we, by way of encouraging him, I suppose, have agreed to ration him & Royalist Greece for the next 50 days with 70% of what was promised so that innocent Venizelists starve on an equal ration with guilty Royalists.

---

[145] See entry 25 Jan. 1917.
[146] Nicolae Mişu (1858–1924), Romanian diplomat; minister at Vienna, Constantinople, London; Foreign Minister, Oct.–Nov. 1919.

[March] 31st [1917]

Russia – marine & advice to.

The Revolution seems to be solidly settling down and discipline to be gradually being reestablished in the army. The Navy is quite different at least 3 Admirals have been shot. Kronstadt is in a state of chaos and 300 officers are being made to do coal fatigues by their men. The navy is tossing on fiery waves. The Polish manifesto may counterbalance some evils, but even the offer there is subject to the consent of a free Parliament. There is a strong feeling abroad for constituting a catholic state of 3 parts – Austria, Hungary, Poland. This I hold foredoomed to failure because Hungary hates the Slavs more than she loves Catholics. Austrian Dualism is essential and trialism fatal to Hungary's interests. Therefore trialism would drive Hungary into German arms.

[April] 1st [1917]

Rasputin[147] – Haig. Today I lunched with some friends and Tom Jones,[148] the latter a friend of L[loyd] G[eorge]'s and pulled from Aberystwith [*sic*] University to grace the Committee of Imperial Defence as a secretary of the War Cabinet. I rallied him – we all rallied him – as the power behind the throne, the unseen hand, finally as Rasputin. 'Well', said he with some humour, 'Mrs. Lloyd G[eorge] has never given me enough encouragement to play that part'.

Then he told the story of Haig and his notorious interview. Journalists – French and glowing ones – dragged words from him as with a corkscrew. Neville Lytton[149] sent the interview to Charteris, then in England, and Charteris passed it without looking at it. Lytton was carpeted and Charteris absolved – sic transit.

[April] 2nd [1917]

Ven[izeli]st Greece Athens. Fr[ench] in Thess[al]y.

---

[147] Grigori Yefimovich Rasputin (1869–1916), Russian Orthodox monk and faith-healer; a close confidant of the Tsarina; murdered 16 Dec. 1916.

[148] Dr Thomas (Tom) Jones (1870–1955), civil servant and educationalist; Professor of Political Economy, Queen's University Belfast, 1909–16; editor *Welsh Outlook*, 1914–33; Deputy Cabinet Secretary, 1916–1930; President of University College of Aberystwyth, 1944–54.

[149] Neville Stephen Bulwer-Lytton (1879–1951), 3rd Earl of Lytton, succ. 1947; military officer and artist; active service on Western Front, 1915–16; General Staff officer (press liaison and censorship officer), Section I (d), General Headquarters, British Expeditionary Force, 1916–18; see his war memoirs *The Press and the General Staff* (London, 1920).

The French have backed down over Zante, disavowed their Admiral, and expelled the Royalists. That is one point to the good. On the other hand Athens is being undoubtedly stirred up against the King, just as Thessaly is – in each case I see the French influence and the hand of Sarrail. What will be the end? We stand passive clinging to our idiotic formula of reconciling Venizelos and the King, which no one except Elliot and the F[oreign] O[ffice] believe possible. The French now with [the] monarchy gone in Russia and Princess George of Greece's[150] lover <[Aristide] Briand> gone in France will urge a speedy resolution, get to Athens, and get rid of Tino by putting him on board a steamer.

[April] 3rd [1917]

On 12/3/17 the F[oreign] O[ffice] asked if the report that the Greek Government had communicated to Germany the names of 23 ships requisitioned for wheat was true. On the 22/3/17 the British minister at Athens [Sir Francis Elliot] replied that the report was true.

On April 2nd Mr Lynch[151] asked the Foreign Secretary whether he is aware that King Constantine is in constant communication with the Kaiser.

Mr. Balfour[:] The answer is in the negative.[152]

Comment is needless.

[April] 4th [1917]

'The ablest head in the Empire' is Asquith's description of General Smuts[153] last time he was over. It has been rumé [?] for some time back. He believes, I understand, that the war will end this summer.

---

[150] Princess Marie Bonaparte (1882–1962), married Prince George of Greece and Denmark (1869–1957); had an affair with Briand, 1916–19; closely linked to Sigmund Freud.

[151] Arthur Alfred Lynch (1861–1934), Irish-Australian civil engineer, journalist and politician; MP (Irish Nat.) Galway Borough, 1901–1902, and West Clare, 1909–18; contested (Lab.) Battersea South, 1918; volunteered in 1914, but did not see active service.

[152] *Hansard* xcii (2 Apr. 1917), col. 885.

[153] General Jan Christiaan Smuts (1870–1950), South African military leader and politician; led Boer Commandos, 1899–1902; Minister of the Interior, 1910–12; Minister of Defence, 1910–20 and 1939–48; Finance Minister, 1912–15; member of the Imperial War Cabinet, 1917–18; Prime Minister, 1919–24 and 1939–48; Minister of Justice, 1933–39; Foreign Minister, 1939–48.

At last there [is] news of the famous insertion of Czecho-Slovaks in the note in reply to Germany's peace-offer. V[ide] Benesh[154] [sic], secretary of the Czecho-Slovak league in Paris, exercised an active propaganda in their favour, got hold of Denis[155] and Eisenmann[156] – the former, somewhat of a lecturer and propagandist Slav – finally secured Briand. There is fairly good evidence that the latter knew little of it or of its tremendous significance. He imposed it rigidly on us, and we, knowing nothing, accepted it. Then, in order to find out, we asked, through Balfour, Professor Oman (a distinguished authority on every other period and people in history except these). So the crazy world is governed. This is from a reliable, authentic source.

There are also prepared Croatian and Czecho-Slovak maps, latter in German, which will be of considerable propagandist use at the correct moment. Milyukoff subsequently in an interview published on the 9th April claimed the Czecho-Slovaks as an independent state. In that case what becomes of the theory of a strong Austria, which some of us so energetically back? All this much strengthens the scheme propounded in my memorandum for mobilising the historians.[157]

5th April [1917]

A last blow at Venizelos – he has not been paid the promised money, so wires to Lloyd George. In the resultant investigation F[oreign] O[ffice] accuses Treasury and Treasury F[oreign] O[ffice]. Each calls the other black – I think both very gray [sic].

C[hief of the] I[mperial] G[eneral] S[taff, Robertson] returns from Italy thinking the General an old man, the troops half-hearted and beaten before they fight, but the Alpini and Bersaglieri as good as the Guards.

Sal[oni]ca. The stinging notes <Memo[randum] of 2nd April>. Condemnation of the failure, from the first, of the improbable results, of the

---

[154] Edvard Beneš (1884–1948), leader of Czechoslovak independence movement and Czechoslovak politician; in exile in Paris, 1915–18; Secretary of the Czechoslovak National Council, and Minister of the Interior and Foreign Minister in Provisional Czechoslovak government, 1916–18; Foreign Minister, 1920–25, 1929–35; Prime Minister, 1921–22; President, 1935–38 and 1945–48; President-in-Exile, 1940–45.

[155] Ernest Denis (1849–1921), French historian of central Europe; took part in defence of Paris, 1870; Professor, Bordeaux University, 1878–81; Grenoble, 1881–96; Professor of History, Sorbonne, 1896–1921; member of Briand's *Comité d'études*, 1917–18, to prepare French policy for a peace conference.

[156] Louis Eisenmann (1869–1937), French historian of central Europe; Professor of History, Dijon University, 1905–13; Paris University, 1913–22; Professor of Slavic Studies, Sorbonne, 1922–37; active on the League of Nations committee for intellectual cooperation.

[157] 'War Notes – Strategy', n.d. [c. 1916], Temperley MSS.

vast amount of sickness, of the use which could be made of 200,000 troops in the West, backed up by an equally strong note from Jellicoe for the Navy, passed by without a sign.

Evidently the P[rime] M[inister] favours neither view but sticks close by Serbia and Venizelos – I wonder if my little book with an inscription to 'the statesman of the greatest empire who <has> understood and interpreted the smallest nations best' had any influence. It was put under his eyes. (v[ide] 11 April)

6th –9th [April 1917]

Rye made me realize the imaginative ability of Ford Mad[d]ox Hueffer[158] in the 'Half Moon' which reconstructs Elizabethan Rye in marvellous fashion, with its slow heavy Dutchmen, its winding ports, its heavy barons, its enterprising Edward Colman first man to be killed in the New World, its mayor's garden on the slopes, its fears, superstitions, ambitious enterprises.

Winchelsea has a beautiful church, Early English fading into decorated. The most interesting thing, however, is the face of Edward I on a tomb,[159] said by those who gazed on his features in 1874 to be a good likeness, though minus the nose. A broad square face, deep-set eyes, a ring-clad wrinkled brow, thick lips prominently forward and iron imperious lines at the mouth's corners – the face of an organiser and a masterful man, not apparently of a genius or a dreamer, still less of the exquisite lover-like tenderness shown in still beautiful memorial at Charing Cross

> 'Her corpse to the tomb be carried
> With grief at his heart's stern core
> And, whenever at night they tarried
> Rise a cross to Eleanore'.

10th April [1917]

F[oreign] O[ffice] blunders – a bunch of sweets. Martens is quoted by the Bulgars to support the enlisting of Serbians east of the Morava in the Bulgar army. The F[oreign] O[ffice] states there is only one Martens, an international jurist of repute and he regards the practice as inadmissible. In fact there are

---

[158] Ford Madox Ford (née Ford Hermann Hueffer) (1873–1939), novelist, poet and critic; employed in War Propaganda Bureau, 1914–15; active service, 1915–18; his novel *The Half Moon* was published in 1909.

[159] That of Gervase de Alard (d. 1310), first Admiral of the Cinque Ports.

3 (v[ide] Sir E. Satow, Diplomatic Practice).[160] Why dogmatically then assert what they could not possibly anticipate?

<Note 18th Ap[ril] glad to hear that this telegram was badly worded and that the F[oreign] O[ffice] really understand that there [are] not 3 but 5 Martens with 19 works to their credit.[161]>

11th April [1917]

I sent L[loyd] G[eorge] an advance copy of my book[162] with following inscription 'To the statesman and leader of the greatest empire who has understood and interpreted the smaller nations best'. This was shown to him by D[avid] D[avies] and he sent a message that he was very pleased and appreciated the compliment. I wonder if he took the advice.

Light from Percy[163] on the original German plan of invasion. The French expected to hold the Meuse and even if the Germans swung round via Brussels etc., to break them in two by la trouée [gap] de Luxembourg by a counter-attack

---

[160] Sir Ernest Mason Satow (1843–1929), diplomat; entered consular service as Japanese student interpreter, 1861; minister-resident and consul-general at Bangkok, 1885–88; minister at Montevideo, 1888–93; at Tangier, 1893–95; at Tokyo, 1895–1900; at Peking, 1900–1906; British plenipotentiary at The Hague peace conference, 1907; author of *A Guide to Diplomatic Practice* (2 vols, London, 1917).

[161] There were in fact three (1) Georg Friedrich von Martens (1756–1821), German lawyer and diplomat; professor of jurisprudence at Göttingen, 1783; Hanoverian envoy to German *Bundestag* at Frankfurt, 1816–21; editor of *Recueil des traites* (7 vols, Göttingen, 1791–1801), *Precis du droit des gens modernes de l'Europe* (Göttingen, 1789); and *Cours diplomatique ou tableau des relations des puissances de l'Europe* (3 vols, Berlin, 1801); (2) Karl von Martens (1790–1863), German international lawyer and diplomat; nephew of G.F. von Martens; Saxe-Weimar minister-resident at Dresden; author of *Manuel diplomatique* (Leipzig, 1823), *Causes célèbres du droit des gens* (2 vols, Leipzig, 1827) and *Recueil manuel et pratique de traites* (7 vols, Leipzig, 1846–57); (3) Friedrich Fromhold von Martens (Fyodor Fyodorovich Martens) (1845–1909), Russian diplomat and international lawyer; entered Russian foreign ministry, 1868; professor of law, Imperial Alexander Lyceum, 1872; special legal assistant to Russian chancellor, Prince Gorchakov, 1874; delegate at The Hague peace conference, 1899; delegate at Portsmouth peace conference, 1905; editor of *Recueil des traités et conventions conclus par la Russie avec les puissances étrangères* (13 vols, St. Petersburg, 1874–1902); *International Law of Civilised Nations* (1884).

[162] *A History of Serbia* (London, 1917); see entry 5 Apr. 1917.

[163] Alan Ian Percy (1880–1930), 8th Duke of Northumberland, succ. 1918, soldier, politician and propagandist, known as Earl Percy, 1909–18; entered army, 1900; active service South Africa, 1900–1902; aide-de-camp to Earl Grey, 1910–11; active service, France, 1914–16; attached to directorate of military operations, 1916–18; financed and directed the diehard, right-wing *Patriot*, 1922–30.

there – they found a trench dug right across all Luxembourg by the busy Huns and recoiled in amazement.

12th [April 1917]

I hear L[loyd] G[eorge] & Painlevé forgathered delightfully. P[ainlevé] shook hands or embraced him every five minutes. Sir H[enry] Norman[164] acting as interpreter, while Jim Butler (the Staff Officer from the War Office – v[ide] the morning papers[165]) stuck pins into the maps to show how we progressed.

Another good thing I hear is that French Thomas[166] of the Mayik head and Labour politics and Munitions achievements, is to proceed to Russia to influence them in the direction of efficiency and sane Republicanism. Prosit amen, say I.

13th [April 1917]

The Serbian rising east of the Morava is now reported by deserters and is probably true. They have excellent cause for they are being conscripted against international law. Moreover in these remote hills and valleys guerrilla fragments of the Serbian army still lurk.

Evidence as to it is also provided by the fact that the <Bulgarian> papers of March 3 published a law for dealing with the extirpation of brigandage.

The Sofia revolution is not so certain but not improbable.

14th [April 1917]

Sent a copy of my book today to Crown Prince Alexander of Serbia, a noble young fellow of a dynasty and people not now too happily placed. [Gerald] FitzMaurice told S[ykes][167] the other day that the crown was already off. I wonder are we all like Ibsen's play whose name I forget – the man who saw a mighty wind blowing

---

[164] Sir Henry Norman (1858–1939), journalist and politician; assistant editor *Daily Chronicle*, 1895–1900; MP (Lib.) Wolverhampton South, 1900–10, and Blackburn, 1910–23; Postmaster-General, 1910.

[165] Clowes, Hickley & Steward to Editor, 'War Office Red Tape', *The Times*, 12 Apr. 1917.

[166] Albert Thomas (1878–1932), French Socialist politician; Under-secretary for Artillery and Munitions, 1915–16; Minister of Armament, 1916–17; resigned over Stockholm Socialist conference, Sept. 1917; Director-General of the International Labour Organisation, 1919–32.

[167] Fitzmaurice and Mark Sykes were old friends, see G.R. Berridge, *Gerald Fitzmaurice, 1865–1939; Chief Dragoman of the British Embassy in Turkey* (Leiden and Boston, 2007), 223.

before which were scattered Kings with their crowns.[168] Spain and Sweden are shaky, Tino totters, Ferdinand fails, Russia is gone – where will it end? In red flags in the Sieges Allee[169] says FitzMaurice where he saw them in prophetic vision early in 1914. There is sane sense in this view that the monarchical principle cannot stand. Serbia has dragged down the Czar – will she lose her King too? America will her boisterous appeal to equality will produce an immense reverberation throughout the world. L[loyd] G[eorge] himself speaks of monarchical swashbucklers and dynastic quarrels as the source of all old wars, and prophesies the downfall of the Hohenzollern. The 'Down' speech as it is called is the bête noir of our Realpolitikers, headed by Milner and Amery.

15th [April 1917]

Apparently the downfall of Asquith was already prophesied in the middle of 1915. Amery, Chamberlain, Milner & Repington[170] of the Times used to meet twice a week to discuss things for the <future> War Cabinet and hatch out the plans.

Aitken did the trick via Bland[171] & the E at the end?[172]

---

[168] *The League of Youth* (1869), act I. The central character, Stensgard, described his dream: 'There was no sun, only a livid storm-light. A tempest arose; it came rushing from the west and swept everything before it: first withered leaves, then men; but they kept on their feet all the time, and their garments clung fast to them, so that they seemed to be hurried along sitting. At first they looked like townspeople running after their hats in a wind; but when they came nearer they were emperors and kings; and it was their crowns and orbs they were chasing and catching at, and seemed always on the point of grasping, but never grasped. Oh, there were hundreds and hundreds of them, and none of them understood in the least what was happening.'

[169] One of the main boulevards in Berlin radiating from the Brandenburg Gate.

[170] Lieutenant-Colonel Charles À Court Repington (1858–1925), soldier and writer; entered army, 1878; active service Afghanistan, Burma, Sudan, South Africa; Military Attaché at Brussels and The Hague, 1899–1902; technical delegate at First Peace Conference at The Hague, 1899; invalided, 1902 (resignation after divorce scandal); afterwards influential writer on military matters for *Morning Post*, 1902–1904, and *The Times*, 1904–18; convicted under Defence of the Realm Act for disclosure of military secrets, 1918; editor *Army Review*, 1911–18; on staff of *Daily Telegraph*, 1918–25.

[171] Presumably Brigadier-General William St. Colum Bland (1868–1950), soldier; entered Royal Artillery, 1887; instructor, School of Gunnery, 1906–1909; Superintendent of Experiments, 1909–13; member, Ordnance Board, 1914; President of Ordnance Committee, 1916–19; Controller of Munitions Design, 1919; commandant, Ordnance College, 1919–20; retired, 1920.

[172] Presumably John St Loe Strachey (9 February 1860–1927), ed. Balliol; called to the bar; editor, *The Spectator*, 1887–1925. A reference to Beaverbrook's campaign against Asquith in the *Daily Express*.

16th [April 1917]

Iliescu's and other Roumanian accusations that Russia deliberately let them down in order to have an excuse for making peace with Germany seem curious but not altogether convincing. It does not appear to be true that Russia presented them with what was practically an ultimatum to force them on but that was natural if not defensible. It is also true that Iliescu wanted 200,000 Russians to occupy Rustchuk before he stirred. <This he had to abandon.> But the actual engagements of the Convention were strictly carried out, except perhaps as regards the transport of munitions. Even in that matter however at the time the French mission at [the] Russian G[eneral] H[ead] Q[uarters] said that the stipulated amounts were going regularly through. As the French now make out the Stürmer was a pro-German traitor all along, this admission is amusing and significant.

The Transylvanian attack plan was approved by Alexeieff[173] who made a somewhat startling change from his original statement that Roumania's intervention would be of no value, and a guaranteed neutrality would be far better.

This is startling and must have been due to political influences. It is also true that the Russians declined to move from Moldavia and even retained cavalry divisions there in the middle of November where they could be of no conceivable use. On the other hand the Roumanians made no serious attempt to join hands with the Russians at Dorna Watra[174] largely because the Toplitsa[175] pass was impregnable.

On the whole it is possible that Stürmer was ready to make peace on the basis of Moldavia to Russia and Wallachia to Germany, but there is not enough evidence to prove it.

17th [April 1917]

In Roumania the Russian Revolution was assuaged by political quarrels. Avarescu and the King, Bratianu and Ionescu are temporarily reconciled. That

---

[173] General Mikhail Vasiliyevich Alekseyev (1857–1918), Imperial Russian soldier; entered army, 1873; Professor of Military History, Nicholas General Staff Academy, 1898–1904; Quartermaster-General, 3rd Manchurian Army, 1904–1905; chief of staff, Galician front, 1914–15; commander, northwestern front, 1915; chief of staff, General Headquarters, Aug. 1915–Mar. 1917 and Aug.–Nov. 1917; led anti-Bolshevik Volunteer Army in Don region in 1918.

[174] Now Vatra Dornei (German *Dorna-Watra*; Magyar *Dornavátra*), in the Carpathian mountains, part of the Bukovina region, northeastern Romania.

[175] Now Toplița in southeastern Transylvania (Romania).

incorrigible optimist Berthelot puts the Roumanian casualties at 400,000 and the existing army at 600,000 with 400,000 effectives. Material conditions, food, sanitation etc., are bad but the morale is improving.

C.B.T[homson][176] makes way for General Ballard[177] directly. Another little 'tea-table scoundrel' or 'Chesterfield in Khaki' relegated to limbo.

18th [April 1917]

The Venizelist shares are distinctly going up. His 2 papers are busy at Athens. Corfu is occupied by his men, Zante[178] has had an exped[itio]n sent by him to it, Leucas and Ithaca have adhered. Corfu will probably do so. Epirus is certainly Venizelist in sympathy for it will have nothing to do with Reservist leagues, which exist only at Janina and Preveza,[179] and old SPIRIDON,[180] Archbishop at Janina, a notorious comitadji-organizer, has found it convenient to go to Athens. In Egypt also Venizelos has had a great triumph. The arrangement as to Consular courts retained them for the Royalists, but allowed Venizelists to put themselves under the protection of the British C[ommander]-in-C[hief]. As 80% of the Greek community has done so in all probability the Royalist jurisdiction there will collapse. V[enizelos] himself as always is moderate but his followers now aim almost openly at Republicanism.

Heard tonight of Maurice's <Maurice Kemp-Welch,[181] 2nd Lieutenant> death at Mouchy[-le-Châtel], the best and truest friend I ever had, or shall have.

---

[176] Major Christopher Birdwood Thomson (1875–1930), 1st Baron Thomson of Cardington, officer and Labour politician; entered Royal Engineers, 1894; Chief Military Interpreter, BEF Headquarters, 1914–15; Military Attaché at Bucharest, 1915–17; Palestine campaign, 1917; member of British delegation at Paris peace conference, 1919; Secretary of State for Air, 1924 and 1929–30; died in R101 air crash.

[177] Brigadier-General Colin Robert Ballard (1868–1941), officer; entered army, 1887; General Officer Commanding 57th Infantry Brigade at the Somme, 1916; military attaché at Bucharest, 1917–18; President, Allied Police Commission, Constantinople, 1920–23.

[178] Now Xanthi in eastern Thrace (Greece).

[179] Coastal town in Epirus, near Cape Actium.

[180] Spyridon Vlachos (d. 1956), Greek Orthodox clergyman; Metropolitan Bishop of Vella and Konitsa, 1906–16; Metropolitan Bishop of Ioannina, 1916–49; Archbishop of Athens and All Greece, 1949–56.

[181] Maurice Kemp-Welch (1880–1917), solicitor; 2nd Lieutenant, 10th battalion, the Yorkshire Regiment; a close friend and contemporary of Temperley's at King's; Temperley was his best man.

19th [April 1917]

An incident relieving monotony at Athens. Deserters are frequent from Piraeus – a sentry was put on to stop them, but followed them in the boat a few minutes after having taken up his post. A number of Greek reservists have petitioned the British Minister (!) to secure their funds in the Bank, as their Government cannot do so.

20th [April 1917]

Tino had an interview with Elliot on the 18th, talked about a Venizelist plot on the 1st & 2nd Dec[ember 1916] and said he personally saw firing from the house of BENACHIS, a feeble old man <a man subsequently so maltreated bu rioters that 'his face resembled that of a corpse'>. He also accused us of bad faith to the agreement of Jan[uary 8th 1917] by which we undertook not to allow the Venizelist movement to be promulgated by force <outside the terr[itor]y it then occupied>. <He> was sharply pulled up by E[lliot] on the ground that we agreed not to allow the movement to be promulgated from Salonica but that this did not apply to spontaneous adhesions such as we witnessed in Zante, Leucas etc. As he still pursued the subject, E[lliot] said he drafted the clause himself.

Tino then discussed a change of Ministry with a view to pleasing the Entente. Mentioned DIMITROPOULOS (whom he did not like as he wished to call the Chamber) KALOGEROPOULOS[182] and ZAIMIS[183] favoured the latter. E[lliot] said he w[oul]d personally like him if only he was strong enough to deal with outside influences as Dusmanis. Tino said he could not send [the] latter away and, later in the day, found that Zaimis would not take office without some addition to prestige as getting the Entente to raise the blockade etc.

One thing emerges – even E[lliot] now seems to think a reconciliation between Venizelos and the King out of the question. As he has also advocated a def[ini]te policy to be decided on immediately, the latter is likely to take place at the ~~Rome~~ Italian Conference.

Tino seemed much afraid of dethronement or invasion of Greece by the French, and with some humming and hawing ~~decided~~ declared he would resist by force. <French proposals to one of our agents previously suggested an attempt to use Salonica as a jumping off ground.>

---

[182] See entry 13 Nov. 1916.
[183] See entry 20 Mar. 1917.

22nd [April 1917]

Venizelos has now his turn – proposes in effect civil war, thinks this two divisions might be usefully employed at Salonica as a base with Athens as an ultimate objective. Asked if he did not think that it was better for Greece to settle her internal affairs without outside help, he said yes but circumstances did not always allow it. The present situation could not go on, either he or the Entente must resolve it. He was willing as always to submit to the Entente. Recently the French gave a categorical refusal to his request to occupy Thessaly. We tried to stop his mobilisation in the islands which is just beginning.

A rumour that Tino was ready to be reconciled to Venizelos was regarded by M. POLITIS[184] as a plot to entrap the latter. M. Venizelos does not altogether approve of POLITIS' circular to his foreign representatives. He says that he personally is anti-dynastic only in the sense that he is anti-Tino. A Venizelist mission has reached Zante, Cephalonia and Ithaca to organize the government there. At Corfu, where Italians and French quarrel, we have resolved difficulties in masterly manner by planting a convalescent hospital there.

23rd Ap[ril 1917]

With ref[eren]ce to 16th [April] att[itu]de of Russia to Roumania. It is not true as Iliescu asserts, so far as I know, that 4 Army Corps were promised by Russia. It is true that in the middle of November the Russian cavalry were kept there in Moldavia where they could be of no possible use, that the offensive from Moldavia, to relieve the situation, was only launched on 2 December after being promised for the 12th November. Also only 2 infantry reg[imen]ts and 1 cavalry regiments [*sic*] were sent to aid Bucharest. These things are true, but it does not follow the Russian judgment was at fault. <In the third week of November> the Roumanians ran from the Alt[185] Valley before one quarter of the numbers to the frank amazement of the Russians. The Russians declined to defend Bucharest and to mix their troops with the unreliable Roumanians whom they utterly despised.

But they immobilised large quantities of Austrian troops and saved the situation when the time came. Of course, Stürmer may have schemed for a peace on the basis of Moldavia for Russia and Wallachia for Germany, but the facts do not prove it. In addition the Russian slowness of movement, which Iliescu ascribed to the treachery to Stürmer, is quite sufficiently accounted for by the negligence and obstruction of the Roumanian railway management, which compelled almost all Russian troops to march.

---

[184] See entry 17 Oct. 1916.
[185] See entry 16 Nov. 1916.

The Roumanian troops, if properly handled, were strong enough to save Bucharest. Iliescu, who messed up everything, naturally invokes treachery of his ally to excuse incompetence in himself.

24[th April 1917]

Ven[izelos] & F[ran]ce Gr[ee]k Press tone. Further evidence accumulates from a French proclamation at Milos that the French attitude towards V[enizelos] is not wholly friendly. Elliot however is incorrigible – he has returned, after a momentary lapse, to his old view that reconciliation between Tino & V[enizelos] is possible. This is supported by the theory that civil war massacres of Venizelists (and possibly detention of Legations as hostages – a powerful argument!) must follow a French occupation of Thessaly or a Venizelist attack from the mainland. The latter is conceivable as V[enizelos] has refused with some well-merited scorn our attempt to delay further his mobilisation of the islands to which we had previously assented.

25[th April 1917]

Bulgaria has not severed relations with the USA, whilst Austria-Hungary has, an interesting and significant fact.[186]

Meanwhile a gleam of intelligence from Elliot. He at last suggests that Greece, Royalist and Venizelist, should be provisioned from India and Egypt instead of America. Thus it saves danger, distance and time. An admirable idea but why not ventilated before? To my certain knowledge D[avid] D[avies] has advocated it for at least 3 months. <Venizelos has done the same – it has only now been forced on by the failure of ships from America.> Also incidentally it would prevent French naval interference such as kept the S.S. Athanasios <a Venizelist grain-ship> for 17 days at Oran[187] though urgently required for Salonica.

26[th April 1917]

Amery's memoir shown by D[avid] D[avies]. According to this thesis to the Prime Minister and Imperial War Cabinet it is a case of Sea vs Con[stantino]ple. We can make certain of the first and the German colonies but not of the second.

---

[186] The USA declared war on Germany on 6 Apr. 1917; the declaration of war on Austria-Hungary did not occur until 7 Dec. 1917.
[187] In French Algeria.

Let us take the first and become so great as an empire that we can afford to disregard Europe and the Balkans and Asia Minor.

I put my finger, when asked, in the vital fallacy. A Constantinople open to German influences means 20 divisions, kept up as a permanent fighting force to defend Egypt and India, where we are vulnerable on land. We have more reason than Napoleon to say when Alexander asked him to give up Constantinople, 'Never – it is the Empire of the world!' If Amery's view is true we are beaten and must go on fighting to get better terms. But it is not true.

27[th April 1917]

L[loyd] G[eorge] notes & on Pref[eren]ce interregn[um].

The Thessalian [*sic*] harvest is a matter now awaking attention. Though it does not begin till early in June, Royalist harvesters are already penetrating there, prepared at the right time to become comitadjis[188], seize the whole harvest for Royalist Greece and thus render it independent of the sea-borne provisions for 7 months. This must be stopped at all costs, but how?

V[enizelos] w[oul]d say by a Venizelist invasion of Thessaly and by an altimate republic of Greece. He has come to think this a possible if not the best solution. He w[oul]d accept at present and impose on his followers the Gr[ee]k Crown Prince, the Belgian K[in]g's 2nd son[189] or best of all an English prince, on the Gr[ee]k throne.

28th [April 1917]

Some suggestion that oil wells at Campina and Buzeu[190] are reopening. If this be so, Norton-Griffiths' famous announcement of complete destruction ad finem which would stop all wells being drilled for at least 8 months is rather an empty boast.

'Empire Jack'[191] is a curious man – he wired in the middle of his exploits to the Whip not to forget him in the Honours. He is one of those who have done much and boasted more.

---

[188] Komitadji, members of secret revolutionary rebel bands in the Balkans during the final period of Ottoman rule in the region, usually associated with the struggle against Turkish authorities in Macedonia.

[189] Prince Charles Théodore Henri Antoine Meinrad of Saxe-Coburg-Gotha (1903–83), Count of Flanders, second son of King Albert I of the Belgians (1875–1934); Prince Regent, 1944–50.

[190] Câmpina, near Ploiești, and Buzău in Wallachia.

[191] Colonel Norton-Griffiths, see also entry 8 May 1918.

29th [April 1917]

Cannot understand L[or]d R[obert] C[ecil] tonight in his answer being asked about the Germans being corpse cannibals.[192] The evid[en]ce is fair for it, yet he made no show at all. There is the German minister's boast to Chinese ministers as the glycerine, the letter from Roumania, referring to the way corpses and dogs were treated and how it surprised the Roumanians (this new and ingenious process!). There is also the mysterious increase of margarine and glycerine in Germany. How & why did the FO remain silent on all these points?

1st May [1917]

L[loyd] G[eorge]'s notes. I understand he spoke as he did on Friday [27 April][193] to check the cut-&-dried Tariff scheme urged on by Milner & Amery at the War Cabinet. He is all for nat[iona]l party, league to enforce peace, democratic diplomacy, and close accord with USA to defeat secret aims of bureaucrats.

Another good source, at Min[istr]y of Mun[itio]ns, his minutes reveal his fiery temperament 'This won't do at all – things must be done quicker' 'Why shouldn't a factory be built from the ground in 3 months, with wooden walls if necessary?' 'Go to S---- to find out how to speed things up – he has made a success of it'. On a contract 'This may be a high price – must be accepted – the cost in human lives will be dearer'.

2nd [May 1917]

The conference at St. Jean de Maurienne[194] showed quite clearly that France was made up her mind about Greece. Ribot[195] said that her conduct was no satisfactory and that further pledges must be exacted from her. Each country reserved the question for reference to their respective Staffs as to what they would do in case of the problem of occupying Thessaly came up. It is pretty clear

---

[192] 'The German "Kadaver" Factories', *The Times*, 1 May 1917; see entries 17 Feb. and 5 Mar. 1917.

[193] Lloyd George's speech at the Guildhall on 27 Apr. 1917, see 'Food And Ships. Mr. Lloyd George On Essentials', *The Times*, 28 Apr. 1917.

[194] The Agreement of St.-Jean-de-Maurienne between Britain, France and Italy, of 26 Apr. 1917, was signed at Sonnino's instigation with the aim of securing Italy's position in the Near East.

[195] Alexandre-Félix-Joseph Ribot (1842–1923), French lawyer and politician; Foreign Minister, 1890–3 and 1917; Minister of the Interior, 1893; Finance Minister, 1895 and 1914–17; Minister of Justice, 1914; Prime Minister, 1892–93, 1895, 1914 and 1917.

however what France will do. In the case of bloodshed at Athens. Ribot said (L[loyd] G[eorge] concurring) that Tino must be dethroned. Both agreed with Sonnino[196] that a constituent assembly was to be deprecated and that republican propaganda should be discouraged. The sands are running down in the glass for Tino, thank goodness. I give the situation a fortnight to clear. In Corfu the clouds have suddenly lifted, Sonnino welcoming a British detachment to keep the peace between France & Italy there.

3rd [May 1917]

Italy must, I think, have been squared possibly by the offer of Smyrna, but to the best of my belief we have offered her a portion south of Smyrna and extending roughly to the Cilician Gates,[197] where France chips in. There must also have been some arrangement by which Italy is to retain some of Epirus. At any rate, Sonnino's cordial tone at St. Jean de Maurienne (19th April) and the marked absence of separation from Entente policy in Greece, which we have seen for the last three weeks or so, must mean something.

4th [May 1917]

Venizelos has at last made up his mind to clear the situation perhaps under the encouragement of the French. He told Granville[198] yesterday he had asked Sarrail if he could occupy Thessaly – was told in reply France could supply only cav[alr]y & art[iller]y & Sarrail had no instructions. V[enizelo]s offered his infantry and said the situation must be cleared, either by the Entente withdrawing the guarantees to Tino or by his own action. Thessaly was in his favour, he could not wait for it to adhere as he had waited for Zante, for the crops (65,000 tons, perhaps of which 20,000 might be maize) would be fried and his adherents massacred. Therefore he must act. He admitted he had changed his mind but even now did not wish to act without our approval and permission.

---

[196] Baron Sidney Costantino Sonnino (1847–1922), Italian politician; Finance Minister, 1893–96; Prime Minister and Minister of the Interior, 1906 and 1909–10; Foreign Minister, 1914–19.
[197] Gülek Pass, connecting the plains of Cilicia with the Anatolian Plateau through the Taurus Mountains.
[198] Granville George Leveson-Gower (1872–1939), 3rd Earl of Granville, diplomat; entered diplomatic service, 1893; agent at Salonika, 1917; minister at Athens, 1917–21; at Copenhagen, 1921–26; at The Hague, 1926–28; ambassador at Brussels, 1928–33.

6th [May 1917]

A somewhat serious report from Roumania. Bratianu, strongly supported by the King, carried his scheme for expropriation of the great landlords in favour of the peasants, and then left for Petrograd (Ap[ril] 29). Take Ionescu, who thought the scheme would make Roumania bankrupt in four years, was with difficulty prevented from resigning. I think he wants to play Lloyd George to Bratianu's Asquith. The latter's popularity is not increased by his appointing a second brother[199] president of the Munitions Commission after his other one Vintila[200] has been suspected of corruption at the War Office and he himself is known to have tried to have saved corn mills in his own interest. Finally his selection of Gen[eral] Presan for the Petrograd mission is thought unfortunate.

In his absence things have got worse. On the 1st May some Russian soldiers, with leave but in the absence of the G[eneral] O[fficer] C[ommanding], attended the celebrations. A drunken sergeant made a speech in which he said that Roumania should enjoy the blessings of freedom but, as she could not achieve it, the Russian soldiers should achieve it for her. The red flag was then carried in procession and a Bulgarian Socialist RADICHOV was released from prison and addressed violent speeches to everybody.

German propaganda is suspected – suspicion increased by the fact the R[omani]a already believed RADICHOV to be in German pay.

7th [May 1917]

There is one serious item in Venizelos' position. His officers do not wish any prince of Tino's house on the throne because in one way or another they fear proscription. Therefore they are for the Republic as indeed are most Venizelists. No one doubts that V[enizelos] can control the people, but it is doubtful if he can control his officers.

On Independence Day <7th April> V[enizelos] spoke to a deputation at Salonica with his usual frankness. He told them he preferred to tell the truth rather than what was palatable – that the day was not one for celebrating memories so much as for deciding to do things in the future. Macedonians had ~~done~~ given one tenth, the islands 9/10ths of the Venizelist army.

---

[199] Dinu (Constantin) I.C. Brătianu (1866–1950), Romanian politician; Finance Minister, 1933–34; Minister without Portfolio, 1944–45.

[200] Vintilă Brătianu (1867–1930), Romanian politician; Minister for Munitions, 1914–18; Prime Minister, 1927–28.

8th [May 1917]

The strong medicine of Venizelos' words has borne fruit. Carlyle[201] says somewhere that what men like is not flattery and praise but appeals to them to sacrifice themselves[202] – that it is there the great leader shines. V[enizelos] has proved it. The islanders mobilise manfully in spite of our fears, 2 more of his battalions have arrived from oversea, 2 torpedoboat destroyers have been handed over to him unconditionally by the French, the Venizelist troops have advanced brilliantly with the French north of YANNITZA[203] and taken a front of over three miles.

Finally a meeting at Salonica, said to number 30,000 (important this because it must include many Salonica Jews who are inclined to be timid and pro-German) met yesterday. It passed resolutions of faith in the National Government, and evinced a resolve to mobilise in Macedonia. Finally, it passed a resolution dethroning Constantine and the clamour of the mob induced the Chairman to add 'and his dynasty'. Then the procession went to Venizelos' house – the great statesman was designedly absent, and subsequently annoyed to hear of the 'anti-dynastic' addition. The word Republic was mentioned by the crowd. It would seem that the hours of Tino are really shut.

At Athens French officers speak openly of his dethronement and General MAS, the second member of the military commission, not only inspires but writes articles to this effect in the Press. It cannot be said however that the Royalist Press is moderate. The Skrip, an organ popular in ecclesiastical circles, has described Greeks who claim indemnities for the events of 1st December, as 'gold seeking nonentities' and 'stinking scum', and says that the only mistake made on the 1st Dec[embe]r was not to kill 'all the monsters'. ZAIMIS also became premier on the 31st December, wishes to be moderate and get rid of the General Staff, but the finding of <concealed> rifles (486) on the same day with the Government mark does not encourage belief in the good faith of the 'dark forces'.

---

[201] Thomas Carlyle (1795–1881), Scottish-born historian and writer; best known for his *French Revolution* (1837), *On Heroes, Hero-worship, and the Heroic in History* (1841), *The Life and Letters of Cromwell* (1845), and *Frederick the Great* (6 vols, 1875).

[202] 'They wrong man greatly who say he is to be seduced by ease ... Not by flattering our appetites; no, by awakening the Heroic that slumbers in every heart, can any Religion gain followers', T. Carlyle, *On Heroes, Hero-Worship and the Heroic in History* (London and Glasgow, s.a. [c. 1914]), lecture II, 94–5.

[203] Now Giannitsa in Thessaly between Thessaloniki and Edessa, until the 1920s surrounded by marshes.

9th [May 1917]

Venizelos is very angry with the Chairman of the meeting for adding "and his dynasty" to the resolution calling for the deposition of King Constantine. He is equally angry with M. POLARETOS, who received the procession at V[enizelos]'s house in his absence, and informed it that the will of the people must prevail. V[enizelos] at once wrote him a letter, censoring him and demanding his resignation. POLARETOS gave the latter in humbly with dignity and devotion. L[or]d G[ranville] remon[strate]d with V[enizelos] for treating him so, but V[enizelos] said the will of the people can only prevail when it is definite, that he was bound to lead, and that his action would serve as a hint to the republican officers to keep within in bounds. He regarded the accession of the Crown Prince as still possible now, but events were moving and even Romanos a staunch Conservative had written to him suggesting a Republic. <He won.> For him the Crown Prince's accession was 'a bastard solution' but he would accept it if recommended by us. It led to the reunion of Greece – his first object in life. He once more declared a reconciliation with Tino impossible, & L[or]d G[ranville] seems to have ended by advising him <so far as he was> personally concerned, that this might do.

News from Roumania still serious.

10th May [1917]

L[loyd] G[eorge] & mun[itio]ns min[iste]r

May 11 [1917]

Our attack today, like that on the 24th April at Douai,[204] successful on left, and a failure on right at Petit Couronne. I am afraid it means heavy casualties. The French and Italian attack on the bend of the Crna, inspite of communiqués, appears to have begun on the 9th. It has certainly done nothing up to date. The Bulgars seem to have counter-attacked us on the left without any good reason, and have probably got heavily smashed on consequence.

---

[204] The fifth Allied attempt to breach the Western Front at Arras, 11–20 May 1917.

12th [May 1917]

S[ecre]t Session. N[oel] Buxton[205] brought up the question of a separate peace with A[ustria]-H[ungary]. L[loyd] G[eorge] replied, as I understand with extracts from a mem[orandu]m written by some friends of mine. It proved shortly that the rights of nationalities, for which we stood, logically implied the break-up of Austria-Hungary, that the emancipation of Russia and the inclusion of USA only confirmed this view. Finally what was more important than treaties and pledges was self-determin[atio]n, the right of each nation to determine its own destiny.

Incidentally, the USA min[iste]r[206] & consul-gen[era]l[207] from Austria-H[un]g[ar]y are here. I understand both absolutely repudiate the idea of a separate peace being possible for Austria.

13th [May 1917]

14th [May 1917]

Nivelle, after a gallant struggle, has fallen because he thought the war would be ended in a fortnight by his methods. Pétain,[208] known to favour the offensive-defensive, is shifted from being Chief of Staff, where he would have been all-powerful, to C[ommander]-in-C[hief] where he will now carry out the plans of

---

[205] Noel Edward Noel-Buxton (1869–1948), 1st Baron Noel-Buxton, politician; MP (Lib.) Whitby, 1905–6, North Norfolk, 1910–18, (Lab) North Norfolk, 1922–30; Minister of Agriculture and Fisheries, 1924, and 1929–30; joint mission to Sofia with his brother, Charles Roden Buxton, to secure Bulgaria's neutrality, 1914–15.

[206] Frederic Courtland Penfield (1855–1922), US diplomat; vice-consul at London, 1885; agent and consul-general at Cairo, 1893–7; ambassador at Vienna, 1913–17. Penfield left Vienna on 7 Apr., the day after the US declaration of war on Germany; on 9 Apr., Austria-Hungary severed relations with the US, though war was not declared until 7 Dec. 1917.

[207] Albert Halstead (1867–1949), US consular official; ed. Princeton (BA, 1889); clerk to surveyor of Port of Cincinnati, 1889–91; Washington correspondent of *Cincinnati Commercial Gazette*, 1891–6, and *Brooklyn Standard Union* and *Philadelphia Evening Telegraph*, 1899–1906; aide-de-camp to Governor William McKinley, 1892–6; editor, *Springfield Union*, 1896–9; consul at Birmingham, 1906–15; consul-general at Vienna, 1915–17; Stockholm, 1918–19; Montreal, 1920–7; London, 1929–32.

[208] Marshal Henri Philippe Omer Pétain (1856–1951), French soldier; entered army, 1876; commanded Second Army, 1915–16 (at Verdun); Chief of Staff, 1917; Commander-in-Chief, 1917–18; Inspector-General of the Army, 1922–5; War Minister, Feb.–Nov. 1934; Minister of State, June 1935; Prime Minister, June–July 1940; Chief of the French State, 1940–44; imprisoned, 1945–51.

Foch,[209] when all is said and done, the best brain in the French army today. If the test of a man's greatness is the gap he leaves, Joffre is a big man. Neither Lyautey nor Nivelle can fill the two half-shares of his work.

On the British front all goes well, and the Italian offensive is promising.

15th [May 1917]

Sal[oni]ca

L[loyd] G[eorge] is a little disconsolate. Ireland and strikes have disheartened him, and breakers are ahead, apart from military difficulties.

I hear however he summarily rejected our offer of Noel Buxton's to negotiate for Bulgaria making a separate peace, on condition that she received all Macedonia, Cavalla,[210] and the Dobrudja, a handsome payment indeed.

16th [May 1917]

The conferences in France of 4th & 5th of this month[211] are very important because they have left the French supreme in Thessaly and at Athens, and given at last a clear policy and coordinated authority. Elliot and Guillemin will both be superseded, and a distinguished French statesman to supersede both and to represent at Athens a common policy, we just having a chargé. Russia and Italy are being invited to cooperate.

Military patrols are to be established at Larissa, Volo etc. Sarrail is to be in charge, and to avoid civil strife and warlike disturbance. At the conference L[loyd] G[eorge] paid a tribute to the loyalty with which Sarrail had abstained from interference.

The total result would seem to be to hand over Greece entirely to France, with our moral support, but without material commitment on our part. It is the greatest step in Greece since Venizelos' departure for Salonica.

---

[209] Marshal Ferdinand Foch (1851–1929), French soldier; enlisted, 1870; Commandant, Staff College St. Cyr, 1907–11; commanded Ninth Army, 1914–15; assistant commander-in-chief, 1915–18; Supreme Commander of Allied Forces, 1918.

[210] Kavala, the principal seaport of eastern Macedonia (Greece).

[211] Inter-Allied Conference at Paris, 4–5 May 1917.

17th [May 1917]

The draft scheme drawn up for control of the Thessalian [*sic*] harvest is to include also control of the surplus of ~~other~~ harvests in other parts of Greece. Royalist and Venizelist Greece are to share alike, and the Allied armies are to purchase their supplies there also. The Allied Board is to create a control over the whole, and to sit at Athens or Larissa as the French rep[resentati]ve shall determine.

18th [May 1917]

The state of Serbia is really serious. The army is discontented and Pašić[212] is striking hard at his enemies, Popovich[213] and the Black Hand.[214] So far as we know only 12 (not 50 as many say) officers are condemned to punishment and that to penal servitude not to death as many say. None the less the situation os quite serious enough. Pašić is the only premier in Europe except Bethmann Hollweg who has not resigned since August 1914. The army is discontented and thoroughly undermined, the Crown Prince perhaps ignorant, Pašić still enraged with the followers of Putnik.[215] A strong military British mission alone can do good.

19th [May 1917]

Potatoes are being exported by Germany to Switzerland in return for iron ore, essential manures etc. At the same time motor spirit is being exported by her to Denmark in sufficient quantities to run the Danish fishing fleet (i.e. to obtain the fish catch). Thus she is exporting food when she is starving at one end and <at the other> [exporting] oil, which she cannot replace, in order to alleviate starvation. This is properly burning the candle at both ends and makes one think that she is now at the last gasp, if one can ever rightly believe that possible.

---

[212] Nikola P. Pašić (1845–1926), Serbian politician; leader of People's Radical Party, 1881–1926; Prime Minister of Serbia, 1891–2, 1904–5, 1906–8, 1909–11, 1912–18; Prime Minister of the Kingdom of the Serbs, Croats and Slovenes, 1918, 1921–4, 1924–6.

[213] See entry 22 Feb. 1917.

[214] Serbian secret society, officially known *Ujedinjenje ili smrt* (Unification or Death), unofficially as *Crna ruka* (Black Hand), formed by Serb military officers in 1901. It was involved in the *coup d'état* of 1903, and trained and equipped the assassins of the Archduke Franz-Ferdinand.

[215] Field Marshal Radomir Putnik (1847–1917), Serbian military commander; entered army, 1863; Professor at Military Academy, 1886–95; Deputy Chief of Staff, 1889–95; forced to retire, 1895; exile, 1899–1903; Chief of General Staff, 1903–16.

21st [May 1917]

Venizelos is much pleased at his return from a 9 days trip in Crete. He was received with almost royal honours, even his opponents in Crete favour mobilization – 1,085 volunteers joined spontaneously, and the total number is 548 above the estimate.

22nd [May 1917]

Today received Order of the Roumanian Crown (Officer)[216] from General Georgescu.

I begin to understand Pope:

> 'Behold the child nature's kindly law
> Pleased with a rattle, tickled with a straw.
> Scarves, garters, gold amuse his riper stage,
> And beads and prayerbooks are the toys of age'.[217]

23[rd May 1917]

Gleichen,[218] Seton-Watson and Alan [sic] Leeper[219] are running the propaganda section of Watergate House for neutrals.[220] They circulate to a select few information about different countries, which consists of rivulets of text and an ocean of commentary, This is, I think, intended as a help to Government

---

[216] 4th Class of the *Ordinul Coroana României* (Order of the Crown of Romania), a chivalric order established in 1881.

[217] A. Pope, *Essay on Man* (1734), epistle III.

[218] Major-General Count (since 1917 Lord) (Albert) Edward (Wilfred) Gleichen (1863–1937), British officer; entered army, 1881; served Sudan campaign, 1884–85; Boer War, 1899–1900; Sudan agent, 1901–1903; military attaché at Berlin, 1903–1906; at Washington, 1906–1907; Assistant Director of Military Operations, 1907–11; commanded 15th Brigade, 1911–15, and 37th Division, 1915–16; Director of the Intelligence Bureau at the Department of Information, 1917–18.

[219] (Alexander Wigram) Allen Leeper (1887–1935), Australian-born British diplomat; employed in British Museum, 1912–15; seconded to Foreign Office, Department of Information, 1915–18; on British delegation at Paris Peace Conference, 1918–20; assistant private secretary of Lord Curzon, 1920–24; First Secretary at Vienna, 1924–28; head of Western Department, 1928–35.

[220] One of the many, ultimately abortive attempts at reorganizing wartime propaganda activities, cultiminating, in Mar. 1918, in the creation of the Ministry of Information.

departments. Inasmuch however as the authors are ardent Jugo-Slavists, ardent Venizelists and advocates of the right of each nation to 'self-determination' they are a little embarrassing and in the fine flush of emotion leave out strategy and diplomacy altogether.

24th [May 1917]

Zaimis jibs somewhat at the draft scheme for purchase of the Thessalian harvest (v[ide] 17th [May]). He wishes only half to go to us and that not to be known, as he fears alarm or open resistance. Elliot thinks this modification sh[oul]d be accepted. The French wish to upset the original scheme and put up a board of Allies, Greeks and Thessalian landowners which they can entirely control.

25th–28th [May 1917]

Two delightful days with Gladys at Kingston, Marlow – wide spaces, lawns, with silver threads cutting them – air and life. 'Two things man should desire, the sun in Heaven and Thames on earth' as Raleigh said.[221]

29th [May 1917]

On my return, the occupation of Thessaly well in hand – on the 28th with four French cavalry regiments and 1 French division well on the way beyond Servia (the town).[222] ~~The Serbs~~ The offensive has broken down, according to Milne[223] for lack of heavy artillery – according to others for lack of being properly pushed by Sarrail.

One thing to me is wonderful. The Serbs were acknowledged by the Bulgars <last November> to be masters of fighting in the mountains & not having losses. We lost 100s at [Lake] Doiran and never sent a single officer or set of officers to learn Balkan mountain fighting from the greatest living masters. We attacked in waves at Doiran!

---

[221] 'There are two things scarce matched in the Universe, the Sun in Heaven and the Thames on Earth', attributed to Sir Walter Raleigh (1552–1618).
[222] Servia-Velventos in western Macedonia (Greece).
[223] See entry 22 Dec. 1916.

30th [May 1917]

Serb losses were heavy, said to be 1,000 in two brigades. The finishing touch on their discontent is said to have been put by Sarrail asking them for a division for Thessaly at the same time as he was withdrawing a regiment from the right flank of their second army. They declined. They have now shifted the seat of their government from Corfu to KIAPHA[224] and fixed a commercial and economic bureau at Salonica.

I understand at the conf[eren]ce we undertook to leave things over till six weeks <after the 1st June> – the French to deal with Tino but by blockade.

Ad[mira]l Troubridge,[225] who comes straight from the Crown Prince, says that, if we do not take care, Serbia will accept JugoSlav autonomy under Austria – very likely indeed in view of their history.

Some light on the inner workings – <War> Cab[ine]t meetings all talk – secretaries occasionally summoned and Cab[ine]t ministers ad hoc. One man, I know, got tired of attending the W[ar] C[abinet] because of the gas. L[loyd] G[eorge] is very patient, C[urzo]n eloquent on trifles, Henderson[226] very sensible in calming down people who do not agree with the P[rime] M[inister]. I think Amery is definitely bust by Philip Kerr – good work.

Northcliffe was with P[rime] M[inister] for 3 hours today, having just received a great rebuff being refused by Balfour for USA. <Subsequently he went to America, having arranged for direct access to L[loyd] G[eorge]. So at this interview, ~~wrongly~~ I was wrongly informed "L[loyd] G[eorge] did not support A.J. B[alfour]" and all-conquering Northcliffe prevailed".>[227]

---

[224] South of Parga on Epirote coast.

[225] Admiral Sir Ernest Charles Thomas Troubridge (1862–1926), naval commander; entered Royal Navy, 1875; Naval Attaché at Vienna, 1901–1902; at Madrid, 1902; at Tokyo, 1902–1904; Commodore Commandant, Royal naval barracks Chatham, 1908–10; Naval Secretary to First Lord of the Admiralty, 1910–12; Commander, Mediterranean Fleet cruiser squadron, 1912–14; head of British Naval Mission to Serbia, 1914–16; oversaw Serb withdrawal to Corfu, Dec. 1915–Jan. 1916; with Serb forces at Salonika, 1916–18; Allied Admiral commanding on the Danube, 1918–19; President of International Danube Commission, 1919–24.

[226] Arthur Henderson (1863–1935), Labour politician; MP (Labour) Barnard Castle, 1906–18, Widnes 1919–22, Newcastle East, 1922–23, Burnley, 1923–31, Clay Cross, 1934–35; Labour leader, 1908–10, 1914–17 and 1931–32; President of the Board of Education, 1915–16; Minister without portfolio in War Cabinet, 1916–18; Home Secretary, 1924; Foreign Secretary, 1929–31; Nobel Peace Prize Laureate, 1934.

[227] Northcliffe headed the British war mission to the United States in 1917.

1st June [1917]

Roumanian affairs seem a little dark. Emancipation of peasants, of Jews, land reform, are to be voted in principle this session by the parliament but deferred in practice until the enlargement and reconquest of our territory, i.e. until Wallachia is regained and Transylvania, I understand as regards these 3 reforms though I do not agree. But I neither understand nor agree that a reform of making permanent the civil service, i.e. removing it from corruption and party, should also wait till the Greek Calends.

I fear Bratianu never intends to honour any of these cheques.

2nd June [1917]

The Serbs have come out def[ini]telly on the war path via Adm[ira]l Troubridge – we chuck the thing & go over to the Central Powers (unless you improve). What will happen, I do not know. They have already refused to lend Sarrail a division and complain that their right wing is exposed near Hurna by the French withdrawal.

Putnik[228] suggested acc[ording to] Sazonoff negotiating with Austria in 1914 on 11 November, at the moment MISHITCH[229] was preparing the glorious counter-stroke in front of Suvotsar, which gave him a marshal's baton and his army a laurel-crown. Pashitch replied to Putnik then that he would resign first before consenting to treat with Austria. Can he resign now? Or can he resist the Vienna-ward trend.

3rd June [1917]

Lord Robert Cecil's mem[orandu]m <24th May> interesting. He ~~agrees~~ expands policy laid down in S[ecret] S[ession] of P[arliament]. Thessalian harvest to be secured, Tino to be forced to abdicate by blockade. These were the two main measures of the Paris Conf[eren]ce of 4th & 5th May.[230] It seems strange that neither Serbs nor Venizelists were consulted there as they were the two parties most directly concerned.

---

[228] See entry 18 May 1917.
[229] See entry 21 Oct. 1916..
[230] See entry 16 May 1917.

L[or]d R[obert] C[ecil] seemed much worried about disrespect to Kings, thought the contempt shown for these persons a great mistake, as notably in the case of Tino and Ferdy at an early stage in the war. He thinks we may offend the Kings of Spain & of Scandinavia. Therefore we must depose only Tino and not his dynasty.

4th June [1917]

The Conf[eren]ce of May 28th and 29th was very fateful for the future of Greece – even now it may not be adhered to Jonnart[231] was to be High Commissioner and above Sarrail, and direct policy of England & France, & of Russia and Italy, if they agree. Now, owing to Sonnino's protests, he has even been secretly instructed to ascertain <as from yourself> if Sonnino w[oul]d be satisfied with a Reg[en]cy & absence of Tino during the war during the war. The same communication adduces evidence to show that Tino is a pro-German throughout, so that the F[oreign] O[ffice] proposal, apart from going back on the Conf[eren]ce, amounts to this: Insist on a non-German regime in Greece during the war, but instal a pro-German there immediately after. Could even the F[oreign] O[ffice] excel this? In addition they propose Percy's[232] comment[:] the Cecils are not straight.

5th [June 1917]

The last desperate plunge of Tino is to work for a reconciliation with Venizelos, in which Zaimis has already made considerable progress! Nothing will, I suppose, induce Sir F[rancis] Elliot to a belief that this is impossible or undesirable. How anyone else can be induced to consider it for a moment passes my comprehension. It so happens that on the 28th May Venizelos <publicly> refused all reconciliation, firmly, flatly, and finally! and Condriotis [sic][233] in his bluffer sailor fashion informed the interviewer that there would be no reconciliation between him and Tino 'in this world or the next'. Venizelos is said to be hardening as he becomes more confident of success. This view is, I think, erroneous. Venizelos meant not to go again under Tino when he first left for

---

[231] Charles Célestin Auguste Jonnart (1857–1927), French politician; Minister of Public Works, 1893–94; Governor-General of Algeria, 1900–1903; Foreign Minister, 1913; Allied representative at Athens, 1917; Minister of Blockade and Liberated Regions, 1917–20.
[232] See entry 11 Apr. 1917.
[233] That is, Admiral Pavlos Kountouriotis, see entry 17 Oct. 1916.

Salonica (v[ide] his letter of Nov[ember] 30 – in diary 8th Feb[ruar]y 1917) Any recognition of this fact is vital to all subsequent history.

When the time comes, I think, one of the most serious counts ag[ain]st the decisions of the London Conference of May 28th – 29th will be that the two parties most concerned were the Venizelos [party] and the Serbs neither of them were consulted and subsequently only informed because we could no longer conceal the facts.

6th June [1917]

A[lbert] Thomas has expressed himself highly pleased with the efficiency and discipline of the Roumanian army. There are 400 French officers with it, and a French courier told me that there was much advantage in this arrangement. An offensive is freely talked about even by the Germans, but the courier thought that it could only be a limited one. Camdolle, from a purely railway point of view, while admitting the improvement in the lines, thinks them unequal to any large operations.

The morale is good. Watts, who has just returned from Roumania, says it was even good in the retreat when for three weeks, beneath his windows the mud was churned up by <the> bleeding feet of a shattered army in torment, when wounded horses squealed as the guns pushed over them, and the dogged peasant toiled stolidly on, tired, hungry, leaderless, but indomitable.

Yet, I wonder, for continuous fighting without ever being relieved Avarescu's army stand[s] unrivalled in the war. How can such worn and weary men ever recover? TCHERBATCHEFF, the Russian commander, seems to have had his men comparatively well in hand.

C.B.T[homson][234] appears to have intrigued with Iliescu for the conquest of Constantinople. At a critical moment he got L[loyd] G[eorge] to whom he claims to have access, to send a telegram of congratulation to Bratianu, which was read with acclamations in the Chamber and momentarily stilled criticism. Also C.B.T[homson] first put up Bratianu and then the King to ask for him to go to England in both a political and military capacity to lay their views before the War Cabinet. The War Office peremptorily declined. Now he has been Stellenbosched to Jamaica, and wishes to enter Parliament. In that classic isle he may exchange his princess for a negress.

A clever bright 'tea table' scoundrel who has become a thorough paced Levantiner by residing in Roumanian corruption for too long. His veracity may be gauged by one single story. He says that he persuaded Bratianu to sign the convention 'that night' – one night when he dined alone with him and the King

---

[234] See entry 17 Apr. 1917.

and Queen. In a letter I have seen he says Bratianu specially deferred signing, when he touched him on the subject, because he was superstitious and wished to put it off till his lucky day. So one of these stories of C.B. T[homson] cannot be true.

June 7th [1917]

Albania. The Independence of Albania, which Sonnino subsequently explained, was of the Albanian race, thus perhaps affecting parts of Serbia and Montenegro, was proclaimed by Italy on the 3rd June. We protested at once and required information, as it was done without our concurrence. The Italians say that it was done because the Austrians were erecting military Governments and the French had proclaimed the autonomy of Koritza. (To the latter announcement L[or]d R[obert] C[ecil] made the weak reply that we had no official knowledge of it, though it happened in December 1916, thus averring to Italy that neither France nor she consulted us in their Albanian policy.) Just before this Italy had refused to be a party to the London Conf[eren]ce of 28th – [2]9th May, which had decided to depose Tino. It subsequently protested strongly against our decisions there as it had not been consulted. At the very same moment it was not consulting in its proclamation on Albania.

This seems the last straw for the Serbs who have always had strategic designs on parts of Albania, and have a heavy load to carry already.

Italy has also demanded the recall of Sarrail, & threatened to leave Salonica if more troops are withdrawn from that front to Thessaly.

June 8th [1917]

Tino. There seems to be a general consensus of opinion, supported by Lebouc, a French army commander, that the last offensive had a good chance of success on the Salonica front if properly carried out. His scheme was to have a proper concentration and to keep the Serb 1st Army, owing to its greater marching powers and endurance, in reserve to pour through the gap made by the other troops. As it was it was a policy of unharmonised pinpricks – no concentration, but ill-concerted local operations which did not materialise. The British at Doiran, with heavy losses did actually advance, and fulfilled their part in attracting some regiments. One of the Serb armies hardly came into action at all, and the Russian regiment broke right <through> to the rear of the Bulgars. The French did little or nothing, and the offensive was ultimately peremptorily stopped.

These considerations moved the W[ar] O[ffice] to bring the matter to the consideration of the Cabinet.

Possibly in consequence of this, we, like Italy, have sent in a demand for immediate recall of S[arrai]l. One of his followers (no less than Ribot, when confronted with the demand) has already described him as 'a general of genius' alluded to 'his large political following' and suggested that his fall would have to be explained as one to the British Government. If we were not prepared for this last, we should not have made the demand.

The Serbs have, of course, put in their protest against Sarrail and being abandoned, I learn that Jonnart spoke reassuring words to the Crown Prince on his visit to Corfu. Jovanović sees L[loyd] G[eorge] today in Eng[lan]d – they have found a champion in Smuts, who has spoken out boldly for their course. I learn that, when approached via W[ickham] S[teed?],[235] he showed no disinclination to take the Balkan command if offered to him. He is said to have refused the Egyptian one.

[June] 9th [1917]

Morgenthau H[enr]y.[236] I wonder that no one notes the interesting development in Cabinet growth which, according to Adams, changes almost weekly. The last interesting development is that the secret minutes and parts of the decision of the Imperial War Cabinet are to be send to Mr. Hughes[237] of Australia, thus tightening the link. Again the Imperial Cabinet is to meet annually, each Premier or representative is against coming to decisions which will be binding on his colony, and which cannot be explained to his Assembly. None the less, there will be progress. Smuts thinks foreign policy must have less finesse, be broader & simpler and capable of being explained to the great democracies. What is in evolution is therefore an imperial Cabinet, a building up on the executive basis – a solution which I advocated in my youthful essay on the Cabinet in 1902,[238] and

---

[235] Henry Wickham Steed (10 October 1871–13 January 1956), journalist; ed. Jena, Berlin, Paris; joined *The Times*, 1896; Berlin correspondent, 1896–97; Rome correspondent, 1897–1902; Vienna correspondent, 1902–13; foreign affairs editor, 1913–19; editor, 1919–22; editor, *Review of Reviews*, 1922–30; a Germanophobe, anti-Semite and strong supporter of the Yugoslav cause.

[236] Henry Morgenthau Sr. (1856–1946), German-born US businessman and diplomat; ambassador at Constantinople, 1913–16; led US mission to detach Turkey from the Central Powers, June 1917; chairman of Special Presidential Committee on Poland, 1919; chairman of League of Nations Refugees Settlement Committee, 1923.

[237] William 'Billy' Morris Hughes (1862–1952), Australian politician; Minister of External Affairs, 1904, 1921–23; Attorney-General, 1908–1909, 1910–11, 1914–21, 1938–41; Prime Minister, 1915–23; Minister of Trade, 1916; Minister of Health, 1934–38; Navy Minister, 1940–41.

[238] H.W.V. Temperley, 'The Growth, Development and Present Position of the Cabinet', unpubl. MS (1902), Temperley MSS.

which was then denounced by academic wiseacres, including John Morley,[239] as impracticable and unripe.[240]

June 11th [1917]

Sonnino appears to have really intended to attend the Conference of 28–[2]9 May but his train was late or unsuitable. Now, while not agreeing with the deposition-policy as regards Tino, he was to meet Parliament in a few days without a basis of policy on Greece to expound. Also a serious ministerial crisis has only just been surmounted by the tact of the King. Bosdari[241] has told Elliot that he at any rate is not going under Jonnart and that the French occupation of Thessaly will be followed by an Italian occupation of the west coast of Greece up to Arta. This indeed has quickly come about. The French moved towards Elassona[242] on the 8th – the Italians entered Janina that day – today they have occupied Preveza and the pass of Metzou, where they are astride the only crossing between Thessaly and Epirus. It appears that they occupied Janina at the request of Zaimis in order to forestal the Venizelists. F[oreign] O[ffice], after sending messages to Rome and Paris to implore them not to be irritated one with the other, inquired if Jonnart w[oul]d sanction a Venizelist rising in Epirus! Truly an admirable method of avoiding inflammation! The rapidity of the Italian advance has fortunately prevented any need for the practical application of our methods of dealing with inflammation by pouring vinegar into the wound.

L[or]d R[obert] C[ecil], with the view of conciliating Italy, put up R[o]dd[243] to ask Sonnino 'as from himself' if he w[oul]d prefer a Regency in Greece,

---

[239] John Morley (1838–1923), Viscount Morley of Blackburn, cr. 1908, man-of-letters and politician; editor, *Fortnightly Review*, 1867–82, *Pall Mall Gazette*, 1880–83; MP (Lib.) Newcastle-upon-Tyne, 1883–95, Montrose Burghs, 1896–1908; Chief Secretary for Ireland, 1886, 1892–95; Secretary of State for India, 1905–10; Lord President of the Council, 1910–14.

[240] '[T]hese pages are not without interest, but they are not *ripe* until the writer has had discussions (in which he would be the learner) with men like Bryce', 'Dr. A.W. Ward's and Dr. G.P. Prothero's Reports on Mr. Temperley's Dissertation', as quoted in J.D. Fair, *Harold Temperley: A Scholar and Romantic in the Public Realm* (Newark, Delware, 1992), 46.

[241] Conte Alessandro De Bosdari (1867–1929), Italian diplomat of Albano-Ragusan extraction; entered diplomatic service, 1891; consul-general at Budapest, 1909–10; minister at Sofia, 1910–13; at Athens, 1913–18; head of Italian delegation at Bern Conference on Prisoners-of-War Convention, 1918; minister at Rio de Janeiro, 1920–22; Governor of Rhodes, 1920–22; ambassador at Berlin, 1922–26; author of *Delle guerre balcaniche, della grande guerra e di alcuni fatti precedenti ad esse (appunti diplomatici)* (Milan, 1928).

[242] In northern Thessaly at the foot of Mount Olympus.

[243] Sir (James) Rennell Rodd (1858–1941), 1st Baron Rennell of Rood, cr. 1933, diplomat and politician; entered diplomatic service, 1884; minister at Stockholm, 1904–1908; ambassador

with return of Tino, whom L[or]d R[obert] C[ecil] carefully explains is fundamentally pro-German, after the war. This I mentioned before. Sonnino contemptuously refused it with the comment 'whatever we compromised, the French would always get their own way'. What a testimony to 'that steel which is the mind of France'.

June 12th [1917]

Dardanelles. About Kitchener – a man I know who did much to prepare the schemes, told me today the true history. He says the real truth is K[itchener] said it could not be done because we had not [got] the men. Then Winston said, 'Alright. The Navy will do it then' – so full steam ahead.

June 13th & 14th [1917]

The fall of Tino was equally long desired and deserved. Russia was not pleased with our decision of 28th – [2]9th May partly it had not been consulted, partly it feared for the Salonica offensive, partly Tino should have gone long ago. Italy was annoyed with France for sending Venizelists to the I[sland] of Leucas and apparently might have attended the Conference had Sonnino caught a train one evening. In addition Sonnino had to meet Parliament in a few days without a considered and announced policy, whilst 3 Cabinet the demand for the recall of Sarrail – Ribot at first met it by saying that the only mistake he had made was his recent marriage. Sonnino says that Jonnart cannot boss Sarrail – the former has not a large political following.

On the 5th June Jonnart arrived at Salamis and subsequently proceeded to Salonica where he impressed on Sarrail the need of acting as pacifically as possible. Elliot, on the 5th, was still mumbling of reconciliations and saying that the bitterness of the opposition was underrated, whilst our M[ilitary] A[ttaché][244] at Athens thought the anti-Venizelists had too much at stake to submit without a struggle. On the 7th Jonnart returned from Salonica and on [the] 8th and 9th troops were embarked from there for an unknown destination. On the 11th French troops occupied the isthmus incidentally cutting the line and thus preventing all news leaving Athens for 48 hours. An action they subsequently

---

at Rome, 1908–19; member of special mission to Egypt, 1919–21; British representative at General Assembly of the League of Nations, 1921–23; MP (Cons.) Marylebone, 1928–32.

[244] Lieutenant-Colonel Edward Abadie Plunkett (1879–1926), soldier; entered army, 1892; active service, Nile expedition, 1898; Military Attaché at Athens, Belgrade, Bucharest and Sofia, 1913–14; chief of military missions there, 1913–22.

explained as 'a mistake'. French troops also moved into Thessaly. On the 11th when the troops were off the Piraeus he presented ZAIMIS with an ultimatum in which he demanded the abdication of the King <in favour of any son except the Crown Prince[245]> and a reply within 24 hours. A Crown Council of ex-premiers etc. was summoned at which ZAIMIS advocated compliance. ZAIMIS tried to get both Jonnart and Elliot to appoint the King's son Alexander as a Viceroy. Each declined to recede from the ultimatum, while expressing a personal opinion favourable to this view. In the evening the King decided to abdicate in favour of Alexander, his second son, and asked for a British instead of a French ship. He sent a letter to the Corporation and announced his intention not to abdicate but to retire from Greece, a significant difference.

Meanwhile, the troops from the Piraeus were disembarked – they included also a British and Russian contingent. Orderly crowds assembled around the palace, but were eventually dispersed. Tino still procrastinated but at last time was not on his side. M. Jonnart on the night of the 13th hinted that his departure would be agreeable and finally on the morning of the 14th he sailed in the Royal yacht, with a suite of 40 (including 5 governesses). An easy dethronement indeed, which we pitiably feared to effect.

June 15th [1917]

Venizelos was unable, for lack of time, to préciser ses idées after the abdication to Jonnart. Now he has done so. In his view Paul would have been better than Alexander but he trusts responsibility may steady the latter's gaiety and frivolity. He wishes at Athens a Ministry of liquidation probably under Zaimis to carry through a Convention with the National Government at Salonica. On two conditions he must insist: (1.) the revision of the constitution to place the monarchy on a <more> constitutional and democratic basis immediately after the war. This is needed because constitutional revision takes place every ten years and six years only have lapsed since the last. (2.) The removal of the provision for irresponsibility of the judges. Certain judges have not behaved well in the crisis and, unless this admitted, he and his followers might be cited anytime for high treason.

While wishing to avoid excesses, he thinks Dusmanis,[246] Goumanis and other pro-Germans must be deported to an island till the end of the war. In addition certain others have committed crimes which cannot be passed over and must be legally cited before the Courts, as some ecclesiastics

---

[245] Alexander I of Schleswig-Holstein-Sonderburg-Glücksburg (1893–1920), King of the Hellenes, 1917–20.
[246] See entry 19 Oct. 1916.

156 *An Historian in Peace and War*

before their own courts. He thinks he may be at Athens in a fortnight. A F[oreign] O[ffice] communic[atio]n shows after 3 years he has come home to us at last: 'Find out the views of V[enizelos] – he is not only the wisest and ablest man in Greece, but our best friend'. Recognition at last. Today the D[irector of] M[ilitary] I[intelligence, Macdonogh] came up and talked to me about the chances of detaching Turkey and Bulgaria – I gave the Dobrudja, Macedonia uncontested zone, & Dibra[247] and Cavalla as their count of terms.

FitzMaurice, who turned up, agreed.

He was impressed by the fear of the Turks for Bulgars and by the telegram of Morgenthau to ~~Waitzmann~~ Weizmann.[248] 'They mean business'. They are two very influential Jews of widely differing parties, now apparently trying to come together. Brandeis[249] too influences Wilson. D[irector of] M[ilitary] I[intelligence, Macdonogh]: 'We're all their tools & pawns'.

June 17th [1917]

Apparently there is evidence now of pro-Germanism in Russia. There was the defeat, almost annihilation, of the 1st Serb Volunteer Division, which fought gloriously in the Dobru[d]ja, after being outflanked and deserted by the Roumanians. After this Stürmer's agents interfered with the recruiting of the 2nd Serb volunteer division at Odessa, hindered the cadres from being formed and the Croat prisoners from joining. Subsequently these difficulties were surmounted and 35,000 men assembled. No sooner were they assembled, in spite of the pro-Germans, than they were assailed by the Revolutionaries. The insidious rules of the Workers and Soldiers' Delegation suggested that the Serbian discipline was strict and even brutal and saved revolutionary propaganda. The Serb C[hief] of S[taff] went off to the British consul, now J. Picton-Bagge,[250] butt of everybody at King's in my day. He interfered, told the Russian authorities that these men had taken [an] oath to the King of Serbia

---

[247] Now Debar (Alb. Dibër), in western Macedonia.

[248] Dr Chaim Weizmann (1874–1952), scientist and Zionist leader; lecturer in chemistry, University of Manchester, 1904–15; Director of Admiralty laboratories, 1916–19; adviser to Ministry of Supply, 1917–18; President of the British Zionist Organisation, 1917–21; President World Zionist Organisation, 1920–31, 1935–46; Chairman of the Provisional State Council of Israel, 1948–49; President of Israel, 1949–52.

[249] Louis Dembitz Brandeis (1856–1941), US lawyer; attorney in Boston, MA, 1879–1916; Associate Justice on the Supreme Court, 1916–39; honorary president, Zionist Organisation of America, 1918–21.

[250] Sir John Picton-Bagge (1877–1967), 5th Bart., succ. 1939, consular official; entered consular service, 1903; acting consul-general at Odessa, 1915–18; on special service at Kiev, Jan.–Feb. 1918; Commercial Secretary for Russia, 1918–19; employed in Department of Overseas

and should not be tampered with. Finally the Russian authorities agreed. The Serb division was purged of 5,000 revolutionists who were released to go their ways. C[ommanding] O[fficer] and C[hief] of S[taff] are excellent men. I have recommended that the Corps or some of it should be sent to (1.) Salonica where they would be free from revolutionary influence and would link up the Serbs or (2.) to France where, in any case, their fighting power would be increased.

June 18th [1917]

I noticed today with interest that a decision was given by B.T. B[uckley][251] which will, in substance, support my views on the Serbs. The Serbs have held to their protest about Albania and, despite advice to the contrary, are circularising the courts of Europe, and reserving the right to raise the question again. The Serbs and Albanians are hereditary foes. In 1878, according to Medo Mijatović,[252] the Toplitsa[253] Valley was full of industrious Albanians. He advised that they should remain. Milan[254] thought otherwise and, to ensure a homogenous Serbia, cleared them all out <without compensation>. Abdul Hamid's[255] reply was to encourage these men and others of the Albanian race to settle in <the> Prishtina-Prisrend-Novibazar area.[256] There they hunted out the Serbs as the brown rats hunted out the black rate of old England. Thus the original cradle of the Serb race was

---

Trade, 1919–28; Director of Foreign Division, Department of Overseas Trade, 1928–37; JP, Norfolk, 1941–61.

[251] Brigadier-General Basil Thorold Buckley (1877–1954), soldier and courtier; entered army, 1894; active service, Nile Expedition, 1898, South African War, 1899–1902; General Staff Officer 1, War Office; Brigadier (Intelligence), Egyptian Expeditionary Force, 1918–19; commanded 1st Bt., Wiltshire Regiment, 1919–20; retired, 1920; His Majesty's Corps of Gentlemen-at-Arms, 1922–49; King's Standard Bearer, 1946–49.

[252] Čedomilj Mijatović (1842–1932), Anglophile, liberal Serbian politician, diplomat and historian; six times finance minister; three times foreign minister; minister at London, 1884–85, 1895–1900, 1902–1903; at Bucharest, 1894–95; at Constantinople, 1900–1902; among his publications are *A Royal Tragedy, Being the Story of the Assassination of King Alexander and Queen Draga of Servia* (London, 1906); *Servia and the Servians* (London, 1908); D. Mackenzie Wallace, Prince Kropotkin, C. Mijatović and J.D. Bourchier, *A Short History of Russia and the Balkan States* (London, 1914), and *The Memoirs of a Balkan Diplomatist* (London, 1917).

[253] Toplica, a tributary of the Morava in central Serbia; a rebellion broke out, in 1917, in the Toplica region against Bulgarian occupation.

[254] Milan Obrenović (1854–1901), Prince Milan IV of Serbia, 1868–82; King Milan I of Serbia, 1882–89; abdicated in favour of his son Alexander Obrenović.

[255] Abdülhamid II (1842–1918), 34th Ottoman Sultan, 1875–1909; deposed 27 Apr. 1909; in captivity in Salonika and then Constantinople since.

[256] That is, in Kosovo.

now, to all intents and purposes, an Albanian land. The balance was somewhat reduced in 1913 by ruthless massacres and forced conversions on behalf of the Serbs.

19th June [1917]

Venizelos is very indignant with Alexander's first speech in which he talks of following his father's brilliant footsteps. He says that this will have to be modified when he comes to Athens. He indicates difficulties in restraining his own republican supporters in view of his provocation. The difficulty is enhanced by the fact that he had decided in principle on the promotion of a number of Venizelist officers, who were aware of this fact. The promotions if made may now offend the Royalists, if not made will offend the Venizelists. His chief remedy is the recall of the Venizelist Chamber of 31st May 1915.[257] The subsequent Chamber he regards as illegal, and his followers abstained from voting. Now you cannot have a general election for 60,000 of his supporters are under arms. Thus we must summon the old chamber. Mobilisation he would not impose at once. He would secure it by a political education tour with his lieutenants when once more installed at Athens.

20th June [1917]

C.B. Thomson[258] <M[ilitary] A[ttaché at Bucharest]> stellenbosched from Roumania, long conversation. A man with sharp nose, close set eyes, scored with lines beneath – brilliant superficial – talked like a Levantiner, cleverly, purposely, tangentially. All the time impressed me as a flash-jack or salon idol.

According to him Bratianu, who 'was a big man', was never so strong. The King who was the most honest man in Roumania now supported him; the Queen[,] who had at first favoured a camarilla against Bratianu, and who carried much weight[,] was now wholly on his side. H.W.V. T[emperley] [']But the reforms promised by Bratianu will not be carried out at best for two or three years. Will not the Roumanian peasant think himself deceived [?'] C.B. T[homson: ']The Roumanian peasant is accustomed to being deceived'. (Yes, but this war is a time when no one is deceived with impunity which Roumanian cynicism will soon discover.) Avarescu was a Bessarabian peasant, implicated in a scandal when Minister of War and forced to resign. A good staff officer but occupied

---

[257] That is, as constituted before the general election brought about by Venizelos' first resignation in June 1915; the new chamber was dissolved by King Constantine in December 1915.

[258] See entry 17 Apr. 1917.

too much in details as writing a trench manual for the front, had blinkers on for other fronts early in the war and would send them no reinforcements. Idolized by the peasants and too strong to be dismissed even when suspected by the King. He swore on his honour to the King that he had not intrigued to be dictator. C.B. T[homson] to King[:] 'Did you believe him?' King[:] 'Not a word'.

He had three German housemaids in his house at the front, each prettier than the other.

Gen[eral] Pressan [*sic*] (O[fficer] C[ommanding] of Northern Army) did well and was always ready to lend divisions to the common cause which Averescu was not. (Have been told that C.B. T[homson] claims to have appointed Pressan [*sic*]. He really got his job – his sister was the King's mistress.)

Gen[eral] Iliescu (of whom he was a sworn pal) he considered very clever, which most Roumanians were not, with plenty of guts (!). He still hoped he might come back and so did the King. The latter sent him a message 'You have my confidence but don't be interviewed any more'.

The interview referred to was no doubt that in which Iliescu claimed that the pro-German Stürmer had betrayed Roumania. This he (C.B. T[homson]) did not believe but thought Alexeieff stupid or slack. The Roumanians went in – according to W[ar] O[ffice] (was it true?) Germany and Austria could bring only abou 10 div[ision]s ag[ain]st them whereas Germany actually produced 16. All very clever but (1.) Thomson was on the French front for 7 months – why did he not tell us that R[omani]a had no big guns? (2.) Why did he never answer any queries. I think he is a man who has made history and made it very badly.

21st June [1917]

A curious pendant to the story opposite[259] – just a year ago, Venizelos left for Salonica on the 24th September, was publicly accused, later in the year, and anathematised by the Metropolitan. Tino was saluted as a hero – he massacred French and British in tens and Venizelists in 5 ones, and called <in a proclamation> on the Marbles of the Acropolis to admire his heroism. Now all is changed. Tino sits in the square at Lugano, is hissed by the crowd and forced to take refuge in a café, and slinks away by a back-door to his hotel. <*A woman in the crowd 'of an abandoned character' threw a stone, and the crowd shouted hurrah for Serbia while Tino was drinking beer.> Venizelos leaves for Salonica last night to arrange for the union of Greece. Poor Tino, he was a sham king up against a real one – and the real King has won.

---

[259] Entry 19 June 1916, inserted at end of volume Jan.–June 1917.

June 22 1917

Insanitary conditions seem to form a large part of the diplomacy of the time. Originally M. Jonnart informed M. ZAIMIS that it had been found necessary to debark Allied troops at the Piraeus owing to the ~~necessity~~ insanitary condition of the ships.

Now Russia, which objected to her troops being released from the Salonica front, has ordered them to return. The excuse is to be the insanitary condition of their camps. So that the same excuse covers disembarkation and withdrawal.

[June] 23 [1917]

R[omani]a. The latest reports are very good of the Roumanian army.

June 25th [1917]

A.J. B[alfour] with Fr[ench] Amb[assado]r[260] on meetings & conf[eren]ces.

Sonnino c[oul]d not be here till 12th or Russian till 15th. S[onnin]o w[oul]d not discuss a sep[ara]te peace with Austria or Russia anything unconnected with [the] offensive at Sal[oni]ca. Conf[eren]ce for revision of Treaties difficult and A.J. B[alfour] clearly shows a desire to adjourn the whole matter.

June 26th [1917]

Saw a large number of intercepted wireless and compiled memo[randum]. They are between Berlin, Sofia and Athens and contain definite proofs of Tino's treachery, e.g. General Staff habitually gave n[umber]s of Entente troops landed, e.g. one of Dec[ember] 9, 1915 to Berlin (Kaiser) states that 'he is too weak to attack Entente' but that if Bulgars advance <into Greek territory> he 'may be driven against his will into the opposite camp'. The Bulgarians distrusted him, but Zimmermann[261] says 'this is an opinion we do not share'. Though dallying with the F[or]t Rupel surrender for months, it seems to have been only ultimately arranged on May 23, 1915, by a treaty which allowed Bulgaria and Germany to occupy

---

[260] (Pierre) Paul Cambon (1843–1924), French civil servant and diplomat; departmental prefect, 1872–82; changed to diplomatic service, 1882; minister-resident at Tunis, 1882–86; ambassador at Madrid, 1886–91; at Constantinople, 1891–98; at London, 1898–1920.

[261] Arthur Zimmermann (1864–1940), German diplomat; entered consular service, 1896; consul at Canton, 1896–1904; head of Far Eastern Department of *Auswärtiges Amt*, 1904–11; Under-State Secretary, 1911–16; State Secretary, Nov. 1916–Aug. 1917.

all Macedonia east of the Struma for military purposes on a pledge of ultimately restoring it, and of not occupying Cavalla, Drama and Serres.[262] This pledge the Bulgars promptly broke, to the great anger of Tino and apparently of the Kaiser. This seems to show the Bulgars will disregard Germany if it is safe to do so.

June 27th [1917]

Venizelos is in the saddle today. He proposes to take the bull at once by the horns as regards Italy and see Bosdari today or tomorrow. He intends to point out that a regenerated Greece does not require an Italian occupation of Janina. If the answer is that this was undertaken in reply to the French occupation of Thessaly he will answer – let there arrangements for mutual evacuation. If that fails he will appeal to the protecting Powers. He points out that his position in endeavouring to get Greece to join the Entente will be rendered difficult if Italy remains at Janina.

June 28th [1917]

The Italians have no match in intrigue. Bratianu in Roumania, taxed by the French Minister there, has been obliged to let 100 Kutzo-Vlach officers and men to go to Macedonia with the apparent view of stirring up ~~officers~~ their fellow Vlachs in Macedonia in the Italian interest and thereby embarrassing Greeks, Serbs and French.

Bosdari sung small when tackled by ~~Bratianu~~ Venizelos, and about Janina, and the F[oreign] O[ffice] has united to ~~give~~ bring pressure to bear on Italy & France for mutual evacuation of recognized Greek territory.

June 29th [1917]

It is curious to reflect on the foresight of Venizelos. He said he would be in Athens in a fortnight and has fulfilled his pledge to the letter and the day. I remind me [sic] that he promised the Allies 60,000 troops at Salonica and has fulfilled his promise. Will he too fulfil the promise of 15 divisions he thinks he can now produce? The Morea is quiet, the deportations of undesirable[s] go merrily on, war is to be declared with the Central Powers and Turkey. Most wonderful of all, the Allied troops leave Athens today and Venizelos is supported only by 400 Cretan gendarmes and by a Venizelist regiment, soon to be increased to a division. The King has shaken hands with Venizelos and promised to summon

---

[262] See entry 19 June 1916.

the Chamber of the 31st May 1915. (This is a curious practice analogous to that in William III's[263] reign, when the last Parliament of Charles II was summoned, it being held or tacitly assumed that that of James II was illegal.)[264]

1st July [1917]

I put in a memo[randum] on the 30th on French and Italian policy in Greece. My points were that Italy intended

> (1.) 'to protect the Albanian race not Albania', i.e. not only extending to DJAKOVA[265]-PRISREND in the north but to Janina and Arta in the South.
> (2.) that this occupation must be internal witness the 4,000 men and guns she has placed at Janina which, while she declares it a temp[orar]y occupation, is anti-liberal and is to remain Italian during the 'temporary military occupation'.
> (3.) that the aims of France are mainly <in the> Aegean. Salonica with its Levantine Jews in relation and with Sarrail & Bonnier[266] and his singular experiments inforced [sic] currency and a Commercial Bureau.

Adriatic. France aims at 'the open door' – shows anger at Italians landing in Corfu – concentrates her fleet there – stirs up Leukas, Paxos, Zante and Ithaca[267] to Venizelist revolt – and sends Senegalese liberators with Venizelist assistants to anticipate Italy in seizing Preveza.[268]

2nd July [1917]

The Russian great haul 8,500 prisoners fine news though I hear that Slav regiments were in front of them, and thus facilitated the move. In view of

---

[263] William III of Orange (1650–1702), *stadhouder* of the United Provinces of the Netherlands, 1672–1702; King of Great Britain and Ireland, 1688–1702.

[264] On 23 Dec. 1688, William of Orange summoned all surviving members of any of Charles II's parliaments and various City of London magistrates to a convention.

[265] Đakovica or Gjakova in western Kosovo.

[266] General (François Xavier Louis Henry) Gaëtan Bonnier (1857–1944), French soldier; commanded 16th Colonial Infantry Division at the Somme, 1916; commander French West African colonial forces, Dec. 1917–Dec. 1919.

[267] Now Lefkada, Paxos, Zakynthos and Ithaka, islands in the Ionian Sea.

[268] On the coast of Epirus, northwestern Greece.

Kerensky's[269] idea that they cannot go on after this year this offensive may have great results. It is the Jemmappes[270] of the infant republic, may it have the same stimulating effects and achieve the same result – the liberation of Russian soil.

3rd July [1917]

G[ree]ce

4th July [1917]

The influence of Russian Jews, clad in uniform, among the Russian army in Roumania, among the Jews of Roumania, and some of the Roumanian troops, is extremely pro-social[ist] and anti-dynastic. Every Jew is of course a natural German spy. The morale of the Russian armies in Roumania has been seriously affected and the Jewish influence is so powerful that Bratinanu, by characteristic political methods, has attacked it by promises of concessions and political rights, which he has not yet embodied in law. Avarescu like a blunt soldier has used bolder methods and shot 32 Jewish spies <(Russian or Rouman?)> in recent times. The serious thing is that some of these Russian Jews appear to be in communication with Kerensky or his Committee.

5 [July 1917]

Rakovski[271] has produced a thunderbolt in the shape of an advocacy of an internationalised Macedonia <and a Roumanian Dobrudja>. As he was released by the Russians from a Roumanian prison, suspected of being a pro-German and known to be a Bulgar, his declaration has caused great consternation in Bulgarian dovecotes. The Socialists in Bulgaria have been – the majority for Macedonia and

---

[269] See entry 26 Mar. 1917.
[270] Victory of French revolutionary forces under General Dumouriez on 6 Nov. 1792 over Austrian coalition army, marking a turning point in the First Revolutionary War and stabilized the republican regime in Paris.
[271] Krastyo (also Christian) Rakovski (née Krastyo Georgiev Stanchev) (1873–1941), Bulgarian revolutionary, Bolshevik politician and Soviet diplomat; collaborator Trotsky and founder of Revolutionary Balkan Social Democratic Federation; organized anti-war Zimmerwald conference, 1915; imprisoned in Romania, 1915–16; chairman of the Council of People's Commissars of the Ukrainian SSR, 1919–21; on diplomatic missions to Berlin and London, 1921–22; Soviet ambassador at Paris, 1925–27; Moscow show trials, 1938; executed, 1941.

Dobruja, and a corridor via Negotin[272] into Austria-Hungary – the minority has been throughout for autonomous enclaves and a Balkan Federation. Rakovsky has provoked the angriest criticism from the Bulgarian newspapers.

6 [July 1917]

Saw submarine figures today for week – the net loss is very small. Unless this is exceptional because a large batch of newly constructed ships has suddenly appeared, or because the Hun submarines were concentrated definitely on sinking American transports, unless this is exceptional, we shall suffer no more than a certain amount of inconvenience during the rest of the year. In addition we do not count the German shipping in American waters, not far off a million tonnage, and the first American standardised ships have not yet been launched. Besides this the distribution of coal, in centres grouped round the pitheads, will save traffic etc. in England and thus relieve <us of> the necessity of importing some new machinery.

7 [July 1917]

War-weariness in Austria is a subject to go to the War Cabinet – the general lines of the paper which I saw was that the letters etc., though melancholy were not decisive, that the morale of the troops though impaired did not suggest a collapse, and that the political situation, though extremely difficult, was not such as to enforce peace this year. A general strike was, of course, possible but that is so in every land. There were interesting details as to recent explosions etc. in Austrian munition works from the SKODA downwards. The conclusion is safe, but, when I look at the figureless Budget, the business ministry, and amnesty to the Czechs imposed by the Emperor on his unwilling ministers, one begins to wonder a little.

9th July [1917]

S[er]bia. A controversy.

---

[272] Town in eastern Serbia.

10th July [1917]

Hear of the fall of David Davies, and can now report his opinion of L[loyd] G[eorge]. 'He has wonderful gifts but is not quite straight'. Apparently, he wrote several hot letters telling L[loyd] G[eorge] that what the country wanted most was one who would run straight. At last L[loyd] G[eorge], who is one who understands a good friend and an honest man, got a little tired. D[avid] D[avies] finally broke with him over the Petrol Committee having fixed up and got L[loyd] G[eorge] to consent to a single committee controlling, he suddenly found himself superseded by 5 committees presided over by Walter Long.[273] Protest – burst bubble – deviating views.

<D[avid] D[avies] afterwards told me that the first he had heard of his ceasing to be L[loyd] G[eorge]'s secretary was a statement in the Press that he was leaving the P[rime] M[inister]'s Secretariat for the front. This was the P[rime] M[inister]'s Press-bureau!>

11th July [1917]

12th July [1917]

13th July [1917]

Today got fairly definite information as to the constitution of a new political section in the W[ar] O[ffice] which I am to head. At present only Burge and a clerk under me. The idea is to study all international movements like Socialism and Zionism and coordinate generally all political knowledge for War Office purposes since the beginning of the war.

---

[273] Walter Long (1854–1924), 1st Viscount Long, cr. 1921, politician; MP (Cons.) Wiltshire North, 1880–85, Devizes, 1885–92, Liverpool West Derby, 1893–1900, Bristol South, 1900–1906, Dublin County South, 1906–10, Strand, 1910–18, Westminster St. George's, 1918–21; President of the Board of Agriculture, 1886–92 and 1895–1900; President of the Local Government Board, 1900–1905 and 1915–16; Chief Secretary for Ireland, 1905; Secretary of State for Colonies, 1916–19; 1st Lord of the Admiralty, 1919–21.

14th July [1917]

Tharp's[274] interview with King of Italy[275] – his chief views were on the absence of British coal – he thought comparatively little of Epirus, and had no belief that anything could be done for Salonica. He knew the country he said. He seemed to be disturbed about the unrest in Spain, and evidently felt a fellow-feeling with the King, and feared for the effect on his own throne. Had complete confidence in his own people.

15th July [1917]

According to [Admiral Sir Ernest] Troubridge the trial of the Serbian conspirators was open, free and fair – the Government was convinced of a serious plot.[276]

16th July [1917]

4 memorials to C[hief of the] I[mperial] G[eneral] S[taff, Robertson] on Germany, Austria, Bulgaria and Turkey. The first of three had all ample manpower, the harvest would save the situation for all three, but the economic strain and lack of fuel would be more serious for Germany and Austria than for Bulgaria. It was to be expected that Germany should come to a definite declaration of policy one way or another. Austria was busy working on the fears of the South German states.

Turkey was showing definite signs of the end of her man-power.

17th July [1917]

Saw D[irector of] M[ilitary] I[ntelligence, Macdonogh] today who interviewed me as to the organization of the new section. I gave my views. He stressed Zionism and the Jews as one of the most important influences in the world today.

---

[274] Lieutenant-Colonel Gerard Prideaux Tharp (1871–1934), soldier; on staff of Governor-General of Canada, 1897–98; active service South African War, 1900–1902; General Staff Officer, War Office, 1914–18; JP, Cambridgeshire, 1919–34.

[275] Vittorio Emanuele III of Savoy (1869–1947), King of Italy, 1900–46; Emperor of Abyssinia, 1936–41; King of the Albanians, 1939–43.

[276] The so-called Salonika Trial against Colonel Dragutin Dimitrijević and several other military officers associated with the 'Black Hand' (see entry 18 May 1917) on the false charge of conspiring to assassinate the Prince Regent Aleksandar I Karadjordjevic in May 1917. Dimitrijević was found guilty of treason, sentenced to death, and executed in June 1917.

18th July [1917]

Bethmann Hollweg proposed a Reichsrath, as intermediary between Government and Reichstag. This was accepted by Bavaria, opposed by Austria, which could not however interfere. The Kaiser opposed it.

On non-annexation, Bethmann was in favour of a declaration – Kaiser, Crown Prince, Ludendorff and Hindenburg all against. Bavaria also supported Bethmann and Austria which declined to listen to U-boat promises. Bethmann resigned last Wed[nesda]y (11th July).[277] Opinions about Michaelis[278] still vary. Von Wiegand[279] regards him as disposed to concessions, and Branting[280] as the reverse. The Kaiser is known to be ready for concessions and von Wiegand thinks Michaelis cannot stay long unless he promises universal suffrage to Prussia and ministerial responsibility to the Reichstag.

England's financial condition highly serious. Despite 4 months of USA the situation is not really relieved as the financial straits of F[ran]ce are such that we supplied a million a day for the last 3 weeks to keep up their exchange. If this falls, the pillar of our financial fabric breaks.

19th July [1917]

More important than any European event my wedding day – the fourth <should be fifth> and the best for me. I brought Glady home some pinks, like those I gave her on her first birthday, first I knew her. Glady had sweets and peaches at dinner, and wore a pink dress, which made her look like a carnation, and Emily and Coxie[281] smiled and were cheerful as if they joined in our happiness. I can say without too much sensibility than [sic] I am happier on the fourth than on the first wedding day.

In the office made progress – the Polish Question seemed to arouse considerable interest and I obtained a report of the Polish Conference at Stockholm and inserted it in S[ecret] S[ervice reports]. This means that, in

---

[277] Bethmann Hollweg resigned the chancellorship on 14 July.

[278] Dr Georg Michaelis (1857–1936), German official and politician; Under-secretary, Imperial Treasury, 1909–15; head of Central Grain Distribution Office, 1915–17; Imperial chancellor, July–Oct. 1917; *Oberpräsident* of Pomerania, 1918–19.

[279] Karl Henry von Wiegand (1874–1961), German-born American journalist.

[280] Karl-Hjalmar Branting (1860–1925), Swedish politician; Leader of the Social Democratic Party, 1907–25; Finance Minister, 1917–18; Prime Minister, 1920, 1921–23, 1924–25; Foreign Minister, 1921–23; Nobel Peace Prize Laureate, 1921.

[281] Two servants in the Temperley household, Miss Cox, the nanny and later cook-housekeeper in Cambridge until Temperley's second marriage in 1929, and Emily Toovey, the cook, see H.N.V. Temperley, 'Recollections of My Father', unpubl. TS, Temperley MSS, fo. 6.

future, we shall be able to get our foot in here, and possibly proceed to other conquests. With Zionism, International Socialism, Poland, Scandinavia, Germany & Austria we should do well.

My own scheme is – myself General, Austria & Germany + Balkans. <u>Burge</u> – Socialism & Scandinavia & Netherlands.

Sumner[282]? ~~Poland~~ ul[tima]tely Germany or Balkans

Webster[283] – Russia & Poland

Skinner – our E[dward]G[rey]ist – Zionism.

The Russian news is bad, but may become better. The capital is disturbed and needs reinforcements, and the Ukraine is in principle independent, and to have produced the crisis.

20th July [1917]

Michaelis comes out as a Junker, or nearly there – ready to admit men into the ministry, but not <make> a parliamentary majority control it. Speaks of a defensive war and no annexations but omits indemnities.

The vague resolution as to no ~~indemnities~~ annexations or indemnities passed the Reichstag by 214 to 116, but the National Liberals had left the Bloc.[284]

The Russian Socialists are making difficulties

> (a.) <u>with Roumania</u> – the Russian delegates in an interview with AZ EST[285] in Hungary pronounced against the Roumanian annexation of Transylvania. Subsequently they declared this interview to be bogus.

---

[282] (Benedict) Humphry Sumner (1893–1951), historian; enlisted King's Royal Rifle Corps, Aug. 1914; active service France, 1914–17; invalided and transferred to War Office intelligence department since 31 July 1917; delegate at the Paris peace conference, 1919; employed at International Labour Office, 1920–22; Fellow of Balliol College, 1925–44; Professor of History at Edinburgh, 1944–45; Warden of All Souls, 1944–51.

[283] (Sir) Charles Kingsley Webster (1886–1961), historian; Fellow King's College Cambridge, 1910–14; Professor of History at Liverpool, 1914–22; commissioned into Army Service Corps, 1915–17; in General Staff intelligence section, 1917–19; seconded to Foreign Office, 1918; Woodrow Wilson Professor of International Relations at Aberystwyth, 1922–32; Stevenson Professor of International History at London School of Economics, 1932–53; head of American section, Foreign Office Research Department, 1942–45; attended inaugural meeting of the United Nations and final session of League of Nations, 1946.

[284] On 19 July, a majority of the Reichstag passed the so-called 'Peace Resolution', calling for a compromise peace.

[285] *Az Est* ('The Evening'), a Hungarian daily newspaper, founded in 1910 by Miklós Andor (1880–1933).

(b.) <u>with England</u> whom they accuse of 'imperialistic' aims and a bourgeois Government. They demand a Conference in September, on war aims which Buchanan[286] thinks highly expedient to grant. <Note. He was right and the British refusal to entertain it did much to produce the Bolshevik revolution and the downfall of Buchanan, 4/1/18.>

21st July [1917]

Was asked today by D[avid] Davies to stand for Parliament against Montagu,[287] who now, after having told a friend of mine that he would not join "those swabs", i.e. the L[loyd] G[eorge] government in December 1916, now gracefully agrees to accept office as S[ecretary] of S[tate] for India. He is a Jew, whose friends and relatives benefited largely from the Silver Currency deal ~~commission~~ when he was under-Secretary of State for India. He of course knew nothing about it when the inquiry was instituted. While under-secretary he sanctioned, or at any rate did not interfere in, those economies <in the military sphere> which produced the Mesopotamia horrors.

Finally, after inquiry, I decided not to stand. If successful I could hardly have retained my place at the W[ar] O[ffice], because it would be said that I was using my position and inside knowledge to oppose the Government.

Had I stood I should have been a 'Win the War' Efficiency candidate, against a discredited place-hunter. Shall I ever have the chance again, I wonder?

My little affairs anyhow weigh as dust compared with those of the nation. I wonder I tremble to record this.

22nd July [1917]

Began to study the Polish question. It is valuable beyond words to find a nation shaking the lid off its coffin and 'hearsed in death' bursting its cerements.[288]

---

[286] See entry 9 Dec. 1916.

[287] Edwin Samuel Montagu (1879–1924), politician; MP (Lib.) Chesterton, 1906–18, Cambridgeshire, 1918–22; Under-secretary of State for India, 1910–14; Financial Secretary of the Treasury, 1914–15; Chancellor of the Duchy of Lancaster, 1915; Minister of Munitions, 1916; Secretary of State for India, 1917–22.

[288] Shakespeare, *Hamlet*, Act I, 4: 'Why they canonized bones, hearsed in death/ Have burst their cerements'.

An interesting point: the Pope[289] entirely denies having stimulated the Austrians to a separate peace, and the Cardinal S[ecretary] of S[tate][290] gave C[oun]t de S[alis][291] to understand also that he had given Erzberger,[292] the leader of the Centrum, no support.

Hindenburg is said to have told them at Vienna that Germany could not have an absolute 'no-annexation' peace, because she would be bankrupt unless she retained at least the commercial control of Belgium.

23rd July [1917]

I admire the way that old fox Pashitch has outmanoeuvred all Europe. Representation at the Paris conference, which deals with the Balkans, was not granted. Roumania and Greece, except in so far as competent officers of each should be called on for advice and information. Pashitch by accepting the invitation for himself, has at once altered the meaning of the concession. Meanwhile, Serbian <and> Roumanian ministers at Paris have protested against the nongranting [sic] to him of representation, and the Russian chargé, though without instructions, has supported them.

I heard a story of Winston Churchill today, which I know to be true; he recommended (after having previously in a magazine article strongly deprecated) a great naval offensive against Germany.[293] This was to be done by an offensive against Borkum, and obtaining a seabase [sic] near the German coast. If it was not possible to obtain it by taking Borkum or something of the sort, then a seabase [sic] must be created. This was to be done by taking out lighters full of stores, mortar and rubble and then sinking them in batches. Am I reading the story

---

[289] Benedict XV (née Giacomo Paolo Giovanni Battista della Chiesa) (1854–1922); archbishop of Bologna, 1907–14; Pope, 1914–22.

[290] Cardinal Pietro Gasparri (1852–1934), Vatican diplomat; Cardinal Secretary of State, 1914–30.

[291] Count Sir John Francis Charles de Salis (1864–1939), diplomat; entered diplomatic service, 1886; minister at Cetinje, 1911–16; at the Holy See, 1916–23; unemployed since 1923; member of 1931 Royal Commission on the Political Situation.

[292] Matthias Erzberger (1875–1921), Catholic German politician; Reichstag deputy (Centre Party), 1903–21; advocate of annexations in 1914; tabled 'Peace Resolution', July 1917; signatory of armistice, Nov. 1918; vice-chancellor, 1919; assassinated by ultra-nationalists, 1921.

[293] Churchill's plans envisaged the capture of two North Sea islands, Borkum and Sylt; flat-bottomed barges were to form the basis of an artificial harbour when lowered to the seabed and filled with sand. The plans never came to fruition until revived in the Second World War (Mulberry Harbour).

of Laputa[294] or the Isle of Bataria?[295] Winston is so determined to overcome difficulties that, if nature opposes him, nature must give way or be remodelled.

24th July [1917]

A general whirl – find a very pettish [sic] fuss has been kicked up by Moreton Murray and Sheppard of the Press-Supplement (Daily).[296] They are apparently afraid of our section and wish to present reports and comments of their own direct to War Cabinet and Prime Minister. I said we would send them our reports for 'vetting' purposes which will, I hope, satisfy them. They seem to me very small-minded, very jealous, not only with us but with Gleichen's information bureau.

Capt[ain] Barber, another of this gang, is a journalist on the Morning Post in private life, and Colonel Wake[297] a very pettish, old dugout Colonel.

25th July [1917]

The Russian situation is not quite so bad as it seems at first sight. The Soviet has been thoroughly sobered, and is now compelled to support the Government. The death penalty has been reintroduced at the front (it should be also at the rear, so that men from the depots may not discourage those at the front by their indiscipline[)].

Kerensky is still optimistic – fears for Finland being attacked from the sea, but believes he can retain south Bukovina and ultimately restore discipline and have an offensive in September after six weeks' strenuous preparation. One thing is certain[:] a separate peace is out of the question.

The Roumanians have started again brilliantly taking 19 guns, and registering a perceptible advance. The eighth Russian army to the north of them should help them.[298]

---

[294] The flying island of Laputa in Jonathan Swift's *Gulliver's Travels*.
[295] The fictional island awarded to Sancho Panza in Cervantes' *Don Quixotte*, and fictional republic in *The Gondoliers* by Gilbert and Sullivan.
[296] *Daily Review of the Foreign Press*, published by the General Staff Intelligence Department, 1916–19.
[297] Lieutenant-Colonel Edward St. Aubyn Wake (1862–1944), soldier; entered army, 1884; active service, Burma 1886 and Tirah campaign; tutor to Maharajah of Bukanir, 1910–13; Red Cross commissioner in France, 1914; General Staff intelligence department as editor of *Daily Review of Foreign Press*, 1916–19; retired, 1919.
[298] The Russo-Romanian offensive on the Sereth (Siret) and around Soveja was repulsed by the Germans, 22–25 July 1917.

[Noel] Buxton made some curious assertions about the Serbs last night in the Commons.[299] He asserted that the unspeakable atrocities committed by the Austrians in Serbia in the winter of 1914 were, in reality, committed by SerboCroats, therefore JugoSlavia is impossible. He was at H[ead]Q[uarters] Kragujevatz and saw and knew. In fact there were only two regiments – Frankist Croats.[300] Serb prisoners were quartered in this anti-Serb district in Croatia from which these Croats came. They became so friendly with the inhabitants that they had to be moved away! So much for the testimony of eyewitnesses.

26th July [1917]

Capt[ain] Jovanovitch came to see me today with a most amusing proposition. He explained that Colonel Nicolaiévitch, the Serbian M[ilitary] A[ttaché], desired to make my acquaintance and to meet me at lunch. As an aside Capt[ain] Jovanovitch explained to me that, while he and his namesake, the Minister,[301] desired to talk much and to inform me of la haute politique, he would prefer that I should just talk generalities to the M[ilitary] A[ttaché]. This was delicious. Colonel N[icolaiévitch] has been described as 'a dear old man'. I think indeed he is nothing else.

27th July [1917]

Venizelos has triumphed again, by laying his demands for the evacuation of Epirus before the Paris Conference – wonderful man. The angle of the Santi-Quaranta road in Epirus[302] is to remain under Italian control but Greek civil administration is to be set up there. Corfu is to be used as a naval base for the Allies but to remain in full sovereignty to Greece. These then are the fruits of his government. Zaimis encouraged the Italians to occupy Janina. Venizelos wins back Epirus and Corfu. Opinions change quickly in Greece – an imprisoned Royalist officer, who fired on the French at Larissa, told a Frenchman that the name Venizelos would be found written on his heart if cut open. An old priest, who preached the Divine Right of Tino on June 3rd, met Sarrail and

---

[299] 'House of Commons: Austria and the Balkans', *The Times*, 25 July 1917.
[300] That is, radical Croat nationalists, hostile to Serbia; named after Josip Frank (1844–1911), a Croatian lawyer and politician in the Party of Rights, and vociferous advocate of Croatian independence.
[301] Jovan M. Jovanović-Pižon, see entry 6 Jan. 1917.
[302] A maritime defile between the northern tip of Corfu and the Albanian coast.

blessed him on July 4th! It reminds me of Clarendon,[303] who, on the advance of William of Orange on James II, found his son [had] fled and wrote in his Diary 'Ah God that my son should be a traitor!' A week later he was one himself. So turns revolution's wheel!

28th July [1917]

Poland again. According to an interview between Ludendorff and a member of that Polish Council of State in April, L[udendorff] was ready to give back the Russian parts of Poland, provided Germany retained the fortified strategic [points?] of Bzierda [sic] –Narew,[304] up Vistula to WLOZLAWEK[305] and Warta.[306] He does not believe in this was being a final settlement. It will be a truce only – we are entering on a period of wars and shall have another one in ten years. He evidently thought it was all they could do to hold out on the Western front.

Apparently, Pilsudski[307] resigned on the 22nd July with 3 other Socialists from the Council of State. There seems to be little doubt from later evidence that he was suspected, probably justly, by the Germans of promoting a rebellion in favour of Polish independence. He was arrested on the 22nd.

29th [July 1917]

R[omani]a non-repr[esentatio]n at Conf[eren]ce – sep[ara]te peace – Kerensky.

Bratianu spoke with great indignation of the fact that Roumania was not fully represented at the Conference, and said that, if there was such conduct at future Conferences, she would refuse to appear. He also complained of the Serbs mirepresenting the Roumanians in London. He declined to admit that

---

[303] Henry Hyde (1638–1709), Lord Cornbury, cr. 1661, 2nd Earl of Clarendon, succ. 1674, politician; MP Lyme Regius, 1660, Wiltshire, 1661–74; Lord Privy Seal and Lord Lieutenant of Ireland, 1685–87; his son Edward, Lord Cornbury (1661–1723), 3rd Earl of Clarendon, was one of the first of James II's supporters to join William of Orange.

[304] The rivers Bzura and Narew, two tributaries of the Vistula. The rivers Bzura and Warta were linked by a canal.

[305] Włocławek on the Vistula in central Poland.

[306] A tributary of the Oder (Ger. Warthe).

[307] Jozef Klemens Pilsudski (1867–1935), Polish military and political leader; Siberian exile, 1887–92; founded Polish Legion to fight alongside Central Powers, 1914; Minister of War in Polish Regency government, 1916–17; imprisoned by Germany, 1917–18; Chief of State and Commander-in-Chief of Polish armed forces, 1918–22; Prime Minister, 1926–28, 1930; Minister of Military Affairs (and *de facto* dictator), 1926–35.

there was any similarity between the Roumanians and others of the smaller powers. Barclay[308] gathered that he was speaking chiefly under the influence of despondency due to the Russian debâcle. A separate peace or evacuation is spoken of as possible. Every care will, however, be taken to grant the King due consideration if evacuation in Russia becomes necessary. The Russian Government has agreed to this.

30th [July 1917]

Kerensky has expressed somewhat despondent views but still hopes to save South Russia, and the rest seem even to think that an offensive in September will be possible.[309] That, of course, depends on conditions no man can foresee. It is thought that the ex-Emperor and Empress will be taken off into Siberia to guard against further eventualities. Interview with Philip Kerr, the P[rime] M[inister]'s sec[retar]y – gave hints as to the speech on Saturday by L[loyd] G[eorge].

31st [July 1917]

Kerensky said by some to be weak – Brusiloff vacillates – Koriniloff[310] is good – Alexeieff and Russky[311] also determined on resistance. Gourko,[312] whom Kerensky disgraced, does nothing but send abusive telegrams to him. <It is not thought too late to save the Russian army.>

The Roumanians attacked with élan and success and are correspondingly depressed by having been compelled to stop their offensive by the orders of the Russians – poor, poor people, the luck's agin them.

---

[308] See entry 18 Oct. 1916.

[309] The Brussilov Offensive had come to a halt on 19 July 1917, and German forces broke through the Russian front in the battle of Zloczow, 19–28 July.

[310] General Lavr Georgi'evich Kornilov (1870–1918), Russian military intelligence officer; Military Attaché, Peking, 1907–11; commander Petrograd Military Distirct, Mar.–July 1917; Commander-in-Chief, July–Sept. 1917; sacked after attempted coup, Sept. 1917; joined anti-Bolshevik forces and killed in action, Apr. 1918.

[311] General Nikolai Vladimirovich Russky (1854–1918), soldier; deputy chief of staff, Kiev military district, 1896–1902; chief of staff, 2nd Manchurian Army, 1904–1905; commander, 3rd Army, Aug.–Sept. 1914; 6th Army, 1914–15 (captured Lviv (Lemberg)); Northern Front, 1915–Apr. 1917; murdered Oct. 1918.

[312] General Vasily Iosifovich Gurko (1864–1937), Russian soldier; chief of staff to General Alekse'ev, 1915–17; Chief of Staff of Imperial Russian Army, Feb.–June 1917.

1st August [1917]

~~L[loyd] G[eorge] &~~ Henderson decided to accompany the Russian Socialists to Paris and selected Wardle[313] and Ramsay Macdonald[314] to go with him.[315] This is likely to occasion great excitement in the country because the War-Cabinet was not consulted. This omits one fact of primary importance, which the public do not know – the War Cabinet was not consulted but Lloyd George was. Also Henderson received instructions so to arrange things that we shall have a main share in running things at Stockholm. If these two facts were known much of the opposition would subside.

2nd [August 1917]

Memo[randum] on Roumania for Capt[ain] Masterson,[316] which I hope he will endorse. The point is that both the reserve and depot part of the army is already depleted in supplies and medicine. Sanitation is also at a discount, there being a small French sanitary mission and a not very efficient Roumanian one. The reserve part of the army has not enough to eat, soldiers are herded together with dysentery, typhus, wounds, and bronchitis, for lack of nails and building materials. The civil population is already emaciated – 20,000 orphans are billeted on villages whose burdens are already intolerable. The harvest of Moldavia is already known to be quite inadequate to its present population. What will ~~therefore~~ be the conditions in the winter? All we do is to dribble out loans, which Bratianu and his friends pocket. Money is useless to a country which has no soap no drugs and too little food & clothing. Take Ionescu himself says that no system of relief can be administered by Roumanians themselves. The Red

---

[313] George James Wardle (1865–1947), journalist and politician; editor of the *Railway Review*; MP (Lab.) Stockport, 1906–18, (Coal. Lab.), 1918–20; acting chairman, National Executive Committee of the Labour Party, 1917–18; Parliamentary Under-secretary, Board of Trade, 1917–19.

[314] (James) Ramsay Macdonald (1866–1937), politician; MP (Lab.) Leicester, 1906–18, Aberavon, 1922–29, (since 1931, Nat. Lab.) Seaham, 1929–35, Combined Scottish Universities, 1936–37; Foreign Secretary, 1924; Prime Minister, 1924, 1929–35; Lord President of the Council, 1936–37.

[315] Following an invitation by Russia, Dutch and Scandinavian Socialists, on 1 July 1917, to representatives of Socialist parties in the belligerent countries; the conference never took place, largely owing to Allied opposition.

[316] Captain Thomas Samuel Masterson (1881–1944), businessman; pioneer of Romanian oil industry; on General Sir John Griffith's staff, 1917–18; director, Phoenix Oil and Transport Co., and managing director, Uniread Co., Ploiesti, until 1935; active service in Balkans and Middle East, 1939–42; War Office adviser, 1942–44.

Cross etc. in Roumania is entirely adequate to the job – all relief agencies only total some £115,000. Our proposal is that £600,000 of the next loan be supplied in kind in stores and medicines, as an incentive to the Roumanian Government. If that fails, a strong distributing commission should take the matter up, and distributed £600,000 in kind.

It will tragic if this [is] not done, and sadly detrimental to British interests. Why we should waste our money in loans, and not spend it productively in relief, I simply cannot conceive.

<Note. This was done but too late. Bratianu told the Allied Ministers (v[ide] 18th Dec[embe]r [1917]) that their present offers of unlimited credit could have been negotiated at banks five months before, i.e. about 5 ½ months from the time I recommended this scheme.

3rd [August 1917]

Soc[ial]ists. As I thought the Press has kicked up hell over Henderson but the real issue is not explained. We are considered bourgeois pirates etc. by Russia. France and Italy will, in all probability, refuse to send delegates to Stockholm. This means that Russians, Germans and Dutch-Scandinavians will have it all their own way. This is the worst evil that could befal[l] us, and yet our press does not seem to see it. Buchanan favours our going, as also having an Allied Conference (Governmental) in September.

4th [August 1917]

Poles & L[loyd] G[eorge].

Some study of the Polish question, after an interview with Zaleski.[317] The facts seem to be these – 5th Nov[embe]r Austro-German decree of Independence[318] was produced because the Huns were not strong enough to impose any other settlement or to recruit on their own. It has drawn all parts of Poland together and the only expressive organ is the Council of State. That fought hard (a.) for control of a Polish army by itself (b.) for control of administration of [the] Polish

---

[317] August Zaleski (1883–1972), Polish economist and politician; representative of Dmowski's Polish National Committee in London; envoy to League of Nations, 1925–26; Polish Foreign Minister, 1926–32; chairman of *Bank Handlowy*, 1935–39; exile in London, since 1939; Foreign Minister in Sikorski government-in-exile, 1939–47; President of Polish Republic in exile, 1947–72.

[318] On 5 Nov. 1916, Germany and Austria-Hungary proclaimed the restoration of the Kingdom of Poland as a hereditary monarchy, and established a State Council but not the new state's borders; the identity of the future king was also left unresolved.

area. It consisted in the main of an Austro-Polish central party, but for long the most important influence was Pilsudski and his 3 comrades of the Republican Left. When they resigned on the 2nd July, the moderates carried the day, and, on the 3rd July, passed three resolutions[:] (1.) summoning a quasi-Senate of 50 to supersede them and undertake administrative functions, until sovereign authority could be handed to a full and free Diet at Warsaw.

(2.) Definition of an oath for the Polish army. This swore them to a King (Carl Stephan)[319] thus excluding a republic, and to a possible 'brotherhood-in-arms' with Austria and Germany.

(3.) issued a recruiting appeal on the 14th July they defined their position more carefully stating [(1.)] that the C[ouncil] of S[tate] must acquire control of army and of national government. (2.) that the army must not be sent anywhere to fight without the consent of the C[ouncil] of S[tate], and that the Polish forces should not be drawn into the whirlpool of war. (3.) that the C[ouncil] of S[tate] wished to be a peace factor, between all parties and with this view could not allow Polish lives to be disposed of outside Poland by foreign powers. This is a cut at the Entente, which favours Dmowski's[320] ideas of raising Polish armies in France, England and USA.

On the other hand the attitude is not wholly satisfactory. The Entente is not to raise Polish forces, and the Polish army is for defence only, but it might be used against Russia in defence, with their good Austro-German comrades.

Thus the mentality is not satisfactory to us because the C[ouncil] of S[tate] may fight Russia, but during this war has practically pledged itself not to fight Austria and Germany.

Looking at the Press tonight at the P[rime] M[inister]'s great speech today [*sic*].[321] I note one or two of my hints carried out – Serbia is praised, and he alludes to Ludendorff's views about wars only beginning (v[ide] the 28th July). On the other hand he put in about the secret deliberations of German and Austrian [governments] beginning early July 1914 'which fired the train'. I should not have recommended this, because I do not think it true exactly in the form the 'Times' revealed it.[322]

---

[319] Archduke Karl Stephan Eugen Viktor Felix Maria of Austria (1860–1933), Habsburg prince; entered Austro-Hungarian Navy, 1879; Admiral, 1901; Grand Admiral, 1911; Inspector of Navy, 1911–18; candidate for Polish regency following Austro-German proclamation of an independent Poland, 5 Nov. 1916; resided in Poland after the war.

[320] Roman Stanisław Dmowski (1864–1939), Polish nationalist and anti-Semitic politician; Member of Russian Duma, 1907–1909; founder of Polish National Committee in Paris, 1917; Polish delegate at Paris Peace Conference, 1919; Foreign Minister, 1923.

[321] Lloyd George spoke at the Queen's Hall on 4 Aug. 1917, see 'Mr. Lloyd George On Victory', *The Times*, 6 Aug. 1917.

[322] See 'July 5, 1914. Fateful Potsdam Meeting' and 'The Potsdam Conspiracy', *The Times*, 28 July 1917, in which it was alleged that at a specially convened 'war council' at

<The Lichnowsky revelations about this Crown Council do, I think, prove that these charges are correct. 29/3/18>[323]

Note. The Times version says that Moltke[324] & von Jagow[325] were not present, Mme Moltke's version that Moltke and Falkenhayn were present and insisted on war.[326] The latter is, I think, correct. v. Jagow in his reply to Lichnowsky did not deny the Crown Council[;] it was officially denied by the German wireless.

6th Aug[ust 1917]

Foch's memoir on Austria-Hungary of 23rd July seems to be a plea written in the well-known French artistic style for a remodelling not a dismemberment of Austria-Hungary. There is to be a Danubian Confederation, of 5 states – Austria, Hungary, Czecho-Slovakia, JugoSlav (less p[ar]t of Bosnia to go to Serbia) Croatia, Transylvania. The autonomy of all these to be guaranteed. It is really therefore a project for the dismemberment of Hungary, not of Austria. Bukovina is to go to Roumania and the Ukraine, and Galicia less Ruthene part to a Poland under a Habsburg prince with strong anti-German guarantees regard the [incomplete].

7th Aug[ust 1917]

Points for L[loyd] G[eorge]'s speech if he goes to the Serbian lunch tomorrow (Wed[nesda]y) which I gave to Philip Kerr at his request –

(1.) Roumania and her good offensive.
(2.) Serbia & Kossovo [*sic*].

Potsdam the German leadership decided on war on 5 July 1914. The story was little more than a compound of different rumours; no such meeting actually took place.

[323] Prince Karl Max Lichnowsky (1860–1928), German diplomat; counsellor at Auswärtiges Amt, 1899–1904; ambassador at London, 1912–14; his revelatory *Meine diplomatische Mission, 1912–1914* (Zurich, 1918) had been in circulation since August 1916.

[324] Lieutenant-General Hellmuth Johannes Ludiwg von Moltke (1848–1916), German soldier; aide-de-camp to Kaiser Wilhelm II, 1891–96; Chief of the Imperial General Staff, 1905–16.

[325] Gottlieb von Jagow (1863–1935), German diplomat; entered diplomatic service, 1897; minister at Luxemburg, 1907–1909; ambassador at Rome, 1909–13; State Secretary, 1913–16.

[326] E. von Moltke (ed.), *Generaloberst Hellmuth von Moltke: Erinnerungen, Briefe, Dokumente, 1877–1916* (Stuttgart, 1922), 380–82. In fact, Jagow was absent. The reference to the Moltke memoirs would suggest that this note is a much later addition to the entry.

Aug[ust] 8th [1917]

L[loyd] G[eorge] did go to the lunch and did use my notes. How much will be seen from the two versions. I know that L[loyd] G[eorge] wanted to get coached by Steed[327] but had not time to see him yesterday, while Kerr and L[loyd] G[eorge], neither of them knew what Kossovo [*sic*] was till they got my typed note on the subject. I have heard that Sheridan[328] used to take the arm of a friend in the lobby and reproduce his ideas in the most glittering phraseology two or three hours afterwards in the House of Commons. This was not quite the same thing perhaps, but it is interesting always to see how genius monopolizes and makes its own the ideas of another

<One serious omission he made – he said nothing of Roumania. Bratianu subsequently remonstrated and L[loyd] G[eorge] had to make two favourable references in speeches, send a special telegram and get the King to do the same, all of which he would have avoided listening to me. 4/1/18>

<u>My note given to 10 Downing Street 7th Aug[ust] 1917</u>
'The most glorious period of Serbian history was in the middle of the XIVth century when Stephan Dushan[329] ruled over nearly all the Balkans. On his death the Serbian Empire went to pieces, and was finally shattered at Kossovo in 1389.

The great defeat has been more celebrated in Serbian song and ballad than any victory. Wandering minstrels, something like the Welsh bards, still sing lays of the death of heroes on the field of Kossovo. The cycle of songs sung in all JugoSlav lands and has done more to make Serbia a nation than any other cause.

The songs are extraordinarily beautiful. In the great defeat of 1915 the Serbian soldiers passed over the field of Kossovo and wept and sang songs of Kossovo as they did so. Serbia's song, like the nightingale's, is 'a song of triumph over pain'. Surely the cry 'remember Kossovo' is one which proves that Serbia is unconquerable. She has drawn victory and national unity from her great defeat in the past and will do so today. Had it not been for Kossovo and its heroic memories she would never have resisted Germany, and – as the Turk failed to restore [*recte* destroy?] her so will the German. My word to all Serbians in the sorrow of today is "remember Kossovo!"'

---

[327] See entry 8 June 1917.
[328] Richard Brinsley Butler Sheridan (1751–1816), dramatist and politician; MP (Whig) Stafford, 1780–1806, Westminster, 1806–1807, Ilchester, 1807–12; Under-secretary for Foreign Affairs, 1782–83; Secretary to the Treasury, 1783–84; Receiver-General of the Duchy of Lancaster, 1804–1807; Treasurer of the Navy, 1806–1807.
[329] Stefan Uroš IV Dušan 'the Mighty' (c. 1308–55), King of All Serbian lands, 1331–46; Emperor of the Greeks and Serbs, 1346–55.

What Lloyd George made of it, 8th Aug[ust] 1917.[330]

'There is one thing about the Serbian nation which always touches me as a Welshman. I believe in a nation which can sing about its defeats. The great event in the history of Serbia is not of triumph, it is not of victory, it is not of glory of Empire, but of a great defeat which submerged it in the deluge of barbarism.

If I may say so, it is almost what has happened in the case of our little nation. Our greatest song is the song of defeat that drove us into the mountains, and we always sang it with hope, and we still live.

And the battle of Kossovo – a battle happening hundreds of years ago, which the Serbian people sang in their mountains about, with a refrain a sadness, but with a certain lilt of hope at the end of it, until the day of triumph came.

Why Serbia Will Emerge

A nation that can sing about its defeat and not lose heart is a nation which is immortal and that is why Serbia will again emerge with victory.

Submerged in the deluge of barbarism, but not destroyed, like a fresco, a beautiful picture covered with the foulness of centuries. Someone comes and cleanses it, and it is fresh and bright as ever – as when it came from the hands of the master.

And this Serbia, a great picture painted on the mountains, was done by the hand of the Great Master and was covered with all the foulness of Turkish barbarism for years. When the heroism of it cleanses its panels, Serbia appears.

Does anyone imagine a race surviving centuries of that degradation is going to die because it has three years of defeat?

That is why I believe in it. It has got, indeed, the necessary grit, endurance, hope, and depth which will make it live, and I fear not what is going to happen in Serbia. (Cheers.)'.

What was said about Belgium – what I ventured to say about Belgium, speaking on behalf of the British Government, I say here again speaking on behalf of the same Government and to the same people of Serbia: Serbians in the sorrow of today 'remember Kossovo!'

9th Aug[ust 1917]

Lunch with Casgrain and Zaleski. The latter is an intelligent man and what few Poles seem in the last analysis – an honest man.

On coming back, a unique experience Casgrain and I had to consider whether our guest should be arrested! The grounds are that he is the accredited agent of the Council of State, which is opposed to be an enemy organization. <I was strongly against it.>

---

[330] Clipping from unidentified newspaper.

10th August [1917]

Dined with Pashitch – a curious impression of benevolence, as of sturdy peasant bonhomie, of bluff directness, pervades him. His massive face, and fine brow and patriarchal beard make him look a little like a rustic Lord Acton. He has the broad peasant humour near the surface, the 'heart's laugh and the smile as of ten thousand beers'. There is something of dignity and power behind it all – his circle obviously hold him in almost slavish reverence, and his long record of heroic resistance to every kind of danger prove it more than ever.

In bits and piecemeal his whole views on politics came out. He was obviously pleased by the great events of Wednesday[331] – I got Ll[oyd] G[eorge]'s personal thanks for my little contribution today, he said he was <very> pleased and that it was just the thing he wanted. He [Pašić] regarded British policy as defined, and therefore the ultimate question of restoration as settled. This seemed to have set his mind at rest. He praised the belle craison de Lloyd George – said he had found his Welsh bards in Serbian guslars[332] and was at once sympathetic and familiar with a small people. Then he turned to past politics – his view always was anti-Austrian and anti-Bulgar. Austria would not let us live – we were not a free state with secret treaties under the Obrenovich[333] – we were tied and bound. Under the Karageorgevich[334] our policy had to change. If I may claim credit it was to have foreseen before, with the Radical party, representing ideas, democratic and modern, that there was no truce with Austria feudal – absolutist. Then with Franz Ferdinand who fell at Sarajevo, his ideal Trialismus or federalised Austria, there was an attack on us – an attempt to detach the JugoSlavs and surround us and isolate us. Had we not resisted, we should have been nothing. Today, in spite of our sufferings, we are something.

As for the grand retreat it was terrible, and I think Sarrail might have done more. We resisted at Katchanik[335] to give him time to come up, but he never came in time to save us.

We stand for modern tendencies – democracy against autocracy, secularism against theocracy, nationality is ours and we are ready to fight and die for it as at Kossovo.

Then I said two words:

'I shall have a finer chapter to write in my book when the war is over', I said – and he beamed. 'Au revoir en Serbie', said I. He gripped my hand twice, and smiled all over – en Serbie, he said.

[331] See entry 8 Aug. 1917.
[332] *Guslar*, a Serb bard of heroic and historical folk poems, accompanied on a *gusle*, a single or double-stringed instrument.
[333] Ruling dynasty in Serbia from 1804 until *coup d'état* of 1903; kings since 1881.
[334] Ruling dynasty, 1903–41.
[335] Kaçanik on the river Lepanac in southern Kosovo.

11th August [1917]

Saw Brigadier-General Phillips,[336] who has returned after having terminated his mission of military control at Athens – burly, cheerful, startling as ever. He was under Camborie, and yet kept his end well up under most trying circumstances, and with perfect serenity. He congratulated himself on not having quarrelled with Canborie for six months.

The next thing he congratulated himself most on was having refused to meet Tino, when under great temptations. Tino offered to meet him near a wood, arranging for a mutual break-down of motor cars. He disapproved heartily of Elliot's policy, but did not think this fair to him and so refused. He was pro-Tino chiefly because he thought our conduct at the Dardanelles made the Greeks pro-German. But on the critical day, the Friday (Tino was kicked out on Monday[337]) he sent through a friend, a Greek intermediary, the hint that the game was up. Tino understood and went off to the Queen, subsequently behave magnificently. (If so, the only occasion he ever did.)

He looked on the future as very gloomy. Venizelos as now hated by the French (whom P[hillips] thought inexpressibly dirty in their methods), faced with dangers of a royalist reaction on one side, and a republican propaganda on the other, unable to fulfil his promises at raising troops.

Incidentally in a characterization he thought Pashitch (whom he knew well) as big or a bigger man than Venizelos, but lacking entirely his charm. <I agree as to charm after seeing Venizelos. 4/1/18>

13th Aug[ust 1917]

Dmowski – Milner

Lord Milner, speaking on Monday to a friend of mine, is all for a separate peace with Austria[:] 'The Austrians are gentlemen'. Incidentally, he had not heard of the Jugo-Slav Conference and agreement at Corfu and, in describing the inhabitants of Hungary to the north, could not put a name to the Slovaks.

This is the man, who is supposed to be our F[oreign] O[ffice] expert and who went on a mission to Russia. He is also, though more pardonably, quite unaware of the difficulties of getting Austria out – the divisional staffs and training centres being largely German and the Austrian divisions mixed between the German like beef between 2 strips of bread.

---

[336] See entry 29 Dec. 1916.
[337] General Jonnart forced Constantine to abdicate on 12 June 1917.

And 'the Austrians are gentlemen', as e.g. Aehrenthal[338] who fathered the Friedjung forgeries,[339] and, when an Austrian court proved them to be forgeries, was raised from a Baron to be a count by his gentlemanly Emperor.

O god, the ignorance in high places.

14th [August 1917]

Dmowski has written a most able pamphlet on European reconstruction, which he has circulated everywhere. Its geist is that Europe is in the mood for reconstruction, that Russia is useless, and that therefore the chief bridle in the German mouth must be an independent Poland, a Poland of 38,000,000 of which at least half are non-Poles extending from the Carpathians to the Baltic, including Posen and Danzig, with an autonomous East Prussia, eastward to include Lithuania, a stretch as far as the Pinsk marshes, thus omitting the Ukraine.[340]

The capital defect of this plan seems to be that Constantinople is not considered a European part or at all and yet the two pivots of the world in East Europe must always be Poland and Constantinople, not onea or the other. An independent Con[stantio]ple throws us back on a Polish Partition.

~~15th~~ \<August\> [1917]

~~Venizelos is certainly in a difficulty. Sarrail is universally hated by the Greek Army, the French faction increases, and the Royalists raise their heads, so that martial law has to be declared in certain areas. The Greeks as a whole show no inclination to fight, and Venizelos after having discovered the German loan made to Greece in the days of the surrender of Rupel~~ [incomplete].

~~The King is gentle and amenable as long as Venizelos is there and got at by Royalists directly he is not there. His affection will pull him this way because, if Tino returned, he could marry the humble girl he loves.~~

---

[338] Alois Lexa Baron von Aehrenthal (1854–1912), Austro-Hungarian diplomat and politician; entered diplomatic service, 1877; minister at Bucharest, 1895–99; ambassador at St. Petersburg, 1899–1906; Foreign Minister, 1906–12.

[339] Dr Heinrich Friedjung (1851–1920), Austrian historian and journalist noted for his liberal and pan-German views; his reputation was damaged when, in 1909, he published purportedly official Serbian documents implicating the Serbian government in terrorist activities, which then were revealed as Austrian forgeries in a trial at Agram (Zagreb).

[340] Reprinted as 'Poland, Old and New', in J.D. Duff (ed.), *Russian Realities and Problems* (Cambridge, 1917).

20th [August 1917]

New light via the Pierce-eye[341] on the origins of the war – not the German conclave of 5th July[342] but the British one of the Friday just before the war [31 July 1914].[343] An informal cabinet of the opposition assembled at Lansdowne House, of Lansdowne,[344] Balfour, Duke of Devonshire,[345] and a few others <u>and and</u> [*sic*] Henry Wilson. Says H[enry] W[ilson] [:] The Germans will be over the frontier tomorrow – says [*sic*] the others we don't believe it. None the less we will support the Government. The word went out to Leo Maxse,[346] who whipped up the Conservatives freely and found Austen Chamberlain playing with his children on an Essex beach. They assembled in scores, applauded Grey's speech on Belgium on the Saturday afternoon to the echo. Thus Leo saved the country. It is even possible that we did. At any rate the wise have owed to the foolish and the intellectuals the brutally energetics [*sic*] a great deal more than they are ever likely to admit.

I am also told that on the same Friday, the majority of the Cabinet decided to stand out <because the industrial worth would not stand war> but, after the temper of the Commons on Saturday, decided to enter in.

21st [August 1917]

Tino's treachery is now evident. The white book shows that he wished to side with Germany but dare not and could not.[347] He was threatening to betray Venizelos in the first days of the war, just at the moment when Venizelos was

---

[341] That is, Sir Henry Wilson.

[342] See entry 4 Aug. 1917.

[343] See also R. Blake, *The Unknown Prime Minister: The Life and Times of Andrew Bonar Law* (London, 1958), 220–24.

[344] Henry Charles Keith Petty-Fitzmaurice (1845–1927), 5th Marquess of Lansdowne, succ. 1866; politician; Under-secretary of State for War, 1872–74; for India, 1880; Governor-General of Canada, 1883–38; Viceroy of India, 1888–94; Secretary of State for War, 1895–1900; Foreign Secretary, 1900–1905; Minister without Portfolio, 1915–16.

[345] Victor Christian William Cavendish (1868–1938), 9th Duke of Devonshire, succ. 1908, politician; MP (Lib. Un.) West Derbyshire, 1891–1908; Financial Secretary of the Treasury, 1903–1905; Civil Lord of the Admiralty, 1915–16; Governor-General of Canada, 1916–21; Colonial Secretary, 1922–24.

[346] See entry 24 Nov. 1916.

[347] *Le livre blanc grec: Les pourparlers diplomatiques, 1913–1917* (Paris, 1917). Politis, the Greek foreign minister, presented the documents to the Greek chamber on 18 Aug. 1917, see 'The Betrayal Of Serbia. Ex-Greek Ministry's Guilt', *The Times*, 21 Aug. 1917.

dreaming of a League of Balkan states and offering the navy and army of Greece to the Entente.

This makes nonsense of enemy contention that Tino really wished us well. Our true and only course throughout was to back Venizelos.

22nd [August 1917]

In consonance with the suggestion I made to Philip Kerr I find that Lloyd George's omission to mention Roumania <on the 9th Aug[ust]> has caused bitter offence to Bratianu.[348]

It has resulted on a congratulatory telegram being sent from the King of England to the King of Roumania.

The winged word would have carried farther and should have reached Roumania sooner. If only my suggestion had been taken.

23rd [August 1917]

The Pope, in spite of his professions, or rather of Michaelis' denials, appears to have been influenced by Germany in drawing up the Papal Note.[349] The evidence is slight but good, so far as it goes. An admission by the Vatican Under-secretary[350] is the chief.

24th [August 1917]

Poland. After studying the situation for some time in Poland I have come to one or two definite conclusions. The decree of the 5th November 1916 was a decree which was epochmaking.[351] No one trusted Russia whose policy was as silly as it was blind, and as brutal as both. Austria demanded in early 1916 Posen, and the Kingdom as compensation for giving up Galicia – the whole to form an independent Poland. Germany wanted a Neben-regierung [parallel government], a mutilated Russian Poland, attached closely, especially in the military sense, to Germany. Austria and Germany disagreed and the Kaiser then broached his

---

[348] See entry 8 Aug. 1917.

[349] Pope Benedict XV issued a note to the belligerent Powers on 1 Aug. 1917, calling for a peace.

[350] Eugenio Maria Giuseppe Giovanni Pacelli (1876–1958), later Pope Pius XII; Under-secretary of State, 1912–17; Papal nuncio to Germany, 1917–29; Cardinal Secretary of State, 1929–39; Pope, 1939–58.

[351] See entry 4 Aug. 1917.

plan to the Austrian Archduke Charles Stephen, a pro-Pole. Charles Stephen turned it down as too dependent on Germany. Then Germany, in desperation, agreed with Austria and proclaimed the freedom of Russian Poland, finding therein compensation. Austria continued with a declaration for enlarging the autonomy of Galicia, thus still making possible the union of the two, with a possible ultimate union of all 3 shattered fragments in a united Poland.

25th [August 1917]

Poland might perhaps be called Piludski-land considering what that man has done. Pilsudski was a refugee from Russia to Galicia where he organized the Sokols[352] and prepared a war-chest for the struggle with Russia. In the early days of August 1914 he raised his legion, drove the Russian patrols and captured Kielce. This made his fame. Austria at once showed suspicion[,] finally allowed him to recruit in Russian Poland, but forbade him to do so in Galicia. Fatal error – by recruiting for Galician Legions on Russian soil he united two parts of Poland and thus brought them more than ever together. During 1915 Austria was hostile but pushed only parties within and Germany without. Pilsudski swelled his legions with recruits, propagandizing for Polish union, republicanism and liberty at the same time. Austria began to support him at the same time as Germany began to suspect him. In September 1916 he demanded a Polish army and national uniforms and badges from the Austrians. After pressure of public meetings etc. they conceded it. At the very same time Germany suddenly asserted herself and dismissed the bold brigadier for insubordination! Happy Allies.

27th [August 1917]

Pilsudski was so mighty that he could not be suppressed. In November Germany, hoping to get voluntary recruits and a subservient council, summoned Pilsudski to help them in forming a Council of State. Pilsudski agreed, and suggested 10 members of the Right Democrats or Dmowski-ites, 10 of the Centre, pro-Austrians, 5 of the Left or Socialists (his own party). Men say he thought Right and Centre would balance and Left hold the casting vote and make him dictator.

He failed and the Right, as eventually constituted included 10 Conservatives not all pro-Germans, 2 or 3 Independents, 7 Centre and 5 Left. As a whole it seems to have been pro-Austrian. Economically it was powerless. By a Bank

---

[352] *Sokól* ('Falcon'), a youth sports movement, originally founded in the Czech lands in 1862, but swiftly spreading across Eastern Europe.

swindle the Germans depreciated the rouble currency, by a customs regulation they controlled the revenue, by a monopoly of grain[,] sugar and coal they exhausted the resources of the country. The peasant grumbled and hated – the Council of State pitifully protested. Pilsudski said the system of requisitions was worse than the treatment of Belgium or Serbia.

29th [August 1917]

Germany is beaten at last for who can hear Wilson's words in reply to the Papal note, and think she can survive them. 'Not the German people but the power that is the ruthless master of the German people'. – 'The intolerable wrongs done by the furious and brutal power'.[353]

Washington or Burke could not have spoken thus, for they would have used more words. As a flame of fire, white and pure, it is unapproachable.

Sept[ember] 10th [1917]

Returned after my second visit to Porlock and Exmoor. Applied my military knowledge to the problem of the Doones.[354] The existence of these freebooters cannot be denied today because parish-registers (which some of the critics do not know) mention persons as having been killed by the Doones. Critics of another sort point out that the Doone valley is not a natural fortress, but is actually defenceless, because it is relatively low, and there is no true Doone gate or waterslide as in Blackmoore's story. But this is a shallow view – a far better defence than choosing a natural fortress was to choose a secluded valley remote from roads. Now, if examined carefully the position of the Doone valley on Exmoor is unique. The modern roads may not have existed but their prototypes in track and by path did. Now Doone valley is the centre of an area of which the four corners are Brendon, Simon's bath [*sic*], Exford and Porlock common, roughly about 5 miles square. In this area there is neither road nor track at all making a through-traverse from side to side of the square. There is no other such trackless waste in all Exmoor – no other place 2 miles square in which tracks do not meet. This therefore was a perfectly ideal centre for a robber band to live. Their valley could not be seen or approached from any important road or track. It was, therefore, ideal for their purposes, because they could sally out straight

---

[353] See 'Reply to the Peace appeal of the Pope', in Scott (ed.), *Wilson's Foreign Policy*, 322–5.
[354] R.D. Blackmore, *Lorna Doone: A Romance of Exmoor* (London, 1869), an historical romance set in late seventeenth-century Devon and Somerset and involving the Doone family, a once noble family now a robber band.

across country, in any direction, and the distance of 5 miles each way gave them opportunity for detecting any advance.

11th [September 1917]

There is a pretty good evidence that both Germany and Austria were behind the Papal Note. Incidentally by the It[alia]n T[reat]y of 1915[355] we are committed, along with R[ussi]a, F[ran]ce & It[al]y ag[ain]st any interf[eren]ce of the Pope in dip[lomati]c arrangements for the peace, or subsequent developments therefrom.

12th [September 1917]

The Korniloff[356]-Kerensky struggle becomes more interesting and perhaps less obscure. A secret point of interest is that Buchanan was approached by a Colonel to countenance a coup d'état in Petrograd. He declined and warned him strongly against it, and was confirmed in his view by the F[oreign] O[ffice].

Korniloff is a cautious man, though a Cossack and probably has more support than was imagined. I incline to back him. My only reason for not doing so is that the 'Times', which has hitherto invariably wrong in its Russian prognostications, is cautiously supporting him.[357]

13th [September 1917]

Buchanan is of opinion that Korniloff's action, however defensible in principle, was none the less 'ill-advised and inopportune'. His practical measures were undoubtedly a failure, because his advance on Petrograd was inconceivably slow. Hence collapse is already in sight on the part of Korniloff.[358] The plot was badly laid – incidentally it seems to prove that, apart from the Cossacks, the Soviet is still supreme in its influence over Russian soldiers, and the result can hardly fail to strengthen its hand, and weaken the Cadets, who have acted an ingenious part, being secretly well-disposed to ~~Kerensky~~ Korniloff.

---

[355] That is, the Treaty of London of 26 Apr. 1915.
[356] See entry 31 July 1917.
[357] See *History of The Times*, vol. iv, pt. 1 (London, 1952), 252–3.
[358] Kornilov attempted a *coup d'état* on 15 Sept. 1917; it collapsed when his soldiers disobeyed his orders.

1917 189

The Amb[assado]rs made representations in the sense of averting a crisis, on the lines of mediation between the two Ks. This was well-meant but probably ill-advised.

There can be no doubt that 'The Times' attack on the Soviets[359] and support of Korniloff will still further increase the anti-English feeling among Russians, and tend to the embitterment of our relations with them. It will cause them to suspect that the offer of mediation was really a blind for letting down the Provisional Government. Kerensky, I believe, does not take this view, but many of his followers will.

Incidentally the result on communications will be terrible, the railway cut at Luga,[360] congestion increased and further disorganization inevitable, a total stoppage of transport threatened in November.

14 Sept[ember 1917]

Going by chance into a room today I found General Corkran[361] there. By inquiry I hear that he proposes to go to the Serbian headquarters as Liaison Officer.

This man is the capitulation of the W[ar] O[ffice] to the scheme of a military mission to Serbia, which I persistently advocated as far back as April. It has now been imposed by the War-Cabinet on the W[ar] O[ffice] largely, I believe, owing to the efforts of Carson.[362]

Meanwhile, British representation at Serbian headquarters at a time their forces were much discouraged and demoralized has been confined to an amateur soldier, so thick that he could not pass the Littlebo and jobbed into a family living without a title.[363]

---

[359] See *The Times*, 5 Sept. 1917.

[360] Town some 90 miles south of St. Petersburg, on the railway line to Pskov.

[361] Major-General Sir Charles Edward Corkran (1872–1939), officer; entered army, 1893; active service Sudan Expedition, 1898, Second Boer War, 1899–1902; Officer Commanding battalion Grenadier Guards, 1914–18; Commandant Royal Military College, Sandhurst, 1923–27; General Officer Commanding, London District, 1928–32; Serjeant-at-Arms, House of Commons, 1932–39.

[362] Sir Edward Henry Carson (1854–1935), Baron Carson of Duncairn, cr. 1921, Irish-born lawyer-politician and Unionist leader; MP (Un.) Dublin University, 1892–1918, Belfast (Duncairn), 1918–21; Irish Solicitor-General, 1892; Solicitor-General, 1900–1905; Attorney-General, May–Nov. 1915; First Lord of the Admiralty, 1916–17; Minister without Portfolio, 1917–18; Lord of Appeal, 1921–29.

[363] That is, Goodden, see entry 19 Sept. 1917.

16 Sept[embe]r [1917]

Saw General Corkran today, a grim tough fighter sent out to the Serbs. He is frankly quite ignorant but is to find out all about them by bluff fraternisation etc. I insisted on several points, the pro-Austrian view of some Serbs, the Black Hand, Pashitch's position etc. He had not heard the latter's name before!

17 Sept[embe]r [1917]

Sir G[eorge] B[uchanan] on Russia – he thinks the Revolution has now come to saty and that Kerensky is honest, straightforward and sincere.[364] The Russian is naturally the most democratic person in the world and there would be no difficulty about maintaining the revolution, if there was community of feeling or organisation. But the feeling of the average Russian rarely rises above his village or at any rate his district, and the Russian peasant seems to have little personal hate for the German as such. In addition the disorganisation of munition factories is great. One of the most important has been blown up, the 12 other big ones may follow.

The Russian does not want peace because he thinks that disgraceful to his part but can he carry on war? Personally I inclined to think that, in L[loyd] G[eorge]'s phrase, we may now be 'at the bottom of the glen'.

18th Sept[embe]r [1917]

Dmowski wins.[365]

19th Sept[embe]r [1917]

Goodden, the educational dunderhead and ex-poison has returned from the Serbian G[eneral] H[ead] Q[uarters]. He confirmed, in general, the news I expressed on the 14th [September 1917]. Like so many however he is extremely ignorant and seems to know only the fringe of the subject.

---

[364] Kerensky proclaimed Russia a republic on 16 Sept. 1917.
[365] A meeting of representatives of the National Democractic and Realist parties at Lausanne in August 1917, presided over by Dmowski, established the Polish National Committee, which was then recognized by France and Britain in September.

20th Sept[embe]r [1917]

Polish men in Petrograd are pressing hard for recognition at the Conference at Paris, which the Russian F[oreign] O[ffice] somewhat deprecates. They wish for representation such as Roumania, a sovereign state had at the Conference at the Conference at Petrograd. The Russian F[oreign] O[ffice] are willing to take them on.

21st Sept[embe]r [1917]

It does not seem possible to safe [*sic*] Korniloff. Kerensky is resolved on purging the army of the traitors throughout. The disbanding of one third of the Army project is, however, very serious for it means let[ting] loose on the defenceless countryside a band of wild, undisciplined savages, without food, order, discipline or mercy.

The F[oreign] O[ffice] held their first meeting today on the economic reconstruction of Serbia. Buckley[366] attended as War Office representative, a complete ignoramus on the subject.

23rd September [1917]

The Pope appears to be much annoyed that the Kaisers twain communicated their reply to the Papal Note to the press before they communicated it to His Holiness who does nto even appear to have received it yet. His Cardinal-Secretary adds, perhaps with irony, that he has no reason to doubt the authenticity of the reports in the Press.

Sir G[eorge] Buchanan in a letter to 'Dear Charlie'[367] repeats his opinions as to Russia. He is also obviously backing Korniloff and says that Kerensky lost ground at the Moscow Conference, as being both nervous and at the same time overbearing. Both men appear to have posed sadly. Korniloff came to Moscow with a Turcoman bodyguard, Kerensky tried to prevent him from speaking and struck attitudes à la Napoléon.

---

[366] See entry 18 June 1917.
[367] Lord Hardinge of Penshurst.

24th Sept[embe]r [1917]

F[oreign] O[ffice] had an absurd blunder on Greece today. Crackanthorpe[368] stated the requirements of Greece for any sorts of wheat, and was promptly called [*sic*] over the coals by the F[oreign] O[ffice] for stating it nearly double. His reply was a masterpiece 'You have apparently taken the figures before 1913 since when Greece has nearly doubled its territory and population'.

25th Sept[embe]r [1917]

Russia & Roumania. Yesterday the F[oreign] O[ffice] at last saw light and adopted in substance Masterson's scheme <(they however on one pretext or another prevented anything practicable being done until the debacle)>, i.e. a plan for enforcing on the Roumanians a scheme of distributing food, munitions, supplies etc., which I drew up with him, and neither our W[ar] O[ffice] or F[oreign] O[ffice] would look at.[369]

The F[oreign] O[ffice] have now realized, of course at the French suggestion, that this must be done at least in so far as it is necessary to convoy them across Russia. It will all result in our having to do the thing, but on an ill-considered plan, and when it is almost too late to do it, instead of in the right way taking timely action boldly.

26th Sept[embe]r [1917]

<u>Serbia.</u> At last Corkran is going with an A[ide] D[e] C[amp] to the Serbian Army. Neither of them know a word about Serbia even in the rudiments of history etc. As Goodden the Liaison Officer is away on leave, there is literally nobody to help the abysmal and colossal ignorance. Incidentally we have not troubled to tell the Serb M[ilitary] A[ttaché] or Legation, though of course they know. Greater folly or lack of consideration I cannot imagine.

Incidentally, however, another scheme is to materialise, which we ought to have taken up and which the French had to suggest before we did. The Serbo-Croat Legion at Odessa has at last been forwarded to England – 3,000 odd of them have arrived in batches from Archangel. It is doubtful if many more will come, but this is a substantial reinforcement of trained soldiers. If any energy,

---

[368] Dayrell Montague Crackanthorpe (1871–1950), diplomat; entered diplomatic service, 1896; chargé d'affaires at Belgrade, 1913–14; legation counsellor at Athens, 1917–18; at Madrid, 1918–19; minister at Guatemala City, 1919–22; retired, 1922.

[369] See entry 2 Aug. 1917.

foresight or intelligence had been shown, 3 times this number could have been got over, as I pointed out in July last. So far as I can discover the W[ar] O[ffice] did absolutely nothing, until the French insisted. This reinforcement will inspirit the Serbs, but it may go against the dynasty.

27th [September 1917]

As a pendant to the ignorance of which an instance was given on the 26th I adjoin the following: Lloyd Jones[370] who is in SR2 is an absolute expert on East Africa and pushed all he could could to get into that section, knowing all about the country and the tribes from years' experience. He did not get there and Major Russell,[371] a man of no knowledge or experience in the matter, was appointed. Again, the Roumanian Minister was not informed that C.B. T[homson] had been dismissed or Ballard[372] appointed. He did not see the latter before he went out.

28th [September 1917]

29th [September 1917]

D[irector of] M[ilitary] I[intelligence, Macdonogh] – ethnographic maps of Balkans. The general conclusions seems [*sic*] to be pre-1913 border of Dobruja to Roumania, Cavalla and Macedonia S[outh] of Uskub to Bulgaria.
  This is a reasonable enough solution I think, if Serbia expands westwards.

1st October [1917]

Paper (D[irector] of M[ilitary] I[ntelligence, Macdonogh]) Germany 17th Sept[embe]r.
  Chief points. Maj[orit]y Soc[ial]ists not real Socialists nut national Deomcrats, i.e. Chauvinists, Minority Socialists partly Jewish & un-German

---

[370] Brevet Major William Lloyd-Jones (1886–1963), soldier; entered army, 1906; served in East Africa; severely wounded at Lake Rudolf, 1913; employed in War Office, 1915–18; retired, 1918; Captain of Invalids Royal Hospital, Chelsea.
[371] Colonel Richard Tyler Russell (b. 1875), soldier; entered Royal Artillery, 1895; Deputy Assistant Director of Equipment and Ordnance Stores, War Office, 1912–17; Assistant Director, 1917–19; retired, 1932.
[372] See entry 17 Apr. 1917.

and therefore less to be feared. Down with Hohenzollern would only result in patriotism.

Food riots, and the rest, though likely to increase, could always be quelled by soldiers from a distance. Therefore in the coming winter there was no likelihood of Germany's collapse. With great deficiency of nickel and rubber, Germany still had copper enough for 3 or 4 years and also cotton.

At present at any rate the front could not be broken. The strategy of Germany in the West was now defensive, but she could always increase her power by shortening her line and thus doing untold damage to the country evacuated.

2nd [October 1917]

3rd [October 1917]

The German oppressions in Poland seem to have particularly fallen upon the Jews, as there are so many big financial swindles going on. The Poles no more friendly to the Jews than before, but the Jews are very much more friendly to the Russians.

4th [October 1917]

A[rthur] Balfour dined with a friend of mine tonight. He was still hopeful as to Austria, but hopeless [as] to Turkey and said Fitzm[aurice] was too. He admitted that in theory it would be good to negotiate with them but did not in practice desire to do so.

He disbelieved a good deal in the Papal menace and thought the Papal note was really in our favour as it stressed the Polish aspect of things.

To switch to another tyke – I hear C.B. Thomson, phased out as M[ilitary] A[ttaché] from Roumania, has reappeared as Colonel of R[oyal] E[ngineers] of 60th Division. This illustrates the great desire of regulars to break a man's fall gently. C.B. T[homson] cannot have had any practical experience of engineering for at least 10 ~~days~~ years during which the whole science has been revolutionised. Yet he is put command the engineers of an active fighting unit.

The W[ar] O[ffice] is as bad as the F[oreign] O[ffice].

5th [October 1917]

The friend, who dined with A. B[alfour], commissioned me to find out from Fitzm[aurice] whether the views attributed to him were correct. Fitzm[aurice] said that the views attributed by B[alfour] to him were correct, We could not make peace with Turkey save by abandoning Armenia, Bagdad and Palestine. That and the Balkan Federation were the defences of Egypt and Mesopotamia.

He said there was rather a conflict about Zionist nationalism in the Cabinet in the last two days. Montagu (anti Zionist) had triumphed but the last word had not been said.

He believed from F[oreign] O[ffice] evidence that the detaching of Bulgaria was nearly settled.

6th [October 1918]

Smuts was absent from the Zionist Cab[ine]t meeting. He has been something of a disappointment. C[hief of the] I[mperial] G[eneral] S[taff] thinks him ignorant and his two suggestions

> (1.) of detaching a strategic reserve from France to defend England or throw into Holland if necessary
> (2.) of bringing aeroplanes back from France to defend us,

were neither very wise or very well received.

As to his ignorance he has had £40 pounds worth of books regularly from Cambridge every month since he left there. Perhaps they were law or transcendental philosophy.

His two recent speeches about Germany being beat one not very happy, yet I still trust and believe in him as our ablest head.

8th [October 1917]

Montagu played about the lowest and dirtiest game conceivable in the Zionist matter. He wrote a letter on the 14th Sept[embe]r to L[or]d R[obert] Cecil, full of the greatest inaccuracies, in which he never once suggested that he was a Jew himself, but always 'I understand that' 'I am informed that' etc. His whole object was to discredit Zionism, and he came out openly for stopping the establishment of Zionism as making the Jews a political factor in Palestine. He spoke for the assimilated Jewry, who looked on England, France etc. as their country. In fact he wished to deny his own nationality and put on ours, a sort of inverted snobbery.

The damning thing is that Rothschild has come out splendidly on the other side, though with more claim to be an International and assimilated Jew than any Jew in all England.

I hope Zionism will prevail[;] it has supporters in R[obert] Cecil, Milner & Smuts.

In any case Zionism will be set in motion by our enemies if we do not do so. There is evidence in the German press about this. Why not then anticipate them? and win the gratitude of the Jews. Anti-Zionists, who have betrayed Zion, will betray us, too.

9th [October 1917]

To dinner with D[avid] D[avies] to the Right Hon[ourable] J.W. [*sic*] Thomas,[373] Sec[retar]y of Railway Union.

Our first meeting was characteristic – through some mistake he was detained outside the frontdoor. When we got to him he said 'Look 'ere, its like 'Enderson was treated by [Lloyd] George.<In his speech after leaving the Cabinet Henderson complained that the War Cabinet, while discussing his conduct, kept him waiting an hour on the door-mat.>[374] I've just been in the mind to smash in the door'. The rest was equally unconventional. He was for an early peace, on terms of full reparation, restoration but not indemnities. He believed in possible revolution both in Germany and in Austria.

Labour was going to pull itself together and have another international Conference. They are going, however, so far as England is concerned, going to disregard minorities, i.e. the <Independent> Labour party which has 30,000 members, will not have as many delegates as the Miners with 1,000,000 etc.

He complained bitterly of the policy of the Government. While he is fighting his railwaymen, they suddenly concede excessive rates of pay to soldiers. Everything rotates in a curious circle of prices & wages. L[loyd] G[eorge] said that other day 'it only means half a crown a week extra', but half a crown in one industry may be millions and millions in several.

Thomas spoke of the views of Smuts, whom [*sic*] he said was the only member of the war-cabinet he could find who had clearly defined ideas or a policy as to peace. First as to Alsace-Lorraine he was at school in Alsace and knew it as a lad.[375]

---

[373] James Henry Thomas (1874–1949), trades unionist and politician; National Union of Railwaymen; MP (Lab., Nat. Lab. Since 1931) Derby, 1910–36; Colonial Secretary, Jan.–Nov. 1924, Aug.–Nov. 1931, and 1935–36; Lord Privy Seal, 1929–30; Dominions Secretary, 1930–35.

[374] See entry 22 Sept. 1921.

[375] Thomas was mistaken; Smuts visited Germany in October 1895 after graduating from Cambridge.

He thought it pro-German (partly or largely) and agricultural like Lorraine was pro-French and industrial. Latter had however 80% (should really be 75%) of steel & iron of Germany. What shocked him was that Germany demanded Lorraine equally with Alsace for this exact reason. Morally this shocked Smuts and determined him in favour of the French view.

For the peace as a whole he looks beyond South Africa. The colonies are not worth a tinker's damn compared with peace. I think the phraseology is that of Thomas not Smuts. That is he himself thought, and thought South Africa would think with him, that East Africa should go back to Germany in the interests of peace, i.e. of a peace wide enough for the whole Empire, a true Empire peace. This is strange and true generosity in the conqueror of East Africa.

10th [October 1917]

Peace. Germany has made a definite offer via Spain to discuss peace with Eng[lan]d.[376] A[rthur] B[alfour] on the 8th summoned rep[resentati]ves of Allies (excluding S[er]bia & R[uss]ia) & told them of it and his proposed reply that Eng[lan]d w[oul]d be prepared to receive inform[atio]n.[377]

This met with general approval, though Cambon[378] indicated that we should not come to a conference, until the main objects of the Alliance were already achieved.

He asked if the letter was dated – awkward pause by Balfour, then amid dead silence 'Yes, a fortnight before'.

<Went to see Adams.> New scheme for military education[;] saw L[loyd] George and Robertson going into Cabinet at 10 Downing Street.

11th [October 1917]

Adams came with me to see Cockerill[379] and talk about the new scheme of military education. It is, in brief, to take hold of young officers, and instruct

---

[376] The German approach was made through Rodrigo, Marquis de Villalobar, the Spanish envoy at Brussels, tel. Villalobar to The Hague legation, 7 Sept. 1917, A. Scherer and J. Grunewald (eds), *L'Allemagne et les problèmes de la paix pendant la premiere guerre mondiale* (4 vols, Paris, 1966), ii, no. 242.

[377] The meeting took place on 6 Oct.

[378] See entry 25 June 1917.

[379] Brigadier-General (Sir) George Kynaston Cockerill (1867–1957), kt. 1926, soldier and politician; entered army, 1886; Intelligence Officer in Indian Army, 1892–99; Deputy Assistant Adjutant General, South African campaign, 1900–1902; technical delegate at Second Peace Conference at The Hague, 1907; retired, 1910, to contest general election; rejoined, 1914;

them in larger aspects of education – International politics, social ethics and aspects of citizenship, economics etc. In short it is to give to the young officer that larger and more liberal education, which Sandhurst and Woolwich cannot, and the Universities are not allowed to give.

12th [October 1917]

~~Imperial munitions board~~ Wilson. From two sources information about Wilson – (1.) Thomas, when Thomas, Bowerman[380] and L[or]d Cunliffe[381] were on tour in America, Wilson did not see Cunliffe though he was governor of the Bank of England, but he saw Thomas, the Labour leader five times. Spring Rice[382] told them all to begin with 'It is no use my suggesting he should see anyone, he doesn't worry to do so' – and 'it's better for me not to'. (2.) Crane,[383] the American millionaire financier, who once ran Albania and now trying to run Russia, said 'I was with Wilson the first hour of his Presidency before his Cabinet came to see him. While talking, he made a note on a paper block and shoved it away. Next morning it made a great stir in the papers – it was to the effect that he would personally see no seekers for political office. A revolution indeed – the whole of a President's time for the first month or two was occupied in that way till then. He is in all respects the opposite of Mr. [Theodore] Roosevelt. He definitely considers that he can serve the state best by keeping in good health. He works only 4 hours a day subject to other interviews with his ministers, who can see him at any time. From 9–1 golf with his doctor, 2–6 work with his ministers. Saturday if possible in the woods, Sunday with his family. Ten p.m. bed except on some occasions. He thinks profoundly on problems and establishes his bases so securely that the never has to draw back when once he has stated his policy. He tries if possible only to do one thing at a time – Mexico he got out of the way before he took up with Germany etc. He never fears opposition, and yet prepares

---

Director of Special Intelligence, 1914–19 (since 1918 with title of Deputy Director of Military Intelligence); MP (Cons.) Reigate, 1918–31.

[380] Charles William Bowerman (1851–1947), trades union leader and politician; President of the Trades Union Congress, 1901; MP (Lab.) Deptford, 1906–31.

[381] Walter Cunliffe (1855–1920), 1st Baron Cunliffe, cr. 1914, banker; Governor of the Bank of England, 1913–18.

[382] Sir Cecil Arthur Spring Rice (1859–1918), diplomat; entered Foreign Office, 1882; minister and consul-general at Tehran, 1906–1908; at Stockholm, 1908–13; ambassador at Washington, 1913–18.

[383] Charles Richard Crane (1858–1939), US financier and philanthropist; supporter of Woodrow Wilson, 1912; member of Root Commission to Russia, 1917; member of US delegation, Paris Peace Conference, 1919; Inter-Allied Commission on Mandates in Turkey, 1919; Minister at Peking, 1920–21; virulent anti-Semite, noted Arabist.

and plans for everything. Set speeches he writes sometimes six weeks beforehand, so that on Gettysburg day he was able to settle a strike before he made his oration. Otherwise he likes to regard his audience before making a speech, and to make his speech as he went along.['] (Though Crane did not say it, he is perhaps the greatest autocrat in the world today and yet is perhaps the only democrat who has quite simply and avowedly taken public opinion for his guide.)

He is so sure of himself that he types his communiqués or despatches with his own hand, thinks them out beforehand, and seldom or never alters a word.

In speaking with Thomas, he said that Liberty was like the Catholic Church in the middle ages – the catholic priest shared authority with the newly ordained priest he had trained up. Each priest had the same celebral powers. [']Now that is democracy[;] it stands for authority divided and shared.

That's what I meant by distinguishing between German Government and the German people. The war will end when the German people see the meaning of liberty. When they see that it is for their good that the system of militarism should be smashed[,] that democracy is good even if they suffer. Democracy must increase in spite of all the mistakes it has made and will make and must make – for democracy divides its authority among the people. Re the question of time. Philip Kerr, who listened to Crane, said that the real difficulty was the Parliamentary – L[loyd] G[eorge] had to consider Parliamentary forms, traditions, speak to Parliamentary persons even when he did not go down to Parliament.[']

He volunteered the suggestion that Asquith did not work over hard. We all know L[loyd] G[eorge] does not overdo it like Gladstone. Kerr told me however he was going to put this up to L[loyd] G[eorge] as a personal touch and that meant much and ought to do good.

13th [October 1917]

I hear that last year in October and this year in August we were very hard put financially. This year in August in Canada the Imperial Munitions Board simply could not raise money – we had enough both in England & in USA but not in the Dominion. The result was nearly a break in British credit, but the danger was tided over by cancelling some orders – save exchange jugglery etc. As however the members of the Board pledged their private credit in the matter, it must have been serious. I had no notion that this (i.e. private credit) could serve nowadays and thought Richelieu[384] at Rochelle was the last who did it.

---

[384] Cardinal Armand Jean Duplessis, Duc de Richelieu (1585–1642), French cardinal and statesman; minister of state to Louis XIII, 1624–29; chief minister, 1629–42. Richelieu besieged and starved into submission the Huguenot fortress of LaRochelle in 1628.

15th [October 1917]

Buchanan today received the greatest power any British ambassador in Russia ever had. Terestchenko[385] proposed that a declaration should be made today (Polish National Fete Day) by England and France with Russia in favour of a "free and indivisible Poland". The F[oreign] O[ffice] consented to this but tried to substitute "independent" for "indivisible" but left Buchanan at his discretion. He has the greatest opportunity to name or aid Poland since Catherine the Great[386] decided to split. By using the word "indivisible" he units it for ever, and the trisected nation is healed.

16th [October 1917]

I hear Pesič[387] [sic] subchief of staff at Salonica has come over with a personal letter from the Crown Prince to the King. I am to see him tomorrow.

17th [October 1917]

Tino. I went through the white book in detail. It entirely confirms the intercepts and other evidence and incidentally proves that Venizelos is as true and honourable a gentleman as Tino, Gounaris,[388] Skoloudis etc. are detestable scoundrels. The Greek-Serbian Treaty is proved by the comments of Alexandropoulos, the Greek minister at Belgrade, to have committed the Greeks to possible action ag[ain]st Powers other than Bulgaria. Tino got alarmed in May because the Bulgars were attacking Greeks at Pangaion,[389] and directed 'in agreement with the P[rime] M[inister][']' the signing of the military convention. Tino's subsequent explanation that the Treaty was 'purely local and Balkanic' was a lie and known by him to be one.

---

[385] Mikhail Ivanovich Tershchenko (1886–1956), Ukrainian-born industrialist and Russian politician; Finance Minister in the Provisional Government, Mar.–May 1917; Foreign Minister, May–26 Oct. 1917; French exile since 1918.

[386] Catherine II of Anhalt-Zerbst (1729–96), Tsarina of All the Russias, 1762–96; she instigated the First Partition of Poland in 1772.

[387] General Petar Pešić (1871–1944), Serb soldier; chief of Serb military mission at Paris peace conference, 1919; Deputy Chief of General Staff, 1919–21; Chief of General Staff, 1921–24, and 1924–9; Minister of War, 1922–24 and 1940–41.

[388] Dimitrios Gounaris (1866–1922), anti-Venizelist Greek politician; Finance Minister, 1908–1909; Prime Minister, 1915 and 1921–22; found guilty of high treason by military tribunal after 'Asia Minor Disaster', and executed, Nov. 1922.

[389] A range of hills near Kavala in northeastern Greece.

Greek Loans were raised by Germany in Jan[uar]y and in May 1916, and the surrender at Rupel was all prearranged by an agreement <on 22 May>, which was flatly denied by Skoloudis in his public explanations.

At Cavalla, there seems to have been a German pledge not to enter Drama, Serres or Cavalla, but the Bulgars appear to have violated it.

I consulted an old friend of mine in early May 1916 – the conclusion then was that Greece was exhausted financially by mob[ilizatio]n and dep[loyme]nt on us unless she could get a loan from Germany. The conclusion was entirely correct – she had already had two loans from Germany. Mutatis mutandis she is therefore now completely in our hands. I rubbed this into the authorities.

18th [October 1917]

The French Amb[assado]r[390] and Terestchenko bullied Buchanan (v[ide] 15th) into substituting 'independent and indivisible Poland' for 'free and independent' which was our aim. Thus we lost out on both counts. Buchanan has since been daily asked as to the meaning of 'indivisible' <(Note 7/11/17)>. The answer was 'indivisible' in the dictionary not ethnographic sense. Why this declaration has not been published I cannot imagine. F[oreign] O[ffice] again I supposed.

19th [October 1917]

Pesič <subchief of Serb H[ead] Q[uarters] Staff>, a cheerful, talkative, very talkative man. He had come from Salonica to get an offensive. He said that in the winter it was possible and that the objective was Sofia. He thought the Greek division on the Vardar[391] good, that near Monastir execrable, numbering only a few thousands. The Greeks as a whole were poor stuff and demoralized. He thought it would be far better to have 5 good divisions than 15 bad ones.

Macedonia

He was extraordinarily moderate on this point, thought that there was much for both Bulgar and Serb and Greek and even for the autonomous Macedonian himself.

Montenegro. He expressed the view (and he was subchief of staff in Montenegro) that the K[in]g of Montenegro had deliberately sold his country

---

[390] Maurice Georges Paléologue (1859–1944), French diplomat and writer; entered Foreign Ministry, 1880; aid to foreign ninister, 1904–1906; agent and consul-general at Sofia, 1907–1909; minister there, 1909–12; political director of Foreign Ministry, 1912–14; ambassador at St. Petersburg, 1914–17; general-secretary of Foreign Ministry, 1920–24.

[391] The river Vardar or Axios rises north of Skopje in Macedonia, flowing southeastwards to debouch into the Aegean west of Thessaloniki.

and that the Montenegrins would be the first to prevent him from returning there. He was saying the King ought to abdicate when Jovanovich stopped him.

21st [October 1917]

Trafalgar Day

22nd [October 1917]

A very curious intrigue of Russian Jews, beginning on 1st May, apparently under the influence of Kerensky, was directed towards overthrowing the Monarchy in Roumania. Subsequently, after the 15th May (when it released Rakovsky,[392] a Bulgar Roumanian imprisoned for pro-Germanism by Roumania) it organized the Society of the RUMCHEROD[393] at Odessa under RAKOVSKY. Recently the RUMCHEROD transferred its activities to Jassy, denounced Kerensky and imported Rakovsky, who presided at a meeting of Russian mil[itar]y Soviets at BOTUSANI.[394] The Roumanian Gov[ernmen]t finally remonstrated at an outrageous interference in their internal affairs, which was sanctioned by Russia. The Allied ministers supported this remonstrance to TERESTCHENKO. TERESTCHENKO decided that Rakovsky had presided at the meeting but disavowed his proceedings and sent off a telegram to Gen[era]l TCHERBATCHEFF [sic],[395] denouncing these proceedings. The general, who has shown somewhat of a disposition to hunt both with hare and hounds, will therefore be compelled to declare himself against the wilder Socialist agitation on his front.

---

[392] See entry 5 July 1917.

[393] *Rumyanskogo fronta, Chernomorskogo flota i Odesskoye oblasti* (Central Executive Committee of the Soviets of Romanian Front, Black Sea Fleet, and Odessa Oblast), a short-lived and self-proclaimed organ of Soviet power in southwestern Russia.

[394] That is, Botoșani in Norther Moldavia.

[395] General Dmitri Gregorevich Shcherbachev (1857–1932), Russian artillerist; entered army, 1894; Major-General, 1903; head of Nikolaevsikaia Voennaia Akademiia, 1907–12; commander, 9th Army, 1912–15; 11th Army, 1915; 7th Army in Bessarabia, 1915–17; commander Romanian front, Apr. 1917–Mar. 1919; fought with White Army, 1918–19; representative of Admiral Kolchak to Allied governments at Paris, 1919–20; French exile.

24th [October 1917]

Jugoslavs & Odessa. In response to Berthelot's remonstrance ag[ain]st the 2nd Jugo-Slav division leaving Galatz our Government has decided to act and insist on the orders being carried out and their being brought speedily away.
     Czernin.[396]

25[th October 1917]

Poles.

26th [October 1917]

Serbian decoration.[397]

27th [October 1917]

Benesh [sic]

30th [October 1917]

Italy – the break-through of Mackensen, the first of the war, is a terrible thrust.[398] I doubt even if the Italians can stand on the Tagliamento [river]. One does not lose 100,000 men as prisoners by fair play. At the critical points they had at least 27 div[ision]s to 10, of which only 5 or 6 were German <and 3 only in the front line>. Cadorna[399] was surprised by the attack on Tolmino, though not by the attack as such. In this he was wiser than [the] French or British, who looked on the whole postponement of the offensive after the 11th battle of the Isonzo as inexplicable, and withdrew the French & British batteries in consequence.

---

[396] Ottokar (Theobald Otto Maria) Count Czernin von und zu Chudenitz (1872–1932), Austro-Hungarian diplomat; entered diplomatic service, 1895; resigned on health grounds, 1898; re-entered, 1913; minister at Bucharest, 1913–16; Foreign Minister, 1916–18.

[397] White Eagle of Serbia, a Royal decoration instituted in 1883.

[398] Battle of Caporetto, the 12th battle of the Isonzo, 24 Oct.–19 Nov. 1917. Temperley was mistaken, however. The German commander was General Otto von Below; Mackensen was still in Romania.

[399] General (Field Marshal since 1924) Luigi Cadorna (1850–1928), Italian military commander; entered army, 1868; Chief of Staff, 1914–17; sacked after the retreat at Caporetto.

31st [October 1917]

Czar telegram. American enterprise – comedy and cinema still live, as the following telegram shows:
   April 1917
   Cinema Company, Philadelphia, to Premier LVOFF,[400] Petrograd.
   Will you please lead Czar to take part in cinema tableaux entitled "The Russian debâcle". Expenses of travel and six weeks profits guaranteed to LVOFF's Government at the rate of $5,000 per week.

1st November [1917]

Henry Wilson is at his subterranean work, seconded by the P[rime] M[inister], and the Harmsworth Press (in all ultimate probability). It does not seem clear from an article in the Manchester Guardian whether Haig or Robertson is aimed at by them.[401]
<(Note. It is announced in the Press of 4th Nov[embe]r that Robertson, Maurice, and Sir Henry Wilson have set off for Italy in the company of Lloyd George.[402]) In general I do not think an Inter-allied Staff a sound proposal – with a Coalition there are some matters, as Salonica, over which there can be no agreement. Any such scheme pivots on France and therefore increases her power, when she is gradually lessening her numbers.>

3rd [November 1917]

R[omani]a. There is a pathetic report from Finlayson[403] as to the Roumanian army and state. The morale, intelligence etc. of the army are extremely high[;] probably no army has ever so quickly recovered from a disgraceful rout and demoralization. Intelligence in the officers, endurance and obedience in the men are the secret.

---

[400] Prince Georgy Yevgenyevich Lvov (1861–1925), Russian politician; Chairman of the All-Russian Union of Zemstvos, 1914–15; Prime Minister, Mar.–July 1917; exile in France since 1918.
[401] 'Changes at Whitehall?', *Manchester Guardian*, 1 Nov. 1917.
[402] Rapallo conference, 5–11 Nov. 1917.
[403] General (Sir) Robert Gordon Finlayson (1881–1956), soldier; entered army, 1900; served European war, 1914–16; Deputy Assistant Adjutant-General, 1 Army Corps, 1916–17; General Staff Officer on special mission to Russia, 1917; Deputy Commander North Russia Forces, 1918–19; Commander-in-Chief Egypt, 1938–39; Adjutant-General, 1939–40; General Office Commanding-in-Chief Western Command, 1940–41; retired, 1941.

Yet despite this high morale, the men are lacking in overcoats and shoes, and starvation is imminent in the whole country by about February 1st.[404]

If they had listened to Masterson's report handed on and partly composed by me on [date missing] the stuff could have been run through by now. As it is they are trying to get them wadded coats from China!

Finlayson was much impressed with the strength of the Roumanian army as a point d'appui, and says that, with 2 or 3 other such, the whole Russian front would be safe.

The Roumanians held up 7 or 8 German divisions under Mackensen, in far worse positions and with far less men and guns than the Italians, who had to face only 3 in the front line <6 altogether>, and were 3 to 1 everywhere.

5th [November 1917]

Zion has won, so FitzM[aurice] tells me. The final vote was last Wed[nesda]y about the time (prospice omen) that we captured Beersheba, the gateway of the promised land. In the end it went through quietly. Bonar Law, well-coached, assented, Milner drove, Curzon hee-hawed, Smuts urged vigorously and L[loyd] G[eorge] said you know my opinion. So it was ~~washed~~ settled, though not public just yet?

The documents relevant were drawn up by Hankey,[405] in a form which undoubtedly favoured the Zionists. The only arguments the anti-Zionists could bring were (1.) That they did not wish a national home for the Jews (2.) That Russia had removed all Jewish grievances.

Fitzmaurice, who has pulled the strings, says that the results are[:] 4 are very small three very big

> (1.) The end of Montagu, whom Zionists will attack
> (2.) Strengthening of the morale of Russia by American Jews
> (3.) Attack via Copenhagen on Germany, loosening the reins and finding the joints in their harness

---

[404] See entry 2 Feb. 1917.
[405] Captain Maurice Pascal Alers Hankey (1877–1963), 1st Baron Hankey, cr. 1939, sailor and civil servant; entered Royal Marines Artillery, 1895; Captain, 1900; coastal defence analyst, Naval Intelligence Department, 1902–1906; Intelligence Officer, Mediterranean Station, 1907–1908; Naval Assistant Secretary, Committee of Imperial Defence, 1908–12; Secretary to Committee of Imperial Defence, 1912–38; Secretary to War Cabinet, 1916–19; Cabinet Secretary, 1919–38; clerk to Privy Council, 1923–38; Chancellor of the Duchy of Lancaster, 1940–41; Paymaster-General, 1941–42.

(4.) The end of Turkey – with manpower drained to the dregs, with Allenby[406] advancing on Jerusalem, and the Jews at last militant for the cross, the crescent is decidedly on the wane.

6th [November 1917]

~~The Serbs extraordinarily afraid that the Germans will send 3 or 4 divisions to Salonica~~ A visit to Gennadius the Greek minister. I talked with him as to the Bulgarian secret obligations to Germany and Turkey. He knew little more than he had already communicated to the F[oreign] O[ffice] – a protocol of May <1917> between Germany and Turkey of which article 12 stipulated for the return of Cavalla to Greece. This was before Tino was dethroned. I have now carefully worked up the whole matter. There were, I think, binding arrangements of a sort between Bulgaria and Turkey in August 1914 (v[ide] Theotokis'[407] telegram in Greek white book). Bulgaria's first obligation to Germany (not absolutely committal) was the loan in March ? 1915. Apparently there was a ~~treaty signed with Tu~~ convention ceding the Maritza railway to Bulgaria July / [19]15, made with Turkey and negotiated by Germany. On Sept[embe]r 25th/ [19]15 there was a treaty of alliance with Turkey signed by Bulgaria and probably also with Germany. This appears to have ceded Macedonia less Cavalla, and possibly the Pirot (and Nish?) are to Bulgaria.

In 1917 Germany negotiated a purchase scheme for the Maritza railway to soothe Turkish susceptibilities. In Oct[obe]r the Kaiser resisted both Sofia and Constantinople and Radoslavoff[408] publicly demanded for Bulgaria in addition to the territory already mentioned, the Dobruja to the Danube and Cavalla. He has probably got both from the Kaiser.

Gennadius enlarged on the wickedness of the Bulgars. How long were they in the [sic] Macedonia – 30 years and we? 30 centuries (a characteristic touch of Hellas!)

---

[406] General (Field Marshal, 1919) Edmund Henry Hynman Allenby (1861–1936), 1st Viscount Allenby, cr. 1919, military commander; entered Army, 1880; served Second Boer War, 1899–1902; Inspector-General of Cavalry, 1910–14; commander cavalry corps, British Expeditionary Force, 1914–15; commander V Corps, 1915–16; commander 3rd Army, 1916–17; Commander-in-Chief, Egyptian Expeditionary Force, 1917–18; captured Jerusalem, Dec. 1917; High Commissioner for Egypt and the Sudan, 1918–25.

[407] Georgios Theotokis (1844–1916), Greek politician; Navy Minister, 1886–90; Prime Minister, 1899–1901, 1903, 1903–1904, 1905–1909.

[408] Vasil Radoslavov (1854–1929), Bulgarian politician; Minister of Justice, 1884–86; Prime Minister, 1886–87 and 1913–18; Minister of the Interior, 1899–1901; in exile in Germany since 1918; sentenced to death *in absentia*, 1922.

In the main he is a scholar and a charming man, and he conducted me to his library – all books bound in Morocco, Aldine editions, beautiful Greek busts and bronzes, and the finest pamphlet collection of the Near East in the world! He caressed <the books> and crooned about their contents 'Ah I have no time now'. Then he showed his relics 'this [is] very precious to us', a faded wreath of laurel which lay on Byron's coffin on its way back to England from Missolonghi.

Poor old man, an ardent Venizelist, a true and generous man, not made for politics perhaps, but worthy to be loved.

7th [November 1917]

The Serbs very alarmed about 4 or 5 German divisions coming down to Salonica. Venizelos thinks that the next two months before mobilization will be the critical ones. After that they will be safe. If that is so, we can, of course, hardly help them, because our divisions are locked up elsewhere.

At the same time, as the German thrust at Cadorna was unexpectedly successful, they may not be able to organize another thrust or drive.

8th [November 1917]

Russia again in motion. Kerensky deposed and in flight – the Soviet under Lenin on top in Petrograd, aided of course by revolutionaries in the navy at Kronstadt.[409] I doubt if the Soviet will succeed in their design of all land for the peasant and a separate peace with Germany. Buchanan thinks the situation could not have been worse. Kerensky declined apparently to take the responsibility of firing early in the crisis, and, though already against the Soviet, still deferred to them in secret. If he now returns, and he probably will, he can only be the mask for a military leader or an irresolute policy, and will probably disappear. The outrageous abuse poured on him in the British Press <of this evening>, however, [will] only do harm.

9th [November 1917]

Pogradetz.[410] The Serbs have had a little incident about this little Albanian town, which I well remember visiting at the extreme South of Lake Ochrida. When the French and Albanian bands pushed out the Austrians from here, the Serbs

---

[409] On 7 Nov. 1917.
[410] Pogradec on Lake Ohrid (Albania).

claimed it on the ground of being geographically separated from Albania and only assigned to her <by Austria> in spite in the Conference of London in 1913. Either way I cannot see the Serbs had any real claim upon it.

G[eneral] O[fficer] C[ommanding] Egerton,[411] SO of Southern Army interview with [H.A.L.] Fisher, Min[iste]r of Education, on the general question of technical education in the army. I understand the Min[iste]r was quite sympathetic but [incomplete].

10th [November 1917]

<u>Poland</u>. D[irector of] M[ilitary] I[ntelligence] asked for a paper on the New Polish schemes today. I gave the evidence [that] Austria undoubtedly wishes to make Charles King of both <Russian> Poland and Galicia. Prussia to have Lithuania and Courland under one form or another. But there seems to be a hitch in the negotiation and Germany has not yet consented.

My own view is that these steps destroy the last chance of a Central Powers' Entente with Poland – Prussia cuts her off from access to the sea, Austria if she wins today, will rule a land crushed by the requisitions and severed from Posen and Danzig. She can only be supported by Conservatives in Galicia & Russian Poland.

12th [November 1917]

The Press has already announced an Interallied Council of 3, with Henry Wilson as one (v[ide] 2nd November).[412]

The Henry Wilson control is, I understand, now very evidently the work of L[loyd] G[eorge] and recognized as such. I understand R[obertson] and H[aig] put the cards on the table some three weeks ago and demanded Westernism pure and simple and the suppression of all side-shows. They were disagreed with and defeated <by French & Wilson>. The last result is that L[loyd] G[eorge] throws on them somewhat of the blame for the German 'breakthrough' [at Caporetto]. It is not quite fair, because 3:1 should be an adequate defence. On the other hand, R[obertson]'s withdrawal of artillery with continued iron roads at the critical moment was very disheartening to Italy. I

---

[411] Major-General Granville George Algernon Egerton (1859–1951); soldier; joined army, 1879; active service Afghan War, 1879–80; Egypt, 1882, and Sudan expedition, 1898; Commander, 52 Lowland Division, 1914–16; at Gallipoli, 1915; General Officer Commanding Sicily and Base Commandant, Mediterranean Expeditionary Force, 1915–16; Inspector General of Infantry, 1916–17; retired, 1919; Colonel of Highland Light Infantry, 1921–29.

[412] See entry 2 Nov. 1917.

find, however, an interesting sidelight on Westernism. Apparently not only G[eneral] H[ead] Q[uarters] France decide on its amm[unitio]n fixing it with the Min[istr]y of Mun[itio]ns but it fixes the percentage of amm[unitio]n to be supplied to each of the sideshows – Galicia, Egypt etc.

In that case, where does the W[ar] O[ffice] come in? I don't blame Haig in the very least for fighting for his own hand, but why should he regulate everyone else's?

<Later. I wonder if this was really true.>

Message on the telephone from L[loyd] G[eorge] over Sir Henry Jones[413] and technical education in the army. Marvellous the man can think of these things at the same time as of Europe.

13th [November 1917]

Jews. The upshot of an inquiry into Bolshevik activities seems to show that many of them are Jewish, that some of them are paid by Germany, that Lenin, though not a Jew, is so paid. But there the matter would seem to stop. The clearest case of anti-Entente Jewish interference is the Rumcherod[414], and Jewish agents in Roumania, who sought to corrupt Roumanian Jews, soldiers and peasants and outrageously interfered with the rights of Jews.

It is probable that the majority of <Russ[ian] & Roumanian> Jews are anti-Entente but mainly on Socialistic grounds perhaps, but certainly also because of previous maltreatment. The Jews is Entente countries, other than Russia & Roumania, have decidedly come out in favour of the Entente. Even in Poland the Jews are now anti-German instead of anti-Russian. Zionism will probably put the finishing touch to the process of winning the Jewish majority.

Italy. We certainly took away our guns from Cadorna with a curtness that was discouraging, when he declined to renew the offensive on the Isonzo. His calculations were wrong but so also were ours.

14th [November 1917]

The Wilson episode is still piquant. Lloyd George made his speech in France, not in England, to save Painlevé,[415] but Painlevé fell today – not a very auspicious

---

[413] Sir Henry Jones (1852–1922), Welsh academic and educational reformer; Professor of Philosophy, Bangor, 1884–91, St. Andrews, 1891–94, Glasgow, 1894–1912; he originated the plan of a 'penny rate' levied by the County Councils for higher education.

[414] See entry 22 Oct. 1917.

[415] See entry 12 Apr. 1917.

beginning for the new scheme of a united council, pooling the requirements of a whole Alliance and representing one united nation in arms.

L[loyd] G[eorge]'s plan I believed to be right in substance – it amounts to technical aid to statesmen in deciding on strategy. This, if properly worked, is an aid not a hindrance and prevents crude plans being sprung on military authorities.

There is however a distinct difference. Foch, chief of French Staff, is also their rep[resentati]ve on the Inter-Allied Council, Robertson our C[hief of the] I[mperial] G[eneral] S[taff] is not our rep[resentati]ve but Wilson is, his known rival.

I believe L[loyd] G[eorge] is sick of France and the West, and wishes victory in Italy. He therefore desires fundamentally to reverse the strategy, probably to break through at Laibach and dictate peace at Vienna.

When some objection was made to Paris as the centre. L[loyd] G[eorge] had an inspiration "Let it be at Versailles. Versailles was the place <from> where the Germans conquered the French, it now shall be the place from where the Allies will conquer Germany".

15th [November 1917]

Anecdote of L[loyd] G[eorge] today – he breakfasted with Venizelos and Reading.[416] With the latter he came to look at the map of Palestine in which the Staff Officer, Jim Butler,[417] stuck pins. He said very well to the progress but "I should like to have seen them go up the Hebron road". Jim Butler said that invaders of Palestine had always relied on the sea. Did Titus?, said Reading, "I think he entered Jerusalem from the North". As Jim said, ["]I did not feel equal to disputing the matter with such an authority!"[418]

16th [November 1917]

The old C[hief of the] I[mperial] G[eneral] S[taff] has played his cards well in this campaign <ag[ain]st L[loyd] G[eorge]>, refusing to resign. I understand that at one of these meetings in Italy he went out for a motordrive, saying 'I don't want to do all this talky-talky'. As it happened Foch wiped the floor with both

---

[416] Rufus Daniel Isaacs (1860–1935), Baron Reading, cr. 1914, 1st Marquess of Reading, cr. 1926, barrister and politician; MP (Lib.), Reading, 1904–13; Solicitor-General, 1910; Attorney-General, 1910–13; Lord Chief Justice, 1913–21; ambassador at Washington, 1918–19; Viceroy of India, 1921–25; Foreign Secretary and Leader of the House of Lords, 1931.

[417] See entry 22 Mar. 1917.

[418] Reading was, in fact, partly right. In AD 70, the Romans entered the New City of Jerusalem from the West, but took Fortress Antonia and Mount Moriah from the North.

Lloyd George and Cadorna. He said to the latter Yes, you gave excellent orders but 25% of orders is in the giving, 75% in seeing them carried out. Cadorna was helpless before him. He is an old man – 71 – too old for modern war.

17th [November 1917]

Venizelos.

<Nov[ember] 17th [1917][419]

A day ever memorable. The Times gives a letter from L[or]d Cowdray[420] today, in which he resigns from the Air Ministry and tells L[loyd] G[eorge] that he ought not to have learnt from Lord Northcliffe's refusal of the Air Ministry the day before (incidentally in terms contumelious and insulting to the P[rime] M[inister]) that it was contemplated to make a change in the Ministry. I understand Northcliffe betrayed a private conversation with L[loyd] G[eorge]. Which is worse[,] Northcliffe or L[loyd] G[eorge] [?]

I turn with disgust to a better level and a greater man – for today was my first meeting with Venizelos. It was at a reception at the Grafton Galleries.[421] He came into the room, slowly, mildly – a small figure, grey beard pointed, white hair, somewhat bold, big spectacles, a beautifully rounded and balanced head, and kind smile – no dignity, no assumption, just the most benevolent and charming of smiles. A great camera was aimed at him as he came down the steps into the room, and he stood simply without affectation in the flash light. Then he passed over to the centre of the hall, while the Greek community shouted Zeto Velizelos![422] G. Marchetti the chairman of the Greek community spoke first – then Venizelos rose. He spoke of the past visit to London – amid thunderous cheers – 'Those were times of pride for Greece', and then his voice broke – his words were dragged out slowly, with painful pauses, and then he suddenly broke down. The contrast of the warmth of the reception, the rush of emotion at <the thought of> the days when he doubled the territory and people of Greece, overwhelmed him and he burst into tears <– some of the audience were in tears

---

[419] On loosely inserted separate sheet. The year may be deduced from the letter, dated 14 Nov. 1917, on the obverse.
[420] Sir Weetman Dickinson Pearson, Bt. (1856–1927), Lord Cowdray, cr. 1910, 1st Viscount Cowdray, cr. 1917, engineer, oil producer, and politician; built up the Pearson construction and engineering conglomerate; MP (Lib.) Colchester, 1895–1910; President of the Air Board, Jan.–Nov. 1917.
[421] Gallery in Bond Street.
[422] *Recte 'Zeto o Venizelos'* ('Long live Venizelos').

too>. He sat down and an old Greek priest with a noble beard took up the word <to denounce>. After an interval he again arose, with the same kind smile, and spoke once more. The first time in a long life that he had broken down, he said, in a public speech. But the moment was such, and the comparison of Greece then and now was such. The misery of Greece was due to one man, and Greece was doomed if that policy were pursued. Greece at the end of the war was doomed if Germany won or Bulgaria remained predominant. It was their duty to save the nation and their task though hard ...[423] the nation. Then he ended amid their cheers of applause. The words were beautiful and the gestures dignified – quick as a flash and wonderful – but most wonderful of all were the tears of Venizelos.

Afterwards he spoke to me, beaming with that wonderful benignant smile – spoke of my book which he had begun to read, of my work etc. All that came from him seemed true, and his manner had indefinable charm, irresistible. I have met some great orators – L[loyd] G[eorge], Apponyi,[424] Andrassy,[425] Roosevelt,[426] Pashitch – none of them has the feeling Venizelos gave you, the feeling of goodness and sincerity. Yet this man carried a rifle in a cave, and dethroned a king. He is now trying to raise a nation from the dead.>

23rd [November 1917]

Back from Winchester to War Office. The first problem set at conference with Cox,[427] Sheppard, Cholerton, Webster, was why did Ludendorff not pursue his offensive in Italy. The facts are that 6 German divisions were assigned to defend

---

[423] Document damaged, words missing.

[424] Count Albert Apponyi de Nagyappony (1846–1933), Hungarian politician; Member of the Hungarian Diet, 1872–1918; Minister of Religion and Education, 1906–10; led Hungarian delegation at Paris peace conference, 1920 (Treaty of Trianon); five times nominated for the Nobel Peace Prize, 1911–32. Temperley, in fact, met Albert's brother, Alexander, 'A Grand Seigneur', 23 Mar. 1909, Temperley MSS.

[425] Count Gyula (Julius) Andrássy de Csíkszentkirály et Krasznahorka the Younger (1860–1929), Hungarian politician; Minister of Education, 1893–94; Minister *ad latere*, 1894–95; Minister of the Interior, 1906–1909; Austro-Hungarian Foreign Minister, 1918; attempted to restore the monarchy in Hungary, 1921, and subsequently imprisoned. Through Andrássy Temperley obtained the services of Josef Redlich as translator of Henrik Marczali's *Hungary in the Eighteenth Century* (Cambridge, 1910), see Redlich to Temperley, 31 Aug. 1910, Temperley MSS.

[426] Theodore Roosevelt (1858–1919), US politician; Governor (Rep.) of New York, 1898–1900; Vice-President, 1901; 26th President, 1901–1909. Temperley met Roosevelt twice in the winter of 1911/12, see Temperley diary, 12. Dec. 1911 and 16 Jan. 1912.

[427] Brigadier-General Edgar William Cox (1882–1918), intelligence officer; joined army, 1900; General Staff officer, 1912–14; active military service Western Front, 1914–16; staff officer to Director of Military Intelligence, 1916–18; head of Military Intelligence Department in France, 1918; suspected suicide.

Trieste. Then in September they knew Cadorna was not coming on any farther. So they changed their tactics, and took the offensive, broke through, by one of the finest strokes of military leadership in the war, and pushed on relentlessly. Why then did Ludendorff not send reinforcements? Only one division has appeared since in the Tyrol and that was probably there already. What is the reason? No one contributed much to that solution.

The most ingenious suggestion was that of Cox, that Germany would not wish Italy out of the war because this would release about a million tons of shipping ~~and possibly also force us to leave Salonica~~. The submarine campaign therefore would then be finally abandoned.

Of course, the Austrian question may be another solution. The Emperor Charles vetoed it, but could he?

Later. I understand that [Alan] Percy, Panouse and C[hief of the] I[mperial] G[eneral] S[taff, Robertson] do not accept this view, and think that the Germans simply did not come on <or reinforce> because they couldn't.

24th [November 1917]

King Alex[ande]r is young and lonely, surrounded by an entourage of old men and pained by attacks on Tino and himself and kingship. Granville to whom he confided his woes, assured him the republicanism was common in Hyde Park and no one attended much to it. Granville deprecates the reprisals on the Gounarists, but Politis has pointed to him that Venizelos is fighting not only his enemies but his own supporters, who accuse him of leniency. The King admitted that he trusted Venizelos.

The Italian Minister Bosdari[428] has complained on the authority of the King, that he (the K[ing]) does not see all official telegrams. At some risk from the unfriendly entourage of the King, Politis and Venizelos had arranged some time ago that he should see them all. Granville tackled the K[ing] on this, who seemed a little uncomfortable when questioned and entered [*sic*] by admitting that he did not see all telegrams.

An attack was made on the King for visiting a regiment and making a speech to the officers. This was the ZIZOSPATHIO, an extreme Socialist organ. Granville expressed his disgust to Politis who promised to prosecute. In general Granville thinks that the K[ing], though given somewhat to brooding over his wrongs, is inclined to play the game and disinclined to surrender his crown to Tino or anyone else.

---

[428] See entry 11 June 1917.

25th [November 1917]

Russia and recognition.

26th [November 1917]

Roumania and Ukraine & France.

The Roumanian situation is more desperate than ever – on the 18th the French counselled retirement on the Pruth.[429] But M[ilitary] A[ttaché] dissented on the ground that it is an indefensible line. Also he believes that it is quite impossible to expect the Ukraine to continue the fight on the grounds of a study of Ukrainian newspapers and leaders, who all long for a separate peace.

The French have sent a reply clear and firm – like that steel which is the mind of France – whatever happens there must be no question of dissolving or disarming the Roumanian army which has been reorganized with such difficulty. Also, France will not recognize or discuss terms with any Russian government that talks of negotiating with the enemy.

Personally I think we still have a chance in South Russia. Kaledin[430] and his Cossacks hold the Don region, and the Ukraine as a whole comprises the best Black Earth Zone, the coal & iron and the guardianship over the oil of Russia. They can be supplied, in all probability, from Vladivostok by railways under American control. In any case there should be no shilly shally. It is not a case of backing a bad horse as of backing the only one we have got.

27th [November 1917]

I understand that Milner has been agitating for a separate peace with Turkey during the last week. It may be longsighted – for us to open the Dardanelles would be to save South Russia and Roumania.

France has, meanwhile, been somewhat rebuffed by our refusal to <agree not to treat with Russia if she> negotiates with the enemy.

---

[429] Russo-Romanian forces continued to resist the German advance at the Oitoz Pass and along the Trotus valley until the armistice of 10 Dec. 1917.

[430] Aleksei Maksimovich Kaledin (1861–1918), Russian cavalry officer; Assistant Chief of Staff, Don Army, 1906–10; commander of 8th Army, 1916–17; dismissed by Provisional Government; *Ataman* of Don Cossacks and head of Cossack Army Government, 1917–18; led *Kaledinschina* rebellion in the Don region; resigned his post and committed suicide after the loss of Rostov, Jan. 1918.

28th [November 1917]

I am afraid Roumania will go. The King asked us, without the knowledge of his ministers, what he should do if he negotiated with Germany, and promised not to do so without telling us first. Since then, building on a kindly message from King George, he has asked us at least to guarantee him his pre-war territories (thereby not even asking for the fulfilment of our pledged word as regards Transylvania and Bukovina).[431]

We have returned a non-committal answer, declining the pledge in substance. Of course, what we should do is to give a pledge to grant them this or its equivalent elsewhere. It seems absolute madness to refuse to give a guarantee on these lines – the only hope to a <country> bravely struggling against despair. Balfour should go for this, and will, I think. It is at any rate quite contrary to the policy of L[loyd] G[eorge], who, after my little hint re Roumania, has fully made amends for his misdemeanours in neglecting Roumania, and is now fully aware of its importance.[432] F[oreign] O[ffice] is counter-working L[loyd] G[eorge].

29th [November 1917]

Lansdowne's letter[433] – a bombshell, though really it is, in all probability, simply his old peace manifesto circulated to the Cabinet at the end of 1916,[434] just before he was kicked out of it on that account. It is ably written and much of it to the point but where it give us a blow in the face is in the statement that all we have fought for is already won, and that nothing justifies the continuance of slaughter and destruction of wealth now going on. That spirit is fatal. The only true spirit is victory first, which, once secured, secures everything else.

(Note. Later on the 14th Dec[embe]r [1917] Kerry,[435] Lansdowne's son, announced that Lansdowne agreed with Wilson (v[ide] 14th Dec[embe]r) and did not think the war had gone on long enough, but that our aims should be defined.)

---

[431] That is, under the Treaty of Bucharest of 17 Aug. 1916, see entry 21 Oct. 1916.

[432] See entry 8 Aug. 1917.

[433] *Daily Telegraph*, 29 Nov. 1917, in which he called for an Allied statement on aims for a post-war settlement.

[434] Memo. Lansdowne, 'The War Situation', 27 Nov. 1916, CAB 37/160/21.

[435] Lieutenant-Colonel Henry William Edmund Petty-Fitzmaurice, Earl of Kerry (1872–1936), 6th Marquess of Lansdowne, succ. 1927, officer and politician; Guards officer; active service, Second Boer War, 1899–1900, and First World War; MP (Lib. Un.) West Derbyshire, 1908–18; member of the Senate of the Irish Free State, 1922–29.

30th [November 1917]

Burrows and [word missing] built up from his and other accounts a view of the present ideas and policy of Venizelos. He was well received by the whole War Cabinet but on his departure last Monday found at the last moment that all these five promises had not materialised in specific proposals from the CIR. He was very angry about this and declared he would speak to L[loyd] G[eorge] and Balfour in the train and, unless he could get satisfaction, would not join the Conference – so I suppose he has got satisfaction.

His views were somewhat as follows:

<u>Food</u> This was the first and prime necessity for Greece and, as the Allies were using some 200 Greek ships, to Greece having the use of 11, it seemed obvious that she had a strong claim. 26,000 tons a month approximately represent Greek requirements and these should be provided at once.

<u>Guns & equipment</u> also should be provided quickly but these are less important.

<u>Propaganda</u> – of a British sort could and should be pushed with vigour in Greece. It would have an excellent effect on both countries in speeding up mobilization and improving relations.

<u>Entente, relations with</u>. Apart from this, he has preserved a studious and complete silence as to French affairs, especially Sarrail. This is probably significant.

<u>Balkan policy</u>. His scheme is a Balkan bloc. Roumania, Serbia and Greece to act together as a Federation to push one another's policies at conferences etc. and generally to form a union solidaire for the war, and subsequently for the peace on terms of complete equality. He does not wish to exclude Bulgaria from this bloc, in fact he desires to include her but it must be upon terms of complete equality, i.e. Bulgaria must not be the Prussia of a Balkan Federation, but only one of four equal states.

The means by which he expects to realize this aim are the policy of a separate peace with Turkey, which he believes could be got on easy terms, and would be of the greatest assistance to the Entente. He believes that the influence of Djemal[436]

---

[436] Ahmet Cemal Pasha (1872–1922), Young Turk leader; Governor of Baghdad, 1913–14; Navy Minister, 1913–14; member of the 'Three Pashas' military dictatorship, 1913–18; Military Governor of Syria, 1915–17; exile in Switzerland since 1918.

& Talaat[437] could be used against Enver[438] to compel the C[ommittee of] U[nion and] P[rogress][439] to back down.

As regards E[astern] Macedonia and the Cavalla area, he thinks this can only be given up by Greece, if she receives compensation in Asia Minor. After the war she will have to receive and deal with Greek refugees from Asia Minor, who can hardly number less than 1½ millions. This will not be the case, if Greece receives compensation in Asia Minor. But of this he now seems not to entertain the highest hope. Hence Cavalla must remain <Greek> to take part of this surplus population.

He was very angry at an anonymous and moderate pro-Bulgar article in the Quarterly [Review] 'It looks as if I am the traitor not Constantine' and he regarded it as a special insult that it was anonymous and published during his visit to England.

Buxton[440] called upon him and was well received.

1st Dec[embe]r [1917]

Spoke with Weizmann on the triumph of Zionism. A man with beautiful brown eyes, and a fine head, who has brought about the new Jerusalem, a practical fanatic. How practical, how fanatical, his words told me! 'The state of Jews under Turkey is dreadful. I have 3 relatives there, a sister, a brother, but that cannot be helped – the cause is won, though there is much to do!' A spirit as of Jepthah[441] [*sic*]. In telling of the Antizionists [such] as Montagu etc. and how they were defeated, he alternated between sheer joy and delight at his subterranean methods. [']I found no opposition from Englishmen – only ignorance and disregard of the importance of things. When we had tunnelled for two years, we suddenly came to the surface and the Anti-Zionists were amazed. Their opposition had to be met. Should we attack frontally or outflank? I chose the latter, and it came off. Incidentally I can prove that the Anti-Zionist argument that the Zionists were pro-German is untrue. Early in 1914 there was a meeting

---

[437] Mehmet Talaat Pasha (1874–1921), Young Turk leader; Minister of the Interior, 1913–17; Grand Vizier, 1917–18; exile in Germany since 1918; assassinated at Stockholm, 15 Mar. 1922.

[438] Ismail Enver Pasha (1881–1922), Ottoman officer and Young Turk leader; Young Turk leader in Salonica, 1908; Military Attaché at Berlin, 1909–11; commander Turkish forces Tripolitania, 1911–12; War Minister, 1913–18; exile since 1918; killed in fighting in Turkestan, Aug. 1922.

[439] *İttihat ve Terakki Cemiyeti*, founded in 1906 as an umbrella organization for underground reformist groups in the Ottoman Empire.

[440] See entry 22 May 1917.

[441] Jephthah, Biblical figure, judge in ancient Israel; said to have sacrificed his daughter, though this is subject to debate, *Judges* 10–12.

in Berlin of Jews (both Zionist and anti-Zionist) to discuss the question of Haifa <school> institute – whether German or ~~Yiddish~~ Hebrew should be taught there. The German Government tried to use pressure, and sent word to the meeting that Zimmermann was waiting for an answer. ~~I got~~ To my mind it was wholly a Jewish matter. I got up and said so 'What has Zimmermann got to do with the matter?' and we voted that Hebrew not German should be taught. Who voted for German? Our own English anti-Zionists.[']

3rd [December 1917]

Bolsheviks, Buchanan's view. He thinks that Russia is morally and materially exhausted that to hold Bolsheviks or any government to the obligations of the Czar is preposterous. He thinks peace is essential to them and that the only thing we can secure is that German economic penetration shall not take place after the war, if indeed we can secure that.

He concludes by serious digs at the F[oreign] O[ffice], that they would do anything for propaganda on the Russian front, and never would discuss war-aims at a conference with new Russia.

5th [December 1917]

Lunch with David Davies, Lord Derby,[442] Maurice, Macdonough [sic] and many distinguished soldiers in the House of Commons to entertain the <officers of the> 1st Serb volunteer division from Odessa.

Speeches. Derby, straightforward and honest, a little blundering when he said 'Serbia must be restored to precisely what she had before the war'. In translating <into Serb for> the Serb-Croats Capt[ain] Jovanovich, the Assist[ant] Military Attaché, added – 'and those people, who wish it, shall be united to her'. Derby, at my instigation, subsequently wrote a letter to the Minister Jovanovitch[443] to explain that this translation of which he had been informed, inaccurate, and that, whatever might be his personal sympathies, he could not pledge the government. He also informed the F[oreign] O[ffice] <of the incident>, an honest, manly speech and letter.

---

[442] Edward George Villiers Stanley (1865–1948), 17th Earl of Derby, succ. 1908, politician and diplomat; MP (Cons.) South East Lancashire, 1892–1906; Financial Secretary to the War Office, 1900–1903; Postmaster-General, 1903–1905; Under-secretary of State for War, July–Dec. 1916; Secretary of State for War, 1916–18, and 1922–24; ambassador at Paris, 1918–20.

[443] See entry 6 Jan. 1917.

Jovanovich's addition was doubtless thought by him palatable to the Serbo-Croat officers. But this, though an indiscretion, was no greater than Derby's, which appeared memorably to pledge Macedonia to the Serbs, and thus cut out all idea of a separate peace with Bulgaria. Both were indiscretions. Derby's verbal, Jovanovitch's moral. Derby must have had the sanction of the F[oreign] O[ffice] I think, in which case Macedonia is to be Serbian and a Bulgarian separate peace out of the question. If so, Venizelos has triumphed.

6th [December 1917]

Capt[ain] Jovanovitch met me today and said he had just had an explanation with Lord Derby. Some persons, who thought that they knew Serbian, had said that he (J[ovanović]) did not exactly reproduce D[erby]'s speech. He had found it hard to translate, though he had taken it down by stenographer. He had apologised for the error D[erby] had pointed out.

All amusing and ironic to me. He did not know I was the culprit, nor that I knew the addition he had made.

7th [December 1917]

Roumania's day – alas in more ways than one. The Anglo-Roumanian Society was inaugurated with a speech by Carson and old General Georgescu comes round almost in tears to tell me that Roumania has had to follow the example of the Russian armies on her front and join in an armistice[444] – poor Roumania, what else can she do? What will become of her? How long shall I wear my Roumanian order?[445] I like to think that I did a little to earn it, by putting up Masterson's report. If its conclusions had been then adopted and pressed, Roumania would now be incomparably better armed, munitioned and supplied. Simply the zest for dolce far niente for doing nothing until it was too late, overwhelmed both F[oreign] O[ffice] & W[ar] O[ffice] in this as in so many other matters. I say, perhaps not in all humility, that if my advice re the Serb divisions at Odessa had been followed, there would not be 5,000 left behind at Galatz today and that, if my advice as to Roumania had been followed, it would not be surrendering today, because the army could then have fallen back on Bessarabia and Odessa.

---

[444] The armistice came into effect on 10 Dec. 1917.
[445] See entry 22 May 1917.

Incidentally also I learn today from the Manchester Guardian of the 28th Nov[embe]r the evidence of Polivanoff,[446] the Russian War Minister, that Roumania's downfall in November 1916 was not necessarily a disaster because it gave Russia the opportunity of putting her under obligations and keeping control over her.[447] As she was aspiring to a population of 13 millions and the headship of the Balkans, this was important to Russia. Thus the old story would seem to be true, though not in the old shape. <The> Russian Government was not pro-German but it was anti-Roumanian.

10th [December 1917]

The case ag[ain]st the F[oreign] O[ffice].

11th [December 1917]

There is a revival of hope – Roumania which seemed so gloomy has bucked up a little. Bratianu's interview with the Allied Ministers on the 8th was of the gloomiest description. The Allied Ministers had been wiring for credits etc. for weeks, with no reply from the F[oreign] O[ffice]. They offered Bratianu unlimited bank credits now (which the F[oreign] O[ffice] should have ordered them to do months ago) when it was too late. No supply depots had been prepared in Bessarabia and evacuation was difficult if not impossible. Berthelot himself in a wire of the 8th regards resistance as plainly impossible and says a capitulation or peace is the only chance, and the only hope lies in getting a peace.

12th [December 1917]

The latest Russian negotiations do small honour to the F[oreign] O[ffice]. Trotsky[448] demanded the release of various Russians in England interned for peace propaganda. We replied that, under the circumstances, it could not even be discussed. Then the War Cabinet intervened, threw over Balfour and released the men in question.

---

[446] See entry 21 Aug. 1916.

[447] 'The Russian Agreements', *Manchester Guardian*, 28 Nov. 1917.

[448] Leon Trotsky (née Lev Davidovich Bronstein) (1879–1940), Russian revolutionary; President of Petrograd Soviet, 1917; People's Commissar for Foreign Affairs, 1917–18; for War, 1919–25; exiled to Siberia, 1927; expelled from Soviet Union, 1929; sentenced to death *in absentia*, 1937; assassinated, 1940.

14th [December 1917]

Wrote a long essay analysing the Peace Terms for the D[irector of] S[pecial] I[ntelligence, Cockerill]. So far as they are public, the French & Italian terms were purely Chauvinistic, with a little about freeing nationalities thrown in, the British ampler and perhaps more genuine, tho[ugh] we say nothing of the colonies, and L[loyd] G[eorge] has said Armenia & Mesopotamia, and Balfour has said Jerusalem will never return to the Turk. Nothing in L[loyd] G[eorge] about the League of Nations except the reference to the effect the democratization of Germany might have on a peace. The only Britisher who has treated it is one who is a Boer, Smuts. He seems to approve but to think it difficult (v[ide] Oct[obe]r 9th).

Germany and Austria have done lipservice to the limitation of armaments and to the principle of compulsory arbitration.

Trotsky has published a <batch of> secret treaties,[449] which reveals England, France and Italy as planning great territorial concessions in Syria and Asia Minor, as handing half of Slav Dalmatia to Italy, and nearly half Magyar Hungary to Roumania, thus violating the nationalistic principle. Russia & France agreed on Alsace-Lorraine going to France, and a neutral state being erected west of the Rhine, thus proclaiming imperialistic ideals. All agreed on Constantinople going to Russia.

Our secret diplomacy is bad, and the public assertions of the Central Powers seem good. I say the 'League of Nations' must be brought forward to convince the working man of the need of a concrete end to the war, of a lasting peace. Victory not as an end but as a means. This is the line and the utterance of Wilson, backed by the tremendous power of the American nation and the stupendous threat of an economic boycott.

15th [December 1917]

L[loyd] G[eorge]'s speech very noble.[450]

---

[449] As People's Commissar for Foreign Affairs, Trotsky began publishing diplomatic documents from the Tsarist archives in the Bolshevik organ *Pravda* on 23 Nov. 1917, starting with the Sykes-Picot; the article was reprinted in 'Russia and the Secret Treaties', *Manchester Guardian*, 26 Nov. 1917.

[450] Lloyd George speech at Gray's Inn, 14 Dec. 1917, see 'Victory or Defeat. "No Half-Way House"', *The Times*, 15 Dec. 1917.

16th [December 1917]

D[irector of] S[pecial] I[ntelligence, Cockerill]'s economic threat.

17th [December 1917]

18th [December 1917]

<The 5,000> JugoSlavs <left behind at Galatz⁴⁵¹> are now to be transported to Vladivostock [*sic*] and thence ferried round to Salonica. So just because my warning and recommendation to the W[ar] O[ffice] was disregarded till too late an immense amount of transport will be used and expenses incurred, which was almost wholly avoidable.

In the same way recently the warnings I made about Roumania have been forgotten were disregarded. Bratianu pointedly told the Allied Ministers that their present financial offer of unlimited credit could have been negotiated at the banks five months ago when he asked for strictly limited credit, whilst now it was impossible.

19th [December 1917]

Telegram today Cossacks disorganized and useless, i.e. the Donetz area.

The Ukraine shows some signs of fight and there is a telegram today that, while we can give no other, we can at least give financial assistance. If so we can put the Ukraine rouble at a value higher than the Bolshevik one and thus help to do down the latter.

All is very uncertain but it seems to me that the transport round Petrograd will be very disorganized whereas that via Samarra⁴⁵² is not.

20th [December 1917]

Ukraine policy.
Sarrail to go.

---

[451] Now Galați (Romania).
[452] Sāmarrā on the Tigris, north of Baghdad.

21st [December 1917]

Asquith spoke straightly to a friend of mine ~~yesterday~~ the other day just before his great speech at Birmingham.[453] Apparently he does not himself believe that we shall get a decision on the west, nor does he think that the audiences, to whom he speaks, count at all. What he does really think is that his speeches count with Germany to whom they were addressed.

On the Lloyd George question A[squith] preserved an impenetrable silence. Mrs Asquith[454] did not and said he [Asquith] had been shamefully treated. She also said she had asked Morley when, in his recently published reminiscences, he said nothing of L[loyd] G[eorge]. 'That's what I think of him', said the literary sage. His omission evidently an ars celare artem.[455]

22nd [December 1917]

Telegram in response to Trotsky's proclamation of a general peace on the lines of national self-determination[456] was sent by Barclay. He said that it had greatly excited feeling in Roumania with regard to the redemption of Bessarabia. Our F[oreign] O[ffice] answered 19th [December], that we should not object to negotiating with Germany on such a basis, if she would add to the category of national self-determination Belgium, Serbia, Alsace-Lorraine, Bohemia, Poland. If this is what they believe why in hell's name do they not proclaim it to the world as a counterblast to the bad effect produced by the disclosure of the secret treaties? In any case advice to the Bolsheviks cannot but be known soon. When shall we realize, as Canning did, the strength of publicity in diplomacy [?][457]

23rd [December 1917]

I should not be human if I was not proud today having had a hand in the message <to be> sent by Allenby to the American troops from Bethlehem on Christmas Eve. It was suggested by me that besides peace and goodwill they should say something as to 'force having its law and law its force'. Finally the D[irector

---

[453] Asquith speech at Birmingham Town Hall, 11 Dec. 1917, see 'A Clean Peace. Mr. Asquith on War Aims', *The Times*, 12 Dec. 1917.

[454] Margot Asquith (née Emma Alice Margaret Tennant) (1864–1945), Countess of Oxford and Asquith, an Anglo-Scottish socialite; married Herbert Henry Asquith, 1894.

[455] 'Art to conceal art'; see also J. Morley, *Recollections* (2 vols, London, 1917), which do not mention Lloyd George.

[456] The offer was made on 28 Nov.

[457] See Temperley, *Canning*, 272–3.

of] S[pecial] I[ntelligence, Cockerill] settled that 'force should not rule law, but law force'. It might make any man proud to have had a hand in a message from Bethlehem.

26th [December 1917]

Behold the Bethlehem message.[458] I cannot restrain my joy [–] not only is the message from the manger of Bethlehem published but the 'Times' sees a new and intensely interesting note 'that contains at once the whole creed of the Alliance

---

[458] Inserted clipping from *The Times*, 26 Dec. 1917:
'From General Allenby to General Pershing.
General Sir Edmund Allenby sent the following telegram to General Pershing, the commander of the American troops in France:–
"The British troops in Bethlehem on Christmas Eve send to their American comrades a message of greeting and of hope that, through the achievement of their common purpose, the law of force may yield to the force of law, and peace and good will reign at length on earth"'.
'There is no such boasting in the Allied peoples, but there is no sign of weakening purpose. On the contrary, there is every sign of new determination and closer accord. Nothing could contrast more completely with the Kaiser's impious boasting than the various messages we publish this morning from the King to his soldiers and sailors and from the British Generals to their troops. All breathe alike the same spirit of gratitude and quiet confidence, and there will be heard among them one new and intensely interesting note in the greeting dispatched to their "American comrades" by the British forces which lay at Bethlehem on Christmas Eve. General Allenby's hope is that "through the achievement of their common purpose the law of force may yield to the force of law and peace and good will reign at length on earth". That message contains at once the whole creed of the Alliance and the secret of achieving it. To those who can survey steadily the events of the last few weeks, with all the disappointments that bulk so large at the end of the year, the greatest event of all has been the practical drawing together of the Western Powers, including that great Republic whose forces are thus for the first time welcomed as comrades in the field. There is no divergence between any of us about our main objects in fighting or about our will to achieve them. President Wilson, Mr. Asquith, Mr. Lloyd George, M. Clemenceau, Signor Orlando – one after the other, in almost identical terms, they have pointed the fundamental difference between a peace negotiated on the basis of German conquests and that permanent democratic peace which involves the destruction of "militarism". Such confused counsels as have sometimes been heard elsewhere are instantly detected, exposed, and abandoned under the pressure of popular opinion. The ideal of the League of Nations grows, but it is recognized everywhere now as the consummation of an Allied victory, not as a subject for bargaining with "the iron fist and shining sword" of Germany'. (Emphasis by Temperley.)

and the secret of achieving it'. Curious that I should be responsible for this and have laid <it> down three years ago in my book on Kaiser Joseph.[459]

For this new note and L[loyd] G[eorge]'s speech on Serbia I may claim to be a source of inspiration.

27th [December 1917]

Most important memorandum of Milner and Robert Cecil on the Ukraine dated 23rd Dec[embe]r and accepted by Clemenceau and Pichon.[460] It proposes to supersede Buchanan on grounds of ill-health and accord unofficial recognition to the Bolsheviks. This is the British policy but they do not necessarily wish their Allies to follow it. Buchanan is too identified with the old regime, Cadets etc. The Bolsheviks are to be informed that we do not favour or desire a counter-revolution but that we must befriend the Ukraine. We are bound by honour to Roumania, and the Ukraine, Caucasus and Armenia must be supported to deal with the Pan-Turanian[461] increase from Turkey.

Officers and agents must be sent to these places to organize and propagandise. The French should take the Ukraine sphere and we the rest.

We are to support the self-determination of nationalities and allow the Poles, Transylvanians etc., Bohemians etc. full play. We recommend the Bolsheviks to insist on these as specific demands in their negotiation with Germany.

We despair of saving the personnel of the Russian army but measures must be taken to prevent guns or South Russian wheat getting to the enemy.

28th [December 1917]

Jellicoe fell yesterday – a friend of 25 years tells me he was very nice, but very conservative and never thought 'a flier'. He was opposed to the Naval War Staff throughout and, being opposed, must go, now that Geddes is in charge. I heard also that things were not well from old Joe Rickman.

I attended D[irector of] M[ilitary] O[perations, Maurice]'s lecture to journalists. His explanation of the campaigns in the East was that they aimed not at land-grabbing but at the defence of Egypt primarily – this was the use of the advance to Jerusalem, while the seizure of Baghdad was to keep the German

---

[459] H.W.V. Temperley, *Frederic the Great and : An Episode of War and Diplomacy in the Eighteenth Century* (London, 1915), 7 and 205–12.

[460] Stéphen Pichon (1857–1933), French diplomat and politician; French minister at Peking, 1897–1900; Foreign Minister, 1906–11, 1913 and 1917–20.

[461] Pan-Turanism, a racialist, political movement propounding the union of all Turkic and 'Turanian' peoples, in its more extreme versions including Magyars and Finns.

agents who had reached Cabul from pouring into India. He is right the soldiers do not wish to be imperialistic and go to Aleppo – Lloyd George does.

29th [December 1917]

Chaos indescribable in Russia. In one case the commander of a regiment has been made a cook and the cook colonel, in another the transport man is the colonel – the Chief of Staff of one division is a private. He declined to sign a pile of documents on the ground that he reserved his signature for the greatest secrets. The secret that transpired was that he could not write. Since the armistice 50% of the troops have gone home.

If peace is not made there will be nothing to prevent the Germans from advancing a few miles and seizing all the guns.

The economic chaos in Russia has struck even the German delegates there with such amazement that they think no single nation however great could restore it and believe that England, France <and> the USA will have ultimately to cooperate with Germany. It is good at least that Germany sees one of the difficulties of her economic policy.

30th [December 1917]

The separate peace with Turkey idea has definitely collapsed. I understand L[loyd] G[eorge] broached it to Clemenceau and Sonnino opposed. I do not know what brought it down, but I fancy it was fear of the Pan-Turanian movement. Talaat's terms as suggested to Pilling[462] were

(1.) recognition of King of the Hejaz
(2.) -"- Jewish Nat[iona]l State
(3.) Autonomy of Bagdad and Armenia
(4.) Ottoman debt to be taken over by us
(5.) Internationalisation of the Straits.

I believe it to have been a profound mistake to refuse because Venizelos advocated it, to some extent against his own interests but immensely in Entente interests.

---

[462] John Robert Pilling (b. 1849), Lancashire businessman and financier with Near Eastern financial and railway interests, *inter alia* the Bank of Syria and the Syrian Ottoman Railway Company. In 1902, he was declared bankrupt.

Meanwhile Turkey having failed, Bulgaria and Austria remain. There is serious business with both. Smuts is in Switzerland to deal with Austria,[463] a characteristic stroke of L[loyd] G[eorge]. He proposed that pourparlers should be held with Austria – Clemenceau hesitated, Sonnino opposed strongly, but L[loyd] G[eorge] finally won. Then, instead of a small F[oreign] O[ffice] going, to the amazement of Clemenceau and Sonnino, a full-fledged War Cabinet minister went. I believe it a mistake for his visit cannot be concealed for long, and he is, I believe, too ignorant of foreign policy to make a great coup, though a straight and masterful and masterly man. Incidentally, there was a real stroke of humour in the Press, where a story was published to disguise from the public his absence from London. He was represented as going to Castle Cary for the New Year, and as having walked 15 miles to save petrol. A good ruse de guerre and perhaps legitimate enough.

As for Bulgaria, her agent is one Shipkoff, who comes forward with Fitzmaurice's old idea that the Bulgars do not wish to harm us and would allow us to evacuate Salonica. Bulgaria would be satisfied with Macedonia and the Dobruja.

31st [December 1917]

As one turns the old year one moralizes – what have we? Some vigour in France[:] Clemenceau has recalled Sarrail and the French Admiral in the Mediterranean, and tackled Caillaux,[464] denounced secret diplomacy and the League of Nations together. Unfortunately, France is deeply discredited by the Bolo-Caillaux scandals and by the revelation of the secret treaty with Russia by which she wished to dismember Germany by erecting a neutral state on the banks of the Rhine. Italy is crushed and war-weary. Russia still tossing on fiery waves of revolution, which seem to be consuming her. Roumania is wasting away, Serbia and Greece are shadows, Montenegro a shadow of a shade. Grim cloudy shapes of nations arising for the first time in Armenia, the Ukraine, Zion, Arabia, fraught with what destinies for the world, perhaps balloons blown up by airy imaginations. Grim realities are an iron still <u>apparently</u> invincible Germany, stronger than ever because freed of the Russian menace, Bulgaria still upright and unbroken, Turkey tottering and Austria strained and suffering. Some hope of failure of the last two, none of the first two. The Entente seems no nearer victory. German rates of exchanges on neutrals have wonderfully recovered and are as high as in January 1917 – no apparent prospect of an offensive likely to

---

[463] Smuts met Count Mensdorff, the former ambassador to Britain, at Geneva, 28–29 Dec. 1917.
[464] See entry 22 Feb. 1917.

be decisive anywhere except against the Turks. In England itself moral is not so high as it might be though not yet low. We still suffer from [the] refusal to view the League of Nations and victory as Siamese twins, that is the great appeal to democracy and the true programme.

Materially things are not good – the casualties on the Western front are approximately French 790,000, British 750,000, German 1,720,000 or higher. We have all the ridges from Champagne to the Passchendaele, which formed the German lines, but we have only had months to dig in and reconstruct, while they have had years. The Germans have brought over 11 divisions from Russia, and the stream is continuing. We shall not have our lines broken, but we shall be sternly pressed. One good thing, the Americans are soon to join up with us, to be between us and the French, thus Anglo-Saxondom will form a continuous line and, even in the case of French defeat or consent to peace, Anglo-Saxondom will not surrender but defend the bridgehead of Calais and, whatever happens, Anglo-Saxondom will war on to victory.

The shipping question is bad[,] approximately 2½ million tons are gone, and only something over 1 million has replaced it. The Americans and Italians make heavier demands than ever on our shipping, and the Salonica expedition demands its toll. Probably with severe economy and American aid, we can pull through, but the fit will be tight. The Americans made a big blunder and lost 3 precious months by trying to build wooden ships. Still the Alliance is now a real thing – we have pooled ships, finance, food, and honour. We shall win of course but the cost is a ghastly one and the end very far off. I see it in 1918, I think.

1918

2nd January 1918

It cannot be said the New Year is opening well. Turkey, and the hope of a separate peace with her, are apparently gone, Russia is negotiating with the enemy, we coquet with Bulgaria, and back up the Ukraine à l'outrance against the Bolsheviks.

At the same time we still are shy about defining our war aims. Gen[eral] Cockerill, in conjunction with me, drew up a statement of war aims which was of high interest and will be worked up into pamphlets and circulated through the army.

The general lines are restitution, security by democracy and the League of Nations, and the principle of national self-determination. So ultimately the army should know in ten minutes lectures all about it. At present many of them seem not to have the faintest idea as to what they fight over.

Saw Trevelyan[1] today. He gives a gloomy but, I fear, true account of Italy. The gist is that, with the contadino, or peasant, the Risorgimento counts nothing, the defeat has been a great one and he sees simply wife and family as the end of the war. Rations for himself and allowances for them are the 2 chief, in fact the only reasons that can keep him in the war. The Italian peasants never counted in peace time[,] now they do. T[revelyan] thinks there is not a rat's chance of their holding on much longer, though he admits that there has been a rally. He says, in any case that the Italian cannot stand up to the German.

I told this view to Capt[ain] Ward,[2] the head of our intelligence in Italy, who hotly denied it on the strength of 30 years residence there. How much he had learnt by it I soon found. He contended that the contadino formed only 30% of the army. I found out by statistics that he formed at least 60% probably 70%. So much for the expert with a generation's experience.

---

[1] George Macaulay Trevelyan (1876–1962), historian; commanded the first British ambulance unit sent to Italy, 1915–18 (see his *Scenes from Italy's War* (London, 1919)); Regius Professor of Modern History, 1927–40; Master of Trinity College, Cambridge, 1940–51.

[2] Major Hon. (Sir) John Hubert Ward (1870–1938), soldier and courtier; active service South Africa, 1900–1901; Private Secretary to Financial Secretary to the War Office, 1901–1902; Equerry in Ordinary to Edward VII, 1902–10; to Queen Alexandra, 1910–26; General Staff Officer, 1915–19.

3[rd January 1918]

Trotsky

6th Jan[uar]y [1918]

Read Lloyd George's war-aims speech,[3] evidently carefully considered.

The D[irector of] S[pecial] I[ntelligence, Cockerill] sent in the war-aims to the F[oreign] O[ffice] 3 days ago, which he and I compiled. I have no doubt that L[loyd] G[eorge] made use of it, as some of his language has traces of it. He has 3 new points – (1.) <to press for> Roumania to extend to Transylvania, (2.) Italians to be confined to Italian districts, (3.) Syria to be severed from Turkey, Thrace to be Turkish (? Including Bulgar Thrace). He touched somewhat too lightly on the League of Nations, of which we made a special point, but he did touch on it.

He made it after consultation with the representatives of the Trades Unions, without the consent of the other Allies because there was not time to consult them, but as he believed in agreement with them.

7th [January 1918]

I hear Clemenceau is in despair about the negotiation with Austria. Leo Maxse met a friend of mine <D[uke] of Northumberland>[4] at lunch – tore his hair at L[loyd] G[eorge]'s speech, which he described as défaitisme, and went roaring off to Northcliffe. Certainly the speech was well-weighed and appealed to all, but it does not seem to be based on the theory of the 'knock-out blow'. It is half way between Empire, in the shape of Carson and Curzon, and Labour, in the shape of Thomas and Henderson.

8th [January 1918]

Weizmann.
Berthelot's new plan.

---

[3] Lloyd George speech to trades union conference, Westminster Central Hall, 5 Jan. 1918, see 'British War Aims. Mr. Lloyd George's Statement. Justice for Small Nations', *The Times*, 7 Jan. 1918.

[4] See entry 11 Apr. 1917.

9th [January 1918]

A friend of mine (D[irector of] S[pecial] I[ntelligence, Cockerill]) met Philip Kerr at lunch today and K[err] confirmed the défaitist[e] view of Lloyd George's speech. The difference between it and his previous speeches is that it goes back on the 'knock-out blow theory', i.e. in other words recognizes the Russian knockout (v[ide] 7th Jan[uary]). Another thing it does (but that is inevitable in the Austrian negotiations to be conciliated) is to go back on the Part of Corfu. The Jugo-Slavs are to be left to the tender mercies of Austria. How tender those are, I saw by an instance today. Oscar Jaszy,[5] the Hungarian publicist, has recently travelled in Serbia and comes back extolling the Austrian administration as ag[ain]st the 'almost pitiless Bulgarian rigour.' Yet on the 7th Dec[embe]r was published a decree in Belgrade which commanded all Serbs to surrender all arms by the 15th. Any man who did not would be shot without trial, hostages would be taken from each village and also shot without trial, and each village fined 10,000 kr[onen] in such case of arms being found anywhere there. One wonder if almost pitiless Bulgarian rigour would not be prefaced. I remember too that about a year ago the Austrian Government at Cettinje issued a proclamation to the General Vesović[6] then in hiding that, if he did not give himself up, that his brother and father, then in prison, would be executed. He did not give himself up, and the Austrian executed his brother and issued a proclamation, extolling their clemency in having executed the father (aged 74) as promised. The Austrian gentlemen! Yet it is with this Machiavellian power that we are now negotiating. Smuts and Philip Kerr went to Switzerland twice and have only just got back the second time. Steed[7] of the 'Times' went to Smuts to find out if he really had gone. Smuts lied like a trooper and talked so volubly of his walk in Somersetshire that he put Steed off the scent. However he went round to the F[oreign] O[ffice] to see Hardinge, who laughed and, laughing, disclosed the secret.

---

[5] Dr Oszkár Jászi (1875–1957), Hungarian social scientist and historian; civil servant in Hungarian Ministry of Agriculture, 1896–1906; published under the *nom de guerre* 'Oszkár Elemér'; co-editor of *Huszadik Század* (*Twentieth Century*); Assistant Professor of Sociology, University of Kolozsvár; co-founder of Országos Polgári Radikális Párt (National Civic Radical Party), 1914; advocate of League of Nations; Minister of Nationalities, Oct.–Dec. 1918; emigration, 1919; Professor of History, Oberlin College, Ohio, 1925–57.

[6] General Radomir Vešović (1871–1938), Montenegrin soldier; entered army, 1871; commanded Montenegrin army in 1912–13 and 1915–16; surrendered to Austria-Hungary, Jan. 1918; interned, 1918; retired, 1919.

[7] See entry 8 June 1917.

10th [January 1918]

The silence of L[loyd] G[eorge] and [Woodrow] Wilson over the JugoSlavs is having a very bad effect on the Serbian army, and explains why Derby disclaimed Jovanovich's addition to his speech, when he addressed the officers of the JugoSlav Division.[8] We are a strange race. Why delay indefinitely to bring the JugoSlavs from Russia? Why having done so <at great expense> take away any incentive they may have for fighting by abandoning their country to Austria?

Wilson spoke recently confidentially to Spring-Rice and Devonshire.[9] He is much pleased with L[loyd] G[eorge]'s speech and also much pleased with the reception of his own reference to 'righting the wrong' in Alsace and Lorraine. He thought it would be badly received and finds it (happy man!) universally applauded. He explains that he was always at heart in sympathy with the Allies but thought it sheer madness to plunge into the fray with a divided and distracted nation behind him, whereas by delaying till the time he did, he secured the support of the vast majority. He realized the importance of shipping and was devoting all the energies of his government to it. He showed excessive keenness on the freedom of the seas.

In conversation afterwards he admitted that he had read many German books and had always a great dislike of German institutions. He might have added (but did not) that he had written about English and American institutions and always shown a great desire (which he afterwards put into practice) to turn the latter into the former, so far as that was humanly possible.

11th [January 1918]

A curious and sinister plot has come across my notice. At the time of the Howell[10] incident, which produced the recal[l] of that officer from Salonica for pro-Bulgar proclivities, the secret was given away in a paper. Sylvia Pankhurst[11] in 'Britannia' published the letter, forced the crisis, and dismissed the General.[12] From where

---

[8] See entry 5 Dec. 1917.

[9] See entry 20 Aug. 1917.

[10] Brigadier-General Philip Howell (1877–1916), soldier; educated Lancing and Royal Military College, Sandhurst; entered army, 1897; General Staff Officer, War Office, 1909–11; Professor, Staff College, Camberley, 1913; *The Times* war correspondent, Balkan War, 1913 (*The Campaign in Thrace* (London, 1913)); resigned over Curragh incident, Mar. 1914, re-enlisted; first battle of Ypres, 1915; Chief of Staff, Salonica Army, 1915–16; killed in action at Thiepval on Somme, 7 Oct. 1916.

[11] Estelle Sylvia Pankhurst (1882–1960), Suffragette leader; enthusiastic supporter of the war effort.

[12] See R.U.B. Howell, *Philip Howell: A Memoir* (London, 1942), 204.

did she get her information? Some people say from L[loyd] G[eorge], I think more likely from some French channel, perhaps from Briand.

Now a similar sinister revelation appears. At the time of General [Sir Henry] Wilson's appointment to the Inter-Allied Council some sinister hints were given in the 'Manchester Guardian' that damaging disclosures could be made, which would affect a very high military reputation, i.e. Sir W[illiam] Robertson. The hint passed for the time[;] now it is arising again. ~~Christabel~~ Sylvia has published, or is publishing <in Britannia>, what she calls a War-Cabinet minute. It is really an extract from a General Staff memo[randum] of 1916. This memo[randum] took the view that it was necessary to maintain Germany as a strong Central Power to counteract the menace and power of Russia. This is now being used by Christabel[13] to prove that a distinguished General (Sir W[illiam] R[obertson]) was consciously treacherous to an ally and therefore should be dismissed.

I wonder if this is really so. At any rate it is true that L[loyd] G[eorge] wants to have W[illiam] R[obertson] out. It is also true to say that L[loyd] G[eorge] spoke to me at a breakfast once about this memo[randum], and said he thought the General Staff must be pretty big men for not wanting to crush Germany. I cannot now remember whether he mentioned the Russian side. I do remember however that there were 2 if not 3 men at that meeting who were not officials and whose discretion was perhaps not to be trusted. Anyhow the secret of his memo[randum] has been given perhaps by L[loyd] G[eorge] by intention, perhaps by accident. Anyhow beyond doubt, the writer of the paragraph in the Manchester Guardian gave the materials to ~~Christabel~~ Sylvia. I saw a letter from Lady Robertson which shows her evident anxiety as to old W[illiam] R[obertson]'s position in this as in other matters, in his contest with L[loyd] G[eorge].

12th, 13th, 14th, 15th [January 1918]

Away on walking tour <chiefly Winchester> – got very wet and found an inn with nothing to eat but bread and jam and a hotel which had had no cheese or butter for a fortnight.

---

[13] Dame Christabel Harriette Pankhurst (1880–1958), Suffragette leader; co-founder of the Women's Social and Political Union; editor of *The Suffragette* (since 1916 *Britannia*); enthusiastic supporter of the war.

16th [January 1918] Thursday

The Montenegrin General Radomir Veshovitch has surrendered to the Austrians. This bald statement covers a tragedy a treason. For over a year he has maintained himself alone with a few followers in the Montenegrin woods, keeping alive freedom's flame. His treatment is another example of the Austrian gentlemen. While originally at liberty, the Austrians issued a proclamation from Cettinje that they would shoot his father and brother if he did not surrender. Veshovitch shot the Austrian officer who brought this message and fled to the woods with 40 comrades. The <Austrian> Government at Cettinje then executed the brother and published a proclamation in which they took credit to themselves for not executing the father as well! Now Veshovitch has been forced to surrender (v[ide] also 9th [January 1918]).

The 11,000 Serb soldiers, who took to the woods in 1915, were rounded up in 1916. The Morava rebellion was crushed in 1917, but a few heroic Serbs still seem to prolong the living breath of freedom, while the Serbs hold Monastir but <for> how long?

Guillaumat[14] is sending the Russians from Salonica because the morale has been sapped by fraternization, in other ways he shows himself energetic enough, but his is a difficult almost hopeless command.

17th [January 1918]

Col[onel] Cox[15] of MI3[16] at the War Office is to be B[rigadier] G[eneral] I[ntelligence] in France at the special request of Haig. He is a good honest worker, with a truly German capacity for application, unrivalled at facts & figures of man-power and statistics. Withal in a somewhat ponderous way is enlightened and <as> genuinely desirous to acquire information as modest in imparting it. Had a devoted and loyal staff, and was generous in acknowledging their help. Hence got excellent results and was a universal favourite. Has had a startling rise – when I was first in the War Office (March 1916) he was still a

---

[14] General Marie Louis Adolphe Guillaumat (1863–1940), French military commander; entered army, 1884; commander, 1st Army Corps, 1915–16; commander, 2nd Army, 1916–17; commanded French forces at Salonika, 1917–18; military governor of Paris, 1918–19; member of Supreme War Council and commander of 5th Army, 1918–19; Commander-in-Chief, Allied Forces in Germany, 1919–26; War Minister, June–July 1926.

[15] See entry 23 Nov. 1917.

[16] Military Intelligence Section 3, a division of the Directorate of Military Intelligence; its subsections in 1914 included: MI3a: France, Belgium, Luxembourg, Morocco; MI3b: Austria-Hungary and Switzerland; MI3c: Germany; MI3d: Holland, Norway, Sweden and Denmark; MI3e: Military translations.

captain and has since risen to <Major>, Br[igade] Major, Br[igade] Lieutenant-Colonel, Br[igade] Col[onel]. He has also, for no special reason, been extremely kind to me – I supplied him with various details on German and Austrian political institutions to show to Haig. I parted from him sadly because he is the living part of intelligence at the War Office. MI2[17] is dying and discredited.

He has always been the right hand of the D[irector of] M[ilitary] I[ntelligence, Macdonogh], who is evidently very sorry that he is going.

19th [January 1918]

Venizelos once again has shown himself a big man. He has not only upheld against our objection the appointment of Bonnier[18] to the InterAllied Commission at Athens, but has decided to appoint him Director of Greek Civil Supplies as well. As he is already Intendant of the Greek Army, he will be supreme Food and Supply controller in Greece. In an interview Granville somewhat questioned this policy and pointed out that some Frenchmen, of whom Bonnier was one, aimed at a <French> protectorate of Greece. He added that Bonnier was known to be dishonest. Venizelos answered with his usual frankness. The crisis for Greece was desperate, as the supply system had broken down. He knew Bonnier in the Balkan Wars when he had supplied both the Greek military and civil population. He had heard that he had taken commissions then, but he had none the less done the work well and saved Greece a good deal of money. He was a wonderful organizer and he had unique local experience, and could save Greece if anyone can. As for his designs to make Greece a French protectorate he (Venizelos) was perfectly aware of them, but he (Venizelos) was the Master of Greece and would never allow anything of the kind.

If England wished he would ultimately replace Bonnier <by an American> but only if England wishes – since then he has announced he will do so.

What a man, what courage and calmness in decision.

On the whole <Greek> mob[ilizatio]n is going a little better and things generally wear a better air than most of us expected.

Italian intrigues in the areas north of the Greek boundary, i.e. in N[orth] Epirus are bad. Albanian brigands are being subsidised, Greek schools suppressed, one high ecclesiastical Gr[ee]k dignitary has died in prison at Argyrocastro,[19] another has been exiled to Corfu.

---

[17] Military Intelligence Section 2, divided into MI2a, covering the Americas (excluding Canada), Spain, Portugal, Italy, Liberia, Tangier, and the Balkans, and MI2b which dealt with the Ottoman Empire, Trans-Caucasus, Arabia, Sinai, Abyssinia, North Africa excluding French and Spanish possessions, Egypt, and the Sudan.

[18] See entry 1 July 1917.

[19] Now Gjirokastër (Albania).

19th [January 1918]

There are 3 new lights on L[loyd] G[eorge]'s war-aims speech,[20] which incidentally show how much (or how little) importance politicians attach to words, e.g. the restoration of an independent indvisible Poland was 'an urgent necessity' subsequently explained by F[oreign] O[ffice[telegram to Russia as 'condition of peace'. 'Reconsideration' for Alsace Lorraine, subsequently explained as standing by France in anything her government demands – "press for justice to men of Roumanian blood and speech" this is explained in F[oreign] O[ffice] telegram as it stood. So that out of 3 utterances two were really different. I suggested to DSI that he should add to his 'origin of the war', and 'war aims' lectures for the troops one on strategic war aims. He said he would be glad and Percy is preparing it.

20th [January 1918]

The Trotski-Kühlmann[21] debate is like that of Luther and Eck[22] – very much so in the temper of the 2 combatants and their previous training. Kühlmann had one scare, when Trotsky was claiming self-determination for nationalities by referendum – Kühlmann said 'Yes, but you have allowed it in the Ukraine by referendum.' 'Yes', said Trotski, 'but I am evacuating Russian troops from the Ukraine.' Kühlmann then became thoughtful and silent and did not take the broad hint that he should do the same. <In the same way when Kühlmann referred to the British in Persia Trotski brought up Belgium.> Trotski's dealings at home in informing the Constituent Assembly that it was to vote that it did not represent anything was the most imprudent suggestion ever heard – more impudent than the subsequent forced dissolution of the Assembly.

Yet, on the whole, the new Russia, though violent and unscrupulous in method, is sincere and based on ideals.

Look at old Tsardom. In 1916 the G[eneral] S[taff] thought it necessary to draw up a memorandum to show that Germany must be preserved as a balance

---

[20] See entry 6 Jan. 1918.

[21] Richard von Kühlmann (1873–1948), German diplomat; entered diplomatic service, 1900; counsellor of embassy at London, 1909–14; minister at The Hague, 1915–16; ambassador at Constantinople, 1916–17; State Secretary at *Auswärtiges Amt*, 1917–18. Since 22 Dec. 1917, Kühlmann was negotiating a peace treaty with Trotsky and Joffe; signed at Brest-Litovsk on 3 Mar. 1918.

[22] The famous 23 days' disputation at Leipzig (4 July–27 July 1519), between Martin Luther (1483–1546), German theologian and religious reformer, and Johann Mayer von Eck (1486–1543), German theologian; Eck was instrumental in securing a Papal bull which declared Luther a heretic in 1521.

to Russia. In that year Tsardom massacred half a million Kirghiz Tartars and kept the fact hidden from the world for twelve months.[23] It also, through its War Minister, advocated no haste to assist Roumania as otherwise she would become a great power in the Balkans. Finally there is some evidence that it was trying to negotiate an agreement with Japan against England and the USA in certain future contingencies. What a crawling, double-tongued, treacherous power, and how cheaply we are rid of it.

I remember a Japanese soldier writing on the Japanese war 'Yes Russian fighters are brave and strong but they did not believe in the Czar's virtue!' or the Czarina's, or the Government's. They had reason not to!

21st [January 1918]

Enclosed cuttings[24] relate to General McEwen's[25] scheme in the Southern Home Army. It has borne fruit and my advice was taken. The good old D[irector of] S[pecial] I[ntelligence, Cockerill] (disinterested patriot) has been financing the scheme up to date and saving the national exchequer. He claims no credit nor do I yet without us McEwen would not have encouraged, advised by Prof[essor] Adams, nor would L[loyd] G[eorge] have know of it. Capt[ain] Egerton[26] who worked out the details is entitled to, and will ultimately received, the bulk of the credit. Still, it was a big thing even to have a small hand in it.

22nd [January 1918]

The resignation of Repington[27] from the 'Times' seems to put the stopper on the intrigue of the Daily Mail to expel Haig and Robertson. The 'Times' is frightened and repudiates the idea that they had an intrigue against one or other or both, and disingenuously insinuates that Repington resigned on man-power

---

[23] In August 1916, the Kirgiz rose up in Pishpek in protest against land expropriations benefiting Russian settlers; the region remained mired in bloody fighting; casualty figures are contested, but about third of the Kirgiz population is estimated to have fled to China.

[24] 'Citizen Soldiers: A Scheme of Training in the Ranks' and 'Education in Khaki', *The Times*, 21 Jan. 1918 (not reproduced here).

[25] Brigadier-General Douglas Lilburn MacEwen (1867–1941), soldier; entered army, 1889; active service South African War, 1900–1902; General Staff Officer, 2nd Grade, War Office, 1910–12; 1st Grade, 1914; active service, 1914–16; retired, 1923.

[26] See entry 9 Nov. 1917.

[27] See entry 15 Apr. 1917.

not on the Haig-Robertson question. 'I hae my doubts.' The Times is intriguing in this sense[.] I am not convinced L[loyd] G[eorge] is.

23rd [January 1918]

With reference to the Austrian.

24th [January 1918]

Saw and lunched with David Davies, after his big speech in the House yesterday evening on the Cambrai incident.[28] He certainly made a good point to me when he said that he brought it forward because the dignity of the Commons suffered, when these matters were discussed in the Press and not in the House.

He said that, to his great surprise, he had recently received an invitation to lunch from L[loyd] G[eorge]. He went there and found the P[rime] M[inister], much bucked with Carson's resignation.[29] The reason he did not know, the fact he did. He said that Kennedy Jones[30] let the cat out of the bag when he said that, at the end of 1916, the Cabinet had desired to sack Haig but could not find enough newspaper support. He said this was true and that he was then in a position to know the truth. L[or]d Rothermore was sent by L[loyd] G[eorge] to act as intermediary with Northcliffe, but Northcliffe had been nobbled by Haig at the time and refused to commit himself. So the campaign collapsed. Now the irony is that Northcliffe is tilting at Haig and Robertson, while L[loyd] G[eorge] perhaps even supports them.

It certainly is a curious fact that, while the Interallied Council, the speech in France, and the elevation of Wilson, were advocated in the press by definitely Lloyd Georgian methods, I am not convinced that L[loyd] G[eorge] is mixed up in this affair, and David Davies agrees. The traces of Northcliffe are there but not necessarily of L[loyd] G[eorge].

---

[28] The government instituted an inquiry into the German counter-attack following the successful operations at Cambrai, see 'Parliament. Cambrai', *The Times*, 24 Jan. 1918.

[29] Carson resigned on 20 Jan. 1918, on the grounds that he wanted to be 'unfettered' in considering any Irish settlement proposal put forward by the convention of representative Irishmen under Sir Horace Plunkett (1854–1932).

[30] (William) Kennedy Jones (1865–1922), halfpenny journalist; editor *Evening News*, 1894–96, *Daily Mail*, 1896–1912; MP (Unionist) Hornsey, 1916–21.

25th [January 1918]

I heard today from Sir George Arthur,[31] the last story of L[loyd] G[eorge] and Asquith. Recently, feeling his insecurity, as witness his lunch to D[avid] D[avies], [Lloyd George] asked Squith to come to 10 Downing St[reet]. 'I'll be damned if I do', said Squith to the intermediary. So L[loyd] G[eorge] Cavendish Square. There he posed as humble almost servile. 'I should be ready to serve under you', said L[loyd] G[eorge]. 'Neither under you, nor over, nor with you', said Squith. (Later this story appeared in the Bystander on the 26th.)

The conversation drifted on to Northcliffe and his hatred of the King, due largely to the fact that the King disliked and hardly ever received him. It is well-known at Court that Northcliffe is anti-King, and it is believed that L[loyd] G[eorge] is a Republican in principle.

The Queen told a friend of mine that she had left her emeralds not to the P[rince] of W[ales] as future King but personally. She thought thus that he might inherit them.

26th [January 1918]

I understand Hardinge is doomed at the F[oreign] O[ffice] – why I do not know, the fact I do. Eric Drummond[32] and Eyre Crowe[33] are fighting for his shoes, the former a Catholic and Vaticanist, the latter with a German mother and wife. Delightful alternative.[34]

---

[31] Sir George Compton Archibald Arthur (1860–1946), 3rd Bt., succ. 1878, soldier and writer; entered army, 1881; active service Egypt, 1882 and 1884–85; retired, 1886, and commissioned into Hertfordshire Yeomanry; volunteered, South African War, 1900–1901; Private Secretary to Earl Kitchener, 1914–16; attached the General Head Quarters, France, 1917–18; see his *Life of Horatio, Earl Kitchener* (3 vols, London, 1920).

[32] See entry 20 Feb. 1917.

[33] Sir Eyre Alexander Wichart Barby Crowe (1864–1925), diplomat; entered Foreign Office, 1885; senior clerk, 1906–12; Assistant Under-secretary, 1912–20; Permanent Under-secretary, 1920–25.

[34] As Viceroy of India, Lord Hardinge of Penshurst was implicated in the disastrous Mesopotamian campaign; he remained Permanent Under-secretary until 1920.

30th [January 1918]

31st [January 1918]

D[irector of] M[ilitary] I[ntelligence, Macdonogh] had me and Buckley down and gave me his views. He said that the war would be decided by Labour in all countries and that personally he had not changed his view that what mattered was not strategic positions being in the hands of the enemy, but whether your neighbours were aggressive or the reverse.

None the less, besides our political ad hoc studies and appreciations, he wished the vital facts of statistics, ~~French-speaking~~ language and treaties to be on hand in all countries – (1.) Belgium, Alsace and Lorraine (2.) Trentino (3.) Balkans (4.) Russia and Poland.

He attached great importance to the international settlement of the colonies and the probable colonial attitude thereto. I indicated we had already worked out some of these problems, as Buckley showed tendency to glide over this. It is curious and amusing that the War Office has at last come round to the view I advocated in a published paper of February 1917. <F[oreign] O[ffice] were moved to it etc. by L[loyd] G[eorge] some time ago, prompted by my agitation via D[avid] D[avies].>

1st Feb[ruar]y [1918]

The Roumanian situation goes from bad to worse – fighting against Bolshevikism and Germans, with a failing and divided Ukraine, and wavering Bessarabia, what hope remains to them? Their army is still strong with a high reputation for military honour but the odds are enormous and supplies are interrupted with Bessarabia. Trotsky has denounced them as the 'Roumanian oligarchy covered with crimes.' The F[oreign] O[ffice] think they should make a separate peace now. Bratianu acquiesces, and Avarescu is believed to do so. Take Ionescu does not, and the King is also opposed but would no doubt consent. Personally I believe in 'no surrender' under all circumstances.

2nd [February 1918]

King's congratulations to the King of Montenegro. The last drops in the Serbian cup.

3rd [February 1918]

5th [February 1918]

Saw Steel[35] who launched forth into a eulogy of the D[irector of] M[ilitary] I[ntelligence] and an attack on the F[oreign] O[ffice] on 2 points

> (1.) Western Persia – he pointed out that for 3 weeks the F[oreign] O[ffice] had been making up their minds that something should be done, had defined the policy but refused to execute it. Now he has drawn up a question that they must answer – are you going to send British troops or no[?]
> (2.) <u>Over Roumania</u> Sir G[eorge] Clerk[36] suggests they should send a reassuring message – much good that is likely to do. The F[oreign] O[ffice] attempt to shore the matter off as a military question is quite futile because the only military question that arises is whether the Jap[ane]s[e] can land at Vladivostok, and that is vetoed on political grounds. Therefore the practical question at once arises – are the Roumanians to be defended or the Bolsheviks to be recognized?

Sound sense enough, after George Clerk's stuff about 'reassuring messages'!

The same day, I hear a conference took place at Balfour's room in the H[ouse] of C[ommons] over Mexico. Incidentally Carranza's[37] shady dealings with L[or]d Cowdray[38] were pointed out. C.N. French,[39] R.B. Carr,[40] A.J. Balfour, Hardinge

---

[35] Sir Arthur Herbert Drummond Ramsay-Steel-Maitland (1876–1935), politician; Fellow of All Souls, 1900; private secretary to Chancellor of the Exchequer, 1902–1905; MP (Cons.) East Birmingham, 1910–18, Erdington, 1918–29, Tamworth, 1929–35; Parliamentary Undersecretary for the Colonies, 1915–17; for Foreign Affairs and head of Department of Overseas Trade, 1917–19; resigned, July 1919; Minister of Labour, 1924–9.

[36] See entry 24 Feb. 1917.

[37] Venustiano Carranza de la Garza (1859–1920), Mexican revolutionary leader; Governor of Coahuila, 1911–13; *Premier Jefe* of Constitutional Army, 1913–15; President of Mexico, 1914–20; assassinated, May 1920.

[38] See entry 17 Nov. 1917.

[39] Lieutenant-Colonel Charles Newenham French (1875–1959), soldier; head of MI 1; liaison officer with Admiralty Intelligence, 1914–18; retired, 1924; director Empire Cotton Growing Corporation, 1924–29.

[40] Lieutenant-Colonel Reginald Blakeney Carr (1887–1963), Australian soldier; 13th Field Company, Australian Engineers; served European war, 1915–19; DSO; retired from army, 1944.

& Sir M[aurice de] B[unsen][41] were present. Sir M[aurice de] B[unsen] gave a typical exhibition of old time diplomatic traditions.
A.J. B[alfour] What is your opinion, Sir M[aurice] de B[unsen] [?]
Sir M[aurice] de B[unsen] gives it.
A.J. B[alfour] I don't agree with you.
Sir M[aurice] de B[unsen] (flustered) No Sir, don't say I disagree with – I have no opinion but that of my superiors, and never have had.
A.J. B[alfour] (collectedly) But I asked for opinion not my own.
So passeth, I devoutly hope, old diplomacy.

6th [February 1918]

Had a useful instance of the supervision of the King or his A[ide] D[e] C[amp] today. A machine gunner arrived, who had been stirred up by George Windsor. The latter found that the establishment of British machine guns per battalion was inferior to the German (in the Supplement to the Summary) and now requires complete explanations, and favours bringing our establishment up to that of the Boche. Good for the King.

I once received a jacket from him <(His Majesty)> on [sic] the Serbian army, which he had kept for eighteen months and was therefore <of> little use to me. This shows a quicker grasp of the situation.

I think I am a Georgian now in preference to a Lloyd Georgian.

7th [February 1918]

Pourparlers via Mackensen have already been taking place. Bratianu is believed to know the German terms, the ultimatum was presented today <or a sort of ultimatum>. Which will it be? The French still refuse to sanction a legal peace, we do not seem to know what to do.

Meanwhile Lockhart[42] wires that in one form or another the Bolsheviks must be recognized. Bratianu has appealed to us to support him, as he attacked the Bolsheviks at our request and apparent desire.

---

[41] Sir Maurice William Ernest de Bunsen (1852–1932), diplomat; entered diplomatic service, 1877; chargé d'affaires, Bangkok, 1894–96; minister at Lisbon, 1905–1906; ambassador at Madrid, 1906–13; at Vienna, 1913–14; on special mission to South America, 1918.

[42] Sir Robert Hamilton Bruce Lockhart (1887–1970), kt. 1943, diplomat and writer; rubber planter in Malaya, 1908–10; entered consular service, 1911; vice-consul at Moscow, 1912–17; special mission to Moscow to establish relations with Bolshevik government, 1918; expelled following involvement with anti-Bolshevik groups, Sept. 1918; commercial secretary at Prague, 1919–22; in banking, 1922–28; on staff of *Evening Standard*, 1928–39; rejoined Foreign

8th [February 1918]

Some hours on the Polish problem since Sept[embe]r last.[43] It seems to me en somme that the bourgeois and the nobles, always of immense power in Poland, have inclined to support the Regency and therefore also the Central Powers, in spite of the bright dream of an independent army, now rest in the Austrian. Curious, how the Council of State fell last August because it failed to release Pilsudski and to maintain the Polish army intact or to prevent the oath of allegiance to the Central Powers, or to relieve the economic situation. The Regency does none of these things and yet grows in power. The reason, I suppose, is that the Bolsheviks have frightened all property in Poland and that the Russian peace and the Italian war have destroyed all hope of Allied victory in the East.

9th [February 1918]

Began for the first time (mea culpa) Froude's[44] history of England. Style the lucid mirror of Victorian thought, unaffected and yet capable of reflecting the deep and the ideal – the exact opposite of Gibbon's[45] also lucid and the mirror of his age, which is fancied artificial and epigrammatic with the glitter of shallow generalisations <e.g. 'The timid are always cruel.'>, the lure of insistent sniggering and the underlying cynicism which makes him incapable of perceiving the heroic or ideal in man, save when, as with Athanasius, it is so evident as to overwhelm.

The tale of Charles V's intrigue,[46] the stirring up of rebellion in Ireland, the forgery of a bull to confound Henry over Catherine, and what I remember

---

Office, 1939; British representative to provisional Czech government in exile, 1940–41; Deputy Under-secretary and Director of Political Warfare Executive, 1941–45.

[43] Memo. Temperley, 'Recent Polish History in Relation to the Baltic Provinces and Ukraine, September 1917 to February 1918', 14 Feb. 1918, Webster MSS, Webster 3/6/83.

[44] James Anthony Froude (1818–94), historian and man-of-letters; fellow of Exeter College, Oxford, 1842–49; Rector of St. Andrews, 1868–71; Professor of Modern History at Oxford, 1892–94; best-known for his *History of England from the Fall of Wolsey to the Spanish Armada* (12 vols, London, 1856–69), and *The English in Ireland in the Eighteenth Century* (London, 1872).

[45] Edward Gibbon (1737–94), historian; Captain in the South Hampshire Militia, 1759–62; MP (Whig) Liskeard, 1774–80; on the Board of Trade and Plantations, 1779–80; best known for his *The Decline and Fall of the Roman Empire* (6 vols, 1776–88), a work of unrelieved pessimism.

[46] Charles V (1500–58), King of Spain and Naples, 1517–55; Holy Roman Empire, 1519–55; abdicated and retired to monastery, 1555. For Temperley's comments on Charles' duplicity see H. Froude, *History of England from the Fall of Wolsey to the Defeat of the Spanish Armada* (12 vols, London, 1870), iv, 67–8, 113–14 and 123–6.

elsewhere, the forgery of the names of Dissentient Electors at [the Diet of] Worms, in order to make the condemnation of Luther unanimous, what are all these? They are not only something old, they are something eternal in the Habsburg blood and policy. The forgeries of Count Forgach[47] in the Friedjung trial,[48] of him again in the ultimatum to Serbia, are not these part of the same web of eternal diplomatic intrigue which Charles V wove for Henry and the new Charles is weaving for George?

11th Feb[ruar]y [1918]

The signing of the peace of the Ukraine,[49] the death of Abdul the Damned,[50] and Trotski's amazing volte face supply enough news for the day – and bring us to Roumania. Avarescu as Roumania's premier will not, I trust, prove a new Görgei.[51] He believes in a separate peace, thinking resistance to be useless or hopeless, but he has pledged his word to destroy the munitions and locomotives. Bratianu's policy is to engage in pourparlers and try and drag them out in the hope that the collapse of Austria or the fall of the Bolsheviks may perhaps free his hands. Our policy is as chaotic as ever – we have not recognized the independence of Finland like France,[52] or been as deeply committed as her to the now useless support of the Ukraine. We have now arrived at the idea of a de facto recognition of the Bolsheviks.

Had a pleasant instance of the King's trouble today and his insight into affairs. A gunner arrived today for a back summary giving details of the <number of> German machine guns allotted per ~~regiment~~ battalion. The gun returns to the King showed the number of British machine guns per ~~regiment~~ battalion and the King, reading his Blue summary intelligently, came to the conclusion that ours were undergunned. They are, and His Majesty is strafing the gunners quite deservedly. After all regulars understand only rules and these decades old.

---

[47] Johann Graf Forgách von Ghymes und Gács (1870–1935), Austro-Hungarian diplomat; minister at Rio de Janeiro, 1905–1907; Belgrade, 1907–11; Dresden, 1911–13; Section Chief Imperial Foreign Minister, 1913–17; representative to Ukrainian People's Republic, 1918.

[48] See entry 13 Aug. 1917.

[49] The peace treaty of Brest-Litovsk, 9 Feb. 1918.

[50] Abdülhamid II (1842–1918), Ottoman sultan, 1876–1908.

[51] Artúr Görgey de Görgő et Toporcz (1818–1916), Hungarian revolutionary military leader; took prominent part in Hungarian revolution; commander-in-chief of Hungarian forces, Feb.–Aug. 1849; War Minister, May–July 1849; *de facto* dictator, July–Aug. 1849; surrendered to Russian army, Aug. 1849; interned until 1867, then pardoned.

[52] On 6 Dec. 1917, Pehr Evind Svinhufvud af Qvalstad (1861–1944), chairman of the Finnish Senate and later Regent of Finland (May–Dec. 1918) proclaimed Finnish independence and secession from the Russian Empire.

Royalty seems to be an improvement on them. Almost thou persuadest me to be a Monarchist. I am a Georgian at any rate in preference to a Lloyd Georgian.[53]

12th [February 1918]

Avarescu has interviewed Barclay – sticks to his policy of a separate peace and swears by all his gods to destroy guns and locomotives. Personally, I am disposed to believe in his good faith and in his Roumanian patriotism. Yet I remember the story of C.B. T[homson], undoubtedly his enemy, that he was charged as Minister of War with malversation which he could only answer by resignation (this is true) and that he keeps three German housemaids, each prettier than the other (which may not be true).[54]

The queen [of Romania][55] has reiterated her wail of passionate complaints at our misdeeds in withdrawing the Serbian division, in not paying the King the money we might have done.

> "Poor Queen,
> Here did she fall a tear, here in this place.
> I'll set a bank of rue, sour herb of grace
> Rue even for ruth here shortly shall be seen
> In the remembrance of a weeping queen."[56]

I remember her in the Coronation procession – the stateliest and <most> beautiful of women. Now she passes across the stage, weeping the fate of her country, sorrowful o'er the death of her little son, his grave in the enemies' hands,[57] perhaps soon to be queen no more, though she can never be aught but a royal woman.

---

[53] See entry 6 Feb. 1918.
[54] See entry 20 June 1917.
[55] Queen Marie of Romania (née Marie Alexandra Victoria, Princess of Edinburgh) (1875–1938); married Prince Ferdinand of Romania, 1893; Queen Consort, 1914–27.
[56] W. Shakespeare, *Richard II*, act III, scene 4.
[57] The Queen's youngest child, Prince Mircea (1913–16) was buried in the grounds of the Cotroceni Palace; the Romanian Royal family was then in exile in Iaşi.

13th [February 1918]

A nasty story. L[loyd] G[eorge]'s defence of himself and his connection with the newspapers was very unconvincing in the Commons. Lord Hugh's[58] fork has 2 prongs, either he <L[loyd] G[eorge]> inspired the press attacks against e.g. Jellico[e], or he was influenced by them.

My comments are

>(a.) The first D[avid] Davies heard of his ceasing to be the P[rime] M[inister]'s secretary was the announcement in the 'Times' that he was joining the forces at the front, inspired of course by L[loyd] G[eorge].[59]
>(b.) The story that L[loyd] G[eorge] wanted to sack Haig at the end of 1916 and could not get Northcliffe's support is stated by D[avid] D[avies] to be true, as also by Kennedy Jones,
>(c.) who disclosed the bargain between Asquith and L[loyd] G[eorge] to the Times, thereby rendering the breach irreparable and L[loyd] G[eorge] premier?
>(d.) The attacks on Robertson and Haig at the time of L[loyd] G[eorge]'s Paris speech could hardly have been uninspired by him. Henry Wilson was certainly cracked up <previously> by him in the 'Outlook' and elsewhere just before H[enry] W[ilson] went to Versailles.
>(e.) It is a fact that Northcliffe was objected to by Balfour, but that, after a two hours interview with L[loyd] G[eorge], he was accepted for the American mission.

Do we need further witness?

Repington is to be prosecuted for his attack on L[loyd] G[eorge] and saying that the latter was trying to get the Alliance into a sideshow at Aleppo (v[ide] Morning Post of 11th [February 1918]).

Repington in his first article in the M[orning] P[ost], after leaving 'The Times' gave away the figures of our casualties in 1917.[60] These I heard the D[irector of] M[ilitary] O[perations, Maurice] give to a dozen pressmen for confidential use but not for publication. Repington was too great a man to be present at this meeting, so obtained the facts privately and <u>published them</u>, which the other pressmen were not allowed to do. Repington was also

---

[58] Lord Hugh Richard Heathcote Gascoyne-Cecil (1869–1956), 1st Baron Quickswood, cr. 1941, politician; MP (Cons.) Greenwich, 1895–1906; Oxford University, 1910–37; Provost of Eton College, 1937–44.

[59] See *The Times*, 12 June 1917.

[60] He did so by circumventing the military censor, see A.J.A. Morris (ed.), *The Letters of Lieutenant-Colonel Charles à Court Repington, CMG: Military Correspondent of The Times, 1903–1918* (Stroud, 1999), 40–41.

obviously furnished with information from the W[ar] O[ffice] to deal with the contentions of L[loyd] G[eorge]'s Paris speech. So there is a leakage to the Press from [the] W[ar] O[ffice], if there is an inspiration to it from Downing Street.

<(Note. Repington was subsequently convicted and fined £100.)>

14th [February 1918]

It seems to me evident from comparisons of the inspirations in the Press that L[loyd] G[eorge] was behind the recent attacks on Haig and Robertson, as well as at the time of the Paris speech. This goes back on my previous opinion. <I learnt after that some think this untrue. The attacks In February embarrassed L[loyd] G[eorge] because he did not like to strike. 18/10/27>

One point of great importance I notice today in the telegrams. Venizelos has at last got rid of all the pro-German elements in the King's entourage. The ministry is purged and strengthened, the only weak point being that EMBIRICOS,[61] the Food Controller, who is himself probably honest, but whose department is 'full of thieves', remains. He is the largest shipowner in Greece and, in a heroic moment, offered the whole of his great fortune to aid the Provisional Government at Salonica when Venizelos left Athens. <(Unfortunately it proved later that Embiricos was himself corrupt.)> Perhaps this is the reward for that constancy in trial. For the rest <exc[ept] some sub-lieutenants of whom 2 were shot>, no officers mutinied at Zaima, a good sign. The King has gone there and to Salonica and made Coudouriotis a Knight of the Redeemer and given Venizelos a signed portrait.

16th [February 1918]

I heard from [Alan] Percy today that the Robertson-Lloyd George struggle had reached a crisis. R[obertson] was not consulted about L[loyd] G[eorge]'s purpose of pooling the reserves and placing them under the Inter-Allied Council. When this was done he took the view that executive responsibility must accompany the disposal of the Allied Reserves, i.e. the representative on the Inter-Allied Council could not be, as he has previously been, 'without executive powers'. The executive power of the C[hief of the] I[mperial] G[eneral] S[taff] was therefore impaired. This was answered by offering to him the post at Versailles and to Henry Wilson that of the C[hief of the] I[mperial] G[eneral] S[taff]. This post he declined on the ground that he was senior to Wilson. Now L[loyd] G[eorge], if dares or can, will get rid of him. He [Percy] spoke bitterly of Derby. I reminded him of

---

[61] Stamatis Embeirikos, of S.G. Embeirikos Ltd., Greek shipowner.

the conduct of the latter's ancestor at Bosworth. He held aloof from Richard III with his forces till he saw how the battle went, and then he joined Henry VII, found the crown beneath a bush, and put it on his head.[62] P[ercy] seemed to think the comparison apt. <(It turned out to be. Derby resigned but withdrew his resignation. HWV T[emperley] 20/2/18)>

Another view I heard from Tharp,[63] who had stayed with H[enry] W[ilson] at Versailles. The latter was in great agitation because R[obertson] steadfastly refused to give an opinion or decision different from that of H[aig]. His view was that, once you did that, you gave the politician a chance. Therefore on many different occasions, he had no opinion. Amery, now political secretary to H[enry] W[ilson] said after 1½ years of R[obertson] in the War Cabinet, that he had no imagination. But Amery had a grudge against him.

Altered view is indicated perhaps in a story Edwards told me, in the summer of 1916. R[obertson] was down at Cambridge with him and smoked a pipe in Pembroke Library. L[loyd] G[eorge] had just become his chief, about a fortnight [earlier]. 'I don't know how I shall get on with him', said R[obertson] meditatively, evidently thinking he might not get on very well.

Some weeks ago, I was entering the front gate of the War Office, and saw old R[obertson] in front of me. Just beneath the clock on the marble stairs was a new bronze bust of Kitchener. R[obertson] just put up. R[obertson] paused beneath it and looked up into the face earnestly for a moment and then passed slowly on. What were his thoughts, I wonder? did he think he might share the fate of K[itchener], supersession by L[loyd] G[eorge] [?]

17th Feb[ruar]y [1918]

The secret is out today. The Gov[ernmen]t issue a communiqué that R[obertson] was offered the job at Versailles, and that he refused it and his resignation was accepted. R[obertson] says that he has not resigned, i.e. he has been dismissed.

~~Edwards told me that R[obertson] smoked a pipe about a fortnight after he had come under L[loyd] G[eorge] as S[ecretary] of S[tate] for War. 'I don't know how I shall get on with him', said R[obertson], puffing his pipe a little doubtfully. Now he does, I much fear.~~

---

[62] The political manoeuvrings of Thomas, 2nd Baron Stanley (1435–1504), were replicated in the Battle of Bosworth (22 Aug. 1485), where he kept his troops out of the fighting until the end; he is reputed to have retrieved Richard III's (1452–85) crown from the battlefield and placed it on Henry Tudor's (1457–1509) head.

[63] See entry 14 July 1917.

20th Feb[ruar]y [1918]

Old R[obertson] sent a moving farewell circular to the W[ar] O[ffice] staff today, frank and direct, like himself.

On the whole, L[loyd] G[eorge]'s explanations are unconvincing, as is the defence in the 'Times'. Panouse says that the exact opposite of L[loyd] G[eorge]'s remarks is true, that the Inter-Allied Council, or at least the French, thought that the C[hief of the] I[mperial] G[eneral] S[taff] would appoint a D[eputy] C[hief of the] I[mperial] G[eneral] S[taff] for France. This was Robertson's own proposal. L[loyd] G[eorge] offered him (1.) the Versailles post, (2.) the C[hief of the] I[mperial] G[eneral] S[taff]-ship, shorn of its powers as redefined for Robertson. He refused both in favour of his own proposal. The affair is unsatisfactory because Sir Henry Wilson is L[loyd] G[eorge]'s candidate. If he was proposed as C[hief of the] I[mperial] G[eneral] S[taff], as he was, what became of Robertson's position? It is incredible that Sir H[enry] W[ilson], being L[loyd] G[eorge]'s candidate, should be ever inferior to anyone else, wherever he is. If he was to be C[hief of the] I[mperial] G[eneral] S[taff] he was to be superior to Robertson; if he was to remain at Versailles, he was to be the same. Whichever way it was "Heads Wilson wins – Tails Robertson resigns." That is the naked fact.

The most charitable construction is that from early in 1917 L[loyd] G[eorge] definitely decided in favour of the constructive imagination of H[enry] W[ilson] against the downright doggedness of W[illiam] R[obert] R[obertson].

In summing up, I hear from one who saw Milner on Sunday, the colleague with him L[loyd] G[eorge] acted in the whole matter, that Milner was absolutely wearied and felt the Government extremely weak. He used a politician's argument about the whole matter. Robertson and Haig had had their way in France in 1917 at a terrific cost of lives, hammering away at the Germans. What have we to show for it? L[loyd] G[eorge]'s thrust at Austria via Laibach in July is what we should have done in 1917. This, I doubt, because it might have brought German divisions into the Tyrol and that would have been the end. Again, Salonica and Palestine – only Jerusalem – only.

All this seems very false and very political. Surely the greatest justification of Haig and Robertson is today. Owing to their efforts we now have all the ridges most favourable either for attack or for defence, when the greatest German force is for the first time prepared to attack them. What we owe to Robertson and Haig is therefore no theatrical triumphs, but the greatest security in the war that we have yet enjoyed.

I hear that Roumania must inevitably make peace. Migné [?] was to send his answer tonight.

I think, in summing up old R[obertson]'s merits and defects, that he had those of a regular. He could not be got to realize that a man, who had been leadcub, should not have another almost equally good job. Thus Cunliffe-Owen[64] dismissed from Salonica M[ilitary] I[intelligence] jumped into that in Mesopotamia, C.B. Thomson sacked from Roumania became C[ommander] R[oyal] E[ngineers] of the 60th in Egypt, Sir A[rchibald] Murray[65] sacked from Egypt gets the Aldershot command, Maxwell[66] retired from Ireland[,] gets increased pay at York, and so ad infin[itum].

Again the Italian business was not happy and his opposition to the Salonica expedition not successful. His failure to take any interests or give any support to Roumania was also a mistake. And yet, and yet, things are very different now – the capture of Jerusalem and Bagdad is a brilliant feat, owing largely to his strategic plans for the defence of Egypt.

The Western front is impregnable thanks to him.

At the W[ar] O[ffice], Intelligence and Operations have both been thoroughly reorganized – the Intelligence is undoubtedly excellent. I am not, however, at all satisfied with the operations nor do I think that General Maurice has been very successful. The operations section is far too small to be of real value, and Maurice does not seem to have been very happy in his management of his team.

Yet Wully Robertson in manly sturdy honesty, directness of purpose and personal force of character, stood out foursquare and colossal.

26th [February 1918]

On my return to the W[ar] O[ffice] I find that Wilson's first act as C[hief of the] I[mperial] G[eneral] S[taff] was to object to our representative at Versailles sending troops to Italy without his advice and consent. Of course he will win because he will be supported by L[loyd] G[eorge]. Equally, of course, in such

---

[64] Lieutenant-Colonel Frederick Cunliffe-Owen (1868–1946), soldier; active service Somaliland, 1903–1904 and Iraq, 1920; Military Secretary's Branch, War Office; General Staff; Military Attaché at Athens, 1912–13; at Constantinople, 1913–14; General Staff Officer, 1915; Civil Administration of Mesopotamia, 1919–22; Refugee Settlement Commission, Greece, 1923–26.

[65] General Sir Archibald James Murray (1860–1945), soldier; entered army, 1879; active service Zulu War, 1879, South African War, 1900–1902; Director of Military Training, 1907–12; Inspector of Infantry, 1912–14; Deputy Chief of Imperial General Staff, 1915–16; General Officer Commanding, Egypt Expeditionary Force, 1916–17; General Officer Commanding-in-Chief, Aldershot, 1917–19; retired, 1922.

[66] General Sir John Grenfell Maxwell (1859–1929), soldier; entered army, 1879; active service Egypt, 1882, Dongola campaign, 1896, South Africa, 1900–1901; Commander of Egyptian forces, 1908–12 and 1914–15; Commander-in-Chief, Ireland, Apr.–Nov. 1916; General Officer Commanding-in-Chief, Northern Command, 1916–19; member of Milner's mission to Egypt, 1920; retired, 1922.

case, Robertson would not have won. It all shows that L[loyd] G[eorge]'s explanation to the world did not fit the real facts.

2 March [1918]

Attended meeting at 3 Great College Street, with Buckley – saw Sir W[illia]m Tyrrell[67] of F[oreign] O[ffice], Parker,[68] F[oreign] O[ffice] Librarian, Prothero[69] their writer and editor etc.

After some discussion, I find that they are proposing to establish (informally) with W[ar] O[ffice], B[oard] of T[rade] & Adm[iralt]y that close liaison for the mutual solution of historical and political questions, likely to arise at the Peace Conference, including cessions of territory etc. This is satisfactory but a lill['] late – if adopted when recommended by me 2nd Feb[ruary] 1917, there would have been a year's work done on these questions.

5th March [1918]

King of Roumania at a Crown Council read a statement in favour of fighting to the end, but said, as a constitutional King, that he w[oul]d accept the ruling of the ministers. The Crown Prince spoke strongly in favour of resistance, probably at the instigation of his mother.

7th March [1918]

Attended weekly meeting at F[oreign] O[ffice]. Tyrrell's points were[:] we are beaten, if Belgium is not in the preamble [and] not in the body of the Treaty.

He disbelieved in an armistice, unless it was preceded by an understanding as to essentials, which all of them would observe.

---

[67] Sir William George Tyrrell (1866–1947), Baron Tyrrell of Avon, cr. 1929, diplomat; entered diplomatic service, 1889; Private Secretary to Sir Edward Grey, 1907–17; head of Political Intelligence Department, 1918–19; Assistant Under-secretary, 1918–25; Permanent Under-secretary, 1925–28; ambassador at Paris, 1928–34.

[68] Alwyn Parker (1877–1951), Foreign Office official; entered Foreign Office, 1900; assistant clerk, 1912–18; Foreign Office Librarian, 1918–19; attached to British delegation at Paris Peace Conference, 1919; resigned, 1919; Director of Lloyd's, 1919–51.

[69] Sir George Walter Prothero (1848–1922), historian; Fellow of King's College, Cambridge, 1876–94; Professor of Modern History, Edinburgh, 1894–99; editor, *Quarterly Review*, 1899–1922; editor, *Cambridge Modern History*, 1901–12; Historical Adviser to Foreign Office, 1917–19; attached to British delegation at Paris Peace Conference, 1919.

It was agreed to discuss (1.) Armistice (2.) African colonies (3.) Alsace-Lorraine-Belgium etc.

8th March [1918]

Yesterday evening at about 12 after we had all 4 + baby come into the drawing room, on hearing the alarms, the ceiling fell suddenly down on us.[70] I jumped up to Gladys, and said 'it's alright darling' – Coxie and Emily seemed on top of the little boy. Recovering ourselves a little we went out into the kitchen, and sat there during the rest of this air-raid. All three women behaved splendidly, and the little boy sat in the kitchen with a plate with some sifted sugar on it, saying 'nicey sugar!' – after a time I looked out – strong fumes were everywhere, the whole of the glass alcove in the drawing room[,] all the glass and beams in the hall were gone, the door alone stood upright, the whole ceiling in the drawing room was down. Every window was shattered. The fence between us and the next house was down, and a tree had been cut off and carried bodily across the garden from one corner to the other. I looked over the fence and a man shouted 'They're [*sic*] several people buried.' This afterwards proved false. In the next two houses the whole fronts were blown entirely in, but of 16 assembled in one room only 1 was at all injured. These poor people knocked at our door but we did not hear them in the clatter. They were taken in by the next house but one. Mr Steel, a carpenter who looked after them. By and bye the police arrived. They did not even take the trouble to inquire if any of us was hurt – the whole idea seemed to be to prevent the 2 vacant houses next door from being robbed. My friend, the naval husband of the district nurse, came to ask after us, and offer us a bed. As it was, Gladys and Coxie and the baby went down to sleep at St. James Terrace.[71] Gladys returned at 2.30, she and I went to bed in 1 room and Emily in the other – the only 2 left <relatively> intact in the house. My own sensations were not those of fear rather of stupidity, a little dulled but not much worried. All the women looked under a nerve strain. The incidents the next day were first a letter from the Estate Agent, informing us that the lease of the house was up on 25th March and did we wish to renew it? 2nd a visit in person from the Estate Agent, saying he had not written this in reference to the raid! <Then Reginald Eves[72] the Society Painter turned up and I offered him to paint me in the ruins and call it the Ypres sector.> Then later in the day I strolled out in a filthy tunic and

---

[70] The Temperleys lived at 41 Townshend Road, St. John's Wood, since 1916.
[71] NW1, just off Prince Albert Road.
[72] Reginald Grenville Eves (1876–1941), artist; educated Slade School; Member of Royal Society of Portrait Painters and Royal Institute of Oil Painter; painted, *inter alios*, Queen of Spain, Lord Leopold Battenberg, Stanley Baldwin and Thomas Hardy.

saw a short man in a brown suit, who looked very hard at me, as if he wanted to tell me my dress was not in order. I was not out for compliments or reprimands, so I slammed the door in his face. Subsequently I learnt the little man was Field Marshal Lord French[73] in mufti. Then Queen Alexandra turned up and the local mayor in a soft hat. The only practical step was taken by the latter, who informed Mr Steel the municipality would cover his expenses. The father and mother of the 16 had to go out and find small rooms to house 16! Gladys fed them with coffee in the morning and Mr Steel housed and fed them throughout <and the naval man gave them a bed>. But, in short, the only practical aid rendered was by people whose houses were injured!

Meanwhile the police took great care to guard 2 houses which were blown to pieces, and even on the Sunday work in cutting boards etc. went on, tho[ough] no helping hand or practical aid was given by them to hungry and homeless refugees.

Shall write to L[loyd] G[eorge] (v[ide] 15th).[74]

11th March [1918]

I hear from S[eton]-W[atson][75] that Beaverbrook's attempt to capture the Dep[artmen]t of Information (Headlam,[76] Gleichen,[77] Saunders,[78] Bevan,[79]

---

[73] Field Marshal Sir John French (1852–1925), Earl French of Ypres, cr. 1915, soldier; joined Navy, 1866; army, 1874; active service Sudan, 1884–85, South Africa, 1899–1901; Chief of the Imperial General Staff, 1911–14; Supreme Commander, British Expeditionary Force in France, 1914–15; of Home Forces, 1915–18; Lord-Lieutenant of Ireland, 1918–21.

[74] Temperley to Adams, 11 Mar. 1918, Lloyd George MSS, Parliamentary Archive, F/77/1/2.

[75] See entry 23 Nov. 1916.

[76] (Sir) James Wycliffe Headlam (since 1918 Headlam-Morley) (1863–1929), historian and civil servant; Fellow of King's College, Cambridge, 1890–96; Professor of Greek and Ancient History, 1894–1900; at Board of Education, 1902–14; employed at Wellington House (Enemy Propaganda department), 1914–17; Assistant Director of Intelligence of Bureau, Department of Information, 1917–18; of Political Intelligence Department, Foreign Office, 1918–19; Historical Adviser to Foreign Office, 1919–28.

[77] See entry 23 May 1917.

[78] George Saunders (1859–1922), journalist; Berlin correspondent, *The Times*, 1897–1908; at Partis, 1908–14; Political Intelligence Department, Foreign Office, 1916–19.

[79] Edwyn Robert Bevan (1870–1943), ancient historian and philosopher; independent scholar; employed in Department of Information, 1914–19; lecturer in Hellenistic history and literature, King's College London, 1922–33.

Leepers,[80] Namier[81] etc.) has failed. He carried it at a committee presided over by Smuts but now 13 of them have resigned, only S[eton]-W[atson], who considers himself under military discipline, remaining.

First check to Beaverbrook. The Dep[artmen]t of Information was to come under the F[oreign] O[ffice] when Buchan[82] and Gleichen retried. Beaverbrook butted in and sought to capture it.

I also heard that Northcliffe is starting proposals for a big anti-Habsburg propaganda today, and that Steed and S[eton]-W[atson] fixed up a working agreement between the Italian deputy Torre[83] and the JugoSlav committee a few days ago.

The state of the F[oreign] O[ffice] seems to be one of acknowledging its nakedness. They have recently handed over to the W[ar] O[ffice] all jurisdiction over maps (having confessed they have no geographical section), annexed from the Admiralty Prothero and his school of historians, and from the Dep[artmen]t of Information the 13 experts in intelligence.

This seems to prove that they are hopelessly lacking (a.) in cartography (b.) in current information (c.) in historical knowledge. Well indeed that they at last recognize. Balfour has not done much at the F[oreign] O[ffice]. Indeed he is seldom there, but he has pressed in this matter, and told Percy that, when he came to the F[oreign] O[ffice], the latter had no maps later than 1870.

---

[80] Allen Leeper see entry, 23 May 1917; and his brother Sir Reginald Wildig Allen Leeper (1888–1968), Australian-born diplomat; Political Intelligence Department, 1917–19; founder of British Council, 1934; head of Political Intelligence Department, 1938–43; Assistant Under-secretary for Foreign Affairs, 1940–43; Director of the Country Headquarter, Political Warfare Executive, 1941–43; ambassador to Greek government-in-exile (Cairo), 1943–46; at Buenos Aires, 1946–48; retired, 1948.

[81] Sir Lewis Bernstein Namier (née Ludwik Niemirowski) (1888–1960), historian; military service, 1914–15; Propaganda Department, 1915–17; Department of Information, 1917–18; Political Intelligence Department, 1918–20; member of British delegation at Paris Peace Conference, 1919; Balliol College, 1920–21; Professor of History, University of Manchester, 1931–53; knighted, 1952.

[82] John Buchan (1875–1940), 1st Baron Tweedsmuir, cr. 1935, lawyer, novelist, and politician; called to the bar, 1901; Private Secretary to Alfred Milner, 1901–1903; commissioned into Intelligence Corps, 1915; Director of Information, 1917–18; MP (Cons.) Combined Scottish Universities, 1927–35; Governor-General of Canada, 1935–40.

[83] Andre Torre (1866–1940), Italian journalist and politician; Senator; Minister of Education, Mar.–May 1920; signed Torre–Trumbić agreement of 7 Mar. 1918, calling for an independent Yugoslavia, a free Adriatic and the division of former Habsburg territories on the basis of the principle of national self-determination.

12th [March 1918]

Northcliffe has demanded material for enemy propaganda from the W[ar] O[ffice] today. I was much strained to provide propaganda against Bulgaria and Austria-Hungary but finally managed to do so, though kept hard at work dictating and writing.

The shadows darken round Roumania and round Avarescu. The latter secretly authorized movements of Austrian and German troops ~~in Bessarabia~~ <through Galatz to Odessa>. Is he a traitor? (v[ide] 12th February). I remember Thomson's story of Avarescu's 3 German serving maids, each prettier than the other, who served the General in his leisure hours.[84] On the financial side Avarescu has always been somewhat weak, and perhaps the Germans have played on this weakness. Of course there is another point of view. Avarescu may be genuinely convinced that peace is inevitable and resistance hopeless and may be making a little money on the way.

13th [March 1918]

D[irector of] S[pecial] I[ntelligence, Cockerill] interviewed me re Northcliffe and the proposed interview. He said he could not consent to much without the D[irector of] M[ilitary] I[ntelligence], but w[oul]d try and not be caught out in knowledge, and w[oul]d play for time. Above all he would insist that there could be no real settlement of propaganda without a settlement of policy. Do we wish to be anti-Habsburg or pro-Habsburg in Austria? etc. All very sound. Northcliffe may yet do good in this matter. Steed I understand gives everything to the J[ugoslav] P[olitical] S[ociety] and this is dangerous and to be avoided.

14th [March 1918]

A.J. B[alfour] on Balkans, paper of Dec[embe]r 1917.[85] <There are merits in> this paper, though dealing a great deal with compensation and balances in the Balkans, and having a little talk at the end weighing out portions of peoples and territory in the approved Congress of Vienna style. Balfour says that, though there are great merits in detailing Bulgaria, we cannot abandon our friends and allies – Greece, Roumania and Serbia. He suggests, however, as an ultimate settlement, Greece less Cavalla area with the Dodecanes and Cyprus, to <the

---

[84] See entry 20 June 1917.
[85] Memo. Balfour, 15 Dec. 1917, Balfour MSS, The National Archives (Public Record Office), FO 800/241.

cession of> which personally he has no objection. Serbia with Montenegro, Bosnia Herzegovina and part of Dalmatia, Bulgaria with Macedonia and the part of the Dobruja taken from her in 1913.

This is about the best to hope for, I think, that the F[oreign] O[ffice] can at present give.

15th [March 1918]

V[ide] 8th March.

Received a letter back from L[loyd] G[eorge]'s sec[retar]y, saying that he had handed my letter of protest about the neglect of the public authorities to L[loyd] G[eorge], and also informed the President of the Local Government Board.[86]

16th [March 1918]

Soveral.[87] The old Marquis and blue monkey of Portugal, a man wise in society, in diplomacy and in the world, delivered himself of sentiments to a friend of mine <Baker-Carr[88]> recently. He said he could not understand the prevailing pessimism. We had lost less [*sic*] men and done more improvising of organisation than any other power. Our immense resources were yet unexhausted, America was bringing yet more to bear. It was only a question of holding and of bringing these powerful forces into play, in order to make certain of winning.

A touching bracing tonic in a world of mist and mystery.

---

[86] William Hayes Fisher (1853–1920), 1st Baron Downham, cr. 1918, politician; MP (Cons.), Fulham, 1885–1906 and 1910–18; Financial Secretary to the Treasury, 1902–1903; Parliamentary Under-secretary to the Local Government Board, 1915–17; President of the Local Government Board, 1917–18; Chancellor of the Duchy of Lancaster and Minister of Information, 1918–19.

[87] Luis Maria Augusto Pinto de Soveral, marquês de Soveral (1851–1922), Portuguese diplomat, nicknamed 'the Blue Monkey'; minister at London, 1891–95, and 1897–1910; Foreign Minister, 1895–97; envoy extraordinary for Edward VII's coronation, 1902, and at Second Peace Conference at The Hague, 1907.

[88] Brigadier-General Christopher D'Arcy Bloomfield Saltern Baker-Carr (1878–1949), soldier; entered army, 1898; served Nile expedition, 1898, and South African War, 1899–1902; Captain, Rifle Brigade, 1902–1906; retired, 1906, and rejoined as army chauffeur, Aug. 1914; instigated Machine Gun School, 1914; commander 1st Brigade Tank Corps, 1917–18; brigade commander, 1918–19; retired, 1919.

17th [March 1918]

C[hief of the] I[mperial] G[eneral] S[taff, Wilson] has apparently some definite views, he is undoubtedly a man of quick imagination. He considers that the German offensive in the West is real but not vital, that they will talk about it a great deal, attract our reserves there, begin it, do what they can and, finally, when they have concentrated all attention there, will strike with a dozen German divisions in the Tirol and drive the Italians down into the plains.

The question of Haig's quarrels with the Supreme Council at Versailles over the reserves has been settled in an amusing way. H[aig] has now discovered there are no British reserves or at least none whom he can allot to the general strategic reserve. The latter has now become a purely French question, and, as such, they can do what they will with it. I am inclined to think that Haig with shrewd Scotch caution has contrived so as to have no reserves <(I think Haig has said truth. I wish he hadn't. 17/4/18)>

18th [March 1918]

The situation between L[loyd] G[eorge], Beaverbrook and Northcliffe deepens. Beaverbrook is still trying to secure the 13 resigned members of Gleichen's dep[artmen]t of Information, who want to go to the F[oreign] O[ffice] which requires their services. After 4 meetings the War Cabinet decided they sh[oul]d not go to Beaverbrook. The latter then demanded that they sh[oul]d not go to the F[oreign] O[ffice], to which the War Cabinet assented. (Is there anything to which W[ar] C[abinet] and F[oreign] O[ffice] will not assent?) Apart from the blustering tyranny of Beaverbrook and his singular methods, the gallant 13 seem quite unsuitable to his job, that of home propaganda.

Meanwhile Northcliffe's scheme of propaganda against Austria-Hungary on an anti-Habsburg basis, i.e. of oppressed nationalities, has been accepted. Meanwhile Lloyd George, though accepting this, has Philip Kerr touring in Switzerland and negotiating on a pro-Habsburg basis.[89] Smuts and Philip Kerr both think it possible to federalise Austria-Hungary as South Africa was federalised. If they but knew! Again Philip Kerr maintains that L[loyd] G[eorge]'s last war-aims speech was both anti-Habsburg and pro-Habsburg. Could there be a greater condemnation? The War Cabinet are anti-Habsburg – L[loyd] G[eorge] is pro-Habsburg.

---

[89] Kerr met Baron Skrzynski (see entry 27 Apr. 1918) of the Austro-Hungarian legation in Switzerland at Montreux on 14 Mar. 1918.

19th March [1918]

Seton-Watson told me today that he is now going to serve under Northcliffe. Steed has gone to Rome to start a public Italo-JugoSlav anti-Habsburg campaign. The War Cabinet sent him, but apparently expected and desired that his mission should fail. S[eton]-W[atson] was to have gone with him but at the last moment was stopped by some mysterious unknown agency.

He is a little unhappy about going to Northcliffe, but thinks that he at least knows what he wants and wishes to run the war. He seems to think that L[loyd] G[eorge] with his double game is a real danger. Northcliffe is suspicious, not confident as to the Government, watching and waiting for a spring, a tiger spring if L[loyd] G[eorge] fails. I asked him if Northcliffe knew of L[loyd] G[eorge]'s two Austrian faces. 'I don't know', said he grimly, 'I think so – anyhow he will know tomorrow when I see him.' I understand N[orthcliffe] was offered the W[ar] O[ffice] & refused because he did not quite trust the Gov[ernmen]t.

A friend of mine was at a dinner party, where old Buchanan was last night. He discussed with great frankness Lockhart's attitude in demanding support and recognition of the Bolsheviks, and his considerable criticism of him (Buch[ana]n). Lockhart was, he thought, a young and relatively inexperienced man. Bolshevikism was, he thought, a dying force, though still very powerful and very far from being dead. The one thing that was necessary was to supply a nucleus of force round which more stable elements than Bolshevikism might gather. The Japanese or the Germans alone could supply this. He acknowledged the grave risks run by bringing in the Japs, but thought that move on the whole to be distinctly the lesser evil.

C[hief of the] I[mperial] G[eneral] S[taff] agrees with this view and wrote a minute recently saying "Lockhart must go". He also says that he was interested to see that Lockhart said in a telegram that "Trotski was very <u>nice</u> to him." Apparently the anti-Bolshevik view is prevailing despite desperate efforts of L[loyd] G[eorge] to the contrary.

C[hief of the] I[mperial] G[eneral] S[taff] also insists greatly on the importance of Armenia, as a bulwark and bastion of India.

20th [March 1918]

Doubts accumulate as to the good faith of Avarescu. He secretly authorized the movements of German and Austrian troops towards Odessa, without the knowledge of King or colleagues. Hence the natural suspicion (v[ide] 12th March [1918]). The French are convinced he is [being bribed?], and Panouse actually asked Gen[eral] Georgescu whether he was. Georgescu did not like the question, and Panouse did not like the answer – 'I have never agreed with General Avarescu, but I would not go so far as to say that!' Perhaps not, but he was defending the honour of Roumania. Poor King and poor Queen. I pity them much. Gen[eral] Berthelot has left, his train several times being interfered with by sabotage. Ballard,[90] our M[iltary] A[ttaché] remains and in this connection I record a fine incident, a ray of light in the gloom. The W[ar] O[ffice] received a telegram for transmission to him. 'Glad you are remaining with gallant Roumania – Wife.'

21st [March 1918]

Our appreciation of the political and economic results of the Brest [-Litovsk][91] Treaty was read on Wednesday at the Conference <of the General Staff> and much appreciated, so I am told. This is good because it means that we are getting our foot in, over Russian affairs, and does something for Webster.[92]

22nd [March 1918]

The first news of the gigantic German offensive is good.[93] So far they claim neither prisoners no[r] guns nor to have done more than take the first line (which nobody ever supposed that they could not do). Their original objective was Peronne on the first day, which they have failed to reach. This does not mean of course that their offensive has failed but it does mean that their programme has not materialised. It is undoubtedly the supreme crisis of the war.

The C[hief of the] I[mperial] G[eneral] S[taff, Wilson]'[s] appreciation of German strategy is as follows. In 1914 they expected to break through, first at the Marne later at Ypres. Having failed to do this, they turned round and tried to knock out Russia, having failed to do this they did knock out Serbia. In 1916 they tried at Verdun – having failed to do this, they partially knocked out Roumania. In 1917 they waited for the submarine to finish us, which, having failed, they partially knocked out Italy, while Russia knocked itself out.

---

[90] See entry 17 Apr. 1917.
[91] The Peace Treaty of Brest-Litovsk of 3 Mar. 1918 forced Soviet Russia to relinquish the Baltic states, Poland, the Ukraine and the Trans-Caucasus.
[92] Memo. Webster (MI2E), 'Some Notes on German Eastern Treaties', 15 Mar. 1918, Webster MSS, Webster 3/5/72.
[93] The last German offensive on the Western Front commenced on 21 Mar. between Arras and LaFère, after a prolonged artillery battle, 1–21 Mar.

Now in 1918 they turn on us and take up the original conception of 1914. They never at any period thought that the Western theatre was not the decisive front, and their efforts elsewhere were of the nature of knock-out blows in minor theatres, in order to release further reinforcements for the supreme front. These they have now obtained and therefore again attack us.

This is, in view of the 50 mile front attack and the 40 odd German divisions engaged. The view therefore <he expressed on> the 17th cannot be sustained. The real thing is in the West.

I cannot help thinking that the situation is rather like that of Treasure Island.[94] We fight, with advantages of position in the Blockhouse of France, against pirates. In one respect it is different – the pirates have discipline as good as ours.

24th [March 1918]

News very anxious tonight[,] could hardly be more serious – breakthrough between 3rd and 5th Armies.

Merval and Sailly ridges taken.[95]

It cannot be much consolation to the P[rime] M[inister] to learn that we have crossed the Jordan. In another sense 'what shall we do in the swelling of Jordan?'[96]

After much anxiety at about 10 tonight I suddenly felt a conviction that the tide had turned. God grant it.

<Note. That was about right. The chief danger was on Saturday when they crossed the Tortelle & threatened to sep[arate] our armies. Later there was similar danger at Martinpont and Courcelette[97] <28/3/18>.

25th [March 1918]

C[hief of the] I[mperial] G[eneral] S[taff]'[s] appreciation of situation is as follows – The offensive on the grand scale will last 9 days, during the first half of this they will throw in 40 divisions, during the 2nd half 40 more.

He also believes that, when thoroughly engaged, we shall have to endure an attack as Italy and subsequently perhaps a violation of Swiss territory.

---

[94] See R.L. Stevenson, *Treasure Island* (London, 1883).
[95] German troops took Bapaume, Combres, Guiscard and Chauny on 24–25 Mar.
[96] '[T]hen how wilt thou do in the swelling of Jordan?', Jeremiah 12, 5 (in the King James version).
[97] Courcelette in Picardie, fiercely fought over during the Somme Offensive in 1916.

26th [March 1918]

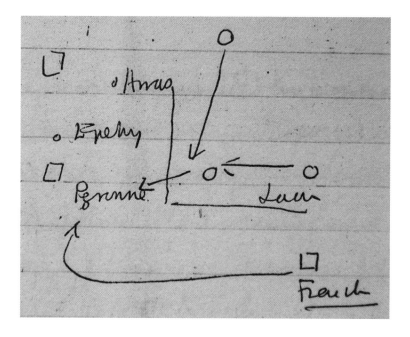

Above diagram proves what the Germans really did with their reserves and why the French have been late in coming.

The appreciation just beforehand suggested that the attack in force was coming north of Épehy.[98] To this extent it was incorrect and the Germans made the best of the re-entrant angle.

27th [March 1918]

I understand Byng[99] and his boys have stopped the rot – this 3rd Army fighting magnificently, the 5th army did not do so well. Haig has been warned against Gough for 2 years but never taken the advice.

Curiously enough no attacks were expected today against Arras to the south and east. None came, which shows that the Germans are exhausted in this area.

---

[98] In the Somme department in Picardie.
[99] Field Marshal Sir Julian Hedworth George Byng (1862–1935), 1st Baron Byng of Vimy, cr. 1921 (since 1928 Viscount), soldier; entered militia, 1879; active service Sudan, 1884–85; South Africa, 1899–1902; General Officer Commanding IX Corps, 1914–15; XVII Corps, 1916; Canadian Corps, 1916–17; Third Army, 1917–18; Governor General of Canada, 1921–26; Commissioner Metropolitan Police Force, 1928–31.

That is good, though they are pressing on and extending their gains, south of the Somme in the Noyon area. When will the French counter-stroke come? At first it was the 29th then the 30th, then the 31st. Not, I hope, the first of April.

28th [March 1918]

Lichnowsky's evidence[100] is absolutely damning and von Jagow's attempts to refute it are of the feeblest description.[101] He asserts (and v. J[agow] does not deny) the genuineness of the Crown Council of the 5th July [1914]. He also asserts the sincerity of our efforts for peace which von J[agow] has grudgingly to admit, as well as our conc[iliator]y efforts to settle Bagdad and African not meet us over the fleet.

Lichnowsky is particularly strong that a hint from Germany would have forced Berchtold to give in on 30th [July 1914]. His reasoning on the Russian mobilization is not equally convincing and von J[agow] scores a point over the Russian mob[ilisatio]n. But L[ichnowsky] asserts (and von J[agow] does not deny) that the German F[oreign] O[ffice] told him <in 1916> that war had to come in 1914 because Russia was not then ready and would have to come in any way in 1916.

Mühlon's[102] revelations as to Krupp & to the Kaiser's personal share in deciding on war[103] are also very damaging and have to be explained on the ground that he is suffering from neurasthenia.

I have seen a good deal of Tyrrell and Parker lately who conducted most of the negotiations with Lichnowsky and Kühlmann.[104] I cannot say that the latter strikes as in any sense the equal of Kühlmann. Tyrrell I think is clever but was <at the crisis>, I believe, for neutrality, a fact which seems to be ~~admitted~~ hinted by Lichnowsky. Hence his comparative fall today.

---

[100] See entry 9 Dec. 1916. His *Meine Londoner Mission* (Zurich, 1918) had been in circulation privately at the turn of 1917–18; it was published also in the Swedish newspaper *Politiken*. It was the subject of committee proceedings in the *Reichstag* in Mar. 1918; a letter by Lichnowsky summarizing his argument was published in the *Berliner Tageblatt*, 21 Mar. 1918.

[101] See entry 4 Aug. 1917.

[102] Dr Johann Wilhelm Mühlon (1878–1944), German lawyer and diplomat; entered diplomatic service, 1907; on secondment to Krupp Works, 1908–14; special commissioner to Balkan states, 1915–16; in Swiss exile since 1916.

[103] See *Revelations by an Ex-Director of Krupp's: Dr. Mühlon's Memorandum and His Letter to Herr von Bethmann Hollweg* (New York, 1918) and *Dr. Muehlon's Diary: Notes written early in the War by Dr. Wilhelm Muehlon, ex-Director of Krupp's* (London, 1918).

[104] See entry 20 Jan. 1917; Kühlmann favoured secret peace negotiations with Tyrrell in the summer of 1918.

29th [March 1918]

The evidence against Avarescu (12th March & 12 Feb[ruar]y) is bad. He, unknown to [the] King of other Ministers, sent a telegram to Misu (then in Paris and waiting to take charge of the negotiations) to detain him there for 10 days, and prevent his interfering. This has succeeded. Avarescu resigned, disclaiming responsibility for destruction of material etc., and the pro-German Marghiloman[105] took his place. Evidently a planned treachery on Avarescu's part.

The greatest farce is now being played – it has been strongly asserted that Foch is to be generalissimo and is probably true.

If this is so, Foch, who has a deputy at the Supreme Council at Versailles, is exactly in the position <for France which> Robertson desired to be in for England. Yet this is the result, the French C[hief of the] I[mperial] G[eneral] S[taff] becomes generalissimo, while the British C[hief of the] I[mperial] G[eneral] S[taff] is dismissed, in each case for advocating the same course. Meanwhile the farce of the supreme council of Versailles disappears. Lloyd George is usually right and true in his objective, false and futile in method and explanation.

(Rawlinson[106] the British member at Versailles commands an army & his place was not filled up for some time.)

30th [March 1918]

Turning over Mignet's[107] Revolution française I found a sentence or two bearing on Germany today[:] 'L'oppression trouva des ambitieux qui la conseillèrent, des dragon qui la servirent, des succès qui lencouragèrent; <u>les plaies et ses gérnissements furent étouffés pas des chants de victoire</u>. Mais à la fin les homes de genie moururent, les victories cessèrent, l'industrie emigra, l'argent disparut, et l'on vit bien que le despotisme épuise ses moyens par ses succès, et dévoire d'avance son proper avenir.'[108] I feel more certain of the underlined passage than of the succeeding one.

---

[105] Alexandru Marghiloman (1854–1925), Romanian politician; favoured neutrality during war; Prime Minister, Mar.–Nov. 1918.

[106] General Sir Henry Seymour Rawlinson (1864–1925), 1st Baron Rawlinson, cr. 1919, soldier; joined army, 1884; General Officer Commanding 4th Division, 1914–15; First Army, 1915; Gallipoli, 1915; Fourth Army, 1916; Second Army, 1917–18; General Officer Commanding-in-Chief, Aldershot, 1919–20; Commander-in-Chief, India, 1920–25.

[107] François Auguste Marie Mignet (1796–1884), liberal French journalist and historian; author of *Histoire de la révolution française depuis 1789 jusqu'en 1814* (2 vols, Paris, 1824–27) and *Histoire de la rivalité de François Ier et de Charles Quint* (1875).

[108] *Recte*: 'L'oppression trouva des ambitieux qui la conseillèrent, des dragons qui la servirent, des succès qui l'encouragèrent; les plaies de la France furent couvertes de lauriers, et ses gémissements

3rd [April 1918]

S[teed] now demands sanction from Northcliffe for a pro-nationalities propaganda.

6th [April 1918]

The sum of the news of this last week is the attempt of Steed and Seton-Watson in their tour in Italy to start a great pro-nationalities and self-determination campaign with the view of stampeding the Austrian army.[109]

The campaign has been fiercely pressed by the Italians and Delmé Radcliffe,[110] by the French, and by Steed. It will, I think, succeed because he says only that we approve of the independence of these nationalities, but do not pledge ourselves to obtain it. This is what both the F[oreign] O[ffices] of Washington and London have carefully explained, with reference to the January definitions of war aims by L[loyd] G[eorge] and [Woodrow] Wilson. They desire to satisfy national aspirations and Serbia and will press them at the Peace Conference but they do not promise more, I have pointed out, in my comment for the D[irector of] M[ilitary] I[ntelligence].

8th [April 1918]

Saw Major Barrett just returned from Roumania. He gave the strong impression that the Central Powers had by their onerous terms wrecked their future opportunity of controlling Roumania. Constanza[111] at any rate is the life of Roumania, and her enemies are (1.) the Bulgarian (2.) the Russian (3.) the Magyar.

Berthelot did magnificently as did his officers and created a fine army out of nothing. Moral in the army was still good, though some had been propagandized.

---

furent étouffés par des chants de victoire. Mais à la fin, les hommes de génie moururent, les victoires cessèrent, l'industrie émigra, l'argent disparut, et l'on vit bien que le despotisme épuise ses moyens par ses succès, et dévore d'avance son propre avenir', François Auguste Marie Mignet, *Histoire de la révolution française depuis 1789 jusqu'en 1814* (Brussels, 11th edn, 1838), 10.

[109] Rome Congress of 'Oppressed Nationalities', 7–16 Apr. 1918, with representatives of Czechoslovak, Polish, Romanian and Yugoslav groups.

[110] Brigadier-General Sir Charles Delmé Radcliffe (1864–1937), soldier; joined army, 1884; Military Attaché at Rome, 1906–11; General Staff Officer, Western Command, 1911–12; Chief of Staff, Third Army, 1914–15; Chief of British Military Mission, Italian Headquarters, 1915–19; Chief of British Military Mission, Klagenfurt, Aug. 1919–Mar. 1920; retired, 1921.

[111] Now Constanţa in the Danube delta (Romania).

Ballard held firmly to the view that Avarescu was alright – he (B[arrett]) did not and he had seen him very often. Berthelot loathed the sight of him, and said once to B[arrett][:] You know the face of Mephisto in Faust? Yes. Is it not that of Avarescu? There is some truth in it – his face is narrow and foxy. <Compare Morley's conversation with Mazzini when they saw a picture of a lion 'is it not a foolish face – is it not the face of Garibaldi?'>[112]

Avarescu's conduct at Marisesti[113] [*sic*] was supicious – he along opposed an advance when the German positions were known to be weak. Why? Was it because he was in relations with Germany already? What, in any case, was his aim? Probably to be regent, with little Nicholas[114] as King.

10th [April 1918]

Commander Myres,[115] straight back from Salonica. He said Greece seemed now to have turned the corner. The coming out of the Goeben and Breslau from the Straits was to have been the signal of a great movement, of revolt at Athens, Lamia,[116] Chalcis,[117] and Larissa. The Goeben came out too early and upset the deeply laid plan.[118] 11 rounds from a mountain battery enabled the Cretans to disperse the Lamia mutineers at Thebes. Arrests and shootings then began. This surprised the Greek regiment and when about to be mobilised, he now says "I may as well be shot in the trenches as at home." The Irishman's cry is the reverse 'I raither be shot in auld Ireland than in France.' It was all a very near thing in Greece but the worst in not over.

---

[112] See J. Morley, *Recollections* (2 vols, London, 1917), i, 79–80.

[113] Mărășești in eastern Moldavia, some 12 miles north of Focșani; site of the last major battle on the Romanian front, 6 Aug.–8 Sept. 1917, which ended in the exhaustion of both sides.

[114] Prince Nicholas of Romania (1903–78), second son of King Ferdinand and Queen Marie of Romania.

[115] Sir John Linton Myres (1869–1954), archaeologist (Cyrpus and Crete) and classicist; Fellow of Magdalen College, Oxford, 1892–95; Student of Christ Church, 1895–1907; Gladstone Professor of Greek, Liverpool, 1907–10; Wykeham Professor of Ancient History, Oxford, 1910–39; Lieutenant-Commander (Acting Commander), Royal Navy Volunteer Reserves, 1916–19, commanding raiding operations on the Turkish coast.

[116] In central Greece.

[117] Now Chalkida, chief town on the island of Euboea (Greece).

[118] The German battle-cruiser *SMS Goeben*, and the light cruiser SMS *Breslau*, both launched in 1911, formed the Mediterranean Division of Imperial German Highseas Battlefleet; both were transferred to the Ottoman Empire on 16 Aug. 1914. *Goeben*, renamed *Yavuz Sultan Selim*, led a sortie into the Mediterranean in an effort to draw Allied naval forces away from the Levant, the so-called Battle of Imbros, 20 Jan. 1918; the engagement was aborted after *Breslau* (now *Midilli*) hit a mine.

11th [April 1918]

Circumstances grave, could in fact hardly be graver. The Messines ridge and Armentières gone, and the Germans within six miles of Hazebrouck.[119] All depends on our firmness, whether we shall decline to move our reserves to meet this strong local attack or not. Foch, as at Verdun, will only strike 'with exact art' at the moment when it can be plucked ripely. But it is weary waiting, with the British still struggling hard as at Waterloo, though now <u>against</u> the Prussians. But we shall pound the largest, I think.

12th [April 1918]

The Press today[120] reproduces the Emperor Charles' letter in which he defines his peace terms, March 1917 and speaks of the French claims to Alsace-Lorraine as just.[121] Curiously enough it appears simultaneously with a telegram, in which he denies to the Kaiser the original charge to Cambon, so Panouse informed me. I told him the story was true 8 months ago.

I am inclined to believe in the genuineness of this letter – it corresponds fairly well to some of his recorded conversations, and it is interesting that he suppressed and vigorously disclaimed Professor Lammasch's[122] version of [it].

13th [April 1918]

Major General Sackville-West,[123] a pleasant cipher and friend of the present C[hief of the] I[mperial] G[eneral] S[taff, Wilson], is to go to Versailles to let the whole thing <slide> down gently and pleasantly along a greased slope to a torpid lake of extinction.

---

[119] The second major offensive south of Ypres, 9–18 Apr. 1918; Messines fell on 10 Apr., Armentières on 12 Apr.

[120] See 'Emperor Charles and Alsace-Lorraine. "Just Claims Of France."', *The Times*, 12 Apr. 1918.

[121] The so-called Sixtus-letter of 24 Mar. 1917, to his brother-in-law, Prince Sixte de Bourbon-Parma, see below entry 16 Apr. 1918.

[122] Heinrich Lammasch (1853–1920), Austrian pacifist jurist and politician; Professor of Law, Vienna University, 1889–1920; advocate of arbitration and league of nations ideal; Minister-President of Austria, 25 Oct.–11 Nov. 1918; signed Peace Treaty of St. Germain, 1919.

[123] Charles Sackville-West (1870–1962), 4th Baron Sackville, succ. 1928, soldier; joined army, 1889; General Officer Commanding 21st Infantry Brigade, 1915–16; 190th Infantry Brigade, 1916; 182nd Infantry Brigade, 1917; attached to General Staff, 1918–19; to Supreme War Council, 1919; Military Attaché at Paris, 1920–24; Governor-General of Guernsey, 1925–29.

16th [April 1918]

The ~~result of the~~ Clemenceau-Czernin scuffle was carefully examined by me today.[124] My conclusions are (1.) that Clemenceau's assertions are substantially correct, though vehement (2.) that Czernin did not know of the Emperor's Alsace letter when he spoke of Clemenceau's refusal to treat on that subject (3.) that the whole affair exhibits the clumsy bungling of Austrian diplomacy. Czernin blundered as to his statement on the 2nd April, when he said that Clemenceau began the overtures, he blundered as to the date of one of Clemenceau's communiqués which he quoted, as 2 days later that it was issued, he blundered in accusing the Emperor's own brother-in-law[125] of forgery, he blundered in referring to Alsace-Lorraine at all. (4.) with all these blunders I don't know that we have triumphed altogether (4.) [sic] Secret diplomacy, unofficial relations etc. are a distinct convenience, and Austria can no longer be detached. I understand Philip Kerr (L[loyd] G[eorge]'s agent) returned in March. (5.) [sic] Austria having been forgiven by Germany, must now slavishly follow her. (6.) [sic] This leads definitely to a pro-nationalities campaign for demoralizing the Austrian army.

This last is what I advocated to the D[irector of] M[ilitary] I[ntelligence, Macdonogh], and what Northcliffe also has steadily advocated.

17th [April 1918]

The chief feature of the situation today is the recovery of west of Bailleux and of Wyteschaete.[126] This gives us a breathing space and a recovery. The D[irector of] M[ilitary] O[perations, Maurice], who has just come back from France today, is more cheerful and hopeful than for some time. He was almost optimistic to the press today. He stays on a little, as I understand, because Radcliffe[127] (very

---

[124] On 2 Apr. 1918, Czernin (see entry 2 Apr. 1918) publicly intimated that a secret French peace initiative had taken place, but that it had failed on account of Clemenceau's insistence on the return of Alsace-Loraine.

[125] Prince Sixtus Ferdinand Maria Ignazio Alfred Robert of Bourbon-Parma (1886–1934); enlisted in Belgian army, 1914; his sister Zita married the Archduke Charles of Austria; used as intermediary by Charles in attempted secret peace negotiations with France, 1917 (Sixtus Affair).

[126] In northern France, between Ypres and Messines.

[127] Lieutenant-General Sir Percy Pollexfen de Blaquiere Radcliffe (1874–1934), soldier; joined Royal Artillery, 1893; active service South Africa, 1899–1900, and France, 1914–18; Director of Military Operations, 1918–22; General Officer Commanding, 48th (South Midland) Division, Territorial Army, 1923–26; 4th Division, 1926–27; General Officer Commanding-in-Chief, Scottish Command, 1930–3; Southern Command, 1933–34.

wisely) cannot undertake so big a job at once. Cox from France sent me a cheerful message today. His chief enemy seems to be L[loyd] G[eorge] not the Germans.

Everything is out of order at the W[ar] O[ffice] since the master-hand of old Wully has been withdrawn. I hear that Derby is going and Milner coming to the W[ar] O[ffice]. Milner says anything that L[loyd] G[eorge] says on the one hand, and draws any information he can from Amery in the other. So Amery will rule the W[ar] O[ffice] at last. Sir H[enry] W[ilson] has sunk to the level of a political general.

I met the Serbian minister [Jovanović] at lunch today. He was dismal and pessimistic, and I sought to cheer him by the Clemenceau-Czernin revelations.

25th [April 1918]

G. Tharp was present last night at a dinner where [there] was the D[uke] of Connaught, General Pershing[128] etc. The chief talkers were Mayer and W[illia]m Waldorf Astor,[129] and their topic was that the "W[ar] O[ffice] was seething with intrigue against Llord George". Lunch for Pershing. Mrs W[aldorf] A[stor][130] also recounted how L[loyd] G[eorge] had said how much he admired old Robertson as the antithesis of himself, dour and downright, and the terrible shock when he realized that he (Robertson) was an intriguer! Terrible indeed, and interesting as showing the madness of the entourage of L[loyd] G[eorge].

An interesting commentary on this is the interlude that took place between the General Staff & L[loyd] G[eorge] last week. His speech at the beginning of the offensive stated that our forces were, if anything, slightly superior to the German. In last week's record <(15th April)>, the statement was made by [Alan] Percy that since then our forces had been reduced and the German increased by 300,000. L[loyd] G[eorge] scanned this with an angry eye and then composed or signed a letter to the W[ar] O[ffice] accusing the General Staff of 'cooking the figures'. An enquiry was held, there was a new D[irector of] M[ilitary] O[perations] (Radcliffe) and Amery and Milner examined the figures and reduced them to 200,000. The C[hief of the] I[mperial] G[eneral] S[taff, Wilson] apparently made no objection, the D[irector of] M[ilitary] O[perations,

---

[128] General John Joseph Pershing (1860–1948), US soldier; Commander-in-Chief, American Expeditionary Force in Europe, 1917–19; Chief of Staff, US Army, 1921–24.

[129] Waldorf Astor (1879–1952), 2nd Viscount Astor, succ. 1919, US-born politician and newspaper proprietor; MP (Cons.) Plymouth, 1910–18, Plymouth Sutton, 1918–19; parliamentary Private Secretary to Lloyd George, 1916–18; Parliamentary Secretary, Ministry of Food, 1918–19; Ministry of Health, 1919–21; a prominent member of Lloyd George's Downing Street 'garden suburb' of advisers.

[130] Nancy Witcher Astor (née Langhorne), Viscountess Astor (1879–1964), US-born politician; MP (Cons.) Plymouth Sutton, 1919–45.

Radcliffe] hardly understood the point. But [Alan] Percy and Kirke[131] stood firm. They pointed out that, if their figures could be revised at the bidding of civilians, the General Staff no longer existed as a separate entitity. After a long discussion they agreed that possibly 40,000 to 60,000 might be taken off but that was the absolute limit. The C[hief of the] I[mperial] G[eneral] S[taff] did nothing in all this. He seems to be there to receive the praise and to do the behests of L[loyd] G[eorge].

I upheld the W[ar] O[ffice] case alone to the F[oreign] O[ffice] over the armistice. Tyrrell pointed out that both Admiralty and W[ar] O[ffice] looked on an armistice as undesirable. But that the Admiralty only admitted two contingencies[,] victory or defeat, while the W[ar] O[ffice] recognized yet another alternative, an armistice forced on the basis of the status quo. Tyrrell highly praised our armistice paper,[132] especially the parts about Frederic the Great and the Seven Years' War. Webster did some of this, but I supplied this instance.

Finding Tyrrell alone for 5 minutes I asked him if it was not unique in his experience of diplomacy to have to deal with an episode like the Czernin-Clemenceau duel. He said that it was, and that the secret, once having been given away via private letters etc., secret diplomacy was over for ever. Peace would be made in public by Lloyd George shouting across the sea to Hertling[133] or Wilson to Burian.[134]

He added that he thought Czernin unequal to his post and was not surprised that he "had got it in the neck."

---

[131] Major-General Walter Mervyn St. George Kirke (1877–1949), soldier; entered Royal Artillery, 1896; active service Waziristan, 1901–1902, Wellaung punitive expedition, 1905–1906, European War, 1914–18; General Staff Officer, War Office, 1912–14; Deputy Director of Military Operations, 1918–22; head of British mission to Finland, 1924–25; President of Inter-Allied Commission of Investigation for Hungary, 1925; Deputy Chief of the General Staff for India, 1926–29; General Officer Commanding-in-Chief, Western Command, 1933–36; Director-General, Territorial Army, 1936–39; Inspector-General of Home Defence, 1939; Commander-in-Chief, Home Guard, 1939–40; retired, 1940.

[132] Memo. Temperley, 'Possibilities of Armistice', 11 Mar. 1918, Webster MSS, LSE Archives, 3/5.

[133] Georg Friedrich Count von Hertling (1843–1919), German philosopher and politician; Professor Philosophy, Munich University, 1882–1912; Reichstag deputy, 1875–90, and 1893–1912; parliamentary leader of Centre Party, 1909–12; life member of Bavarian Upper House, 1891–1918; Minister-President of Bavaria, 1912–17; Minister-President of Prussia and Imperial Chancellor, 1917–18.

[134] Stephan (István) Baron (since 1918 Count) Burián von Rajecz (1852–1922), Austro-Hungarian diplomat and politician; consular career before transfer to diplomatic service, 1886; minister at Sofia, 1887–95; at Stuttgart, 1896–97; at Athens, 1897–1903; Austro-Hungarian Finance Minister, 1903–12 and 1916–18; Foreign Minister, 1915–16 and Apr.–Oct. 1918.

27th [April 1918]

600,000 casualties is the figure given to the French M[ilitary] A[ttaché] at Copenhagen as that of the German losses in the offensive to date. This corresponds to some extent to the <earlier> figure given by the German M[ilitary] A[ttaché] in Spain. If true it may supply a good deal of explanation as to the pauses in the German advance. Panouse seemed to be particularly hopeful now. Amiens and that area were perfectly alright – only the north was still troublesome.

28th [April 1918]

Kerr & Skrynski[135] [*sic*]. I saw signs today of the negotiation carried on in the first fortnight of March by Philip Kerr in Switzerland for the benefit of Lloyd George above the heads of the F[oreign] O[ffice] and perhaps the French.

He apparently sent a memo[randum] to Skrynski, sec[retar]y of the Austrian Legation, in which he apparently mentioned the Trentino-Trieste and Alsace-Lorraine. He was answered by Skrynski in a memo[randum], which is stated to have come direct from Czernin. After vague generalities on all these three subjects, it ended[:] The Entente would be in a better condition to discuss the disposal of these territories, if they were actually in possession of them. This was a heavy blow. I cannot think why he was sent. Smuts' mission in January was a failure confessed, the Austro-French negotiations broke down on Alsace-Lorraine at the end of February, where then was the opportunity for Philip Kerr early in March?

29th [April 1918]

A royal romance.

30th [April 1918]

L[loyd] G[eorge][136] on <the> Nelsonian qualities of Trenchard.[137]

---

[135] Ladislaus Ritter von Skrzynno-Skrzyński (1873–1937), Austro-Hungarian diplomat; entered diplomatic service, 1900; legation secretary at Stockholm, 1905–1908; at Brussels, 1908–1909; at Paris, 1909–11; at The Hague, 1912; at Berne, 1912–18.

[136] 'Air Debate', *The Times*, 30 Apr. 1918.

[137] Air Marshal Hugh Montague Trenchard (1873–1956), 1st Viscount Trenchard, cr. 1936, officer; entered army, 1893; Assistant Commandant Central Flying School, 1913–14;

1st [May 1918]

French revelations in Monday's Manchester Guardian are of high interest.[138] They appear to substantiate that not only Ribot[139] but Poincaré[140] were in the Alsace negotiation with the Emperor Charles and it was, on the French side, a genuine one until Clemenceau came along, who by his direct methods saved the situation.

2nd [May 1918]

I hear that Harrington[141] in lecturing yesterday on the Western front stated that the actual situation was that the Germans started with 40 divisions up, and we now only 17 down.

3rd [May 1918]

[Alan] Percy returning from Windsor where he saw the King informed me that the latter is outspoken to the point of indignation as regards the dismissal both of Trenchard and Robertson. He had greater confidence in the latter, as man was entirely direct in his methods.

5th [May 1918]

The Vatican has denied all knowledge of the Bishops' united protest against conscription in Ireland. It may be so, as Sykes[142] said, no one suspected it of

---

Officer Commanding Military Wing, Royal Flying Corps, 1914, First Wing, Royal Flying Corps, 1914–15, Royal Flying Corps, 1915–18; Chief of Air Staff, 1918, and 1918–30.
[138] 'Austria's Overtures in 1917: M. Poincaré Demands More Light on the Facts', *Manchester Guardian*, 29 Apr. 1918.
[139] See entry 2 May 1917.
[140] Raymond Nicolas Landry Poincaré (1860–1934), French politician; deputy, 1887–1903; Senator, 1903–34; Education Minister, 1893, 1895; Finance Minister, 1894 and 1906; Foreign Minister, 1911–13 and 1922–24; Prime Minister, 1911–13. 1922–24 and 1926–29; President, 1913–20.
[141] General Sir Charles Harington Harington (1872–1940), military commander; Deputy Chief of the Imperial General Staff, 1918–20; General Officer Commanding-in-Chief, Northern Command, 1923–27; Aldershot Command, 1931–33; Governor-General of Gibraltar, 1933–38.
[142] See entry 8 Feb. 1917.

inspiring Cardinal Mercier's[143] protests in Belgium. The Irish bishops too are nearer the priests than we can imagine in England.

De Salis drew Cardinal Gasparri[144] on the subject of the Vatican view of Austria. It regarded a strong Austria as an essential to counterbalance German influence. It did not believe that any number of small states could perform this office, and was very doubtful as to Jugo-Slavia being formed.

This view is possible but I do not think that it will really be practicable now. An ended Austria is better than a mended one.

6th [May 1918]

I hear that three weeks ago a certain person was with the King and threw doubts on the authenticity of the letter of the Emperor Charles to Prince Sixte. 'My dear fellow', said the King to him, 'he read it to me in this room.' S[ixte] has been once, and I think twice in London, so it is possible and my source was excellent <(I have forgotten who)>.

7th [May 1918]

I read with amazement Gen[era]l Maurice's letter in the paper today in which he accuses Lloyd G[eorge] and Bonar Law of erroneous statements to Parliament on 3 heads.[145]

His charges are true and will, I hope, be substantiated though I much doubt if 2 judges will understand the technical points of ration-strength etc. on which the whole thing turns.

Unfortunately personalities enter into the matter, and some points of principle. But he is certainly, as he claims, a democrat and does not wish a military conspiracy. He is also, like old Robertson, a poor man and acting under a sense of overpowering duty. Still it is a breach of discipline and government would become impossible if servants can arraign their superiors and demand Government inquiries at critical times. It will give Milner the opportunity to show that he really exists, which I personally doubt. The real underlying principle is that L[loyd] G[eorge] wishes to blame the soldiers, and Maurice to point out that the shortage of manpower was the real thing. It is true that the rifle strength had fallen by 25% when the German offensive began.

---

[143] Désiré-Félicien-François-Joseph Mercier (1851–1926), Roman Catholic clergyman; Archbishop of Mechelen, 1906–26; Cardinal since 1907.

[144] See entry 22 July 1917.

[145] 'Ministerial Statements', Maurice to the Editor, *The Times*, 7 May 1918.

The news from Ireland is very bad, could hardly be worse. A Connaught ranger was landed from a <German> submarine like Casement.[146] He had been given £50 and, when found, had drunk away £10 of the total.

8th [May 1918]

Lunch with Cockerill and Norton Griffiths – the first time I saw 'Empire Jack', a bluff burly coarse-natured man, with a genius for action, and none for speech and council. He fought his victories over the Roumanian oilfields again – one story was good. He told me that he attended a council, at which were Barclay, C.B. Thomson, himself and Bratianu. At the council Bratianu came to the definite and final decision, with which Barclay and C.B. T[homson] agreed, that the destruction of the oilwells should cease. 'Empire Jack' said nothing whatever but when the conference was over, he said to C.B. T[homson] 'I am going on destroying for my orders are only from the War Office and if you want them changed you must apply to them.'

He thought ill of Bratianu as corrupt as might be and well of Avarescu. He said Avarescu was a true Roumanian and really cared for his troops.

The Maurice affair he settled in a few words. 'People say it affects the honour of Lloyd George and Bonar Law – that doesn't affect me in the least. I don't care about it at all but <what> I do care about is a government that will win in the war. If we turn this [one] out we put in 'Squith'. That's what I am going to say in the Commons tomorrow.'

À propos it is curious, but he from one point of view, and Raymond Greene,[147] a chevalier sans peur et sans reproche – from another, both agree that ministers tell lies in the House of Commons. Old Colonel Churchill[148] in the W[ar] O[ffice] quoted to me also two instances of this in days gone by, referring to military matters. Strange that MPs and soldiers in their private moments admit what the public never understands or admits. There is, however, a very

---

[146] Sir Roger David Casement (1854–1916), consular official and Irish nationalist; postings in the Belgian Congo and Brazil; retired, 1913; co-founder Irish Volunteers, 1913; negotiated with German chancellor, 1915; captured and hanged for treason, Aug. 1916.

[147] Lieutenant-Colonel Sir (Walter) Raymond Greene (1869–1947), 2nd Bt., succ. 1920, soldier and politician; served South Africa, 1899–1900, and with 9th Lancers, France, 1914–15; Lieutenant-Colonel 2nd/3rd County of London Yeomanry, 1915–16; General Staff Officer, 1918; MP (Cons.) Cambridgeshire, Chesterton Division, 1895–1906, Hackney North, 1906–23; member of London County Council, Hackney North, 1907–10.

[148] Colonel Arthur Gillespie Churchill (1860–1940), officer; entered army, 1880; Military Attaché at Tokyo, 1898–1903; Chief Staff Officer, Western Command, 1904–1905; General Staff Officer, Scottish Command, 1905–1909; retired, 1909; General Staff Officer, War Office, 1914–18.

dangerous fallacy in the N[orton] Griffiths' view of ministerial honour. If we are fighting for freedom and truth and our ministers are tyrants and liars – we have no ideals for which to fight. To suppose that ministerial honour and national honour have no connection is absurd, and national honour is our highest national efficiency. Without efficiency truth and justice may triumph – without honour they never will.

The situation on the Western front is that the total Brit[ish] casualties are 240,000[,] French 100,000.

Divisions unused to date 61 French 8 British corresponding German 74 at most, some probably unusable. Americans will arrive at the rate of 120,000 a month. The direction of attack not accurately known, but there will be pegging away in the Kemmel area,[149] and a heavy assault somewhere on the southern end. All freshwater inundations in the Ypres area have already begun, those at the coast, the seawater ones, are in preparation but will only be used in the last extremity.

9th [May 1918]

Interview with Benesh. He is apparently quite satisfied with the Czech-Slovak Convention signed between Italy and Stefanik[150] on the 21st April. He believed (a little optimistically) that Italy would recognize an independent Czecho-Slovak, JugoSlav, and Transylvanian State as soon as England and France did so. This does not accord with our information (though it is perhaps what Orlando[151] told him). Orlando told us that Italy would not declare for the dismemberment of Austria because of clerical and internal intrigues.

Benesh also claimed that the Congress of oppressed nationalities of Rome of the 9th April had demoralized the Austrian army in Italy and stopped the offensive, and caused Slav troops to be moved from the first line into the rear trenches. All this is doubtful and open to dispute. He had an interesting story as to the Emperor Charles' 2nd letter. It was to the effect that he said that Italy was intriguing against France with him, and that, if France would give up Italy, he would work for Alsace-Lorraine. Clemenceau wished to publish this but Sonnino did not.

---

[149] German forces had captured Kemmel ridge to the east of Messines, on 29 Apr. 1918.

[150] General Milan Rastislav Štefánik (1880–1919), Slovak astronomer and politician; at *Observatoire de Paris-Meudon*, 1907–14; enlisted in French army as aviator, 1914; co-founder of the Czecholslovak National Council, 1916; Czechoslovak War Minister, 1918–19.

[151] Vittorio Emanuele Orlando (1860–1952), Italian politician; Minister of the Interior, 1916–17; Prime Minister, 1917–19; President of the Italian Chamber of Deputies, 1919–20 and 1945–46.

He spoke well also of Vatican. The Vatican did not want to break up Austria, because an Austria incorporated in Germany would not Catholicise Germany, whereas Austria-Hungary at present was almost wholly Catholic. The argument is sound and was confirmed from another source by Cardinal Gasparri.[152]

10th [May 1918]

Poor Maurice could not answer for himself in the Commons last night[153] and L[loyd] G[eorge] cut him up in fine style. One point was really good that Maurice was not at the Supreme Council at Versailles when the decision was taken, but only in a room hard by.

On the other hand the other parts were broadly correct in his statement, viz. that our numbers were reduced just before the offensive. L[loyd] G[eorge] says that M[aurice] never corrected the figures he (L[loyd] G[eorge]) gave on the 9th April. This is not true and L[loyd] G[eorge] by his letter (v[ide] 25th April) knows that it is untrue. Still, on the whole, I think that his conduct was wrong and L[loyd] G[eorge]'s figures, if wrong, should not have been corrected in the newspapers by a retiring subordinate. The true danger is "amateur strategy" and civilian interference in the military province. This has, if anything been intensified by the debate. L[loyd] G[eorge] however has certainly secured a great moral triumph.

As at the Vatican Council, unity meant more to many than did truth, and L[loyd] G[eorge] put the same question as Pio Nono[154] to the discontented[:] "Amas me?" The answer was the same in both cases.

11th [May 1918]

I find that the specific facts as to L[loyd] G[eorge]'s speech were as follows

> (1.) 'The very small percentage of (white) troops in black divisions' was 64% in Egypt 27% in Palestine & Mespot.
> (2.) The <2> divisions referred to by L[loyd] G[eorge] as under orders to go in Egypt were not actually so ordered until after the offensive, i.e. after the date of the statement given by Maurice.

---

[152] See entry 5 May 1918.
[153] *Hansard* (5) cv (9 May 1918), col. 2312–3.
[154] Pius IX (née Giovanni Maria Mastai-Ferretti) (1792–1878), Roman Catholic clergyman; Pope, 1846–78; convened First Vatican Council, 1869–70, which decreed papal infallibility.

The figures and facts of Maurice were correct but Henry Wilson said there were 3 not 4 or 5 div[ision]s in Egypt in addition to 3 white div[ision]s in Egypt[;] in addition 3 white cav[alr]y div[ision]s are not reckoned in at all.

> (3.) The figures quoted by L[loyd] G[eorge] in his speech referred throughout to ration strength not to combatant strength. In combatants the white troops were at any rate 140,000 down in 1916.
> (4.) The supreme council at Versailles decided to continue the offensive in Palestine the same time as the campaign in France.

13th [May 1918]

I am told very confidentially that Maurice broached some of his project of writing to Sir W[illiam] Robertson who did his best to dissuade him altogether. Sir H[enry] W[ilson] thinks he was badly treated by Maurice. In days gone by they had a great row, while in France in 1915, which rendered it impossible for them to get in well in the future together. But though he desired Maurice to go, H[enry] W[ilson] thought that he treated him with gr[ea]t consid[eratio]n, in especial in continuing him at full D[irector of] M[ilitary] O[perations]'s pay for a month, after Radclyffe [sic] arrived. Maurice said nothing whatever to him about the letter before writing it.

Sir H[enry] Wilson is more and more obviously a political general. Milner wrote recently to Lawrence,[155] Haig's C[hief] of Staff saying that he had heard from a staff officer that there were no reserve garrisons behind the line in France and that this was neglecting an obvious precaution. Lawrence's reply was good. The German calculation of the space required for a divisional front was 4,000 yards preferably 3,000. The British had to occupy lines with divisions from fronts ranging from 5,000 to 8,000 yards. This consequently left no room for reserve garrisons of which in theory he approved.

It seems strange that Milner should write on a purely military matter of this sort direct to the C[hief] of S[taff] France without consulting the C[hief of the] I[mperial] G[eneral] S[taff] here.

I understand also that the D[irector of] M[ilitary] I[ntelligence] reports daily to Milner <direct>, which the C[hief of the] I[mperial] G[eneral] S[taff] would not stand if he was a real man.

---

[155] General Hon. Sir Herbert (Alexander) Lawrence (1861–1943), soldier; entered army, 1882; staff captain, Intelligence Division, War Office, 1896–99; on active service South Africa, 1899–1902; retired, 1904, and recalled, 1914; active service Dardanelles, 1915, Egypt, 1916, France, 1917–19; Chief of Staff, Headquarters, British Armies in France, Jan. 1918–19; retired, 1922; managing partner Glyn, Mills, Currie & Co., 1919–34; chairman, 1934–43.

14th May [1918]

The attitude of Wilson has hardened over intervention in Siberia, and he is less convinced than ever, despite the G[eneral] S[taff] memo[randum]. This is a serious matter because it is not only a difference of opinion, but a rift in the Entente lute. Murmansk will have to be defended by 20,000 Czechs and 3,000 Serbs, we do not know about anything else. Siberia certainly cannot be defended except by the Jap[ane]s[e].

Lockhart appears to have now come round to the view that the Jap[ane]s[e] should intervene whether the Bolsheviks invite them or no. It would seem that Knox[156] and Buchanan (v[ide] 19th March) were right after all.

15th May [1918]

Maurice is in the papers again, and to be war correspondent of the Daily Chronicle.[157] He now writes to say that he did not notice L[loyd] G[eorge]'s speech of the 9th at first being occupied and in France – on the 20th he left the W[ar] O[ffice]. On the 30th he wrote calling the attention of the C[hief of the] I[mperial] G[eneral] S[taff] to these statements, a fact which L[loyd] G[eorge] omitted to give in his speech <and Wilson in his private defence. Maurice> does not mention, as he might have done, that the correct figures were supplied in the weekly report and were interpreted by L[loyd] G[eorge] as a correction (v[ide] 25th April). L[loyd] G[eorge] did not mention this either. <Maurice's letter was censored in the Press.>

L[loyd] G[eorge] was at the W[ar] O[ffice] today. I don't know whether it was this or about the Mexican business in which the W[ar] O[ffice] policy conflicts with the F[oreign] O[ffice].

The present strength sit[uatio]n on the Western front is that we are some 7 or 8 to the good in fresh divisions but that an attack may still be made with 70 or 80 divisions by the Huns. Foch thinks not so many but our intelligence was righter than his before.

16–17th [May 1918]

Brentwood camp. To see the educational scheme of the 23rd Army Corps.

---

[156] Lieutenant-General Sir Alfred William Fortescue Knox (1870–1964), officer and politician, kt. 1919; joined army, 1891; General Staff, War Office, 1908–11; Military Attaché at St. Petersburg, 1911–18; retired, 1920; MP (Cons.) Wycombe, 1924–45.

[157] A Radical half-penny paper, generally supporting Lloyd George.

I find that G[eneral] H[ead] Q[uarters] Home Forces printed 60,000 copies of the "Origin of the War" which was especially written and done up for the educational scheme, but did not circulate to the 23rd A[rmy] C[orps] the one unit which would have profited most by it. So runs the Army away from all intelligent guidance or sustentation of moral.

19th [May 1918]

F[oreign] O[ffice] have made a champion blunder, in direct opposition to my advice. Lansing[158] asked us if the USA should declare war on both Bulgaria and Turkey, stating that Bulgaria being a Christian country, they could hardly declare war on that alone, and leave Turkey out. Passing by his edifying but not convincing method of reasoning I recommended declaring war on Turkey, as we could not get her out, and might frighten Bulgaria and induce more friction between these 2 choice Allies. The F[oreign] O[ffice] rejected this advice, and intend to declare war on both together simultaneously.

<(FitzM[aurice] told me today that he made the same recommendations to F[oreign] O[ffice] and that they appeared to accept it. Harold Nicolson[159] somebody went behind – 'The hidden hand'! 22/5/[18])>

20th [May 1918]

Wilson again, evidence from G.G. Butler[160] and Lord E[ustace] Percy.[161] Both think W[ilson] one who thinks too much of women – 'The Merry Wives of

---

[158] Robert Lansing (1864–1928), US international lawyer and politician; advised State Department on arbitrations matters, 1892–1914; counsellor to State Department, 1914–15; Secretary of State, 1915–20; member of US delegation at Paris Peace Conference, 1919.

[159] Sir Harold George Nicolson (1886–1968), diplomat, writer and politician; entered diplomatic service, 1909; member of British delegation at the Paris Peace Conference, 1919; legation counsellor at Tehran, 1925–27; embassy counsellor at Berlin, 1928–29; resigned, 1929; MP (Nat. Lab.) Leicester West, 1935–45; Parliamentary Under-secretary at the Ministry of Information, 1940–41; BBC Governor, 1941–46.

[160] Sir (George) Geoffrey Gilbert Butler (1887–1929), historian and politician; Fellow of Corpus Christi College, Cambridge, 1910–29; employed in Foreign Office news department, 1915–17; director of British Bureau of Information, New York, 1917–19; MP (Cons.) Cambridge University, 1923–29.

[161] Lord Eustace Sutherland Campbell Percy (1887–1958), 1st Baron Percy of Newcastle, cr. 1953, diplomat and politician; entered diplomatic service, 1911; private secretary to Lord Robert Cecil, Jan.–Mar. 1919; delegate at Paris peace conference, 1919; joint secretary of the Inter-Allied Commission on the League of Nations, 1919; resigned, 1919; MP (Cons.) Hastings, 1921–37;

Wilson' and 'McAdoo about nothing' are 2 old Washington japes.[162] This is a curious trait, common, I fear, to great leaders.

They also think that W[ilson] did not see very far, and was not pro-Entente from the first, but moved by events. This they seem to consider a flaw – I think it the reverse. From the insular part of view it is true, I think, that W[ilson] was not pro-Entente from the first. That however I regard as an advantage. He avowed himself the instrument of the people, and was it. As he moved so did they. This is the popular government. Even in the Presidential election he was still saying this was the last great war America would be kept out of. Then came his definite offer of good offices, the German U-Boat ruthless [*sic*] campaign. Then he and [the] USA were stung into action, and the war followed. To me this Pilgrim's Progress is a noble one, and it seems to me insular to regards it as otherwise. He was 'too proud to fight' for the selfish interest of [the] USA but, as he says now, 'he is proud to fight for mankind.'

21st [May 1918]

Sal[oni]ca.

22nd [May 1918]

The German offensive still inexplicably hangs fire – perhaps the record number of 224 <tons of> bombs dropped behind their lines may in some way account for this.[163]

23rd [May 1918]

Went to [the] doctor [and] learnt I have got varicose veins – a legacy of weakness from my illness at the Dardanelles. I cannot complain – others have greater troubles, though I shall never be the same again.

Parliamentary Under-secretary, Board of Education, 1923; Ministry of Health, 1923–24; President of the Board of Education, 1924–29; Minister without Portfolio, 1935–36.

[162] Woodrow Wilson's daughter, Eleanor Randolph Wilson (1889–1967), married in 1914, William Gibbs McAdoo Jr. (1863–1941), the US Treasury Secretary, 1913–18.

[163] The third German offensive, in the sector between Soissons and Reims, commenced on 29 May.

26th [May 1918]

I got some fresh light on the Maurice crisis today as I saw the true figures, worked out in the closest detail.[164] L[loyd] G[eorge] is approximately right on the western front, though less right on March than on January 1917, and 1918. But the real gravamen is that, while the forces in France remained stationary, those in Mesopotamia and Palestine practically doubled in 1917 – that is what it [is] to have 3 Orientals in the War Cabinet – L[loyd] G[eorge] a little Bethelite, Milner an Imperialist, Curzon a sultan. As old Robertson said, you will be caught with your extra divisions out in the East when they really should be in the West. This is too sadly true.

28th [May 1918]

The offensive has begun, the real thing, I fear. We are caught somewhat unprepared on the Soissons-Reims line. 24 of our divisions are attacked there, sent there <u>because it was a quiet part of the line</u>. Curiously enough I was looking at the map of the German forces on the 26th and thinking that it would be just as easy for their reserves to descend to the South as to the West.

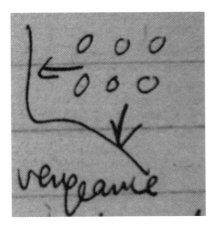

They have done [so] with a vengeance and what makes it worse is that it is the Crown Prince's[165] army.

---

[164] See entry 7 May 1918.

[165] Prince (Friedrich) Wilhelm (Victor August Ernst) von Hohenzollern (1882–1951), German Crown Prince and Crown Prince of Prussia, 1888–1918; commanded German 5th

29th [May 1918]

News not very reassuring, though the French have recaptured Soissons.[166]

Fitzmaurice came to see me today[.] I am afraid that it will be difficult to rescind the telegram of the F[oreign] O[ffice] to [the] USA advising declaration of war on both Bulgaria and Turkey but I am sure it is the foundation of our policy and the beginning of wisdom, and have strongly advised in this sense (v[ide] 19th May).

At the same time Heard[167] is going out under the Northcliffe propaganda to start a propagandist campaign – 69 Bulgarian prisoners etc. I greatly doubnt if this is wise, because the only propaganda we can start is that of a Social Revolutionary propaganda. Can we extend this in the Balkans? Even if successful in Bulgaria, it might not ultimately benefit us for it would affect the dynasties of Serbia, Greece, Bulgaria, all of which we desire to support. There seems to be no guiding or directing policy at the back.

1st [June 1918]

<u>Armistice paper</u> 30th [May 1918] accepted by D[irector of] M[ilitary] I[ntelligence], who thanked me much for the work I had put into it.[168] I certainly think that what I did was worth it, and we have now worked out a reasonable paper which will set the standard, I hope, to both Admiralty and F[oreign] O[ffice]. The latter have not yet interfered in the matter.

2nd [June 1918]

3rd [June 1918]

The romance of King Alexander[169] and Mlle Manos[170] nears completion. On the 21st May Granville had an interview with them, the Duke of Connaught having previously acted the part of Cupid's footpad. M[ademoise]lle was

---

Army, 1914–16; commanded Army Group *Kronprinz* during 3rd offensive of 1918.

[166] The Germans captured it again on 29 May.
[167] See entry 24 Feb. 1917.
[168] Memo. Temperley, 'Possibilities of Armistice', 11 Mar. 1918, Webster MSS, LSE Archives, 3/5.
[169] See entry 13–14 June 1917.
[170] Aspasia Manos (1896–1972), Greek commoner; married King Alexander in secret civil wedding, Nov. 1919; Consort of the King of the Hellenes, 1919–20.

reasonable, the King was not. Granville demanded that she should not be Queen and at one point the King threatened an outburst. Since then Venizelos has objected and shown signs of ~~recalibrating~~ withdrawing from his position of support. In an interview the other day he showed definite signs, and Granville even thought him incorrect in statement. V[enizelos]'s position is that he will yield to pressure from England but not unless it is known. We have advocated a morganatic marriage and pressed it from the first. The Greek army has done well against the SRKA bi LEGEN and taken 1,700 prisoners.

4th [June 1918]

Hear today that a General (Blow) and a G[eneral] S[taff] O[fficer]3 are going out to France to form a liaison for the Czecho-Slovaks. I wonder if the history will be the same as Corkran[171] with the Serbs – to send out a general well-intentioned but totally ignorant, and finally to have to supersede him with somebody else. I shall lend what help I can, of course.

The disgusting Maud Allen[172] [*sic*] trial ends with the acquittal of Billing[173] – strange champions of purity he and Spencer,[174] who wrote a phrase so filthy that no paper has yet been induced to print it.[175] It is a combination of motives which has worked on the jury – the attraction of unnameable vices linked up with the wildest cat stories of Germany. The acquittal will have the worst effects on foreigner and will convince them that 47,000 of the highest in the land are sold to Germany or blackmailed by her. Spencer is an avowed lunatic, who, among other things, thinks and has said in private that I ordered an offensive at Salonica! Unfortunately he did not know that I never had the power or position to do so. All I can say is that Maud Allen is an artist, Billing an adventurer and Spencer a lunatic, both the latter of the most infamous character. If these are thy champions, virtue, vice itself might be preferable. To adapt Burke, virtue itself

---

[171] See entry 14 Sept. 1917.

[172] Maude Allan (née Beulah Maude Durrant) (1873–1956), Canadian-born actor and dancer; her version of the 'Dance of the Seven Veils' gained her notoriety before 1914; she lost the libel case against Billing.

[173] Noel Pemberton Billing (1881–1948), aviator, publisher and politician; volunteered Second Boer War, 1900; MP (Indep.) Hertford, 1916–23; his journals *Imperialist* and *Vigilante* circulated conspiracy theories during the war, including that of the 'Black Book', said to contain the names of 47,000 British aristocrats blackmailed by the enemy.

[174] Captain Harold Sherwood Spencer (b. 1890), US-born activist and writer; volunteer on staff of Prince Wilhelm von Wied, as King of Albania, 1913–14; commissioned into Royal Field Artillery, 1915; invalided on grounds of mental instability; anti-Semitic and homophobic writer afterwards.

[175] 'Acquittal Of Mr. Billing', *The Times*, 5 June 1918.

loses half its goodness when it gains all this grossness.[176] <Note. Later – the chief woman witness who professed to see the Black Book was convicted of bigamy and perjured herself in court.>

5th [June 1918]

Lord Robert Cecil, in answer to a question in the House of Commons, showed what an outrageous liar Spencer is.[177] He was not employed by the F[oreign] O[ffice] in 1913, and he did not send them a confidential report. Incidentally he was then the paid servant of an alien enemy, the Prince of Wied. These are our Gods, o Israel! <Subsequently Adm[ira]l Troubridge who, according to Spencer, saw and reported officially on the Black Book, published a letter denying the statement.>

There was no special light on the offensive in the Conference today. Prince Rupprecht's[178] divisions have not appeared in the Marne sector yet.

6th [June 1918]

The Declaration of premiers at Versailles, taken on the 3rd June,[179] binds us (1.) to [the] creation of a united and independent Poland with access to [the] sea (2.) to give an expression of earnest sympathy with the American declaration in favour of the nationalistic aspirations towards freedom of CzechoSlovak and JugoSlav peoples.

So Austria again escapes.

8th [June 1918]

Sir W[illiam] Tyrrell sent for me today to the F[oreign] O[ffice] and told me, for my private information, what happened at the Conference of Premiers at Versailles. England and France strongly favoured declaring independent Czech

---

[176] 'Vice itself lost half its evil by losing all its grossness', E. Burke, 'Reflections on the Revolution in France [1790]', in *The Works of the Right Honourable Edmund Burke* (12 vols, London, 1837), iii, 332.

[177] *Hansard* (5) cvi (5 June 1918), cols. 1557–58.

[178] Field Marshal Rupprecht Maria Luitpold Ferdinand von Wittelsbach (1869–1955), Crown Prince of Bavaria, 1913–18; commanded German Sixth Army, 1914–16; Army Group Rupprecht, 1916–18; a strong critic of Ludendorff's conduct of the war.

[179] Allied Supreme War Council meeting, 1–4 June 1918.

and JugoSlav states. Sonnino opposed it, declaring that not 5% [of] JugoSlavs wanted JugoSlav independence.

Is this true?, said Tyrrell – Will you answer me? give me a paper. I have no one here who could do it. I said I would. I could not keep feeling flattered at their thinking that I had the knowledge on this subject.

12th [June 1918]

Saw an extract from War Cabinet conversation of June 10th. The Prime Minister drew attention to the fact that the Germans were very clever at using information behind their own lines to hearten their own men. Could we not do something more of this sort? Talk about the Americans coming up etc. Sir Henry Wilson (C[hief of the] I[mperial] G[eneral] S[taff], Wilson) said that he fancied our men had got into the habit of reading the enemy communiqués and paying no attention to our own.

The Prime Minister drew attention to the fact that there appeared to be some leakage from the General Staff to the papers, and that there was much dissatisfaction in France at the suggestion in the 'Star' that Frenchmen had not fought well. C[hief of the] I[mperial] G[eneral] S[taff] said that the very reverse was the case – the D[irector of] M[ilitary] O[perations, Radcliffe] had said the opposite to the Pressmen and you could not protect yourself against abuse of that sort.

Note Lord Milner (not C[hief of the] I[mperial] G[eneral] S[taff]!) undertook to submit to the Prime Minister copies of the D[irector of] M[ilitary] O[perations]'s statements to the Press.

This is a blinding flash of light – the autocrat is certainly not the C[hief of the] I[mperial] G[eneral] S[taff].

14th [June 1918]

Finished my armistice problem – Jugo-Slav problem.[180] The latter as requested by Tyrrell. My own view is that they have, since 1918, shown both in Croatia and Slovenia a new spirit and desire for independence, sufficient to make Sonnino's statement absurd and an Allied declaration in favour of their independence justifiable. Will Austria escape for ever? I begin to hope not.

---

[180] Memo. Temperley, 'The Jugo-Slav Problem', ? June 1918, TNA (PRO), FO 371/3135/11631.

Heard confidentially that I had received a Serbian decoration.[181] I have avoided an English one – the OBE, for which relief much thanks.

How we are governed. The papers announce that Gulland[,][182] Chief Whip to Asquith had resigned owing to illness. At the [Reform] Club I heard a man today saying "Hullo Gulland, sorry to hear that illness has made you resign." "I hadn't heard it" said Gulland wearily. I infer a press intrigue to upset him. I remember him well a burly cheerful man in 1910, who told me long before it was public that the king had consented to create peers. Now he looked worn and anxious and the press is trying to destroy him. I understand it was some counter-faction in the Liberal party.

June 15th – 2nd July 30th [1918]

Breakdown Spanish influenza – away at Thorney[;] cure consisted of drinking cider and browning in the sun.

1st July

Events in my absence are

>   (1.) Further definition of position of Japan,[183] which suggests that
>   (a.) they will not move without full American consent
>   (b.) they wish the supreme undivided command
>   (c.) they did not engage to go further west than Eastern Siberia unless the military situation demanded it.

Not very encouraging. Balfour had some pretty rapier play about the meaning of "engage" with the military attaché. Of course he scored heavily but I don't know that it was worth it.

---

[181] Order of the White Eagle of Serbia.
[182] John William Gulland (1864–1920), politician; MP (Lib.) Dumfries Burghs, 1906–18; Parliamentary Secretary to the Treasury, 1915–16; Chief Whip, 1915–18.
[183] In July, President Wilson had requested Japanese support for an Allied intervention force to rescue the Czech Legion stranded at Vladivostok, and to secure Allied war materials there.

1st July (cont[inue]d)

The situation between L[loyd] G[eorge] and the General Staff seems as lively as ever. L[loyd] G[eorge] (nominally Sir Maurice Hankey) has sent a series of demands, strongly protesting against the Adjutant General's assertions as to the demands for man-power, as made by the G[eneral] S[taff] in 1917. The substance of L[loyd] G[eorge]'s reply is that

> (1.) The state of the country did not allow the number of men to be raised in 1917[.]
> (2.) The shortage due to the Ypres offensive, which was undertaken against the advice of the War Cabinet. In fact, of course, the War Cabinet advised the sending of greater forces to Italy and Palestine and, had this advice prevailed, the result would have been to weaken the defensive in France of today.

Incidentally Amery by some private manoeuvre, has managed to delay the despatch of the 54th division from Palestine.

L[loyd] G[eorge] at the end of January at the Versailles Conference stated that we (the Entente) had always been overinsured in France. What is the only way to end the war? by knocking out Turkey, i.e. by sending more troops to Palestine, and this not seven week's before Gough's débâcle!

L[loyd] G[eorge] has also had another struggle with the General Staff, or rather has not had one because of his professed opionions. Northumberland compiled some statistics for the "very secret" weekly summary as to British Divisions to which L[loyd] G[eorge] Milner objected on the ground of too wide a circulation and of L[loyd] G[eorge]'s objection thereto. N[orthumberlan]d then suggested that this should be made the basis of a paper to the <Imperial> War Conf[eren]ce, to which Milner agreed. When however he saw the final draft he said that the P[rime] M[inister] would not like it and declined to sanction it. In other words there is practically an agreed conspiracy on the part of [Lloyd] George and Milner to keep the true military facts from the Conference. They say, however, that Australia's Hughes[184] is smelling a rat and that he is inquiring into military matters, more especially into this dismissal of old Robertson.

---

[184] William Morris 'Billy' Hughes (1862–1952), Australian politician; Minister for External Affairs, 1904, 1908–1909, 1921–23 and 1937–39; Attorney-General, 1908–1909, 1910–13, 1914–21, 1938–41; Prime Minister, 1915–23; Minister of Trade, 1916; Minister of Health, 1934–35 and 1936–37; Minister for Repatriation, 1934–35 and 1936–37; Minister for the Navy, 1940–41; leader of Labor Party, 1915–16, National Labor Party, 1916–17, Nationalist Party, 1917–23, Australia Party, 1930–31, United Australia Party, 1941–43.

At a recent Cabinet [Lloyd] George spoke strongly in favour of not treating German proposals to negotiate with too much brusqueness. He stated that the French were strongly of this opinion especially the Socialist parties there. The evidence, so far as it goes, is totally against this view, and I suppose [Lloyd] George was voicing his own thoughts and personal wishes in the matter. It is worth noting that, in the secret negotiations with the Emperor Charles in 1917, [Lloyd] George was more anxious either than France or Italy to procure a peace and prolong the negotiation. I cannot help thinking that he does, for some reason, wish to secure peace on terms less justifiable than we should have.

3rd <July 1918>

Saw a F[oreign] O[ffice] paper on the Austrian question, whether to promote a revolution there or not, and, if so, how? It was from Tyrrell's department, chiefly Namier,[185] I think, and is to go before the War Cabinet. My comments were – overstress upon the social motive as against the national, and therefore damning the real motive force in Austria and Hungary, i.e. the oppressed nationalities rather than the oppressed proletariates [*sic*].[186]

The Military suggestions for armistices, stampeding of JugoSlavs & CzechoSlovaks on the Italian front were incredibly crude. They show incidentally that the F[oreign] O[ffice] does not understand the rudiments of strategy.

4th [July 1918]

Bouboloff. This Bulgarian negotiator who declares that MALINOFF[187] (the present premier) belongs to his revolutionary, i.e. anti-Ferdinand, organization, and that an upset in Bulgaria is possible – has imposed a good deal on F[oreign] O[ffice] and on D[irector of] M[ilitary] I[ntelligence, Macdonogh]. The F[oreign] O[ffice] conclusion, viz. that a reolution is possible or likely is, in my opinion, wrong. Their action to send him to Bulgaria is right or at least will do harm.

<Note. Subsequently this affair transpired and Greek and Serb ministers both saw – the latter thought badly of him.>

---

[185] See entry 11 Mar. 1918.
[186] Memo. Temperley, 28 June 1918, TNA (PRO), FO 371/3135/103498.
[187] Aleksandar Pavlov Malinov (1867–1938), Bulgarian politician; Prime Minister, 1908–11, June–Nov. 1918, June–Oct. 1931; critical of German alliance and favoured a separate peace.

5th [July 1918]

According to Panouse the decisions of the Conference are as follows[:]

> (1) USA can go on supplying troops at the same rate as last month 276,000 and the Admiralty can arrange contingent shipping.
> (2) Even the USA representative agreed in principle to Japanese intervention in Siberia. Wilson therefore still remains, though he recently declared himself in favour only of an economic commission, possibly guarded by or accompanied with troops.
> (3) Sonnino agreed not to ~~fight~~ oppose volunteering <for Serb army> of the 22,000 JugoSlav prisoners in Italy. He agreed to form a JugoSlav unit to fight in Italy (~~CzechSlovak~~ Croat Slovene?)

6th [July 1918]

7th [July 1918]

The Archbishop of Chicago[188] is stated on fair authority to have addressed a private Irish meeting telling them to put the softpedal on before talking about Sinn Fein.[189]

10th [July 1918]

Venizelos had not been very happy lately, for, in a despatch about rationing the Greek troops, he took the part of the French against us, and spoke of their 'well-known generosity.' As a matter of fact their generosity was with our goods. But he rose to his full height in an interview with Granville recently. He began by saying that Avezzano[190] (who replaced the late Italian min[iste]r to Greece, C[oun]t Bosdari) had made a good impression on him and that his instructions were to bring about a basis of definite understanding between Italy and Greece.

---

[188] George William Mundelein (1872–1939), US Roman Catholic clergyman of German-Irish descent; Bishop of Brooklyn, 1909–15; Archbishop of Chicago, 1915–39; Cardinal, 1924.

[189] Irish nationalist and republican party, founded in 1905 by Arthur Griffith (1872–1922).

[190] Baron Camillo Romano Avezzano (1867–1949), Italian diplomat; legation secretary at Peking, 1901; minister at Athens, 1918–23; ambassador at Washington, 1923–30; Senator, 1922–43; member of the Italo-Greek Conciliation Commission, 1930.

He outlined the possibilities on general lines. Italy might retain STAMPALIA[191] or another port in the Dodecanese but otherwise must retire from there. In Northern Epirus and Koritza[192] he asked for no more than was guaranteed by treaty of 1913 (Note. This [is] obscure and probably erroneous.) He said nothing of Cyprus or of Cavalla. But he said Greece could not put up with [an] Italian monopoly of Albania or with the predominance of a Great Power strong enough to do her mischief so near. Albania might go under an international commission and only then, if proved incapable of <self-> government, should she be partitioned.

As regards Turkey he did not doubt the final ultimate triumph of the Entente, but he did think that at present it might not be practicable politics to put an end to him [sic]. He thought Constantinople must be internationalised (moderate for a Greek!). In Asia Minor he thought neither Turks, Kurds, Armenians or Greek had enough numbers of justify sovereignty over a single district, the Armenians in especial were nearly exterminated. He did not think that Italy should be allowed intercede there, but, if internationalised Government was impossible, they might have an <internationalised> Governor for a period of years, who might prepare the way. (One thinks rather of the Governor in Crete who led to Greek domination there.)

There is a Balkan Conference at Paris this week, where no doubt this plan may come up. Like few other men Venizelos knows the Balkans and sees deep and far.

11th [July 1918]

Wilson has at last capitulated on the 9th. An expedition of 14,000 can start from Vladivostok to save the CzechoSlovaks, 7,000 Americans, 7,000 Jap[ane]s[e] – no Allies, though the latter are to appear in the proclamations.

Lloyd George not very pleased and sent a long telegram in private to Reading.[193] He says that it is a race between Germans and us for Western Siberia, and that this small expedition of Wilson's is really 'preposterous'. It entails grave risks like those which left Gordon of Khartoum and may have as disastrous results.

Reading on the other hand is pleased. He looks not to what is actually proposed but to the complete change of policy, to which Wilson has been brought.

---

[191] Now Astypalaia, an island in the Dodecanese.
[192] Now Korcë in southeastern Albania.
[193] See entry 15 Nov. 1917.

Northcliffe has at last attacked the F[oreign] O[ffice] with an article on "Our wonderful Foreign Office" re the Dutch Convoy.[194]

Panouse told me that at least 2 interviews had been held, with a view to peace, by a representative of Ludendorff with a French representative in Switzerland.

12th [July 1918]

Venizelos and Pashitch. An interesting correspondence has taken place between these two leaders recently, because P[ašić] is going to the Paris Conference, and wishes to agree, so far as possible, with V[enizelos]. P[ašić] suggested

> (1.) joint diplomatic action to which V[enizelos] agreed
> (2.) in view of the state of Bulgar morale in the army and state the USA should be approached, and corrected as to propaganda on the 'principles of nationalities'. This brought a sharp passage from V[enizelos] who said that no peace could be based on a violation of that principle, and that Greece and Serbia would lose all credit, if they advocated it. P[ašić] promptly explained that he had not wished to attack the principle of nationalities but only the Bulgar misapplication of it.

My memo[randum] on JugoSlavs[195] was asked for in a hurry by [Sir Rennell] Rodd[196] to enable a public statement to be made.

16th [July 1918]

The Hun offensive has not been very successful to date.[197] Foch, whom Du Cane[198] saw at 1.30 <today> was pleased and confident, and satisfied. His staff compare the situation to that of the French offensive of May 1917, when further operations could only have been pushed forward with enormous losses. The time and place of the offensive were almost exactly known owing to admission

---

[194] See the leader 'The Dutch Convoy', *The Times*, 10 July 1918, calling into question 'the nerve and the sound judgment of the Foreign Office, if not of the Government'.
[195] See entry 14 June 1917.
[196] See entry 11 June 1917.
[197] The fifth German offensive on the Marne and in the Campagne, 15–17 July.
[198] Sir John (Philip) Du Cane (1865–1947), military officer; commissioned into Royal Artillery, 1884; Commander Royal Artillery 3rd Division, 1911–14; General headquarters, 1915–16; Ministry of Munitions, 1916; Commander XV Corps, 1916; Master-General of the Ordnance, 1920–23; General Officer Commanding-in-Chief for Western Command, 1923–24; British Army on the Rhine, 1924–27; aide-de-camp general to George V, 1926–30.

of prisoners and deserters, and there was thus no surprise. The French staff estimate 40 divisions as engaged but, so far, only 26 have been identified.

L[loyd] G[eorge] has not emerged scatheless [*sic*] from the test. He pulled Milner and the C[hief of the] I[mperial] G[eneral] S[taff] [Sir Henry Wilson] up in the middle of the night and had them off to Brighton the other night. When they got there they found him in a great state of excitement because Foch had taken 4 British divisions away from the British front. Why? What did this mean? Was it safe? etc. Milner and Wilson found it difficult to explain that he did more than any other to secure the supreme command. If so he 'built better (or does he think worse) than he thought.'[199]

L[loyd] G[eorge] has also been putting questions savouring of amateur strategy to the Staff recently, e.g. [h]ad the General Staff ever considered what would happen if the Germans suddenly transferred large numbers of divisions to the East – could we pursue them, or transfer similar quantities by sea? Still harping on the old string – getting out to Asia.

<"His army each day growing bolder & finer
With the Turcoman tribes he subdues Asia Minor
Goes on to the East through Turkmans & Tartars
Chokes the wretched Mogul in his grandmother's garters.">[200]

Another question of supremely absurd character was recently put to the G[eneral] S[taff]. "Why should not Great Britain resume its historical role of operating on the outskirts of the theatre of war?", i.e. got to Palestine or Salonica in force. Northumberland[201] has written a long memo[randum] to show that this role is not historical, that the War of Spanish Succ[essio]n was war in Blenheim and Flanders, that the Seven Years' War is not an exception because the balance of power was never endangered in Europe, and that in 1793 we committed grave faults in attacking the West Indies when a joint Allied march on Paris might have been decisive. I don't suppose L[loyd] G[eorge] will care – a volcano throwing out rubbish and sometimes scorching and brilliant fire.

---

[199] 'He builded better than he knew;/ The conscious stone to beauty grew', R.W. Emerson, 'The Problem', in D.H.S. Nicholson and A.H.E. Lee (eds), *The Oxford Book of English Mystical Verse* (Oxford, 1917), no. 77.

[200] 'His army each day growing bolder and finer,/ With the Turcoman tribes he subdues Asia Minor,/ Beats Paul and the Scythians, in journey previous/ Cross the Indus, with tribes of Armenians, and Jews,/ And Bucharians, and Affghans, and Persians, and Tartars;/ Chokes the wretched Mogul in his grandmother's garter,/ And will hang him dry in Luxemburg Hall/ 'Midst the plunder of Carthage, and spoils of Bengal', [G. Canning, J.H. Frere, G. Ellis and W. Gifford], *The Poetry of the Anti-Jacobin* (London, 4th edn, 1801), no. XXXIII, 220; cf. H.W.V. Temperley, *George Canning* (London, 1905), 59.

[201] Earl Percy as was, see entry 11 Apr. 1917.

17th [July 1918]

~~The JugoSlavs~~ Rhondda.[202] I saw Loveday[203] today who told me the story of R[hondda]. His 3 ablest assistants (of whom none <u>mirabile dictum</u> have yet received a decoration) – one Wintour,[204] Lloyd[205] and Wise.[206] The last has a presence, imaginative ideas, the last but one, organizing capacity, the first no presence but imagination & organizing power. The 3 have solved the food problem between them. R[hon]dda, they think, never recovered from the catastrophe of the Lusitania (H.W.V. T[emperley]. None the less in the fall of 1916 he did some very good work over contracts in America.) He was, think the 3, an able man with a scientific brain, but he never showed himself in his full stature at the Food Bureau. His strength, his brain, were both weakened, his backbone remained and he was distinguished by absolute loyalty to his subordinates. In the War Cabinet (which wished to get rid of him) he could not frame intelligible arguments, but he said things must be done, and they were. L[loyd] G[eorge] who likes talkers above all, did not care about him and thought of getting rid of him.

---

[202] David Alfred Thomas (1856–1918), 1st Viscount Rhondda, Welsh colliery owner and politician; MP (Lib.) Merthyr Tydfil, 1880–1910, Cardiff, 1910; special mission to USA, 1915–16; survived sinking of *Lusitania*, 1915; Minister of Food Control, 1917–18; died 3 July 1918.

[203] Alexander Loveday (1888–1962), economist and civil servant; ex-pupil of Temperley's; lecturer, Leipzig University, 1911–12, Cambridge, 1913–15; employed in War Office, 1915–19; in League of Nations Secretariat, 1919–31; Director of League of Nations Financial Section, 1931–39; of Economic, Financial and Transit Department, 1939–46; Warden of Nuffield College, Oxford, 1950–54.

[204] Ulrick Fitzgerald Wintour (1877–1947), civil servant; entered Imperial Chinese Customs Service, 1898; transferred to Board of Trade, 1904; Director of Exhibitions branch, 1908–14; Director of Army Contracts, 1914–17; Permanent Secretary, Ministry of Food, 1917–19; Controller, H.M. Stationery Office, 1918–19; with Inter-Allied Trade and Banking Corporation, 1919–20; director-general of British Empire Exhibition at Wembley, 1920–23.

[205] Commander Edward William Lloyd (1855–1946), sailor; passed into Navy, 1868; on staff of Director of Naval Ordnanance, 1889; resigned, 1889; joined W.G. Armstrong, Whitworth & Co., 1889; Commander Tyneside Royal Naval Volunteer Reserves, 1904–14; Ministry of Munition, 1915–19.

[206] Edward Frank Wise (1885–1933), economist, civil servant and politician; junior clerk, House of Commons, 1907–12; called to the bar, 1911; Acting Principal Clerk, National Insurance Commission, 1912; Secretary, Anglo-Russian Supplies Committee, War Office, 1914–15; Assistant Director of Army Contracts, 1916–17; Principal Assistant Secretary, Ministry of Food, 1917–19; Second Secretary there, 1919–22; Assistant Secretary, Board of Trade, 1922–23; delegate on Supreme Econmic Council, and Chairman of Sub-committee on Germany, 1919; economic adviser in respect of foreign trade to All-Russian Central Union of Consumers' Cooperative Societies (Centrosoyos), 1923–29; MP (Lab.) Leicester East, 1929–31.

18th [July 1918]

JugoSlavs. Rodd reported that the JugoSlav question was taken a much broader view of by Sonnino, who had proposed that those of Serbian race should be allowed to volunteer, but that Croats and Slovenes should remain in Italy. This is to divide the JugoSlav race by a truly Machiavellian stroke.

I got the D[irector of] M[ilitary] I[ntelligence] to write a letter to the F[oreign] O[ffice] denouncing it. <Since then I found out that, on 3rd July, the Supreme Council of Versailles 'took note' of these proposals. Ll[oyd] G[eorge] & Milner walked out of the room when Sonnino discussed the proposals and Balfour went to sleep – hence all this pother.>

21[st July 1918]

America has now definitely asked Japan to intervene and allowed a Japanese general to command. The situation is however still anxious as nearly all the CzechoSlovaks are leaving for Vladivostok for Irkutsk, and Vlad[ivosto]k is really exposed to a destruction of stores etc. until Jap[anese]-Americans arrive.

22[nd July 1918]

Today D[irector of] M[ilitary] I[ntelligence, Macdonogh] recommended me to represent W[ar] O[ffice] on the Committee for revision of Treaties (F[oreign] O[ffice], W[ar] O[ffice] & Adm[iralt]y.
  These comprise

> Agreements with Norway 1907–8 & Scandinavia[207]
> Neutrality of Switzerland 1815[208]
> Suez Canal Convention[209]

---

[207] The North and Baltic Sea agreements of 1907 between the states of the region affirmed the status quo, including the demilitarization of the Åland Islands.

[208] Swiss neutrality was established by the 'Act on the Neutrality of Switzerland', part of the Treaty of Paris of 20 Nov. 1815.

[209] The Convention of Constantinople of 2 Mar. 1888 confirmed as international law the guaranteed right of passage of all ships through the Suez Canal during war and peace.

24th [July 1918]

Dealt with telegrams from R[obert] C[ecil] to Wiseman,[210] a very important decision for shortening the war via the USA by getting out a certain power and fixing a time limit to action when she can formulate terms.

25th [July 1918]

Heard Balfour for the first time at the meeting at the Mansion House for statement of JugoSlav War-aims. The great idea of Wickham Steed[211] and other speakers was to commit us to the dismemberment of Austria. Balfour evaded <in words> this issue, but seemed morally to be committed by it. His main thing was that Austria was the Vassal, the plaything, the victim of Germany, just as Esthonia [sic] or Lithuania. He also dwelt long on the theme that Austria and Turkey between them had stifled or destroyed either nationality or union in the Balkans as occasion required. He made one serious slip, stating that the CzechoSlovaks and JugoSlavs had the same language, an error discreetly omitted from the Times Report of today (26th) but otherwise was good.[212] He gives an impression of wide philososophic grasp, as well as of moral feeling.

Steed, far more applauded as a speaker, made a contrast, full of points, some very good (as the three international forces which supported Austria – the Gold International finance, the Red German Socialism, the Black – international clericalism. Black-Gold-Red the colours of the Pan-German League[213]) – but it was that of an advocate, theatrical and fevered, every time he insisted on the need for dismembering Austria he turned round to A.J. B[alfour] to catch he eye. A.J. B[alfour] staff sat immovable as Buddha but no doubt thought the more. It seemed a parable of the relation of Northcliffe to the Government. If only Balfour had not slept on the 3rd July! <28th July>

---

[210] Sir William George Eden Wiseman (1885–1962), 10th Bart., intelligence agent and banker; military service, 1914; transferred to military intelligence; head of SIS branch in New York, 'Section V', 1915–21; liaison officer between President Wilson and British government; member of British delegation at the Paris Peace Conference, 1919; general partner of Kuhn, Loeb & Co., New York, 1929–60.

[211] See entry 8 Aug. 1917.

[212] 'An End To Austrian Tyranny. Yugo-Slav Aims', *The Times*, 26 July 1918.

[213] *Alldeutscher Verband* (Pan-German League), an ultra-nationalist, proto-racialist organisation, founded in 1891, with the aim of pursuing a Greater German empire, replete with a large fleet and colonial empire.

1918 295

26[th July 1918]

28th [July 1918]

The crisis is now nearly over.[214] Foch and his tanks has [*sic*] done splendidly, but he could not break through the salient, and so has been forced to smash in the end and the Germans back on the line of the Vesle. It is, however, all in all a masterly stroke, which has reversed the fortunes of war, and the 4 British divisions of L[loyd] G[eorge] (v[ide] 15th July) have been used to some purpose. Tanks and improvised attacks have also played a great part. It is strange that the partial failure of Cambrai[215] has showed the way to victory, the tank overcoming the machine gun, and the improvised attack succeeding better than the most carefully prepared offensive, both British ideas in origin. Northumberland thinks the Boche is definitely beat and that though the Crown Prince[216] has used 62 divisions, there are only 22 left with Rupprecht[217] and that these cannot be risked in a final attack just now, because Germany will then be defenceless until her 1920 class comes in in October. The French are only calling up their 1919 class[;] ours is in already.

A new instance of carrying economy too far. D[irector of] M[ilitary] I[ntelligence] received a letter from Clive Wigram,[218] A[ide] D[e] C[amp] to the King today[:] 'Following envelope enclosed. This would not matter except that, as it contains the confidential summary, it is opened by His Majesty with his own hands. I think, you will agree with me that this is not a very dainty address to set before the King.' The envelope enclosed contained the previously written and used address of "J.M. Saunders, Esq., National War Savings Committee." This had been crossed through with a pen and, instead, there had been written <u>in pencil</u>

His Majesty the King,
   Buckingham Palace.

---

[214] Foch's counter-offensive started on 18 July; by 26 July–3 Aug., the Germans had withdrawn behind the Marne and Vesle.
[215] British attack on *Siegfried Line* using large-scale tank formations, 20 Nov.–7 Dec. 1917.
[216] See entry 28 May 1918.
[217] See entry 5 June 1918.
[218] Col. Sir Clive Wigram (1873–1960), 1st Baron Wigram, cr. 1935, courtier and soldier; commissioned in Royal Artillery, 1893; aide-de-camp to Viceroy of India, 1895–97, 1899–1904; active service on Northwestern Frontier, 1897–98, South Africa, 1900–1901; Military Secretary to General Officer Commanding-in-Chief, Aldershot Command, 1908–10; Assistant Private Secretary and Equerry to King George V, 1910–31; Private Secretary, 1931–35; to Edward VIII, 1935–36; resigned, July 1936; to George VI, 1936–37; Keeper of the Royal Archives, 1931–45; permanent lord-in-waiting and extra equerry, 1937–45; retired 1945.

I heard a story of H[is] M[ajesty] the other day. A man called Burrows was introduced to him, whom he, from previous but inaccurate information, imagined to be Dr. Burrows[219] [,] the famous Venizelist champion. The King began <(it was in 1916)> 'I believe you are a great friend of Venizelos. Yes, oh yes, I know you are a great supporter, but I think there was a good deal to say on the other side, indeed. In some ways Constantine was quite right.' The poor pseudonym of Burrows was left standing on the spot, gasping and not daring to explain.

30th [July 1918]

The Pope of Washington [President Wilson] has made another of his great utterances but this time not in public. Even if Germany wished to retire from Belgium and restore Alsace Lorraine, on condition of a free hand in the East, the USA would not consent – a satisfactory and reviving tonic to the weak.

The strike, which threatened to burst on Monday [29 July], has been averted, partly, I suppose, by public opinion, partly by the threat of calling out the strikers.[220] Winston [Churchill], who saw his career trembling in the balance, was in a state of indescribable excitement on Sunday evening, and wore out 3 secretaries during the day. Even when Seeley[221] [*sic*] came back from Woolwich to report a partial qualified success, he almost jumped with joy.[222]

His tackling of strikes argues well for the future, though, in view of the Dardanelles catastrophe a strike which shoved Churchill out might be a national benefit.

31st [July 1918]

The divisions question. There are 186 Allied to 201 German, and in total numbers a difference of only 20,000. <71 German div[ision]s used in the last push.> The balance of fresh divisions, available for fighting is 27 German and 35 ours, so that the odds are again weighted in our favour. I do not, however, anticipate anything

---

[219] See entry 7 Dec. 1916.

[220] The so-called 'embargo' dispute, see 'No General Strike', *The Times*, 29 July 1918.

[221] Major-General John Edward Bernard Seely (1868–1947), 1st Baron Mottistone, cr. 1933, soldier and politician; called to the bar, 1897; active service South Africa, 1900–1901; MP (Lib.) Isle of Wight, 1900–1904, 1904–1906 and 1923–24, Liverpool Abercromby, 1906–10, Derbyshire Ilkestone, 1910–22; Parliamentary Under-secretary for the Colonies, 1908–11; for War, 1911–12; Secretary of State for War, 1912–14; active service European War, 1914–18; Parliamentary Under-secretary, Ministry of Munitions, 1918–19; for Air, Jan.–Dec. 1919.

[222] Workers at the Woolwich Arsenal decided nevertheless in favour of a strike, 'Gen. Seely's Appeal To Woolwich Men', *The Times*, 29 July 1918.

of serious importance in the way of a grand offensive, on either side, again this year. There may, however, be exceedingly important local offensives, which will serve the purpose of wearing out the enemy. Foch has therefore again in this second battle of the Marne turned back the German hordes with a composite force and with inferior numbers. Best of all the prestige of the German General Staff is seriously shaken.

Probably they will have a try at Italy or Salonica with a few divisions as a diversion.

2nd August [1918]

Venizelos. Venizelos has undoubtedly accomplished a very fine performance with the army. 6 divisions are already in the field and there will soon be 10. This is entirely due to the great man. He has, of course, made enemies and some think that his popularity is on the wane. This however Granville doubts – he says that the opposition is largely personal and partisan, due to his autocratic and severe methods, and to the fact that he is a Cretan. On the other hand he does represent what few men in Greece have ever represented – principle and personality together. All opposition is anti-Venizelist[;] it is not purely that of principle. But this is confined to the comparatively narrow circle of partisans – he is emphatically the people's man, the national premier who stands in their eyes for the greatness and the future of Greece. He is much worried at present by the fact that the Bulgarian peace offensives become more and more persistent towards the Entente.

3rd [August 1918]

F[oreign] O[ffice] meeting – present Sir Wilbraham Cooke[223] [*sic*] of the Admiralty, Mr. Hurst[224] and Ollivant[225] of F[oreign] O[ffice], self – subject Revision of Treaties.

---

[223] *Recte* Sir Philip Wilbraham Baker Wilbraham (1875–1957), 6th Baronet, lawyer and ecclesiastical administrator; called to the bar, 1901; chancellor of the Diocese of Chester, 1913; Truro, 1923; Chelmsford, 1929; Chancellor and Vicar-General of York, 1915–39; served in Naval Intelligence Department, 1915–18; Secretary of National Assembly of the Church of England, 1920–39; First Estates Commissioner, 1939–54.

[224] Sir Cecil James Barrington Hurst (1870–1963), lawyer and civil servant; called to the bar, 1893; assistant legal adviser to Foreign Office, 1902–18; Legal Adviser, 1918–29; delegate at the Paris peace conference, 1919; editor of *British Yearbook of International Law*, 1919–29; judge of Permanent Court of International Justice, 1929–46 (president, 1934–6); chairman, United Nations War Crimes Commission, 1943–44.

[225] Sir Lancelot Oliphant (1881–1965), diplomat; entered diplomatic service, 1905; Assistant Under-Secretary, 1928–36; Deputy Under-secretary, 1936–9; ambassador at Brussels, 1939–44;

The Declaration of 1907 re Norway and of 1908 re integrity of North Sea passed without much discussion. Ollivant is the barber's assistant type of F[oreign] O[ffice] man, Hurst apparently one of the chosen, a man with a hawk nose and eye, quick, precise, able, impressive.[226] The renewal of the Suez Canal Convention produced a long discussion. Apparently, we have had long talks with France over Morocco and Egypt, in which she has not once mentioned it. The position of the Sultan for Khedive and of British protectorate for British occupation appears to make little or no difference. Commercially, it seems that renewal is desirable, politically this is more doubtful, and it is recognized that military and naval considerations come first.

Stress is laid on the fact that free passage, and not neutrality are is the great defences point in the original agreement, and that internationalization is was not contemplated. If revived it would or might create as great difficulties with our allies as with our enemies. Hurst says Wilson has not observed as exact a neutrality with the Panama Canal and that neutrals have many reasons to be grateful to us. The Panama Canal agreement was modelled on the Suez, but the original is safer because of equality of tolls. It may therefore be worth retaining because it may serve as the model or the Dardanelles Convention.

Personally a good deal seems to me to turn on the question as to whether permanent fortifications may be erected. Art[icle] XI says no but art[icle] VIII seems to give the Khedive power to do so in case of necessity. I believe he can.

5th [August 1918]

Amery & Marros.

7th [August 1918]

Two friends (Baker-Carr[227] and N[orthumberland]) saw Old Robertson lately. To B[aker-]C[arr] he said that he had always thought the Germans the finest soldiers, but he could not on any grounds explain their latest strategy which laid them open to Foch's counter-stroke. The leaving of an exposed flank was an elementary military blunder and he could not explain it. (Note. The probable explanation is that they despised the French too much – they attacked Gouraud[228]

---

interned in Germany, 1940–41.

[226] Hurst was, in fact, not Jewish but an Anglican from a long line of Anglicans.
[227] See entry 16 Mar. 1918.
[228] General Henri Joseph Eugène Gouraud (1867–1946), French soldier; joined marines, 1890; commanded French Expeditionary Force, Dardanelles, 1915; Commander,

with 30 division, and but for their heavy defeat there by new tactics, might have attracted the French reserves there.)

To N[orthumberland] W[illiam] R[obertson] said that there was properly no strategy in the West. Some 400 miles of front was manned on each side, there was no room for true manoeuvre – it was a question of better armaments, better communications, better scientific appliances, exhaustion of manpower. Then he spoke of Henry Wilson – he will not, in the end, get on better than I. There is no agreement with the War Cabinet.

8th [August 1918]

There was a recent discussion of the G[eneral] S[taff] memo[randum], which advocated concentration in the W[est] for purposes of decision there in 1919. There should be an entente superiority of 400,000 rifles and therefore [a] good chance of success. Sal[oni]ca and Palestine would be reinforced with Black troops.

Milner stated that USA troops would prove a great drain on our shipping. It would therefore be better to send 10 or 15 divisions to Palestine or at any rate to the East. (NB In Palestine this force would have to go 400 miles before striking a vital point (Aleppo), their maintenance would be most costly, and much more difficult than in the West, while the supply and transport would have to pass the worst danger zone of all U-Boat areas.)

M[ilner] added however[:] 'I quite admit that the ultimate decision will <only> be reached in the West (i.e. the war will last till 1920).

L[loyd] G[eorge] in the same strain.

Hughes said 'What have we done by our Eastern expeditions, Salonica for example[?]'

L[loyd] G[eorge:] 'Well at any rate we have saved hundreds of thousands of men from being engulphed [*sic*] in the mud of Flanders.'

Smuts argued that he was much struck by possibilities in Palestine.

Borden[229] and Hughes alone supported the scheme.

The War Cabinet turned down the proposal and said they would do something elsewhere. Where? Oh that is for the G[eneral] S[taff] to decide.

Now these conclusions indicate important fallacies – (1.) The G[eneral] S[taff] is obviously counted as little worth. (2.) There is no

---

Fourth Army on Western Front, Dec. 1915–Dec. 1916 and June 1917–Nov. 1918; French Army of the Levant, 1919–23; Military Governor of Paris, 1923–37.

[229] Sir Robert Laird Borden (1854–1937), Canadian politician; Member of the Canadian House of Commons (Cons.) Halifax, 1896–1904, Carleton, 1905–20; Leader of the Conservative Party, 1901–20; Prime Minister of Canada, 1911–20.

counterproposal in the true sense. 'Doing something in the East' means nothing at all. There are 3 points in the East[:] Siberia, Turkey, Bulgaria. They cannot be equal in political value and therefore it is for the statesman to determine their respective political value, and the G[eneral] S[taff] to say what action is then possible. It is absurd to expect the G[eneral] S[taff] to decide political objectives in the first instance.

C[hief of the] I[mperial] G[eneral] S[taff] said little and plays deep, so say Butler and Northumberland, hoping to manage and rise, where Wully [Robertson] failed. Perhaps he will but I hear that L[loyd] G[eorge] was quite rude to him the other day[:] 'The G[eneral] S[taff] is woodenheaded and cannot get a new idea into their heads.'

9th [August 1918]

2nd meeting with Hurst at the F[oreign] O[ffice] and Sir P[hilip] Wilbraham[230] of the Adm[iralt]y.
 It was decided to recommend the renewal of the integrity of
 Switzerland Treaty (of 1815) where we found Hall[231] out in a blunder,
 of the 2 Scandinavian integrity Treaties,
 finally we dealt with the Suez Canal.

13th [August 1918]

3 Papers on the Colonies all of great value. Balfour's of May was gloomy, almost defaitist [sic], and assumed that we might be compelled to give back the German Colonies, not to Germany but to our Allies, in view of developments elsewhere, i.e. our desire to control Persia.

The general thesis was sharply criticized by Walter Long,[232] I hear. Smuts' (15th July) was nobly worded and sincere, especially when he spoke of it as

---

[230] See entry 3 Aug. 1918.

[231] Hubert Hall (1857–1944), archivist and scholar; archivist at Public Record Office, 1879–1921; resident officer there, 1891; literary director, Royal Historical Society, 1891–1938; Secretary of Royal Commission on Public Records, 1910–18; an expert on international treaties.

[232] Sir Walter Hume Long (1854–1924), 1st Viscount Long of Wraxall, cr. 1921, politician; MP (Cons.) Wiltshire North, 1880–85, Wiltshire East, 1885–92, Liverpool West Derby, 1892–1900, Bristol South, 1900–1906, County Dublin South, 1906–10, Strand, 1910–18, Westminster St. George's, 1918–21; Parliamentary Under-secretary to Local Government Board, 1886–92; President of the Board of Agriculture, 1895–1900; President of the Local

incumbent to preserve the British Empire as the greatest institution for the promotion of human liberty.

Strange words these from a Boer pen.

He finally suggested that the tropical colonies might go under an International Board, to prevent Germany from erecting a great central or Mittel Africa.

Curzon put up a reply on the 27th July with a cloud of epigrams and a thunder of denunciations, but at the end seemed to accept the principle of international control as a possible solution for East Africa.

16th [August 1918]

The Times today contains an article on the Eastern front,[233] obviously preparing is for an adventure there inspired by Amery, and expressing the ideas of Milner and L[loyd] G[eorge], tending to prepare one <and direct> public opinion <for campaigns in the East, i.e.> against the opinion of the General Staff (v[ide] 8th) and probably against that of our Allies, notably France and USA. [President] Wilson has recently shown unmistakable signs of restiveness under our persistence at sending a force to rescue the Czecho-Slovaks. The Japanese may not force his hand.

Amery's methods are interesting – two days ago he brought in Sidebotham[234] of the Times to introduce to Northumberland. The latter told me all about it. His (S[idebotham]'s) mission was not to obtain information from N[orthumberland], but to convert him from the G[eneral] S[taff] to the L[loyd] G[eorge] view. Artistically Amery made a serious blunder – if he had brought Sidebotham a little earlier, or if S[idebotham]'s article had appeared in the Times a little later, it might have made a difference.

Government Board, 1900–1905 and 1915–16; Chief Secretary for Ireland, Mar.–Dec. 1905; Colonial Secretary, 1916–19; First Lord of the Admiralty, 1919–21.

[233] 'The Eastern Front. From Murman To Siberia. A General Survey', *The Times*, 16 Aug. 1918.

[234] Herbert Sidebotham (1872–1940), journalist; called to the bar, 1912; on editorial staff of *Manchester Guardian*, 1895–1917 ('Student of War'); co-founder of British Palestine Committee, 1916; on editorial staff of *The Times* ('Our Correspondent on the War'), 1917–20; political adviser to *Daily Chronicle*, 1920–23; thereafter on staff of *Sunday Times* ('Scrutator').

17th [August 1918]

Today there was a meeting at the F[oreign] O[ffice] re the CzechoSlovaks.[235] I did not attend. Benesh[236] submitted a project of a Convention, which I criticized. It was chiefly on the lines of recognizing them as independent following upon Balfour's recent declaration, recognizing them as an Allied nation and as a sovereign Council, but not as independent. Benesh tried to settle the matter shortly by saying they should be placed on a footing similar to that of Serbia. This I pointed out, would commit us formally to independence at the peace, and therefore to the dissolution of Austria-Hungary. Faced with this alternative Lord R[obert] Cecil shrank back and substituted a less ambitious term.

18th [August 1918]

Summarised our recent controversy with Norway. We demanded on the 5th that the N[orwegian]s should stop the Huns sending submarines through their territorial waters and do by this mining them, in which process we offered to cooperate, if desired. After a good deal of humming Foreign Min[iste]r and Adm[ira]l both took the line that they could increase patrols, and bid them fire on submarines but not lay a mine. The King[237] also took this line to Findlay[238] in private and sent a message to [King] George. Findlay pointed out that to fire on submarines was more dangerous than to lay mines, and that Denmark and Sweden did the latter without breaking their neutrality. The King dissented but appears subsequently to have urged this view with force on his ministers. The formal reply of the 12th was contentious and unsatisfactory. Italy, France and USA (but independently) have supported our measures. It is curious that the K[ing] complained that he ought have expected such treatment from the Americans but was surprised at it from us. However, the W[ar] C[abinet] for once took a strong line on the 18th and have insisted on the mines being laid, in one way or another, i.e. either by us or by them, though they give Norway privately a fortnight in which to comply. I hope they will comply. At present our note is secret, and therefore the Huns don't know, and Norway can lay the mines because of the presence of submarines of unknown

---

[235] See Minutes of Interdepartmental Conference, 16 Aug. 1918, TNA (PRO), FO 371/3136/148362.

[236] See entry 4 Apr. 1917.

[237] Haakon VII (née Christian Frederik Carl Georg Valdemar Axel of Schleswig-Holstein-Sonderburg-Glücksburg) (1872–1957), Prince of Denmark; offered crown of Norway 1905; reigned as Haakon VII, 1905–57.

[238] Sir Mansfield de Cardonnel Findlay (1861–1932), diplomat; entered diplomatic service, 1885; minister-resident at Dresden, 1907–1909; minister at Sofia, 1909–11; at Christiania, 1911–23.

origin. This might not offend Germany, and Findlay thinks Hintze[239] does not want to attack Norway. He is sure that Norwegian patrols will not fire on German ~~torpedos~~ submarines, as the result would be war. The Norwegian Admiral openly admitted that he would sit on the fence as long as possible, but wished to come down the right side when he did.

Coercion <by us> of a small power, because she cannot or will not resist a greater, reminds me of Canning and Denmark at the Treaty of Tilsit period.[240]

19th [August 1918]

A footnote to history. October 1915 was, I think, the most critical month for England, incidentally for me also, I believe that there has ever been. A war policy (really manpower) Board was created by the Gov[ernmen]t[241] and consisted of Curzon, Winston [Churchill], Henderson, Balfour, Runciman,[242] McKenna.[243] It heard evidence really re conscription. Runciman & McKenna together proved, by figures, that Eng[lan]d w[oul]d be bankrupt in 6 months, and could not spare a man from home for war-services abroad. Winston & Curzon riddled these contentions and wanted 100 divisions in the field. McKenna answered that £200 per year was the product of each man in England. Curzon pointed out that the product of 70,000 actors was different from that of munition workers or jewellers – advocated, with a large view, the most drastic prohibitions on luxuries. Winston likewise breathed fire and nosed around everywhere for figures and statistics to refute them. Balfour denounced conscription for Ireland, as morally bad and politically inexpedient as it would lead to rebellion. K[itchener] appeared to give evidence and said that we had promised France 70 divisions, that he had done it in the presence of Asquith who had not said to him no, and that it was an obligation of honour from which we could not draw back. Asquith wobbled as always, Henderson feared revolt, of the last public

---

[239] See entry 5 Mar. 1917.
[240] See Temperley, *Canning*, 72–9.
[241] Minutes of Cabinet meeting, 21 Oct. 1915, TNA (PRO), CAB 37/136/26.
[242] Walter Runciman (1870–1949), 1st Viscount Runciman of Doxford, cr. 1937, politician; MP (Lib.) Oldham, 1899–1900, Dewsbury, 1902–18, Swansea West, 1924–29 and Cornwall St. Ives, 1929–37 (Nat. Lib. From 1931); Parliamentary Under-secretary to Local Government Board, 1905–1907; Financial Secretary to the Treasury, 1907–1908; President of the Board of Education, 1908–11; President of the Board of Agriculture, 1911–14; President of the Board of Trade, 1914–16 and 1931–37; Lord President of the Council, 1938–39.
[243] Reginald McKenna (1863–1943), banker and politician; MP (Lib.) Monmouthshire North, 1895–1918; Financial Secretary to the Treasury, 1905–1907; President of the Board of Education, 1907–1908; First Lord of the Admiralty, 1908–11; Home Secretary, 1911–15; Chancellor of the Exchequer, 1915–16.

appeal were not made to labour. This was done by Derby's[244] scheme, after which conscription was inevitable & came 25th May 1916.

Note Interesting that, in all man-power calculations, Serbia was omitted. <L[loyd] G[eorge] said that the Russians never had more than <one &> half a million rifles, & that conscription must be done to save France, as for two years we must wait till Russia was rearmed.>

20th [August 1918]

H[enry] Wilson saw Northumberland today. He said the War C[abinet] were coming round to his views (v[ide] 8th) probably under the influence of the successes of the last fortnight which conveys to them the impression that a decision may be reached in the West next year.[245] Possibly also in view of Woodrow's [Wilson] public announcement to the same effect & Foch's obvious determination.

He added that Germany would not send aid to Italy because of the friction between her and Austria, and that the Austrian division on the Western front was sent there because it could not be trusted in Italy. These last things are purest folly. The <Austrian> division in France is half Roumanian, half Magyar, and more to be trusted than half the divisions of Austria, and as for friction dividing Austria from Germany, friction will not prevent a drowning man from clutching the outstretched arm of an enemy. These errors are so ridiculous as those of the War Cabinet.

23[rd August 1918]

The views of Venizelos. I was asked for these today and put them as follows:

   (1.) Internationalized Constantinople.
   (2.) E[ast] Macedonia or Smyrna.
   (3.) Probably Koritza and Ersek to LIASKOVICS[246]
   (4.) West of LIASKOVICS to HIMARA[247]
   (5.) Internationalized, i.e. not Italianised Albania

---

[244] See entry 5 Dec. 1917.
[245] On 8 Aug., Allied troops breached the German lines along the Amiens–St. Quentin road, and the Germans retreated between Oise and Aisne, and Scarpe and Somme.
[246] Now Korcë, Ersekë and Leskovik in southeastern Albania.
[247] Now Himarë on the Ionian coast of Albania

(6.) Italians holding ~~Gibraltar~~ <Valona[248]?> as a sort of ~~Albania~~ Gibraltar, and P[or]t Stampalia[249] as one of the Dodecanese.

27[th August 1918]

A very sad day, poor Cox[250] was drowned while bathing last night. He has done infinitely much for me and for the War Office, for Haig and for England. No man knew more, or as much, of the German army in every detail of its organization. Without profound imagination he had a great breadth of view, was extraordinarily modest and enlisted one's sympathy by appearing to learn from him [sic]. I only met him a few days ago just when, after a short illness, he was returning to France looking the picture of life and strength. I shall never forget that I told him what he did not know, after a few days' absence, that an Austrian division had appeared on the Western front. Very few have been able, ever, to tell him anything about the Western front.

I got a tribute to his work the other day from Happold,[251] who told me he owed his captaincy to Cox. I asked how. 'Oh', said he, 'Cox came down and inspected us <(i.e. aeroplane photo-lieutenants)>, and said, at once, that our status must be raised. Therefore now we are all captains.['] So also with the intelligence officers of the divisions & also as to his <entering> cooperation between the economic, military and political sections. Everywhere he let in light, bristle energy, with his immense driving power.

They cannot replace him for if, by any chance, they got a man with the same capacity, they could never get a man with the same knowledge. He has worked with a truly giant's energy, ever since the start of the war at the German army, first under the D[irector of] M[ilitary] I[ntelligence], next under himself. How sad that a tremendous energy and unique experience should be ended by so sad an accident. Personal loss we all feel<, the military and political loss we cannot estimate. He had differences with H[aig] whom he described as 'an extraordinarily stupid man with a very dominating personality.' He also suggested something of the German crack in France recently.>

---

[248] Now Vlorë (Albania).
[249] Now Astypalaia (Greece).
[250] See entry 23 Nov. 1917. Cox's death was a suspected suicide.
[251] Captain Frederick Crossfield Happold (1893–1971), soldier and school-master; studied at Peterhouse under Temperley; active service in northern France and Belgium, 1914; General Staff Officer 3 on Instructional Staff, Intelligence School Harrow, 1914–19; Assistant Master, Perse School, Cambridge, 1920–28; lecturer, Cambridge University, 1922–28; Headmaster Bishop Wordsworth's School, Salisbury, 1928–60; Pilot Officer, RAF Training Branch, 1941–46.

28th [August 1918]

The Italians have abandoned Fieri and Berat and fallen back on the Malakastra range.[252] Ferrero[253] is stated by the Commando Supremo to have taken both entirely unauthorized and they decline to support him. He has 12,000 men and (8,000 bayonets) out for fighting in the open.

28th [August 1918]

Designs of Venizelos.

Boche manpower is waning – in the Ypres-Passchendaele campaign of last year we took 24,000 prisoners for 49% casualties <in 1917.> In our sector alone we have taken 47,000 prisoners for 20% casualties in 1918, and not done yet. Tanks, aeroplanes, and cooperation between the two are one explanation.

29th [August 1918]

Some lights on Russia from Keyes[254] who has just returned after a hundred dangers. He now advocates intervention and has done so since March, and a lot of it. He thinks if employed earlier that it would have already overthrown the Bolshevik. In the 3rd week of July he was arguing over this with the P[rime] M[inister] and with Milner via Amery. He saw the P[rime] M[inister] for an hour, the latter seemed fairly well posted about Russian affairs. Talked about possibilities of assassinating Lenin and Trotsky, without any sign of disfavour though not, of course, of direct stimulation. What would Acton say? Keyes at any rate debarred him from Lenin whom he thought honest and, serving a useful purpose. Keyes

---

[252] Now Fier, Berat and Mallakastër in southwestern and south central Albania.

[253] Lieutenant-General Giacinto Ferrero (1862–1922), Italian soldier; served at Dolomite front, 1915–16; commanded Italian Expeditionary Force at Durrës, Feb. 1916; commanded 23rd (Palermo) Infantry Division, 1916; commander, Italian Occupation Forces, Dec. 1916–May 1917; commander, XVI Army Corps, May 1917–Apr. 1919; issued proclamation of Albanian independence under the protection of Italy at Argyrokastro, 3 June 1917; commanded Italian troops to prevent d'Annunzio from entering Fiume, 1919.

[254] Admiral of the Fleet Roger John Brownlow Keyes (1872–1945), 1st Baron Keyes, cr. 1943; naval commander; entered Royal Navy, 1884; Naval Attaché at Rome, 1905–1908; Inspecting Captain of Submarines, 1910–14; Chief of Staff to Vice-Admiral Carden (Dardanelles), 1915; Second-in-Command, 4th Battle Squadron, 1917–18; commander Dover Patrol, 1918; Deputy Chief of Naval Staff, 1921–25; Commander-in-Chief, Mediterranean Station, 1925–28; Commander-in-Chief, Portsmouth, 1929–31; MP (Cons.) Portsmouth North, 1934–43.

described modestly his own share in bringing about a coalescence of Russian parties under Alexeieff.[255] He explained that Denikin[256] was a splendid man, Alexeieff's Chief of Staff, and that, with much difficulty, he had arranged their cooperation with Savinkoff,[257] the extreme Revolutionary, who was also a friend of Korniloff. He said that even <many of> the S[ocialist] R[evolutionaries][258] were now monarchical in principle. Miliukoff[259] he believed discredited and without much influence since March, while the Cadets as a whole were still of weight.

He thinks that the Murman[sk] Railway will be cut by the Germans and consequently that a division at least is required at Archangel, for it will be six months in the air and blocked with ice from December to May.

He is one more confirmation of the sinister influence of Amery on Milner and also on Lloyd George. I found an instance of him today trying to obtain information from a subsection (in which there was a girl clerk) as to the total French casualties, a thing he has no business to do except via the D[irector of] M[ilitary] I[ntelligence].

30th [August 1918]

I find that BENESH has told Lord R[obert] Cecil that his news from Austria indicates that a rising is at last seriously possible either Christmas or April. He says that it has been organized among Czechs, Jugo-Slavs and Poles and begs for assistance from us for this purpose. This does not fit in with his previous interview of May, and seems indeed to be inconsistent with it. It is a fundamental

---

[255] See entry 15 Jan. 1917.

[256] Lieutenant-General Anton Ivanovich Denikin (1872–1947), White Russian commander; active service, Russo-Japanese War, 1904–1905; Chief of Staff, Kiev military district, 1914–15; commanded VIII Corps in Romania during Brusilov offensive, 1916; involved in 'Kornilov Affair', 1917; commanded White Army in Russian Civil War (White Terror), 1919–21; exile in France, 1926–45, USA, 1945–47.

[257] Boris Savinkov (1879–1925), Russian revolutionary writer and terrorist; one of the leaders of the armed wing of the Socialist Revolutionary Party; involved in various assassination plots against senior government officials, 1905–1906; exile in France; active service in French army, 1914–17; Deputy War Minister, July–Aug. 1917; exile from 1918; murdered on return to Soviet Union.

[258] The Party of Socialists-Revolutionaries, a moderate socialist party, founded in 1902; in office after the February Revolution, it won a majority of the votes cast in the elections to the Russian Constituent Assembly, but soon split and then destroyed by the Bolsheviks.

[259] Pavel Nikolayevich Milyukov (1859–1943), Russian politician; founder and leader of Constitutional Democratic Party (*Kadets*), 1905; advocate of conquest of Constantinople during First World War; led Progressive Bloc in Duma; Foreign Minister, 1917; in French exile, 1921–43.

change of policy and apparently for an inadequate reason. I suspect he wishes to force our hand as on the 17th (q.v.).

I had an interview with <Capt[ain]> Jovanović today, who was greatly excited about the attack on Pašić in the New Europe.[260] He asked me if it was S[eton-] W[atson]. I said I did not know but that it might be. He also asked me about the representative Serbs – again I said I did not know. Indeed I could not tell.

Then he asked me as a friend of Serbia to give good advice. I said that, while disclaiming a desire to interfere in internal affairs, I thought that it would be better for all sides for Pašić to either [*sic*] agree with the Opp[ositio]n (the position now being uncon[stitutiona]l) or to strengthen himself from outside. That could only be done by associating some such men as Trumbić[261] with them, in the way Smuts was associated with the British Cabinet, not interfering in internal affairs but representing the British <race and> Empire. Similarly Trumbić would represent the JugoSlav race as distinct from the Serbian. What I said made an impression, I think, it will be interesting to watch further developments.

1st September [1918]

I spoke to D[irector of] M[ilitary] I[ntelligence, Macdonogh] on [the] subject of Benesh, and he got me to draft a letter on the subject to Lord R[obert] C[ecil], which he subsequently signed. The general line was that B[eneš] see be out for a big political coup and was adjusting his information ad hoc.

2nd [September 1918]

There are two great surprises[.] D[irector of] M[ilitary] I[ntelligence, Macdonogh] is going to replace Cox in France, and Panouse is leaving as French M[ilitary] A[ttaché]. I think I have spotted the reason of the latter. In the midst of the Cz[echo]Sl[ovak] business he sent a telegram from London misrepresenting our attitude. It was most unfortunate and will have had to be explained away. Of the D[irector of] M[ilitary] I[intelligence] I will say nothing except that he has the distinction of being the only British officer praised by Lloyd George. For

---

[260] 'Serbia's Choice', *The New Europe*, 22 Aug. 1918. The author was Seton-Watson, see *R.W. Seton-Watson and the Yugoslavs: Correspondence, 1906–1941* (2 vols, Zagreb, 1976), i, app. 3.

[261] Ante Trumbić (1864–1938), Croat politician; mayor of Split, 1905–1907; leader of Yugoslav Committee, 1914–18; Foreign Minister of the Kingdom of the Serbs, Croats and Slovenes, 1918–20; leader of Croatian Federalist Peasant Party, 1926–29; opposed to the 1921 constitution, and after 1932 advocated Croatian secession from Yugoslavia.

culture and contact with the F[oreign] O[ffice], and wide grasp, he was and will be unique.

Thwaites,[262] his successor, is a friend of Amery's. I draw my conclusions accordingly. Milner, who regarded him (D[irector of] M[ilitary] I[ntelligence]) as indespensible in February has now changed his mind.

3rd [September 1918]

Saw Trevelyan. He was, of course, a little shamefaced after his very drery prophecies early in the year (v[ide] on the 2nd Jan[uary 1918]). But he said that in April the Italians were in great alarm and anything might have happened then. Since then they had won, to some extent deservedly, great credit in the repulse from Piave.[263]

He complained much of the absence of effective British army propaganda, bands, marching etc.

The Americans had done this effectively, and enjoyed enormous prestige accordingly. The Red X [Cross] and distributive organs also had done much to relieve distress.

5th [September 1918]

I wrote somewhat under pressure a lengthy monograph on the Czech Anabasis and Odyssey in Siberia. At points we do not always emerge well as the French wished to get them away to fight in France and we to leave them behind to produce intervention in Russia.

It seems, however, that they did not consciously act with the <counter-> revolutionaries but, so far as was possible, did act with neutrality. They had to purge their ranks of Bolsheviks and may have had a disciplined soldier's contempt and prejudice of them but on the whole acted very well. Their miracle and discipline were magnificent. No illiterates <50& higher education 30% secondary education. While living in the trains they taught themselves Swedish

---

[262] Major General William Thwaites (1879–1947), soldier entered Royal Artillery, 1887; special employ and Staff Captain, Intelligence, Army Headquarters, 1905–1906; General Staff Officer, War Office, 1906–15; Brigade Commander, June 1915–July 1916; Divisional Commander, July 1916–Oct. 1918; Director of Military Intelligence, Oct. 1918–22; Director of Military Operations and Intelligence, 1922–23; General Officer Commanding, 47th Division, 1923–27; General Officer Commanding-in-Chief, British Army on the Rhine, 1927–31; Director General, Territorial Army, 1931–33.

[263] The Austrians withdrew from Piave on 24 June 1918.

drill to relieve the monotony, and organized classes of French lessons. Is anything impossible to such men?>[264]

16th [September 1918]

Return. Czecho-Slovaks rescued. Austrian peace-move etc.

18 [September 1918][265]

Light on the D[irector of] M[ilitary] I[ntelligence]. I find my conjecture of the 2nd does not appear confirmed. It is H[enry] W[ilson] not the W[ar] C[abinet] who desired to get rid of him. He complained to W[illiam] R[obert] R[obertson] that H[enry] W[ilson] wanted him to play the war-game with the D[irector of] M[ilitary] O[perations]. As he effectively said, however, it is not possible – D[irector of] M[ilitary] O[perations] knows what Foch is going to do, I do not know what the Boche is. So his moves will always be correct and mine always conjectural. It is true, I think, that D[irector of] M[ilitary] I[ntelligence] was cautionary, while H[enry] W[ilson] likes a splashing imaginative treatment of everything. Perhaps also the fact that he is a Catholic and H[enry] W[ilson] a black Protestant makes a good deal of difference.

21 [September 1918]

The Serbs have again accomplished marvels in their offensive of the last few days.[266] They have broken right through the Bulgar defensive line, captured Dobropolye[267] and Vetrenik [?] each 5,000 feet high, torn a bulge 375 square miles in extent in the Bulgar line, and are now across the Crna at Radowye and Dunye[268] in the direction of Prilep and within 6 miles of the vital Vardar line at Negotin[269] with their cavalry. It is an achievement as wonderful as unexpected – 5,000 prisoners

---

[264] On loosely inserted sheet.
[265] The date can be deduced from the reference to the fall of Haifa and Acre (see entry 23 [September]).
[266] On 15 Sept., Anglo-French and Serb forces launched a major attack against Bulgarian positions along the Struma, followed by the collapse of the Bulgarian front.
[267] The nine-day battle of Dobropolje (now Dobro Pole, Macedonia), beginning 14–15 Sept. 1918, led to Franco-Serb forces under General Louis Franchet d'Esperey breaking through the Bulgarian lines; revolt spread through the Bulgarian army afterwards.
[268] Dunje in southern Macedonia.
[269] Negotino on the Vardar in southern central Macedonia.

and 90 guns, and the enemy flying in all directions before them. The JugoSlav division has done the best, but the whole Serbian rifle strength is only 40,000!

A French division suffered 1,800 casualties on the Serb left but these wonderful men of the mountains have suffered almost no material loss, owing to their cleverness in improvising tactics and concealing themselves in the advance. They have broken through the defences prepared for 2½ years. The only fly in the ointment is that they may not have enough troops or support to win a complete victory. It is the old fallacy of an offensive without enough men, partly owing to the fact that the front is so enormous in its length. If we can push the advantage the Bulgars are irretrievably ruined. If! None the less there has been serious blundering for us. We attacked with 3 divisions and some ~~French~~ Greeks – the attack north of Lake Doiran was a total failure – that west of Lake Doiran failed before the grand advance but gave us an advanced line in a line with Doiran town. It also gave us 40,000 casualties[,] a very heavy toll indeed.

Politically, the results are already apparent. There will be a stronger hold (politically) of the Serbs on Macedonia. I see they are already saying that the soldiers of new Serbia (i.e. Macedonia) are deserting from the Bulgars. The latter also will be encouraged by the defeat of the British. At the same time Allenby's[270] defeat of the Turks in Palestine will encourage the Bulgars.

23 [September 1918]

The Serb effort is more and more wonderful. They hold Gradsko to Krivolak[271] <and also west of the Vardar> and have cut the Gradsko line north of Prilep.

Milne[272] is west and north of Lake Doiran, and sending the British cavalry to Strumnitza[273]. If they get there the Bulgar army will be cut in three, whereas a separation in two is usually deemed sufficient. Prilep seems likely to fall shortly.

I worked out a scheme of possible Bulgar defence – so far as I can see the line USKUB-KRIVA[274] river to BREGALNITZA[275] and GRLENA-TSAREVO SELO-JUMAIH is about the only true line. But we may get to Uskub and stop that.

The chief reason of Serbian success was that the Bulgars valued positions and points like PRILEP and the GEVGELI-DOIRAN-HUDOVO[276] triangle, and

---

[270] See entry 5 Nov. 1917.
[271] Gradsko and Krivolak, both on the Vardar, in eastern central Macedonia.
[272] See entry 22 Dec. 1916.
[273] Strumica in eastern Macedonia.
[274] Now Skopje.
[275] Bregalnica river, a tributary of the Vardar.
[276] Gevgelija, located on the Vardar and border with Greece; Lake Doiran; Valandovo, in southern Macedonia.

not the front. Half a division in reserve 10 miles north of Dobropolye would have saved the situation, or an attack, prepared beforehand, north of DZENA, on the Serb right flank might have restored the day. As it is the Bulgar disaster seems irreparable. They must lose all their guns in the GEVGELI area, I think. It is the old story of the cordon system, small bodies of men strung out along an arc.

Allenby's success goes on increasing. HAIFA and Acre have fallen. In time, after resting, his cavalry will proceed to Damascus and Aleppo, perhaps in three weeks. It reminds me of the advice to Hannibal after Cannae – "Only send me the cavalry", said Mago, "and in five nights they shall sup in the Capitol."[277] Hannibal did not take the advice, Allenby has. We shall see the results.[278]

I must try and work out a Zionist frontier again. Already a Turkish division on the way to Tabriz has been stopped.

A note of wise warning was sounded by Maurice in the D[aily] C[hronicle] the other day. Do not think that you can knock out Germany, Turkey, and Bulgaria is a single day and at the same time. Certainly it was politically bad strategy to attack Bulgaria and Turkey at once. In the military sense, as our communications lengthen, our obligations and shipping increase.

Percy[279] suggests the sending of more divisions for to Salonica, there to finish the job. There is no question that great possibilities are there.

25 [September 1918]

A wire from Milne pleading hard for reinforcements. He says, in his opinion that the French G[eneral] S[taff] gave themselves far the easiest jobs and put us and the rest to the hardest. The British assault should have been delayed 48 hours as in effect it crippled us, and prevented us making the pursuit as effective as it otherwise would have been.

---

[277] During the Second Punic War (218–203 BC), the Carthagenian leader Hannibal (247–182) destroyed a Roman army in the battle of Cannae in 218, but then overstretched his supply lines and become bogged down in Italy; Mago(n) (243–203 BC) commanded the centre of the Carthagenian army at Cannae; after the battle he was despatched by Hannibal to Southern Italy.

[278] Allenby broke through the Turkish front on 19 Sept., and entered Aleppo on 26 Oct.

[279] That is, the Duke of Northumberland.

26th [September 1918][280]

The Serbs have turned the Balima,[281] always the idea of Mishitch,[282] captured Veles.[283] How well I remember it in the old days! and also captured STIP[284] and are thus in control of the road system, of which it is the junction. 30 miles and the Serbs reckon 4 days from USKUB. It is curious that I have been considering various lines of defence for the Bulgars. Three of them were based on the Veles-STIP line holding. This I (wisely as it proved) thought would not hold. This throws the Bulgars back on a last line of defence – USKUB-KRATOVO-Bregalnitza-GRLENA-TSAREVO SELO. If the Serbs reach Uskub the strategic centre is forced, and the army must fall back on the defence of Sofia. Meanwhile it cannot improve their moral[e] that the British have captured KOSTURINO, i.e. have mastered the BELESH range, and actually entered Bulgaria.

27th [September 1918]

Strumitza entered by British – KOZANA by Serbs – armistice asked for yesterday of Milne by TODOROFF,[285] G[eneral] O[fficer] C[ommanding] Bulgars. Laus Deo.

30[th September 1918]

A happy entry for the end of this book[:] Bulgaria out of the war,[286] surrendered unconditionally. LIAPCHEFF[287] talked on the way to Milne, very gloomy. Apparently even before the armistice Bulgar soldiers threw down their arms. 3 motors filled with French are on the way to push via Sofia.

---

[280] On two separate sheets, loosely inserted in diary in different places.
[281] Velika river.
[282] See entry 21 Oct. 1916.
[283] Veles on the Vardar in northern central Macedonia.
[284] Štip in eastern Macedonia.
[285] General Georgi Stoyanov Todorov (1858–1934), Bulgarian soldier; served in Russian army, 1877–85; joined Bulgarian army, 1885, but dismissed in 1886 on account of his involvement in the deposition of Prince Alexander of Battenberg; reinstated, 1887; commanded Second Army, 1914–18; dismissed, 1919.
[286] The armistice between Bulgaria and the Allied Powers was signed on 29 September.
[287] Andrey Tasev Lyapchev (30 November 1866–6 November 1933), Bulgarian politician; Minister of Trade, 1908–10; Finance Minister, 1910–11 and June 1918–19; signed 1918 armistice; Prime Minister, 1926–31.

1st October [1918]

The new D[irector of] M[ilitary] I[ntelligence] Gen[era]l Thwaites came to see me today – and went round the section. He praised highly my little monographs on Austria and the Balkans[288] – as concise and compact and well written.

A good, honest, frank soldier not knowing or pretending to know much beyond the German army.

B[rigadier] G[eneral] I[ntelligence] Buckley[289] from Egypt sent a letter to late D[irector of] M[ilitary] I[ntelligence, Macdonogh] of date 31st Aug[ust 1918], with an appreciation of the situation in Palestine. He thought the Turks would retire on a line from Deraar west by Lake of Galilee to the sea – and that we should be unable to catch them in their retreat! Under the circumstances it was exquisitely ludicrous – a power of imagination equal to that of a flea.[290]

2nd October [1918]

U.S.A. and wool-clip. A nasty incident. Weir[291] and Goldfinch[292] of the Army Contracts had bought the woolclip of Australia – U.S.A. said they wanted some of it – but it must be at cost price. Weir and Goldfinch agreed but ultimately charged 10%. The U.S.A. found out and complained. Austen Chamberlain[293] interviewed W[eir] & G[oldfinch] on behalf of the War Cabinet. They had only this excuse that they thought in business you must make a profit. Quite frank no one impugns their personal honour or thinks that they understand (though they may care for) the honour of the nation. In France some of the U.S.A. troops

---

[288] *Inter alia* mema. Temperley, 'Proposed Settlement of Albania (D.7)', 17 Sept. 1918, 'Notes on the Claims of Bulgaria to an Outlet on the Aegean Sea (D.9)', 1 Oct. 1918, 'The Czecho-Slovak Problem – Political (I.1)', 14 Apr. 1918, Webster MSS, Webster 3/7.

[289] See entry 21 Sept. 1917.

[290] Allenby occupied Nablus, Nazareth and Haifa in September.

[291] William Douglas Weir (1877–1959), 1st Baron Weir, cr. 1918, industrialist; chairman, G. and J. Weir, Glasgow, 1910–53; Scottish director of munitions, 1915–16; Controller of Aeronautical Supplies and member of Air Board, 1917–18; Director of Aircraft Production, Ministry of Munitions, 1918; Secretary of State and President of the Air Council, 1918; Chairman of Advisory Council on Civil Aviation, 1919; delegate at Imperial Conference, Ottawa, 1932; adviser on national defence, 1937–38; Director-general of Explosives at the Ministry of Supply, 1939–41; Chairman of the Tank Board, 1942.

[292] Sir Arthur Horne Goldfinch (1866–1945), wool merchant; partner in Duncan, Fox & Co., General Merchants, 1903–13; Director of Raw Materials, War Office, 1917–21; Chairman of London Board of British-Australian Wool Realisation Association, 1921–26.

[293] Austen Chamberlain, Minister without Portfolio, Apr. 1918–Jan. 1919; see entry 7 Dec. 1916.

showed some inexperience not far off Cambrai.²⁹⁴ They did not "mop up" and the result was that Australians some way behind found themselves attacked by machine guns (concealed) and prisoners (released) whom the U.S.A. fondly imagined that they had settled for ever. In result there was no 'leapfrogging' and some damage to the Australians.

The U.S.A. and Czech attitude is now of considerable interest. The former have definitely and finally come to the conclusion that they will not support an advance beyond the Urals. This is partly done on military grounds. Curiously enough Benesh [sic]– in a recent interview reported by Spiers²⁹⁵ seems not disinclined to the prospect. He thinks Bolshevikism more firmly established than was actually realized. Consequently he thinks the Czechs should establish themselves behind the Urals till the spring when they can attempt the reconstruction of European Russia.

He then went on to make some very strange remarks as to the number of Czechs in Russia being 200,000 – and the Czechs being the one Slav race akin in sympathy to the Russians and able to assimilate with them – I should say that the Army virus is working, the latter suggesting colonization in Siberia as an equivalent for Austria-Hungary.

3 October [1918]

Went to see P[hilip] Kerr about P[ašić] who has just arrived. I find he did now know that the New E[urope] had made a recent attack on Pasic.²⁹⁶ I therefore explained the situation, which was one of for the P[rime] M[inister] There were serious quarrels between P[ašić] and the Opposition, partly quarrels over place and political intrigues, partly also over a ministry of concentration and coalition. That I said was a purely internal affair between Serbians with which we had no right to interfere. But when the question dealt with JugoSlavia it was different. The whole affair then was bound up partly with the Alliance as a whole – and here we could say something. P. was for a great Serbia or a Serbian Imperialist as P[hilip] K[err] preferred to call him. The larger and more liberal view was a Federal JugoSlavia. Here I thought L[loyd] G[eorge] could step in and say – with perfect truth and justice – that, in proportion as the JugoSlav

---

²⁹⁴ Allied forces were pushing towards the *Siegfried* line between Cambrai and St. Quentin since 8 Sept.

²⁹⁵ Major-General Sir Edward Louis Spears (née Spiers) (1886–1974), 1st Bart, soldier and politician; entered army, 1903; liaison officer between General Sir John French and French Fifth Army, 1914–15; between French Ministry of War and War Office, 1917–18; MP (Nat. Lib.) Loughborough, 1922–24, (Nat. Cons.) Carlisle, 1931–45; Prime Minister Personal Representative to French Prime Minister, 1940; to Free French, 1940–44.

²⁹⁶ See entry 30 Aug. 1918.

316   *An Historian in Peace and War*

cause gained ground, we should be pleased. Also he might go a step further and say he had done the same – and he was a British Empire man and had proved it by putting Smuts in the Cabinet – so P[ašić] could prove himself a JugoSlav man by putting – say – Trumbic in the Cabinet. P[hilip] K[err] listened and seemed greatly impressed.[297] I told him also that, in any case, P[ašić] would raise the question of getting the JugoSlav volunteers from Italy (the 22,000) and this would provide a good opportunity for the rest.

P[hilip] K[err] said he would put the P[rime] M[inister] in touch with the situation.

4th October [1918]

Gub brought out a communiqué on the evacuation of Baku, attributing the cause to the failure of the Armenians to support the British. This has caused great excitement in Armenian circles ever since [something missing] from the Manchester Guardian to Mark Sykes. Finally, an Armenian deputation, headed by Lord Bryce,[298] waited on Lord Robert Cecil, who, in moderate phrase, threw over the W[ar] O[ffice] communiqué.[299] This is another blow to the W[ar] O[ffice] and not wholly a deserved one – the Armenians in that area did parley with the Germans, though elsewhere they did not e.g. under Aubranik they are still maintaining heroic resistance.

On the general situation on the Western front I have had 3 interesting opinions in the last 2 days. Northumberland, Cornwall,[300] [A.G.] Churchill.[301]

---

[297]   Temperley had made the suggestion before, see entry 30 Aug. 1918.

[298]   James Bryce (1838–1921), Viscount Bryce, cr. 1914, historian and politician; called to the bar, 1867; Professor of Jurisprudence, Owens College, Manchester, 1870–75; Regius Professor of Civil Law, Oxford, 1870–93; MP (Lib.) Tower Hamlets, 1880–85, Aberdeen South, 1885–1906; Parliamentary Under-secretary for Foreign Affairs, 1886; Chancellor of the Duchy of Lancaster, 1892–94; President of the Board of Trade, 1894–95; Chief Secretary for Ireland, 1906–1907; ambassador at Washington, 1907–13.

[299]   'Armenians and Baku. War Services to The Allies', *The Times*, 4 Oct. 1918.

[300]   General Sir James Handyside Marshall Cornwall (since 1927 Marshall-Cornwall) (1887–1985), soldier; commissioned into Royal Artillery, 1907; Intelligence Officer, British Expeditionary Force, 1914–15; General Staff Officer, Intelligence, Army Headquarter, 1915–18; War Office, 1918; delegate at Paris peace conference, 1919; with Army of the Black Sea, 1920–23; delegate Thrace boundary commission, 1924–25; Shanghai Defence Force, 1927; Military Attaché at Berlin, Stockholm, Oslo and Copenhagen, 1928–32; head of military mission at Cairo, 1936–38; General Officer Commanding, III Corps, 1940; General Officer Commanding-in-Chief, Western Command, 1941–42; with Special Operations Executive, 1942–45; retired, 1945; editor-in-chief of captured German Foreign Office documents, 1948–51.

[301]   See entry 9 May 1918.

All agree that the Germans are fighting delaying actions with the view of getting to the Meuse this year, probably minus Antwerp and Brussels. The Hindenburg line, which they meant to hold, is wholly gone, Lille is going and the coast shortly. N[orthumberland] looks at it from the point of view both of Allied and enemy strategy, C[ornwall] purely from the German side, Ch[urchill] from a different angle still – the character of the recent fighting, failure of German counter-attacks, yielding of ground etc. I am afraid we shall witness two things, as the German scale is slowly weighed down – sham democracy on the part of Germany, and a rise in our territorial demands re Colonies etc. for the peace. This should be resisted – we do not want a Germanized E[ast] Africa, but we do want an internationalized one.

JugoSlavs. I am afraid over the recent party struggle in Italy that Sonnino[302] has won a complete victory. He says probably with truth that the forecast of the Times of Sept[embe]r 13[303] that the JugoSlav legion in Italy should take an oath to King Peter,[304] as King of JugoSlavia, was 'an invention of Mr. Steed.' Orlando[305] and Nitti[306] were too weak to oppose him. His latest card is that there are many Slovenes of Trieste in the JugoSlav prisoners and that an oath to King Peter would compromise Italian claims. I assisted to draft a strong letter to the F[oreign] O[ffice] on the subject.

7th October [1918]

Went with Cornwall to see the Serbian Minister [Jovanović] and Trumbitch. The former, who is usually depressed, took a very much more cheerful view of things than usual – as indeed well he might. Trumbitch showed himself singularly moderate, sane and sound. He considered that an armed rising of JugoSlavs in Austria-Hungary was out of the question unless the Entente armies were at the gates. Even then an Italian army was not what was desired, and should be accompanied by British or French. He suggested the armed bands could be made use of by propaganda etc. and might possibly be assembled at convenient places – by aeroplane direction, with a view to military cooperation. But in this he did not place very much reliance. He thought something might be done by a visit to Sebenico of a Brit[ish]-Italian fleet, combined with an invasion of Bosnia from N[orth] W[estern] Serbia.

---

[302] See entry 2 Mar. 1917.
[303] 'The "Yugo-Slav Nation." Recognition By Italy', *The Times*, 13 Sept. 1918.
[304] Petar I Karađorđević (1844–1921), King of Serbia, 1903–18; King of the Serbs, Croats and Slovenes, 1918–21.
[305] See entry 9 May 1918.
[306] Francesco Saverio Vincenzo de Paola Nitti (1868–1953), Italian economist and politician; Minister of Trade, 1911–14; Finance Minister, 1917–19; Prime Minister, 1919–20.

He spoke enthusiastically of the JugoSlav legion and bitterly of Sonnino's attitude towards the JugSlav prisoners in Italy. He also added (what seemed to be reasonably true) that Sonnino's latest attitude seemed a desire to save Austria.

8th October [1918]

The Times has a leader today really directed against Pasic (v. 3rd Oct[obe]r) rather on the lines I advocated to P[hilip] K[err] but going a good deal beyond them.[307]

9th October [1918]

Several important interviews. At lunch at the R[eform] C[lub] I sat at a table with Harold [*sic*] Spender[308] of the <u>Westminster Gazette</u> and Lord Buckmaster,[309] two arch-pacifists, if there are any. Both slightly regretted the evacuation of entente territory demanded by [President] Wilson of Germany, as they thought the latter might consent. Both seemed to think, however, that Germany in the military sense was beaten, which I confess I do not. Both however attached most important to what the 'Westminster Gazette' of this day calls the fifteenth point i.e. the democratization of Germany, which Wilson appears to demand by asking Max[310] who or what he represented. They did not think that Germany could accept that, or frame a satisfactory answer to it. I am not certain of the latter, though I am of the former. [Admiral] Keyes[311] told me some queer stories

---

[307] 'The Prince-Regent of Serbia', *The Times*, 8 Oct. 1918.

[308] That is, (John) Alfred Spender (1862–1942), journalist and author; leader writer, *Echo*, 1886; editor *Eastern Morning News*, 1886–91; on staff of *Pall Mall Gazette*, 1892; assistant editor, *Westminster Gazette*, 1893–96; editor, 1896–1922; President of the National Liberal Federation, 1926–27. Alfred's brother (Edward) Harold (1864–1926) was on the staff of the *Daily News*, 1900–14, and thereafter a freelance writer. Alfred was a member of the Reform Club; Harold was not.

[309] Sir Stanley Owen Buckmaster (1861–1934), Baron Buckmaster of Cheddington, cr. 1915, 1st Viscount Buckmaster, cr. 1933, lawyer and politician; called to the bar, 1884; took silk, 1902; MP (Lib.) Cambridge, 1906–10, Keighley, 1911–15; Solicitor-General, 1913–15 (since Aug. 1914 also Director of the Press Bureau); Lord Chancellor, 1915–16; member of Inter-Allied Council to Co-ordinate the Purchase of War Material from the USA, 1917; chairman of the political honours scrutiny committee, 1929–33. In Dec. 1917, Buckmaster publicly supported the 'Lansdowne letter'.

[310] Prince Max(imilian Alexander Friedrich Wilhelm) von Baden (1867–1929), German politician; titular Grand Duke of Baden, 1928–29; German chancellor and Prussian Minister-President, Oct.–Nov. 1918.

[311] See entry 29 Aug. 1918.

of Milner, whom he knew well, interviewed often after his return from Russia, and described as a charming man personally. He had experience of him in three directions

> (1.) he proposed certain modifications at the Eastern Committee, with which M[ilner] entirely agreed. M[ilner] consulted L[loyd] G[eorge] who appeared favourable and brought them before the War Cabinet. Curzon said nolumus mutari leges hidiae and L[loyd] G[eorge] suddenly veered round [,] threw Milner over, and downed the project. The sole result was to add Gen[eral] Smuts to the Committee.
> (2) The next point was with reference to Bolshevikism. Keyes got the idea of getting Julius West[312] (the Fabianized Jew) to write up Bolshevikism as the sin against the Holy Ghost of Democracy. This was considered by Keyes to be a necessary antidote to British Bolshevikism, in which incidentally Comrade [Lloyd] George is so strong a believer. Milner, after considering the matter, finally expressed the view that the British working man was a very sound fellow, who didn't trouble about Bolshevikism, and that there was nothing to be done in the matter. He displayed great apparent ignorance or indifference in the matter and seemed to think (somewhat à la Bismarck) that machine guns were the best remedy for industrial unrest. Julius West went out to Switzerland and the best remedy for counter-propagan to British Bolshevikism vanished with him.
> (3) The last story is that Keyes did not want to go under Beaverbrook to the Min[istr]y of Information. Milner told him that he could rely on him that he would not go. He is however now there. I think M[ilner] is something of a legend like Sir Bedivere[313] 'Alas for this gray shadow, once a man.'[314]

---

[312] Julius West (1891–1918), Russian-born British writer, Chekov translator and journalist; clerk in Board of Trade, 1906–1908; clerk at Fabian Society, 1908–13; on staff of *New Statesman*, 1913; freelance writer thereafter; witnessed Bolshevik revolution, 1917–18; mission to Switzerland, 1918. His *History of the Chartist Movement* (London, 1920) was published posthumously. Of Jewish descent, he was, in fact, confirmed in the Church of England, and married an Anglican clergyman's daughter.

[313] A figure in Arthurian legend; knight of the Round Table, who returned Excalibur to the Lady of the Lake.

[314] Alfred, Lord Tennyson, 'Tithonus' (1859): 'Alas! for this gray shadow, once a man—/So glorious in his beauty and thy choice,/Who madest him thy chosen, that he seem'd/ To his great heart none other than a God!'.

10th October [1918]

JugoSlavs 4 prisoners Austria Addison[315] & Recon[structio]n.

Plunkett[316] writes of the Serbian advance that the JugoSlav division, which did the best, was somewhat rough in its methods and took only 4 prisoners (!) during the first week.

I made out a memo for the Min[istr]y of Reconstruction on Recon[structio]n in Serbia. My chief points were the French commercial designs in Greek and Serbian Macedonia of which I adduced proofs from the Sarrail era and the urgency of such relief owing to the devasted condition of Serbia. Afterwards I received a request for Addison to use it in his memo to the War Cabinet.

11th October [1918]

The Allied Gov[ernmen]ts have put in a strong note to [Henry] Wilson re evacuation[,] pointing out that, in the opinion of Foch, an armistice is most undesirable, at least at present and that [incomplete].

13th October [1918]

Received and forwarded an extract from Mlle Christitch as to reconstruction in Serbia. According to her the greatest need was boots – then corn – and semolina puddings. The real population of Serbia were those left behind and they had not been well treated by Pasic and relief agencies and expected a Great Serbia not a Jugoslavia to which, as they disliked the Croats, they were hostile. I think, however, that much will be decided by the few Serb warriors who remain. They have reached Nish today so that the German dream of the gateway to the East is gone forever. Ferdinand's meeting with Wilhelm at Nish in 1916 seems very

---

[315] Dr Christopher Addison (1869–1951), Baron Addison, cr. 1937, 1st Viscount Addison, cr. 1945, medical doctor and politician; MP (Lib.) Hoxton, 1910–22, (Lab.) Swindon, 1929–31 and 1934–35; Parliamentary Secretary to Board of Education, 1914–15; to Ministry of Munitions, 1915–16; Minister of Munitions, 1916–17; Minister of Reconstruction, 1917–19; President of the Local Government Board, 1919; Minister of Health, 1919–21; Minister without Portfolio, 1921; Parliamentary Secretary to Ministry of Agriculture and Fisheries, 1929–30; Minister of Agriculture and Fisheries, 1930–31; Dominions Secretary, 1945–47; Lord Privy Seal, 1947–51; Paymaster-General, 1948–49; Lord President of the Council, 1951.

[316] See entry 13–14 June 1917.

far away when Ferdy addressed Wilhelm as 'miles et gloriosus'. Ferdy is now a crownless exile and I expect Wilhelm to follow suit shortly.[317]

Venizelos has intimated that with the present action Greek obligations as regards Serbia ended and that, if his troops continue fighting, he will expect some concessions in Thrace and Serbian Macedonia. This is a little disappointing for V[enizelos] should be moderate and the boundaries of 1913 are very favourable to Greece. When his carriage entered Serres the other day the people buried him in flowers and kissed his hands. Perhaps this has intoxicated him. He has triumphed splendidly but should be moderate in the hour of victory.

The French ambassador at Rome[318] reported Sonnino on the 4th October as saying that Serbia and Greece should not be allowed to parcel out Bulgaria. On the same day, the US chargé presented to Balfour a note intimating that the USA did not think it desirable to have a premature and separate Balkan peace settlement, as that area was most likely to be the future seedpot of war. It should form part of the whole settlement at the Peace Conference. Balfour intimated to him that, subject to the P[rime] M[inister]'s assent, he thought it likely that England would concur in this. I am not sure if France will. When Murphy[319] [,] the USA Consul-General at Sophia [sic] suggested a separate negociation [sic] of USA mediation at the time of the armistice with Bulgaria [,] Clemenceau promptly intimated that the USA, which had had no part in the war with Bulgaria, could not have any part in the present dealings.

15th October [1918]

I was informed that I must go to Serbia on Friday [18 October]. Wilson's reply is the death of autocracy and the greatest event since the [incomplete].

---

[317] Ferdinand I of Bulgaria (see entry 11 Mar. 1917) abdicated on 3 October in favour of his son Boris; Emperor Wilhelm II abdicated on 9 November.

[318] Camille Barrère (1851–1940), French lawyer and diplomat; entered diplomatic service, 1879; consul-general at Cairo, 1883–85; minister-resident at Munich, 1889–94; minister at Berne, 1894–97; ambassador at Rome, 1897–1924.

[319] Dominic I. Murphy (1847–1930), US lawyer and consul; commissioner US Pensions Office, 1896–97; editor, *The New Century*, 1903–1905; secretary, Isthmian Canal Commission, 1904–1905; consul at Bordeaux, 1905–1909; at St. Gall, 1909–14; at Amsterdam, 1914–15; at Sofia, 1915–17; at Stockholm, 1917–24.

16th October [1918]

Ostend, Lille fell and Bruges & Thielt[320] [*sic*] and Milner preferred or professed to believe in German democracy rather than face Brit[ish] Bolshevism.

17th October [1918]

Off. Bless dear Glad[ys] and the boy.

17 [October 1918]

Adm[ira]l B. spi – arr[ive] Bord[eaux] SWH – lively girls – calm passage – no LBS

18 [October 1918] Saturday

Havre – big, dirty, commerce – Chi[efly?] Belg[ians] Brit[ish] – Brit[ish] G[eneral] S[taff], USA, V[oluneteer] A[rmy] O[fficer]s, W[omen's] A[rmy] A[uxiliary] C[orps].
    Officers Club. Boots tight – Ord[onance] scoop.
    Lucky mistake over Hotel de St. Lazar.

19 [October 1918] Sunday

Ride in amb[ulan]ce, decayed gen[era]l. Serb troops. French review in rain ending at Bastille.
    Imp[eria]l Club 6 Rue des Capucines.

20 [October 1918] Monday

Turin – fine, large colonnades & magnificent tram system.

---

[320] That is, Tielt in west Flanders.

22 [October 1918] Tuesday [*sic*]

Eternal City – St. Peter's very wonderful – half-classic and reverential, but too small. Saw Shoebridge.

Wonderful restaurant, just by colonne de Trajano – old Roman house, yellow wine.

The view of St. Peter's from Colonna Palace very fine, and the forum, with its picturesquely disposed fragments, the finest sight I ever saw – in an amber twilight.

23 [October 1918] Wednesday [*sic*]

Taranto, a sleepy Levantine town, fine only for its harbours, outer & inner. Embarkation on Fr[ench ship] v[er]y picturesque – the blackamores in blue & blue helmets, like Saracenic knights. An Australian girl, fat and expressionless eyes, the only lady on board – in Serbian army, with a medal 'for bravery' and costume to match. Now running a canteen, smokes cigarettes & plays cards very well.

24th [October 1918]

At sea at ITEA,[321] a little rough, no events exc[ept] a flash, and the Saracenic knights, disturbed on deck, came and slept in the passage outside my room so that I felt like a sultan amid guards.

25th [October 1918]

Saw an old scene – a glassy blue bay, framed in surrounding hills – this was ITEA – found an old F&F man, then by lorry through magnificent scenery, rather bare studded hills, olive groves in valleys, for 50 km to BRALO – men on donkeys, some of Albanian type – then to AMPHISSA,[322] thence leaving Delphi and Parnassus[323] on the right – to the summit of the pass 2,900 feet – beyond that a true green mountain grove, oaks of real beauty. Before we got to it, there was a distant glimpse of 5 rows of mountains, with a faint blue touch of

---

[321] Itea, Greek town on the northern shore of the Gulf of Corinth, in the southeastern part of Phocis.
[322] Amphissa and Bralos, towns in Phocis and Phthiotis (Greece).
[323] Delphi on the southwestern flank of Mount Parnassus in the Phocis valley.

sea beyond. BRALO is near the ancient Doris,[324] which is now being explored by a professor with occasional aid from fatigue parties.

26th [October 1918]

The way lies at first thro[ugh] the same type of rather bare rugged hills <& plateaus> – there is a faint glimpse of sea, where Thermopylae[325] once was and the junction comes ~~with Pharsalis and Pisades~~ <near DERILI>. The scenery is peculiarly lovely – soft hills rounded and green, with delightful little valleys and rifts in the hills. Similar scenery is with us all the way to the Pharsalis-Pisades junction. Near it on the right a big blue shimmering lake. The sky was lovely at sunset as clouds just touched the peaks – one part of the horizon swam in a multitude of gold feathers, like a sheen on an angel's wings, the rest of the clouds being dark and light dove-colour. Then gradually the gold turned scarlet and rose, and faded into dingy grey. Finally at last, the stars came out – Orion being low in the East, the sky all dark, save for a pale lemon-coloured streak behind the hills in the west. I wished much for the pen of Ruskin[326] to describe it all as he has done. <Mod[ern] Painters, vol. I, p[ar]t II, Sec[tion] III, c[hapter] IV.][327]

28th [October 1918]

Arrived about 9 at Lambert Station Salonica – found gr[ea]t ign[oran]ce and badly veiled opp[ositio]n in a certain quarter – was left stranded till 3.30 and after a thousand adventures got my baggage safe. The certain quarter knew nothing of me, so I went off to Capt[ain] A, A[ide-] D[e-] C[amp] to Gen[eral] P[lunkett][328] and now serving his turn at malaria in the 48th Hospital.

29th <Oct[obe]r> [1918]

Saw Col[onel] Jovanović at Serbian G[eneral] H[ead] Q[uarters] and delivered my credentials and letter to Col[onel] Pešić,[329] subchief of General Staff. He

---

[324] In the Pindus valley (now Apostoliá); see Herodotus, *Histories*, book viii, ch. 31.1.

[325] Mountain pass to the coast in antiquity; site of many battles, most famously that of 279 BC.

[326] John Ruskin (1819–1900), Victorian art critic and patron of the arts; see his *Modern Painters* (5 vols, London, 1843–60).

[327] J. Ruskin, *Modern Painters*, vol. I, *Of General Principles and of Truth* (London, 1843).

[328] See entry 13–14 June 1917.

[329] See entry 16 Oct. 1917.

was genial and reported the Serbs at MLADENOVATZ, 40 kilo[metre]s from Belgrade <and POZHAREVATZ>.[330] He promised to do what he could to get me transported to Uskub. Subsequently saw Min[iste]r of [the] Int[erio]r BADJOURITCH, very quick and pleasant. He laid stress chiefly on scarcity of food, of leather, clothes and ag[ricultura]l materials. The food was bad especially in the towns, and in the Bulgarian occupied part of Serbia.

He put Serbian prisoners in Bulgaria at 50,000 originally, since reduced by deportation to Asia Minor, disease and malnutrition, first to 30,000 and then to 20,000. But officer stated 6,000 in Sofia, 500 in Philippopolis.

Casualties of Serbs stated to be 3,000 out of 28,000 rifles. The war is now a species of guerrilla warfare. Jovanovich described the war as new, a species of guerrilla war, and Austrians and Germans as both demoralized, and fleeing before small parties of Serbs.

General Bridges[331] saw me, and praised my book[332] and gave me my orders. These I was glad to see as there was nothing but verbal instructions.

Crown Prince drove by – very dark and rather handsome. I put in a card and J[ovanović]'s letter of recommendation.

30th [October 1918]

Plan air raids – M des – modified by G[enera]l Franchet.[333]

A day of disappointments ending in promises of support from Strutt with the French.

---

[330] Mladenovac, 29 miles south of Belgrade, Požarevac in eastern Serbia.

[331] Lieutenant-General Sir (George) Tom (Molesworth) Bridges (1871–1939), soldier and colonial administrator; entered Royal Artillery, 1892; active service during Boer War, 1899–1901; Military Attache, The Hague, Brussels, Copenhagen and Christiania (Oslo) 1910–14; Commander 4th Hussars, 1914; head of military mission with Belgian Field Army; Commander, 19 Division, 1915–17; Controller of Trench Warfare, Ministry of Munitions, 1917; Military Member of Arthur James Balfour's Mission to Washington, 1917; Head of British War Mission to USA, 1918; Head of British Mission to Allied Armies of the Orient, 1918–20; Commander, British Military Mission to Constantinople and Smyrna, 1920; Governor of South Australia, 1922–27.

[332] *A History of Serbia* (London, 1917).

[333] General Louis Félix Marie François Franchet d'Espèrey (1856–1942), French soldier; entered army, 1876; commanded French Fifth Army, 1914–16; Eastern Army Group, 1916–May 1918; Commander, Allied Armies at Salonika, 1918–19; Allied forces in Hungary, 1921; *Marshal de France*, 1921.

Accounts differ a good deal, as to the cause of the Bulgar demoralization. Heywood[334] seemed to think defic[ienc]y of supplies the great cause, and the cert[aint]y that they would not spend another winter in the trenches. He admitted however that the military success had come as a surprise to everyone and far exceeded expectations. He was charged with bombing the dumps and succeeded to perfection, especially in the Kosturino Pass. (An airman told me he saw dozens of lorries wrecked and men and beasts strewn and scattered over the whole pass.) Then H[eywood] passed with 2 cars right up to Sofia. His car broke down just in front of an advance guard of Germans, a battalion. They glared at him. When he got to Sofia, the found the 217th German div[isio]n there just arrived from the Ukraine. The Bulgars took charge of him and posted 40 men as guards over him. The whole interesting if not unique experience. He found from the Bulgar C[hief] of S[taff] that the Austrian Commander at Sofia was anxious about the fate of 2 guns and a batt[alio]n. 'Oh that's alright', said H[eywood] cheerily, 'we captured them this morning.'

The counter is put by a doctor, whom I met, who got up as far as Strumitza. He saw enormous quantities of supplies, timber & munitions, abandoned almost without fighting. Then also he saw of food great quantities of corn, and vegetables growing everywhere, while fodder was also abundant. H[eywood], on the other hand, asserted the defic[ienc]y of transport.

31st [October 1918]

C'est la vertu. F[ranchet] d'E[spèrey] asked Gen[era]l Bridges, when he saw Col[onel] [Heywood?] how old he was, and when he saw the A[ide-] D[e-] C[amp] with a Mons star, 'were you born then?' Gen[eral] B[ridges] explained that 'in England it was the life that made the man keep young.' 'Ah, ha!', said F[ranchet] d'E[spèrey], 'C'est la vertu!', an expression at which an Eng[lish]man w[oul]d be amused and a Frenchman insulted – worthy to be a classic.

Saw Dinant[335] FM – nothing doing.

---

[334] Lieutenant-Colonel Thomas George Gordon Heywood (1886–1943), soldier; entered army, 1886; active service, Western Front, 1914–16; General Staff Officer, 1916–17; General Staff Officer 1 (Chief Intelligence Officer), Salonika, 1917–18; British military mission, Turkey, 1920– ; Military Attaché at Paris, 1932–36; Chief of British Military Mission at Athens, 1940–41; killed in aircrash in India, 1943.

[335] Could not be identified.

1st [November 1918]

Interesting news re advance of S[er]bs to W[est] via N[ovi] B[aza]r to B[o]snia, and via SIENICA to Scutari.[336] Serbo-Fr[ench] force ordered to stop advance by l[an]d to Scutari.

It[alian] sphere acc[ording to] Fr[ance] the Drin [River]. Malyi now beyond both at Alessio & S[an] G[iovanni] de [sic] M[edua][337] & advancing without F[ranchet] d'E[spèrey] having power to prevent.

2nd [November 1918]

Serb forces – Boyovich,[338] Drina & Morova [sic].[339] 1st Army entered Belgrade little resistance.

J[ugo]S[lav] Div[ision] – Priština.

3rd [Army?] to approach Podgorica.

3rd [November 1918]

Night left Sal[onika]. Gen[eral] Bridges offered me champagne & promised me his support and insisted on my drinking his port.

4th [November 1918]

Arrive Monastir,[340] indescribably shell-shattered. Turkish barracks almost wholly wrecked, hospitals in cellars just emerging – all the old Turkish picturesqueness gone, children largely wounded by playing with bombs – visited Serbia Relief Fund hospital, very good not attended or visited by any Serbian auth[orit]ies.

Pro-Bulgar sentiments – many B[ulgar]s uncounted in the hills.

---

[336] Now Novi Pazar (western Serbia), Sienica and Shkodër (northern Albania).

[337] Lezhë on the river Drinit, and Shëngjin on the Albanian coast.

[338] *Vojvoda* (Field Marshal) Petar Bojović (1858–1945), Serbian military commander; Chief of the General Staff, 1905–1908, 1916–18; Chief of Staff, 1st Army, 1912–13; member of Serbian delegation at London ambassadorial conference, 1913; commander, 1st Army, 1914–16 and 1918; Chief of the General Staff of the Yugoslav Army, 1921–22; Assistant to the Commander-in-Chief of the Yugoslavian Armed Forces, 1941.

[339] The Drina forms the border of Bosnia-Herzegovina and Serbia; Moravica in western Serbia.

[340] Now Bitola.

Much material uncounted here. Gradients round Babuna[341] differ from old, making a diff[eren]ce of 3 km – 25 to Babuna instead of 28.

5th [November 1918] <Tuesday>

On to Veles – aerial railways not working, road good. Decauville[342] only p[ar]t working N[orth] of Prilep. Veles still contains strong pro-Bulgar elements, reported intense at STIP and Bregalnitza.

German lorries iron wheels – knocked road about. Ox transport problem. The problem of how 112 b[attalio]ns were fed from Prilep as a centre still unresolved, unless subsid[isin]g supply lines from TETOVO & OCHRIDA.[343]

6th [November 1918] Wed[nesda]y

Road from VELES to KAPLAN good, from KAPLAN rather bad & spongy. Acc[ording to] Tudor, transport prep[aratio]n for Serb offensive was wholly inadequate and, in the end, till the 30th little beyond ammun[itio]n was supplied. Tudor says rail from VRANYE[344] will be restored shortly (3 weeks) to within 3 or 4 kilo[metre]s of USKUB. R[ai]lw[a]y bridge there only slightly damaged and can be restored.

Reported arrival KUMANOVO[345] by wire.

7th [November 1918] Thursday

Road very bad from parts along from Kumanovo-Bozanevce.

Many Turks in Kumanovo (market day). Turks thro[ugh]out Vranie – Germans behaved well. Austrian prisoners starved by S[er]bs – food plentiful. <Germans behaved well> Sniping during retreat – report of assassination of Franchet d'E[spèrey] at Sofia & move of a Serb div[isio]n there.

Approach to Vranya very fine, poplars & willows, long plateau, framed in faint blue hills.

---

[341] River near Veles in central Macedonia.
[342] System of portable trench railways, made of prefabricated light, narrow-gauge track fastened to steel sleepers.
[343] Tetovo and Ohrid in northwestern and southeastern Macedonia respectively.
[344] Vranje on the Morava in southern Serbia.
[345] Kumanovo in northern Macedonia.

8th [November 1918] Friday

Dzep[346] bridge intact – romantic defile.
   Guzla Cargul Kustendil.[347]
   Canal Sultan Tepe.
   Turkovce 56 children & schoolmistress.
   Leskovtzy

9th [November 1918] Saturday

Mishitch[348] – a grey or pale eyebrow, moustache and hair, a wild almost savage expression. Conversation. Letters of compliment from Troubridge[349] and Bridges, which he was clearly very pleased to receive. He spoke of his friendship with Laffan[350] and his desire to educate his son at Eton, as that would be of great importance to him in the future. He stated how much he had opposed the taking away of two British divisions from Salonica, and declared that it had always been possible to pierce the front. When it was done, he was almost astonished. He spoke of the necessity of Entente opinion, winning back Jugoslav lands – Banat, Bačka, Temesvár,[351] all Jugoslavia. The Magyars were the most formidable enemy and concentration would be chiefly against them.

---

[346] Village in southeastern Serbia.

[347] Kyustendil in western Bulgaria.

[348] *Vojvoda* (Field Marshal) Živojin Mišić (1855–1921), Serbian military commander; commanded First Serbian Army on the Salonika Front, 1916–18; Chief of Staff, Serbian Army High Command, 1918–20; Chief of General Staff, 1920–21.

[349] See entry 30 May 1917.

[350] Robert George Dalrymple Laffan (1887–1972), historian; ordained into the Church of England, 1911; fellow and chaplain of Queen's College, Cambridge, 1912–33; temporary Army Chaplain, 1914–18; attached to Serbian Army, 1916–18; MI2(e), 1918–19 attached to legation at Belgrade, 1919; university lecturer, 1927–53; converted to Roman Catholicism, 1933; Senior Bursar, Queen's College, 1935–39; at Chatham House, 1939–43; Foreign Office Research Department, 1943–46.

[351] The Banat and Bačka (Hung. Bácska) are part of the Pannonian Basin. The former is limned by the Mureș in the north, the Tisza in the west and the Danube in the south, and the Carpathian Mountains in the east; the latter is flanked by the Danube to the west and south and the Tisza in the east. Temesvár (now Timișoara (Romania)) was the historical capital of the Banat.

10th [November 1918] Sunday

Nish. Interview with Adm[ira]l T[roubridge], now Adm[ira]l of Danube, gave him my book on D[anube?]. He pointed out diff[icult]ies of getting to BP 493 km from Smed[erov]o[352] – 6 days prob[abl]y allowing for rests at night and barges in which men w[oul]d have to go – practical diff[icult]ies greater. Orsova[353] bend was strategic knot to cut. Met mayor Teodorovich,[354] a cav[alr]y man, and large prop[rieto]r of woods on Bosnian frontier – a fine singer whose song a paraphrased.

>\<On the shores of Lake Romola
>In weather fine or wet
>For sixty years Alexander
>Has cast his net
>Beside her sue [?] Alexia
>Whitebreasted like a the swan
>The fairest Slava's daughter
>
>The sun e'er looked upon.
>Weep, weep for fair Alexia
>She listened to love's tale
>Before the twilight purple
>Had changed to morning pale.
>Down fell the storm in thunder
>Wild rolled the waves and high.
>Is this the wind a-howling,
>Is that a human cry?
>At dawn so pale & troubled
>Alexander fishes yet
>What gleams so white & lovely
>In the meshes of the net?
>No fishes' scales nor swanbreast
>E'er gleamed so white and fair!
>The father's hands dropped trembling
>Alexia was there!

---

[352] Smederovo, some 35 miles east of Belgrade.
[353] Orşova on the Danube in southwestern Romania.
[354] Temperley may have been mistaken here. The mayor of Niš until the end of November 1918 was Nikola Uzunović (1873–1954), Serbian politician; mayor Niš, 1910–Dec. 1918; Prime Minister of Yugoslavia, 1926–27 and Jan.–Dec. 1934.

12th [November 1918] Tuesday

Started from Stari Alibegovac,[355] our car decked with flowers by the children – road unspeakable – some attempt at repairs near (about 10 km) from Smederovo, but otherwise unspeakable. The fine square towers of the old fortress by Smederovo where George Branković[356] made the last Serb stand for freedom are impressive.

13th [November 1918] Wed[nesday]

Belisch[357][*sic*], C[hief] of S[taff] of 1st Serb army said to a g[rea]t chauvinist – gr[ea]t Serbia and a large extension in Roumania.

Boyovich, genial, modest – saw Flora Sandes.[358] 40 kilo[metre]s was the most travelled by any Serb reg[imen]t. 6th reg[imen]t Roi Pierre was the first to enter Belgrade.

The armistice signed on the Champ de Mars. Wilhelm is in flight in Holland and Germany in revolution, and my old theory that lack of bread and of men w[oul]d bring down the Hohenzollern is proved to be true.[359]

14th [November 1918]

The ruins of Belgrade are not very serious. I found an inscription in the fortress of Belgrade 'erobert 9/10/15' with 7 Magyar names below and a copy of Jokai's *Die Dame mit den Meeraugen*.[360]

---

[355] Stari Alibegovac near Petrovaradin on the Danube ('the Gibraltar of the Danube').

[356] Dzuradz (George) Branković (1377–24 December 1456), Serb king, 1427–56.

[357] General Vladimir J. Belić (1877–1943), Serbian soldier; Chief of Staff, 1st Army, 1917–18; Deputy Superintendent, Military Academy, 1924–27; retired, 1936; recalled, 1941; General Officer Commanding, 7th Army Rear Area, 1941; Prisoner of War, 1941–43.

[358] Sergeant-Major Flora Sandes (1876–1955), Red Cross volunteer; volunteer in St. John's Ambulance in Serbia; officially enlisted in Serbian army during retreat in 1914 (the first woman to do so in the Serbian army, and the only British women officially to enlist during the First World War); co-founder of Fund for Promoting Comforts for Serbian Soldiers and Prisoners, 1916; ran Serbian military hospital, 1916–22.

[359] See entry 13 Oct. 1918.

[360] Original *A tengerszemű hölgy* (1890), English translation by Robert Nisbet Bain, *Lady with the Eyes like the Sea* (1893); see also entry 25 Oct. 1916.

15th [November 1918] Friday

17th [November 1918]

NOVISAT[361] rest extraordinary – Magyar and Austrian officers walk about the streets unguarded and but for some remaining swagger almost unnoticed. Austrian or Magyar privates are in the hotels, Serbs are everywhere ordered [*sic*] and quiet, occasionally asserting themselves but not bullying and domineering. They give one the idea of natural gentlemen, compared with finished and civilized villains. The Civil Gov[ernmen]t is now in JugoSlav hands, but some of the old Magyars still remain in Novisat – the bulk of the population is Serb – it is otherwise in other places as SZABADKA.[362] M[iši]ch[363] the G[eneral of] D[ivision] told me he had occupied the whole BAČKA with his division without difficulty and there no unrest except the Hungarian papers which still spoke of <recovering territory>. Magyar officers on the boats conduct the steamers quietly and without protest.

We obtained our room from the military authorities and were confirmed in it by the mayor. While I was out, P[lunkett?] was sleeping on the couch when some 40 Serbs burst in. 'This is our room.' 'We have paid 40 crowns for it tonight etc.' One unslung his rifle to emphasize the argument – finally P[lunkett?] pacified them by informing us [*sic*] that we were British officers. They said it was particularly annoying because they had prepared a Slava[364] for the night. P agreed but held to the room. Later on I appeared and noticed 2 Serbs in the doorway. They had come to say they had arrested the proprietor. I said 'At night that doesn't worry me, as long as you leave the room alone.' They did.

1 woman I spoke to, a Hungarian, told me she didn't care either way whether Hungarians or Serbs were on top. For the rich such a question ought to have interest for the poor not. 'I have lost 1 brother, and the 4 little children and the wife of the other are dead of privations. For me nothing matters now, except peace and bread.' It seemed like the voice of the world speaking.

18th [November 1918] Monday

Semendria[365] with Admiral T[roubridge]. Touched at Pancsova,[366] where there seemed plenty of rolling stock. Talked to a nice Serbian girl on board the boat,

---

[361] Now Novisad.
[362] Now Subotica, in the northern Serb province of Vojvodina.
[363] See entry 9 Nov. 1918.
[364] A ritual feast of veneration of a family's patron saint.
[365] Now Smederevo.
[366] Now Pančevo on the Tamiš in Vojvodina.

Mlle Nikolić. She knew and spoke French, German, English as well as Italian and was learning Japanese. As a cultivated person she was an ardent suffragist, and much in favour of the rights of the women of Serbia. She said they had no legal rights, they could inherit property but in practice the father never left it to them. A peasant could put away a barren wife and take another, and the first was sometimes forced to serve as a servant where she had been mistress. She quoted an old ballad to prove her point – the mother says 'My Alexia' and the father interrupts and says 'No, she is not yours at all – she is mine!' I remembered also how Marko Kraljevich[367] hews a woman to pieces, as dispassionately as he would hew a man. Also she said how when they went to market the women walked and the men rode, and, when the man entered the house after his day's labour, the women had to kiss his hand.

She then turned to the occupation during which she had been [word missing?] part of the time until sent away to Zagreb for tuberculosis. Many girls were now suffering from it. She herself was doomed, as was thought, in two years.

She said the average rate for the bourgeois in the Austrian occupation was 100 Kr[onen] per day, allowing for 3 or 4 persons and one meal with meat and one with soup. <For the poor it was better because they could smuggle things in from the villages.> An incident showed the spirit not only of the Serbs but the Jugoslavs during the darkest period. At her sanatorium at Zagreb news came of the death of Francis Joseph. Immediately a concert was organized for that night, a firm comment indeed.

19 [November 1918] Tuesday

Belgrade. Serb Staff.

20th [November 1918] Wed[nesda]y

En route for Fiume <with a French officer> by ferry to Semlin, by motor to Batjovica [*sic*],[368] then some waiting. Tresić Pavičić,[369] the famous Reichsrat-Abgeordneter, whose speech last year made such a sensation, and who was one of the national Council of Croatia, accompanied us. His views were strongly in

---

[367] See entry 21 Nov. 1916.
[368] Now Zemun, opposite Belgrade (until 1918 Hungarian), and Batajnica, near Zemun.
[369] Ante Tresić Pavičić (1867–1949), Croatian politician; Member of the Austro-Hungarian *Reichsrat*, 1907–18; envoy of the Kingdom of Serbs, Croats and Slovenes at Madrid and Washington. His *In Darkest Europe: Austria-Hungary's Effort to Exterminate her Jugoslav Subjects. Speeches and Questions in the Parliaments of Vienna and Budapest and in the Croatian Sabor (Diet) in Zagreb* (London, 1917) caused a stir.

favour of unity. At Mitrovitza,[370] there was a deputation to meet him, headed by Kostić, Governor of Syrmia.[371] They threw flowers at him, and gave him a large bouquet of chrysanthemums. They presented the French officer with a flag and me with a ribbon, each of course bearing the Slav tricolor [*sic*]. (It is ingeniously vowed to represent Slovenes, Croats and Serbs). T[resić] P[avičić] then made a speech, punctuated by rapturous Zhivvios – his chief points were that everyone must work for the future in his own home and that the KaraGeorge dynasty[372] was the symbol of unity. Personally, he was a Republican but the real thing to look at was the spirit. In England there was a monarchy, which had proved compatible with the utmost extension of democracy. In Jugoslavia there could be one, too. There was much reference to the fact that freedom could not have achieved without the aid of France and England, whom Carbonnier and I in our unworthy persons represented – about 12 midnight several shots were fired at the train and answered by our soldiers. It appeared to be deserters. I did not trouble to get up and see. < The French commandant was sleeping in one carriage with Pavičić and I with Angelineff the poet. Both seized their revolvers. The soldiers came back and reported 'We have shot two'. They did not bring home the scalps however and it is doubtful if [incomplete]. >

Railway Information 8 engines and trains per day. Batjovica [*sic*] to Indija – 76 at Brod.[373] 3 or 4 k[ilo]m[etre]s still needed repair betw[een] Batjovica [*sic*] and Semlin. When dual there w[oul]d be through connections with Fiume[374] – capacity 60 trains per day. The question is difficult, complicated by Hungarian personnel and poor materials, owing to iron shortage in Germany. There seems no sort of system about it.

Slavonia has still considerable stocks of food. We heard of 40 truckloads at Vinkovce[375] which they meant to send to Dalmatia, but didn't seem to have quite decided. Henceforth the artery of Jugoslav life will be the Fiume-Semlin line.

---

[370] Now Sremska Mitrovica in the western Vojvodina.
[371] Region south of the Drava and Danube, from Vukovar in the west to Neo Beograd in the east, since 29 Oct. 1918 part of the State of Slovenes, Croats and Serbs (SHS).
[372] Karađorđević, the ruling dynasty, 1903–41.
[373] Indija in Vojvodina, half-way between Zemun and Petrovaradin.
[374] Now Rijeka (Croatia).
[375] Vinkovci in eastern Croatia.

21st [November 1918] Thursday

<u>Baker</u>.[376] Arrived Zagreb[377] – breakdown en route because of the special train, which Tresić Pavičić had ordered, disorganizing [the] line. Subsequently, in conversation with Stationschef at Zagreb I ascertained that no arrangements were really being made to run the railway. Coal and material were bad, the railways had 4 years of war, and the coal came from Germany. Another difficulty was the relations with Italy at Fiume, as they had a considerable amount of rolling stock etc. There is however enough to run the railway given agreement and central control.

Korosics[378] [*sic*]	Pres[ident]	Slovene
Pavlević[379] [*sic*]	V[ice] P[resident]	Croat
Pribicević[380]	V[ice] P[resident]	Serb Commissars
Priča, Admiral	Marine	
Dr [Srdjan] Budisavijević[381]	Interior	[Serb]
Dr Brandt	Finance	
Trumbić[382]	Foreign	
Dr [Mate] Drinković	Guerre	[Croat]
Csorvin Dr	Public Works	
Dr Baday	Justice	

---

[376] Lieutenant-Colonel (Bernard) Granville Baker (1870–1957), soldier, travel-writer and artist; entered army, 1890; served in 9th Prussian Hussars Regiment, 1894–1900; active service South Africa, 1900–1901; on Staff, Indian Corps in France, 1914–15; 1st Army staff, 1915–16; British Commissioner for Propaganda in Enemy Countries on Italian and Salonika Fronts, 1918; member of Supreme Economic Council's mission to Central Europe, 1919; retired, 1919.

[377] On 6 October, a National Council of Slovenes, Croats and Serbs was organized at Zagreb, a *de facto* government of the Yugoslavs in the dissolving Austro-Hungarian state.

[378] Dr. Anton Korošec (1872–1940), Slovene priest and Yugoslav politician; member of Austro-Hungarian *Reichsrat*, 1907–18 (advocated southern Slav state within the Austro-Hungarian monarchy); President of the National Council of Slovenes, Croats and Serbs, 1918 (elected 19 Oct. 1918); Minister of the Interior, 1924–7; first Prime Minister of Yugoslavia, 1928–29.

[379] Dr. Ante Pavelić (1869–1938), Croatian dentist and politician; member of the *Sabor* (Croatian diet), 1906–18; Vice-President of National Assembly, 1918; speaker of the Yugoslav Senate, 1932–38.

[380] Svetozar Pribićević (1875–1936), Croatian Serb politician; leader of Croatian-Serb coalition in *Sabor*, 1906–18; Vice-President of National Council of Slovenes, Croats and Serbs, 1918; Minister of the Interior, 1918–20 and 1921; imprisoned, 1929–31; in Czech exile since 1931.

[381] Srđan Budisavljević (1883–1968), Croatian-born, pro-monarchist Serb politician; involved in Zagreb (Friedjung) trial, 1909; member of National Council of Slovenes, Croats and Serbs; leader, Indepent Democratic Party, 1936–41.

[382] See entry 30 Aug. 1918.

Dr Reilos	Education
Dr Markovics	Santé public [*sic*]
Dr Wilder	Railway
Dr Petričić	Public Eco[nomy]
Dr Marković	Food
M Akačić	Posts etc.

70 Nat[iona]l Council

The Jugoslav National Council fully installed in the Ban's house, interesting literary much talent but little organisation – an Adm[ira]l without a fleet, a Min[iniste]r without control of railways, a Nat[iona]l Council, a sort of Jugoslav Versailles, without recognition from the latter. The triumvirate was good idea and will have a great effect, as each man represents a nation. Zagreb and all Croatia is perfectly tranquil and there is no sabotage on the railway. The Ban Mihalović[383] still exists but the Sabor[384] is dissolved and he is now simply the local administrator of Croatia. Talk of course entirely turned on the Italian question which is, I suspect, at bottom more on of the disposal of the Austrian fleet than of the disposal of Austrian territory.

There was subsequently a delightful dinner at which there were 4 kinds of wine, of bread and of meat, sugared cakes in abundant variety, and speeches on the necessity of political union in great variety – or rather in great sameness. Several of the ministers were present. I thought of Dalmatia and the Star Chamber. The best was the V[ice] P[resident] of the Croatian Ag[ricultura]l Soc[iet]y – his wife the heiress to great estates, charming and amusing. As we were going she flung down a bunch of flowers for the C[omman]d[an]t and myself, as representatives of England and France, which we bore off in triumph, while she waved her handkerchief from a balcony.

Zagreb retains its distinct individual character of culture – the new library built in a quasi-Assyrian style is very fine, with owls of wisdom looking down from the gables, the interior is finely decorated with frescos. In front of the theatre, which I well remember in 1906, is a wonderful composition of Mestrovics,[385] a fountain known as the waters of life, a strange history of man, his sins, follies and desires over which I could have mused for hours. The cold did not permit by compensation the snow on the hills made Zagreb look more beautiful.

---

[383] Antun Mihalović (1868–1949), Croatian nobleman; *ban* (viceroy) of Croatia, 1917–19.

[384] Croatian diet.

[385] Ivan Meštrović (1883–1962), Croatian and Yugoslav sculptor with a preference for religious themes; in exile, 1914–18; member of the Yugoslav Committee; renewed exile since 1941; Professor at Syracuse University, 1946–55, Notre Dame, 1955–62. The fountain is 'The Sources of Life' outside the Croatian National Theatre in Zagreb (1905).

A new Serb regiment (the 25th) independent is being formed here consisting of 4 companies of returned prisoners. Some attempt is being made to form demobilised Croats into regiments but there was not the same enthusiasm here. The town was gay and lively as it always has been, and the university has continued throughout the war.

17th [November 1918]

Evac[uatio]n [of Fiume]

19th [November 1918]

22 [November 1918]

23rd [November 1918] Sat[urda]y

Conference. Italian General DI SAMBRANO, Italian Admiral Rainer,[386] General Gordon,[387] L[ieutenant-] Col[onel] Everson,[388] USA Command.

The line was taken by Commodore Dumesnil that the thing was fait accompli. His account of the facts was substantially supported on all sides, viz. on the 18th trouble began [in Fiume] and the Serbs said that there w[oul]d be trouble if Italians entered.[389] On the 17th, after a previous meeting between Col[onel] Maximovitch[390] and Adm[ira]l Rainer, it was arranged that Serb evacuation should take place <and no more troops should enter the town>, and the Serbs agreed to evacuate by 4. This was agreed to with some shuffling by Admiral Rainer, in the presence of a British and French officer, C[omman]d[an]t

---

[386] Admiral Guglielmo Rainer, Italian sailor; commanded the Italian squadron at Fiume.

[387] Major-General Lochinvar Alexander Charles Gordon (1864–1927), soldier; served in Royal Artillery; on staff in France, 1914–15; active service in Mesopotamia, 1915–17; eastern Mediterranean, 1918; Serbian decoration; retired, 1919.

[388] Major-General William G. Everson (1879–1954), US clergyman and soldier; ordained Baptist minister, 1901; entered militia, 1898; active service Spanish-American War, 1898, and Italy and Balkans, 1917–18; represented USA at Fiume and supervised food distribution in Austria, 1918–19; discharged, 1919; Brigadier in the Reserves, 1922; Chief of National Guard Bureau, 1929–31; retired, 1945.

[389] The Austro-Italian Armistice of Villa Giusti, Padua, of 3 Nov. 1918, paved the way for the Italian occupation of the Austro-Hungarian littoral.

[390] Colonel Voja Maksimović, commanded the Serb forces at Fiume in Oct.–Nov. 1918.

DUHAND-VIEL[391] and Forster.[392] Rainer sent them to see that the evacuation was taking place, and, meanwhile, the Italian Gen[era]l, on the pretext of seniority, advanced troops from Trieste. When Forster and DUHAND-VIEL returned they saw the troops being disembarked from Italian ships. When he heard this on arrival Dumesnil sent word that it was not necessary to call a French officer to witness the fact that an Italian admiral was breaking his word. He considered that this action had made his officer commit an unworthy act.

He then referred to the fact that the latest order of the Italians had commanded all ex-Austrian troops to be expelled from the town within 48 hours.

In the course of the conversation it appeared to be established that the Italians had abolished or pulled down all flags except their own in Fiume, and oppressed all but Italian propaganda. The newspapers also had been suppressed or heavily censored. In a subsequent interview with Gordon the Italian General denied all these charges, except that about the expulsion of the Austrian troops which Gordon did not ask him. He admitted however that there were intelligence agents in the town and indirectly of course that they [incomplete].

24th [November 1918] Sunday

Before I left today I had the pleasure of seeing a tug depart carrying Admiral Rainer who is to be replaced by Adm[ira]l Ruggiero. Even Italians disgrace a man who has broken his word. I understand now the agitation displayed by Rainer yesterday – why he could not keep still a moment, and fluttered in his talk like a bird. I confess I have little sympathy with him – 'a man lies facile and lies faible' said my French colleague. I don't think that I disagree with either view.

It is said that the Jugoslav flags at SOSAK[393] were to be hung today. Superb panorama driving from Fiume to Kraljevica and thence to PLASE[394] – long lines

---

[391] Vice-Admiral Georges Edmond Just Duhand-Viel (1875–1959), French submariner; commanded torpedo boat in Adriatic, 1918; director, École de Guerre and Centre des Hautes Études Navales, 1927–29; commander, 1st Squadron, 1929–31; chief of naval staff, 1931–37; retired, 1937; director of Suez Canal Company.

[392] Major Edward Seymour Forster (1879–1950), classicist; ed. Wellington and Oriel College, Oxford; Assistant Lecturer, University College of North Wales, 1904–1905; Lecturer in Classics, University of Sheffield, 1905–21; Professor of Greek, 1921–45; commissioned as 2nd Lieutenant, 1915; active service (attached General Staff, Intelligence) with British Salonica and Black Sea forces, 1915–19; Major, 1918; a noted translator of Aristotle, also author of *A Short History of Modern Greece, 1821–1940* (London, 1941).

[393] Sušak, a suburb of Rijeka.

[394] Kraljevica (It. Porto Ré) on Croatian coast between Rijeka and Crikvenica; Plase in hinterland of Kraljevica.

or walls of hills stood up in tiers from the azure sea with flat green-yellow valleys in between. To Zagreb at about 2 am Royal hotel.

25th [November 1918] Monday

<u>Videm Krsko</u> Weisskirchen Reichenburg[395] nat[ional] costume.

1 French battalion arrived yesterday and another is expected. 1 British battalion is expected tonight.

Saw Smodlaka[396] in the morning. He is one of the representatives of the provisional government of Dalmatia – come to ask the S[lovenaca] H[rvata i] S[rba][397] [authorities] of Zagreb for food. He has had a terrible time – first imprisoned then a common soldier in a Strafcompany [*sic*], finally released released after the amnesty of July 1917. He confirmed all my views as to the inefficiency and inability of the existing Jugoslav Government to run the FIUME-BEOGRAD railway and suggested an International Commission as the sole or at least the best remedy. He related an incident at Zebenico[398] by which the Italians induced the inhabitants to appear pro-Italian but did not know that they had refused except to those who signed a document.

We left Zagreb at 3.30 for Laibach[399] which we reached at 9. Thrice on the way we were held up by deputations, one at VIDEM KRISKO where they waved flags, held candles and sang the national anthem to us ending by cheering for England and France and again at REICHENBURG where girls appeared in national costum and shook us by the hand and where a lady gave me a bunch of beautiful roses. A Trappist father came forward at this latter place as the representative of the town and addressed us in excellent French. I replied as follows 'I bring you the greetings of England which, like France, is a friend of freedom. England which rules the free colonies rejoices to see the free states of Jugoslavia, Slovenia, Croatia and Serbia uniting in one. Zhivela Jugoslavia', and we glided off amid cheers, songs and flags, one of the latter flew in my face, so I kissed it, which evinced cheers.

So, amid high living to Laibach by special train.

---

[395] Videm near Krško in eastern Slovenia; Weisskirchen in the Murtal district, Styria; Brestanica (ex- Rajhenburg) in eastern Slovenia.

[396] Josip Smodlaka (1869–1956), Croatian politician; Member of the Dalmatian diet, 1901–1909; of Austro-Hungarian *Reichsrat*, 1911–18; mayor of Split 1918 and 1943.

[397] State of Slovenes, Croats and Serbs (*Država Slovenaca, Hrvata i Srba*), short-lived state that seceded from Austria-Hungary on 29 Oct. 1918 and consisted of the southernmost parts of the Habsburg monarchy; not recognized internationally; acceded to the Kingdom of the Serbs, Croats and Slovenes on 1 Dec. 1918.

[398] Now Šibenik on the central Dalmatian coast at the mouth of the Krka river.

[399] Now Ljubljana.

26th [November 1918]

LJUBLJANA – LAIBACH

A French woman who had not seen a French officer for 35 years, came up to greet us. She was greatly moved as I was a little.

We passed on to see Jeglić,[400] the great Slovene Bishop. I had previously ascertained from various sources that all the stories about him are true, i.e. to say he was in a position, being a Bishop, to say things which no official dared to say, though he risked not only the resentment of Austria but of Rome. He said them openly, at the critical time and won over the peasant population and the priests. In Croatia the latter have not been very patriotic, here they have been the chief supporters of the movement.

After a few moments we were admitted to the Prince Bishop's presence. His appearance was a great surprise – a mild old man, with a merry eye and great benevolence and simplicity in his appearance, with an air of simple goodness and benevolence that could not be resisted. We could not speak much because the French commandant did not know German, and the Prince Bishop knew very little French. We each made a speech of compliment, Carbonnier ended by comparing him to Mercier,[401] and I to Stroessmeyer.[402] My phrase did not stick and the interview only appeared in the paper the next day. Carbonnier was promoted to the rank of General and the phrase the 'Jugoslav Mercier' was used. He said very simply to me that it was not he but the people, who had done everything. He also spoke of the great danger now threatening his people from Italy.

After leaving him we proceeded by auto to the Land Rat. The President and his Cabinet were in session and we sat down on his right and his left. The President addressed a speech of welcome in which he said that he welcomed us as the first representatives of the Entente and as a sign of the good will of France and England towards the Slovenes. We replied expressing our delight at being able to witness the birth of a nation but saying we had no duty or mission but that of observation.

Subsequently, the President Pogačević talked to me a good deal and made clear what they wanted – 100 English soldiers to chase the Italians from some of the territory which they had taken over. That would be enough with the Slovene

---

[400] Anton Bonaventura Jeglić (1850–1937), Slovene Roman Catholic clergyman; entered priesthood, 1873; Professor of Theology, University of Laibach, 1881–97; Prince Bishop of Laibach/Ljubljana, 1898–1930.

[401] Cardinal of Mechelen, see entry 5 May 1918.

[402] Josip Juraj (Joseph Georg) Stroessmeyer (1815–1905), Croatian Roman Catholic clergyman and politician; entered priesthood, 1838; bishop of Djakovo, 1848–1905; leader of the Croatian People's Party, 1860–73; supported federalization of the Habsburg monarchy.

levies. This is, of course, preposterous but I made it clear that we should be glad to hear anything they could tell us of the conditions and to report it.

To Zagreb and the theatre in the evening. Ljubljana is a beautiful place and the castle overhanging it and its broad parks must make it delightful in the summer. I shall think coming away the scenery for three quarters of the journey is that of small hills, with the deep green river running beside it, the Save. Cheers were raised for us again at the Café as we left, and the manager came to express a regret that they could only play 'Rule Britannia' as 'God Save the King' was the same as the German 'Heil Kaiser dir' and apt to create misconceptions with the crowd. I was glad of the warning because shortly afterwards I recognized the tune.

27th [November 1918]

There was rather an amusing pendant to our interview with the Italian General at Ri[j]eka.[403] French batt[alio]n landed from Venice on the 24th, another reached there on the 25th and a British one also. The difficulties of sending a goods train from RIJEKA so insurmountable on the 23rd were waived on the 26th for a passenger train which conveyed a French colonel to Zagreb in SIX hours! The Croat press remarked with some humour that neither Italians nor Magyars received this feat with much enthusiasm.

We left today in a special train with a deputation carrying a crown, for the National Council of S[lovenaca,] H[rvata i] S[rba] had declared for a united Jugoslavia with Alexander as Regent, and the deputation was carrying the news and the crown to Belgrade.

28th [November 1918]

During the night we arrived very fortified at Semlin – the stretch of the railway has now been repaired from BATAJNICA[404] and we went smoothly to Semlin. We were received with Zhivvios[405] and with a bodyguard of red-shirted Sokols,[406] who carried falcon's feathers in the Astrakhan hats. They invited us to a banquet at 1 am but commandant and I refused. Afterwards we were glad for they sang until 7 am. ANGELUVOFF, the dear little doctor, whom I call my Englishman because of his whiskers, presented me with a copy of his poems printed the day before. There were 3 Bosnian delegates with red fezes aboard, who distributed

---

[403] That is, Fiume; Temperley generally used the Italian version Fiume.
[404] Batajnica, some 20 miles west of Belgrade.
[405] *Zhivio* (Serb) 'long live'.
[406] See entry 25 Aug. 1917.

their home products in the shape of cigarettes. A picturesque, white-bearded old man was Vladan Georgevich[407] with a good-looking daughter and two lovely children (to represent the rising generation, I suppose). He was stately and looked wise, and was vain – he was an Obrenovich premier and is said to have been designed by the Austrians to constitute a pro-Austrian Serb government while Austria was still in occupation. His vanity was great and he nearly fell into the trap but not quite, and now Georgevich is a KaraGeorgevich.

29th [November 1918]

Dine with General Henrys,[408] the C[omman]der of the Army of the East. A very pleasant quick bright man, with grey moustache and small alert movements. One of his officers in attendance was Capt[ain] Murat,[409] a descendant of the beau sabreur,[410] said to be the first officer to enter Monastir on its fall. He modestly disclaimed the honour. I believe the report wh[ich] appeared in the newspapers was quite untrue. Heavy and a little dull, tho[ugh] agreeable, he did not remind one much of the King of Naples. If the latter was an ancestor, he is certainly a descendant.

General Henrys' talk ranged over the whole field of action of which he had clearly a wide grasp. He was evidently keenly interested in occupying Budapest, for which purpose a division of Frenchmen is already at Novisat. It is unlikely to proceed farther as the Brit[ish] forces have been sharply stopped on the Danub[e].

30th [November 1918]

Saw Admiral Troubridge. He made the rather interesting suggestion that river peoples, like those on the Danube, never moved from the river, winter or summer never knew what was going on outside the river, or cared except whether the river rose or fell as much. He said it was the same on the Broads, among the Junk peoples of Canton and Hong Kong, and of course on the Danube. That is why

---

[407] Dr Vladan Đorđević (1844–1930), Serbian physician and politician; Minister of Education, 1888–91; Minister at Athens, 1891–94; at Constantinople, 1894–97; Prime Minister and Foreign Minister, 1897–1900; interned by Austria-Hungary during the war.

[408] General Paul Prosper Henrys (1862–1943), French soldier; Commanding Officer, 17th Army Corps, May–Dec. 1917; Commander-in-Chief, L'Armée d'Orient, Dec. 1917–Apr. 1919; Chief of French Military Mission to Poland, 1919–20; retired, 1924.

[409] Joachim Murat, 6th Prince Murat (1885–1938), French soldier; served in cavalry regiment during the war.

[410] Prince Joachim-Napoléon Murat (1767–1815), French soldier; Marshal of France, 1804; Grand Duke of Berg and Cleves, 1806–1808; King of Naples, 1808–15; executed, Oct. 1815.

he said you can employ with perfect safety Hungarians and Germans to navigate the steamboats. 'A Brit[ish] Gen[era]l the other day told me he had chucked out the chief engineer because he found he was a Boche. I told him he was a damned fool and that, if he did this, we should have no one to work the boats, and shoved the man immediately on another boat. The sentiment of riverine populations makes it safe, while the absence of personnel makes it essential to act thus. It is with the Magyar stationmasters on the Fiume railway – foolish to dismiss them, though they have no riverine sentiments. One told me they were no politicians.[']

1st Dec[embe]r [1918]

Several pathetic cases come before our notice. We can do nothing but summon our hearts. A half starved Serb soldier came and begged me for bread, a beautiful woman who was wife of the secretary of the Austro-Hungarian legation, came and begged for the protection of us and our Government for her and her husband, and woman with 6 small children wrote to say her money was exhausted and she had not heard from her husband for months, who was in English employ, could we help? Of course, we could not – there would be no end of appeals if we satisfied any.

Today, Wettmann, the former police Chief at Belgrade during the occupation, was brought here from Temesvár. I saw him sitting in a carriage with a Serb officer beside him and small boys hanging on behind and the crowd booing. He is said to have struck every woman who ever came to see him and to have caused the death of 2,000 Serbs.

2nd Dec[embe]r [1918]

Today Adm[ira]l Troubridge told me that he had dined with the Prince last night, when the deputation offered him the rule over all Jugoslavia and turned a ruler of 4,000,000 men into a ruler of 13,000,000. The Prince made an excellent reply saying Jugoslavs desired only self-determination as expressed by Wilson and peace with their neighbours such as Italy.

The Adm[ira]l said he was glad to be the first Englishman to congratulate him on being the new ruler, whereupon the Regent, much moved, rushed into his bedroom, and brought out his KaraGeorge order (2nd class) saying 'its dirty, but it is my own – will you have it.' The Admiral showed it to me with pride the next day and by that time it was cleaned up.

Proposal for disarmament.

3rd [December 1918]

Mishitch's plan.

4th Dec[embe]r [1918]

Dine at Offiziers Klub – fine singing, many French and Serb officers. The Prince led off with the first Kolo[411] danced for 4 years, perhaps for 7, in Belgrade. For the honour of England I joined up, with Jedan Nikolić, a fair flower of a girl who will die in a year of tuberculosis, with whom I had tea this afternoon. As the slow graceful dance wound round the Prince came opposite me and smiled. I bowed politely, but my spurs and hobnailed boots made the evolution less graceful than it would otherwise have been. Afterwards I spoke with him a few words of compliment, and said to him – 'Highness the last time I saw you, you were regent of 4 millions and now of 13 – my felicitation.' He bowed greatly pleased. He was more excited with the General when he spoke of the Italians and came to the point of saying that Serbia had no representation at Versailles while Italy had and he feared she would not have backing. It is difficult to know our policy as Protitch[412] told a friend of mine yesterday that he feared another Power (<u>who</u>?) would not stand by Serbia.

The Prince reminded me of Charles Stuart[413] and the balls at Holyrood, though his fate is the happier. He certainly has a gracious unaffected manner. The whole assembly was charming, everyone seemed to know everyone else and was simple unaffected and national. It was half a large country house party, a quarter of a political assembly and a quarter of a military dance.

5th [December 1918]

Off to Pancsova[414] – mist on stream which delayed us 4 hours and caused us to draw heavily on our provisions. Carbonnier and I are going to Temesvár – owing to the mist we did not reach Pancsova till 2, and the only train left at one. Consequently, we had to stay there till the next day. I was put up with a charming

---

[411] A folk (circle) dance popular in Serbia.
[412] Stojan M. Protić (1857–1923), Serbian journalist and politician; deputy, 1887–1923; Minister of the Interior, 1903, 1904–1905 and 1906–1908; Finance Minister, 1912–18; Serbian representative on Yugoslav Committee, 1917–18; Foreign Minister of the Kingdom of Slovenes, Croats and Serbs, 1918; Prime Minister, Dec. 1918–Aug. 1919 and Feb–May 1920.
[413] Charles Edward Louis Philip Casimir Stuart (1720–1788), the 'Young Pretender', led the 1745 uprising.
[414] Now Pančevo.

family, of which the niece spoke English well. They talked of nothing but the dear English and clung on my words as if I was a prophet and asked countless questions about me and mine. If it was not that I knew all this was intended not for me but for the country, I should feel proud. I awaked some enthusiasim by telling them that I had been at Pancsova before in the days that were gone, 1909, I think, to be correct.

At night there was quite a revel in the hotel. Of course, the Kolo was danced, and walses [sic], and, of course, I was called upon, in knee boots of the trench order, to represent my country. I did what I could – there were two quite nice girls, one a Montenegrin. The morning of the 6th, we went round the town, nothing much to see, but an interesting Church in the Byzantine style with fine modern Serbian paintings, spoilt by heavy plaster outside, representing red and yellow alternatives of stone, and by the imitation of marble within. The religious pictures were a little force but the historical were not, and the picture of Knez Lazar[415] before the field of Kossovo was really noble.

I talked with the town council about the revolution. They said it took place very peacefully, on the 1st November after several days of excitement – a national council of Serbs was formed. It took place quite peacefully at first, though they were armed – the Hungarian officials also had arms, including machine guns and a gendarmerie. After several days' tension a motorboat sneaked off unnoticed to Belgrade where it brought the news and asked for help. Boyovitch at once sent a battalion of the 2nd regiment, the famous iron regiment, and it entered the town on the night of the 8th and 9th. After that there was no more trouble.

<There is a strong Serb majority.> There are also Germans, but there is undoubtedly a strong Serb feeling in the town as a whole. There was no mistaking the fervour of the celebration in the hotel, when we danced the Kolo, or the enthusiasm at the songs. The family with whom I stayed said they did not know what they had done to deserve the gratitude help of the English, who had educated their children, saved their soldiers and liberated their country. The company at the hotel was headed by a priest Davidovich, who had suffered in gaol for his principles, who danced the Kolo, and who kissed me on both cheeks. I am afraid that I did not represent my country very well with the family of Nikolics, for they told me that they had entertained a compatriot, Flora Sandes,[416] the famous English woman sergeant in the Serbian army and that she had ate, smoked and drunk more than I did.

---

[415] Lazar Hrebeljanović (1329–89), Serbian nobleman; as Stefan Lazar, Prince of Serbia, 1371–89; fell in battle of Kosovo Polje against Ottomans, 28 June 1389.

[416] See entry 13 Nov. 1918.

6th [December 1918]

To Temesvár by special train with Col[onel] Sokolić and wife, and with Mme Subotić and Carbonnier. The chief feature was the lateness of the train in arriving and the magnificence of the dinner set before us by the Bishop Letić.[417] He entertained all our party, a French general Gambetta,[418] and several priests. There were 5 kinds of wine, including champagne and magnificent courses of meat, including venison, pheasant and turkey. The Bishop spoke a little English – he read British theological books, knew the Illustrated London News, Christmas number, took in the Guardian (not Manchester)[419] and read a part of his speech in English.

<B[isho]p Letić's speech v[ide] 6th Dec[embe]r

I am very happy to have [the] opportunity to express in a few words my wishes sincere and true, who fill this day my heart with abundance, to the English noble nation and English army.

May God in heaven grant his perfect bliss upon England and [the] English army, covered with glory, which fighting in this war of independence bring to the whole world fraternity liberty parity culture and durable peace.>[420]

His meal and air did not give me the idea that he had suffered much persecution but he informed me that two of his priests had been put in gaol in the earlier part of the war. The portraits of his predecessors were shady or stern or sensual.

7th [December 1918]

Went to the National Council of Serbs at Temesvár. I understand their whole numbers are 4,000, but the proportion of educated is high. There are 27,000 Germans[,] over 20,000 Magyars, and the rest Roumans. Total 75,000. The Roumans in this area are simply ignorant peasants – they are giving great trouble in the country districts by pillaging and massacring the inhabitants. In the town the Serbs have not the Government, but a representative from Novi Sat had come over to address them, who proposed to me that the Serbs of Temesvár should link up with Bačka and Baranya[421] and make a common offer of the Crown to Regent Alexander. The actual situation in Temesvár

---

[417] Dr Gheorghe Letić, Serb Orthodox bishop of Temesvár.
[418] General François Léon Prosper Jouinot-Gambetta (1870–1923), French soldier; entered cavalry, 1888; member of Algerian-Moroccan boundary commission, 1904–1905; commanded cavalry of the Armée d'Orient, 1917–18; captured Üsküb (Skopje), 29 Sept. 1918.
[419] *The Guardian*, a Church of England weekly paper.
[420] In the original entered following the entry for 30 Oct. 1918.
[421] Region between the rivers Danube and Drava.

and in the adjoining counties of Krasso and Torontal[422] (the last pure Serb) is extraordinary. They are all ruled by a Socialist regime, installed a Temesvár on the 1st November,[423] and presided over by a Magyar Jew Dr Rot.[424] The Germans, Magyars and Serbs have all acquiesced in this arrangement and the Serb troops have tactfully left the matter alone. It is not however a situation which can be eternal. A French general is also here with a cavalry brigade of Moors. Pesics[425] informed me later that Serbs had been asked to advance beyond Arad but had refused as it was against the armistice terms. I cannot say that I am impressed by the Serb argument that Temesvár was serb some 60 or 70 years ago. Generally I do not understand why the frontier was moved from S[outh] of ARAD[426] to the Lippa-KARANSEBES-ORSOVA line,[427] unless there was a reason with the Roumanian bands who have inaugurated a regular Jacquerie[428] and are pillaging landowners. It does not necessarily appear that the Roumanian Government is inciting them but it is playing its own game in North Tansylvania Maro Vorsarkely and threatened Koloszvar.[429]

8th [December 1918]

Versecz.[430] We returned to Versecz after a heavy lunch, from Col[onel] Georgevich, where we drank red wine given by a German archbishop to Mackensen and obligingly left behind by the latter. We thanked both for their gift. At Versacz we found the famous Morava division, the best in the whole Serbian army. I saw only however the General and his C[hief] of S[taff]. In the evening there was a great banquet in honour of the French major and myself, the first Entente

[422] Krassó-Szörény and Torontál, two administrative counties in the Kingdom of Hungary, the former between Danube and Timiş, the latter now in the Eastern Vojvodina (Serbia).
[423] The short-lived Banat Republic, proclaimed at Temesvár on 1 Nov. 1918, the day after the dissolution of Austria-Hungary, and suppressed by Serbian forces on 15 Nov. In 1919, the Banat territory was divided primarily between the Kingdom of the Serbs, Croats and Slovenes and Romania.
[424] Dr Otto Roth (1884–1956), leader of the local Hungarian Social Democratic Party; civilian People's Commissar of the Banat Republic.
[425] See entry 16 Oct. 1917.
[426] Arad, then the capital of the Hungarian county of Arad, now in western Romania.
[427] Now Lipova in Arad county, Caransebeş in southwestern Romania, and Orşova, just above the 'Iron Gates' on the Danube.
[428] A peasant rebellion in northern France in 1358; *jacquerie* later became synonymous with peasant uprising in general.
[429] *Recte* Marosvásárhely, modern Târgu Mureş in northern central Romania; and *recte* Kolozsvár (Klausenburg), now Cluj-Napoca in Transylvania.
[430] Now Vršac in the Vojvodina (Serbia).

officers to be there. There were the usual songs and enthusiasm at the banquet in the evening. At the end the air seemed full of 'Vive Carbonnier' and 'Hip, hip, hurray for Major Temperley.' Starojević, a jovial John Bull sort of fellow, our chief host, outdid everyone in enthusiasm. An amusing instance of Serb tolerance took place.

In the middle a Magyar got up and began attacking the Entente saying we talked a great deal about freedom, but it should be freedom for all, Hungarians as well as Slavs or French or British. This speech was squashed by cries of Zhivela Inglezka – Zhivela Francuzka! However nothing daunted he returned to the charge and his second speech was more moderate, and he said all the woes of Hungary were due to the Habsburg. The mere fact that he was not thrown out the first time shows the general liberality of the Serbian rule at present.

The fun waxed more and more furious – we sweated in the Kolo. On one occasion 5 Serb officers gave a special display, very complicated, but graceful and beautiful. I danced with a pretty Montenegrin girl most of the time, though Carbonnier, as always, secured the prettiest girl in the room.

At the end the applause became absolutely deafening and Starojevich, who had long ago discarded his glass, wildly waved a bottle in response to all toasts – we finally got away about one 30 – there was tremendous applause as we left and, one man came out and, of course, kissed me. Even then the students would not leave us alone and escorted us to the house, singing songs, and shouting so loud, that we had at last to appear on the balcony, before the applause subsided. Next morning a young lady brought four bottles of very good red wine, and the ladies of Versecz gave us bouquets. As Starojevich said, Pancseva was good, Temesvár was better, Versecz is best.

16th December 1918

Ceremony of celebration of the birthday of Regent Alexander, first the service at the Catholic Cathedral impressive and short, many canons and one archbishops, then the Greek Church ceremony, then the parade. There were six battalions of Serb troops, some Jugoslavs and some guns – all prisoners of war; considering this is the 5th year of the war and most of these were half-starved prisoners their bearing was very fine, their step time was good and many swing their arms well. Afterwards there was a reception at the palace of the Banus, who was grandly attired in the original national costume, brown velvet, gold bars and fur collar with white plume in his fur kolpak, and topboots. Some of his attendants were even more gorgeously attired in what, I believe, are the original hussar uniforms, borrowed by Louis XIV from Hungary and Croatia.

The reception was splendid, many Serb and Austrian uniforms making it very picturesque and the priests lending a touch of crimson and purple. The Banus made a speech to the effect that Croatia and Jugoslavia were one and inseparable under the sceptre of Alexander. Subsequently, after seeing whether I could say goodbye to the Banus[431] I found him dancing in the square – the Kolo – white plume and all, among Croat women and Serb men. It is the first time any Ban ever has, but MIHALOVIC came from Slavonia where he learnt the Serb Kolo as a boy. It was a masterstroke and he was cheered and chaired to the echo. I danced too with Admiral ~~Joch~~ Koch but left a little too soon. The engineer colonel also came out and danced and was widely cheered. This is the entrance of the Serbian democracy into Croatia, humorous and gentle, yet moving. I cannot imagine the Lord Mayor of London and Admiral Beatty dancing with me in any kind of ceremony. Yet this unselfconscious method of proceeding is the salt of life. It reminds me of Chesterton,[432] whom Mr. Joseph McCabe[433] denounced for treating with levity religious subjects and dancing about them as in an Alhambra ballet. Chesterton replied that dancing was a religious ceremony and that the tragedy 'is not that I dance in the Alhambra ballet, but that Mr. McCabe does not dance with me.' So with me – it is really a comedy not that I dance the Kolo with the Banus and the Admiral, but that the Admiral Beatty and the Lord Mayor do not or would not dance with us.

18th [December 1918]

Attended a funeral today, Mazura, the last helper of old Strossmayer. I also saw a sculptor who spoke to me both of Rački,[434] the spiritual soul of Strossmayer,[435] and of the great bishop himself. The latter he described to me as a 'man with a lovely face – in fact a genius.' The former he had already limned in stone on a tablet which he showed me, a gentle spiritual determined face.

---

[431] See entry 21 Nov. 1918.

[432] Gilbert Keith Chesterton (1874–1936), poet and novelist; creator of the detective-priest Father Brown (1911). The reference is to *The Alhambra*, a music hall on Leicester Square, 1854–1936.

[433] Joseph Martin McCabe (1867–1955), writer and secularist speaker; entered Franciscan order, 1882; ordained priest, 1890–96; thereafter writer on religion and science; included in Chesterton's *Heretics* (London, 1908).

[434] Dr Franjo Rački (1828–94), Croatian Roman Catholic clergyman and historian; entered priesthood, 1852; author of several works on mediaeval Croatian history; Member of Croatian diet, 1861–65; Chairman of the Croatian Academy of the Sciences and Arts, 1866–86.

[435] See entry 26 Nov. 1918.

20th [December 1918]

Spoke with a doctor just come from Vienna. He said that the food problem was terrible and the allowance of meat per week was now 120 grams per person. There was still railway connexion with Budapest but it was very bad and no food could be obtained that way. The regime in Vienna was Socialist Jew, and the National Guard kept such control as existed. The nobility remained shut up in their houses. These did not appear yet to be pillaged. Up to date there had been only raids on banks and foodshops. A revolution is of course feared.

The informant professed to have following from a good source – details as to the Kaiser [Charles I]. At the end of October, two or three days before the beginning of the offensive, he told the Papal Nuntius, who expressed pessimistic views, that the situation was good and that the Italians would never get to Trieste.

On his first arrival at the villa where he now lives there was only a bed for the children and the Empress, and Karl slept on straw wrapped in a cloak. He is allowed two autos, but one was stopped by the National Guard and has been taken away. The Empress is stated to be in a state of great depression and has lost 20 kilos. There appears to be no feeling of hostility to the Ex-Emperor, rather one of compassion or comtempt. Lights go out at 4 p.m. and tramways are cut off.

I had a curious confirmation today from a Croatian (Serb) lady of the atrocities committed in Serbia during the first year of the war by the Croatian regiments. She was serving in the hospital early in 1915 and personally heard a Croatian soldier boasting to his comrades of spitting babies on bayonets and pulling them asunder. When challenged by her as to these horrible atrocities he said[:] "Well what could we do? We were ordered to do so by our commanders and, in any case, what could we do? We could not leave the babies when fathers and mothers were both killed.["] A very nice commentary which tends to show that the denunciation by Dr. R.A. Reiss,[436] the Swiss neutral, of Austro-Hungarian atrocities in Serbia was true. At the same time I asked whether there atrocities were confined to the Frankist or anti-national Croats, but was told that they extended to all of them.

Called today on the Burgomeister who was chiefly interested in Croatian history, though he demanded coal etc. from England. He spoke of the Velina Gora, where there is a peasant nobility and everything like a Highland clan. I gather it is entirely surrounded and cut off from the world.

---

[436] Dr Rodolphe Archibald Reiss (1875–1929), German-born Swiss forensic scientist and writer; professor of forensic science, University of Lausanne, 1906–15; volunteered for the Serbian army, 1915; propagandist for Serbia; member of Serb delegation at Paris peace conference, 1919; resided in Belgrade until 1929. The reference is to his *Report upon the Atrocities committed by the Austro-Hungarian Army during the First Invasion of Serbia* (London, 1916).

I also visited Anton Bauer,[437] the Archbishop, a genial rather worldly man. Not like the saintly Jeglic,[438] but interesting and reputable. He was much interested in discussing the Italian Secret Treaty, which is now almost wholly public. They do not know this here as the Agramer Tageblatt said the other day, and interesting testimony to the slowness with which new penetrates here from the outside world.

22nd [December 1918]

Received wire today to go to Montenegro – evidently there were one or two [telegrams] before which I could not decipher. Frightful rush but did just get away, at the cost of breaking 3 engagements. My dear hosts, the Cuks, equipped me with marmalade (delightful), 4 eggs, and huge hunk of white bread, sent their servant to the station – all for me, it was very nice and I shall long remember it. Their hospitality is that best of all, which is enough for itself and neither desires nor expects reward. Had the satisfaction of writing to Plunkett – "Your wire received – left in 1½ hours" – scribbled a note to Mme. Raičević with whom I had promised to go to tea, and caught the train on the hop. I shall miss Mme R[aičević]'s friend Mme Semse, who goes to Budapest on Tuesday – a woman with no special looks but lovely speaking eyes. She was very nice indeed to me, and, as she spoke perfect English, I shall miss her on my return. The voyage was uneventful until I reached Brod – Bromich and Slavonisch Brod are 2 dirty towns amid flats – but from the railway bridge over the river Save there is a really beautiful prospect. Lunched with the local officers, very nice and journed to Sarajevo. A dismal one-armed officer was in my carriage, who came from Odessa, had been 5 times wounded and had been in 400 fights. He was[,] I think[,] a Jew as he asked about Zionism and Anti-Semitism in England.

23rd [December 1918]

Sarajevo. A short and hurried visit, arrive early in the morning, saw among other things the monument just at the bridge where Franz Ferdinand and his wife were killed. The monument is of dark-gray stone, portraits in relief of the two, beneath a virgin with a Pieta, and a date. On the whole a simple and dignified memorial. You do not want for thoughts if you stand on the place where the war began. A change was provided by an inscription on a triumphal arch, waiting

---

[437] Anton Bauer (1856–1937), Roman Catholic clergyman; entered priesthood, 1879; titular Bishop of Pessinus, 1911–14; Archbishop of Zagreb, 1914–37.
[438] See entry 26 Nov. 1918.

for the Crown Prince – "Welcome White Eagle – hundred years has Bosnia waited for you." Serajevo itself is a fine town but rather squeezed in between the hills. There is a fine mosque, with faience work and an interesting bazaar. The Catholic cathedral is cheap and bad. I found the Scottish women in trouble there because there were German doctors in the hospital to which they were assigned[,] who desired to continue to exercise control over them. They asked me what they should do and I advised an ultimatum, as the Serbs continued to put off the affair. The ultimatum to the voivode was to expire by 3.30, but I left about that time and do not know the result. The scenery was fine, though Herzegovina is full of stones and I missed most of it in the night, especially Mostar. From Hutovo (197 m[e]t[re]s) the Popovopolye valley [is] watered by the Trebnjčica [sic],[439] an appearing and disappearing stream – at this time the effect was particularly fine because of it and overflowed its banks at certain points. The result was a series of deep green[,] pale lakes extending for miles, like a necklace of jade on a dull green string. The land owing to this flooding is of extraordinary fertility. It is said that, in 1906, some of it produced 110% profit. Unfortunately till now the policy of the government has hindered the Koneti from acquiring their land, and so discouraged real cultivation.

The line runs on with magnificent glimpses of the sea at the rents in the stony walls. Ridiculous picturesque little cottages cluster on the hillside at points but few countries can be less populated.

24th [December 1918]

Wound down among the hills to Castelnuovo, where, amidst most picturesque castle ruins, with oranges growing in the open air and a sparkling blue sea beneath. I met a Serbian Colonel,[440] the commandant of the place and the brother of Simovich at Zagreb. He was a pleasant fellow, gave me the dispositions of the Serb troops and pointed out to me Ponto Ostro,[441] with a true poet's feeling. He said, it is a very sharp point descending steeply to the sea, fortified very strongly, but there are always the first roses and the first oranges. He provided a steam launch to take me to Cattaro, and, ad interim, the French Command[an]t in the Bocche,[442] in which the latter desired to control a certain telegraph station but Simovich intimated curtly that it belonged to the Serbs not the French.

---

[439] Popovo Polje, a valley in Herzeogovina, bisected by the river Trebišnjica.
[440] General Dušan T. Simović (1882–1962), Serbian soldier; entered army, 1900; active service Balkan Wars, 1912–13, and First World War, 1914–18; Chief of General Staff, 1938–40 and 1940–41; led *coup d'état*, 1941; Prime Minister, 1941–42.
[441] Cape Oštro on the Prevlaka peninsula at the entrance to the Bay of Kotor.
[442] Bocche di Cattaro, now Bay of Kotor.

A crowded day – went by boat to Cattaro, with a Montenegrin captain, who exclaimed – Lovtchen[443] – with ecstasy as he saw the first glimpse of its snow silver-white in the evening light. Subsequently he talked with less ecstasy of how Nikita[444] had betrayed Lovtchen. The Bocche was as beautiful as when I traversed it with Gladys in 1913, and only required her presence to make it perfect. I was put up in a house under the gateway, after having first drunk raki and coffee with two old dames, called Stepanovitch, who were described to me as the oldest of Serbian families in Cattaro.

25th [December 1918]

Christmas – a trying day – could not get off anywhere. Went to Cattaro to keep Christmas with a family – on the way called on the French Admiral Caubet, who was polite and agreeable to the utmost. Ristic[,] the Serbian Col[onel] in command at Cattaro, and over Simovich, referred to the telegraph incident. Caubet was bland & polite but carried his point without difficulty. Ristic threw over Simovich and the incident came to an end. This was, unfortunately, not the case with the Christmas dinner, which contained 2 liqueurs[,] 3 kinds of wine[,] 4 kinds of cakes and 5 kinds of meat, all of which tried to shirk consuming. Up to a point I had succeeded in getting the party off to the boat – we stopped halfway down at the grand niece of our entertainers. This meant more cakes and wine and effectually spoilt any Christmas day bliss I might have enjoyed by giving me indigestion. Subsequently, on the way back, we called on the Veronique,[445] the only British vessel in the Bocche, here again I had to submit to the inevitable two cocktails. I hear from the commander the Yankee navy is teetotal and he wonders how it can get along without. I don't. Dinner with the Serbs was too much for me. I frankly cut it and spent the last part of a very strenuous day with the commander of the American force at Cattaro, and his 2 sub[altern]s. The former, Scanlon,[446] seems a great man. At any rate one who knows his own mind. On the 22nd Nov[embe]r the Italians made an attempt, after a previously unsuccessful one – to reach Cettinje. This time they had an American advance guard, and said that Montenegro desired an

---

[443] Mount Lovćen in southwestern Montenegro, overlooking the Bay of Kotor.
[444] That is, King Nicholas of Montenegro, see entry 6 Jan. 1917.
[445] That is, HMS *Veronica*, sloop of the Acacia-class, launched in 1915 and adapted for escort work, minesweeping and as a Q-ship.
[446] Brigadier-General Martin Francis Scanlon (1889–1980), US soldier; entered army, 1912; temporary major, 1918–19; transferred to Air Service, 1920; Assistant Military Attaché at Rome, 1924–27; at London, 1929–34, and 1936–41; at Headquarters, US Air Force, 1941–42; retired, 1948.

interallied occupation. They were stopped at Nyegush[447] by a Serbian major and a civil deputation, who stated that they welcomed the U.S.A. but did not want Italian troops. The USA captain refused to move further and asked for instructions. The bold major promptly gave them – they were not only not to move further but to come away and bring the Italian troops with them. This he did finally on the 26th. As a last resort, the Italians asked Major Scanlon to leave a platoon at Nyegush, while his Italian b[a]t[talio]n remained on the boundary. The Major not only refused this, but went further and declined to recognise the Italian General as interallied C[ommander]-in-C[hief], although[ugh] his USA troops formed part of [the] Italian army. This truly American method of cutting the Gordian knot apparently succeeded. On the 12th Dec[embe]r a French battalion and on the 17th a French General arrived. The latter was finally recognised as C[ommander]-in-C[hief] by the American major. Since then the Italian troops have drawn in their horns somewhat and are encamped very low down the hill and not far from Cattaro. So much for the effects of a little sound disobedience. For a human touch to soften this the USA Red X man gave me a Xmas present.

26th [December 1918]

Met General Milutinovic,[448] Serb C[ommander]-in-C[hief] in Montenegro who had just come from Cettinje. He was off in a motor boat to Teodo and I accompanied him and then went off to the Veronique to send off a telegram, which I did. I allowed the motorboat to return to Teodo[449] for lunch on the strict promise of the lieutenant in charge that he would return. He did nothing of the sort. I was stranded, but the commander of the Veronique came to my rescue and took me off to the Gloucester.[450] The commander there informed me that his instructions were not recognize the Jugoslavs or their flag in any way. He allowed me to get ashore in a motor launch, where I found Ristic waiting in a state of great excitement. He and the General had found out the lieutenant's perfidy in deserting me, and asked the Jugoslav admiral to send a motorboat for me. Ristic apologized deeply and promised to sack the lieutenant. I thought it was a very proper punishment.

[447] Njeguši, a village on the slopes of Mount Lovćen, the home of the ruling Petrović dynasty.
[448] General Dragutin Milutinović (1865–1941), Serbian soldier; Commander-in-Chief, Montenegro, 1918–19; Inspector General of Infantry, 1919–22; member of Military Council, 1925–27.
[449] Teodo on the Bay of Kotor.
[450] HMS *Gloucester*, a Town-class light cruiser, launched in 1909; took part in the hunt for SMS *Goeben* and *Breslau* in August 1914; posted to the Adriatic, in December 1916, as part of the 8th Light Cruiser Squadron.

I had been fairly well into Cattaro politics by now. The chief point is of course the government by ideologues and professors, to this here they add priests (Greek and Catholic). The wife of a businessman called on the American major, and remonstrated because professors and priests formed the national Council and not businessmen. <Would he not interfere?> The major sympathized but shook his head.

The revolution ran the usual course here. Between the 24th and 30th Oct[obe]r the last remaining Austrian troops disappeared, very humbly at the end as shown by the fact that officers, riding to the station at ZELENICA,[451] when told by privates to dismount and give up their horses, did so. Then the usual national Council began to appear, and on 29th October the independent Jugoslav state was proclaimed, and arms[,] war material etc. were later handed over by Austrians to Jugoslav authorities <who gave them a receipt for it>. This was all previous to the Armistice with the Allies, which came into force on the 4th November.

A national guard was formed and order kept with the aid of Czechslovaks (800) and Jugoslavs. On the 2nd or 3rd November (whichever is a Sunday [3rd]) there was a thanksgiving service for the departure of the Austrians and a national Assembly of 1000 nominated a Committee of 5 for the National Council. This was to be under the control of the Dalmatian Government who sent a deputy[,] Dr. Vukotic[,][452] for the purpose. On the 18th the Serbs arrived and were received with enthusiasm[;] that for the Italians, real for the moment, cooled in a day. A protest against Italian action was addressed to Admiral Caubet who arrived on the 20th, and found it necessary to assure the Jugoslav authorities that the Italians had no bad intentions.

On 22nd December, however, the Jugoslavs showed that they no longer believed this, and arrested a certain Baldacci at the request of the Montenegrin Government.

27th [December 1918]

Proceeded to Cettinje – noticed with some amusement that on the hill opposite to Cattaro,[453] the Austrians cut a huge K with a Hungarian crown above the rock. It seemed unnecessarily ironical now. About one third of the way up, I suddenly heard a bump, and turned my head just in time to see the front near wheel of the car bounding down hill. It leapt higher and higher like an ibex

---

[451] Zelenika, Montenegro, on the Gulf of Kotor.
[452] Stevo Vukotić, Montenegrin politician; President of the Executive National Council, Nov. 1918–Apr. 1919.
[453] Now Kotor.

and finally disappeared from sight after a peculiarly colossal leap. The American chauffeur swore strong oaths but finally put it right. We arrived about midday at Cettinje and put up at the British Legation where the old dame welcomed me crying with pleasure. There was in addition a scoundrelly and useless old cavasse, and a gendarme turned up to look after me who turned out to be an impostor, who tried to pass himself off on me as a guide the last time I was in Cettinje and said he was an American. He now said only he was born in America. He proved inefficient as I expected, so I told me next morning to go to the devil. I much doubt if the latter will find him a better servant than I did.

I called first on the Provisional Government of 5 men – 4 of the lawyer type – and the last, the brother of the Queen, a huge and gross relic of heroic Montenegro, Voivode Vukotić,[454] old General and War Minister and great patriot. He had taken the most prominent part in dethroning the King or perhaps was put most prominently forward for the purpose. The Provisional Government seemed to be doing nothing, except sit there all day, and suppress all opposition. There was no rationing system, and no apparent attempt to create one, or to organize a service from Cattaro. They seemed also to be very ill-informed about the state of communications in the country, and indeed about everything outside Cettinje. They had just arrested another Italian emissary[,] Marko [sic] Miushkovic[,][455] at Virpazar[456] but did not seem to know whether he was an Italian or Montenegrin subject.

I was visited in the evening by one of the rival camp[,] Jovo Popovitch.[457] He declared that everyone represented as a traitor anyone who had supported the King. He said everyone was for Jugoslavia and against two dynasties. Now that Nicholas was gone, he said that they were republican, i.e. anti-Karageorge. He said Nikita still had supporters in Njegush, among the Mussulmans, and everyone except the towns. He denied utterly that his friends and he wanted to introduce Italian influences and seemed much surprised that his good friend MIUSKOVICH had been arrested. Ingenious but unconvincing I thought. He, doubtless truly, said that all freedom of press and movement was suppressed, and the fact that he came and left by the backdoor tends to prove this.

---

[454] General Janko Vukotić (1866–1927), Montenegrin soldier; ed. Military Academy Modena, 1886; Brigadier, 1902; War Minister, 1905–1907, 1911–12 and 1913–15; Commander, 1st Division, 1910–11; Prime Minister, 1913–15; Foreign Minister, Aug.–Dec. 1915; prisoner of war, 1916–18.

[455] Mirko M. Mijuskovic, Montenegrin politician; Minister of Education, 1913–14; Minister of Finance, Aug.–Dec. 1915; Representative of the Foreign Minister, Sept.–Dec. 1915; President, Montenegrin Party (Federalist), 1924–28.

[456] On the northwestern shore of Lake Scutari.

[457] Jovo Popović, Montenegrin official; minister at Constantinople, 1909–10; at Paris peace conference, 1919; Chairman of Advisory Council, Apr.–July 1941; see his *Un aperçu sur les affaires monténégrines; memorandum adressé à la Conférence de Paris* (Paris, 1919).

I also had a visit from Radovich[,][458] President of the Montenegrin Nat[iona]l Committee in Switzerland, a clever rather well-bred man, who took the line that the whole affair was over.

My other visit was to the Archbishop of Cettinje, Ban,[459] a little old man from Cattaro, who talked very fast and seemed very old and feeble. He was a striking contrast to the fierce bearded Vladikas[460] of old. He seemed much disappointed that I had not visited him when I was in Cettinje in 1913, said that I was very young to be a major, and said that personally he regretted breaking with Nikita, but the general will and the national good came before everything. He is said to have been intimidated and I can well believe it. He was a gentle[,] kindly old man [and] was very much interested that I had seen Letić,[461] the Greek Bishop at Temesvar, and provided me with a glass of raki, almost as good as his friend's wine. When he saw I appreciated it, he made me drink a second glass which highly amused his particularly gigantic servitor.

After leaving Njegus, the view of the North Albanian Alps is really marvellous. Long tossing crests of mountains, snow white with pale blue, hyacinth and lilac tints on the slopes below. For the rest rain shrouded the hills or mist and turned the white limestone into shimmery black. Anyone who has seen Tsrnagora[462] on a day like this understands why it is called black. But they have not usually and therefore do not understand.

28th [December 1918]

Riding on the rim is not a new experience for me on a bicycle, on a motor that is. After a very short time on the way from Cettinje we lost the outer tyre – then we proceeded on the inner tyre and finally 8 kilo[metres] from Podgoritza,[463] the outer rim departed for an adjoining field and left us to walk the rest of the way in. At Podgoritza I was accommodated in one of the best houses in the

---

[458] Andrija Radović (1872–1947), Montenegrin and Yugoslav politician; Finance Minister, 1905–1906 and Jan.–Apr. 1916; Foreign Minister, Feb.–Apr. 1907; Prime Minister, Jan.–Apr. 1907 and May 1916–Jan. 1917; established Geneva-based, pro-Yugoslav 'Montenegrin Committee for National Unification', Mar. 1917; delegate at Paris peace conference, 1919.

[459] Mitrofan Ban (1841–1920), Montenegrin, Serb-Orthodox clergyman; entered monastic order, 1865; active military service against Turkey, 1876–78; Metropolitan of Montenegro and Exarch of the Patriarchate of Peč, 1885–1920.

[460] *Vladika*, prince bishop; Montenegro was ruled by prince bishops, 1516–1697, when power was to the Petrović-Njegoš dynasty.

[461] See entry 6 Dec. 1918.

[462] Crna Gora ('Black Mountain'), the country's name in most West European languages dates from the period of Venetian hegemony in the eastern Mediterranean.

[463] Podgorica, now the capital of Montenegro.

town belonging to one of the 10 Montenegrin women millionaires <(Gjanjevic Karageorgevitch Ulicza)>.

Nothing much that night as we arrived late, but, of course, I came across two things, one a Peace play – Jazarać pred Sudom – an amusing take off of Austrian officialism [*sic*] by a Serb peasant. This I had seen twice before, and the Kolo.[464] I had forgotten how often I had danced this. The scene was made better by some fine Montenegrin costumes – the red plush zouave, embroidered with gold, the wife's veil, and the lightblue under-jacket are really superb. Most of the women were rather afraid to dance, for Turkish traditions still keep them very quiet in Montenegro. As I was leaving the assembly suddenly woke up and shouted ZHIVELA INGLESKA – the first intimation that they knew there was one there.

29th [December 1918]

On the road to Niksić[465] early morning – rode out on horses[,] the first time I have bestrode a horse since Sept[ember] 1915. We saw, among other things, the house of Stephen Nemanja,[466] where the first King of Serbia was born. I did not know it was here. Also I came across among a heap of stones[,] designed for building, 2 stones with fragments of Roman inscriptions. I pointed this out to the young officer I was with and he promised to send soldiers to preserve them from further damage. I imagine most of the inscription is already a heap of stone. The views on the way to Niksic are very beautiful, first a series of rounded pumicestone hills scattered well in the bottom of the Moratcha[467] valley, and entered between high mountain walls on each side. Next these rounded hills assuming an oblong shape, and looked like gigantic petrified saurians, laying on the bed of a now dried up valley. Then what strikes the eye is the vast wall of rock to the right after Danilograd,[468] just below it is the monastery of Ostrog,[469] once heroically defended against the Turk by Mirko, I think by 20 against 2,000 or 500 against 20,000, I'm sure I don't know which. The valley this side is subject to irrigations, and in spite or because of this is rich and fertile. We wound among

---

[464] See entry 27 Jan. 1919.

[465] Nikšić in central Montenegro

[466] Stefan Nemanja (c. 1113–99), Grand Prince of Serbia, 1166–96; later canonized by the Serbian Orthodox church; his son Stefan Nemanjić (c. 1165–1228), was the first official king of Serbia, 1217–28.

[467] The river Morača cuts a deep gorge north of Podgorica, before flowing south to debouch into Lake Scutari.

[468] Now Danilovgrad in central Montenegro, founded in 1870 by King Nicholas I.

[469] A seventeenth-century mountain monastery, defended, in 1853, against the Ottomans by Mirko Petrović-Nejgoš (1820–67), father of King Nikola I.

the stony heights round to the left and finally reached Niksic at 7 p.m. There, to my great astonishment, was a deputation with flags and torches awaiting me. The kmet[470] made a speech of welcome saying all Montenegro owed their freedom to the great British nation. I replied with a slight variation of my usual answer – ZHIVELA TSARNOGOROKA l Srbiya 1Jugoslavia which provoked much applause. I then moved on preceded by torches and cheers to the Hotel Amenca, small boys singing and the crowd shouting for Clemençeau – Zhivvo Lloyd George and Velika Britannica. There was a reception afterwards in the house, which was now national property and had once been Nikita's. It seemed a good joke to dance in the house he built for himself. In addition he had annexed a large wood and great property without paying anything to the dispossessed. Hardly had a I entered when a man who spoke English came up to me and said 'Whichever she's you like you take.' I had not had time to cast my eye around the assembly but my first essay was not fortunate, for I asked two girls in succession who had lost brothers and therefore did not dance. The scene here was much more dazzling than at Podgoritza – there were more girls and less orientalism. Curious variants of the red and light blue national dress appeared, one a black variety which is peasant, the other a light blue undercoat very handsome. I selected the two stateliest women, with the best embroidery, and struck luck. One was Madame Jankovitch Niko Martinovitch,[471] a niece of the Queen, and the daughter of old Vukotitch, as refined, graceful and slender, as he is rough, clumsy and fat. She had charming manners and pretty though slightly affected air. She told me her story very simply. She was educated for 8 years at the Cettinje institute and was a good testimony to it. She had never travelled except a little in Italy. During some months of the war, she had been attached to her father, the old Voivode. But she never fired a shot – she married later in the war a doctor, and resided near Nikshitch. She thought her own folk 'tres bon' but sometimes wished to see the great world. She knew the old King well and she thought him a personage 'tres drôle'. Altogether a charming[,] unaffected girl, as shown by the fact that she said she had been 'enchanté' to see him and hoped to do so again. By her side equally stately, a better dancer, and more matronly, was a dame Sotchitza, wife of the son of the last Voivode of Piva and head of the Nikšić Pleme.[472] The national costume made all the women look beautiful in this assembly, but they didn't need it. In spite of the hunger and ravages of war, the faces of Montenegrin women are as regular and beautiful as ever, the profiles pale and pure, and their bearing dignified. They show a natural dignity

---

[470] *kmët* (Serbian), village elder, mayor (from Latin *comes*).
[471] Vasilija Vukotić (?), acted as a courier during the Battle of Mojkovac (6–7 Jan. 1916).
[472] *Pleme* (Serbian), clan. The Nikšić clan was one of several that populated the Piva region in the southwestern highlands of Montenegro, since 1878 the Old Herzegovina region of Montenegro.

when you visit them in their cottages which could not be surpassed. <They have a fierce strain in them which Miss Durham[473] noticed. I saw an instance one day, with the daughter of Madame Dangević. As I was looking into the henyard, she suddenly caught up a chicken, there was a twirl of graceful fingers, a gleam of light and an agonized cluck. Then the next instant the chicken's head was in the cat's mouth a stream of blood running from its severed neck and the body jerking convulsively. As she looked she said – 'I wish it was an Austrian.'> I am sure too that they have most of them been able to resist the rude embraces of the Austrian soldiers. 'Add not unto your cruel hate yet more cruel love.'[474]

30th [December 1918]

I made some visits of personal enquiry, with CHALOVITCH Novitza, a journalist and student, mild in appearance and a great lover of children. He has had adventures, his journal SLOBODA at Niksic was an opposition one, and so Nikita sent soldiers who smashed the factory and the Press. He was concerned or believed to be concerned in the Bomb plot of 1908[475] against Nikita and spent some time in prison, along with Radovitch. Old Lazar Sotchitza,[476] head of the Piva Pleme suffered a similar fate – he was imprisoned for ten months for signing a petition of protest against Nikita. He was one of the last of the old heroic voivodes. He led a revolt in Herzegovina of the Piva pleme in 1875, and was presented by the inhabitants of Ragusa[477] with a silver boar's head for his bravery. Then subsequently he headed the Nikšić pleme – of 2,500 soldiers. In the Sotchitza house we saw his portrait, his zouave and his weapons. The latter, by a characteristic Austrian touch, had had all the sabres removed from the scabbards and all the locks from the pistols. The whole Sotchitza room was interesting[;] it was strewn with rugs (Turkish) and bearskin – and adorned with portraits of all Montenegrin royalties signed, except the King, and Madame Sotchitza apologised for retaining that of the Queen, because she was her aunt. Madame Sotchitza looked a good deal more stately in ordinary dress than in

---

[473] (Mary) Edith Durham (1863–1944), artist, traveller and writer; closely associated with Albanian aspirations and best known for her *High Albania* (London, 1909).

[474] 'But, by the shades beneath us, and by the Gods above,/ Add not unto your cruel hate yet more cruel love', T.B. Macaulay, 'Lays of Ancient Rome. Virginia', *Lord Macaulay's Essays and Lays of Ancient Rome* (London, 1892), 859.

[475] Part of the political struggle between the autocratic Prince Nikola I and reformist groups in Montenegro; intercepted bombs, smuggled in from Serbia, were used as a pretext for the Prince to persecute his domestic opponents.

[476] Lazar Sočica (1838–1910), Montenegrin politician; head of the Nikšići clan; played prominent role in 1875 Herzegovina uprising.

[477] Now Dubrovnik.

Montenegrin costume. Her husband was no longer the Voivode of the pleme. The title and office had perished with her father.

I had an experience of the horrible present, as well as the heroic past. I visited first a weaver's cottage, one of the lower class bourgeois. There were three women in two rooms, 1 purely a kitchen. They took 3 days to weave one coarse coloured scarf, and got 70 Kr[onen] for it at the end. They had a certain amount to eat, not starving.

I visited also a more well-to-do bourgeois, an old Herzegovinian who had been interned during the war. He was a fine old fellow, and told of how he had fought in different ways, 30 years for Montenegro, but that during this war, the Austrians detained him on the pretext that he must prove himself not to be an Austrian subject, for 2½ years in Austria. His wife was simply dressed, but as always dignified. She showed us 4 rooms, all they had, well but plainly furnished and clean. The bedroom had one small bed – for 2 large persons. It is all very simple, she said, it was but impressive all the same.

The peasant houses were very different. I saw three at Nikšić, the first was [with a] tiled roof and had 2 rooms, one being the kitchen and 7 persons being in the other. The man earned 100 Kr[onen] a month by being curator of the school. They had enough for one meal per day but not always for two. He had not worked for anything from the town authority. He said he could bear his hardships for since the Austrians left 'I have opened my eyes for the first time for 3 years!'

The next case was one of 2 rooms for 3 persons, thatched with straw and very cold. They had a few cobs of maize as reserve food, and 3 or 4 handfuls of coarse flour. They received ½ kilo of flour or bread per week per person from the town authorities. The man said: 'We have suffered, but today we are free and that is better than plenty.'

The last case was particularly painful[,] a filthy hovel consisting of two of the smallest rooms I ever saw, so low that they pitifully pushed forward stools about 8 inches high for us to sit on. 2 women were there clothed in the barest rags – there was one bed covered with filthy sacking & some rugging – 8 people slept in this room. They had 2 kilos of flour at this time and did not know where to get any more. I said I did not think that England would let them starve, and one poor thing kissed my hand as I said goodbye.

So far as I can make out from prices and wages, the town populations have not a living wage. They must therefore be slowly being starved to death by malnutrition, i.e. the poorest classes. This tends to confirm the stories that numbers are dying of hunger. I saw one woman gathering weeds and grass and round she was going to boil it up with other vegetables and mix it with flour. It was worse than anything recorded by Arthur Young[478] of the miseries of French peasants. Yet these poor creatures neither complain nor beg.

Coming back from Nikšić there was a wonderful view beyond and by Danilovgrad.[479] The little town is surrounded to the south and east by great walls and tiers of mountains ending in the North Albanian Alps. As I looked at them[,] the upper heights turned luminous purple, like heather seen from a great distance in the sunlight, while bluish transparent mists spread their veils over the lower slopes. Above the purple were the snowpeaks, and above them again floated rosy clouds. As the latter melted away, the purple turned dark black, and the long line of snow peaks above looked like the tossing of the crests of miles of foam-breaking over dark rocks, such as you might see on the Cornish coast in a storm. It is not often such a sight could be seen in the world but I thought the Montenegrins pay dear for their beauties of scenery.

31st [December 1918]

Podgorica. I spent the morning in enquiries as to prices and looking into dwellings. I woman told me that she earned 2 cr[owns] a day and ½ kilo bread, by washing clothes and could obtain no milk for the children as even inferior milk was 4 Kronen a litre, a fact I afterwards verified in the market. I went into the Turkish quarter over the river, tho[ugh] there are many Serbs there. A large otherwise empty building is used as a sort of workhouse, one family had lived in a corner of one of these vast rooms for 15 years – in another corner were two women wretchedly clothed, one was lying on straw, covered with a rug made of paper-cloth with a stone covered with a cloth for a pillow. She was sick in the stomach, and her sister gave her vinegar to cure it. When I asked why she said she had nothing, but me a friend in the marketplace with some vinegar. I cannot imagine anything worse except prussic acid. Usually I give nothing to these people because, if you give one, you must give to all. I asked the sick woman if she would like some good food. She said 'No, it is better to die because then I should not suffer.' I said 'in England one does not die until one is dead' – and she smiled faintly. I went away and returned with 2 tins of condensed milk and some Bovril lozenges, enough to keep her alive for a week or ten days. Unfortunately her sister had only the vaguest ideas of cooking, the water was not hot and I

---

[478] Arthur Young (1741–1820), farmer, agricultural reformer and writer; Secretary to the Board of Agriculture, 1793–1808; best known for his *Farmer's Tour through the East of England* (1770), *Political Arithmetic, Containing observations on the present state of Great Britain and the principles of her policy in the encouragement of agriculture* (1774), and *Travels during the years 1787, 1788 and 1789, undertaken more particularly with a view of ascertaining the cultivation, wealth, resources and national prosperity of the kingdom of France* (2 vols, 1792)

[479] Danilovgrad, a town in central Montenegro in the Zeta valley.

spent 2 Bovril lozenges in making her a soup where one would have sufficed. She seemed better and much appreciated the warm food, and spoke no more of death. However, I much doubt whether the milk or Bovril will even be properly warm for her.

In making some enquiries in a shop I saw a tobacco box with the portraits of the 4 central sovereigns – Kaiser, Francis Joseph, Ferdinand and the Sultan. I bought the box for 5 Kronen and then stamped on it. This greatly impressed the spectators – one said 'it was a magnificent manner', another that the Entente had treated the Central Powers in the same way, another thing that impressed them was that I hung out of my window at Podgorica the particularly enormous flag that I had with me. This, they said, showed that they were under British protection.

A curious little incident came to us the night before. Chalovitch discovered 2 little boys, and brought them in to sing to us at dinner, which they did most sweetly, all sorts of Serbian national songs. It appears that they had a history.

There is a curious and interesting little play given at Belgrade, which I saw there, which turns on the fact that, during the Austrian occupation, 4 officers, a Serb, Czech[,] Slovene and Magyar are quartered in a Serb house and that the son of the house gradually works on the other Slavs' sentiments by playing national Serbian airs. Finally he does so completely that the Czech major quarrels with the Magyar over the affair and shoots him. Consequences are averted by the Serbian re-entry into Belgrade in December 1914. This little history seems made up, but these two lads are an interesting collaborative piece of evidence as to how affected Slav officers were. During the Austrian occupation of Podgorica they were hired from 12 crowns by Croat and Czech officers to sing national Serb songs in the streets. They did so, were promptly arrested and got 3 months imprisonment. One of them got very severe rheumatism in prison and still had a badly swelled leg. The names of the 2 little lads were Velimir Perković aged 15, Jovan Jovanović aged 14. They had wonderful voices and lived by singing in cafes. Chalovitch gave me another instance of the sympathy of Slav officers with the Serbs. He says a Czech officer, who saw him after the surrender of Lovtchen,[480] wept and said 'Why did you do it?' Another Czech officer, who presided over courts martial at Podgoritza, winked at many offences.

---

[480] On 10 Jan. 1916.

1919

1st [January 1919]

I visited the hospital in Cettinje[,] beautifully appointed, in days gone by, with elaborate operating apparatus – Rontgen rays, radium etc. Some of it left by the Austrians but all taken away, and diabolical ingenuity shewn in destroying the pans and apparatus of the latrines. There are about 70 patients, lying on mattresses stuffed with straw – ventilation insufficient and drugs very small, and no anaesthetics at all. There is no possibility of real central heating apparatus, because there is very little coal. More beds are being prepared but there is a great danger from lice, which were left behind by the Austrians. There are a few nurses and orderlies and 5 doctors. Outside the hospital no drugs at all can be bought by the poor people because the prices are too high for all except a few. In one ward which I entered ventilation was very bad.

3 or 4 persons were arrested at midnight last night on various charges – Rista Popovich[,] father of Jovo (who came to see me by night), Lampa (who wrote me a petition), while Jovo Popović has fled to Cattaro and Jovan Plamenatz[1] is gone to Virpazar – they say to the Italians. All is important at the moment.

2 little interesting traits of Montenegrin character before I leave it. On the way from Nikšić I saw a sad looking woman in an inn, with deep marks of suffering in her eyes and her face defaced with small scars. I found on enquiry that she had torn her hair and face with her nails because of her brother's death. Another pair of girls in Niksic sat melancholy all night refusing to dance the Kolo because their brother had been killed in 1915. As of old the love of brother is the most tender feeling in a Serbian woman's heart and the custom pobratim[2] the most sacred and ennobling bond.

Chalovitch told me that the sense of poetry was very strong in the peasant and that, on one occasion he had been talking to an old man about a recent affray in the mountains, and asked for a plain account. The old man answered in verse, improvised for the occasion and quite good [*sic*]. He said also that the peasants

---

[1] Jovan Simonov Plamenac (1873–1944), Montenegrin politician; Minister of Education, 1907–1909; of the Interior, 1909–10 and 1912–13; joined 'Green' opposition to Yugoslav unification and led 'Christmas Rebellion', Jan. 1919; Prime Minister of government-in-exile, 1919–21; returned to Yugoslavia and supported Pašić; executed by Tito's partisans for collaborating with the Italians, 1944.

[2] *Pòbratim* (Serbo-Croatian), meaning 'blood-brother'.

still believed in vampires and that in wartime they believed they appeared in the battle in the form of a whirlwind and dealt out wounds and death. He has been collecting legends and songs for four years among the peasantry and ought to know. As we came down the mountain Lovcen had his cap of cloud and looked black beneath it, thus justifying his name Montenegro, a name travellers wonder at when they see him gleaming like frosted silver in an August sun.

I arrived in time to take part in somewhat uproarious New Year festivities with my Yankee friends.

2nd [January 1919]

On board Gloucester – ordered to Dalmatia – Pendants to Montenegro – Gov[ernmen]t Comitadj[i] I must give 2 pendants to Montenegro – (1) the Government truly are more incompetent than it is possible to imagine. The poets, professors and lawyers of Zagreb were not ideal, but they were much better than the peasants and lawyers of Cettinje. I suppose there is no governing class and never has been in Montenegro and that the King's success was due to the fact that he governed himself and was cleverer than the rest. Certainly these people have not an idea in their heads except talking about liberty and practising tyranny. They arrest, they terrorize almost at random and do nothing to feed the people or build up a good administration. They feast on the fat of the land themselves. I know because of the meals they gave me. But Vukotić (not Stevo) [,] the man who accompanied me as their representative[,] had so little interest in local conditions that he always absented himself when I enquired into them, while Chalovitch, the literary man, was always present. They were as pleased as schoolboys with having deposed the King forgetting, as old Phillips[3] said to me once, that the King was such a magnificent scoundrel as to endear himself to a primitive race by his very vices. One thing I am quite certain that is that the existing regime cannot last long with Nicholas partisans, Italian agents and starving villagers thundering at the doors. I am sure the new Government are afraid because their local press is full of allusions to the tranquillity all round and the Cettinje news says, à propos of me, that I found tranquillity wherever I went. On the contrary I found all the signs of an imminent revolution or upheaval.

[(2.)] I had thought the heroic age of Montenegro had passed, certainly the sophisteris [sic] and calculators are in office. But I found a representative. Bishko Boyovics is a Comitadji chief who took me back to the days of Vladika

---

[3] Sir Perceval Phillips (1877–1937), journalist; war correspondent for *Daily Express*, *Morning Post* and *Daily Graphic*; with Bulgarian army, 1912–13, Western Front, 1914–18; special correspondent, *Daily Mail*, 1922–34.

Danilo.[4] He was 6 feet 6, tanned a deep brown, brown eyes, firm and calm, well-cut regular features, black beard and moustache. He spoke a little English, a fact which rather detracted from his picturesqueness. Apparently he had been on the northern frontier at the time of the surrender of Mount Lovtchen and with one or another comrades had gone into the hills, and remained there the whole three years. He told me at first he had thought it a case of only two or three months and so he always told his followers. As time went on his invention was taxed and he had to invent stories about the French marching across Albania and the British on Jumaia. He had at one time over 300 followers together and there were usually supposed to be 4,000 altogether. They claimed to have kept 30,000 Austrians in Montenegro. The people were entirely in league with them and supplied them with food and clothing at all times. Their method was as follows – whenever they heard of any outrage or cruelty by the Austrians, they at once attacked a post in the vicinity and wiped it out, sometimes with the aid of local inhabitants. I heard of one such affray near Bogatić[5] where 12 comitadjis fought 300 Austrians with machine guns for 5 hours, and where women armed with axes assisted them. This was in October just before the end. Boyović's biggest action resulted in an Austrian colonel and several field officers being killed. He wandered along into Herzegovina and Bosnia at times, and sent agents both into Bulgaria and Serbia. One of the comitadjis was a woman, who developed a great affection for him and married him at the close. The people, who regard him rightly as a hero, have saluted him with the title of Voivode – the old name for a successful robber chief in Montenegro. A painter was painting his picture. I asked him what his future would be, and he said 'Damn if I know'. He told me he had greatly admired Vesović[6] for his resistance to the Austrians but, after he surrendered, he would kill him if he saw him. He had probably been bought and found it convenient to go to Belgrade. It would be equally dangerous, he said, for King Nicholas, the other traitor, to come to Montenegro.

---

[4] Prince Danilo I Petrović-Njegoš (1826–1860), Prince-Bishop of Montenegro, 1851–52; Prince, 1852–60; transformed Montenegro into a secular state, 1852; assassinated, 1860.

[5] Either Bogatić in the Mačva district of northwestern Serbia, or Bogatić in the Valjevo district of western central Serbia.

[6] General Radomir Vešović (1871–1938), Montenegrin soldier; entered army, 1887; War Minister, 1913–15; killed Austro-Hungarian officers during attempted flight in 1916, whereupon the Habsburg authorities hanged his brother Vlajko and associate Sava Radulović; surrendered and interned in Austria, Jan. 1918; opposed to unification with Serbia; arrested, 1919; tried treason and acquitted, 1921.

4 [January 1919]

Reached Split on board Lowestoft[;][7] found a magnificent room prepared for me at the hotel and a Serbian colonel[,] the Commandant of the place[,] waiting for me on the dock. I went off at once to the Government House over which floated the new Jugoslav Tricolor – Blue-white-red – and ingenious permutation of the three previous tricolors (Serb-Croat-Slovene). With singular lack of tact the Italian cruiser here is moored within about 100 yards of the building. One day ago there was a bad incident – songs deprecatory of Jugoslavia or shouts that Spalato[8] was Jugoslav were set up and shouted from the deck of the ship. When the USA commander here brought this to the notice of the Italian C[ommanding] O[fficer] he said 'I begged and prayed my men to be silent'. The USA said nothing, but repeated it to me. What I say is – either the crews were Bolshevik – or the C[ommanding] O[fficer] instigated or allowed the demonstration. The atmosphere is certainly hot.

5th [January 1919]

The Government here seem fairly effective in restraining the demonstrators, but feeling runs high and the women are more enragé than the men. Every few days there seems to be an incident of one kind or another – with explosive mixtures. The commodore of the Lowestoft[9] is a good man who knows his own mind and speaks straight to both sides. He takes care not to commit himself and is acting very well. One little incident is instructive. The Jugoslav Government asked him to go across the bay on an expedition to a vineyard. He scented a demonstration and held off. On the other had he has accepted an invitation to the French circle and the Boxing Day dinner of the Serbs.

Retribution has followed swift on the incompetence and callousness of the M[ontenegri]n Gov[ernmen]t. I hear there was an outbreak at NJEGUŠ and that Interallied troops, including of course Italians and the bold American Major Scanlon are in Cettinje. The outbreak is stated to be Republican and Jugoslav – some doubt as to whether it is against Nicholas or not. It is certainly anti-Serb and against absorption by Serbia.

---

[7] HMS *Lowestoft*, a town-class light cruiser, launched in 1913; assigned to the 8th Light Cruiser Squadron operating in the Mediterranean since 1916.

[8] That is, Split.

[9] Captain the Hon. Bertram Thomas Carlyle Ogilvy Freeman-Mitford, 3rd Baron Redesdale (1880–1962), 3rd Baron Redesdale, succ. 1958, sailor; entered Royal Navy, 1894; acting commander HMS *Lowestoft*, 1918–19; Naval Attaché, 1919–22; retired, 1922.

6 [January 1919]

Dined with Smodlaka.[10] He has a dear old mother and I heard the whole story of his internment. About 250 Dalmatians were taken away at once at the beginning of the war by Austria. He was for a time with wife and family but also at times isolated. The harder thing[,] he said[,] to bear was the doubt and despair at having no news. He had always believed that the Austrian Government could not last but it seemed to him to last unconscionably long. He is undoubtedly broken and marked for life by his sufferings. There is a painful strained look in his eyes that is really sad to see. His whole family were also interned generally at Vienna and it has had the result of making his wife thinner and also enabling her to speak German which she could not do before. His eldest son, who shared his troubles, was less attractive as a young man than as a boy.

7th [January 1919]

There was an evening at the Cercle Sociale where I met dear old Dr. Bulić[11] again, the great antiquary of Split. He was unconquered as ever and held forth a great length on the history of Dalmatia. It was certainly rather interesting that the earliest classical inscription here is Roman and contains some complaints about the inhabitants speaking Greek. For Roman read Italian, and for Greek Slavonic and you have the existing situation. Only I do not think it will end the same way. There is a very spiritual portrait of Bulić, by Bukovac,[12] with his head on an antique statue, and a background of marble reliefs with Star motifs.

There was the usual Kolo, which I danced to the admiration or perhaps to the pleasure of all. In the first Kolo my partner was a nice girl with a pleasant smile[,] short skirt and a complexion like a gipsy. She is called by all her friends Carmen.

---

[10] See entry 25 Nov. 1918.

[11] Dr Frane Bulić (1846–1934), Croatian Roman Catholic clergyman, archaeologist and historian; curator of archaeological museum, Split; led several excavations in Croatia and Dalmatia; author of numerous historical works, including (with S. Rutar) *Guida di Spalato et Salona* (1894); member of Dalmation diet, and Austro-Hungarian *Reichsrat*, until 1918.

[12] Vlaho Bukovac (née Biagio Faggioni) (1855–1922), Croatian painter of mixed Italo-Croatian ancestry; educated at Paris; Professor at Academy of Fine Arts, Prague, 1893–1902.

8th [January 1919]

The general attitude of the Italians there seems to be provocative. The most definite incident is that which took place on board Poerio[,][13] the Italian destroyer [*sic*] here (the first arrival was on 20th Nov[embe]r). On the night of the 2nd they sang songs insulting to Jugoslavs on board it and shouted Spalato is Italian. This is only one incident – they asked the American commander to be allowed to take off a wounded man in a destroyer from Trau.[14] They have also tried to establish a civil department for authorizing citizens her to pass to Sebenico[15] via the Labin railway.[16] The authorizer was to be Martinelli, lately Italian consul, and a well-known propagandist. The tendency of these incidents is obvious – and there are many more – the wish to establish themselves by one means or another in a permanent capacity at Trau or Split or both. I am sorry for these things because Smodlaka, whose judgment I really trust, has said he thinks it must come to a conflict. We must at least do all we can to avert it.

9th [January 1919]

Italians have consented to restart the SPLIT-LABIN-SEBENICO railway and arrangements have been made by which papers of persons desiring to go to Sebenico can be visaed by an Italian and an American – on board ship – <u>not</u> on land. There was a charming Boxing day (Serbian style) dinner today. We were waited on by Carmen and her friends in national costume. One thing a little destroyed the illusion – their costumes were so hot that they had to leave them before the dancing began. Carmen promised me the first Kolo, but I treacherously deserted her, as I had to leave for Sebenico the next morning at 6.30 a.m. The dinner was presided over by General Miloš Vasić[17] who has just arrived, a genial cultivated old man. He is the hero of the Kaimakchalan[18]

---

[13] *Alessandro Poerio*, Italian scout cruiser, launched in 1913, and named after the Neapolitan poet and revolutionary Alessandro Poerio (1802–48).

[14] Now Trogir to the west of Split.

[15] Now Šibenik on the central Dalmatian coast at the mouth of the river Krka; occupied by Italy at the end of 1918, and evacuated in June 1921 in accordance with the Italo-SHS Treaty of Rapallo, 17 Nov. 1920.

[16] Labin, about half-way between Split and Perković on the so-called '*Dalmatinerbahn*', built in 1876. Not to be confused with Labin (It. Albano) in Istria.

[17] General Miloš Vasić (1859–1935), Serbian soldier; appointed general, 1916; Minister of the Army and Navy, Jan.–Nov. 1922.

[18] Kajmakčalan, a mountain to the southeast of Bitola (Monastir), fiercely fought over by Serbs and Bulgars, 12–30 Sept. 1916; the costly Serbian victory was neutralized by the onset of winter.

capture. The local population were very glad to see him, and one old Serb from Belgrad who had resided there for 30 years, came to see him last night, cried, kissed his hand and was kissed on the cheek in return.

10th [January 1919]

6.30 a.m. in saloon to KNIN.[19] In the last 2 days I have visited the local school of industrial art, and seen the embroideries. It is perfectly marvellous how the peasants can do them and the director assures me that, after 5 years' instruction in the schools his pupils never do as well as the peasants. They carry in their heads the general plans of the embroidery from tradition and work them out as occasion arises varying at will or pleasure. This seems to create no difficulty with them though it calls for great artistic skills. The designs – geometric or wavy – the colours, the harmonies, the patient work are all their own. It is just the same with the shepherds – they play their pipes, and carve exquisitely everything, water bottles, handles for scythes, the wooden cases in which they hang their whetstones. It is all national unconscious mentality. Thinking of this one gets hold of some idea of the Serbian peasant and history. He carries in his memory and his brain the songs and heroisms and histories of the past – as he desires or feels these sentiments come to the top and shape themselves in his actions so that he is ready. In the same way with military tactics. He appears to possess none because they are not written in books and appear to be improvised. But this is not really so – soldiers with six years of war behind them have had unequalled experience. In their brains and minds there is a wealth of military lore, which no tactical handbook ever contained. This expresses itself quite naturally as occasion arises. They know what to do in an attack – in defence – in envelopment or in retreat, because they have the memory in their heads of the formations required for the purpose – experience has no doubt produced a national – <u>unconscious</u> – effective action.

10th [January 1919]

Proceeded to Knin, most of the country is barren and stoney to the last degree but the peasantry were extremely picturesque, women with bright red caps, and black zouaves. The women as usual with kerchiefs and embroidered dresses. The hand of Italy is obviously heavy – there was a brigade – newl;y arrived at DRNIS[20] – another at Knin. It seemed clear from enquiry that Serb soldiers were really captured at Drnis, tho[ugh] they may possibly have been on leave, but

---

[19] Knin near the source of the river Krka in the Dalmatian hinterland.
[20] Drniš in the Dalmatian hinterland, half-way between Šibenik and Knin.

not likely. There was therefore probably some incitement of the local comitadji bands against the Italians. On the other hand at Knin it seens to have been a genuine local uprising against Italian oppression – some 40 of the DRNIS people and some 200 of those of KNIN fled up into the hills and over onto the Serb side of the armistice line. I saw some villagers at KNIN, after visiting the commandant, but they had not much to say except that they hated the Italians. 2 Jugslav leaders[,] Dr. Bogic and Bavic[,] followed me into the Roman Catholic Church and then into the vestry. I did not stay there long but, on coming out, saw 2 Italian soldiers devoutly praying. I have no doubt they were really acting as spies on me. Spent the night in the railway carriage but reached Sebenico by about 8.30 in the evening – slept in railway carriage.

11th [January 1919]

Visited Jugoslavs, Dr. Smolčić etc. Their story was a little pathetic: from 29th Oct[obe]r when the Magyars left till 6th Nov[embe]r when the Italians arrived, we were free. Since then flags, Serbs & Jugoslav[,] have been suppressed[,] right of association except privately forbidden[,] letters and newspapers from the outside world impeded. Several of these men had been in Austrian prisons and it seemed rather hard that they should now be threatened with Italian ones. The public reading of a telegram from the Regent Alexander was prevented as was also a Te Deum at the church. Bread and food generally had sometimes been distributed gratis especially at the beginning – now it appeared to be distributed sporadically among the Italian supporters and with the view of propaganda. They were too vague in their language as to deportation or imprisonment – "hundreds" is valueless. As contrasted with the district of Knin, where a regular rationing system has now begun, Sebenico is interesting. Police surveillance is very close – a guard and a major watched me while talking to the Jugoslavs. Subsequently I went down to the quay and found the Lowestoft there and discovered that the captain was visiting the Governor. I decided to wait for his return but the Governor was in a hurry and sent for me first. Admiral Millo[21] is a stronger looking man than most Italians. He spoke guardedly about the Jugoslavs and subsequently, I hear, complained to several people that I had seen them. His general line was that he was purely there for keeping order and acting in the name of the Entente. I discussed with him the DRNIS incident, and he said Serb soldiers were there. I agreed that required explanation. I think it also requires explanation why the title on his card is "Governor of Dalmatia".

---

[21] Admiral Emilio Millo (1865–1930), Italian sailor; entered navy, 1884; led Italian torpedo boat raid on Dardanelles, July 1912; Senator, 1912–30; Minister of Navy, 1913–16; Governor of Italian-occupied Dalmatia, 1919–23.

12th [January 1919]

Went with Allied Commanders to the Italian advanced line at GIZDAVAC[22] due north of Spalato and about 20 km from it. Found them 3 km north of it, having retired a little. Also found a poor schoolmistress of MUČOVAC – she is a ZIČEVIĆ – she had been dismissed from her school because she could not speak or teach Italian, and, finding life insupportable there, had fled over the mountains without anything the night before. The local population were very excited in our favour, an old woman bowed, boys shouted and threw in their caps, returning we were fired on from a cart, but it proved only foi de joie and the inmates yelled loudly as we came by.

13th [January 1919]

Trip to Trau with Allied Commanders, on report that Italians had reached SEGHETTO[23] beyond armistice line. This appeared incorrect and we also went to BOSSIGLINO[24] at the end of the Trau gulf. The most ridiculous and contradictory rumours obtained at Trau, among others the most ignorant were the burgomaster and the Serb commandant. They could not agree as to dates[,] numbers or places where Italians would be or had been found. Finally my best sources proved to be an old woman, a local mayor, and a charming duchess <Medini> who spoke English well. The old woman first spoke, and had seen an Italian patrol on the 9th at St. ILIJA about 3 kilometres away – the Mayor then proceeded with his grievances. The Italians had occupied PRGOMET[25] on the 6th and begun to terrorize the inhabitants. So far the countess [sic] interpreted, then her eyes bulged and filled and she could not go on. I said 'We are here to help you and put everything right'. She then told me that the priest was a Jugoslav at Prgomet and had been confined in a stable, and that the inhabitants were given food and being compelled by hunger to sign their names in a log book, giving assurances of loyalty to Italy. For such wise I left – not, like the rest, seeing the beauties of the church and the loggia which I well remember with Gladys, but having, I hope, performed a duty better at the moment. Coming back I was glad to find Americans unloading lard and 6 sacks of haricot beans for distribution of food and counterpropaganda to the Italians. We went to SEGHETTO having ascertained that there were no Italians there beforehand. We missed this point

---

[22] Gizdavac, near Muc in the Dalmatian hinterland.
[23] Seget Donji, a fishing village on the Dalmatian coast, one-and-a-half miles from Traù (Trogir).
[24] *Recte* Bossiglina, now Marina to the west of Trogir.
[25] Prgomet, a village in the Dalmatian hinterland, half-way between Split and Metković.

and so went on to BOSSOGLINA [*sic*][,] a curious little village at the end of the Trau Bay. It consists of little more than a wharf and a few tumble down houses. The priest and a few others told me that they had little bread and less milk and depended chiefly on distribution from Spalato. I went and looked into one house where chickens seemed chiefly to reside. I was promptly conducted upstairs to a bedroom and entertained with a pancake (which I could not eat)[,] a glass or rather jug of good wine and cup of coffee. An old man with rings in his ears, Josip Cvitanovic and his son, both master mariners, talked to me and entertained. As we left the whole population shouted and waved their hats. An Italian aeroplane had brooded sulkily above us, as we ate our picnic lunch aboard the subchaser that took us to Trau. I could not help remembering that the last time I had a picnic on the Adriatic, it was an eagle and not an aeroplane which had witnessed the lunch between Glady and me at Ragusa.

On board subchaser,[26] which will now (c-m) remain at Trau, one officer told me that he had witnessed a shocking incident at Curzola[27] on the 15th Dec[ember]. As the American boat approached the population came down with Jugoslav flags and a band welcomed them. As they did not disperse quick enough they used bayonets. This officer saw a man and an old woman bayonetted.

14th [January 1919]

Went on board the Israel[28] today at the request of Cap[tain] Barker[29] of USA and attended at the investigation of an alleged plot by comitadjis against the Italians of Spalato, as to which the new Italian captain had requested our investigation (Capt[ain] Baishout [?][,] his feeble predecessor[,] was the hero of the demonstration incident and also I think the victim of it 4th). 4 persons were cited as being the victims of this plot[,] two Italians and 2 renegade Jugoslavs. Each was first asked separately by the captain if he knew anything of a plot. The first was then asked if he had anything to say and proceeded to make a long rambling statement as to certain incidents – his life had been threatened

---

[26] One of 36 American 'submarine chasers' stationed in the Adriatic since the middle of 1918, 110-feet-long wooden vessels with listening devices and depth charges, J. Corbett and H. Newbolt, *Naval Operations* (5 vols, London, 1920–31), v, 286n.

[27] Now Korčula, one of the main islands off the Dalmatian coast.

[28] USS *Israel*, a *Wickes*-class destroyer, launched in 1918; since November 1918 operating out of Venice and Split; named after the US naval officer Joseph Israel (c. 1780–1804).

[29] Lieutenant-Commander George N. Barker, US sailor; entered US Navy, 1903; commanded USS *Grayton*, 1917–18; USS *Israel* and Commander of US naval forces in the eastern Mediterranean, 1918–19; Director of Naval Academy, 1919–22; aide of Commander of Destroyer Squadron, 1922–25; Commander, Naval Yard, Portsmouth, NH, 1929–32; Professor of Naval Sciences and Tactics, 1934–37 and 1940–44; Commander, USS *Houston*, 1937–39.

by some Serb soldiers, but he could not remember the day etc. 200 Jugoslavs were banded together against Italians etc. etc. Captain Barker, who had listened with some impatience to this rigmarole, now ordered the production of a Bible. No. 1 demurred. 'According to my instructions by my Admiral I cannot submit statements to him unless sworn'. No. 1 said it was an affront to a gentleman to ask him to swear. 'It is all good form to be observed', said Capt[ain] Barker. No. 2–3 & 4, when equally asked to swear, declined. 'I thank you very much'[,] said Capt[ain] Barker and bade them goodbye.

Just then the Italian captain turned up. He said not a single word of any of the incidents mentioned by the 4 liars, but referred to the fact that, on the 11th Jan[uar]y, a comitadji named Ilić of Knin had left Spalato for Knin. He omitted to consider him as an inoffensive person, but the whole bottom was already knocked from this preposterous story.

Subsequently in the afternoon I paid a call on this Captain MENINI.[30] He elaborated 2 theories (1) that the Jugoslavs had done nothing in the war – (2) that the great nations, Italy-England-France and America were superior in culture[,] civilization etc. and should do everything. The whole discourse was interesting. The Jugoslavs were traitors to Austria and had done nothing in the war – quite different from the Czechs who had demoralized the Austrian army and had fought in Siberia. On this last head I pointed out (1) that 1 Jugoslav division had covered the Russian retreat and been annihilated on the Dobruja[;] (2) that another had broken the Salonica front; (3) that information as to the Austrian offensive on the Piave was given by Jugoslavs. On the political question I said I was not allowed to have any politics, which rather impressed him.

15th [January 1919]

Trau

16th [January 1919]

---

[30] Captain Giulio Menini, Italian sailor; commanded torpedo boat *Puglia*; see his *Passione Adriatica: Ricordi di Dalmazia, 1918–1920* (Bologna, 1925).

17th [January 1919]

SINJ.[31] Italians have now tried to do something by fraternization. The Italian Col[onel] from NEORIĆ[32] requested permission to call on the Serb Colonel at SINJ and asked leave for Italian soldiers to come over the mountain and buy food there. His argument was that the two were allies and friends. I pointed out that, in such cases[,] Italy had better recall the rule made the Serbs, travelling in Italian occupied territory, should travel disarmed. There is an interesting little chapel on a height above SINJ where the Turks received a great defeat in 1715.[33] The rest of the country is a wilderness of stone – varied by marsh to the east of SINJ.

In coming back from GIZDAVAC at night I was greatly impressed by the wonder of the scene, especially after leaving Clissa.[34] The mountains lifted their pure foreheads to the heavens – and the solemn shadows hung bleakly around them. In the daytime, without sunlight the effect is not so great, a dull grey light like a petrified haze, is the effect of the mountains.

SINJ and district were suffering a good deal from lack of food – 20 out of 36 villages had not enough. <Their houses are dreadful, one on the hillside near the chapel had a thatched roof, and the bare rock of the hillside for a floor.>

18th [January 1919]

Roddolo left today, the Italian ex-consul at Spalato and notorious agent provocateur. He was probably closely connected with the celebrated plot of the 4 liars (14th Jan[uar]y).

At the same time Admiral Millo has given up his attempt to establish a passport visa station here and proposes to place it at Labin, which is occupied by both Serbs and Italians. The attempt to place it here was undoubtedly to secure a basis for propaganda, agitation and permanent lodgement in the town. It looks therefore as if the plot was collapsing.

19th [January 1919]

Heard the ac[count] of hauling down the American flag on an interallied requisitioned ship – on 15th Jan[uar]y our captain's sworn statement.

---

[31] Sinj in the *Cetinska krajina* in the Dalmatian hinterland.
[32] Neorić, a village in the Zagora district near Sinj.
[33] The Marian shrine Our Lady of Sinj, in the vicinity of which a Turkish army was beaten back on 15 Aug. 1715 prior to the 6th Austro-Turkish War (1716–18).
[34] Klis, mountain fortress and village in central Dalmatia.

On the 16th Mr Juraj Duboković, the Mayor of Jelsa,[35] on the 15th SS Dinar[a], Capt[ain] Kankovic, arrived was stopped by Italian capt[ain] – at Jelsa – and flag hauled down.

20th [January 1919]

I hear that a chevalier BUONFIGLIO[36] has succeeded Roddolo as agent provocateur. Certainly they will require a good fig leaf to cover their diplomatic nakedness here.

21st [January 1919]

I had the pleasure of seeing B[uon]F[iglio][,] the new agent provocateur. I hear his name does not mean good fig but good son. He certainly is a worthy one of his spiritual father. He is a fat greasy jelly of a man, cleanshaven, and bald like a tonsured priest. In fact he looks like a priest who has retired from business because he could not help getting drunk on the sacramental wine.

3 incidents have again arisen and I hear there is a fourth in the offing. One of the incidents is exactly similar to the one related by Dr. Taković in the 4 liars drama, and by a singular coincidence Dr. Taković has been visiting the Italian boat in the harbour.

We had a railway conference with the Jugoslavs today, which was based on a letter of complaint they had written as to its working. The conference resembled a chattering of monkeys, and had it not been for the fact that we had prepared a series of questions, nothing would have been elicited. As it was we found that they had made a great fuss about mere trifles, and had not mentioned at all the principal point that no freight trains had ever run through at all.

Some vignette views on Montenegro from Colonel Wallis, USA in command of all American Adriatic detachments[,] who had just returned from Cattaro. Apparently scrapping began on the 3rd and 4th Jan[uar]y in the Njeguš district and was over on the 13th. The chief intermediary was an American captain of the company ordered up to cooperate. He went to and fro between the rebel and Government forces with a white flag, and was alternately cheered by each. It appears doubtful to others and to themselves, as to what the Montenegrin rebels were fighting about. Their connexion with the royalist party was obscure. They declined to surrender in response to an ultimatum from the French general. There were about 500 in all and about 250 of these fled down to Cattaro, where

---

[35] Jelsa (It. Gelsa) on the island of Hvar (It. Lesina).
[36] Presumably Roberto Buonfiglio, Italian journalist on the staff of the *Corriere d'Italia*.

they were protected by the Americans and employed in unloading ships. After 2 days work, they petitioned for their woman folk, not for the pleasure of their society, but in order to make them do the work. However, when they were offered the alternative of no work, no food, they used their magnificent muscles to some effect.

1 co[mpan]y French, 1 Am[erica]n garrison Cettinje, 1,000 Italians at NJEGUŠ. Col[onel] Wallis said he had advised recall of American troops as they acted merely as shock-absorbers and might get in trouble any time.

22nd [January 1919]

5 a.m. after sleeping on board DINARA, left, without knowing it, for Brazza, and Lesina.[37] Slept in the old valise and only woke to see through my tiny porthole the dark faces and blue caps of Serbian soldiers at Brazza. We touched at several places at Brazza, at one of which I was treated to a really good coffee with milk and splendid cakes – 1 goat cream. Lunched off beefsteak and red wine. The little ports are all the same, red roofs, stone fronts, green blinds, a little church, a little quay, all wedged against somewhat barely clothed hills, and surrounded with a few vineyards. One striking difference there was, people were merry and happy in Brazza, but directly we reached Jelsa there was a change – cordon of <Italian> troops, as many officers as men, no Jugoslav emblems or flags and atmosphere of constraint, remarkable among so free and lively a people.

So from Jelsa to Verboska[38] [sic] and Verboska [sic] to Citta Vecchia or STARIGRAD.[39] I met several persons on the boat who spoke to me of the deeds on the island of Lesina and these I investigated for myself.

There is nothing much in the town, a Venetian campanile[,] a big Croat school still functioning and an Italian one newly installed. There is a distinctly cowed air about the inhabitants but the only specific thing I could find out was, that the town council of Citta Vecchia had resigned because 6 Italians had been introduced into it, and that there had been a deportation of an old man, variously described as 62, 64, 66 and 70, who was the author of a brochure known as European Tripoli (released & sent to Spalato 28th on intervention of Barker).

The food distribution is used of course as a means of Italian propaganda and the food tickets bear the title VIVERI Italiani – Italian Provisions.

---

[37] The islands of Brač and Hvar.
[38] *Recte* Vrboska.
[39] All on the island of Hvar.

24th [January 1919]

Departure of George, the faithful, to Lipa where he had not seen his family for ten years, having been a copper miner in Canada before being snaffled by Milan Pribrievic for the Jugoslav Legion. He was rich and did not want money even if I had dared to offer it him.

27th [January 1919]

SVETI SAVA[40] – Children's festival night at the theatre, a Serbian custom introduced not for the first time into Dalmatia. The general threw bouquets to the various children who recited, and made himself generally agreeable. I personally thought the little children charming. There was a repetition of Jazarac pred Sudom for the fourth time,[41] but here, for both actors and reception, it was comparatively a failure. On the other hand a camp fire scene of Serb soldiers, singing and dancing was received with a furore of applause.

It was reported by rumours in cafes and by snatches of conversation of Italian soldiers that the 28th was the true "Der Tag"[42] when Split, long defended by the wiles of Barker, would fall and Italians occupy it. We did not believe it as regards Split but thought it might perhaps be true of Trau, where the population was considerably alarmed. We found them much satisfied with our visit, and the troops were under arms, because we tried, and failed, to get them to dance the Kolo. The people also refused – only the mountain people did that, said they, not the fishers.

We also made the little harbour of Seghetto, an ideal of fishing village. We were received with open arms. We tried to make them dance the Kolo, but they said only the mountain-folk not the fishers do this. Fishers are in great distress because the price of their net twine is expensive owing to scarcity and thereby raises the price of fish. One policeman entertained us regally on almonds and red wine, both home grown and as good as the other. His wife and little baby to whom the duchess[43] was godmother were approving spectators. The almond blossom already out in patches, in the early spring 'when the flush on the almond

---

[40] St. Sava (née Rastko Nemanjić) (1174–1236), second son of Stefan Nemanjić (see entry 29 Dec. 1918); first autocephalous head of the Serbian Orthodox church; his feast day is celebrated on 14/27 January.

[41] See entry 28 Dec. 1918.

[42] Originally 'der Tag' (the day) marked the beginning of the last German offensive on the Western Front on 21 Mar. 1918.

[43] See entry 13 Jan. 1919, the Duchess of Medini.

announces the earth a bride'.[44] Leghetto must be a dream, a blue gulf, a white and red village, lying gracefully upon it, smothered in pink and white blossoms.

Got back late to find Col[onel] Jelusevich saying goodbye. We drank his health many times, and dances the Kolo to celebrate the occasion. The Serb orderlies did the celebrating by stealing my last 2 pairs of gloves, which I had foolishly left in my mackintosh. The only thing they ever do steal.

4th Feb[ruary] 1919

Left on board the Veronica for Curzola which we reached about 12.30 p.m. We landed in the afternoon, a pretty town with an overhanging fortress, which once was in English hands in 1813, a church in the centre of the town, surrounded by long narrow mediaeval streets, with exquisite vignettes through them. Many of the older houses are roofless, burnt through the plaque of the 16th century. What remain are lovely – Venetian architecture and the lion of St. Mark are everywhere, and by one exceptionally picturesque gateway there is a miniature pillar, surmounted by a miniature green lion, a little copy of the famous one at Venice. Big dance at night.

5th [February 1919]

A beautiful church and convent at Badia,[45] about a quarter of an hour by motorboat. There is a small square cloister, with beautiful painted Venetian arcades like the window in the Doges. <The church is uninteresting except the Christ on the crucifix looks different from 3 positions – Christ suffering, Christ dying, Christ weeping – the expression changing with the angle of vision. Impressive but trick not depth> – 2 amiable Franciscans showed us over. They live there on a small island surrounded by water, supported by alms[,] 'the world forgetting[,] by the world forgot'.[46] They are Jugoslavs but did not even brighten when addressed in their own tongue. In the afternoon to a wonderful old man <Anton Boski> shewed us over his antiquities collection. He had everything from a British cannonball which fell into his garden, to relics of bishops who lived in his house. Incidentally, they had a secret staircase both up to the roof and down to the street, concealed behind unsuspicious cupboards. One of his

---

[44] The opening line of M.H. Hewlett, *The Life and Death of Richard Yea-and-Nay* (London, 1900), ch. VIII: 'Long before the pink flush on the almond announced the earth a bride, on all Gaulish roads had been heard the tramp of armed men, the ring of steel on steel'.

[45] Boi on the island of Brač.

[46] 'The world forgetting, by the world forgot', line 208 of Alexander Pope's 'Eloisa to Abelard' (1717).

ancestors was a cardinal, and nearly a pope. He left him a series of priceless saints reliquaries, toenails, hair, skin etc. Every room was crammed with curiosities – only after seeing 3 I was exhausted and went elsewhere.

The other house – very beautiful – is that of Arneri,[47] the ex-mayor, who has found it convenient to go to Spalato, because the Italians know he is a patriot. A beautiful courtyard filled with tropical plants, the walls covered with statues and coats of arms, and a gigantic and wonderful bronze knocker on the door. It was taken down in the war to avoid confiscation and had just been replaced. The daughter of the house was a lovely girl[,] a little saddened by the recent death of her brother – the mistress, a stately matron in black silk looked like a tragedy queen straight out of the fifteenth century. For tragedy is everywhere, and blood runs as free and hot in the islands as in the streets of Verona and the tragedy of Dobrilo and Milenka[48] was not the only one. I spoke to an Italian officer of the story of Margerita Spoletano, the Dalmatian Hero[ine], who swam the Canale of Meleda[49] nightly to meet her lover and who was discovered and drowned by her brothers. "Ah" said he "the land here is full of tragedy". Which was true with a meaning and a sense that he did not understand.

There were not only love tragedies – either there were pirates, Turks, and Venetians to oppress the islanders and it is hard to say which oppressed most. The islands were the nests of pirates, as in this war of submarines, which the organized power of Venice found it difficult to uproot. I think the Turks were the worst because there are still festivals commemorating their defeats – there is a Byzantine ikon of a Madonna of Badia, which is reverently visited on a certain day by thousands, because the Virgin is supposed to have caused a great defeat of the Turks in the sixteenth century. In Curzola too is the figure of a Madonna – with a cannonball between her knees. It is supposed to have been miraculously attracted there, during a Turkish bombardment.[50]

6th [February 1919]

Suddenly summoned by wireless to Lissa,[51] where an incident with one of the British requisitioned ships occurred on the 4th. The ship put in from stress

---

[47] Originally from Dubrovnik (Ragusa) the Arneri Lords of Korčula were the dominant family on the island since the fifteenth century.
[48] Dramatized by Maciej Ban (1818–1903), the Dubrovnik-born playwright ('*Dobrilo a Milenka*').
[49] Now Mljet Channel between the island of Mljet (It. Meleda) and the Pelješac (It. Sabbioncello) peninsula.
[50] Possibly a reference to the defeat of a Turkish fleet by the combined fleets of the Holy League under Don John of Austria (1547–78) at Lepanto, off Korčula, on 7 Oct. 1571.
[51] Now Vis, eponymous capital of the island of Vis.

of weather, was not allowed to make fast nor were crew or captain allowed to land. When we were approaching we were met by HMS Cyclamen,[52] which had already visited there on her own. The Italian commander, whose Christian name was most inappropriately Hector proved interesting. He first said the incident was a puerility. To this it was replied that there were several puerilities which had occurred. He then said that they had not been allowed to land because of an outbreak of smallpox, but this did not apply to officers. On the medical weakness of this being pointed out he had no answer. He said that the smallpox was also a Curzola. We said we had just come from there and the C[omman]d[an]t had not thought it worth mentioning. He was then asked if he had notified the outbreak of this disease to the Allied commanders. He replied in the negative and started a new attack. He then stated that the incident was due to the fact that Jugoslavs landed letters to their colleagues in the town. It was pointed out to him that this boat had visited the town twice before and such action had not been necessary. As they only put in this time under stress of weather, it was unlikely they would have them this time. At this point he endeavoured to create a diversion by dilating on the sardine industry at Lesina. Brought back he was asked point blank if he wished to prefer a complain ag[ain]st the captain and said he did not. He then proceeded to say that he explained everything satisfactorily to the captain of the Cyclamen. The latter's signal was then read – 'The Nidzor did not receive the ordinary courtesies of the harbour'. This proved a great difficulty – finally he said that possibly the interpreter had misinterpreted his conversation to Captain of Cyclamen, or that the latter had been misled by the Jugoslavs who had subsequently visited him. This concluded the case for the prosecution – and old Gregory,[53] assuming an air of terrific dignity, stated that it would be a deplorable thing if incidents like this necessitated the stationing of interallied boats at Lissa. The captain agreed, and said that the best thing would be to have a British officer or sailor aboard requisitioned ships. He had <had> such a dressing that I spared him a last thrust, to the effect that my presence at LESINA on board of requ[isitione]d ship Jadrai had not prevented the USA flag from being lowered (v[ide] 22nd Jan[uary]). We concluded to close the incident and landed, though the c[omman]d[an]t had previously told us he feared a demonstration as a French captain, who landed, had been carried shoulder high. However, no such fate awaited us. We called on the captain, received much politeness. Gregory was presented with a vast bouquet of mimosa by an Italian lady. We expressed a desire to thank her in person, but she could not

---

[52] HMS *Cyclamen*, launched in 1916, an *Arabis*-class Fleet minesweeper of the Flower-class sloops.

[53] Presumably Captain George Gregory (1872–1929), sailor; entered Royal Navy Reserves, 1888; in merchant navy, until 1914; Royal Naval Transport Service, Eastern Mediterranean, 1914–19; divisional transport officer, Syrian coast, 1917–18; an Elder Brother of Trinity House since 1919.

be found. As the said lady could only have known some half hour of our arrival this was remarkable.

Ultimately we were carefully escorted round the place by the commandant and a military officer and so politely prevented from seeing anything. This did not prevent others however and ultimately we secured an order signed by the commandant of the 24th December prohibiting the import of Jugoslav food into Lissa. This seems a definite proof of food stoppage.

7th [February 1919]

Left Lissa early – visited Spalato – and then entered the gulf of the Narenta.[54] We did the last 11 miles to Metkovic[55] up the narrow channel in a motorboat. It was rather ghostly sailing up there at night. This was the place which Stephan Dushan[56] came in 1351 and hurriedly recalled overland to Salonica. The Serb officers received us uproariously and we danced the Kola again, a new and original one.

8th [February 1919]

Very cold journey to Sarajevo, tho[ugh] the Vale of the Narenta is lovely enough – the Bora[57] was strong and howled fiercely all the way. Left at 5 and arrived at 1.30 conveyed by motor to my hotel by 2 very amiable Scotch women, who did not seem to mind having been kept out of bed.

9th [February 1919]

Train again to Ragusa.[58]

---

[54] *Recte* the Canale della Narenta, now Naretjanski Channel, off the delta of the Neretva river, between the Pelješac (Sabbioncello) peninsula and the island of Hvar (Lesina).
[55] Metković on the river Neretva, some seven miles upriver.
[56] See entry 8 Aug. 1917.
[57] A strong north/northeasterly kabatic (drainage) wind along the Adriatic littoral.
[58] Now Dubrovnik.

10th [February 1919]

Arrived 3.30 p.m. from Uskoplje[59] – the view is very lovely, opening on the sea and the arms of the Ombla.[60] Found a room in the hotel Okda, a dream of a place perched on the eastern extremity of the town opposite Lacroma.[61] I remember looking at it from the city gate, when it was being built in 1913, and saying to Gladys 'Next time we come we will stay there'. I little dreamt how and in what circumstances, as a requisitioning officer. It fulfils more than any place I know the line 'magic casements opening on the foam of precious seas in faery lands forlorn'.[62] Everything is picturesque, and the snow, which is very rare, really adds to the beauty.

11th [February 1919]

Saw Batistić,[63] the singer – he accompanied me on a walk round the battlement at sunset. The scene is one, then, of really magical beauty, especially towards the east. The <dark> green that fringes the point to S. Giacomo gives way to the blood red of the cliffs and then a long promontory of purple thrust out into the sea – above a single snowcapped peak – beyond the hyacinth blue of the water[,] the tender greens of Lacroma <and the pale blue of the horizon> – to the west, the pale blue was laced and shot with fire, beneath which the cream white fortress of Porte Pille[64] and the wooded slopes of Lapad stood up clear and distinct. There is a lover's tragedy here too – 2 lovers drowned as they fled to Pettini, a little isle beneath which the sun set. I thought no death could have been more beautiful than to sink into the sapphire sea bathed with golden light. I wish some great writer had surrounded Ragusa with the beauty and tragedy Victor Hugo wove into "les Travailleurs de la Mer".[65]

The whole scenery and situation of Ragusa is more enchanting than I realized before. Every corner of the streets shows you a new view, a wrought knocker of bronze green, a fountain or a gallery of priceless beauty. Even the new houses, as

---

[59] A small town northwest of Dubrovnik in the Dalmatian hinterland.

[60] A small river to the northeast of Dubrovnik.

[61] Now Lokrum, a small island off Dubrovnik, famed for its botanical gardens, established by Archduke Maximilian of Austria (1832–67), the ill-fated Emperor of Mexico.

[62] 'Charmed magic casements, opening on the foam/ Of perilous seas in fairy lands forlorn', in John Keats' 'Ode to a Nightingale'.

[63] Josip Batistić, Croatian tenor and actor, who performed under the nom de plume Kokotić (Delphinium).

[64] The Pila Gate, one of four gates in the city walls, a complex fort with multiple gates.

[65] Victor Marie Hugo (1802–85), French writer; his *Les Travailleurs de la mer* (1865) is an idyll of passion, adventure and self-sacrifice.

in Nurnberg, have caught and are based on the model and inspiration of the old. The hotel Odak, where I stayed, and the General's house adjoining are both new and beautiful, built of fair white stone. It is curious how at every point Ragusa reminds one of Italy but prevents one thinking of Venice. <There are several Titians> but there is no Lion of St. Mark, for the winged Lion never flew here. Ragusa has stamped on it the ineffaceable mark of its originality.

Saw Črugruja – a delicate[,] highly cultivated man – difficult to get much out of him – remembered me – admitted difficulties with French but professed optimism. I am inclined to think that he knew more than he cared to say. General Dokić,[66] the Serb general, a cultivated man, seemed excited about the relations between the French and the Serbs, though he said they had improved since Franchet d'Esperey's[67] recent visit. A line of demarcation had been established, the French in the port of Gravosa,[68] and the railway control, and the Serbs the city. The general said the French had taken all the matériel de guerre, and wood amounting to millions of Kronen. He said the interest of the French in the port could not be commercial because the railway was strategic (capacity stated by the French subsequently at 300 tons a day maximum). It might be historic and sentimental. He seemed to think that the French were far better agreeing with the Italians now than before. I had an opportunity of seeing this in conversation with the French Colonel Lellouche and the 2 French naval commandants. The two latter showed quite clearly that France had no intention of sending cruisers or destroyers to visit the Italian occupied islands. The French colonel thought that all danger of an Italian advance on Ragusa was now past and said that, when the population threatened an Italian torpedo boat on the 16th Jan[uar]y, he had told them it was an act of war and would not do. He had considerable difficulties with the Serbs, & with Stepanovitch,[69] but things were better now with Dokić.

A few words of my old friend Radović[70] and Montenegro. The former has distinguished himself by stealing a French motorcar from the capt[ain] of the Algérien[71] here and taking it off to Antivari.[72] I should much doubt if it is the

---

[66] General Đuro Dokić (1873–1946), Serbian soldier; Commander 1st Brigade, 1916–17; aide-de-camp to Chief of Staff, 1917–18; Commander Serbian forces in Dalmatia, 1919–20; Inspector of Infantry, 1922–25; General Officer Commanding 1st Army District, 1926–30; honorary aide-de-camp to king, 1930–31; retired, 1931; Minister of Transport, 1941–44; sentenced to death for high treason, 1945; executed, 1946.

[67] See entry 30 Oct. 1918.

[68] Now Gruž, a summer resort for Ragusans and an Austro-Hungarian naval base.

[69] *Voivode* Stepa Stepanović (1856–1929), Serb soldier; entered artillery, 1874; active service, 1876–78, 1885 and 1912–13; acting Chief of Staff, 1914; commanded Second Army, 1914–15 and 1918; Commander-in-Chief of Serbian armed forces, 1918–19.

[70] See entry 27 Dec. 1918.

[71] French destroyer of the *Arabe* class, launched in 1917.

[72] Now Bar on the Montenegrin coast.

greatest of his acquisitions, because he is interesting himself much in the food distribution in Montenegro. This is being done under Serbian supervision. Lieut[enant] Bell had seen and talked with large numbers of the 25 Montenegrin rebels, who sought refuge in Cattaro. Some of them admitted to have been stirred up by the Italians – others were supporters of Nicholas – other did not know why they fought – and all were very vague about the Republic. They seemed to think the great thing was to protest ag[ain]st the Serb dynasty – v. 21st Jan[uary].

13th [February 1919]

Arr[ive]d Split.

17th [February 1919]

Rec[eive]d orders to leave for Zagreb – could not go on 18th because destroyer was full.

18th [February 1919]

General Vassić heard news of my departure with great regret, and telegraphed to War Minister at Belgrade, asking that I should remain. This was a compliment.

19th [February 1919]

Saw some more American food officers from Montenegro – found they had found my list of price and wages and that also it was confirmed by their subsequent study. The plan of food distribution is also mine, but it is improved by a new connection from Rizano.[73] 1000 tons of flour have been distributed already[,] much more in future. Aerial railway[74] Cattaro to Cettinje could prob[abl]y be repaired by a few mechanicians. The American contingent under the redoubtable Major Scanlon[75] has received orders to withdraw. Situation now quiet.

---

[73] Now Risan in the innermost part of the Bay of Kotor.
[74] A cable car-type transport system.
[75] See entry 25 Dec. 1918.

16th night [February 1919]

Visited Bossoglina [*sic*],[76] with the USA subchaser, to distribute food. The local mayor and his son, whom I had seen before, received us with open arms. They gave us wine to drink, like furniture polish, and a hare as big as a young hound. It is curious to be distributing food and receiving it at the same time, but it would have been a mortal insult to refuse either his furniture polish or his hare. The food, chiefly flour, was unloaded from the boat by women, while the men sat around smoking. As we left the population shouted and waved handkerchiefs. I saluted them through the megaphone with Zhivela J[ugo] S[lavia], which provoked uproars of Zhivela Ingleska. That night we spent at Trau, the enchanted city, which I saw, as I feared, for the last time. Capt[ain] Tarbell of the subchaser fairly excelled himself. Even in his English (or rather American) he is original, and he was more original than usual today. The Duchess as usual was charming, and the Duke (quorum pars minima fuit[77]) as dull and dumb as Dukes usually are. The Capt[ain] related that, on one occasion when he was present at a large party, a song in Spanish was sung – the burden of which was 'She was sold – for an old man's gold/ And married a money bag'.

The company applauded, laughed, and some persons even pointed out the appropriateness to the Duke, who seemed somewhat put out. <u>O tempora, O mores</u>. There was a delightful dance in the evening attended by all without distinction, one of the Duchess' friends, a very handsome girl, danced all the time with an American sailor, and some peasant girls with red handkerchiefs and national costumes danced with us. My last appearance in Trau was with the Duchess on one arm and the Duke on the other. I need hardly say that I felt unequal to the part. The parson in Seghetto, accompanied everywhere at Trau and seemed to take no interest in his parish. He tried to be a naval chaplain on board an Austrian ship during the war. His beautiful parish, smothered in almond blossom the last time I saw it, was barren and dead, all the blossom killed by the Bora. Interesting to find that in 1875 Franz Joseph wrote his name in the Visitors' book at the cathedral at Trau as "Francesco-Guiseppe". It was more Italian then than now.

20th [February 1919]

Last day at Split. I was very sorry to leave because I had made many friends there. The nicest and most interesting was a girl, a musical genius of 22, though she looked like 15. Her name was Jelka Carlovacz and she kept one mother and

---

[76] See entry 13 Jan. 1919.
[77] 'Whose role was minimal'.

5 brothers by teaching music. She was a most clever and interesting girl and, I fancy, a good representative of the younger generation. Her history and name were romantic. Originally her ancestor had been a Croat rebel of noble family called ZABOROVIĆ. He had rebelled against Maria Theresa[78] and finally had to flee into Herzegovina. He fetched up at Cattaro, married a peasant girl, and called himself Carlovacz after the Croat town[79] where he had lived. Eventually he went to Brazza,[80] and from Brazza the family landed at Split. All rather interesting as a bit out of the past.

That afternoon I gave a small tea party[,] all the old friends. To my great embarrassment the American commander made a speech in my honour. I replied feebly. The Serbian officers had a little entertainment for me at 9 p.m. and passed a book round for their signatures. One of the wrote: Uspomena-dragom majoru ingleskom – in memory of our dear English major.

21/22 [February 1919]

By destroyer French, with excellent cuisine to Fiume. Fiume quiet.

23rd [February 1919]

Reached ZAGREB, 10 a.m. I left SPLIT confident that it was quiet on the Italian side, and that nothing further is being planned by them. This can be seen in several ways, e.g. on the 18th I visited NEORIĆ, in company with a French officer. We find the Italian Colonel in the kitchen, an old whitebearded mean – and the battery once at NEORIĆ had disappeared – Distribution of food very small – is taking place among local inhabitants. There are no signs of an advance, quite the contrary. Generally my impression is that the Italians have abandoned the idea of entering Split and, failing some untoward event, they will not now do so.

27th [February 1919]

The untoward event has occurred.[81]

---

[78] Maria Theresa von Habsburg-Lothringen (1717–80), Holy Roman Empress, Queen of Hungary and Archduchess of Austria, 1740–80.

[79] Karlovac, a fortress in central Croatia, part of the Austrian 'military frontier' against the Ottomans.

[80] The island of Brač.

[81] On 27 Feb. 1919, Baron Sonnino refused to accept President Wilson as arbitrator in the Italo-Yugoslav frontier dispute.

28th [February 1919]

Interview with Milan Pribičević.[82] He told me of the success of his tours in Croatian villages, converting peasants from Radić[83] and Republicanism to Karageorge and Monarchy, on the platform of Agrarian Reforms.

3rd March [1919]

Frightful atrocities reported from Syrmia[84] by Frančuk early in the war. At Beška,[85] a schoolmistress was found saving a piece of white linen, which the Austrian patrol declared to be part of a Serbian flag. She was arrested and was so frightened that she tore her hair up by the roots. This did not save her, or the notary and another official of the village from execution. 18 young girls were brought to Zagreb from Syrmia, accused of having danced with Serb soldiers. They were originally captured by soldiers, who fired their rifles at random threw [sic] the doors, and killed or wounded some of the party. They were then shut up in Zagreb in a house, and fed only by the kindness of Serbian inhabitants here. They were 18 months without trial. Other women from Syrmia lay on straw in the middle of winter, and one old women of 80 shewed to a friend who gave her a white linen chemise, the one she wore, browner than coffee with filth. Serbian male prisoners were shot secretly in prison here, and in Slavonian Karlovicz[86] there is a great mound where prisoners, men and women, were shot and buried in a grave they had been forced to make themselves. It can be seen from the railway.

8th [March 1919]

Rec[eive]d orders to leave for Belgrade. Left that evening by slow train.

---

[82] Milan Pribićević (1877–1937), Yugoslav nationalist politician; leader of the proto-fascist *Organizacija Jugoslavenskih Nacionalista* (ORJUNA), 1921–29.
[83] Stjepan Radić (1871–1928), Croatian politician; founder and leader of Croatian Popular Peasant Party (*Hrvatska pučka seljačka stranka*), 1905–28; member of Croatian diet, 1908–18; opposed creation of the Kingdom of Serbs, Croats and Slovenes; imprisoned, Mar. 1919–Feb. 1920; assassinated by Serb MP, Aug. 1928.
[84] See entry 20 Nov. 1918.
[85] Beška, a village in the Voivodina, near Srem.
[86] Now Sremski Karlovci, on the left bank of the Danube some five miles from Novi Sad, the traditional, political and cultural centre of the Voivodina.

9th [March 1919]

Arrived Indija[87] – Serbian interpreter told me and an American courier there was 20 minutes to wait, so we went across the road to get some coffee, and in 5 minutes the train, which required to be turned, had gone. This remarkable celerity surprised us much. The next train was at 7 p.m. and a freight one. The Serbian commandant surpassed himself in lying. He first said that he could get us a fiacre, then that it had arrived while we were away at lunch and gone away again. Finally he admitted that it did not exist. After a great deal of trouble we rang up the French commissionaire at SEMLIN,[88] and after about 3 hours got a lorry. Just before we left, the c[omman]d[an]t came in and said a carriage had arrived and we could have it. We said alright but it never turned up. We then bumped into SEMLIN – proceedings somewhat hindered by an officer (Fr[ench]) taking his lady friend in the car who took a wrong turning – short cut of course. After dinner, we went to some rooms supplied by the French and entered the chamber reservé des officiers. To our amazement two negroes sat up in bed, and gave a salute touching their woolly curls. We indicated that these were not the kind of officers we wished to sleep with and finally found salvation in a room reservé pour des capitaines. The American courier remarked[:] "Well, that's odd, a couple of coons coming up to salute in bed". I suspect that they were reliefs for the guard, thought no-one was coming, and slipped into bed to be surprised there by the unobtrusive stranger.

10th [March 1919]

To Belgrade next morning at 8. Our interpreter distinguished himself by saying boat at 8.30 and it was only by the merest accident that we got it at 8. The interpreter was one of those persons whose interpretations you could do without like St. Bernard on the Song of Solomon.[89]

At Belgrade I was nominated a member of the Commission of Styria and Carinthia. Pres[ident] Col[onel] Dehove[,][90] my old friend of Ragusa. The object of this Commission was not at all to delimit the Styrian frontier. This had already been done, and it had been done by the French in a sense ethnographically favourable to the Slovenes. It was not, therefore, unnaturally supposed by some persons that the Carinthian frontier would be delimited upon the same lines.

---

[87] See entry 20 Nov. 1918.
[88] See entry 20 Nov. 1918.
[89] St. Bernard of Clairvaux (1090–1153), Cistercian monk; in his 86 sermons in *Cantica Canticorum* he offered an allegorical and mystical exposition of the Song of Solomon.
[90] Colonel Dehove, head of the Commission for Styria and Carinthia.

This however was denied by the French who said the object of delimiting the Carinthian front[ier] was purely military. This I took the liberty of doubting, though the American attaché did not quite agree with me.

Radića.

14th [March 1919]

Proceeded to Laibach.[91]

17th [March 1919]

Laybach [*sic*].

26th March 1919

The Regent [Prince Alexander] asked me where I had been. I said shortly. He was much interested. Then he asked me about Lyublyana [*sic*] and the Slovenes. I said they were a people diff[eren]t from the Serbs, This excited him. How? I said they were a little as the Scotch are from the English. A little stiff, but very patriotic – peutêtre l'influence catholique.

What was your impression of Split? Very good patriots, but the peasants very ignorant and sauvage.

Cavić – a tres non Jugoslave but went to Italy in an Italian ship.

H[arold:] perhaps because of the Italian – he evidently knew all about it. Everywhere in Dalmatia an Allied officer is well rec[eive]d. H[arold:] except, I suppose, an Italian.

Tell me truly about Montenegro.

Well, I said the chief difficulties are in Njegush, where the old King was born[,] where it is poorest, and where the Italian money and influence are. He knew about the Italian intrigues in Njegush and the Baldacci incident[92] and was very excited about the poverty of the people – extremely poor. <He said he was born in Cettinje, and I told him an incident about the little old woman at the British Legation who remembered about him.>

Amused greatly, especially by my story about the Italian lady at Lissa, who was supposed to have presented me with a bouquet. When I asked personally to

---

[91] Now Ljubljana (Slovenia).
[92] See entry 26 Dec. 1918.

see her, and thank her, I was informed by the Commandant that she was away. Personally I wonder where she was ever there.

He ~~did not say much about~~ alluded to the French-Italian rapprochement, and evidently knew and feared it.

Ragusa and its aspirations for independence, backed by France evidently had not occurred to him and somewhat disturbed him. He said the most important thing was recognition – decline of prestige of local gov[ernmen]t etc.

The regent said. [']Few know as much as you do about Jugoslavia?['] I said 'I don't know, but perhaps it is because of my interest in it before the war'. Finally he ended by saying 'Je vous remercie bien'. <10 May. I think I can say I deserved this.>[93]

2 April [1919]

> In many lands I wander
> In many towns I dwell
> Well Ljubljana knows me
> Dubrovnik knows me well
> In Temesvár and Versecz
> I drank till dawn of day
> From Cattaro and Nikšić
> I wandered by the way
> At dawn in sunny Zagreb
> I saw the market folk
> In Sinj saw I the ploughman
> His two stout oxen yoked
> In Vis I watched the sunset
> Dying in the golden sea
> In Metković the shadows long
> Fell o'er my boat and me.
> By Trogir moon fell lovely
> O'er church and loggia old
> At Split – I saw the sun at dawn
> His laughing ray unfold.
> But by the Grdelica
> Is my dear native home.
> There for the night I came to fight.

---

[93] See entry 9–10 May 1919.

4th [April 1919]

Left by train for Marburg.[94] The situation here has always been odd – the town itself is almost wholly German, the surroundings almost wholly Slovene, the problem of ultimate destiny very difficult to solve. General Meister,[95] the Slovene commander here for all his German name, solved the present situation in a sufficiently drastic manner. When Col[onel] Miles and the American Boundary Commission were here – while they were lunching – a great German crowd assembled and began to call for Col[onel] Miles.[96] At first he said he would not go, but, when General Meister spoke of danger, Miles said "Well, I shall go out on the balcony because otherwise they'd say I was afraid". So he went out and was received with applause and with songs, chiefly the "Wacht am Rhein". Shortly after he went in again, a conflict arose between the Slovene troops and the crowd, and when Miles left in his motor, one of his officers told me that long trails of blood could be seen in the snow. General Meister gave his word of honour that there would be no reprisals after that, but, according to Miles, he did not keep it.[97]

He is a cold stern man, very tall, with strongly marked features and [a] long black moustache. He is very amiable to me, but – it seemed – a little by an effort. They entertained me royally, a little royally in fact on the local wine which is good and yellow.

5th [April 1919]

Slept long, as very tired. I forgot to record yesterday that I saw my old friend Col[onel] Kvaternik[98] in the train. He is a very energetic, highly trained

---

[94] Now Maribor (Slovenia).

[95] General Rudolf Maister (1874–1934), Slovene soldier and poet; entered Austro-Hungarian army, 1894; District Commander Marburg/Maribor, 1917–18 and 1919–23; took control of Maribor on 23 Nov. 1918; retired, 1923.

[96] General Sherman Miles (1882–1966), US soldier; entered US army, 1901; Military Attaché to Balkan states, 1912–14; observer, Argonne offensive, 1918; field member of Coolidge mission to former Austria-Hungary, 1919; military attaché at Ankara, 1922–25; at London, 1939–40; Assistant to Chief of Staff, 1940–41; retired, 1946; Member (Republican) of the Massachusetts House of Representatives, 1947–52.

[97] Maister's pro-Yugoslav Slovene volunteer force killed thirteen ethnic Germans during the events of 'Bloody Sunday' on 27 Jan. 1919.

[98] Marshal Slavko Kvaternik (1878–1947), Croatian soldier; entered Austro-Hungarian army; aide-de-camp to Field Marshal Boroević; joined Council of Slovenes, Croats and Serbs, Oct. 1918; Chief of Staff, Oct.–Dec. 1918; commanded Croatian troops against Hungary, 1919; transferred to Yugoslav army, 1921; co-founder of Croatian *Ustaša* movement; Minister of Home

Austrian staff officer, son of the famous Croatian revolutionary who was shot in 1870. He himself was an Austrian till the last moment but was taken on by the Serbs for organizing work in the 4th Army. He had one disadvantage, that he was the husband of a Frank, the daughter of that famous reactionary. This far outbalanced the fact of his paternity. It was amusing for me, knowing this, to read on one of the parcels in the train the name of Frank, and still more amusing to find that he crossed it out when I was not looking. He has had some difficulty or other with the Serbs, and was retiring to his estate at CILLI.[99] There he told me he meant to work in the garden from dawn till dusk, and spend his evenings reading military literature. I asked him if he would not write it and he said he was always too tired to do that.

His comments on affairs were interesting. He was evidently a great admirer of England and, as he had been frequently in France as well as in Italy, his opinion was worth something. He admired the methodical advance of the British on the Piave, and foretold its success. But he put down the demoralization of the Austrian army less to national propaganda, though there was plenty of that, than to lack of food and clothing. He admired still more in England the system of government, and its self-government above all. He is a great enemy of Chauvinism, which he said was a Slovene and Serb defect but it was a fault from which Croats were free (he is a Croat). His hopes in Jugoslavia were moderate but real. He expressed some doubts as to whether Serbian administration was equal to the task of organizing a large army. He said theirs was a peasant organization and they showed no signs of altering it. He spoke without bitterness but there is no doubt something behind this accounting for his retirement. It is as great loss to Jugoslavia for he is a first class scientific soldier trained in a good staff school.

5th [April 1919][100]

In the morning was convoyed in motor round the town. Prices very high – beef 36 kr[onen] kilo – eggs 1–2 kr[onen] each. Beef very scarce. It was curious that, while the whole town is obviously German, the people in the market were obviously nearly all Slovenes. Marburg is a pretty little town, surrounded by low, but steep, hills, which rise up from the flat with a startling abruptness, two of them by a park in the middle of the town. It must be lovely in summer when these hills are clothed in vines and the trees with foliage. There are two

---

Defence, 1941–42; Croatian Minister of Armed Forces and Deputy Head of State, 1941–43; retired, 1943; tried to treason and executed, 1947; married to Olga Frank, daughter of Josip Frank (see entry 25 July 1917).

[99] Now Celje, in the lower Savinja valley of the Lower Styria region of Slovenia.
[100] Second entry under that date.

picturesque bridges. The population is rather given to wearing green Tiroler hats but that is not confined to Germans.

In the afternoon via St. Egidi to STRASS.[101] The way lies through lovely valleys, low hills, with green well-cultivated sides to them, with roomy well built cottages, and on every eminence, a crucifix or a Pièta, for the folk are truly devout. I crossed over the Mur[102] with a French officer to STRASS which is held by the Germans. The only German soldier I met had a Slovene name and also spoke Slovene, he was of course one of the 'traitorous Slovenes'. The burgomeister, on whom we called, was a typical German Austrian of the old delightful type. His wife was similar but more pronounced in German tendencies. He set the inevitable wine before us and plaintively said that 2 of his vineyards lay over the Mur, that all the beef, and most of the food came from Marburg in ordinary times. They had beef (much cheaper than in Maulsor 8–10 kr per kilo) once a week now, and had no bread for 13 or 14 days, though meal arrived yesterday. Potatoes were also scarce, wine-growing being the chief industry. They were allowed 40 kilo of coal per cooking per month. There was a certain amount of food distribution from LAIBNITZ[103] [*sic*] but it could not be relied on. The country was fairly quiet but for some Bolshevist elements in returned soldiers etc., who got excited when food was scarce. They evidently hated the Slovenes much. He explained that there was a great military school in the neighbourhood but this had been closed down by the Serbs and materials and pupils sent to Wiener Neustadt. I had an amusing dialogue with him over the Slovenes.

I[: ']I see there are some in the neighbourhood?'

He: 'Absolutely none'.

I: [']But I saw there are some Slovene names on the doors of the shops here.[']

He (quickly): [']Well of course there are some but I sent a circular note round for signature. Everyone was to sign himself German or Slovene. No-one signed as a Slovene.[']

That I can quite understand, for the signer would at once have found his way to a gaol. If some had signed as Slovenes I should have believed that the whole district was German. Because none did I don't believe. It is like the Grand Skuptchina,[104] which unanimously deposed old Nicholas. If it had not been unanimous I should have believed in its unanimity. We are back again in

---

[101] Now Šentilj (Ger. St. Egidi in Windischbüheln), on the Austro-Slovene border opposite the Austrian town of Spielefeld, and Straß in Steiermark.

[102] The river Mur (Slovene/Croat Mura) rises in the Tauern mountains and joins the Drava near Legrad in Croatia.

[103] *Recte* Leibnitz in Lower Styria (Austria).

[104] The Skupština, Montenegro's parliamentary assembly, was specially convoked, in November 1918, to depose Nicholas I and to join Montenegro with the new Kingdom of the Serbs, Croats and Slovenes.

the middle ages both in Montenegro and German Styria for we do not have a decision by a majority but a forced – sometimes reinforced – majority.

Directly we crossed the Mur, we came to the priest of St. Egidi, a very different type – the opposite – one of the greatest fighters and champions of Slovene ideas. He gave us excellent wine but his talk was still better. St. Egidi had been the bulwark of Slovene nationality against the Germans and the latter had therefore concentrated their attention on it, seeking to drive the Slovene element out. They went to all lengths of propaganda with the famous Deutsche Schul Verein,[105] but the pastor seems to have kept up his end. With a view of further dividing the people from the pastor they even imported Protestant Würtembergers [sic], so that the German Catholics should not assimilate with Slovene ones. From Graz the German centre poured out literature and money. But, after 20 years, the day of deliverance was come – <since the day of the Armistice> the pastor preached in Slovene, and most of the valley came to hear him. So he went on talking, his glasses falling over his eyes, thumping the table, <his voice> rising and falling with emotion.

We came back by a slightly different route to Marburg through ravishing scenery. Little valleys clustered with houses, beautifully green, waving firs and hills, clad with vinepoles.

6th [April 1919]

Journey back uneventful, but, before leaving, found out some interesting things about the Italians. The two representatives there had been visited by a British officer a few days before my arrival and had been informed by him of the decision of the Generals' Conference at Ljubljana that these two Italian officers must quit Marburg, i.e. because they had intrigued with the Germans there. This officer doubtless thought that I had come to witness or insist upon his final departure. I visited him without success yesterday, and sent me a letter by his soldier regretting his absence. I acknowledged his letter at once by a carte de visite given personally to his soldier. In the evening the Italian officer came to my Slovene attached officer, and asked him if I had received the letter, and then asked where I had been that day. He said to me himself next morning – did you go to Spielefeld?[106] I said 'Yes' – but did not say that I crossed the German lines to Strass. He had previously said he was going to Vienna, but now admitted

---

[105] Founded in 1880 in Vienna, the *Deutscher Schulverein* was a cultural association for the promotion of the German culture and language; after 1919 it operated under the name *Deutscher Schulverein Südmark*.

[106] Austrian border town, opposite Šentilj (St. Egidi in Windischbüheln).

that he would stop some days in Graz, a notoriously Bolshevist centre, where no doubt he hopes to fish in troubled waters – O perfidia plus quam Italica.[107]

I received this morning a visit from two German notabilities of the town, with pamphlets and propaganda galore. I said that I and my government were fully informed of the ethnological situation of Marburg. They then said that there was an economic connection with Graz, and the following dialogue took place.

I: 'I think I may as well at this point inform you what English ideas are. We had no quarrel with Austria, but they made war on us.[']

They: [']We did not make the war – we were compelled.[']

I: [']I must remind you that you acted during the war as our enemies while the Jugoslavs acted as our friends. In Dalmatia the first day of the war 250 persons were put into prison, and many <Jugoslavs> here also.[']

They: [']But, Sir, they were traitors.[']

I: [']Traitors to what – to the Government you yourself condemn as having unjustly made against your own wishes. If you had had the manliness to protest in the same way, you would be better treated than you are now.[']

They: [']But England is a chivalrous nation and will treat us well.[']

I: [']I desire no compliments. England has a million dead in this war, and is resolved that none of those powers, who made the war, shall have power to make another.[']

They: [']But our economic interests should be upheld.[']

I: [']Only in so far as they do not conflict with the aim I have indicated. We intend to show you it does not pay you to make war against England, and any material loss you may suffer will be due to the fact that you supported the war. We do not come in any spirit of enmity or revenge, but to deprive you of the power of working us ill in the future. The fate of Marburg will depend upon whether or no its retention by the Jugoslavs is essential in the triple interests of national security, consent of the governed, and international law.[']

They: [']But Wilson's 14 points.[']

I: [']These were not meant to say that every particle of land, which belongs to one nation, should be reunited to that nation. In such case, the Germans of Gottschee[108] <a small German enclave surrounded by Slovenes.> ought to be an independent state. Moreover Wilson's points have nothing to do with the economic interests but with the wishes of the majority of a community. If there was a clear and intelligible frontier here there would be no difficulty. But you can be quite sure that we shall not concern ourselves to preserve to the Germans

---

[107] Cf. Livy's diatribe against Hannibal, 'Has tantas viri virtutes ingentia vitia aequabant, inhumana crudelitas, perfidia plus quam Punica, nihil veri, nihil sancti, nullus deum metus, nullum ius iurandum, nulla religio', Livy, *Ab urbe condita*, 21.4.8–9.

[108] Now Kočevje on the river Rinža in southern Slovenia.

a corridor of territory running into the heart of Slovenia merely to satisfy a pedantic zeal for ethnological rectitude, still less in order that you may fill your pockets. We shall act on principles of justice, but we do not think that you have deserved or will receive anything more than that. You should have thought of that before you made the war. We go on the principle of supporting our friends, and giving our enemies nothing more than what is necessary to prevent hardship.[']

10–11 night [April 1919].

Left for Paris by arrangement on Zagreb train. Had to pay both for Jeremia and myself – £33 – 906.60 fr[an]cs – or about 3600 kronen.

11 [April 1919]

Vienna – people looked fairly tranquil – gendarmerie and firemen about, no defacing of public monuments or imperial insignia. The people a little pinched & thin, but prices in the shops seemed to compare favourably with those of Zagreb and Belgrade. Food and lighting seem scarce.

12 [April 1919]

Met P[rin]cess Bib[esc]o[109] in train – evidently a dame politique, quite interesting, defended Std [?] who, she says, got 70,000 kr[onen] from Sturdza [*sic*] wh[ich] was stopped by Bratianu – hence arose trouble. She thought Std was merely marketing his brains and that the price was not high of he had really advertised R[omani]a.

She thought cond[itio]n of R[omani]a itself extremely serious and evidently disapproved of much of the Chauvinistic Imp[erialis]m now so pop[ula]r.

13 [April 1919]

Paris. Arr[ived.] W[ilso]n said to block everything – a good many people are actually of the opinion that they are running the Congress, but I have not found anyone who thought he was running W[ilso]n.

The great four are not especially pop[ula]r, and the time seems to have come for political decisions.

---

[109] See entry 18 Jan. 1917.

Everyone seems to understand the Bolsh[evik] danger and the peril of further delays. None the less everyone has agreed to the payment of enormous sums by Germany. Obviously, if she does not want to pay them, she will become Bolsh[evik].

I put up forcibly the case of the spread of Bolsh[evik] influence from the Prekmurye[110] to Strasz, west of Radkersburg, and Graz.[111] Little attention likely to be paid.

Naked truth force fails everywhere and the 26th Div[ision] leaving Dobrudja for Egypt – Odessa has already been evacuated and Berthelot who advised going there will be relieved.

Kisch[112] has done well for Poland – there has been a fierce fight betw[een] Czechs and Poles over Teschen,[113] resulting ultimately considerably to the advantage of the Czechs, who were briefed by Webster.[114]

The latter has evidently had much power, and occupies the place I should have had before I went to Jugoslavia. I am very glad of it, because he is a sound man, and my own choice. The basis of the whole British Peace Conf[eren]ce appears to have been the papers – prepared under my supervision in MI2E,[115] which supplied the groundwork of solid information to coach our delegates.

The ethnographical map also is largely based on our designs. Certainly I laboured but I do not complain that others have reaped. The W[ar] O[ffice] had become insupportable to me, and I could not have borne to be England on the declaration of peace. And what could have been better and finer for me than the Jugoslav Odyssey, with 70 beds in six months – a free wild life and wanderings among simple children of nature. For that I would surrender all Congresses of the world.

Saw L[loyd]G[eorge] at dinner – radiant and genial, looking without a care.

---

[110] Prekmurje (or Transmurania), a geographically, linguistically, culturally and ethnically defined region in northeastern Slovenia, between the Mur river and the Rába Valley in Hungary.

[111] The latter three in Austrian Styria.

[112] Brigadier-General Frederick Hermann Kisch (1888–1943), soldier; entered Royal Engineers, 1907; served in India, 1909–14; active service, France, 1914–15, Mesopotamia, 1916; General Staff Officer (Intelligence), Sept. 1916–19; member of British delegation at Paris Peace Conference, 1919; retired, 1922; Chairman Palestine Zionist Executive Committee in Jerusalem, 1923–31; rejoined army, 1939; Chief Engineer, Eighth Army; killed by landmine in Tunisia, 1943.

[113] Teschen, town in Austrian Silesia on the Olza river, divided in 1920 between Poland (Cieszyn) and Czechoslovakia (Český Těšín).

[114] See entry 19 July 1917.

[115] MI2, Military Intelligence Section 2, which specialized on gathering intelligence from and concerning the Balkans.

14th [April 1919]

Home – satis bene.[116]

15th [April 1919]

London. Cyrano de Bergerac – last time I saw this was in Zagreb in 1906 – striking enough in its way, almost great, and very French.

18th [April 1919]

Back to Paris – everything in great confusion, and most people away. Great excitement here, as in England, at Ll[oyd]G[eorge]'s attack on Northcliffe.[117] When I was last in England they stuck closer than brothers. All say that L[loyd]G[eorge] is very wild – for instance the Times attack on him re Poland[118] is quite true. He decided ag[ain]st all the experts that Danzig sh[ou]ld not be Polish apparently: he thought he knew more history than they. He decides by inspiration – Wilson apparently be a similar process, always moreover on principle rejecting the advice of anyone in uniform.

19 [April 1919]

L[loyd]G[eorge] going to visit the Somme battlefields at 5 p.m. this afternoon but postponed.

20 [April 1919]

Spent a good deal of time today on a FIUME memorandum[119] – one a memo, to show that Serbia could fight in 2 or 3 years with 800,000 to 1,000,000 men whereas today only with 250,000. Secondly that it was the universal opinion that FIUME would mean war though not now. This was embodied also in a short letter for the P[rime]M[inister].

---

[116] 'It is well enough'.
[117] 'Mr. Ll. George's Speech. Paris Criticisms. "The Times" The Friend Of France', *The Times*, 19 Apr. 1919.
[118] 'The Prime Minister's Apologia' editorial, *The Times*, 17 Apr. 1919.
[119] Memo. Temperley, 'Memorandum on Fiume', 19 Apr. 1919, Temperley MSS.

Dined with Princess Bibescu[,] interesting as ever – very deep as a thinker, but not yet deep as a woman.

Easter Sunday.

21 [April 1919]

My letter got up to the P[rime]M[inister] about 5 minutes before he went to confer with the French and Italians on the question of FIUME. I hope it worked properly. Wilson has withdrawn from the Conference. I supposed because he does not desire to be tainted with the [1915] treaty of London.

I saw Philip Kerr at lunchtime and pitched into him my several points

(1) FIUME means war in 2 or 3 years.
(2) Dalmatia means comitadji.
(3) The Croats.

These points will, I am sure, have their effect, as the P[rime]M[inister] is approached by 2 roads.

Note My more detailed mem[orandu]m[120] was submitted to Hardinge[,][121] Balfour and the P[rime]M[inister] on the 22nd April. H[ardin]ge noted it as very [incomplete].

22 [April 1919]

Thought yesterday was my birthday owing to G[lady]'s letter, find that day before ~~today~~ yesterday really was. This is a noticeable achievement forgetting one's own birthday, not because I am forty years of age. It makes one feel a bit ashamed to think how little I have done at this age. What is before? Dunno. What is behind? I don't regret – certainly since December of 1914 every moment devoted to my country. It has brought loss of vigour, health, amusement, brightness – and brought what, not happiness, but contentment with my conscience. Whatever happens now I can never forget these years were not selfish. Happiness I had before with Gladys – strength in myself – success in my career. Such things I

---

[120] Memo. Temperley, 'Recent Tendencies in Italian Military Policy', 22 Apr. 1919, Temperley MSS.

[121] See entry 8 Feb. 1917.

cannot have again in equal measure, unless perhaps with perfect rest and leisure to think or rather to play. 'O duty – what crimes are committed in thy name'.[122]

23 [April 1919]

Dined with Haskins,[123] Seymour,[124] Day,[125] Lord,[126] and heard American gossip. All much elated at Wilson's pronouncement on FIUME and Dalmatia.[127] All down on Italians as having consistently played a bad game of blackmail and bluff. They threaten to withdraw.

Teschen committee hung up again for revision.

24 [April 1919]

Wilson's statement re FIUME very noble & very determined. The Italians leave at 2, but deferred till 8. I wonder if they really will go then. L[loyd]G[eorge] tried

---

[122] Cf. Madame Roland's reputed final remark before she died on the guillotine in 1793: 'O Liberté, que de crimes on commet en ton nom!'

[123] Charles Homer Haskins (1870–1937), US mediaevalist; educated Johns Hopkins University; Professor of History, University of Wisconsin, 1892–1902; at Harvard, 1902–31; advisor to President Wilson at the Paris Peace Conference, 1919 (chief of the Western European division).

[124] Charles Seymour (1885–1963), US diplomatic historian; educated King's College Cambridge; instructor at Yale University, 1911–18; member of US delegation at the Paris Peace Conference (chief of Austro-Hungarian section and on Czechoslovak, Romanian and Yugoslav territorial commissions), 1919; Stirling Professor, Yale University, 1922–37; President of Yale University, 1937–51.

[125] Clive Hart Day (1871–1951), US economic historian; educated Yale, Berlin and Paris universities; instructor in history, University of California, 1902–1905; at Yale, 1905–1907; Professor of History, Yale University, 1907–22; Know Professor of Economics, 1922–36; member of the US delegation at the Paris Peace Conference, 1918–19 (chief of the Balkan division).

[126] Robert Howard Lord (1885–1954), US diplomatic historian and clergyman; educated Harvard, Berlin, Vienna, Moscow; instructor at Harvard, 1910–24; Professor, Harvard University, 1924–26; resigned and ordained in Roman Catholic church, 1926; Professor of Church History, St. John's Seminary, Brighton, MA, 1929–44; Professor of Modern European History, Regis College, Weston, MA, 1929–44; pastor at St. Paul's church, Wellesley, MA; member of US delegation at Paris Peace Conference, 1919 (technical adviser on eastern Europe); chief of Inter-Allied Commission on Poland, 1919.

[127] On 23 Apr., Wilson issued a public statement, emphasizing the importance of Fiume to Yugoslavia, and appealing to Italy 'to exhibit to the newly liberated peoples across the Adriatic that noblest quality of greatness, magnanimity, friendly generosity, the preference of justice over interests', 'Mr. Wilson's Appeal to Italy', *The Times*, 24 Apr. 1919.

to pour oil on the troubled waters by saying that he was the only one of the four, who did not care about his personal dignity. It is true but his attack on Northcliffe seemed to show that he had no particular reason to do so.

P[rime]M[inister] in great fettle[,] thoroughly determined about FIUME, and spoiling for a fight.

24th [April 1919]

Wilson communication very noble[,] reminds me of his reply to the Pope and is as effective in its ultimate result.

Dr Zsolger[128] interviewed me today – quick, bright, alert, decisive, a true Slovene of grit and determination. He was pleased at Wilson's utterance but seemed to think it only the beginning. The Italians, after saying they w[oul]d leave today at 2, finally left, only one of them that mattered, i.e. Orlando, at 8 – Nunc Dimittis.

25th [April 1919]

Balfour and Clemenceau drew up a statement today, which Wilson also signed very strangely, as one phrase was 'we are bound by the Treaty of London'. It was able, diplomatic, temperate and beautifully phrased in true Balfourian style. It put the F[oreign] O[ffice] people in a state of mild ecstasy but it lacked the grand simplicity of Wilson's large utterance. The more the latter is studied the more the former will be appreciated.

Orlando replied by a long note to Wilson on the possibility of human error, and the dangers of publicity which, however, as he threatened, might well be a double-edged weapon.

---

[128] Ivan (Ritter von) Žolger (1867–1925), Slovene lawyer and official; educated Vienna University; lecturer, 1900–18; full professor, 1918; entered Austrian Education Ministry, 1902; Section chief, 1911–15; Minister without Portfolio (for constitutional reform), Nov. 1917–May 1918; drafted constitution for transition to SHS state; representative at League of Nations, 1920; Professor of Law at Ljubljana University, 1919–25.

26th [April 1919]

In council with Nicholson[129] [*sic*], Leeper[130] and R.W.S[eton-]W[atson] immediate occasion – Italian envoy[131] came to see Balfour last night and, after being completely intransigent for some time, he suddenly said Italy would be prepared to consider a compromise on the whole matter. We have tried to work out one. I offered them the strategic line to the West, of the Arsa,[132] skirting the lower slopes of Mte Maggiore[133] to protect Fiume, giving Idria[134] to the Jugoslavs and Adelsberg.[135]

The F.O. proposal is a series of graded offers – Lissa,[136] Lussin,[137] sov[ereign]ty in Albania, or concessions in Asia Minor.

27th [April 1919]

Dined R.W. Seton-Watson. Got nothing very new from him. He said L[loyd]G[eorge] was not direct <As an old naval captain said to me 'He can no more be straight than a rattlesnake on the move'.[138] At the same time as he attacked Northcliffe, he made Rothermere a Viscount.> and had had negotiations with Bolshevik agents, and infected P[hilip] K[err], so that the latter said the thing that was not over the Karl-Smuts negotiation.[139] Am in general agreement with him.

---

[129] See entry 18 May 1918.
[130] See entry 23 May 1917.
[131] Guglielmo, marchese Imperiali di Francavilla (1858–1944), Italian diplomat; entered diplomatic service, 1885; agent and consul-general at Sofia, 1903–1904; ambassador at Constantinople, 1904–10; at London, 1910–20; delegate at Paris Peace Conference, 1919; Italian representative at League of Nations, 1921–22; retired, 1922.
[132] Now the river Raša in western Istria, often used to demarcate regional boundaries.
[133] The Učka mountain range along the eastern coast of Istria, near Opatija (It. Abbazia).
[134] Now Idrija in western Slovenia, known for its mercury mine.
[135] Now Postojna in southwestern Slovenia.
[136] Island of Vis (Croatia).
[137] Island of Lošinj in the Gulf of Kvarner in the Northern Adriatic (Croatia).
[138] See entry 18 Apr. 1919.
[139] See entry 30 Dec. 1917.

28th [April 1919]

Worked hard on Albanian boundary. Recognition proposed for SHS.[140]

29th [April 1919]

Recognition not accepted by French to date – that and Clemenceau's telegram about 'scraps of paper' very foolish.[141]

Saw Barnes[142] in the evening – the War Cabinet minister a fine plain honest man. He had two good impressions.

(1.) that English policy in the things he knew, i.e. Labour Commission and the League of Nations, had beaten all others out – [(2.)] that the French and Americans were not really practical in details though he admitted Clemenceau was a fine man and Wilson a stern idealist.

He particularly mentioned Leon Bourgeois[143] as futile and said Lloyd George said to Clemenceau the other day 'that man was P[rime]M[inister] of France?' C[lemenceau]: 'Yes'. L[loyd]G[eorge]: 'How?' C[lemenceau]: 'Lack of material'. A sad confession always, I think. He said Wilson – Henry, not President – thought the Italians should remain in Fiume. This he must be beat out of.

30th [April 1919]

Masterpiece by Hankey. Recognition of Jugoslavs 'cleared up', which means that they recognize their credentials as those of SHS but not publicly.

---

[140] *Kraljevina Srba, Hrvata i Slovenaca* (Kingdom of Serbs, Croats and Slovenes), the official title of the Yugoslav state, 1918–29.

[141] See tel. Clemenceau to Luzzati, 27 Apr. 1919: '[T]here can be question of dishonouring our mutual engagements. The policy of France is not that of "scraps of paper"', 'Annexation of Fiume', *The Times*, 28 Apr. 1919.

[142] George Nicoll Barnes (1859–1940), trades unionist and politician; General Secretary of the Amalgamated Society of Engineers, 1896–1908; MP (Lab.) Glasgow Blackfriars, 1906–18, (Nat. Dem. and Lab.) Gorbals, 1918–22; Minister of Pensions, 1916–17; Minister without Portfolio, 1917–20; Chairman of the Labour Party, 1910–11.

[143] Léon Victor Auguste Bourgeois (1851–1925), French politician; Minister of the Interior, 1890 and 1895–96; Education Minister, 1890–92 and 1898; Justice Minister, 1892–93; Prime Minister, 1895–96; Foreign Minister, 1896, 1906 and 1914; President of the Chamber of Deputies, 1902–1905; Minister of Labour, 1912–13 and 1917; Minister of State, 1915–16; President of the Senate, 1924–25; delegate at The Hague peace conferences, 1899 and 1907; Paris Peace Conference, 1919; strong advocate of the League of Nations.

1st [May 1919]

Passed off fairly successfully – only a few cavalry charges, a great many wounded police and one dead Bolshevik.[144] Vertical rain and horizontal hosepipes, apparently attributed much to cooling ardour.

2nd [May 1919]

1st interview with C[hief of the] I[mperial] G[eneral] S[taff, Wilson]. Went to see him re the Jugoslav attack on Klagenfurt.[145] He first began by offering me a cigarette – my first experience of this with a general. He then asked who I was. I said 'a Don' after which he always addressed me as 'Mr.' – a humorous Irish dog, out to impress me and pull my leg at the same time. He said – [']well what about you – you study you'll never write it. How can anyone write the History of this Congress – even Maurice Hankey often isn't in the room with the great four!'

Then – on the situation in Carinthia, mountaineers fighting well – [']what can we do? What will they say?

Do you know ever since 11 November I have said one thing – You are trying to run a League of Nations, on a basis what of – not of force – 'You can't!' What is our role [?] For the first time in our history we made war, i.e. really went into the scrum, i.e. reversed our historic role. What do we do now? What can we do now? Get out! Get out of the scrum and pick up the mufflers, one muffler in S[outh] W[est] Africa, one in East Africa, one in Mesopotamia.

I am for this little island, and for the taxpayer. Do you know what we pay for our sideshows? At Murmansk[,] at Archangel[,] at Baku[?] £180,000,000 a year. Why should we pay it, you and I?[']

Why should we be in Fiume in trouble and danger. I shall have another go at the P[rime] M[inister] tonight.

5 [May 1919]

After seeing Glady off returned to find myself half an hour late for C[hief of the] I[mperial] G[eneral] S[taff] and P[rime] M[inister] – went off and found them walking in the garden, talking about Bulgaria and Turkey – Philip Kerr in attendance with despatch boxes. They wanted to know all about the situation. I had maps and

---

[144] See 'Paris May Day Disorders. Processions Broken Up By Cavalry', *The Times*, 2 May 1919.

[145] SHS troops had occupied Klagenfurt in southern Carinthia in early January 1919, and remained in partial occupation until the 1920 plebiscite.

books with me as if I was a beast of burden. L[loyd] G[eorge] sat down in the sun on a bench, but there was a little old woman there. 'Let's try a free one' said the C[hief of the] I[mperial] G[eneral] S[taff]. They sat down and I stood up, expounding the map. Then L[loyd] G[eorge] thought it too windy. 'Let's move on to the President' – so on to the President we moved; 'Georgie' as H[enry] W[ilson] calls him – L[loyd] G[eorge] went straight in. <Not quite before he went in he said to me [']Who occupies Bulgaria?['] H[arold] T[emperley] [']A strong Italian Division.['] L[loyd] G[eorge] 'Who put them there?['] H[arold] T[emperley] 'Franchet d'Esperey.['] L[loyd] G[eorge] (sharply) [']Franchet d'Esperey's a fool then.['] H[arold] T[emperley] 'I agree'.>

I remained outside with H[enry] W[ilson] still expounding the map to him. 'Ah' said he 'the French divisions are very good or very strong. Is it not so, M. Pichon[146][?]' – and he turned round to an old gentleman with a white walrus moustache. 'I don't know' said the aged diplomat who had come into the room behind us unobserved. Then a ferret nosed foreigner came in, seeking President Wilson and looking agitated. It was Imperiali.[147] The door opened again, and a soldier – not Foch – came out, but before it closed the face of the Tiger [Clemenceau] looked out of the door – 'solemn and calm' I thought. Imperiali came out again with Lloyd George in tow and they turned us out of the room for a few minutes. So we came back. <After Imperiale left,> L[loyd] G[eorge] whispered a few words to P[hilip] K[err]. P[hilip] K[err] talked on the telephone and then said to us 'The organgrinders are returning on Wedneday. They will demand the Treaty of London and give up FIUME.[']

Then the C[hief of the] I[mperial] G[eneral] S[taff, Wilson] went into the Conf[eren]ce. We waited just a few minutes long, and then a tall man with hooked Yankee nose, and grey trousers, suddenly popped out and said 'good morning' to me. It was President Wilson looking much agitated. He went back into the room in a moment.

Then after half an hour, C[hief of the] I[mperial] G[eneral] S[taff] came out looking radiant. <Going out we passed 6 sentries USA who all saluted and many detectives. H[enry] W[ilson] 'It looks like a pool'. H[arold] T[emperley] 'or like a harem'. 'Children' said he [Wilson] to us, me & Mcindoe. 'How many divisions will occupy the Straits [of] Con[stantino]ple and Armenia[?]' We've fought Wilson. I said to him[: ']are you an American or a European? If the one[,] go back, if the other[,] take over the mandate for Con[stantino]ple and Armenia. It is tied up with the League of Nations and agreed. But they'll never go there.[']

---

[146] See entry 27 Dec. 1917.
[147] See entry 26 Apr. 1919.

6 [May 1919]

Spoke with W[illia]m Sutherland[148] very friendly. He seemed to think the P[rime] M[inister] was only concerned with Germany and not with Austria at all. He said the P[rime] M[inister] had spoken to him that day about Italy. They were quite clear on one point, he and Clemenceau, i.e. Fiume &c might or might not be Jugoslav, but it should never be Italian.

The Italians rage against Wilson. L[loyd] G[eor]ge says that he published his famous statement at 2 p.m., instead of, as he promised, at 6, and that these last 4 hours might have produced a settlement by negotiation. It was not honourable of him to do this, if he promised, but I doubt the difference it would have made or not made.

Venizelos has now resolved to send a division to Smyrna,[149] which he will now get. There are 7 Italian warships there who may give him a lively time.

8 [May 1919]

Went to the meeting of the <Five> Foreign Secretaries today – to decide on the frontiers of Austria-Hungary. Balfour started characteristically by asking what Austria-Hungary meant. Sonnino[150] corrected – Austria and Hungary. Lansing,[151] who, in the intervals of making bright remarks, knocks off admirable sketches with his left hand <A case of your left hand not knowing what your right hand doth>, said he would like to have a commission to decide on a possible frontier between Austria and Hungary, of that question arose. He said he was not competent to decide the question <and wanted a subcommittee>. Sonnino at once jumped on this and said, if we are not competent, how can the committee be? For a foreigner a very clever misuse of words – competence in the sense of knowledge and competence in the sense of powers. Out of all this arose a proposal by Sonnino to ~~design~~ discuss the triangle of the railway between the following points – Feistritz, Radmannsdorf, p[oin]t 1370 and on the west the old provincial boundary, northwards to a point on the railways west of Wurzen.[152] Sonnino said this ought to be either Italian or Austrian. Sonnino

---

[148] Sir William 'Bronco Bill' Sutherland (1880–1949), political fixer and fundraiser for Lloyd George; MP (Liberal) Argyllshire, 1918–24; private (press) and then parliamentary private secretary to Lloyd George, 1915–20; a Lord of Treasury, 1920–22; Chancellor of the Duchy of Lancaster, 1922; see also entry 28 Aug. 1921.

[149] Now Izmir.

[150] See entry 2 May 1917.

[151] See entry 19 May 1918.

[152] Windisch Feistritz now Slovenska Bistrica in northeastern Slovenia; Radmannsdorf now Radovljica in the Upper Carniola region of Northern Slovenia; Wurzen now Podkoren, and

with a genial smile, and a twinkle of his coffee-coloured eyes, said he wanted to settle it then and there. 'We are competent'. Then ensued the verbal passage above alluded to. <Lansing got one thrust in 'I want more knowledge for Baron Sonnino is much better prepared than the rest of us'.> Finally it was referred to a committee not to fix the frontier but to assemble the information of a statistical, ethnographic & economic character. The Committee, quorum pars magna fui, withdrew at once to report. The discussion went on most unsatisfactory lines, of which I strongly disapproved. The Italians (Martino,[153] the chief) claimed that the Austrians should have it, and M[artino] said [']<u>entre nous</u> we fear the Jugoslavs, and a possible concentration at Radmannsdorf.['] When challenged with favouring the enemy at the expense [of an ally], he said Gen[era]l Pechitch said the same thing as to possible war in claiming a frontier ag[ain]st Roumania. Crowe[154] countered by saying that in such case the Jugoslavs must have Klagenfurt. The Americans declined to agree at all without further discussion, and the meeting was adjourned for tomorrow.

Roumanian boundary approved. 2nd meeting.

Further notes – Sonnino, when the question of Vorarlberg was raised, and its possible voting itself into the Swiss Fed[eratio]n did his best to stifle the discussion. 'So far as I am concerned it is a part of Austria. I have no knowledge of this territory as an independent unit. Its recognition would lead to <the secession of further pop[ulatio]ns> [and] endless confusion'. In the same way Sonnino did his best to avoid the raising of any readjustment of territory between Austria & Hungary.

Lansing took a strong popular line over the question of Roumania and Hungary, quite in accordance with the traditions of the 'bird of freedom'.[155] He asked why the blue boundary line was drawn as it was. Tardieu[156] said the population was much mixed and the blue line represented an equitable compromise. Lansing thrust at once – 'Is there anywhere west of the blue line

---

the Wurzen Pass (Korensko sedlo (Slov.)) in the Karawanken mountains between Arnoldstein (Austria) and Kranjska Gora (Slovenia).

[153] Giacomo de Martino (1868–1957), Italian diplomat; entered diplomatic service, 1891; agent and consul-general at Cairo, 1907–11; Secretary General of Foreign Ministry, 1912–20; delegate at Paris Peace Conference, 1919; ambassador at Berlin, 1920; at London, 1920–22; at Washington, 1923–32; retired, 1932.

[154] See entry 26 Jan. 1918.

[155] That is, the bald eagle as a representation of the United States.

[156] André Pierre Gabriel Amédée Tardieu (1876–1945), French journalist and politician; foreign affairs editor, *Le Temps*; enlisted, 1914; aide to Clemenceau at Paris Peace Conference, 1919; Minister for the Liberated Regions, 1919–20; Transport Minister, 1926–28; Minister of the Interior, 1928–30; Prime Minister, 1927–Feb. 1930, Mar.–June 1930, and Feb.–June 1932; Agriculture Minister, 1931–32; War Minister, 1932; Foreign Minister, 1932; Minister of State, 1934.

a preponderance of Roumanians?' 'Yes'. 'Let's see it'. At this critical moment I produced an ethnographic map, on which rested the august eyes of the British and American Foreign Secretaries. Then Lansing thrust again – 'What are the numbers?' '25,000 Roumanians west of the line – 600,000 Magyars east of it'. Lansing – 'This distribution does not seem very fair, as the decision seems to go, in every case, against the ~~Roumanians~~ <Hungarians>'. The explanations that the railway line between N[orth] & S[outh] Transylvania w[oul]d be cut, and much else, did not seem, under the circumstances, very convincing. However, after having made everyone very uncomfortable, Lansing suddenly withdrew his objections. Balfour characteristically had never made any. One priceless thing, omitted from the official report, shall not be omitted here. Lansing was told that the Committee was unanimous in their opinion. He said a unanimous opinion did not always mean harmony <as far as Romania was concerned>, e.g. the Allies were unanimous in restricting Roumania to a certain line in the Armistice. This line she promptly violated, and, as a consequence, she has received an enormous extension of territory. Balfour said this was not due to that cause but to consideration of the whole matter. He added blandly[:] 'All that we can say is that unanimity of opinion causes less difficulties than difference of opinions'. Lansing, having acted as Transpontine 'enfant terrible', withdrew.

9 [May 1919]

L[loyd] G[eor]ge told me 2 stories of his papa at lunch yesterday. A propos of Brockdorff-Rantzau,[157] he says that he is the second Junker he's met, and he is of the same old type. The previous one was Metternich[158] in 1911. He said to him one day, if you go on like this I shall go down to the H[ouse] of C[ommons] and ask for £100,000,000 for defence. M[etternich] 'Ships aren't enough'. L[loyd] G[eorge] 'In that case we should get a conscript army'. M[etternich] 'Do you think we'd wait for you?' L[loyd] G[eorge] 'Well, we shall see any way we shall keep the ships up'. Shortly after he went down and made the Agadir speech.[159] M[etternich] then act[uall]y tried to suggest his dismissal to Sir E[dward] G[rey] but the latter cut him short. Curiously enough I could see

---

[157] Ulrich Count von Brockdorff-Rantzau (1869–1928), German diplomat; entered diplomatic service, 1893; consul-general at Budapest, 1909–12; minister at Copenhagen, 1912–18; Foreign Minister, Jan.–June 1919; attended Paris Peace Conference 1919; ambassador at Moscow, 1922–28.

[158] Paul Count Wolff Metternich zur Gracht (1853–1934), German diplomat; entered diplomatic service, 1882; ambassador at London, 1901–12; at Constantinople, 1915–16.

[159] On 21 July 1911.

this. After Agadir, Metternich came to Cambridge to get his degree,[160] and stayed with A[dolphus] W[illiam] W[ard].[161] A[dolphus] W[illiam] W[ard] said that he was certain he was in disgrace and painfully humiliated. Which contributed most? L[loyd] G[eorge] in public or in private [?]

L[loyd] G[eorge] had another story about Bethmann Hollweg. He sat next to him at a dinner at which after wine B[ethmann] H[ollweg] became extremely communicative. He wished he had taken it all down, but he remembers clearly that B[ethmann] H[ollweg] said, in case of a war, Bavaria would go against Prussia and social revolution would break out.

Spoke with Adam[162] of the 'Times' who sat next to L[loyd] G[eorge] last night at the press dinner. L[loyd] G[eorge] was ragged and baited in 15 speeches by different pressmen and finally rose to his feet, stable, thrilled and made what A[dam] described as one of the best speeches of his life. He said, as in one instance he knew, L[loyd] G[eorge] was apt to see Northcliffe in which he was not. But he gave the show away when he spoke of his relations with Northcliffe, and finally said, [']well anyhow, if I am criticized for the peace terms by the press everybody will put it down to personal spite against me['] – very right and clever.

10th [May 1919]

Before leaving the meeting yesterday I discussed the triangle of railway <(the Assling triangle[163])> with Major Johnson (USA) and its possible cession to Austria. He said he thought it strategically a danger as bringing the frontier of Austria close to Laibach and not far from the Sea. I said I would like to have the technical military opinion of General LeRond,[164] one of the best men in

---

[160] This seems doubtful; only Dominion prime ministers received hon. degrees at Cambridge.

[161] Sir Adolphus William Ward (1837–1924), historian; educated Germany and Peterhouse; Professor of History and English Literature, Owens College, Manchester, 1866–97; Principal, Owens College, 1890–97; co-founder Victorian University, Manchester; Vice-Chancellor, 1886–90 and 1894–96; Master of Peterhouse, 1900–1924; editor-in-chief, *Cambridge Modern History*, 1901–12.

[162] George Jeffreys Adam (1883–1930), journalist; Reuters correspondent in Paris; contributor to *Continental Daily Mail*; assistant Paris correspondent, *The Times*, 1912–14; Paris correspondent, 1914–21; European editor, *New York Herald* and *New York Sun*, 1921–30; a confidante of Briand.

[163] Assling, on the river Drau in Eastern Tyrol (Austria).

[164] General Edouard Louis Henri LeRond (1864–1949), French soldier; entered artillery, 1886; military attaché at Tokyo, 1912–14; active service, 1914–18; aide to Marshal Foch, 1918; delegate at Paris Peace Conference, 1919; chairman of Inter-Allied Commission for Upper Silesia, 1920–22; Commander 9th Military District, 1923–26; retired, 1926.

France on frontiers, who was sitting at a Polish Committee in an adjoining room. LeRond was much impressed and said that, in the case of a joint Italo-Austrian attack, Jugoslavia would be helpless. This was very serious. I went into it again in the evening – with Col[onel] Henniker,[165] our railway expert, and Col[onel] Twiss.[166] The latter did not take quite the same strategic view. He said Laibach was indefensible anyhow. That, however, seemed to me no reason for giving it to Austria.

Finally, I saw Mance[167] – Gen[eral] – the head of all railway experts. He pointed out (1) that the railway triangle was the most important route to Vienna[;] that there was a second by Tarvis[168] – not so good – and a third by Pontebba,[169] possibly costly – but one which the Italians thought they could build as shown by previous negotiations with the Austrians.

It was a bad solution to have 3 powers on the same railway and our railway policy was, everywhere, to knock out the third power. Therefore, from the railway point of view, this railway triangle should be Italian or Austrian – and not Jugoslav – but, and it was the biggest of all buts, this most important of all railway solutions was our trump card in all negotiations for FIUME – SEBENICO – DALMATIA etc. Therefore we must play for keeping this trump card up our sleeves.

The position was thus very difficult. We had to play for keeping this trump card, and, on the face of it, could not bring in the FIUME area, because we were limited solely to defining the Austrian boundary.

Then a bright idea occurred to me – why not draw the boundary from point 1370, up to which it had already been defined, westwards along the Karawanken[170] to Tarvis – to say that north of this was the Austrian frontier

---

[165] Colonel Alan Major Henniker (1879–1949), soldier; entered Royal Engineers, 1889; active service, South Africa, 1900–1902; Chief Instructor, School of Military Engineering, 1908–12; Assistant Director of Railway Transport, War Office, 1914–Oct. 1915; Assistant Director of Railways, Oct. 1915–May 1917; Assistant Director of Transportation, May 1917–19; cf. his *Transportation on the Western Front* (London, 1937).

[166] Brigadier-General John Henry Twiss (1867–1941), soldier; entered Royal Engineers, 1885; Assistant Director of Railways, South Africa, 1899–1902; Director of Railway Transport, 1914–21; retired 1921.

[167] Brigadier-General Harry Osborne Mance (1875–1966), soldier; entered Royal Engineers, 1895; active service, South Africa as Railways Staff Officer, 1900–1902; Staff Captain, War Office, 1912–15; temporary Director Army Railway Department, War Office, Jan.–Apr. 1915; temporary Assistant Director of Railway Transport, Apr. 1915–Sept. 1916; Director of Railways, Light Railways and Roads, War Office, Sept. 1916–19; adviser to Ottoman Bank; Member of Transport and Communications Department, United Nations, 1946–54.

[168] Now Tarvisio in the northeastern part of Udine province (Italy), until 1919 Carinthia.

[169] Pontebba in the Friuli-Venezia-Guilia region of Italy, 30 miles north of Udine.

[170] The Karawanks, an Alpine mountain range along the Austro-Slovene border.

but not to adjudicate as to whether the triangle at present or Tarvis was either Jugoslav or Italian. This was necessary to in the interest of the All[ian]ce.

I filled [Allen] Leeper up with this, who promised to instruct Sir E[yre] Crowe in time for the next meeting at 9 a.m. the next day.

I got there early [10 May] – bounced 8.45 a.m. by mistake into the Rubens Hall and found old walrus-moustached Pichon already at work.

On the morning of the 10th Johnson opened the ball by pointing out the strategic dangers of letting the Austrians over the Carawanken [sic].

The Italians talked as wildly as before – the military representative being especially indiscreet – he said for them Austrians and Jugoslavs were equally enemies and that the Italians had nothing to fear from Austrian concentration here. Sacro egoismo did not allow them to say that it did not matter what the Jugoslavs had to fear.

After some other observations I took the field. I observed that the strategic danger to the Jugoslavs of permitting the Austrians to cross the Karawankens was obviously great. That, so far as I knew, it was the first instance of a terr[itor]y predominantly consisting of allies or friends being handed over to an enemy, and giving that enemy strategic advantages. Such a principle contravened ethnic justice and was difficult to defend in public.

I proposed therefore drawing the Austrian frontier westward along the Carawankens [sic] <to above TARVIS> and not deciding <at the moment> whether or no the railway triangle should be Jugoslav or Italian. A formula sh[oul]d, in all cases, be found to safeguard Italian free passage.

Sir Eyre Crowe expressed himself as frappé by that observations and strongly supported it.

The Italians grew wilder and wilder in their protests and wasted the whole morning on them. My proposal was embodied in writing and known as that of the British Delegation. The Italians, who became almost tearful, declined to accept it quoting their instructions. French, USA & British embodied their results in a formula, giving as little as possible offence to Italy in words, but making the intentions greatly clear. The Italians left very sorrowfully.

At 4 p.m. the Foreign Secretaries assembled in the Great Rubens Hall. Balfour spoke first, having had only 40 minutes coaching. He spoke finely – but as usual with blunders. He called the Carawanken [sic] the Alps, and said the Assling – Trieste rail[wa]y was double-tracked, and that there had been no strategic discussions at the Sub-committee. But he said we cannot hand over thousands of Slovenes to an enemy without very grave reasons. We are in this case against <bringing the enemy over> the natural line – the Karawankens – and at the same time violating ethnic justice, i.e. neglecting at the same time ethnology and topography. In the case of the Brenner[171] we agreed to neglect

---

[171] Brenner Pass, one of the principal Alpine passes along the Austro-Italian border.

ethnic considerations, in other cases topographic – but never at the same time. In case where strategic necessities have overcome ethnic justice, the arg[umen]ts have always been stronger, e.g. the Danzig question where Danzig is the single life line and harbour entrance to the Polish state. Now we must not violate both at once, and place an enemy in possession. Admirable despite blunders.

Lansing supported him very briefly saying we were bringing the Austrians down nearly to salt water and making them remember it again (only 20 km nearer said Sonnino[)]. He looked a little old and half asleep – the coffee brown eyes half closed – but every now and then he woke up and fired in a retort interrupting both Balfour and Lansing frequently. In a passage with the latter he had rather the best of it, in one with Balfour a little of the worst. He said the Slovenes were Austrians[.] 'Our friends, we have recognized them', retorted Lansing. The French representatives spoke hardly a word.

At last the proposals were read and put forward. 'I will accept', said Sonnino. There was a gasp of wonder – people did not realize even now that his great powers of resistance were at an end over this matter. He strove desperately however to secure that the Tarvis line should be hallmarked as Italian. This Balfour refused, saying free passage – not territorial right. Sonnino gave way again but, in a small explanation with Lansing, in which the latter, as he said was trying to help not hinder, Sonnino lost his temper and finally said, 'such an enmity to all our designs surprises me'. 'I must protest against that', said Mr Balfour – 'and I' said Lansing.

Sonnino gradually recovered balance. I picked up one of Lansing's fallen sketches – 2 gargoyles grotesque heads, got him to sign them for me – and said I would show it to the Jugoslavs when I returned there, as a memorial of the great victory won today by American aid.

In passing out Sonnino shook hands with me. 'If age but knew'.[172] He would not have done had he known my triumph to the full, I must say.

Everyone speaks of it as the British proposal – no one will know that it was really mine, though of course Mance helped me.

11th [May 1919]

Nothing today. P[rime] M[inister] told a friend of mine 3 days ago that the D[irector] of M[ilitary] I[ntelligence, Thwaites]'s letter – i.e. my letter – re Fiume came at a very important time, and assisted him in making up his mind. That and yesterday constitute my 'Nunc Dimittis'. If I do no more for Jugoslavia, I will still have done much to deserve well of her.

---

[172] Cf. *'si jeunesse savait, si vieillesse pouvait'* – 'if youth but knew, if age but could'.

12th [May 1919]

Went to the final Council for settling the boundaries of Austria-Hungary. P[rime] M[inister]s and Foreign Secretaries all present. Sonnino pleaded hard and ably for the Tarvis area to be assigned to Italy before the Austrian boundary was settled. He was opposed blandly by Balfour, and forcibly by Wilson. The latter fenced not altogether to his advantage with Sonnino. Sonnino said that thousands of Germans had been assigned to Czechs – and thousands of Magyars to <both Czechs and> Roumans – also with long stretches of railways. Wilson seemed surprised – and said 'recommended but not decided', which was either purely a verbal quibble or a revelation that he did not realize what had been happening. <Subsequently he said something about some mines in Assling which neither he nor anyone else understood.> Then arose a contest as to what numbers were involved in the Travis and triangle areas.

Then Clemenceau struck and [came] straight to the point with Sonnino. [']Do you move, or do you not move, that the decision as to the Austro-Hungarian boundaries be carried?['] Sonnino demurred – 'it is my wish that the this question <be> decided first'. Clemenceau pointed with his arm – 'Do you move that the Tarvis area be settled first?' 'No', said Sonnino. 'Ah well, let us vote on the other', said Clemenceau.

Lloyd George suddenly intervened, taking no notice whatever of the fact that Sonnino had at last been brought to assent without reservation. 'I am interested in this Klagenfurt question. It appears that there will be an inquest or plebiscite there, and that it is separated by a narrow ridge from the triangle area – the Rosenbach Tunnel[173] etc. Now if the people in the triangle voted for Austria, and the people in Klagenfurt for Jugoslavia, you would have an extraordinary situation, for the narrow ridge between is, I gather, Jugoslav. I think all this should be decided first before we vote the boundaries of Austria.[']

Pale grew every face in the British representation – this meant hanging up the whole thing, and Sonnino beamed. Balfour leaned over and spoke earnestly to L[loyd] G[eorge] and the rest of delegation whispered hurriedly. L[loyd] G[eorge] was so delighted with his own original observation that he had forgotten the real point. Order was speedily restored, and discussion began again.

M. Tardieu was now put up to explain that the recommendations of the committee were unanimous The gap was awkwardly bridged and L[loyd G[eorge] finally agreed not to press his point.

Then M. Cambon was put up to explain the Czecho-Slovak boundaries. This he did in the dullest possible manner and L[loyd] G[eorge]'s boredom

---

[173] Rosenbach, a village in central Carinthia at the northern entrance to the Karawanken Tunnel, linking Austria with Slovenia.

was increased by the fact that our delegation was provided with only one map without lines in red, and not the French map with additional details in blue and green ink. This, and his hurried inquiry behind, was quite enough to convince L[loyd] G[eorge] that it was impossible to understand this question and better to settle it at once – even though, by this process, our rulers handed over thousands of people to alien rule – on 'recommendations' of which Wilson <had previously> professed to know nothing, and of which L[loyd G[eorge] did not seem to know the maps. Incidentally, Clemenceau also said showed he did not really know what was going on. Thus Sonnino raised the point that, in settling the boundary of Austria, we did not mean that it was permanent. Clemenceau – a well-known anti-Austrian – at once said 'Yes', thus betraying ignorance of the experts. Wilson, however, now came out strong. He said that what we meant was that Austria ceded all points, beyond the defined boundaries to Jugos the Allied and Associated Powers. This did not mean that the latter could not give them back – or rather a part or piece of them, but that they (and not Austria) must decide on that. This hit the nail on the head, and was agreed to.

Then a somewhat futile discussion arose as to whether Austria and Hungary should have a revision of the boundary between them. L[loyd] G[eorge] said they were 2 states. Wilson said they had, under the Ausgleich,[174] shadows uniting them and it was desirable to lay these shadows. 'Let us therefore', he said, 'take the boundaries of 1866 – or whatever was the date before the Ausgleich – and leave them to claim rectifications, as I understand Austria to do'. Agreed.

Finally, someone elaborated the theory that all the Great Four had to do was to decide and not to discuss, i.e. if the recommendations of the committees were supported by the Foreign Ministers. L[loyd] G[eorge] promptly supported this – and the whole Austro-Hungarian boundaries were forthwith voted.

This means that the Great Four or Five had no powers, if their reporting Ministers and Committees were unanimous. If that be so, why did they talk all the afternoon?

A minor excitement was got up by the point raised by me with Mr Balfour that the frontier <of Austria was continued along> of the Carawankens was continued to a point n[orth] w[est] of Tarvis, which some thought was the Treaty of London. Crowe said it was 'to the Italian frontier'. It isn't, but no one cared. <A.J. B[alfour] leaning over the chairback backwards said airily – 'I had always realized with sorrow that I should never be able to spend my summer holidays again in Germany or France. Now I am afraid, after today, that I shall have to add Italy to the number.[']>

---

[174] The constitutional compromise of 1867 between the Austrian and Hungarian halves of the Austrian Empire that transformed the Habsburg monarchy into Austria-Hungary.

13th [May 1919]

There has been some dirty work recently over Asia Minor. It was discussed thoroughly in the absence of the Italians. In fact – it is a fact that the Great Three were actually discussing sending the Greeks to Smyrna, when Orlando walked into the room – 'What are you discussing', said he. 'Reparations', said the only one of the four [sic] who retained his presence of mind.

During the last fortnight Venizelos has had deep speech with everyone and won practically all his points. Wonderful man – too good for his country. L[loyd] G[eorge] helped him, but his victory was not difficult. L[loyd] G[eorge] Nicolson went to see L[loyd] G[eorge] the other day with a coloured map, the mountains done in fawn and deep brown[,] the river basins in green, and the Greeks coloured ethnographically in Asia Minor in dark green. This appears to have been the undoing of L[loyd] G[eorge]. He pointed out, saying are 'There are numbers of Greeks at Smyrna'. 'Yes' – 'and in the Meander[175] Valley'. 'Yes' – 'Ah, but there are lots more at Adana'. 'No, Sir, very few'. 'But how's that, aren't they green?' 'Yes, Sir, but not dark green'. 'What is the light green, then?' 'Rivers and flats, Sir'. 'H'm well, the next time you bring a map you ought to put some hills in it'. 'They are here, Sir, light and dark brown'. (I expect he thought they were Turks). 'Well, I see – I don't understand this'. (The only profound thing he said).

I understand there was a meeting today for the final disposition of Asia Minor. Somebody spoke of moral considerations. The Italians promptly laughed – so did L[loyd] G[eorge], but A.J.B[alfour] kept a straight face.

Then they got to business. Greece got Smyrna – Italy Koneh and Adana[176] – France the interior – USA mandate for Con[stantino]ple and Armenia. Nobody seemed to mind or know what the frontiers really were to within ten miles or so. The Turks are stuck on a high plateau, without means of subsistence and surrounded by deadly enemies.

15[th] [May 1919]

I was informed that I must be present tomorrow at the Serbo-Bulgar frontier and coach A.J.B[alfour] before it.

I prepared in case it was questioned a correction of the geographical mistakes in this area – maps and notes -.

---

[175] Now Büyük Menderes, a river in southwestern Turkey, reaching the Aegean near the ancient city of Miletus.

[176] Konya in central Anatolia, and Adana, on the river Seyhan in southern Turkey.

The initial and most disputed area is that of Tzaribrod, where the Serbs want an advance – to protect themselves against the approaches to Pirot.[177] They must not have too much for that would threaten Sofia and the compromise agreed upon was one which left the GINTSI and DRAGOMAN passes[178] in Bulgar hands, but improved the Serbian capacity for defence. The Americans had formulated objections to this, as being purely strategic and, of course, the Italians. I saw Johnson, however, in the evening, and he informed me that he was going to advise Lansing tomorrow morning – to accept this without qualification. This was a very useful piece of information.

16th [May 1919]

Proceeded with Crowe, Nicolson & Gen[era]l Mance to A.J. B[alfour]. The latter received us with great amiability – first Crowe explained about the proposed rectification of the Dobruja in favour of Bulgaria, but said it was a suggestion of Roumania. 'I don't dissent from that', said A.J. B[alfour] languidly stretching out his legs on his easy chair and putting up his pale white fingers together, 'but I should have thought Roumania is getting more out of the war than anyone else and consequently we could ask her to do this'. Crowe said the French were very jealous of interference, and we could hardly do it without agreement with them.

Next to the Greek question <Greek-Bulgar boundary>. A.J. B[alfour] found it difficult to understand the hopelessly confused map which Nicolson produced – and the equally confused manner in which he explained it, did not mend matters. However, after being satisfied that Adrianople was Greek, A.J. B[alfour] sailed ahead, only dropping one bad egg, when he asked if there was any Serb-Bulgar <difficulty in Thrace>. On the Serb-Bulgarian frontier, I first expounded the Strumitsa[179] salient. 'Who are the inhabitants?' 'Undoubted Bulgars'. Why – 'Well, Sir, Strumitsa is surrounded by a ring of mountains, which enabled comitadjis in old times to defend it – so the Serbs never expanded here.['] Then we got to Vranje,[180] which he passed over easily. The Tsaribrod – Dragoman pass position took much explaining, but he finally grasped it well – and his questions were intelligent. He returned to the Strumitsa question but I said the best proof – the essential justice of this rectification was that the Italians raised no objections to it. He agreed that there was much in this.

---

[177] Now Dimitrovgrad in southeastern Serbia, in the district of Pirot.
[178] Gintsi village near the Kom Peak in the Western Balkan mountains on the Serbo-Bulgarian border; Dragoman, a town in southwestern Bulgaria, the nearby pass was the site of battles in December 1443 and November 1885.
[179] Strumica on the eponymous river in eastern Macedonia.
[180] Vranje, a city in southern Serbia.

As we were going out Crowe got on the question of including Belgium in the Turco-Bulgar Treaties by name, as she was not at war with them and might be left out or disregarded. ['] Haven't you forgotten another similar power', said A.J. B[alfour] smiling, 'the United States – also not at war – with either'. 'She doesn't seem to mind', said Crowe. 'Perhaps she's big enough not to', said A.J. B[alfour].

At the meeting of the 4 Ministers for Foreign Affairs – amid the gorgeous Rubens tapestries on a sweltering day – after heavy lunches[:] 'The diplomats' dinners take place in fine weather. And they cut up their mutton and Europe together'.

Sleep was evident in the first ~~half~~ hour and little was done. It was decided not to touch the Greek frontier in Thrace for the moment – and not to approach Roumania in the fashion desired by Balfour. The latter finally said – 'We have been here an hour and decided nothing'. 'Can we not decide something', Sonnino grinned. Tardieu briefly explained the reasons for the desired strategic rectifications. Only one really mattered – the Dragoman pass area. Sonnino – suddenly solicitous about handing over one race to another – enquired if the inhabitants were not Bulgars. Tardieu said 7,700 only and race not very important. Balfour then spoke – as usual not expressing 'a strong view'. ~~Strong frontiers~~ 'There was no important question of population changing their sovereignty. The purpose was not to make a more defensible frontier. Strong frontiers, as a whole made for peace. The new frontier rendered Jugoslavia more defensible and did not imperil Bulgaria'. After an interval and a few questions, White and Pichon agreed – and Sonnino said 'Je ne m'oppose [pas]'.

I can claim a little credit for our sticking to our guns, by finding out beforehand that the USA would support us.

18th [May 1919]

On Friday night the Jugoslavs came with a great offer to the Americans and [Allen] Leeper, i.e. to give up frontier claims to the Klagenfurt basin – if they could have a line stretching from a p[oin]t s[outh] of St. Johann, just east of Klagenfurt and Villach[181] asking that it sh[oul]d be definitive and without plebiscite. Personally I disapprove of this because I doubt if any of the Klagenfurt basin is really pro-Jugoslav, and by this means the J[ugo]S[lavs] secure command of Klagenfurt and Villach and the respective railways, without imperilling their position by obtaining these essentially German towns. However, the

---

[181] Sankt Johann im Saggautal, near Leibnitz in Styria; Klagenfurt, capital of Austrian Carinthia; Villach on the river Drau (Drava) in southern Carinthia.

J[ugo]S[lavs] offered it – they claim also the PREKOMURJE[182] [*sic*]. On this I am heartly with them and also with some rectification of river areas.

19th [May 1919]

We came to a preliminary discussion with the diff[eren]t Allies on the subcommittee as to the Klagenfurt offer. Martino, the Italian, promptly raised a point of principle that he had only seen the map that morning, whereas others had several days. Tardieu genially responded with a thumping whacker to the effect that he had only heard of it the night before, which can only be true in the official sense. Martino announced that he wished to settle everything on the compromise basis, not on the ethnic, but on a mixture of economic, ethnographic and political necessities, in other words, so as to justify the Italian attempt to grab Tarvis and so many Slovenes in the west. The meeting was adjourned for detailed discussion to the next day, when it was arranged that the Jugoslavs should be heard in person.

20th [May 1919]

The Jugoslav deputation turned up in fine form. Trumbić[183] asked for an extension of the frontier in the Backa Crijic, in the Baranya-Vestnich, in the Prek Murye [*sic*] and Zholger [*sic*] in the Klagenfurt area. They spoke well and to the point on the whole and shortly, the latter a suggestion of Zholger. Afterwards I entertained Popovich and Zholger to lunch with Curtis,[184] in order to deal with the problem of South African Union from the standpoint of Jugoslavs. They listened with great attention to Curtis, who argued, on general principles, for a Central Assembly with an unlimited right of interference in local affairs. He argued strongly for the preservation of local autonomous assemblies on the ground of time, local particularism and specialised interests.

In the afternoon we settled in principle that no further rectification of the Serbo-Bulgar frontier or the Banat or Bačka should take place, but that some

---

[182] See entry 13 Apr. 1919.
[183] See entry 21 Nov. 1918.
[184] Lionel George Curtis (1872–1955), academic and public servant; called to the bar, 1902; volunteered for service in South Africa, 1899–1900; assistant imperial secretary to Sir Alfred Milner as Governor-General, Cape Colony, 1900–1901, and subsequently prominent member of 'Milner's Kindergarten'; assistant colonial secretary, Transvaal province, 1903–1906; founder-editor, *The Round Table*, 1909; Beit Lecturer in Colonial History, Oxford, 1912–13; Fellow of All Souls, 1921–55; member of Lord Robert Cecil's League of Nations section at Paris Peace Conference, 1919; co-founder, Royal Institute of International Affairs, 1919.

changes should be made in the Baranya,[185] and in the Prekomurje. I settled the case for the latter by quoting some statistics showing its predominantly Slav character.

21st [May 1919]

Details of above were worked out at a Committee, General LeRond presiding. The Prekomurje [*sic*] **went** through without difficulty though the General was not very pleased at my reference to this as a prime defect of the previous report.

We drew a line at the Baranya not altogether as I wished over the crests of vineclad hills, just south of the 2 sub-centres Baranyavar and Kisfalud.[186] I had sought vainly the night before and that morning to get information as to viticulture, though I had all the agricultural statistics. No-one in the Jugoslav delegation could inform me. Then at last, while I was in a meeting, and too late to alter the decision, they brought a priest round, ironically enough an inhabitant of Kisfalud. He said the properties of the vineyards lay on the north for the most part. Poor devil, he little knew we were signing away his birthright at the moment.

I went back to the meeting and tried to get some reconsideration[,] taking the line a little north of the hills.

The French wanted a strategic line higher up, the Italians said these hills, if going to the Jugoslavs, would be entrenched and form a basis of concentration. Knowing I had had a verbal interview they demanded documentary proofs of the properties. Finally I withdrew from my position. The next line prevented Jugoslav aggression and I had already laid down as a basis that this affair was simply to draw a good frontier, because the Danube shifted its bed and that the ethnographic basis could not be taken. My words were true – the most Serbian part was excluded, and districts chiefly Magyar and German included. From the ethnographic scientific point of view, however, justice was done.

22 [May 1919]

Saw the results of Montagu's meeting with the Frocks <The Great Four>, when he brought Hindus and Mahommedans together to protest against the turning of the Turks out of Con[stantino]ple and Asia Minor. He required some bolstering up before this meeting, and the nurse told me she was to give him

---

[185] Baranja, geographical region between the Danube and Drava, now divided between Hungary and Croatia.

[186] Baranjavár, now Branjin Vrh, and Kisfalud, now Branjin, in the Croatian part of Baranja.

Bovril and a hypodermic of strychnine. I implored her in the interest of British Empire to inject the Bovril and give him the strychnine to drink.

23 [May 1919]

Final meeting to settle with 4 Foreign Secretaries transfer of Bukovina,[187] <Transylvania> & Banat to Roumania. Lansing took up hotly the question of the Dobruja. In the southern part there are 60,000 Bulgars, 50,000 Turks, 867 Roumanians. There was a certain old world fervour in his attitude which was strange to the others. But tactically he was unfortunate in trying to make the cession of the Banat depend on the retrocession of the S[outhern] Dobruja. Balfour, tho[ugh] I know he approved of every word Lansing said, supported him feebly.

25 [May 1919]

Was told in great secrecy today that the Frocks had determined to recognise Koltchak.[188] I pointed out that it was all in the 'Daily Mail' of this morning. This is interesting because only the great Four and Philip Kerr knew, outside the military.

On the whole a fruitful week something really done to settle the Russian question, decisions to assist the Esths [*sic*], progress made with Austrian treaty, much done in Syria.

C[hief of the] I[mperial] G[eneral] S[taff, Wilson] has a map story. The other day he assisted at a conference of the Four. L[loyd] G[eorge] partly sat on our map, partly trampled on it, and pointed out the importance of Mogador[189] to the other three. 'Mogador' said they all, looking at the map on the table. 'Where is it?' None of them could find it. Finally, L[loyd] G[eorge] turned to C[hief of the] I[mperial] S[taff][:] 'Where is it?' 'If you take your great foot aside you'll see it'. He did!

---

[187] Bukovina, region on the northern slopes of the Eastern Carpathians and the surrounding plains, traditionally centred on Czernowitz, now Chernivtsi (Ukraine).

[188] Aleksandr Vasili'evich Kolchak (1874–1920), Russian sailor; entered navy, 1894; polar expedition, 1900–1902; on active service, Russo-Japanese War, 1904–1905; Vice-Admiral commanding Black Sea fleet, Aug. 1916–June 1917; on mission to Britain and USA, June 1917–Jan. 1918; minister in Siberian Regional Government, Jan.–Nov. 1918; Supreme Ruler of Russia, Nov. 1918–Jan. 1920; executed, Feb. 1920.

[189] Essaouira on the Moroccan Atlantic coast.

26 [May 1919]

On 21st Winston wrote a fine memo[randum] ag[ain]st occupying Germany, in favour of reaching a peace settlement. 'The same crowd that is now so vociferous for ruthless terms of peace will spin round tomorrow ag[ain]st the Gov[ernmen]t if a military breakdown occurs thro[ugh] the dwindling forces at our disposal. It is quite another thing to spread these young troops we have over large areas of Germany holding down starving populations, living in houses with famished women and children, firing on miners and working people maddened by despair. Disaster of the most terrible kind lies along that road and I solemnly warn the Government of the peril of proceeding with it. I consider that we shall commit a political error of the first order if we are drawn into the heart of Germany on these conditions. You cannot carve up and distribute at pleasure the populations of three or four enormous Empires with a few hundred thousand war-weary conscripts and 150,000 slowly organising volunteers.

Now is the time, and it may be the only time, to reap the fruits of victory "Agree with thine adversary while thou art in the way with him". ... The British Empire is in a very fine position at the present moment and we now require a peace which will fix and recognise that position. Let us beware lest in following too far Latin ambitions and hatreds we do not create a new situation in which our advantages will largely have disappeared. Settle now while we have the power or lose victory perhaps forever the power of settlement on the basis of military victory'.

27 [May 1919]

Went at 10 to see Jugoslav Commission. The Italians had a few proposal to make, with regard to the new adjustments of the Klagenfurt are, the Prekomurye, and the Baranya. It really had nothing to do with them and concerned simply the point that they had only agreed to this on the principle of compensation and that they w[oul]d agree to it unless they got Tarvis they w[oul]d not agree to anything. They had 3 speakers each with a different and mutually destructive line of argument. (1) Tarvis was vital to them <and had not been claimed in the last demands of the Jugoslavs>. (2) It was in the Treaty of London. (3) It was in the armistice which was an interpretation. After the Am[erica]n Delegation and Crowe had shown their hands, Tardieu genially observed to Martino that he thought personally Tarvis might go to them but that it was only within the competence of the 4 to settle such a question. We then left and went to Balfour. Crowe explained his policy as that of signing the Treaty of London but nothing more, while he knew America w[oul]d not sign the treaty.

Balfour seized on the point that the omission of the Jugoslavs to ~~seize~~ claim Tarvis had wrecked their claim on the Klagenfurt, Prekomurye [*sic*] and Baranya. He added wearily 'The Italians make me sick, perfectly sick – they are worse than the Fr[ench]'.

<u>Afternoon</u> A meeting of the Great Four & Foreign Secretaries to settle the frontiers of Austria. <It was at Wilson's house, a fine room with magnificent paintings and bric-à-brac cabinets and deep red carpets & curtains.> Wilson spoke, and very finely, stating that there were strong reasons over the Klagenfurt basin from not departing <the principle of maintaining> an economic unity. Just as we have fixed the natural walls of Italy on the basis of giving her 750,000 Slovenes, on the ground of a natural frontier, so we had to consider the natural frontier of Austria in the Klagenfurt basin. The slopes of the Carawanken were steeper on the south than on the north and consequently <it was> harder to go north than to come south from the crest.

So he ended – the result was extraordinary <– complete collapse>. We did not want to give up Klagenfurt, without a struggle or a plebiscite, because it might advantage the Italians. A.J. B[alfour] said sotto voce to L[loyd] G[eorge] 'Nothing is bad enough for them.['] Ll[oyd] G[eorge] sat back in his chair, and called us up. I said 2 things to him[:] (1) that Tarvis was our most valuable pawn in the whole box[;] (2) that Wilson wanted to give the Austrians the Klagenfurt basin without conditions, because he thought the Slovenes were not very pro-Jugoslav. [']Oh is that so['], said L[loyd]G[eorge][, ']then we have material for a bargain.['] Then Tardieu came up and said[:] 'I have a plan to settle the Adriatic question in 24 hours'. '24'[,] said L[loyd]G[eorge] blankly[,] 'you're optimistic'. Then L[loyd] G[eorge] went off to Clemenceau, and spoke 'Let's keep them here – we shan't want the experts and adjourn the meeting. <The true solution of the Klagenfurt basin, I have just thought, is to give the Austrians a mandate there. I should like to see our little Mr. Hughes there, I really should like to see him.['] Clemenceau groaned.> Then Mr. Balfour in very bad French began dissenting.

'I want to keep my friend Sonnino' said Clemenceau and both [Clemenceau and Lloyd George] laughed uproariously. Then they and A.J. B[alfour] and Tardieu got together talking about Tarvis and Assling. 'Don't let the Italians hear' said A.J. B[alfour].

L[loyd]G[eorge] 'We'll disagree – get into your most disagreeable mood' and they laughed uproariously like schoolboys. Then L[loyd]G[eorge] rushed off and talked earnestly to Wilson, then he drew Orlando aside and spoke in the embrasure for a few minutes earnestly with him.

Meanwhile A.J.B[alfour] was chaffering with Clemenceau on the merits of peasant proprietors, as stable and good fighters but as impossible in England. L[loyd]G[eorge] came back to Clemenceau and Clemenceau spoke about the arrival of Paderewski[:]¹⁹⁰ 'I believe Paderewski when I don't see him' said L[loyd]G[eorge]. 'I don't believe him when I see him' retorted Clemenceau. 'Now we'll adjourn and do without the experts' said L[loyd]G[eorge]. 'I am glad that we can do that' said A.J. B[alfour] 'because I shall get some good tennis' – then sotto voce to Crowe 'that is good – when the premier adjourns a thing it means he is beginning to take an interest in it'. The Ten remained behind – the compromise proposal will be known tonight and the result Prosit Jugoslavia! I fancy it is to make a Saar valley¹⁹¹ of the Fiume-Tarvis-Assling triangle.

I had an interesting interview with Lansing before the meeting opened. He said he greatly disliked the Italians. But he said he thought it a great mistake to try and force Austria and Germany apart. Even if successful politically it would not be successful practically. They would find some way of linking up. Far better to give them the power and hope they won't do it.

29 [May 1919]

'A unique occasion today at which I congratulate you on being present'[,] said the spruce secretarial Mr. Norman¹⁹² to me on leaving. It was no less that this – the Great Four summoned the experts to Wilson's House at 11 to discuss the Klagenfurt basin – they however rejected the Foreign Secretaries. Lloyd George met us on the stairs, demanding maps, and entered into the conclave. The usual interval followed – then suddenly Wilson appeared, radiant behind his glasses, and carrying a large map, which he spread on the carpet and, kneeling down, expounded to the experts. 'We have decided'[,] he said[,] 'to make the whole Klagenfurt basin one area, where there shall be a plebescite after six months, during which International Commission shall administer affairs there with the local authorities. The Sexten valley¹⁹³ is ceded to Italy. Tarvis is ceded to Italy, otherwise we follow the Treaty of London line in the area.['] The Italian expert at once scented a rat in the Rosenbach tunnel area. According to the old

---

¹⁹⁰ Ignacy Jan Paderewski (1860–1941), Polish pianist, composer and politician; international musical career before 1914; member of Polish National Committee, 1916–18; Prime Minister and Foreign Minister, Jan.–Dec. 1919; ambassador to the League of Nations, 1920–22; returned to musical life; head of Polish National Council in exile, 1940–41.

¹⁹¹ The Saar territory in southwestern Germany was occupied by France under a League of Nations mandate for a period of 15 years, its coal industry nationalized and administered by France.

¹⁹² Herman Cameron Norman (1872–1955), diplomat; entered diplomatic service, 1894; transferred to Foreign Office, 1906; secretary to London peace conference, 1912–13; secretary of legation at Buenos Ayres, 1914–15; counsellor of embassy at Tokyo, 1915–20; member of British delegation at Paris Peace Conference, 1919; minister at Tehran, 1920–21; *en disponibilité* since 1921; privy chamberlain of sword and cape to Pope Pius XI, 1925–55.

¹⁹³ Sextental, in South Tyrol, near Innichen and Toblach where the river Drau (Drava) rises.

definition the tongue of land lying to the north and including the north end of the Rosenbach tunnel was to be Austrian, with the curious result that if the Klagenfurt area went Jugoslav and the Assling triangle went Jugoslav they would be separated by an intervening tongue of territory. This was the subtlety which had attracted Lloyd George on one occasion, and this no doubt was the reason it was now to be set right.

The Italians intervened, Vannutelli Rey[194] and Pariani.[195] 'There is one little point, Mr. President'. Mr. President beamed amiably behind his glasses. 'It is a very small matter but this bit of tunnel should remain Austrian'. 'Oh no'[,] said he[,] 'we've thought a good deal about that. We've decided it shan't be, unless the plebiscite decides it shall'. Then among the Italians reigned consternation. The next point that followed was, is the Assling triangle to be under the plebiscite? Accounts differ as to what Wilson said, and no stenographer was there. <He did however certainly say north of the Rosenbach tunnel is Austria's business, south of it is none of her business. Also, when the Italians said it's a very small concession, he said 'I am not here to give concessions but to find out what people want'. This with a steely shimmer in his eye.> So we went away. Wilson was so radiant and Lloyd George knew that Tarvis was our most important pawn so that I cannot believe they have surrendered it without gaining important quids pro quo. As the previous negotiations broke down over Zara and Sebenico,[196] which the Italians wished to retain, I infer that they have given way at least over Sebenico. Ll[oyd] G[eorge] looked genial and drank mineral water.

The Italians gave some trouble in defining the boundary when we adjourned to the Quai d'Orsay. Both insisted that Wilson had said that there was to be a plebiscite in the Assling triangle in 6 months. This was important because it would deprive us of yet another pawn in negotiation. Leeper and Johnson said they w[oul]d see Wilson at lunch time and bring his words in writing.

They did, but in going to the Quai d'Orsay I missed my way and got into the Plenary Session of Powers to receive the Austrian Treaty. Wilson said good afternoon very genially, Clemenceau nodded, and for the first time I saw the dark melancholy eyes of Foch. I got away as soon as possible. Lloyd George was absent.

---

[194] Luigi, Count Vannutelli Rey (1880–1968), Italian diplomat; member of Italian delegation at Paris Peace Conference, 1919; minister at Prague, 1928–30; Warsaw, 1931–32; ambassador at Brussels, 1932–36.

[195] Alberto Pariani (1876–1955), Italian soldier; commanded 6th *Alpini* regiment, 1917–18; delegate at Paris Peace Conference, 1919; Chief of Operations, Army General Staff, 1925–26; military attaché and head of the Italian military mission at Tirana, 1927–33; Deputy Chief of General Staff, 1934–36; Chief of Staff and Under-secretary, War Ministry, 1936–39; retired, 1939; recalled as commander of Italian forces in Albania, 1943; arrested and imprisoned in Germany, 1943; imprisoned in Italy, 1945–47, but acquitted, 1947.

[196] Now Zadar and Šebenik on the northern Dalmatian coast.

Leeper and Johnson returned with a categorical statement of Wilson's views. Leeper said he had been most genial. He absolutely denied the Italian assertion as to the plebiscite in the Assling triangle. They sustained however that an unofficial minute of Hankey's[197] intialled by the 4 supported their view. They argued with heat, and gradually we realized that they were asserting that Johnson & Leeper were liars, but of course behind the veil. The advent of Tardieu however put an end to this, who ruled that there was no such question implied. The Italians spent the rest of the afternoon in quarrelling about particular peaks. I instructed Ogilvie[198] to do his best to keep them on the crests of hills and not to give offensive military advantages to them.

1st June [1919]

I heard a good deal about the plenary session from Leeper, none of it like the papers. M. Tardieu did not introduce a general description of the treaty as they say. On the contrary he spoke only a few words. Bratianu[199] opened by complaining that he had not received his copy of the Treaty on Thursday, but on Friday at 6 p.m. – consequently, instead of having 48 hours to study it, he had only 18. Clemenceau at once rudely interrupted him denying his facts and saying he was insulting the Peace Conference. After this furious breeze Bratinau proceeded. He objected to the Bukovina frontier being decided, because the representatives there (<sotto voce> when no Ruthenes were consulted) were unanimous for cession to Roumania. Then he touched on the clauses for protection of minorities of other nation[ali]ties to be absorbed in Roumania, whose rights were protected by the Great Powers. This he said was an insult first because their rights were safe, second because the Great Powers, and not the League of Nations, were the guarantors. Here again Clemenceau interposed furiously[:] 'It's not the Big Powers but the League of Nations'. 'Oh no'[,] said Bratianu blandly[,] 'let me read the article'. He did and even Clemenceau was silenced. Poor old man, the pain in his body affects his temper at times. Bratianu followed this up with some ridiculous promises about the Jews.[200]

---

[197] See entry 5 Nov. 1917.

[198] Captain Alan Grant Ogilvie (1887–1954), geographer and soldier; entered Royal Field Artillery, 1911; demonstrator in geography, Oxford, 1912–14; active service, France, Dardanelles and Salonika, 1914–18; Staff Officer in Geographical Section, War Office, 1918–19; technical delegate at Paris Peace Conference, 1919; Reader in Geography, Manchester University, 1919–20; Lecturer then Reader, Edinburgh University, 1923–31; Professor of Geography, 1931–52; cf. his *Some Aspects of Boundary Settlement at the Peace Conference* (London, 1922).

[199] See entry 19 Dec. 1916.

[200] The treatment of Romania's Jewish minority had been an issue of Great Power politics since the Congress of Berlin, 1878.

Trumbić followed also protesting ag[ain]st the minority clauses, saying that Jugoslavia was willing to submit to them but not the Kingdom of Serbia (i.e. including Macedonia). This made the worst impression on all concerned.

Paderewski followed, declaring he could not suffer Poland to put up with these minority clauses.

Wilson then made a long and rather fine speech saying, among other things, that the U.S.A. might, under certain circumstances, send an army to Serbia to protect her territorial integrity, but it c[oul]d no do so, unless assured that justice w[oul]d reign in Jugoslavia, and that he hoped his friend Dr. Trumbić w[oul]d not press these clauses.

2 June [1919]

Notes of meeting of 1st June of British Empire Delegation.

Smuts impossible – to sign it a real disaster not only to Brit[ish] Empire but also to the world and this disaster comparable in magnitude only to the war itself. It was meant to be a 'Wilson Peace'. The Allies must keep their agreement. 1. They must not end the war by making the armistice agreement another scrap of paper. 2nd point. War aims of Jan[uary] and Sept[ember] 1918 bedrock. 3rd Doc[umen]t itself was 'not just and c[oul]d not be durable'.

Far too much of the French element in the Peace. It was called an English peace but it was nothing of the sort; mil[itar]y occupation for 15 years was indefensible. Internat[ionlizatio]n of German rivers a gr[ea]t mistake. 'Poland was an historic failure and always w[oul]d be a failure'. As the doc[umen]t stood he c[oul]d not sign it.

Massey[201] agreed with very little of Smuts. G[erman]y caused the war, lost the war and sh[oul]d be compelled to pay as far as possible. Immunity from punishment encouraged.

Ch[urchill] agreed largely with S[muts] and said weapons of blockade and occupation were mutually exclusive. The hatred of France for Germany was something more than human "split the difference peace".

["Billy"] Hughes[202] agreed largely with Wilson's points, confirmed by P.M. In favour of conceding nothing. Germans a nation of liars whose words could not be trusted.

Milner We sh[oul]d restrain France now as we did Prussia in 1815.

---

[201] William ('Farmer Bill') Ferguson Massey (1856–1925), New Zealand politician; MP (Conservative, since 1909 Reform), Waitemata, 1894–96, Franklin, 1896–1925; Prime Minister, 1912–25.

[202] See entry 9 June 1917.

Barnes[203] agreed with Smuts. Finance impossible and Labour thought it bad and dangerous.

Montagu said Hughes objected to the Armistice since the 14 p[oin]ts did bind the Allies – there was a good deal of rather discursive talk in which Austen C[hamberlain] figured not very brightly – and Milner heavily intervened.

L[loyd] G[eorge], who had ably held the chair, kept himself to the last.

A.J. B[alfour] contributed some bright remarks chiefly on the 14 Points and how it came about that they were accepted. 'There had to be an armistice. Time was the essence of the matter. They had no option but to take the 14 Points. They made some corrections in them and they were supplemented by some perorations' – 'the 14 p[oin]ts were incapable of being treated in a strictly legal manner, and e.g. in case of Italy Presid[en]t Wilson had not kept them himself'.

Re Poland all agreed with P[rime] M[inister]'s suggestion (plebiscites in certain areas). 'Poland had behaved quite abominably and mismanaged her affairs'. 'But why should there be faith in Germany altering her course, and no hope – he would not go so far as to say confidence – in Poland behaving as a reasonably civilized state?!' Then he wandered off into a financial morass.

L[loyd] G[eorge] 'disc[ussio]n very creditable to British Empire. It has taken the form of an earnest and sometimes a passionate plea for justice for the fallen enemy.['] He thought they erred rather on the side of consideration for the enemy. There was no note of vengeance. He thought it an extraordinary tribute to the temper of the British Empire that under such circ[umstance]s there could be a discussion in such a spirit. He was sure that the Germans w[oul]d not have believed it to be possible.

The first thing was to have an absolutely just peace. <They must have no hesitation in admitting that they were wrong, and they must modify our terms> but they must also see that the terms were expedient as well as just. Justice was a question which the Germans are at liberty to raise but expediency was a matter for the Allies to consider not the Germans.

Eastern frontiers. Allies had gone too far and that sh[oul]d be put right. (Views app[arentl]y accepted) Army of Occupation – a question of expediency rather than of justice.

He wished not to press on the Saar valley question on L[eague] of Nations. <He> w[oul]d take an indulgent view of admitting Germany to League, if she would sign.

On compens[atio]n gr[ea]t diff[icultie]s – he w[oul]d like to make the Germans do the reparation without naming the sum, and paying[,] say[,] £3,000,000,000 to cover the rest – this to be divided acc[ording] to casualties.

Re Army of Occup[atio]n <for 15 years> – not a mil[itar]y prop[ositio]n at all. Foch wanted really 30 or 40 years. 'The French w[oul]d give up nothing

---

[203] See entry 29 Apr. 1919.

unless forced – the hatred of the French for the Germans was something inconceivable – it was savage and he did not blame them for it. He had seen most of the devastated areas, but he did not think the British Empire w[oul]d allow the future of the peace of the world to be tied to the chariot of French fury. When in his speech at Versailles Rantzau spoke of an atmosphere of hatred he had said a thing that was terrible but true. The French w[oul]d not concede anything unless we c[oul]d say to them[:]

(1) Unless the French agreed to the proposed concessions no British troops w[oul]d advance to Berlin[.] (2) No British ships w[oul]d be employed to starve the Germans. It was sometimes necessary to starve women and children as an operation of war, but it was poor business at best. We were entitled to say that we c[oul]d not inflict these horrors on the pop[ulatio]n to enforce anything we thought was unjust or unfair. Was the British Delegation prepared to adopt that attitude? W[oul]d his colleagues support him if he said that he c[oul]d not ask the British Parliament to sanction the nec[essa]ry measures for an enforcement of the Treaty unless the French w[oul]d make def[ini]te concessions in that direction. It was no use his going to the Four next day and saying his colleagues said so & so. If he merely said that[,] M. Clemenceau w[oul]d say he c[oul]d not help it and that he was going on.[']

Churchill said 'already it was the greatest triumph in the history of the world'.

L[loyd]G[eorge] pressed for unanimous support. Clemenceau was a man with a sense of justice but he was in a position of very great difficulty in view of the opinion which was behind him, but if he knew he had to face his own extremists or to march forward without the British Empire he w[oul]d be willing to discuss.

Gen[eral] Botha[204] was against occupying Berlin but was for the P[rime] M[inister] and for getting Germany to sign. [']If the Germans refused to sign they w[oul]d be getting towards the position in which they w[oul]d be able to dictate to the Allies.['] He understood the position and the feelings of the Germans because he had had to make peace.

L[or]d Milner would remember that it was exactly 17 years on that day when peace was signed in S[outh] Africa. On that occasion it was moderation which had saved the South Africa for the British Empire and he hoped on this occasion that it w[oul]d be moderation that saved the world.

Res[olutio]ns

(1) modification of E[astern] Frontiers.
(2) Some sort of promise re League of Nations.
(3) modif[icatio]n re forces and duration of Army of Occupation.

---

[204] See entry 21 Aug. 1916.

(4) Rep[aratio]n (1.) to be effected by Germans themselves, & then lump cash sum to be offered.
(2.) In case of recalcitrance <on part of France> – full weight of British Empire even to extent of refusing services of British army in advance.
(3.) services of British navy in Blockade.

H.A.L. Fisher, like [Henry] Wilson, attended this great debate but without speaking, except on finance, thus missing his only real chance of making as well as writing history.

5th [June 1919]

A recent mot of Clemenceau's is that, while Orlando was absent, he found it difficult to work with two men, one of whom he thought was Napoleon and the other Christ – the old rascal.

J.T. Davies[205] told me today how Napoleon (L[loyd] G[eorge]) prepared his speeches, i.e. when they were set ones[:] (1) He wrote down himself or dictated every word at full length usually at night. Then he threw it over to a secretary who typed it and put it under his bedroom door. About 6 a.m. he often woke up and revised it carefully in detail, changing and striking out everything. This was again corrected by the typist. Finally he reduced every paragraph to about 5 words – and threw away the material, and retained only the main heads. Just before the prep[aratio]n of a speech he was always anxious, irritable & absorbed. J.T.D[avies] also told me that, when he was first secretary, he discovered 9 or 10 old sacks of papers, many of which contained L[loyd]G[eorge]'s speeches of old, written out in his own hand, containing the minutest corrections over and over again. So the principle of the conservation of energy still holds.

6th June [1919]

Another meeting of the Jugoslav territorial Commission on the eternal Klagenfurt question <& the plebescite>. The proposal which found most favour was to divide the Klagenfurt basin into 2 areas – A & B.

A area that claimed by the Jugoslavs (v[ide] 18th May). B area that claimed by the Germans <and considered undoubtedly German>.

It was considered that the best plan was to put district A under Jugoslav administration and district B under German. The Jugoslav International

---

[205] (Sir) John Thomas Davies (1881–1938), private secretary to Lloyd George, 1915–22; British government director of Suez Canal Company, 1922–38.

Commission was to have the general and supreme control over both until the plebiscite was taken. The time as to the plebiscite varied – 3 years is probably the least the Jugoslavs will accept. An amendment on these lines was drafted.

The Italians suddenly objected, saying that the original instruction of the Great Four to the Committee was vague and general. Tardieu blandly asked them to point out defects in details. They refused – then he said it was impossible to criticize the Four, but the Italians c[oul]d send up a special memorandum if they thought good. Then the cloven hoof appeared. Vannutelli Rey proposed to sever the Klagenfurt basin not laterally along the Wörther See, but vertically. This corresponded, he said, to the wishes of the inhabitants (the first time since I have seen any Italian solicitude for them) and, more important, gave to Austria the north end of the Rosenbach tunnel. Crowe, prompted by me, interposed and stated that, at the meeting of the 29th, Vannutelli Rey had asked Wilson that very question and he had definitely said that that was included in the plebiscite area (v[ide] 29th [May 1919]).

Vannutelli Rey blushed but did not deny it. Martino whisperingly pleaded to give this span of railway, 10 kilometres only, which was vital to Italy.

However, the Committee maintained its view – thereupon Martino added a long protest and suggestion on behalf of Italy.

Finally, Martino summed up rather in the style of Sonnino on another occasion (10th May). 'I regret in conclusion that, in all proceedings, I have observed enmity to Italy and a parti pris taken by all the other nations. I except you personally, Mr. Chairman' (looking at Tardieu). Tardieu [']I regret your opinion. We have all tried to respect your views.['] Martino 'I speak against none of you personally, I speak pour l'histoire'.

This was too much – the various delegates fell back in attitudes of ease and peals of laughter ran round the room. One polite Frenchman rushed into the other room and came out with a large bottle of port and a glass which he offered to Martino, to cool his fervour. We all laughed greatly, even Martino himself. Afterwards it struck me 'the noblest answer unto such'[206] had been given. None of the 3 delegations thought it worth while refuting him. As for history and the accusation of the parti pris by us or America or even by France, history will regard Italy as the Irishman who disagreed with the rest of the jury, and then said "Until now I never saw eleven more obstinate men in my life".

---

[206] 'The noblest answer unto such,/ Is kindly silence when they brawl', Alfred Lord Tennyson, 'The After Thought', *Punch*, 7 Mar. 1846.

8th [June 1919]

<The Hungarian Bolsheviks are everywhere driving back the CzechoSlovaks.> After many attempts to raise the Bela Kun[207] question, which emanated largely from my room tho[ugh] more from Twiss than from me[,] L[loyd] G[eorge] finally took it up. There was a full dress discussion by the 4 with military experts at Versailles. As a result a telegram was despatched to Bela Kun of an amazing character (1) saying that it had been intended to invite him to the Conf[eren]ce[;] (2) saying that the Roumanians had twice been stopped from smashing him[;] saying that it was the inflexible will of the Allies that he sh[oul]d at once cease hostilities. This contained 3 blunders[:] (1) it in effect gave Bela Kun recognition[;] (2) it admitted Roumania had done wrong[;] (3) it threatened without real power to enforce.

9 [June 1919]

Today L[loyd]G[eorge] and the other gr[ea]t Four and some Generals held a meeting about Bela Kun. Wilson asked for information of a military character. Gen[eral] Wilson gave it and said Czechoslovak sit[uation]n vis-à-vis Hungarians was very bad, but that Czechoslovaks had just overstepped the line.

L[loyd]G[eorge] then intervened quoting a person just returned from Budapest (i.e. Ashmead Bartlett).[208] He complained that the Roumanians had overstepped two boundary lines fixed by Franchet d'Esperey, ag[ain]st his orders, and the result had been to madden the Hungarians. The CzechoSlovaks also advanced to seize the coal basins of PECS,[209] the only coal-bearing area remaining within the <new> state of Hungary. <Double error. He meant Miskolcz.[210] Pecs is far to the south and in Jugoslav hands, and is not the only coal area.> The fault lay entirely with the Roumanians.

---

[207] Béla Kun (née Kuhn) (1886–1938), Hungarian revolutionary; journalist before 1914; active service, 1914–16; Prisoner of War in Russia, 1916–17; founded Hungarian Communist Party, Nov. 1918; proclaimed Soviet Republic, 21 Mar. 1919; People's Commissar for Foreign Affairs, Mar.–Aug. 1919; in exile in Vienna, 1919; in Moscow, 1919–38; leading figure in Comintern; executed during Stalin's purges, 1938.

[208] Ellis Ashmead-Bartlett (1881–1931), journalist and politician; on active service, South Africa, 1900–1901; war correspondent, Russo-Japanese War, 1904–1905; Reuters war correspondent, 1901–11; war correspondent, *Daily Telegraph*, 1912–18; National Press Association representative at Gallipoli, 1915; special mission to central Europe, 1919; involved in anti-Kun intrigues in Hungary; MP (Cons.) Hammersmith North, 1924–26; special correspondent, *Daily Telegraph*, 1926–31.

[209] Pécs in the Mecsek mountains in southwestern Hungary.

[210] Miskolc, an industrial city in northeastern Hungary.

He said Slovaks had become Bolshevik.

'Roumania defied the Four' – 'The Paris writ was not running'. Consequently, all supplies should be stopped until they came to heel. In the past the small Balkan states had defied every order issued from Paris and, having got themselves into trouble, invariably appealed to Paris to extricate them from their difficulties. He agreed with President Wilson that the question should be settled by the Council of Four without consulting the small Powers concerned.

10th [June 1919]

Ashmead-Bartlett's views <to L[loyd] G[eorge]> were quite interesting. He is a reactionary of reactionaries, and thinks the Magyar and Austrian aristocrats should be restored. He carried with him, among other things, a statement signed by the counter-revolutionary government at SZEGEDIN[211] making certain promises, as the calling of an assembly etc. This he showed with gr[ea]t triumph to L[loyd] G[eorge], who seemed to be profoundly impressed, and pocketed the original petition. Ashmead Bartlett came away thinking he had won L[loyd]G[eorge] over to his views completely. It is a lesson in disillusionment, for L[loyd] G[eorge] simply used his information to support the argument for voting for Bela Kun. I don't know whether A[shmead] B[artlett] or L[loyd] G[eorge] were responsible for the howlers about the coalbasins of Pecs.

11th [June 1919]

Meeting of the 5 today which I attended. We were instructed by the Four to communicate the terms of the treaties to Czechoslovakia and Roumania. Bratianu astonished even the hardiest of us by saying that the boundaries had only been communicated to him at 10 a.m. that day. Crowe, by no means sotto voce, ejaculated behind Balfour's chair 'What a lie'. Lansing asked him point blank. Have you not had unofficial knowledge of the decisions, and seen the maps? <u>Bratianu</u> Very conflicting reports. <u>Lansing</u> What kind of conflicting reports? <u>Bratianu</u> All kinds. Some went further, some fell short of the boundaries actually now indicated. The limits of time necessary for consulting Bucharest were astronomically fixed and would last 10 to 12 days. We all gasped at this hardy imitator of Italy. Bratianu at any rate refused to give a definite answer.

---

[211] See entry 23 Nov. 1916; Szeged was briefly occupied by Romania in 1919.

12th [June 1919]

Supreme Council <of Four> put us some rather nasty questions this morning[:] <Mr. Balfour expressed his great disgust at the previous meeting's waste of time. He did not get up out of bed to this one and, after keeping everybody waiting for half an hour Hardinge finalled appeared to represent him.>

(1) Why were frontiers between Roumania and Hungary, approved by the 10 on 12 May, not communicated to Roumania or other states concerned? The Five responded smartly to the Four that they had no such powers, as seemed to be indicated by the fact that the Four instructed them to make such a communication the day before. Also the only exception was when Belgium received a communication about her frontiers, but this came direct from the Four (not the Five). The Five therefore thought they had the precedents on their side and state that in future they will abide by the rule of non-communication unless the Four direct to the contrary. After this little passage of arms, the Five refused to alter the Roumanian frontiers as requested by Bratianu but made the rectification of the railway junction of Vorpona railway with the Komaran Lorincz[212] railway, thereby altering the agreed line in favour of the Czechs.

14th [June 1919]

Rather an interesting talk with Sutherland.[213] He said Haig & Robertson were both second-rate men quite incapable of talking about or appreciating strategy and their one idea, when Foch or others spoke to them[,] was to avoid committing themselves. He said L[loyd]G[eorge] looked on his sojourn at the W[ar] O[ffice] as the most profitless 6 months he had spent in the war. He said Russia in the war had always been hopeless and that he had sent her £800,000,000 worth of munitions. Lindley[214] <intervened hotly> but denied this & put it at between £300 and £400,000,000 (NB It turned out ultimately to be 550,000,000).

---

[212] Komárom, on the Danube to the west of Budapest; Szent Lőrincz, half-way along the railway line from Barcs to Pecs.

[213] See entry 9 May 1919.

[214] Hon. (Sir) Francis Oswald Lindley (1872–1950), kt., 1926, diplomat; entered diplomatic service, 1896; appointed clerk in Foreign Office, 1897; embassy secretary at St. Petersburg, 1915–18 (in charge, Mar. 1918); consul-general for Russia, 1918; delegate at Paris Peace Conference, 1919 (with rank of minister plenipotentiary), 1919; high commissioner at Vienna, 1919–20; minister at Vienna, 1920–22; at Athens, 1922–23; minister at Oslo, 1923–29; ambassador at Lisbon, 1929–31; at Tokyo, 1931–34; retired, 1934.

18th [June 1919]

A meeting of the Council of Five – the first question turned on Poland and the Ukraine. Sonnino came out as a strong pro-Pole and wished to give all E[astern] Galicia in full sovereignty to the Poles (a strange argument from a Power which is at the same time supplying arms to Bela Kun). Balfour stuck by a Mem[orandu]m of his own, appointing a High Comm[issione]r under the League of Nations and giving military control to the Poles. The Five were greatly embarrassed because the Committee dealing with the subject had been asked to make suggestions, but to give no advice. Consequently Balfour's Memo[randum] had to be written in haste.

Finally a breeze came. Mr. Balfour asked Sonnino what the autonomy offered by him meant. Sonnino – 'I mean "Administrative self-government". There are various degrees of self-government. You know what I mean when I speak of self-government for example for Ireland – you want to give self-government to Ireland'.

Mr. Balfour, interrupting[:] 'I don't'.

Sonnino: 'But there are various degrees'.

Mr. B[alfour][:] 'But perhaps I should say I am merely expressing my own opinion'.

The rest of the debate then turned on a dispute between Lansing and Balfour as to whether the Ruthenians and Poles were really friendly. As this was not one that could be settled offhand, nothing else was done.

Then came on the question of the Klagenfurt basin and the plebiscite. We had met in the morning, with a letter from the Four (who had all gone away in their motor cars for two days) of the 17th June of which the contents were very important. The SHS[215] force having been reported to have pressed forward & occupied Klagenfurt. In these circumstances the Council decided that a demand should be made for the evacuation of the entire district of Klagenfurt by the forces of both SHS and of the Austrians. It was agreed that the Council of Foreign Ministers sh[oul]d be asked to approve and send a telegraphic despatch to the Governments of the SHS and of the Austrian republic demanding the evacuation of the Klagenfurt basin by both contending parties. It should be premissed that the Four had already sent a telegram to the belligerents <on the 31st May>, demanding the mutual evacuation of the basin.

The Committee on Boundaries had already considered this in the morning – 2 questions[:] (1) the plebiscite[;] (2) the letter. It is a striking fact that on the 12th June the Italians made an excuse to avoid meeting on the plebiscite question and the same day they despatched a telegram 'enforcing and

---

[215] *Kraljevina Srba, Hrvata i Slovenaca* (Kingdom of Serbs, Croats and Slovenes), the official title of the Yugoslav state, 1918–29.

amplifying' the 31st May telegrams for evacuation. The telegram, a purely bogus invention of the Italians, so far as we know, greatly befogged the 4 Allied military men who had been requested to attend the armistice negotiations between SHS and Carinthians. On the 6th an armistice was completed and signed by the two belligerents; on the 8th, encouraged by the Italians, the Austrians broke the armistice. On the 10th 4 military men (InterAllied) arrived in Klagenfurt and found themselves with nothing to do and no armistice to arrange. Consequently on the 12th the Italians forged a telegram to the Four, constituting these 4 military men an InterAllied Commission to make the SHS evacuate the basin. Gen[eral] Walker,[216] the British Military representative, interpreted these orders as overriding his own, which were to be present at an armistice but not to undertake arrangements for evacuation of the basin.

Consequently, we arrived at the morning meeting with some knowledge of the circumstances – (1) That the Italians were exploiting the demand for the evacuation of the basin in order to introduce Italian troops there[;] (2) that it was <now> therefore highly desirable if possible to avoid evacuation.

The Committee under Tardieu took a bold line and their only possible one. This was to assume that, in view of the new proposal to withdraw the Czechoslovak and Ruman[ian] troops behind their permanent boundaries[,] it w[oul]d be better to withdraw the Jugoslav and Austrian troops only to the limits between zones B & A in Wilson's map and not to make them evacuate the basin entirely. This was a bold scheme, because contrary to the policy of the Four, but it was put up.

(2) The plebiscite was also regulated. Zone B Jugoslav administration[;] Zone A Austrian[;] plebiscite in B 3 months, in A 3 weeks after <u>result</u> in B made known.

We did not get farther than (1) in discussion with the 5. 3 diff[eren]t opinions were expressed and expounded by Tardieu. (1) Franco-British as above. American half and half. Italian opposed – such was the Com[mitt]ee's policy. Sonnino began with a curious exposé. He said the Four had decided to evacuate the basin on the 31st May. This reached Belgrade on the 3rd but on the 5th the Jugoslavs advanced on Klagenfurt. On the 6th there was an armistice forced on the Austrians, but it was subsequently broken. The Allied generals on the spot informed the Jugoslavs of the order of the Council (NB prompted thereto by the forget telegram of June 12th). The Allied off[ice]rs thereupon asked for the instructions of the Council. He (Sonnino) had brought up the question before the Four. The Four had decided on the 17th that a telegram should be despatched

---

[216] Major-General Sir George Townshend Forestier-Walker (1866–1939), soldier; entered army, 1884; active service, South Africa, 1899–1900, East African campaign, 1902–1904, Somaliland, 1904–1905; Chief Staff Officer and Adjutant Quartermaster-General, Intelligence, Somaliland, 1903–1904; aide-de-camp to George V, 1907–15; Brigadier, General Staff, 1914–15; commanded 21st and 27th Divisions, France and Salonika, 1915–19; retired, 1920.

by the Five, requiring the evacuation of the basin. Sir M[aurice] Hankey added in his letter that the Comm[issio]n on Jugoslav affairs sh[oul]d determine the frontiers behind which they should retire, but these frontiers were already settled on the 31st May. The Commission had put an entirely different construction of this, on the assumption that military lines should also be political frontiers, but this was not a case of political frontiers but of plebiscitary lines. TARDIEU[:] [']If so we have nothing to do and the Commission was asked to deliberate under a misunderstanding. PICHON said that there was a contradiction in the letter of the Four, one part said that the basin was be evacuated, another that the boundaries were to be fixed.

Balfour: 'I'm not sure I know what is meant and, if I do, I disapprove. Are we to "approve" without discussion? If so, it means that we are to empty the basin and leave no one in there. If so I disapprove. If we are asked merely to draft a telegram that is not our business.

Sonnino repeated his points, and said 'a repetition of the telegram of 31st May is required'.

Balfour[:] 'It must be more than that. If it's a mere repetition why can't the Four repeat their own orders? What we have to find out is, first is the letter the decision of the Four and, if it is, what it means'.

Tardieu[: ']It's quite certain the boundaries weren't defined because the Jugoslavs tried to include the Miessthal'.[217]

Sonnino went on explaining – Lansing interrupted sharply[:] 'Are you to blame for all of this? I move we adjourn'.

Balfour[:] 'I'm not going to draft telegrams' and glided imperceptibly out. As he passed Crowe, the latter who had laughed a good deal said 'an impasse'. 'Perfectly unimportant anyway'[,] said Balfour airily. Sonnino made a desparate effort[:] 'I know what the Four meant'. Lansing rose hotly and passed out saying not very softly 'I'm not going to stay here to be fooled by Sonnino'. In the official minutes 'the meeting then dispersed'.

19th [June 1919]

We met again. The Five, or rather Four of them, had a difficult case to argue or to meet. A.J. B[alfour] began by stating that he did not approve. 'We are to empty the whole basin and leave nobody in it. Well, the Four may approve but I don't.[']

---

[217] The Mießtal, now Mežica Valley, with the town of Unterdrauburg, now Dravograd, was ceded to the new Kingdom of the Serbs, Croats and Slovenes in the Treaty of Saint-Germain of 10 September 1919; the future of the remainder of southeastern Carinthia and the Klagenfurt basin was left to be determined in a plebiscite in October 1920. After the predominantly Slovene Zone B had voted for adhesion to Austria (59.1 per cent), the plebiscite in the ethnically German Zone A was never held.

Lansing[:] 'I don't either'. Then he picked up the famous instruction. We are asked 'to approve, and despatch. Well, I don't approve'. Sonnino – ['] There is no question of approving in that sense as it was agreed that the Council of Five should be asked to approve'. A.J. B[alfour] & Lansing[:] 'But we don't approve'.

Sonnino – 'Simply to ask advice of the military gentlemen there'. Lansing[:] 'There must be some mistake, for the natural course is to inquire of military men first and approve afterwards'.

A.J. B[alfour] at this point remarked audibly to the Japanese[, ']Have you a view on this point?[']

After further discussion Lansing brought forward a motion that the <Jugoslav & Austrian> forces should remain on the purple line as marked on President Wilson's map. This gave ⅔rds of the basin, but not Klagenfurt, to the Jugoslavs. It utterly defeated Sonnino's plan of beguiling the Four into evacuating the basin.

That night Sonnino got one of the British Secretaries on the telephone and said that Sec[retar]y Lansing had meant not the purple but the green line. (If it meant the latter the basin w[oul]d have been evacuated.) The Secretary replied that he had accepted the resolution as passed by 4 foreign ministers and could not alter it at the suggestion of a fifth, who had dissented from the resolution. That night also Sonnino learnt that he was no longer Minister.

Lansing and Balfour <had> quibbled absurdly and Sonnino was right in the interpretation of the meaning of the Four. What he was wrong about was that he deluded and misled the Four, and the Five defeated him on account of that. Someone pointed out that it was the only meeting in which Balfour had not gone to sleep or in which Lansing had not drawn pictures. As regards the latter he was wrong for he drew one, which I made him sign as a memorial of the day.

21 [June 1919]

The Four met to consider the matter – fortunately L[loyd] G[eorge] was not present and Balfour had been well briefed. I can claim a little credit for the whole affair, for on the 19th he had a memo[randum] of mine on military consequences of the evacuation of the Klagenfurt basin and on the 20th a summary of all the transactions, showing quite definitely that the Italians ahd sent a bogus telegram on the 12th June, which deceived Gen[eral] Walker into constituting an entirely unauthorized InterAllied Commission to make the Jugoslavs evacuate the basin. B[alfour] was thoroughly primed and sound.

Meanwhile Johnson had been attending to President Wilson by a Memorandum. He opened the proceedings by saying that there were 3 points to decide

(1) The occupation of zones A & B by Jugoslavs and Austrians

(2) Determination of time at which plebiscite should be taken 3 months or 6 to 18 months as the Italians [propose]
(3) Date of qualified voters – 1914 or 1905

On (1) said Pres[ident] Wilson [']I coincide with the majority, which is, I believe, in favour of such mutual occupation.[']

<u>Sonnino</u> 'You can have an InterAllied Commission or local police'.

<u>Wilson</u> 'You will have a Commission in any case'.

<u>Sonnino</u> then began his old story of how the Italian General tried to get into touch with the Austrians and Jugoslavs, how an Armistice was forced on the Austrians which they subsequently refused.

<u>Wilson</u> 'Is it your judgment then that an entire evacuation would now be safe?'

<u>Sonnino</u> 'If inadequate we could have other arrangements'.

<u>Wilson</u> 'Would you consult with the military men?'

<u>Sonnino</u> 'I didn't understand that the military men were to prejudge anything about the settlement'.

<u>Wilson</u> 'Their duties were limited merely to cessation of hostilities and arranging an armistice'.

<u>Sir M[aurice] Hankey</u> 'I wish to explain here that the telegram I wished to send in my letter was repeated for information only (but that they were to receive no special instructions). Someone here said that Italian troops were in the basin'.

<u>Wilson</u> 'Are they?' <u>Sonnino</u> 'I don't know'. <u>Clemenceau</u> 'Why not?'

<u>Wilson</u> 'Isn't it important you sh[oul]d find out?' <u>Sonnino</u> 'Owing to the message sent on 12th June the 4 military gentlemen have taken on themselves to recall the troops (Jugoslav)'. <u>Wilson</u> (gravely) 'If they have[,] they have done a very serious thing'. <(Sonnino blushed to the top of his head.)>

M. Tardieu here intervened and explained that, as Chairman of the Commission, he had drawn up a report suggesting that the lines of military occupation sh[oul]d coincide as far as possible with the future political frontiers. This was adopted by the Foreign Ministers except Baron Sonnino.

<u>Sonnino</u> 'I think the precedent does not hold good. These are plebiscite lines, not permanent political frontiers'.

<u>Wilson</u> 'I want to state as a premise that it would not be safe to clear these areas of troops. If this were accepted who w[oul]d occupy this area? It is out the question for any other troops except Italians or Jugoslavs to occupy it. They only other forces at hand (looking hard at Sonnino) are Italian forces and Italy is known to have conflicting claims with Jugoslavia as regards the general settlement. Her occupation would be a mistake and would lead to trouble'.

<u>Sonnino</u> (whose bald crown had pinkened) 'Not a large force'.

<u>Wilson</u> 'There are no American nor British near and no French to be spared'.

Tardieu 'I wish to say that the purple line has been accepted as the limit for the plebiscite. I am unable to understand why we are looking for a different one'.

Wilson 'Is Baron Sonnino willing to waive this point?'

Sonnino bows sulkily.

A.J.B[alfour] 'I wish it to be laid down quite clearly that the Commission should be the controlling Power as to the distribution of forces in the basin'.

After this plain speaking other points were easily settled. 3 months was fixed for the plebiscite in Zone A and 1912 for no reason selected as the qualifying period for voters.

Sequel at drafting committee

At the drafting committee a new difficulty suddenly arose. On examination it was discovered that President Wilson's map included in the plebiscite area a piece of territory granted to Austria in the Treaty, that between Mittagskogl and Malestiger.[218] The Italian representative said that, as this piece was granted to Austria in the Treaty, we could not contemplate taking it away from her by including it in the plebiscite area. It was pointed out to him that all parts of the Treaty relating to Jugoslavia and including the basin had been reserved, and not presented to Austria and that consequently the question did not arise. However, having created this technicality, he stuck to it and declined to agree to the despatch of a telegram that night. The Four could not be consulted so it meant putting off the whole thing till Monday the 23rd. In the middle of this discussion Sonnino arrived, obviously very excited, and took Tardieu aside. The latter said afterwards Sonnino was very excited and said he could not have this dishonour inflicted upon him on the last day he should be present at the Congress.

(Note: On the 23rd [June] at a discussion at which I was not present the Big Four brushed aside Sonnino's objections and dispatched the telegram without the smallest regard for his 'honour'.)

22nd [June 1919]

I could not help being amused yesterday because, before our business came on, the Big Four discussed the despatch of a letter, the third "last word" to Germany, informing her that the concessions granted in our final reply (our first last word) were binding. After having decided this they then spent some ¾ hour discussing what they had decided.

---

[218] The Techantinger Mittagskogel (Trupejevo poldne) the Mallestiger Mittagskogel, (Maloško poldne), near the village of Mallestig, two peaks in the Western Karawanks between Villach in the Carinthian Drau Valley (Austria) and Jesenice in the valley of the Sava Dolinka (Slovenia).

The German reply to the first last word came today. It was to the effect that they could not accept two articles, one asserting their responsibility for the war, two demanding the extradition etc. of the Kaiser. They offered to sign with these reservations. L[loyd] G[eorge] at once summoned Wilson, Clemenceau & Sonnino to the Rue Nitot at 6.30. They sat till 8 and drafted a reply really composed by Wilson, in which they rejected both demands and insisted on immediate compliance. L[loyd] G[eorge] very excited and invited everyone to dinner – none of the 4 went – and Balfour had to go without it, as he was drafting a despatch. Clemenceau says they won't sign, L[loyd] G[eorge] says they will. Anyhow we shall see by 7 p.m. tomorrow.

23rd [June 1919]

At 5.30 the Germans sent a message that they agreed to sign.

28th June [1919]

Today I saw the Huns sign. The entrance to the Galerie des Glaces was up two lines of stairs, <guarded by a> a line of troopers with blue uniform, steel breastplates and helmets with long horsehair plumes, making a splendid appearance. In the Salle des Glaces itself there were too many women and civilians to make it really impressive. At 3 pm there was suddenly a tense interval and silence, and preceded by four armed officers the Boches appeared. One <Müller[219]> pale, <bowed> with glasses like a student, the other <Bell[220]> next, head erect and hair like an artist's.<Immediately after, I suppose by design, the cuirassiers all suddenly sheathed their swords. I suppose a symbolic and conscious act. The atmosphere of hate was terrible. They advanced and sat down on the fourth side of the square – near the table of rose and almond wood – on which lay the Treaty. In a minute or two Clemenceau got up speaking in a sharp clear musical voice, like a succession of strokes on a gong, said 'We are in complete accord. I have the honour to ask (Mantoux translated 'I ask') Messieurs the German

---

[219] Hermann Müller (1876–1931), German trades unionist and politician; press secretary, Social Democratic Party (SPD), 1906–18; 'unofficial SPD foreign minister' before 1914; *Reichstag* deputy, 1916–18, and 1920–31; member of National Assembly, 1919–20; Foreign Minister, June 1919–Mar. 1920; *Reich* chancellor Mar.–June 1920 and June 1928–Mar. 1930.

[220] Dr Johannes Bell (1868–1949), German lawyer and politician; member of Prussian diet, 1908–18, and Prussian *Landesversammlung*, 1919–21; *Reichstag* deputy, 1912–18 and 1920–33; member of National Assembly, 1919–20; Transport Minister, June 1919–Apr. 1920; Minister of Justice, May 1926–Jan. 1927.

Plenipotentiaries to sign'. At this point the 3[221] Huns got up and bowed low. They were asked to sit down again and the speech was translated. After this they came forward and signed slowly amid a tense hush. Then came Wilson etc. Lloyd George, who smiled broadly as he finished, the Colonial Premiers and the Maharadjah of Bikanir,[222] looking magnificent in a pale khaki turban. After that Clemenceau with Pichon and Tardieu – behind them Sonnino. The last days of his reign – and then the minor plenipotentiaries. As Paderewski with his tawny mane and stage bow signed the guns began to boom outside. The ceremony ended soon. The Huns were carefully escorted out and Clemenceau came down the Hall slowly beaming, shaking hands as he went. As he went out the old man reached me his hand – or rather the hand covered as always in a grey glove. 'Felicitations', said I. 'Mille remerciments', said he. In the park the water was playing in the fountains for the first time since the war. Wilson, Clemenceau, Lloyd George and Sonnino walked down to the Tapis vert, were uproariously cheered and with difficulty protected from the crowd. <Immediately after, I suppose by design, the cuirassiers all suddenly sheathed their swords – I suppose a symbolic and conscious act. In a word a great moment but I fear a peace without victory just as we had a victory without peace.>

3rd July [1919]

Committee of 5 on Bessarabia – Maklakoff[223] (a Russian representative) and Bratianu to be heard before them.

Tardieu was in the Chair, Clemenceau and Pichon being absent. Balfour began by saying – a remark which was not reported – that he had been speaking with Clemenceau, and asked him what Treaty we could construct including Bessarabia. I thought none. M. Clemenceau answered 'That is good logic but what is good logic is not always practical policy'. Mr. Lansing had then pointed out that no resolution could be adopted, and no-one dissented.

Mr. LANSING: [']Furthermore I have no full powers to discuss anything unless it related directly to peace. The President had perfect latitude, I haven't.[']

---

[221] The third German representative was Ulrich Count von Brockdorff-Rantzau, see entry 9 May 1919.

[222] Maharaja Sir Ganga Singh (1880–1943), Indian prince; ruling Maharaja of princely state of Bikaner, 1888–1943; entered Indian Army, 1898; commanded Bikaner Camel Corps, France, Egypt, Palestine, 1914–18; represented India at Imperial War Conference, 1917; member of Imperial War Cabinet, 1917–19; delegate, Paris Peace Conference, 1919; Chancellor of Indian Chamber of Princes, 1920–26; Indian delegate, League of Nations, 1924.

[223] Vasili Alekse'evich Maklakov (1869–1957), Russian lawyer and politician; *Duma* deputy, 1907–17; ambassador at Paris, Oct. 1917–24 (though never accredited); French exile thereafter.

TARDIEU said it was unfortunate to leave a frontier gaping and suggested Maklakoff sh[oul]d be heard.

Lansing agreed but said he would take no share in a resolution. Maklakoff was then admitted.

His views were the usual rechauffé of dubious history and ethnology. He said the body which had voted for union to Roumania was the Sfatul Tseri[224] and only 46/160 members voted.[225] It was originally a Soviet Committee and a revolutionary committee was not likely to vote for adherence to a monarchy except under compulsion etc. (exit) Enter Bratianu –

Tardieu. The members of the Council have studied thoroughly the ethnological question. They would like to know what degree of sincerity and authority M. Bratianu attributed to the vote of the SFATUL TSERI.

Lansing. It doesn't matter how that vote has been obtained. What I want to know is how the consultation of the people can be carried out in future.

Balfour & Tardieu both interposed.

Bratianu The vote, I think, was given in full freedom and expressed the will of the people etc. Mr. Lansing had suggested a plebiscite but Bessarabia was a Roumanian country attached by force to Russia for 100 years. The difficulty did not arise about nationality, the social question caused all the trouble etc.

Lansing. I wish to put a plain question to M. Bratianu. Would he object to a plebiscite? and aside Yes or no[,] that's all I want to know.

Bratianu. Yes I do. I do so because the choice offered to the people is between Bolshevism and order. On the borders of disturbed Russia it was dangerous to offer such a choice. If the Roumanian troops withdrew there would be endless tumult in the country.

Lansing. Would M. Bratianu, if given possession of the country, agree to a plebiscite in two years?

Bratianu. No, because only revolutionary agitation would result from the knowledge that a plebiscite would be taken.

Lansing. Will you object to a plebiscite at any other specified time in the future?

Bratianu. (now dusky red, <voluble> and a little heated) No, because however long a period, so long would the agitation be prolonged. (At this point Lansing rose muttering not very softly and turned his back.) The possession of Bessarabia by Russia was an anachronism. It had been a step on the road to Constantinople and could no longer serve that purpose. Russia was largely

---

[224] Sfatul Ţării, the National Assembly of Bessarabia, which proclaimed the independent Moldavian Democratic Republic in December 1917, and then, on 27 Mar./9 Apr. 1918, the union with Romania.

[225] In the final vote on 27 Nov./9 Dec. 1918, only 44 members of the Assembly cast their votes.

responsible for Roumania's misfortune, and therefore owed her a great debt. The best way of discharging it was by ceding Bessarabia. (At this point, to quote the official record, 'the Roumanian delegates withdrew'. Bratianu shook hands all round – whether to repair his damaged reputation or because he was retiring permanently I don't know.)

4th [July 1919]

Tittoni[226] made it clear to 4 that he disapproved of sending It[alia]n troops to Asia Minor and w[oul]d not send any more and w[oul]d withdraw those sent when it c[oul]d be done without humiliation to Italy. Terr[itoria]l acquis[itio]ns in Asia Minor were of little value to Italy – coal & raw material were her real need, not territory. Coal could come from Heraclean coalfield[227] not already occupied by French Col[umn], and a full & fair share of oil in Lake Van.[228]

Clemenceau said Italy having landed troops in Anatolia in flat opp[ositio]n to Allied policy, now wished to be rewarded for not advancing them beyond positions they ought never to have occupied by getting the right to plant a ring of new Italian coalmines round the one the French were already working.

Lansing showed sympathy for Italian desire for Turkish coal but not for Armenian oil.

A.J.B[alfour] suggested Italian question sh[oul]d be considered as a whole not piecemeal and raised the Adriatic. Mr. Lansing[,] 'who is nothing if not a lawyer'[,] asked Tittoni without further preamble whether Italy stood by the Treaty of London or whether she did not. If she did all Italian claims on Fiume must obviously be abandoned. If on the other hand Italy maintained her claim to Fiume she hereby tore up the Treaty of London and had no right to appeal to it on any other point. Tittoni, poor man, was a good deal embarrassed by a question which however he must certainly have foreseen and for obvious reasons forbore <I thought it not opportune> to ask Mr. Lansing whether if the Italians did fall back on [the] T[reaty] of L[ondon] the Americans were prepared to accept it as it stood. Lansing in his wisdom said this was a second question which could most properly be dealt with after the first question had been answered. The matter c[oul]d not be left there.

---

[226] Tommaso Tittoni (1855–1931), Italian politician; deputy, 1886–97; prefect of Perugia, 1897–1900; Naples, 1900–1902; Senator, since 1902; Foreign Minister, 1903–1905, 1906–1909 and June–Dec. 1919; Prime Minister, Mar. 1905; Minister of the Interior, 1906–1909; ambassador at London, Mar.–May 1906; at Paris, 1910–16; President of the Senate, 1919–29; President of the Royal Academy of Italy, 1930–31.

[227] Karadeniz Ereğli, on the Black Sea coast of Turkey, known in Hellenic times as Heraclea Pontica.

[228] Lake Van (Turk. *Van Gölü*) in eastern Turkey.

He told Tittoni that tho[ugh] Italy had shown no great respect for provis[io]ns of T[reaty] of L[ondon] that it was not for E[ngland] or F[rance] to say it had lost all validity. It must be perfectly clear that the Americans w[oul]d not accept [the] T[reaty] of L[ondon] as it stood. Now a settlement which Am[eric]a did not accept was no settlement at all and it seemed to me that the first thing for Tittoni to do was to come to an agreement with Mr. Lansing.

Clemenceau said Orlando had never made proposals. Tittoni should make them. He (C[lemenceau]) had originally desired [the] 1814 frontier for France but yielded to Wilson and had finally obtained a compromise not unfavourable. He trusted T[ittoni] might do the same.

The latter claimed in the last resort to fall back on [the] T[reaty] of L[ondon]. Clemenceau. In such case we would be no nearer [an] agreement.

8th [July 1919]

Accounts of great anti-French riots at Fiume.[229] I suspect the Italians are at their old game of provocation. It seems to me the foreseen and inevitable result of the Allied policy at FIUME, i.e. permitting the Italians to conduct a campaign of propaganda unchecked in the town for 7 or 8 months.

11th [July 1919]

On the Greek Committee. The Eastern Thrace line, which gives so much to the Greeks, came up for consideration, or rather for reconsideration. After infinite delays it had at last been agreed to give this line, and Venizelos had been informed and the Greek newspapers rejoiced accordingly. Now, just because Coolidge[230] and Johnson[231] have taken up the reins of government in the American Delegation, the whole has to be revised.

---

[229] Cf. 'Trouble at Fiume. Franco-Italian Dispute', *The Times*, 7 July 1919. French and Italian soldiers brawled after the French had paraded through the streets, with a trumpeter blowing the Italian retreat; in street fighting on 7 July 10 people were killed, 'Fiume Street Fighting', *The Times*, 8 July 1919.

[230] Archibald Carey Coolidge (1866–1928), US historian; educated Harvard, Berlin, Paris and Freiburg; secretary at US legations at St. Petersburg, 1890–91, Paris, 1892, and Vienna, 1893; instructor in History, Harvard University, 1893–99; assistant professor, 1899–1908; Professor of History, 1908–28; Director of Harvard Library, 1910–28; member of the 'Inquiry', 1917–18; mission to Russia, Feb. 1918; headed 'Coolidge Mission' to Austria, 1919; delegate at Paris Peace Conference, 1919; organized humanitarian aid to Russia, 1921; editor, *Foreign Affairs*, 1922–28.

[231] Douglas Wilson Johnson (1878–1944), US geographer; educated, Denison University, Granville, OH, University of New Mexico, Albuquerque, Columbia University; instructor in

16th [July 1919]

Heard Venizelos today, explaining the situation in Asia Minor. He was plausible, pleasant, agreeable, frank, impressive. But he had a bad case. He said the 4 had asked the Greeks to go to Smyrna 'and that various incidents had arisen. It was necessary to protect the local inhabitants against the Turks and therefore it was difficult to remain within the limits originally contemplated. The Greek advance did not imply political claims and there was nothing definite or settled about the proposed frontiers. We have nine divisions in Macedonia and 5 in the Smyrna area – it is too much and we would gladly withdraw some, if we could. What we really want is security['] – and smiling at Tittoni, to whom he came over and spoke earnestly of 'collaboration'. 'Certainement', murmured Tittoni weakly. So the great man.

A.J.B[alfour] intervened with some cold douches of common sense. 'I don't propose to go into the history of the whole affair. That is difficult and perhaps impracticable, anyway undesirable. We have got to envisage the situation. There are three armies in this area, Turkish – Greek – Italian. These have created a mutual distrust and suspicion. How are we to put that right? I gather that the Turks do not, in all, number more than 60,000'.

21 [July 1919]

Gr[eek] Comm[ission].

22 [July 1919]

Baranja.

23 [July 1919]

Orders to go as A[llied] M[ilitary] A[ttaché] Serbia.

---

geology, Massachusetts Institute of Technology, 1903–1907; assistant professor, Harvard, 1907–12; at Columbia University, 1912–43 (since 1919, professor); Newberry Professor of Geology, Columbia, 1943–44; chairman of executive committee, American Rights League, 1916–17; author of *Topography and Strategy in War* (New York, 1917); served with Intelligence Division of US Army (with rank of Major), 1917–19; member of the 'Inquiry', 1917–18; chief of boundary geography division, US delegation, Paris Peace Conference, 1919–20.

24 [July 1919]

Sous commission Szegedin.

25 [July 1919]

Szegedin. R[omani]a Bukovina.

26 [July 1919]

Philip K[err]. Bulg[ari]a. Fiume.

27 [July 1919]

Dinner Balfour. Decad[en]ce – what is it? Kaiser punishment binding to all. Maint[enan]ce of int[ernational] l[aw].

28 [July 1919]

Tardieu began his report on the latest Serbian claims in the Bazias[232] & Banat, Szegedin, Baranya & Prekomurje [*sic*]. After a short discussion, which only reached or dealt with the first three, A.J. B[alfour] suddenly intervened – [']As to this apparently we are not going to give the Serbs anything, but we are going to give them something elsewhere, I believe (looking hastily at me) in the Baranya. Now we know how they are behaving at Klagenfurt, refusing to retire or to give up war-material. Why should we give them something elsewhere when they are behaving like this?[']

Clemenceau: 'Why indeed?'

Mr. White[233] & Tittoni also added remarks.

---

[232] Baziaş, in western Romania, where the Danube enters Romania.

[233] Henry White (1850–1927), US diplomat; educated in France and Britain; entered US diplomatic service, 1883; Secretary at Vienna, 1883–34; Second Secretary at London, 1884–86; First Secretary at London, 1886–93 and 1896–1905; unofficial agent for Secretary of State Richard Olney during Venezuela Boundary Dispute, 1896; ambassador at Rome, 1905–1907; at Paris, 1907–10; US delegate at Algeciras conference, 1906; Chairman US delegation, Fourth Pan-American Conference, 1910; retired, 1910; member of US delegation at Paris Peace Conference, 1919; retired, 1920.

Finally Mr Balfour said 'I propose we don't proceed further until they obey our orders elsewhere'.

Clemenceau: 'Une tres bonne attitude', and then to Tardieu: 'Eh bien, nous ne discutans pas'.

Tardieu: 'Eh bien, j'ai fini'.

Clemenceau: 'Moi aussi'.

(Applause)

Tardieu: 'One question I will deal with – <it does not affect> the Serb question – of the isle of Ada Kaleh,[234] a little island east of Orsava, which was forgotten in the Treaty of Berlin 1878. It was annexed by the [Hungarians]'.

Clemenceau: 'Why should we not give it to [the] Italians? They want ten. Why sh[oul]d we? I give it to Mr. Balfour. He had no island'.

Tardieu: 'It is a valuable island – it has a restaurant on it'.

Clemenceau: 'I suppose they play the guitar' – pretending to strum.

August 1. 1919

Saw Foch yawning magnificently in the antechamber as we entered. He went in first and we stayed behind.

Then we entered. I was our chief interpreter with Balfour. The Prekomurje and the Baranya, with the 7 villages I gave to Serbia, were settled – extension was refused in the Banat. Permission to occupy Prekomurje given. Then came up the question of the old boundary of the Bukovina, less the junction. Balf[ou]r suddenly woke up – R[omani]a insists on disobeying us[;] why sh[ou]ld we oblige her. She has not been very nice or very wise.

Move to postpone.

Clemenceau (with a sure win) [']Mr Balfour moves to postpone till R[omani]a has a reasonable gov[ernmen]t'.

<Balfour: 'A reasonable gov[ernmen]t as unlike as Mr B[ratianu]'s as possible'.

---

[234] Ada Kaleh, a small island in the Danube, some 1.8 miles below Orşava, mainly inhabited by Turks. A notorious smuggler's nest, it was of some strategic significance in the seventeenth and eighteenth century. It was submerged during the construction of the Iron Gates hydro-electric dam. The island was, indeed, forgotten at the Congress of Berlin in 1878, when the surrounding areas were ceded by the Ottoman Empire. In consequence, it remained *de jure* Turkish territory, and its inhabitants were exempt from taxation and conscription. In May 1913, it was annexed by Austria-Hungary as Újorsova; in 1919, Romania proclaimed her sovereignty over the island; and, in the 1923 Treaty of Lausanne, Turkey formally ceded it to Romania (arts. 25 and 26).

It plays an important part in Mór Jókai's novel *Arany Ember* [*Man of Gold*] (1872), in which it is called 'No-one's Island' and serves as a quasi-mythical symbol of peace and seclusion.

Clem[enceau]: 'Do you think there is a chance to obtain [it]?'>
Balfour: 'till the Greek Calends'.

6th [August 1919][235]

Called Col[onel] Calafatovic[236] and explained boundaries – then saw Mishitch,[237] looking very well & more impressive than ever. I began by the subject of FIUME – he interrupted me with considerable passion. Why do the Allies allow all this? The whole hinterland, the whole country, except some of the inhabitants of FIUME, are Jugoslav. Why permit them to rule there? I explained it would internationalised. [']Why internationalised?['] said he brusquely. I said there were difficulties. 'What difficulties' said he. [']Italy[']. [']Ah, Italy['], said he grimly, [']ces diables.['] I said that I had told the authorities that, if Italy had FIUME, there would be war with Jugoslavia. [']Quite true['] said he – and slowly and with emphasis – 'Je desire une guerre avec Italie'. When, said I? [']Ah['] said he grimly, [']not too soon, of course, we are tired, we have too much to do, we need boots, clothes, munitions – let us say 3 or 4 years.[']

Besides there is the internal question. 'You mean social disturbances?' said I. 'Yes, if we leave the Italians to Italy perhaps it will be needless to fight'.

<u>Albania</u>. What about Scutari? commercial not political rights. He said Scutari was an old Serbian city, about which there was a famous song. Don't you know it 'the Building of Skadar'.[238] I said I didn't think you could argue from too old history.

As regards the rest of Albania he said we do not want it – but we should like some tactical points as we must maintain a police force there to deal with raids, esp[ecial]ly between Djakova and Prisrend,[239] where he wanted the crestline. We do not want Albania now but we want no-one else to go there except an international protectorate, we should be very pleased to see that. <He said the Italians had intrigued at Cettinje, Plava & Gusinje[240] – and Montenegro was still in a state of grave unrest. Consequently it was always against Serbian interests for Italians to be in Albania.>

---

[235] Temperley arrived at Belgrade on 30 July 1919, see tel. Thwaites (DMI) to Temperley (no. 80118, secret), 30 July 1919, Temperley MSS.

[236] General Danilo Kalafatović (1875–1946), Serbian soldier; Commander-in-Chief Rear Area Command, 1941; Chief of General Staff, 1941; prisoner of war, 1941–45; died in Germany, 1946.

[237] See entry 21 Oct. 1916.

[238] That is, Shkodër (Scutari).

[239] Now Đakovica and Prizren (Kosovo).

[240] Now Plav and Gusinje (Guci, Alb.) in northeastern Montenegro; they constituted an Albanian Catholic tribal area that resisted Montenegrin rule for much of the period, 1878–1912.

I asked him if Serbs had evacuated at LYUMA[241] and elsewhere. He said 'Yes. We intend everywhere now to obey the Congress.['] I said [']did you at Klagenfurt[']. He said – [']we had beaten ces diables les Autrichiens and consequently it was difficult to make our troops retire. However now we are satisfied.['] I referred to the Preko Murje [sic]. He said the troops had already been ordered to occupy it. (I believe they had begun to move in before.) He asked about the Baranya, and if the Serbs would get Mohacs.[242] I said I thought it unlikely. 'But it is the key of the Baranya, and without it we are nothing. We ought to have as far as we conquered, i.e. to Pecs'. He then enquired as to the rest of the frontiers. I said they were now all defined as regards Hungary and Austria. He showed some discontent as to BAZIAS.[243]

But the main thing he said is to decide on a policy and adhere to it and impose it all round. That is the right policy for this part of world and especially for the Roumanians.

Bulgaria not demobilised but we have assembled a force in Macedonia. The situation is dangerous because we cannot rely on the Greeks.

7th [August 1919]

I saw H[is] R[oyal] H[ighness, Prince Regent Alexander] – first my old friends Col[onel] Simović[244] and Major Dimitrievich. H[ighness] lives in a little summer residence up by Toptschider[245] – very simple and unassuming. He began by asking me where I had been. I told him at Paris for 3 months. He asked me about the whole situation there. I told him what I could discreetly. He was much interested in FIUME and seemed to be content with its internationalisation, but very anxious about there being no Italian sovereignty. <I told him when pressed a little incident.> He then asked about Dalmatia – said the Jugoslavs could not possibly give up Sebenico, but seemed to think Zara, Lissa & Lagosta[246] did not matter. He seemed to be quite convinced of the friendliness of England. Then I went at his suggestion over the points Prekomurye [sic], Bacska, Baranya. He seemed reasonably satisfied with the concessions there. He said the Bacska was a very rich interesting land and that he had been well received there. He said also that on the 5th or 6th Sept[ember] he hoped to visit Zagreb. He asked me about

---

[241] Lume, near Kukës in northern Albania.
[242] Mohács on the Danube in Southern Hungary; the site of two battles: 29 Aug. 1526, which led to the partition of Hungary; and 12 Aug. 1687, which reversed the outcome of the earlier battle.
[243] See entry 28 July 1919.
[244] See entry 24 Dec. 1918.
[245] Topčider Palace in southwestern environs of Belgrade.
[246] Now Zadar on the Dalmatian coast, and the islands of Vis and Lastovo.

the Croats, about whom he seemed anxious. I told him that, in my opinion, the great difficulty was to orientate them towards Belgrade. In the old time they had oriented towards Vienna and, as that was not Budapest, their attitude was even patriotic.

He said that the great difficulty was the Slovenes who were forceful and never satisfied.

'I thank you for all you have done for Jugoslavia'.

10 [August 1919]

Avala.[247]

11 [August 1919]

Went along the Save to within 5 km of Obrenovatz.[248]

12 [August 1919]

Pancsova.[249] Left Belgrade at 11. The view of the Danube was beautiful and unique as ever, wooded hills on one side and willowed flats on the other, and a broad space of stream between unequalled except – I suppose – on the Volga. On arriving at Pancsova we, that is Radcliffe Mooney, the Radio Agent, and I no motor waiting for me and took the postal wagon. About 3 km out we encountered the motor, which should have been at Pancsova at noon. We boarded the motor and progressed 12 km, at the end of which our brilliant specimen of chauffeur informed us that the petrol was at an end. He had just enough to take us back to Pancsova. This seemed suspicious, and I suspect he preferred the demimonde of Pancsova to the demi-monde of Nagy Kikinda.[250] I cannot imagine why we stopped en route at Jakova[251] – all march to the telephone and encountered a German Magyar who informed us that Hungary had been a culture state while Serbia was a Balkan one. He produced various charts coloured by himself of Baranya, Bacska, Banat etc. I did not let him know that the boundaries of Jugoslavia as coloured in by himself were defensible on ethnic grounds, for the

---

[247] A mountain, some 10 miles southeast of central Belgrade.

[248] Now the Sava river, which flows from northwestern Slovenia to join the Danube at Belgrade. Obrenovac, some 20 miles southwest of Belgrade.

[249] Now Pančevo, 10 miles northeast of Belgrade.

[250] Now Kikinda in the Voivodina, northern Serbia.

[251] Jakovo, some 15 miles southwest of Belgrade.

grand majority of the lands included in Jugoslavia were Jugoslav according to his figures. I tackled him about the elementary schools and said that the Magyars were not liberal. No, said he, but otherwise there was great freedom. Credat Judaeus Apella.[252]

It was a not inept commentary on this great freedom and its results that the family I lived with in Pancsova before had a son who came under the law of 1908, by which it was enacted that in all schools, Magyar was to be taught first. The result was that, tho[ugh] born of Serbs, he cannot speak Serb properly. I visited them again[;] they received me with great gladness and astonishment and were especially pleased that I had spent an hour trying to find their house (Nicolić Starčevaya Ulica 34).

There was a circle of linguists that night who, when the mist was clear, walked out in the park, teaching one another languages. This I did with them. It is a nice park and I met cultivated persons.

13 [August 1919]

En route to Nagy Kikinda. We stopped ay Nagy Bacskerek[253] en route. All towns and villages are the same in this area. A village is a large street obviously muddy in winter, with trees planted along the side of it. A town is a series of three or four streets running at right angles to the long street. It is something of a testimony to the culture and administrative ability of the Magyars, which is also seen in the care of agriculture. The population is everywhere very mixed.

Nagy Kikinda is a large town but I am truly sorry for General Delobit[254] [sic] and his staff who have to stay there. Nothing to do, and nothing to see. The General was amiable and did me the honour to consult me on Roumanian affairs – particularly their alleged armistice with Hungary. I said the terms were so extraordinary that it was impossible to believe the Five would allow Roumania to impose them. He appeared satisfied.

I subsequently discovered that he had been at Koritza[255] as governor, had shot Ghermandy,[256] the President of that ill-fated republic, and had subsequently

---

[252] *Recte* 'Credate Judaeus Appella, non ego' ('Let the Jew Appella believe, not I'), Horace, *Satires*, book I, 5, 100–101.
[253] Now Zrenjanin in the Eastern Voivodina.
[254] General Paul Joseph Jean Hector de Lobit (1860–1938), French soldier; Commander of the Allied l'*armée de Hongrie*, Mar.–Aug. 1919; l'*armée du Danube*, Sept. 1919–Jan. 1920.
[255] Now Korçë in southeastern Albania.
[256] Themistokli Gërmenji (1871–1917), Albanian nationalist leader; police prefect of the French-proclaimed 'Autonomous Albanian Republic of Korçë', Dec. 1916–Nov. 1917; sentenced and executed at Salonika for cooperating with the Central Power, Nov. 1917.

advanced in the valley to Tomovica[257] with great success, having eventually to fall back because the Italians ran away. He dwelt on their incompetence, lack of organisation, observation or transport. He also spoke of the value of the lignite and mines at Koritza, the latter new to me.

An old lady told me much of the Serbs here, how they had strafed various people who opposed them and how they had maltreated some of the lower though not the upper classes. She said when the Prince Regent came here some Hungarian girls wished to bring him some flowers and make a loyal speech of address but were prevented by the Serbs. It appears however that H[is] R[oyal] H[ighness] remarked something for he said in a speech to notabilities – I notice that nationalities are not treated with tolerance and on an equality here – that is not right. It is better to feed these people with sugar than Essig <'vinegar'>.[258] Ristich especially distinguished himself by his gaucherie, I gather.

14 [August 1919]

My car was late, but my driver was a genuine sportsman and, despite two breakdowns, went all out for catching the boat. We started 1 ½ hours late and with two breakdowns arrived only 1 hour too late for the boat killing two turkeys on the way. Then I went to my old friend Nikolic & Mme & Miss Grigovic at 34 Starcevaya Garsa Panisova to spend the night. I played tennis in the afternoon, the first time for 5 years, and maintained the prestige of the British name by drawing two deuce sets with a bad partner against 2 local cracks.

15 [August 1919]

Morning 6 a.m. by boat to Belgrade.

16 [August 1919]

Received officially from Calaftović notice of a telegram sent from Gen[eral]s Gorton[259] (Brit[ish]) & Brandholz[260] (American) – Generals Commission at

---

[257] Mount Tomori in central Albania, some 10 miles east of Berat.
[258] *Essig*, Ger. for vinegar.
[259] Brigadier-General Reginald St. George Gorton (1866–1944), soldier; entered Royal Artillery, 1886; active service, Miranzai expedition, 1890, Chitral, 1895, South Africa, 1900–1902, European War, 1914–18; Chief of British Military Mission to Hungary, 1919–22; retired, 1922.
[260] Major-General Harry Hill Bandholtz (1864–1925), US soldier; Provincial Governor on Philippines, 1902–1907; Chief of Philippines Constabulary, 1907–13; Chief of Staff, New York

1919 455

Budapest. After fulminating in a pompous manner ag[ain]st the Serbs for having crossed the boundaries prescribed by the Armistice of Nov[ember] 13th 1918 they said they were authorized by the Five to give such commands. You have no authority 'for such occupancy'. 'It is trusted and believed that the report in question is an error or if not that it is due to mistaken instructions or to excess of zeal on the part of a subordinate and that you will rectify same immediately'. Every word of this is a masterpiece of buffoonery – (1) The Serbs did not occupy the Prekomurye [*sic*] on the 8th but on the 11th. (2) I was present (v[ide] Aug[ust] 1) at the meeting where the Five gave the Serbs authority to occupy the Prekomurye[.] (3) This has since been in the papers and the Serbs replied by quoting Pichon's official telegram to them.

The only people who erred by 'mistaken instructions' and the only [']excess of zeal on the part of the subordinate' were shown by the 2 ridiculous generals who signed the note. Further they addressed it to the C[ommander]-in-C[hief] Serbian forces, who happens to be the Crown Prince, and who, as constitutional monarch, cannot be addressed directly. Further the telegram was sent in English and en clair, and not through the Minister or Attaché here, to whom no copy was forwarded. 'How not to do it' tips packed onto a short space – I do not know it has ever been done better.

17 [August 1919]

Left Belgrade for ult[imat]e tour to Uskub, Prisrend & Skoplje[261] – joined up with American journalist on the way & Spalajković,[262] the celebrated diplomat & min[iste]r of Serbia to Russia. He described an interesting interview with Lenin, which he and the rest of the dip[lomati]c corps paid to Lenin when the latter had arrested Diamandy,[263] the Roumanian min[iste]r. The doyen (I think

---

National Guard, 1913–17, on service in Mexico; Commander 58th Brigade, 29th Division, 1917; US Army Provost Marshal General, 1917–19; US representative, Inter-Allied Military Mission to Hungary, 1919–20.

[261] Temperley made a mistake here: Üsküb and Skoplje denote the same town, now Skopje, the capital of Macedonia; Prisrend, now Prizren in Kosovo.

[262] Dr Miroslav Spalajković (1869–1951), Serbian diplomat; entered diplomatic service, 1900; secretary of legation at St. Petersburg, 1900–1904; consul at Priština (Prishtinë), 1904–1906; Under-secretary, Foreign Ministry, 1906–11; minister at Sofia, 1911–13; at St. Petersburg, 1913–19; Minister without Portfolio, 1920; acting Foreign Minister, 1922–23; minister at Paris, 1923–35.

[263] Constantin Diamandy (1868–1931), Romanian diplomat; entered diplomatic service, 1892; secretary of legation at Sofia, 1910–12; at Rome, 1912–13; minister at St. Petersburg, 1913–19; High Commissioner in Romanian-occupied Hungary, 1919–20; minister at Paris, 1924–31.

Spal[ajković] explained that the offence was unheard of and against all public law. Lenin smiled & replied – that is the bourgeois and capitalistic one. We have another – it is this. The offences of Roumania against us would justify us in declaring war on them, but because we do not believe that <the> Roumanian people sh[oul]d suffer for the offences of the bourgeois … . Spal[a]j[ković interrupted[:] 'Assez menteur traité. You speak well with your sophisms against war but you do not remember the martyrs of Salonica in the trenches, who are suffering while you make peace at Brest-Litovsk'. Lenin found it difficult to answer this. S[palajković]'s report seems to have been as much out of the ordinary course of things as Lenin's original action.

18 [August 1919]

Stopped at Vranja Branska [*sic*][264] because the bridge was broken just beyond – said to be by Bulgar comitadjis and for 2 or 3 k[ilo]m[etres].

Their chief point of interest was with regard to the latest atrocities Comm[issio]n 'The Enemy in Serbia'. Acc[ordin]g to them and their work covers anything within a radius of 100 k[ilo]m[etres] the statements as to injuries etc. have not been verified by medical men. Some of the injuries described must have resulted in death, and were due to syphilitic scars or tuberculosis sores. They had never had any instances in the hospital of proved Bulgar atrocities in the way of mutilations. Some of the people said these things under the influence of hallucinations, others under that of the wish to divert blame from themselves. A number of Serb women (they had definite instances) had lived with Bulgar men. There had also been a strong Bulgar propaganda in the schools, which had had much success. Pretty good this from a pro-Serb source.

19 [August 1919]

Examined the bridge between Vranje and Vranja Branska [*sic*] – cannot say I am convinced that it was done by Bulgar comitadjis as has been suggested.

From evidence, I find 20 out of 80 older men remain undemobilised in one area, and many students, after being called up, are being released. 5,000 in whole Vranje district were called up, many being physically unfit.

As regards atrocities: 1 hand cut off of a child [at] Kumanovo,[265] eyes of a woman gouged out [at] Vranje.

---

[264] *Recte* Vranjska Banja, opposite Vranja on the river Morava in southern Serbia; see entry 19 Aug. 1919.

[265] Kumanovo (Alb. Kumanovë), in northern Macedonia.

Ristovać[266] [sic] – number of men shot in cold blood by Bulgars.

The other day there was a man murdered mysteriously and no family quarrels explain this. Was this by Bulgars?

20 [August 1919]

Saw Serbian troops reviewed.

21 [August 1919]

Rail to Ferozović[267] [sic], motor to Prisrend – a veritable dream of delight – though rather a hot one – first up the Kačanik defile[268] where the Serbs fought so bravely, then across wooded mountains, and through gorges to Sukareca. It lies beautifully surrounded by poplars, and by beautifully wooded flat-topped hills with the firm pale blue outlines of the overtopping them in the distance. It is very Serb. Then to Prisrend, beautifully picturesque with winding streets, through which the river flows, bazaars and shops, where Albanians in fezes & white caps sit very stolidly – up to my house in a perfect position, with a balcony. Opposite on the right on the hill overlooking the town is the white and grey fortress of Stephan Dushan.[269] The hills fold round, the houses picturesquely climbing almost to the top of the hill. Straight ahead the red roofs of the town are separated from one another by masses of green, only the white mosque and minarets towering above the green. Beyond a circle of poplars which stand like sentinels all round the town, stretches a broad flat fertile plain to the foot of the mountains, which grow high and stern in the west, where the sun is sinking redly behind them.

At supper we met Col[onel] Katanić,[270] whose knowledge of Albanians corresponds to Strickland's[271] knowledge of India, & whose methods are very similar. He lives with his wife in Prisrend and has studied Albania for 15 years – he is usually surrounded by hadjis and by blood-brethren, and smokes infinite

---

[266] Ristovac, small village near Vranje.

[267] That is, Ferizović, now Uroševac (Alb. Ferizaj), small town on the Belgrade–Salonika railway, some 24 miles south of Pristina (Kosovo).

[268] Kačanik Gorge, between the town of Kačanik and the Macedonian frontier, with the Lepenac river running through it; it was the site of repeated fighting during the late Ottoman period.

[269] See entry 8 Aug. 1917.

[270] Colonel Milutin Katanić.

[271] Sir Walter William Strickland (1851–1938), 9th Bt., succ. 1909, naturalist and scholar; settled in Java in 1890s; supporter of various anti-imperial and left-wing causes; a friend of T.G. Masaryk, he became a Czechoslovak citizen in 1923.

cigarettes – 17 before 11 am one day, pro patria for he cannot refuse one from an Albanian.

Beside him was a typical Colonel of the Shumadiya[272] who commands the battalion in the town. He had the big moustache of the fire-eater and a Gascon way of talking. He said there were reported Bulgar comitadjis everywhere in Macedonia (he had just left Prilep[273]) and that they were not supported by the natives. He had one story of Bulgar atrocities which did credit to his imagination at least. At Prilep the Bulgars arranged to have balls to which the parents and daughters of the place were invited. It was also arranged that warning sh[oul]d be given by bell and that all lights sh[oul]d be extinguished when a French aeroplane turned up. This happened once, and the Bulgars took advantage of the darkness and their partners, if not before the eyes, at least in the presence of the parents. This seems to be a modern version of what the pagans said the Christians did at their religious ceremonies, and of the practices ascribed by the orthodox to Bulgarian heretics, which resulted in the creation of an objectionable expression.[274]

Prisrend has 1,500 Serb houses, but the streets are strictly guarded with sentries and Albanian is the general character of the town. There are a few twins.

We wound up by going to see the American mission, where there was a lovely girl, Dr Stevens. She said they never slept because they were tormented by animals, but had a good time riding and bathing. All Prisrend wants to complete its beauty is a veela,[275] but the vision of an American nymph bathing in a mountain stream seemed out of place.

22 [August 1919]

By ford to Djakovitza[276] – country beautiful, we oriented very close to the border. The high Albanian mountains look down on the plain, where is an abundance of corn and cattle – no marauding people could possibly keep their hands off it. In turning the corner to Djakovitza we walked over Stamsky most, an old bridge, crossing where the Drin[277] emerges from a defile of high rocks and most lovely views – the water 20 feet deep and jade green and the rocks wild and

---

[272] Šumadija, a heavily wooded region south of Belgrade; in the eighteenth century a refuge of Hajduks (bandits) who fought the Ottomans.
[273] Prilep, in central Macedonia.
[274] A reference to Bogomilism, a tenth-century Gnostic sect that emerged in Macedonia as an anti-feudal reaction. The English word 'buggery' evolved from Bulgar/Bogomils.
[275] Vila, a Slavic version of nymphs.
[276] Đakovica (Alb. Gjakovë), a town in western Kosovo.
[277] The White Drin (Alb. Drini i Bardhë), one of the headwaters of the river Drin.

picturesque. A darker interest attaches to it because it was here the Serbs cast away their guns during the great retreat [in 1915].

We went further on the way, seeing a vulture, a stork and a heron in the air and being told that deer and boar haunt the neighbouring hills. Sleepy buffalos lay wallowing everywhere in the Drin, sometimes only their noses and horns above water.

Finally we left the Drin and followed the line of the Erenik[278] to Djakovitza. There we were received by a young Albanian, about 23, who was the sous-prefet of the district and also the chief of the local clan. He seemed very malleable in Katanić's hands, wore a Serbian white eagle, and professed to admire and support Essad Pasha.[279] He was surrounded by 7 or 8 gigantic retainers and seemed very frail beside them but he was Chief. Tzena Bey[280] conducted us to his house[,] a round building of thin Roman bricks, with iron bars to the windows and heavy wooden shutters behind them (half the thickness of a tree) to keep out rifle bullets. He showed us his state dress, magnificently embroidered with pure gold & yellow. He also dictated a telegram which he said he wished published in the papers to the effect that he hated the Italians and loved Essad Pasha and the Serbs. Katanić told us this morning that a general offensive had been started that day by the Albanians, south of the Drin by 4 tribes including the Mirdites.[281]

Tzena Bey said he was going to use all his efforts to further had begged Katanić to give him guns & munitions for it without success. He said he personally intended to go in, fight for a month, and then go to lay his country's cause before the Paris Conference. Apparently like many others he thought a peace-breaker always acceptable at a peace conference. Before leaving he entertained us as usual of course. Turkish dinner – rather a poisonous ordeal in more senses than one.

Finally we went on our way, leaving the tangle of narrow streets and red roofs behind. The Metoja basin,[282] while gradually narrowed, is of inconceivable richness, green grass, such as one seldom sees on the continent, yellow corn, green maize, willows.

---

[278] A tributary to the White Drin.

[279] Essad Pasha Toptani (Alb. Esat Pashë Toptani) (1863–1920), Ottoman soldier and Albanian politician; Young Turk deputy in Ottoman parliament, 1908–12; commanded Ottoman forces at Scutari, 1912–13; established Republic of Central Albania at Durrës, Oct. 1913–Mar. 1914; Prime Minister of Albania, 1914–16; delegate at Paris Peace Conference, 1919; assassinated in Paris, June 1920.

[280] Ceno Beg Kryeziu (1895–1927), Albanian politician; brother-in-law of Ahmed Bey Zogu, the later King Zog I (1895–1961); Foreign Minister, 1922–24; Minister of the Interior, 1925; minister at Belgrade, 1925–27; assassinated in Belgrade, Oct. 1927.

[281] A semi-autonomous clan in the Mirditë region of northern Albania, which had retained its Catholic faith.

[282] Now Metohija (Alb. Rrafshi i Dukagjinit), a large basin in western Kosovo between Peć and Prizren.

Finally, after a detour, we came to the famous Detchanski[283] monastery built to commemorate Urosh's[284] victory over the Bulgars, in which Dushan played a hero's part. It is a well constructed building, Byzantine in style, of white and pink marble, with some pointed windows and a lovely round east window, with lovely tracery. A little small.

The Archimandrite,[285] the only representative left, as the Russian monks had all been interned, had had the bad taste to die two days before, and the Church was in consequence locked up.

There really are a few Serbs in this place, practically the first I've seen since entering Montenegro, and a smart scene of Serb soldiers better guardians of Dečanski than Russian monks.

There is a spring of mineral waters and the place is set in a magnificent grove of horse chestnuts, with vast framing rocks one side where a pass leads to Plava and Granje. <We made two jokes. (1.) It was rather inconsiderate of the Archimandrite to die so soon. (2.) As this had been erected for a victory over the Bulgars, we must now build a second one.>

Thence to Peć – counted about 60–70 soldiers patrolling the road, the who[le] country here a farmer's paradise.

Saw the Prefect, and Dožić,[286] the Metropolitan of Peés [*sic*], the latter a genial man of about 40, who seemed newly oppressed by the burden of his office. He had a keen political interest – enjoyed his joke, his wine and his cigarette, fasted a little at supper to show he was a priest, but seemed a real bonhomme. He spoke scornfully of King Nicholas & more scornfully of his daughter Xenia[287] & his song. He explained also that he was against sudden or forcible conversion of the Moslems, tho[ugh] his ideas had been somewhat different when he was appointed in 1914. You must trust to culture, school & real agrarianism and not any other means. I think he was sincere in this view because he was extremely agitated about the Agrarian Reform question, which would equally hit the great

---

[283] Visoki Dečani, a major Serbian Orthodox monastery in Kosovo, some seven miles from Peć; founded by Stefan Uroš III Dečanski in 1327, who was buried there.

[284] Stefan Uroš III of Dečani (c. 1285–1331), King of Serbia, 1322–31; defeated the Bulgarian Tsar Michael Asen III in the battle of Velbuzhd, 1330; dethroned by his courtiers in favour of his son Stefan Uroš IV Dušan and killed at the castle of Zvečan, 1331

[285] Archimandrite Leontije Ninković, abbot of Dečani monastery; cf. his *Srpska lavra Visoki Dečani* (Peć, 1928).

[286] Dr Gavrilo Dožić (1881–1950), Serb Orthodox clergyman; Metropolitan of Raška and Prizren, 1911–13; of Peć, 1913–20; interned in Hungary, 1915–18; member of Grand National Assembly, 1920; Metropolitan of Cetinje, 1920–38; Patriarch of Serbia, 1938–50; incarcerated at Dachau Concentration Camp, 1941–45; exile in London, 1945–46.

[287] Xenia (also Ksenija) Petrović-Njegoš (1881–1960), eighth daughter of Prince Nicholas I of Montenegro and his consort Milena Vukotić (1847–1923); in French exile since 1918.

Albanian landowners in the Djakova-Peć area. He said, quite truly, that Poljak,[288] my friend of the long speeches <and drinks> at Zagreb, was a Croat who knew nothing of the problems here and a special commission should be sent. All very sound sense in its way, I thought.

The Archbishop confirmed the view that there were coalmines near Peć, and also that there were hot mineral springs. He gave me the impression of being a bit of a bonhomme, and of his small library I saw only 4 books, the Bible, a French dictionary and Jokai's 2 books, the 'Green Brook' and 'Black Diamonds'.

23 [August 1919]

Mitrovica.

24 [August 1919]

Uskub.

25 [August 1919]

Uskub.

26 [August 1919]

Nish.

27 [August 1919]

Belgrade.[289]

---

[288] Franjo Poljak (1877–1939), Croatian and Yugoslav economist, poet and politician; editor, *Hrvatska Misao* (Croatian Thought), since 1897; SHS Minister for Agrarian Reform, Apr.–Nov. 1919.

[289] Temperley returned to Britain in September 1919 to resume his academic duties at Peterhouse.

1920

27 [July 1920][1]

Tour to Plevihić.

30 [July 1920]

Dined with Vinčić lost 9 dinars.

31 [July 1920]

Saw 2 Jovanovićs.

1st August 1920

Lunch Vesnić.[2] Crown Prince [Alexander] present, arrived half an hour late owing to absurdity of 1st Secr[etary']s[3] who tried to enciper a telegram and then lost the way.

Had conversation with the C[rown]P[rince]. He was most cordial. Afterwards he played auction bridge, and lost most of the time as I did. Unfortunately I played with him. He was not a very good, but a very amiable, player, his manner unassuming and delightful as always, a little shy, I noticed.

---

[1] Temperley returned to Yugoslavia as Assistant Military Attaché to report on the political conditions in Montenegro and Albania, see 'Minutes concerning Mr. Temperley's Trip to Montegro', 17 July 1920, FO 371/4695/1489.

[2] Milenko Radomar Vesnić (1863–1921), Serbian politician and diplomat; Professor of International Law, Grande École, Belgrade, 1893–99; Minister of Education, 1893–94; imprisoned for *lèse majesté*, 1899–1901; minister at Rome, 1901–1904; at Paris, 1904–20; delegate at London ambassadorial conference, 1912–13; Paris Peace Conference, 1919; SHS Prime Minister and Foreign Minister, 1920–21.

[3] Edward James Hope-Vere (1885–1924), diplomat; entered diplomat service, 1906; first secretary at Cairo, 1919–20; at Belgrade, 1920–21; at Buenos Aires, 1921–22; at Christiania, 1922–24.

I agreed to pay Petrović 80 dinars, while the Prince offered Mme. Vesnich an emerald bangle.

A ministerial crisis on, Vesnić just resigning. He told H[ope]-V[ere] that he had returned his mandate. Both C[rown] P[rince] and he looked gay and happy as if care never came near them.

The one solid result of the Vesnić regime is the foundation of an Anglo-Serb tennis club due solely to the energy of Mme Vesnić, who drove out the gendarmes from a place that Jovanović[4] (Min[iste]r of War), present at the dinner, had sworn they sh[oul]d occupy.

2nd [August 1920]

Adm[ira]l Troubridge.[5] Long conversation – very much for suasion and ag[ain]st force on the Danube, leaving policing of waters to each nation.

5th [August 1920]

Lunch Gen[eral] Gorton[6] & Troubridge when the former invited me to Budapest. Dined Crown Prince [Alexander] – very fine silver plate, dinner on the terrace. The Crown Prince appeared first riding a beautiful white Arab, then he delayed a few minutes to speak with Ninčić,[7] the Foreign Minister [*sic*], whom he took by the arm, then he hurried off to wash. We dined on the terrace with a fine vignette of Belgrade in the distance. He spoke ordinary conversation. He was very much interested in matters Albanian about which he spoke frequently and excitedly.

---

[4] General Branko Jovanović (1868–1921), Serbian soldier; SHS Minister of War, 1920–21.
[5] See entry 30 May 1917.
[6] See entry 16 Aug. 1919.
[7] Dr Momčilo Ninčić (1876–1949), Serbian and Yugoslav politician; entered Finance Ministry, 1899; Professor of Law, Grande École, Belgrade, 1902–19; Finance Minister, 1915–16; SHS Justice Minister, 1920; Minister of Trade, 1920–21; Foreign Minister, 1922–24 and 1924–26; President of the League of Nations assembly, 1926–27; Foreign Minister, Yugoslav government-in-exile, 1941–43; died in Swiss exile.

9 [August 1920]

Democrats under Drasković[8] met today and drew up a doc[umen]t insisting (1) on Agrarian reform (2) on limited compens[atio]n (3) on export. This busts all hope of a compromise if insisted on. It was sent off to Vesnić tonight.

10 [August 1920]

C[rown]P[rince Alexander] still trying to form a Gov[ernmen]t. He intereviewed every member of the Cabinet separatism and tried to persuade them to join – situation very difficult.

11 [August 1920]

Jov[anovi]ć telephoned that the situation was very bad – that complete failure had ensued, and that the Regent [Alexander] was depressed. At one time hopes of a compromise were entertained and the decree establishing the ministry w[oul]d, it was thought, be signed tomorrow. Now c'est fini. Alternatives are a Cabinet which cannot last, or a business (or neutral) government which will put through an electoral law and hold elections in due form.

12 [August 1920]

Informed C[rown] P[rince Alexander] would see me tomorrow at 5.

13 [August 1920]

H[is] R[oyal] H[ighness, Alexander] received me on his balcony – gave me 2 cigarettes, which he lighted with his own hands. There is a superb view of Belgrade and Semlin[9] from the windows. I remarked on this – he said that, when one side was Hungarian and the other Serb, war was inevitable. I said the present solution was a better one. He seemed amused at this.

He then asked me about my proposed journey, listened in considerable detail, and made a few suggestions.

---

[8] Milorad Drašković (1873–1921), Serbian politician; Minister of Public Works, 1915; opposition leader to Pašić; Minister of the Interior, Jan.–July 1921; assassinated, July 1921.

[9] Now Zemun, opposite Belgrade.

I spoke first about Dalmatia and he stated the difficulty of Italy holding it. He seemed to think it simply a question of time when they would abandon it. He said in the military sense he could see no possibility of their defending it.

Then he went on to Montenegro and spoke of the situation there. He said he regarded it as much simplified and practically looked on the settlement as a <u>fait accompli</u>. There would still be troubles but no real trouble was expected since the departure of the Italians. He said they were a very good people and was much amused at two or three anecdotes I told about them.

As to Albania in which he was much interested he said that the present frontiers were impossible, that you must go forward or back. The North Albanians had no national sentiment and the territory was very sparsely populated north of the Drin river, the valley of which he had traversed in the great retreat. He seemed to favour strategic rectifications rather than annexation. He looked on the Scutari Prizrend railway as very desirable, but recognizing the expense of building and the difficulty of defending it. The question of Scutari itself was very difficult but [a] commercial route must be preserved. He said was with the Albanians was certain in September as it was their usual custom and instanced Dibra.[10]

He then pointed out the advance and the Western frontier. His working map contains only Macedonia & Albania. I could see the idea of a protectorate.

Mesopotamia – 'un bon morçeau'.

Bolsheviks – no result, open mind.

On general questions he seemed very hopeful and said the outlook was much better than last September[11] when I talked with him. The Slovenes and Croats were, he admitted, very different from one another and the Serbs, despite similarities of language. In particular the customs of Slovenia resembled greatly the German. He had been very pleased with his reception there, and evidently expected a less favourable one. Everybody thinks me very happy, and I was much deferred to in the antechamber.

14 [August 1920]

I heard Pribičević[12] on telephone ask for interview with Regent.

15 [August 1920]

Ministerial crisis has practically been arranged.

---

[10] See entry 15 June 1917.
[11] In fact, the meeting took place in August, see entry 7 Aug. 1919.
[12] See entry 21 Nov. 1918.

16 [August 1920]

Saw J[ovanovi]ć. Hear P[rince] R[egent, Alexander] was very pleased with my visit and thought I had made an excellent sketch of my journey, of which he thoroughly approved. Saw Pešić,[13] who agreed to arrange details and admitted the advance on the western frontier. I showed him a postcard, on which was a photograph of himself in a review. He seemed much pleased and so I offered it to him. He said he w[oul]d send it to his wife. I wonder how many members of the G[eneral] S[taff] w[oul]d crack jokes with the Regent, present a picture postcard to the sub-chief of the General Staff or, as I once did, give a brandy bottle to the Chief of Staff, a pair of gloves to a General, and in each case make a friend for life.

18 [August 1920]

Arrive Zagreb. Cuks as ever – wonderful.

19 [August 1920]

Exhibition of embroidery and peasant work. Some is beginning to degenerate, I saw, into the crude colours etc. of old English cottage work. I noticed this particularly in Slovenia. I did not sleep well because I introduced my colleague to the Cuks, which I regret, as he spent most of the night turning on the electric night and striking matches to find a small population.

20 [August 1920]

Left for Bakar[14] at 8.50 a.m. Curiously enough rather cold on the journey, climbing round by Ogulin[15] etc. among the tops of firs, until near the coast we came to the bare boulders of the Carst [sic]. At Bakar the absurdities of the existing situation are well illustrated. The Italians occupy the direct road to Bakar and part of the village just outside Bakar called Krljevo. There sentries face each other [on] each side of the road, the church is Italian – the cemetery Jugoslav. The result is to force on Jugoslavs (and incidentally on myself) a detour

---

[13]   See entry 21 Oct. 1918.
[14]   Bakar (It. Buccari), a coastal town in western Croatia, some two miles east of Rijeka (It. Fiume).
[15]   Ogulin in northwestern Croatia between Rijeka and Zagreb.

of some 11 kilometres before the harbour can be reached. It is a bad road instead of a very good one, and I am told a wagon of meal can only be transported from the station to the harbour for 8,000 kr[onen] = 2,000 dinar = £24 – 6 and even 8 horses being required at certain parts of the road.

The military situation is quite ludicrous – the regulars of the Italian army have surrounded FIUME interposing a wide zone or band between D'Annunzio[16] and the Jugos[lavs]. Constant tension has produced a sort of weary boredom, the very reverse of exciting.

Got on board leaving for SPLIT after seeing Milan's brother-in-law.[17]

21 [August 1920]

Saw Adm[ira]l A[ndrews].[18] Chief points of interview – no def[ini]te evid[en]ce re 11 July incident – points, at one point Italian subchaser was struggling desperately to escape – the hand grenade which exploded came from the land not the sea. It did not look next day as if the Italian machinegun had been fired.

Events began by the incendiary speech of a blind Serb captain; they were subseq[uent]ly aggravated by Italian off[ice]rs entering a house, pulling down a Jugoslav flag & carrying it off. The Italians deny that this had time to affect the issue, but this is improbable. Next 2 Italian petty officers and then 2 officers were attacked. When the firing act[ual]ly took place, there was a crowd in thousands & armed gendarmerie on the quay, and the Italians knew that many of the crowd had revolvers. One of the Italians however may have lost his head and fired.

The consequences were interesting. Not only did the captain of the Puglia[19] lose his life but the Italians have lost all desire to land in Spalato. As long as they

---

[16] Gabriele d'Annunzio (1863–1938), Principe di Montenevoso, cr. 1924, Italian writer and adventurer of Dalmatian extraction; served in war against Austria, 1916–18; organized raid on Bakar, Feb. 1918; seized and held Fiume/Rijeka, Sept. 1919–Dec. 1920; an early advocate of fascism.

[17] Presumably Ioniță Keşco, the only brother of Queen Natalie of Serbia (1859–1941).

[18] Vice-Admiral Adolphus Andrews (1879–1948), US sailor; commissioned into US Navy, 1901; junior naval aide to President Roosevelt, 1903–1906; aide to Prince Axel of Denmark, 1918; Assistant Chief of Staff, Atlantic Fleet, 1923–26; US delegate at Geneva armaments limitation conference, 1927; Chief of Staff, US Naval War College, 1931–3; Chief of Bureau of Navigation, 1935–38; commanded anti-submarine operations on the Eastern seaboard, 1942–43; retired, 1945.

[19] Captain Tommaso Gulli, commander of the torpedo-boat *Puglia*, was killed on 11 July 1920 during street fighting between Italians and Yugoslavs.

do not, no trouble is likely. According to the Admiral they were much impressed by ~~Nedić~~.[20]

He told me 2 stories one of which interested and the other amused me – one[,] the captain of the Puglia had been talking to him on the 11th. Adm[ira]l A[ndrews] had just returned from a journey thro[ugh] Bosnia, Slavonia and Voivodina. He said – I saw three millions of hogs, geese, turkeys and grain in abundance. I hear you have to import all these things from Western Europe at Chicago stock market prices. Why don't you make it up with the Jugos[lavs] and have your food at a decent price? Poor Gugli [*recte* Gulli] spent his afternoon composing a despatch on the merits of conciliating the Jugoslavs, and at 10 p.m. rushed out on the submarine chaser to the post where he met his death.

Adm[ira]l A[ndrews] told me about his tour, how at Karlovci[21] he had met the Archbishop, a little man, who had entertained him royally, and finally made a speech carefully prepared in English. The first time he had spoken it he had learnt it from books. He was delighted with the little chap. So was I, and with the story. For the little chap had made a speech once before and in my presence. He was Letić[22] of Temesvár, who read the 'Guardian' not 'Manchester' and spoke of the Entente supporting 'Parity, Liberty and Fraternity'.

25 [August 1920]

Went to Almissa,[23] a little town placed flat on the shore with a fine green gorge behind it showing like a funnel through a mass of rugged hills. The upper falls, though very low, were magnificent unwinding like white wool from a very narrow passage in the rocks. North west and east were very rugged walls of rock, to the south the opening towards Almissa green and terraced and cultivated. The highest and barest mountain here is Mosor[24] – Mons Aureus – between

---

[20] General Milan Nedić (1877–1946), Serbian soldier and politician; commissioned into army, 1904; General Staff Officer, 1915–16; aide-de-camp to King Peter, 1916–18; commanded infantry brigade on Salonika front, 1918; Commander, Drava Division *oblast*, 1919–23; Chief of Staff, 1934–35; Minister of the Army and Navy, 1939–40; Prime Minister of the Government of National Salvation, 1941–44; committed suicide, Feb. 1946.

[21] Sremski Karlovci, in the Voivodina, some five miles south of Novisad; in Habsburg times the seat of the Serbian Orthodox church.

[22] See entry 6 Dec. 1918.

[23] Now Omiš, on the Dalmatian coast, some 16 miles southeast of Split; a notorious pirates' nest in the sixteenth century.

[24] A mountain range in the Dinaric Alps.

the eagle's nest fortress of Clissa[25] and Almissa. Under its shadow and between these 2 spots was a little republic, up to the end of the eighteenth century, of shepherds and fishermen, which sternly battled against Ragusa and everyone else who tried to deprive it of liberty. It was really a sort of Montenegro, with a golden instead of a black mountain to overshadow it. The old villages here are all built about 2 or 300 feet above the sea, because of the pirates, Moslem ones are practically on the sea shore there being no tide. At sunset the light brings out the brown tint of the earth and the red hues in the granite and bathes the heights of freedom in gold. The line of the Mosor is straight & regular as a wall.

27 [August 1920]

Very rainy day. Read and digested the latest Jugoslav evidence, the findings of the judicial court on the events of 11 July. I think they omit some points of considerable value but there is no definite evidence that the Jugoslavs fired first.

Dined with the General. Dr. Krstelý, the President of Dalmatia also present. He seemed very cheerful – it turned out that he had resigned that day which was perhaps the cause. I doubt if the Belgrade Gov[ernmen]t will accept his resignation. The admin[istratio]n is extraordinarily difficult tho[ugh] he is a long-suffering man. German has been abol[ishe]d in the schools but French is not being properly taught owing to lack of instructors. In the lawcourts the greatest confusion prevails as illustrated by one interesting incident. The Agrarian Law was proposed to be applied here by decree from Belgrade & not as everywhere else with the greatest difficulties in practice. Admiral Andrews, the Adm[ira]l Admin[istrato]r, declared it did not apply to Dalmatia. Some judges acted on this, some did not, so that greater confusion was created; finally the High Court at Zagreb declared it ultra vires because it was the project of a law and not a law in the proper sense, but declared that Adm[ira]l Andrews was wrong in interfering. Juridically I cannot see that the Belgrade Gov[ernmen]t had a right to issue the decree, nor the Zagreb court the right to annul it. Adm[ira]l Andrews was the most nearly correct. I remember hearing Presid[en]t Wilson discuss this very point, at a meeting of the Ten, with reference to the territory south of the Karawanken. He said that he supposed this territory belonged to the Allies ad interim after the Treaty was signed and might conceivably be assigned to Italy, Jugoslavia or Austria. All agreed. Most judges etc. will not admit this and say they act in the name of King Peter. This, however, is wrong as they themselves

---

[25] The fortress of Klis, best known for its role in the defence against the Ottoman invasions in the sixteenth century.

have proved. For in case of insults being publicly given they do not proceed against the offender as a case of Majestäts-beleidigung.[26]

Another proof is that in the American sphere the Serbs have not yet conscripted anyone though they have in the Cattaro[27] area.

28 [August 1920]

Left for Cattaro.

29 [August 1920]

Arrive.

30 [August 1920]

Arrive Cettinje from Cattaro – 42 [kilometres]. Kipling says everyone has 3 or 4 pictures in his eye finer than any painter ever made. I should like to fix this one. I am sitting beneath a fig tree, the blue sky shining above its graceful fronds and tinting <the upper half of> the fruit lemon yellow, the lower half an exquisite <yellow> velvety paleness. Right left and rear wave the slender pale green leaves, and slender grey branches of young ash trees. Through them, wherever I look, I reach eventually the huge grey mountain walls, which look down on Cattaro on every side – walls grey and solemn, splashing silver to the sun, only occasionally touched with green, whether of wood or grass, more like lichen in the sun than anything else. In front are the tall lines of firs in the cemetery, numerous and erect in my picture like Las Lanzas of Velasquez.[28] Next the sideways view of the cross crowning the graveyard's gateway. Beyond and to the right the grey stones and red roofs of a few cottages and the bay a dazzling sheet of turquoise, cut asunder into 3 by a mole, and by trees obstructing the view. The town of Cattaro I hardly see at all, but above is a wide belt of wood, and above that again climb stoney lichened heights up to the blue heaven.

---

[26] That is, *lèse majesté*.
[27] Now Kotor.
[28] Better known as 'The Surrender of Breda' by Diego Valesquez (1599–1660), in the Prado.

31 [August 1920]

Saw Glamazić, prefect of Cettinje. Chief interest metropol[ita]n police 20,000 he pointed out all Mont[ene]g[r]o was policed with 1,000 which was the same number as the City [Police]. He had been reading an article on this subject. He was lame and a man with a severe energetic type of face, obviously more competent than the famous Provisional Government of five that his predecessor superseded. He is said to have shown some sharp practice recently in imprisoning political opponents, just after the summer session of the courts closed. Hence they c[ou]ld not be tried for 3 or 4 months until after the reassembly of the court. There certainly is some efficiency about e.g. the Food Controller, Novaković, whom I met on the road to Podgorica, is a man of high character and has done very well. He is now reporting at Belgrade. The prefect of Podgorica was superseded recently, Vučović[29] succeeding Boyović,[30] both were excellent men and Montenegrins. One tendency I note and it is important. Everyone repudiates the title of Governor of Montenegro – there is no head of the admin[istratio]n, simply a collection of prefects. Another point of importance, though there are plenty of political prisoners, the prisons at any rate, at Nikšić and Podgorica,[31] <under water!> described once as being very bad, have recently been inspected and are now tolerably clean. The population is gradually being clothed by the Red X. One sees that even in remote villages. Some of the clothes were made by the Montenegrins themselves, and a great deal of food has been imported and distributed. It appears, however, that the harvest, at first with great expectations, has turned out badly. Certainly the maize was wretched and at present it is not known that there is any reserve of food for the winter. So far as I can make out no taxes are being paid at present to have been for four years except through monopolies. Evidence for supporters of King Nicholas is very difficult to find, especially among the Red X people I have met.

There are comitadjis in Nikšić, who killed the gendarme the other day, but otherwise it is hard to find them – and comitadjis are always agin the government!

This day was a busy one – drove from Cettinje to Podgorica evening, 3 breakdowns – 42½ km, and 11.30 p.m. started for [Antivari].

---

[29] Jakov Vučović, member of Dalmatian Autonomist Party.
[30] See entry 2 Nov. 1918.
[31] Nikšić in central Montenegro and Podgorica, the capital, in the southeast.

1 Sept[ember 1920]

Podgorica to Antivari (77 km) Antivari – Scutari[32] (36) = 113 km, a wonderful all-night moonlit ride, the river by Rijeka,[33] which looked wonderful in the daylight, looked even more wonderful at night; and beyond Riyeka we passed Zabljak[34] in the distance between two peaks, low on the marshy flats, where Ivan Czernojević[35] kept his gold and his state and judged the people 'sitting on a silver settle'. Thence over the mountains in soft moonlight to Virbazar.[36] This little Turkish town lies on the lake practically in a marsh, nothing very much to be seen of it at night. There is a small island near where was once an underwater prison for special torments. After leaving we plunged directly down through the gorge of the Sotomore[37] [*sic*] pass towards Antivari. The dawn refused to break and the black-blue of the sky seemed lined with threads of red gold, for all the world like tiles of blue enamel fixed into the sky with fiery coloured cement.

On arriving at Antivari at 6 a.m. the 3 American Red X girls could not find the Italian steamer which sh[oul]d have taken them to Bari. We therefore went to sleep, some in the car and some on the quay. At 10 a.m. we woke up and drove round to the 3 hotels the place contains – or rather does not contain. Finally the 3rd surrendered at discretion and produced beefsteak and eggs. After eating this we whiled away the time drearily. I never realized how or why an azure sea & fine surrounding mountains could be insufferably boring yet it was so. Finally at 2 p.m. I suggested adjourning to the villa of ex-Crown Prince Danilo[38] as I expected to find General Mihailović arrived there. Danilo's villa was interesting, it was planted with tropical palms etc. and there was a tennis court, with electric light, for playing at night – a luxury of princes. Certainly Nicholas' family chose out the stars and plums for their own special use in the way of buildings. The villas and palaces are now curiously enough in every case converted either into barracks or hospitals, at any rate turned from private and dynastic to public purposes.

I saw General Mihailović, a fine man with a dark grey moustache and that sense of controlled power which all Serbian military authorities give you when you find in them anything to respect.

---

[32] Now Bar, on the Montenegrin coast, and Shkodër.
[33] Rijeka Crnojevića, between Cetinje and Podgorica.
[34] Žabljak, a small village on the shores of Lake Scutari.
[35] Ivan Crnojević ('John the Black') (d. 1490), Lord of Zeta, 1465–90; the principality was Serbian crown land but *de facto* independent since 1389, and covered much of Modern Montenegro. Crnojević fought variously against Venetians and Ottomans.
[36] Virpazar, a village on the western (Montenegrin) shore of Lake Scutari.
[37] Sutomore, a small coastal town near Bar; until 1797, part of Albania Veneta (Ven. Spizza).
[38] See entry 2 Jan. 1919.

3 Sept[ember 1920]

Saw Dr. Burnham of White X. Even by his own account he is an unconscious humourist of a high order and, though he has only recently been expelled from Dulcigno.[39] My only surprise is that he was not expelled some time ago. He came as a Red X man and appears at the suggestion of the Americans to have indulged in schemes for enabling American subjects in Montenegro to leave the country, in spite of having been forbidden to do so by the Serbian Gov[ernmen]t, and of the fact that he was sending them to Italy. A letter describing his activities fell into the hands of the Serbs and was censored in the ordinary post. As he gradually fell under suspicion he was watched and took to making his journeys to Scutari and, when asked why, declined to say anything except 'personal business'. He naively mentions the help and support he had received from the Italians in all things. He seems in short to have assumed the role of a political Don Quixote out to redress injustice and without any regard for the fact that Red Xs should be impolitical [*sic*].

I also attempted to clear up the perplexing affair of Baerlein[40] & Gibbons.[41] Both are British subjects – first however a German Jew – and pronounced Jugoslavs. They apparently at once began a violent pro-Serb propaganda here, insulted the Archbishop[42] and the Franciscan Superior and generally gave everyone the idea they were comic brigands. The fact that they wore camouflaged British uniforms was, I think justly, used as an argument against their authenticity. Without them, however, I believe they would have been shot. The Gov[ernmen]t were considerably surprised at my intervention and offered to bring them back from Medua.[43] This however I refused.[44]

---

[39] Now Ulcinj on the Montenegrin coast.

[40] Henry Baerlein (1875–1960), journalist and travel-writer specializing in eastern Europe and the Near East; cf. his *The Birth of Yugoslavia* (2 vols, London, 1922) and *A Difficult Frontier* (London, 1922). He was not a German Jew, as Temperley surmised, but born in Manchester, educated at Charterhouse and Trinity College, Cambridge; his father, Otto Baerlein, was honorary Serbian consul at Manchester, 1896–1920; his brother Harold succeeded him in 1920.

[41] John Gibbons (1882–1949), journalist and travel writer; author of, *inter alia*, *London to Sarajevo* (London, 1933), *I wanted to Travel* (London, 1938), *The Keepers of the Baltic* (London, 1939), *The Soviet Union and Its Western Neighbours* (London, 1946).

[42] Jacob (née Jakë Serreqi), Roman Catholic archbishop of Shkodër-Pult, 1910–21.

[43] Now Shëngjin.

[44] Cf. tel. Temperley to Buchanan (ambassador at Rome), 3 Sept. 1920: 'Two British journalists Baerlein and Gibbons were removed from Scutari on grounds of utterances and actions calculated to excite population. Two independent witnesses confirm this. Have received assurances from Albanian Government as to their securiy of life and property. Their uniforms occasionsed much comment.'

4 [September 1920]

Left Scutari for Tirana <112 km>. Beautiful scenery, at first by the side of the Drin, then with grand walls of rock, not bare stone like the Dinaric Alps but well vegetated, on one hand and reeds and bushes stretching out flat to the invisible sea on the other great hills, bare at the top like a rampart, but clothed with trees well up the sides. Kruja,[45] a famous haunt of tribesmen, is the finest of all.

5 [September 1920]

<u>Tirana to Scutari</u>. Saw Gov[ernmen]t Suleiman Bey[46] & Tourtoulis Pasha[47] and return Scutari from Tirana (120 km).

Following conversations with Albanians, at the crossing of the Mat Ep.[48] Who do you belong to? A[nswer]: Kastorini tribe. How many fighting men have you? 2,000. Do you ever fight anybody? No. Why do you carry arms? Because there are sometimes cattle-thieves about. Don't you ever fight the Matya (next tribe)? No, never. Have you been to fight the Serbs? No. Why not? We've so many men as gendarmes and soldiers already, that there was no need for the whole tribe to go. You must really fight other tribes – who are the ones south of you? The Kruëzez. Don't you fight them? No. The Shkrela,[49] don't you fight them? Yes, sometimes. Are you Mohammedans? Yes. Where is your chief town? Miloti.[50] I see on the map there is a church there. How can that be if you are

---

Neither man later mentioned the incident in his memoirs, see H. Baerlein, *Travels without a Passport* (London, 1942) and J. Gibbons, *I Wanted to Travel* (London, 1938). Temperley met Baerlein again, by coincidence, in Sofia in 1933: 'The only good thing about Sofia was that Baerlein, whom I met in the train, got out there. The Anglo-German-Jewish journalist buttonholed me in the train and bored me with his inconceivably boring sermons on everything. When he was in Scutari, in 1920, shut up in prison by the Albanian Revolutionary Government, I got in a boat and rode [*sic*] over from Montenegro and pulled him out at the risk of my life, for Albanian sentries levelled rifles at my breast as I rode [*sic*] over. It is remarkable how one resents sermons from a person for whom one has risked [one's life]', Temperley diary, 'Near East, Sept.–Oct. 1933', entry 15 Sept. 1933.

[45] Krujë, a town in northern central Albania, some 15 miles to the north of Tirana, between Mount Krujë and the river Ishëm.

[46] Sulejman Bej Delvino (1884–1932), Albanian politician; Albanian representative at Paris Peace Conference, 1919; Prime Minister, Mar.–Dec. 1920; took part in the overthrow of Ahmet Zogu, 1924; Foreign Minister, June–Dec. 1924.

[47] Dr Mihal Turtulli Bej Korçë (1847–1935), Albanian oculist and politician; member of the High Council, Jan.–Dec. 1920.

[48] Mat, river in northern Albania, which debouches into the Adriatic near Fushë-Kuqe.

[49] A tribe in northwestern Albania.

[50] Now Milot, a town four miles north of Laç.

Mohammedans? There are also Catholics in our tribe. How many? About half and half. Are there two chiefs? Yes. Where does the Mohammedan chief live? Also in Miloti. Do you pay any taxes except the dime? Yes. What did you pay last month? 87 gold napoleons. From 2,000 men? Yes. Do you like paying it? No. Would you pay any more? No.

Interview 2. With an Albanian north of that river [Mat].

What tribe do you belong to? Plana tribe. What is its central town? Plana.[51] What are you in religion? Catholics. How many fighting men have you? 60 houses, 460 fighting men. Why do you carry arms? Because there have been Austrians and Turks in the land. But are there any now? No but there are Italians & Serbs. Have you sent any men to fight the Serbs? No! Curious that they had no relations with & no knowledge of the Kastorini tribe though only divided by a stream. They also had no use for the Matya tribe to which they belong.

Dr. Bourcart,[52] a Frenchman, residing at present in Tirana, professedly on the pretext of studying geological phenomena of Albania, gave me a good many details of the tribes, chiefly Mirdite and Matija. He said a regent – Mala [*sic*] John[53] – governed the Mirdites from Oroshi,[54] that his position was that of a chieftain, who was practically an autocrat. The tribe was very large and important. They were friendly to the new government but paid neither taxes <exc[ept] the dime[55]> and sent no soldiers to it. The Matija on the other hand were purely feudal, divided into 4 tribes or subdivisions. All are Moslems. Food was at present insufficient in both tribes. The Dukagini[56] he knew less about but they are a very strong commercial tribe on the route Scutari to Prisrend, and are great cattle breeders.

6 Sept[ember 1920]

Visited chef de police and saw a number of refugees from Hoti, Gruda & Gusinje[57] coming into the town, or encamped on its outskirts. Afterwards

---

[51] Pllamë, in northwestern Albania.

[52] Jacques Bourcart (1892–1965), French geographer and marine scientist; active service, 1914–18; PhD, 1922; research director, Sorbonne, 1925–50; professor, 1950–55; Professor of Physical Geography, 1955–61; a specialist on the Albanian and Moroccan littorals, cf. *L'Albanie et les Albanais* (Paris, 1921).

[53] Kapidan Gjon Markagjon (1888–1960), Albanian tribal leader; led Mirdite rebellion, 1921; President of the Republic of Mirdita, 1921; clan chief since 1925; pacified northern Albania, 1926–28; led anti-Communist guerrilla, 1944–46; in exile in Rome since 1946.

[54] A small town in northwestern Albania, the traditional seat of the Mirditë chief.

[55] Fr. *la dime*, tithe.

[56] Dukagjini tribe in northern Albania, to the east of Skodër and north of the river Drin.

[57] Hoti, clan area in the region Malësia along the Albano-Montenegrin frontier; Grudi in the Malësia region of southern Montenegro, to the north of Lake Scutari; Gusinje (Alb. Guci) in

strolled through Scutari bazaar in company with chef de police and 3 American girls who seemed to embarrass the former considerably. He ordered a carriage for the girls to take them back to the town, and sent them off on a circuitous route, and then seated me and himself in a second, and went off on the direct road, thus saving his dignity by preceding the women. Afterwards I visited the school or clearing house for refugees, as the public schools have already begun to exist. I examined first into the tribes from which the refugee children came. They were 20 Hoti, 4 or 5 Gruda, 2 Shkreli, 2 Rugova, 1 Klementi, 20 Kastrati, 1 Koplika,[58] 2 from other points beyond the border. I do not find any Djakovitsi or Krasnich, Mestini or Niray. This seems to indicate that some tribes are pro-Serb.

The children did some dances, one representing get up in the morning, brushing the hair[,] powdering the face etc. Another a Scutari dance rather like the Montenegrin dance waving the hands above the head etc. Curious that the Serbians sing beautifully, the Albanians tolerably, while Montenegrins can only howl like tone-deaf wolves. The Montenegrins have a very wild sword dance rather Albanian in type, and a sort of lover's dance, which should, but for reasons of modesty[,] end in a public kiss between the two.

7 Sept[ember 1920]

Return Scutari <36> – Antivari <77 km> – Podgorica 113.

8 [September 1920]

Nikšić & back 119 km – and then Cettinje 42 km 151 km.

Saw again in Nikšić M. & Mme. Soličista [sic], head of the Piva clan.[59] M[ada]me looked statelier and sadder than ever and gave me & American Red X girl the most delicious confection of stewed figs ever tasted. The carpets in this house are priceless especially a pale blue motif from Novibazar.[60] Nothing else to note in Nikšić.

I am impressed more than ever by the extraordinary misery here, round about Podgoritza the hovels are terrible – one room, no chimney, a chain from

---

southeastern Montenegro.

[58] Škrijelj, a clan in northern Albania and southern Montenegro; Rugova, a clan in western Kosovo; Klementi (Alb. Kelmendi), a Roman Catholic clan in the north; Kastrati, a clan to the north of Shkodër; Koplik clan from Koplik on Lake Scutari in northwestern Albania.

[59] Piva (or Pivljani), a Serb clan from Old Herzegovina in Montenegro. The Sočica were a prominent family in Piva, cf. Voivode Lazar Sočica (1838–1910), who took a prominent part in the 1875–76 war against Turkey.

[60] The Sandjak of Novipazar, an Ottoman district between Montenegro and Serbia.

the roof for the kettle, cattle and pigs living in the house to warm the inhabitants and three or four families in a room, that is the worst – or rather not the worst. For the poorest live in caves under the overhanging banks of the Moratcha.[61] One little boy <now> at the orphanage lived there with his mother and her 2 sisters, and all three lost their lives one stormy night trying to find their way down to the cave by a rutted track. In some of the caves three families live, and in others the damp streams from the roof on the dwelling. We are really back in the age of troglodytes.

9 [September 1920]

Return from Cettinje to Podgorica 42 km.

Stoyanović,[62] the SHS finance minister arrived here today – it is said to enable the SHS Gov[ernmen]t to distribute and issue the financial credits. What information he can get I do not know, from prefects who know only their petty local affairs – and how he can get any conspectus of the total wants of Montenegro is still more mysterious. There appears to be some financial control independent of prefects etc.

Visit to Junior Red X orphanage. I understand there are 93 orphans here and between 2–3 at Danilovgrad.[63] Altogether there are 7,000 in Montenegro, i.e. without both parents and 17,000 deprived of one. There are also a number, the children of women who marry again. Such children can be, and often are turned adrift, by command of the second husband. The magisterial authority of the father therefore triumphs maternal instinct. In the orphanage is one remarkable sight. Militza Perunovic, as matron, a tall strong rather boyish but not masculine looking girl, who was a famous comitadji leader in the war. Seven Austrian officers are said to have been her victims and now she controls little children under the direction of a small American girl half her height and one quarter of her strength. Wondrous are the ways of the Red X and still more wondrous those of comitadjis. One curious fact – the orphanage includes both Montenegrins & Serbs – they distinguish between the two by calling the former dark and the latter fair. As a generalisation it is true, I think, though since I heard I have kept seeing Montenegrin women with brown and not black hair.

---

[61] Morača, a river in northern Montenegro that flows past Podgorica and empties into Lake Scutari.

[62] Ljubomir Stojanović (1860–1930), Serbian historian and politician; Professor of History, Belgrade, 1891–99; Minister of Education, 1903, 1904, 1906 and 1909; Prime Minister, 1906.

[63] See entry 30 Dec. 1918.

10 [September 1920]

Left Podgorica for frontier at 7 a.m. Cijena[64] [*sic*] brook with very steep banks, but no water. Fine old castle at Sipčovik. 28 kil[metres] good road to the top of Ličeni [*sic*] Hotit.[65] First we took carriage to Hulm [*sic*], then rowed in a metal pontoon across a sort of lake,[66] covered with water lilies and wild-fowl. The Austrians had bridged this lake but afterwards artistically destroyed a part of the bridge and taken out a plank or two of what they had not destroyed at intervals of every two yards. For artistic destruction no-one ever equalled the Austrians. Then we took horses. I had a fine black one, and wound slowly up the arms of the Ličeni [*sic*] Hotit to point 178, just opposite to and commanding it. The Colonel and officers received me with all the old Serbian hospitality and, seeing me look sleepy, forced me to lie down for 2 hours after lunch. On arising I had a superb view from the nest. By Han Hotit[67] just below point 178, the Albanians broke through. The Serbs have now seized and fortified Boudza and Velečiku[68] and dragged up cannons. By this means, if the Albanians advance again, and it is the only way here they can advance, they will be exposed to fire from 3 quarters without effective possibility of reply. I am told the last time they tried this game – that was on 23rd Aug[ust] – there were no infantry on the spot, but the artillery held them well in play, and they retired with heavy losses.

It must be terrible to remain here up hill 178 – all water to be carried by hand every day, no food except from Podgorica, no amusements for the troops, only bivouacs, terrible in ice, snow & wind when winter comes. What soldiers in the world will stand this, except Serb soldiers, but these soldiers are not all Serbs & being Croats, Dalmatian etc. I wonder if their morale will be as good. The Albanians attacked fiercely twice, and with some success for a while. But they never got as far as Tuzi.[69]

Tuzi is a wonderful and curious old town, very old and very Turkish. It was taken by a coup de main by the Montenegrins at the beginning of the war of 1912. It contains of course the usual Turkish barracks now used by the Serbs.

---

[64] Cijevna, a small river near Podgorica.
[65] Lićeni Hotit, the northwestern extension of Lake Scutari leading up to the town of Hani Hotit.
[66] The Humsko Blato, a shallow, marshy lake a short distance to the north of Lake Scutari.
[67] Hani Hotit, on the Montenegrin border.
[68] Bozaj, a Montenegrin border point.
[69] Tuzi, a town to the northwest of Lake Scutari, half-way along the main road between Podgorica and Hani Hotit.

11 [September 1920]

Had a curious and unpleasant experience of the official class today. A Montenegrin now a British subject naturalised in Canada since 1911, Stepan Stepanović – Steve Stevens – came to me and said that the authorities had detained his passport for some time. He said he thought they had no right to do so. I went to see the Prefect.

Q[uestion]: There is a small matter here about a British subject who sh[ould] receive his passport.
A[nswer]: Who is he? Details given –
Q: Why has his passport not been given him?
A: We cannot give anyone their passports until they leave the country.
Q: That I know to be inaccurate because American citizens have received their passports before leaving the country and in any case I refuse to accept this as a principle of international law.
A: No answer, but is this man really a British subject?
Q: Of course he is – look at the passport. I see that it says there 'formerly a Montenegrin citizen' – this has been viséd by the Serbian Government Consul in London – both Governments attest to this statement, do they not?
A: According to our laws it is necessary to have a certificate as well.
Q: Here it is (giving naturalization paper). You could have had it from the man any time. I do not, however, admit, in view of the visés given, that it is necessary. Will you not give the man his passport?
A: There are other matter against him. We have some suspicions about him. It is not the same if he were a British citizen only. He was a Montenegrin officer and fought in 1914–5.
Q: Will you give me a statement of these suspicions in writing?
A: We are not prepared to do that.
Q: Will you then give the man his passport? You have the right to expel him but not to detain his passport.
A: Yes, as soon as he appears and signs his name for it.

In private I heard that they told the man that a British subject might mix in politics, but an American w[oul]d not, and that is why they had detained his passport. If they do these things to British subjects what will they do to M[ontenegrin]? (He got his passport on Monday.)

In the book shops here there is a curious atmosphere. A work full of insults to old N[icholas I] is sold in the street once called Königl Nikolagasse by the Austrians in curious reference to him, and now Sloboda Ulica (Freedom Street). They deny that they have any collection of Montenegrin Nat[iona]l Songs, only Serbian etc. All the signs of pressure.

Saw Col[onel] Martinović, the Serb Commandant here, a man of boisterous, irritable Prussian type – what Canning would call 'a downright grenadier with no politics but the drumhead & cat-o'-nine tails'.[70] He began by denouncing the wickedness of D'Annunzio's seizure of Fiume. He went on to ask for an exactly similar action at Scutari. He said the situation was impossible and would be worse in the winter. He had in the last 2 months been called out of bed 20 times with rumours of Albanian attacks. They were a savage people who understood nothing but pillage and robbery. The only law they understood was the baton. He had enough of politicians and was sure the local population would help him to take Scutari by force. He was determined to do it and would not delay much longer.

Q[uestion]: But I thought you disapproved of D'Annunzio?
A[nswer]: Yes, what then?
Q: Why should you seek to imitate him?

M[artinovic]: found difficulty in replying. Among items of information he communicated the fact that he had received an offer from the chief of the Clementi to put all his resources at his disposal. He also said that all the Gruda were on his side, which is only partially true. I suspect the baton may have something to do with this. M[artinović] seemed to be a true Potsdam type and, unlike Gen[eral] Mihailović showed no sign of control or of power.

12 [September 1920]

Danilovgrad. This is a pleasant home for little orphans, also a state experimental farm which still exists, tho[ugh] diminished in value & utility. This school & that at Podgoritza will ultimately take about 400 children. I saw a certain P at D[anilovgrad]. I was informed by him and at least one other reliable witness that he held a meeting a few days ago in which he quite openly advocated a republic and denounced the P[rince] R[egent Alexander] on these lines. If he reigns he will marry and have children and you will have to pay for all these. There appears to have been a great crowd and much applause. The chef de police, a Serb, attempted to interfere with some gendarmes. The result however alarmed him because the local organization[,] the Omladina,[71] supported the speaker & went to get their guns. So he subsided and no arrests were made. There are

---

[70] Canning's characterization of Prussia in 1818, see H.W.V. Temperley, 'The Foreign Policy of Canning', in A.W. Ward and G.P. Gooch (eds), *The Cambridge History of British Foreign Policy* (3 vols, Cambridge, 1922–23), 54.

[71] A political youth movement in Montenegro.

many such Omladina, notably in Zeta and Kolasin[72] – all are Jugoslavs but now apparently for a republic, or at least anti-Serb. There are 3,000 in the district between Danilovgrad & Ljekopolje, 1,000 in Zeta.

13 [September 1920]

Cettinje <42 km>. C[oul]d not see General no time coming out – 1 breakdown – coming back 4 punctures, last at the 13th kilometre from Podgoritza. I have three times visited Podgoritza in an auto and 3 times broken down. Lost my stick & recovered it – also an important letter & ditto.

Capt[ain] Whiting told me he expected to feed 16,000 children this winter if he stayed on – probably there were 21,000 needing it. The minister Stoyanovic is said to have been much struck by poverty here and to have said it was the poorest part of all Jugoslavia.

I gathered some details as to the volunteer levies raised in July to meet the Albanians. Bojović, a Montenegrin, commanded them. The Omladina sent detachments[,] that of Danilovgrad 150. All were very dissatisfied and very badly fed. There was in consequence a great demon[stratio]n ag[ain]st Bojović in Podgorica. The Serbs patrolled the streets but did not interfere otherwise.

14 [September 1920]

Podgorica – Plavnica[73] – 18km – ~~boat~~ vedette to Suoktar[74] thence back to Scutari. Decided to revisit Albania – got transport from Red X to Plavnica – right across a flat plain and right of Žabljak.[75] Stopped at Golubovci[76] some minutes and conversed with a lusty lad.

> Q[uestion]: Are you all Montenegrins in Zeta?
> A[nswer]: All.
> Q: No Albanians?
> A: None.
> Q: What about the Hoti district?
> A: Not Albanians. Catholics.
> Q: What about the Gruda? Aren't they Mussulmans?

---

[72] Zeta plain, which stretches from Podgorica to Lake Scutari; Kolašin, a town in eastern central Montegro.
[73] A village on the northern shores of Lake Scutari.
[74] Presumably Seoca, a village southeast of Virpazar on Lake Scutari.
[75] A small village half-way between Virpazar and Podgorica, on the Morača river.
[76] Golubovci, a small town, 10 miles south of Podgorica on the main road to the coast.

A: Yes, but Serbian Mussulman.
Q: At this rate is not all Albania Serb?
A: No.
Q: How much [of] it then?
A: I don't know.

I saw some signs of foreign literature at Podgorica finding the only two English authors represented were Elinor Glyn[77] and Oscar Wilde.[78] Here I surprised a Serb soldier reading – Pierre Loti[79] of all people.

15 [September 1920]

Scutari to Tirana 67 km. Nothing special to note. Scutari lake in all its moods is wonderful, its grand grey fortress flanked by Tarabosh[80] red and grey on one side, and on the other the Albanian mountains, the highest marking where, say the villagers, the ark of Noah rested instead of on Ararat – and the glassy blue lake between. At dawn an exquisite grey film floats over the lake – seen in the distance, as at Tuzi, it turns a delicate robin's egg blue. In the full sun, seen from Tarabosh or a corresponding height the lake is less glassy – green-blue like a serpent – and at evening a pale cold blue like steel, until just as the last light dies it turns lilac and last of all a cold aluminium grey. I saw it thus last night from a little way above the old Venetian bridge. There we picnicked frying eggs and bacon and eating it under the moon. When that went out, I lighted a bush, and the glorious blaze 'streamed like a meteor to the troubled air'.[81] On the way out I was shown a little conical hill where King Nicholas sat to await the tidings of the fall of Scutari. Strange destiny for him – to dream in youth and to embody in noble verse the dream of adding Scutari to Montenegro, and in age twice to capture Scutari and neither time to retain it above two or three weeks. Vile as the man is – vile as he once was noble – one cannot help pitying him in this.

---

[77] Elinor Glyn (1864–1943), Anglo-Canadian popular writer of racy novels for a mass readership.
[78] Oscar Fingall O'Flahertie Wilde (1854–1900), Irish poet and epigrammatist.
[79] Pierre Loti (pseud. Julien Viaud) (1850–1923), French naval officer and writer, famed for his descriptive powers.
[80] Taraboš, a mountain west of Shkodër.
[81] See Thomas Gray's 'The Bard': 'With haggard eyes the poet stood/ (Loose his beard, and hoary hair/ Streamed like a meteor to the troubled air'. On taking up his fellowship at Peterhouse, Temperley occupied the rooms once belonging to Gray, overlooking the churchyard of Little St. Mary's.

16 [September 1920]

Tirana to Scutari – important interview with Tourtoulis and Suleiman Bey. They said that there were 30,000 refugees and 50,000 of them fighting men, so that a very serious situation was created. Sh[oul]d they negotiate? I thought that, placed as they were, their situation could hardly be injured by negotiation, and might be improved. They reflected on this for some time and finally said nous prendrons. Very remarkable conversation of Tourtoulis subsequently on revision of the Treaties – as a whole – which w[oul]d include a revision of the Balkan world on the lines of ethnic justice, bring the Bulgars to Vodena and Monastir[82] and redrawing the 1913 frontiers against the Greeks & Serbs. Gr[ee]k triangle Chamouria.[83] Consequently the Albanian question w[oul]d again come up and Djakova, Novibazar, Prisrend, Ipek[84] & Pristina must return.

I said that this implied that the Conference Treaties had been planned on the basis of injustice which I did not think the Powers w[oul]d admit, that such a revision as had been made or, so far as I knew, was contemplated was on the expect[ation] of making Germany pay certain sums, that there was no question of revising territorial decisions and that, even if there was, this did not apply to the decisions of 1913 preceding the war.

17 [September 1920]

Scutari

18 [September 1920]

Scutari to Plavnica.
   Nikšić – protect[tora]te – Balkan League.

19 [September 1920]

Cettinje & back. Saw Gen[eral] Jov[anovi]ć. Min[imu]m & max[imu]m come frères – re Mart[i]nović.

---

[82] Now Edessa in northern Greece, and Bitola in southwestern Macedonia.

[83] Alb. *Çamëri* (Gr. *Τσ(ι)αμουριά*), Albanian-speaking area in northwestern Epirus and in the region around Preveza. The Chams (Alb. *Çamë*) are a distinct ethno-cultural group.

[84] Now Peć in western Kosovo.

I said that he made serious statements to me on taking Scutari by a coup de main with the aid of comitadjis, that this was a serious matter and asked him as a friend to see to it that no rash act of this kind should take place before the decision of the conference was announced. He agreed with me and promised to see to it that such an attempt should be rendered impossible. <Evidently some notice was taken of this, for a dementi was issued from Belgrade on the 21st that any such reports were without foundation and was reproduced in the papers (Nova Doba[85]) 22nd.>

21 [September 1920]

Cettinje, Ragusa, good road all way.

22 [September 1920]

Slano.[86] Three hours by boat. This is a lovely place, surrounded by hills with a perfect bay in front and my dear Milan at home in his own place. I went out this evening, and saw an old man looking out of his window at the sunset. His wife died a year ago and since then he has lived alone in a big house which he manages entirely himself.

> Q[uestion]: How are you?
> A[nswer]: Very well.
> Q: How long were you in America?
> A: Nearly half my life.
> Q: Did you like it?
> A: Yes.
> Q: Why did you leave then?
> A: Because I was a damn fool.
> Q: Why don't you go back then?
> A: Because I am a damn fool.

Near Slano there is a curious cave known as the bridal cave. A wedding parting, consisting on the return journey of a bride & a husband, accompanied by other boats, put off to return to Ragusa. Weather interrupted them. The other boats put back and the bridal boat put into the cave where it remained six hours until it was dark. The only joyful one of the legends of Dalmatia which tell always of

---

[85] That is, 'New Era'.
[86] Slano (It. Islana), a small village on the Dalmatian coast, 17 miles northwest of Dubrovnik.

sad and not of joyous lovers. The only other cave adventure I remember is that of Aeneas and Dido, but that was not a happy one.[87]

Saw T[rumbić]. He seemed ready to compromise about Albania provided there were rectifications to protect Prisrend, Dibra & Hani Hotit. He said that Italy c[oul]d not demand the 1913 frontier if Sasseno[88] [*sic*] remained to her.

Re FIUME he thought the L[eague] of N[ations] a British invention.

On Schneeberg[89] it was impossible to compromise, but he might accept the Scialoja[90]-Nitti[91] line 20th March, which leaves [it] out. 'Something very modern and yet romantic, something stupendously resolute. Going whither? At any rate, going magnificently somewhere. That was the power of it. It <u>was</u> going somewhere'. So Wells in Joan & Peter of Germany (p. 491)[92] contrasted with the helpless Russia. I cannot help thinking of Jugoslavia contrasted with helpless Italy. The P[rince] R[egent] is modern, yet romantic, his G[eneral] S[taff] stupendously resolute – it is going somewhere. Italy is in the trough, enduring a moral and political Caporetto. Is she going anywhere, and if she is, that is the weakness of her. She is heading for anarchy.

30 Sept[embe]r [1920]

Heard a curious instance today illustrating old, haphazard <and anarchic> Mont[ene]gro. A new order to effect that bullock carts must not enter a market place at Podgorica. A villager, who had not heard [of] or disregarded the order, parked his bullock cart. The prefect sent a gendarme to remove it – the villager refused to go – the gendarme then took away his revolver. Incensed at the insult to his honour, the villager appealed to his fellow villagers. These came thick around the gendarme and forced him to give up the revolver.

This incident shows the temper of the people – village and clan can still prevail over municipal & civil law.

---

[87] In Henry Purcell's opera *Dido and Aeneas* (1688), Act 2, scene 1, which is set in the cave of the sorceress who is plotting the destruction of Carthage.

[88] *Recte* Saseno, now Sazan, a small island in the Straits of Otranto at the entrance to the Bay of Vlorë.

[89] Now Snežnik (Ger. *Schneeberg*; It. *Monte Nevoso*), a karst plateau in the Dinaric Alps of southwestern Slovenia, some 17 miles from the Adriatic coast.

[90] Vittorio Scialoja (1856–1933), Italian lawyer and politician; Professor of Roman Law, Rome University, 1884–1931; Senator, 1904–33; Minister of Justice, 1909–10; Propaganda Minister, 1916–17; Foreign Minister, 1919–20; delegate at Paris Peace Conference, 1919; at League of Nations, 1921–32; Minister of State, 1927–33.

[91] See entry 8 Oct. 1918.

[92] H.G. Wells, *Joan and Peter: The Story of an Education* (London, 1918), one of Wells' lesser novels.

3rd Oct[obe]r [1920]

Gov[ernmen]t has ordered 4,500 waggons <to be delivered via Bakar> of food for relief of Dalmatia in winter. As the maximum clearance is 15 wag[gon]s a day, 300 days will be consumed before the food is delivered.

8 Oct[ober 1920]

C[onference of] A[mbassadors]
USA declines to sign Bessarabian Treaty 'in view of their persistent refusal to approve a policy tending towards dismemberment of Russia'. Reject German Gov[ernmen]t's applic[atio]n (6th Oct[obe]r) for special militia E[ast] Prussia. Russian & German war material in Austria to be destroyed.

Austrian Comm[issio]n of Control (Gen[eral] Zoulong). Mil[itar]y Conf[eren]ce of Versailles instructed to draw up scheme <either by destruction> in case of material allotted to G[reat] B[ritain], or by removing without delay to various Allied Countries to whose Gov[ernmen]ts it allotted them.

15 Oct[ober] 1920[93]

I am prepared to admit some modifications of the Wilson line.

Q[uestion]: W[oul]d you accept the T[reaty] of L[ondon] line?
A[nswer]: Why should I? Nitti & Scialoja offered us something better in March.
Two points we c[oul]d not, in any circumstances accept (showing the map). Schneeberg[94] (here p[oin]t 1796, and M[oun]t Blegas[95] (p[oin]t. 1596) have both been claimed by Italy. These two points threaten the two roads to Laibach and would ensure its speedy fall, in case of war. So far from accepting them we could not even discuss them, and discussion of them would break off the negotiation.
Q: What about FIUME?

---

[93] This entry summarizes an interview with Ante Trumbić, see memo. Temperley, 'Notes on Conversation with Dr Trumbić', 15 Oct. 1920, Temperley MSS, file 'Despatches as Assistant Military Attaché Belgrade'.
[94] See entry 22 Sept. 1920.
[95] Now Mount Blegoš, west of Škofja Loka (Ger. *Bischoflack*) between the Poljane Sora and the Selca Sora rivers, in Slovenian Carniola.

A: Sušak[96] with port Baross must remain Jugoslav. But the larger harbour of FIUME is essential to us also for deep draught ships and railway communication.

[Q]: Would you accept an independent sovereignty of FIUME?

A: Yes, provided it was inalienable.

Q: Why would you not accept the League of Nations as a guarantee for communications?

A: (hesitating) Some people say the League is a British device.

Q: I believe the Italians did not at first suggest, certainly have never favoured, the L[eague] of N[ations] solution of the communications of FIUME. This looks as if there were advantages in Jugoslavia having this solution.

T[rumbić] had no fears about Dalmatia.

He seemed very pessimistic about the whole negotiation as did General Resic.

17 October 1920

Lunched with Prince Regent [Alexander]. Met also Princess Hélène,[97] who was very amiable – nobody except myself and Janković,[98] General Zevković and Major Dimitrievič.[99]

Talk – first about my tour. H[is] R[oyal] H[ighness] asked me about it. I said that it was a hard time. He said he believed so. He was much astonished to find that there was a road from Scutari to Alessio and thence to Arana traversable by motors. He seemed pleased that I had been there and that the thrust for Tirana had caused the Gov[ernmen]t such fear. He seemed to have great contempt for the Gov[ernmen]t of Tirana & to doubt whether it had any control over Valona.[100] I said I thought it had but not over the northern parts. I said that when they mobilised at Tirana they had shut up the shops – 'on n'a pas eu beaucoup de confiance', said he amusingly.

---

[96] Sušak, the eastern suburb of Rijeka; under the Treaty of Rapallo (12 Nov. 1920) it was part of the Free State of Fiume.

[97] Princess Jelena (Helen) Karađorđević (1884–1962), daughter of King Peter I of Serbia (r. 1903–21); married Prince Ivan Konstantinovich Romanov (1886–1918), who was killed by Bolshiviks in July 1918; in exile in Sweden, later France.

[98] Presumably General Radivoje Janković (1889–1949), Serb soldier; Chief of Army Operations, 1941; aide-de-camp to King Peter II of Yugoslavia in exile, 1941–49.

[99] General Aleksandar Dimitrijević (1884–1963), Serbian soldier and courtier; Chief of Operations section, General Staff, 1923–26; Military Attaché, 1926–27; Marshal to the Royal Court, 1927–34; Deputy Inspector for National Defence, 1932–34; retired, 1934; recalled, 1941, as General Officer Commanding 22nd Division; prisoner of war, 1941–45; US exile, since 1945.

[100] Now Vlorë (Albania).

He then asked me about Montenegro – what do they think of the Gospodar? (roi Nicholas). I said that his partisans in my opinion had greatly diminished and gave instances to prove this. I said the bulk of the population appeared to be Jugoslav in one form or another – but he showed some disinclination to go further here. He asked about the internal condition of Montenegro – de faim [i.e. starvation]?

After lunch H[is] R[oyal] H[ighness] shewed me a silver sword from Sarajevo graven with the Serb victories. He said he was much pleased with his reception. I said that I read he had been called seven times out on the balcony. He 'Yes'. I 'Even the most celebrated prima donnas could not exceed that'. He laughed. <I said I supposed he was the only sovereign for 5 centuries who had visited Serajevo without fear.> He then made me read out and translate a very embarrassing article on himself by H.C. Woods.[101] It was to the effect that he was the link between Serbs, Croats & Slovenes, that he read history, botany, astronomy – 'I only know the great Bear', he interrupted – and social science (He looked a little dubious). That he knew maps and topography very well and sometimes corrected his general staff (He looked pleased). That he loved bridge which he learnt to play at Salonica, and riding and shooting but at the latter was so excited that he sometimes forgot to fire well (much excitement). Then that he did not go into society much because of its jealousies (tension) but was a truly democratic ruler, who loved talking with peasants and giving them a lift in his car. One passage referring to the fact that he seemed to have had no youth being a Crown Prince at 21 seemed very sad and, to judge from his expression, <u>true</u>.

Princess Hélène, who spoke good English, began by saying that she had heard I was a very great friend of Jugoslavia. I said I had deserved that title. <You speak Serb, I think? Yes, but not as well as you do English.> 'Do you not think it is very sad about him', pointing to the P[rince] R[egent]. 'He wants so much to marry somebody nice. It was nearly arranged that he should marry the youngest daughter of the Czar, but then the tragedy came. He would like to marry an English Princess. Q. Is he intending to visit England? A. Yes, but he would like to be invited, because then he would know he would be welcome, and it would make a great impression on the people here. Q. I don't think there would be much difficulty about that. When would he like to come? About February when the elections are over but he would like to have the invitation before.

---

[101]   Henry Charles Woods (1881–1939), journalist and writer; entered army, 1907; active service, South Africa, 1900–1902; forced to resign on the grounds of inefficiency ('Woods Case'), 1907; appointed vice-consul at Adana, 1910, but did not proceed; war correspondent, *The Times*, 1911–12, *Evening News*, 1912–15; contested Winchester (Ind.), 1916; lecturer, Lowell Institute, Boston, MA, 1916–17; special correspondent, *Daily Telegraph*, 1927–28; cf. his *The Danger Zone of Europe: Changes and Problems in the Near East* (London, 1911) and *War and Diplomacy in the Balkans* (London, 1915).

Then the Prince said goodbye. He ended by addressing me as 'mon cher Commandant'.

P[rincess] H[élène] was very charming and courteous – black hair and a pink complexion. She wore a black dress and is a widow, her husband having been murdered in Russia. She seemed sweet, gentle and well-bred. She told me she would send her son to Eng[lan]d.

23 Oct[ober 1920]

Recommend[atio]n of geographical committee. The Conf[eren]ce decided that frontiers defined in a treaty by a watercourse cannot be altered by a Boundary Commission except by a unanimous vote.

25 [October 1920]

Had a talk with another friend.[102] 2 hours.

> (1) Bulgaria – no good to talk of reunion with Jugoslavia as Stambuliysky[103] had done. He did finally admit that S[tambuliysky] had returned half the material for Kragujevatz. With that they began to execute the terms of the Treaty, e.g. out of 2,000 carriages and material for Kragujevatz and a hundred other things – coal. The Reparation Comm[issio]n was not const[itut]ed but he hoped they w[oul]d not put an Italian at the Head as they had with the Military Commission as that w[oul]d result in innumerable difficulties.
> (2) Alb[ani]a. Personally he did not care about it being sep[arate]d from the Adriatic [questions]. The Serbs did but that was since the situation had changed and the Serb mentality had not. Scutari and the Drin were the favourite idea of Pasic.

It was very doubtful if the Scutari railway would work <or could be built>, for Medua could not, for technical reasons, be made a port.

Prisrend was the most dangerous point since the Vardar and the railway was [*sic*] threatened.

---

[102] General Pešić, see entry 16 Oct. 1917; see also Temperley's 'Notes', n.d., Temperley MSS, file 'Despatches as Assistant Military Attaché, Belgrade'.

[103] Aleksandur Stoimonov Stamboliyski (1879–1923), Bulgarian politician; leader of Agrarian party, 1908–23; imprisoned for opposing Bulgaria's entry into the war against the Entente powers, 1915–18; instrumental in deposition of King Ferdinand, 1918; Prime Minister, 1919–23; overthrown and assassinated, Apr. 1923; a consistent advocate of a South Slav federation.

Dibra did not matter so greatly. The rectification by the Klementi was very desirable.

The future of the country was not in Albania but on the Adriatic, probably ultimately in Dalmatia, but now FIUME was a necessity as the only debouchure.

The gr[ea]t idea – owing to the sacrifices demanded we could not do much by direct negotiation with Italy but we c[oul]d accept an imposed settlement which left the essentials, i.e. free comm[unicatio]n FIUME-Schneeberg-Blegas-Dalmatia, to Jugoslavia.

Why not intervene and offer good offices?

Pressure on I[taly] via coal. Wished to end it.

Serb maladm[inistratio]n partisan, in effect not sufficiently intellectual in equipment when outside Serbia. Admin[istrati]ve aut[onom]y – exc[ept] in matters like railways. Promising Instr[uctio]n Civil Laws etc.

He thought Ll[oyd] G[eorge] had a wonderful insight into political situation but no sense of detail, e.g. on 11 Jan. 1920 he pointed out Sebenico to him and said it had been the nest of all the submarines attacking Italy. In reality there were no submarines & no naval base there, it was the commercial port.

Central Europe was very disturbed. Fr[ench] policy there was very capitalistic, at any rate in H[ungar]y.

Nov[ember] 2nd [1920][104]

Heard Hankey[105] on diplomacy by Conference.[106] He said he had attended 488 general conferences since the war. Lecturing beneath an enormous chart of war organisation in Nov[ember] 1918. He began by sketching the beginnings of such conf[erenc]es in the war – said L[loyd] G[eorge] wished one in March 1915 at Lemnos, of Russian, French, British & neutral Balkan diplomats and thinks, if it had occurred, the war might have proceeded differently. According to him the principle was well established by 1916, and says that L[loyd] G[eorge] had intended to go to Russia with Kitchener but was stopped because of Ireland. He offered to go again 3 weeks before he threw Asquith out on the mission on wh[ich] Milner actually went. Immediately after his PMship he developed a perfect rage for Conferences, the most important was, he thought, that at Rome early in 1917 when L[loyd] G[eorge] insisted on a plan for coop[eratio]n with Italy being worked out, which proved extremely useful after Caporetto. The

---

[104] Temperley returned to Britain on 29 October, see Temperley to Young [minister, Belgrade], 29 Oct. 1920, Temperley MSS, file 'Despatches as Assistant Military Attaché'.

[105] See entry 5 Nov. 1917.

[106] The Chatham House lecture, in fact, took place on 3 Nov., see S. Roskill, *Hankey: Man of Secrets* (3 vols, London, 1970–77), ii, 194–5.

presence at Sarrail[107] & Milne[108] from Salonica tended to coordinate strategy. He went on to speak of a previously unknown meeting at the Chequers in Sept[ember] 1917 where Balfour, L[loyd] G[eorge], Foch, Robertson, Painleve & Viviani[109] were present. It was here that L[loyd] G[eorge] broached the outline of the schem afterwards expounded in the Paris speech not of 'stitching strategy together' but of having a permanent coordination. After this he went on to the supreme command decision, one which he said nothing new.

On the peace he said the difficulties of the Ten were leakage and formality, that of the Four met these difficulties. He thought that the time when Mantoux[110] was alone with the Four was not wasted (3 weeks). They became intimate and blocked out the lines of the Treaty. But he left us to infer the later period he was taken on as secretary was equally necessary. He gave instances of the pressure on the Four. In 101 days they had 206 meetings and took 674 decisions.

<Dangers of Conf[eren]ces illustrated by fact that on one occasion L[loyd] G[eorge] & he might have been killed by bombardment had not L[loyd] G[eorge] decided to spend the night at Abbéville.>

His general conclusions seemed to be that for such Conf[eren]ces you required

1. Intimacy & friendship of principals.
2. Absence of formality (and the larger the numbers the greater the formality)
3. efficient secretarial work
4. each man spoke best in his own language.

On publicity he was very reticent though he seemed to approve.

Lord Robert Cecil made a few pertinent comments. He said that the success of Conf[eren]ces depended on the pressure and definition of ends, e.g. in war time the Allied Maritime Transport Council worked well. At the Conference he did not think the Supreme Economic Council did because it was largely vague.

He also thought a Conf[eren]ce or Supreme Council meant <u>force</u>.

---

[107] See entry 19 June 1916.

[108] See entry 22 Dec. 1916.

[109] (Jean Raphaël Adrien) René Viviani (1863–1925), French politician; Minister of Labour, 1906–10; Education Minister, 1913–14 and 1916–17; Prime Minister, 1914–15; Foreign Minister, 1914 and 1915; Justice Minister, 1915–17.

[110] Paul Mantoux (1877–1956), French historian and official; Professor of French Civilization, London University, 1912–14; interpreter in Territorial Army, 1914–15; aide to Albert Thomas (French Munitions Minister), 1915–18; interpreter for Clemenceau at the Paris Peace Conference, 1919; co-founder of the *Institut de hautes études internationales et du développement*, Geneva (under the auspices of the League of Nations), 1927; see his *Les délibérations du conseil des quatre 24 mars–28 juin 1919: Notes de l'officier interprète Paul Mantoux* (Paris, 1955).

Nov[ember] 12 [1920]

Sent in Memo[randum] to Crowe, recommending recognition of Tirana Government as that of Albania. Objections were (i) Gov[ernmen]t could not control tribes north and northwest of Scutari. To this I answered – nor had anyone else, the Serbs or the Italians. When in occupation of these territories they were incorrigible.

Arguments for were (i) Strengthening the existing gov[ernmen]t which was rep[resentati]ve of all interests & religions (ii) Further delay would make matters worse and make the Gov[ernmen]t dependent on Italy. Lord C[urzon] returned with a note 'we clearly cannot recognize'.

[15 November 1920][111]

Saw J[ovano]v[i]ć. He said Regent [Alexander] approved of Treaty.[112] He is right.

Dec[ember] 3 [1920]

Saw Philip Kerr. He said 'we have just had another instance of the futility of Wilson. He has given his arbitration on [the] Western boundary of Armenia – and includes both Trebizond and Erzerum which probably cannot be defended and in neither case included more than 25% of Armenians. Poor President, thought I.

He asked about Montenegro and I told him the facts. Two parties pro-Serb and anti-Serb, both for Jugoslavia – and a dwindling third party for King Nicholas.[113]

I had some words with him about Albania, and said that I thought the government should be recognized and gave old reason (v[ide] Nov[ember] 12). He listened carefully. I spoke also of proposed visit of Regent to Eng[lan]d to which he seemed favourable.

---

[111] The date can be deduced from memo. Temperley, 'Interview with Dr. Jovanović', 15 Nov. 1920, Temperley MSS, file 'Despatches as Assistant Military Attaché, Belgrade'.

[112] The Italo-SHS Treaty of Rapallo of 12 Nov.

[113] See memo. Temperley, 'Memorandum on the Situation in Montenegro', 12 Oct. 1920, *Parliamentary Papers, Miscellaneous No. 1 (1921), Report on Politicial Conditions in Montenegro (Cd. 1123)* (1921).

1921–1939

12 Jan[uary 1921]

To I[nstitute of] I[nternational] A[ffairs] to hear [H.A.L.] Fisher on the League of Nations. It was curious to see him, as he stood before us – the man whom I had introduced to Lloyd George and, in that sense, placed him where he now stands.[1] Of course, I was only the connecting wire of the telephone, but even that humble instrument has its uses.

His last points which I will take first was Albania.

Lord Robert Cecil in subsequent discussion said that Albania had been recognised in this way. The British were doubtful, the French not opposed, if, said they, the Serbians are not. Mr. Rowell[2] of Canada got up and pleaded for Albania, and attacked the Treaty of London 'as unjust and immoral' but, as he paid a tribute to Italy elsewhere, he was, no doubt to his own surprise, thanked by the Italian representative. At the last moment, however, the Greek representative asked for 'further inquiry'. That enquiry seems to have been satisfactory and the Serbs gave way, following them the French, next the English. Lord R[obert] C[ecil] used this as an example of the small States controlling the Big.

Fisher at the end rose serenely – 'during the last few years I have noticed that the history of events of different people will always be different. Certainly my history would be quite different from that of the noble lord. The British Delegation were uncertain. I spoke to Mr. Balfour about it. Later on, however, I saw the Bishop of [blank] and after a conversation with him I decided we ought to favour it – that is my history of it'.

Personally I think the whole history was different again. We knew at an early stage (by the secret channel) that Greece saw the admission was going to be carried and therefore decided not to oppose it. Serbia saw it too. I don't believe big nations count when there is a majority vote.

---

[1] See entry 9 Dec. 1916.

[2] Newton Wesley Rowell (1867–1941), Canadian lawyer, Methodist churchman and politician; leader of Ontario provincial Liberal Party, 1911–17; left party over conscription and joined Unionist Party, 1917; Member of the Canadian House of Commons (Un.), Durham Riding, 1917–20; President of the Privy Council of Canada, 1917–20; Minister of Health, 1919–20; Canadian delegate at League of Nations Assembly, Nov. 1920; co-founder of League of Nations Society of Canada.

Apart from this Fisher was fairly optimistic. He said the Secretariat was good, and it was very difficult to construct one which was 'cosmopolitan and competent'. This had been done and would be very important in the future.

At the moment, of course, there had been some confusion. Still things had been done.

The Aaland Islands[3] was an instance of a nationalisation which no-one doubted would be successful. But here the limits of the subject were defined.

It was more doubtful in the case of the honour of a country. But here the International Court was of great importance in removing resentments at an early stage etc.

The Vilna-Poland controversy[4] was difficult but not impossible. Some progress had been made. The chief difficulty was the fear of Bolshevist invasion in the spring for which the French General Staff vouched. This was not for publicity. The serious danger thus implied affected the question of proposed limitation of armaments. Also the commission of enquiry had only succeeded in meeting and examination of the questions a fortnight before.

There was some difference between British and French Delegations here which ended in an amended resolution.

Otherwise the Assembly was ruled in the main by France and England. One objection to the whole meeting was that it was often dull.

This was, to some extent, irremediable especially in the Council, for the public debates of the Council were not debates. He well remembered a most interesting debate between Paderewski and [blank] of Lithuania <at the moment of strife between the 2 countries>, punctuated by telegrams arriving every quarter of an hour the contents of which were reflected on the countenance of the two protagonists. No-one could ever forget that. What a pity it could not be made public.

He made some interesting remarks on the proposed admission of Germany. Switzerland was in favour, the Scandinavian and most of the South American states. (Lord Robert said that Motta,[5] the Swiss, with gr[ea]t courage proposed it, and was fallen on by the brilliant orator Viviani[6] at once, but that the idea made progress.)

---

[3] Åland Islands in the Gulf of Bothnia off the coast of Finland; demilitarized after the Crimean War in 1856; constituted as an autonomous, Swedish-speaking region under Finnish sovereignty by the League of Nations, 1921.

[4] On 9 October 1920, Polish troops seized the Vilnius district and proclaimed the Republic of Central Lithuania, which was duly annexed by Poland.

[5] Giuseppe Motta (1871–1940), Swiss lawyer and Conservative-Catholic politician; President of the Swiss Federal Council, 1915, 1927, 1932 and 1937; head of Political Department, 1920–40; President of the League of Nations, 1924–25.

[6] See entry 2 Nov. 1920.

One great difficulty was the need in the Assembly for unanimity of resolutions, though this did not apply to voting for admission of states into the League.

The League had 42 states but was necessarily very imperfect without America and Russia. Perhaps Article X could be modified for the former. Lord R[obert] Cecil – followed first vehemently about U.S.A. The American journalists had arrived with instructions to report the Assembly and the League dead, but he had been struck by their consternation and the life in the Assembly. Possibly Article X might be amended, but we must be very careful. The Covenant was now a living thing and it was much harder to amputate a limb than to amend a clause in a draft. America wished only a court and a talk. This would be bad for the rest of the world. If we wanted the U.S.A. to come in we had better stop talking about it because they thought it a trap, if we kept saying how much she was missed[.] (Fisher had said that no attempts to get her to come in had yet been successful. She had not even sent advisers to the Disarmament Comm[issio]n though asked, and, though President Wilson had arbitrated on Armenia, he had only done so personally – I noticed by the way that Fisher's reference to Wilson, as the author of the League <as the selector at Geneva> and the message of the League to him, produced no effect on the audience. Thank God! However, if Wilson is dead, Wilsonianism is still alive.)

'The noble lord representing the air washed spaces of the veldt', as Fisher called him [Robert Cecil], went on about the admission of Bulgaria. The sub-committee contained a Serb (I think Zholger[7]) 'a man with large shining eyes' which shone and swelled as he spoke about Bulgaria. However, on certificated evidence that Bulgaria was fulfilling the Treaty Greece proposed and Serbia seconded Bulgaria's admission.

He then went on to advocate publicity. It did not do any harm, e.g. Viviani in his impassioned attack on Germany said 'let her pay her debts'; realizing that this meant 30 or 40 years he drew R[obert] C[ecil] aside (who was to speak next) and said – 'You see I didn't quite mean that, you won't say anything about it, will you?' Lord R[obert] C[ecil] did not quote the phrase or refer to it and noticed later with considerable interest, that the official text of the speech was equally polite in its omissions. 'I think it a good tribute to publicity'.

He also suggested somewhat unkindly that one desire of the Council for secrecy was that the various representatives often said things in the first half hour of examining a question because they had not properly apprehended the point through ignorance of the subject matter.

Fisher had said that he had no fears for the Assembly but he had for the Council. In future it would meet every two months – premiers could not possibly attend especially at Geneva – and you needed commanding personalities. Lord Robert said that you must have a Minister. You must also coordinate

---

[7] See entry 24 Apr. 1919.

the 3 different agencies – the P[rime] M[inister], the F[oreign] O[ffice] and the Council representative. To my amazement Fisher said that he had no access to the F[oreign] O[ffice] information, so that I endured disease and danger to get information which nobody used or attempted to use.

1 Feb[ruary 1921]

Returned to F[oreign] O[ffice] and did my best to stir up the Montenegrin question.[8]

14 Feb[ruary 1921]

Communication made to Italy and Yugoslavia that we (G[reat] B[retain]) unreservedly accepted the Treaty of Rapallo[9] – due indirectly to my suggestion. It must eventually be published.

22 Feb[ruary 1921]

Today Montenegro ceased to exist, on receiving a report communicated by me that Gjonovic[,] the Montenegrin Republican Delegate on the Con[stitutiona]l Committee had proclaimed his adhesion to the Yugoslav union idea, despite his Republicanism, and it was also reported that all the Montenegrin (deputies), including the Communists, had taken the oath on the Constitution.[10]

France had already discontinued (30 Dec[ember]) diplomatic representation. Our rep[resentati]ve had left on 24th August.

It is however a sad thing that a country should lose its independence of 300 years by the cancelling of an exsequatur to 4 or 5 consuls scattered over the world.

This night there was a debate on the policy of the Internat[iona]l Inst[itute]. It was of no importance, but in ref[eren]ce to 'policy' we had some revelations of the past. Sir M[aurice] de Bunsen,[11] who rep[resent]ed us at Vienna till the war – he contributed some senile reflections: 'we are always told we sh[oul]d have a policy, but I am not certain that it was an advantage and that our advantage has

---

[8] See memo. Temperley, 'Memorandum on the Situation in Montenegro', 12 Oct. 1920, *Parliamentary Papers, Miscellaneous No. 1 (1921), Report on Politicial Conditions in Montenegro (Cd. 1123)* (1921); see also 'Political Conditions In Montenegro. Large Majority For Yugo Slavia', *The Times*, 15 Feb. 1921.
[9] The Italo-SHS Treaty of Rapallo of 12 Nov. 1920.
[10] See Baerlein, *Birth of Yugoslavia*, ii, 253.
[11] See entry 5 Feb. 1918.

not lain in not having one. When I went to Vienna in [1913] I don't remember that I heard that a great war was likely. I heard a great deal about the disputes of the C[anadian] P[acific] R[ailway] with Austria, but nothing about the imminence of a European crisis. This was the old order, each dipl[omatic] representative left free to his own devices – and to find out things for himself. I am not certain it was a bad one'. I am.

23 Feb[ruary 1921]

Here is a flower:

> Our mil[itar]y officers in Germany have shown except[iona]l pol[itical] act[ivit]y and it is notorious that just as poets long to be thought to excel in prose and great beauties hanker for the reput[atio]n of intelligence the soldier is apt to consider that his real bent is for politics and that he possesses an insight denied to the civilian.
>
> C[urzon]

I understand that recently C[urzon] sent a wire that our ships were not to salute Tino's[12] (i.e. 'His Majesty's ships' in wire). The K[ing] at once rang up C[urzon] and objected to this strongly as not having been consulted first. C[urzon] kicked up hell with Crowe. Crowe sent for the telegram and showed C[urzon] his initial at the bottom. C[urzon] said – Well I have so many things to do – I can't be responsible for every telegram I initial.

3 March [1921]

Poor old Nicholas died yesterday (no 1st March)[13] – just about the time we were cancelling his consular exequaturs. A chequered career, the longest and for forty years the most glorious in the history of his country. The change from the poet and warrior to the stock exchange dabbler and double-faced diplomat was not only from youth to age, I fear. But it took long indeed to find him out. I hope my report did not hasten his end – we received a protest from his P[rime] M[inister] the other day naming me by name. The King, like a gentleman, though rather embarrassingly for us, has insisted on sending a telegram to his widow, a truly noble lady, like all true Montenegrin women.

---

[12] See entry 19 June 1916.
[13] King Nicholas I of Montenegro died on 1 Mar. at Antibes on the French Riviera.

4 M[ar]ch [1921]

Telegram sent re rumours as to possible Greek action in S[outhern] Albania crushing these reports without foundation.

Poor [Sir Henry] Wilson goes tomorrow – or rather today. So much glory and so much discontent and shamed today. I think history will judge him more charitably than his opponents.

I heard from Reynier who was present at the Foreign Journalists' interview with Briand, immediately after L[loyd] G[eorge]'s speech to the Germans as sort of exposition by him of his methods with the Welsh wizard. He had, in case of difficulty, only to mention the devastated areas, and 'on voit briller dans les yeux de Lloyd George l'éclair de justice'. Very likely.

7 March [1921]

Spoke with W[ilson?]. Received pretty definite evidence on all the German transactions – and at Paris.

It seems clear here that Ll[oyd] G[eorge] told the Brit[ish] auth[orit]ies to make out as big a bill for damages as possible and returned the bill once – and was disappointed that they could only get a little over half his demand even at the second time of asking.

The legal authorities were unable to do much in making out breaches of the Treaty and even that they had to be gingered up considerably to do. So far as I can see no-one really approves of our action, exc[ept] for political reasons.

12 March [1921]

The Turkish compromise is really eye-wash as regards the Straits, but is intended to make concessions to the Turks in Asia Minor, in the zone, but not in the town of Smyrna.[14]

It appears to be true that the Sèvres Treaty was based on Constantinople ultimately falling to Greece.

Quantum distat ab illo[15]!

Tino is said to want to abdicate, as his prop[er]ty is quite gone. They latter may be true, the former cannot be.

---

[14] On 12 Mar., the last session of the London conference on a Graeco-Turkish settlement took place, see 'Proposals of the Allies', 11 Mar. 1921, CAB 24/120.

[15] Cf. Horace, *Odes*, book iii.19: 'Quantum distet ab Inacho/ Codrus, pro patria non timidus mori,/ narras ...', as denoting distance in time.

14 March [1921]

Comical element supplied by Plamenatz[16] informing us that Danilo, having abdicated, Prince Michel,[17] eldest son of Mirko,[18] was King.

(Princess Nathalie[19] (now C[oun]tess Dudzelle[*sic*]) intimated that she didn't want him to accept. Now at Eastbourne aid Bro School, in spite of the fact that the Min[iste]r of Justice offered to wait on her.)

15 M[ar]ch [1921]

Made strong push for the publication of documentation of 14th Feb[ruary] re Rapallo. As all the terr[itor]y involved belonged leg[all]y to the Allies not to Italy – & Yugoslavia – our formal published argument [?] is essential – no-one saw this point, but I planted, Nicolson watered and Crowe yielded.

18 March [1921]

Montenegrin consuls' exequaturs cancelled – Finis Montenegro [*sic*] M[ar]ch 17.
The concessions to the Austrians are probably real, and may help their credit.

18 March [1921]

H[an]k[e]y. Meanwhile I saw a letter of Hankey to Crowe of 19 Feb[ruar]y describing his impressions of Italy.[20] They may be summed up as indicating the aptness with which Giolitti[21] seized the opp[ortuni]ty to pay homage to Lloyd George. Giolitti, that ex-pro-German and neutralist, is now apparently Ll[oyd] G[eorge]'s warmest admirers and loads H[ankey] with favours, and his

---

[16] See entry 1 Jan. 1919.
[17] Prince Michael Petrović-Njegoš (1908–1986), Prince of Montenegro; pretender to Montenegrin throne (as Mihailo I), 1921–29; renounced claims and declared adhesion to Yugoslavia, 1929; in German internment camp, 1941–45; *chef de protocol*, Yugoslav Foreign Ministry, 1946–47; in French exile since 1947.
[18] Prince Mirko Dimitri Petrović-Njegoš (1879–1918), second son of King Nicholas I.
[19] Natalija Konstantinović (1882–1950), married Prince Mirko, 1902; divorced, 1917; she married, in 1920 at Eastbourne, Gaston Count Errembault de Dudzeele, a Belgian diplomat.
[20] Hankey to Crowe, 19 Feb. 1921, CAB 63/31.
[21] Giovanni Giolitti (1842–1928), Italian politician; Chamber of Deputies, 1882–1928; Treasury Minister, 1889–91; Minister of the Interior, 1901–1903, 1911–14 and 1920–21; Prime Minister, 1892–93, 1903–1905, 1911–14 and 1920–21.

wife with bouquets. I hae my doots. G[iolitti] at any rate has a sound view on Reparations. He thinks the French hotheads and the attempt to get much out of Germany for 30 or 40 years (written on 19th February!) quite impracticable, because Germany will not pay when she is strong enough to refuse and that means war. A short period and a large sum summarise his ideas. In internal politics he is no doubt at the moment the man of destiny and to this he devotes all his attention. He seems serene but perhaps not as serene as he appears, e.g. recently he gave a young colleague at a Cabinet meeting a tremendous 'dressing down' and he thought of resigning but at the end of the meeting Giolitti completely reconciled him by saying he (aet. about 80) was still too young always to restrain his feelings.

Giolitti accounts to our ingenuous H[ankey] for the attacks on England in the Italian press by saying that he is personally poor and has only 80,000 lire a month for propaganda.

All this venom is apparently due to the rich friends of Nitti,[22] who want to discredit the government and therefore attack England through them. <All very pawky.>

I confess I don't understand how anyone can be taken in by all this.

19 [March 1921]

Had a very interesting interview with Miss Durham,[23] the famous queen first <of Montenegro and then> of Albania. She had read and approved of my report on Montenegro, which pleased me as well. She knew much Serb history and taught me some, e.g. that Vladika Peter II of Montenegro[24] died of consumption, which Mirko no doubt inherited; that no Montenegrin man w[oul]d water his land[,] that being a woman's work.

22 March [1921]

Was summoned to Parl[iamentar]y Under Sec[re]t[ar]y (Harmsworth[25]) to explain as to some questions of Serbs pillaging cattle in Albanian villages. He

---

[22] See entry 4 Oct. 1918.
[23] See entry 29 Dec. 1918.
[24] Petar II Petrović-Njegoš (1813–1851), the last Vladika (Prince-Bishop) of Montenegro, 1830–51; died of tuberculosis.
[25] Cecil Bisshopp Harmsworth (1869–1948), 1st Baron Harmsworth, cr. 1929, politician; MP (Lib.) Droitwich, 1906–10, South Bedfordshire, 1911–22; Parliamentary Under-secretary for Home Affairs, 1915; member of the Prime Minister's secretariat, 1917–19; Parliamentary Under-secretary for Foreign Affairs, 1919–22; member of the British delegation at the League of Nations, 1922.

seemed not very able to get to the point, but very amiable and anxious to give Parliament the full truth. Personally delightful – politically – but in all ways a gr[ea]t contrast to Northcliffe.[26]

After redrafting the question I submitted it once more – in the absence of L[or]d C[urzon] (still week-ending) Mr H[armsworth] sent it down to Sir E[yre] C[rowe]. The latter asked to see me. The first form of the question was – whether the Jugoslavs looted 79,227 sheep and goats 4,584 etc. I wished to answer we had no exact information as to numbers. C[rowe] said that all I knew (first hand from the Prefect of Dibra[27]) was that houses or villages had been destroyed not cattle. In the letter correct and ingenious, so the final answer was thus 'In the course of disturbances which arose in these border districts a number of villages were destroyed (Sir E[yre] C[rowe] improving on C[ecil] H[armsworth]). H[is] M[ajesty's] G[overnment] have received no reports as to what may have been done with the animals belonging to such villages (Sir E[yre] C[rowe]). It should be observed however that part of the Dibra district, including the town of Dibra itself, is within the Kingdom of Serbia and cannot be described as Albanian (H.W.V. T[emperley]) in whatever way that country and its boundaries may at present be defined (H.W.V. T[emperley]) with some correction by Lord C[urzon] before he weekends).

Q. 'Whether these (cattle) will be returned before any cattle are required for Jugoslavia from Austria'.

'The Answer to the second part of Question 51 is a matter for the Supreme Council' (H.W.V. T[emperley] with advice from Harold Nicolson and [Sir Francis] Lindley,[28] our Minister to Austria. <Hans[ard] vol. 139, pp. 2226–7. 21 Mar[ch 19]21.>

<u>Tantae molis erat</u>[29] an interesting specimen of a revised authorized and corrected version of a syndicated answer – or of answers – to questions in Parliament.

Ap[ril] 7 [1921]

Hardinge gave an interview to Geddes.[30]

---

[26] See entry 2 Nov. 1916; Harmsworth was his younger brother.
[27] See entry 15 June 1917.
[28] See entry 14 June 1919.
[29] So little was the difference.
[30] Sir Auckland Campbell Geddes (1879–1954), academic, civil servant and politician; active service, South Africa, 1901–1902; lecturer in anatomy, Edinburgh University, 1906–13; Professor of Anatomy, 1913–14.

Viviani except for certain demands as[,] e.g. entry into L[eague] of N[ations] & French cancell[atio]n[,] had talked 'mere rhetoric about blood & gathering of spears of Huns to heart of France' (pleasant reading for L[loyd] G[eorge] who said the same once about the Contemptible Army 'which gathered the spears of Prussia into its breast and in perishing saved Europe'.[31]) V[32] said 'These damned Frenchmen have completely messed things up for themselves and for him.['] So long as he was Pres[ident] he w[oul]d not accept any resp[onsibilit]y for T[reaty] of Versailles or for entering L[eague] of N[ations]. USA was pract[icall]y at peace, techn[icall]y at war with Germany. He proposed to make peace by res[olutio]n though he did not himself think this the best way.

He rush[ed] to ratify Treaty with sweeping reserve[atio]ns but Viviani's mission had stirred up so much mud as to make this impossible.

Re German colonies cables etc. 'We have not given and we do not intend to give up any of our rights as victors nor our share in poss[essio]n of any spoils of war exc[ept] in return for advantages or benefits'.

Am[eric]a is determined that Wash[ingto]n [*sic*][33] sh[oul]d pay rep[aratio]n to limit of her capacity. S[upreme] C[ouncil] c[oul]d arrive at prov[isiona]l dec[isio]ns & refer to Wash[ingto]n for endorsement.

G[eddes] He did not picture this.

H[ardinge] Some machinery perhaps a comm[itmen]t 'all ag[ain]st publicity during neg[otia]t[io]ns'. Say his action misconstrued. Asked to say that Am[eric]a had no political interest in Ireland and w[oul]d not encourage. 'I could not say that politically it would be impossible, but it is true'. 'Very difficult' to speak of disarm[amen]t.

18 April 1921

21 M[ar]ch Milner's a[c]c[ount] given to C[o]m[mit]tee.

On Sunday 26 Haig asked for a Supreme Command.

Milner & Wilson crossed over – made stops – they saw Haig at night & early next morning (Monday) Clemenceau.

Motored to Compiègne where owing to bad staff work Haig not present. On Tuesday they met at Doullens.[34] Haig & Pétain spoke – Haig that he must have reinforcements, Pétain that the enemy's full attack had not been delivered, and that it would come in Champagne, near to which he must hold his reserves.

---

[31] In the House of Commons on 29 Oct. 1917, see 'Thanks to the Services: Mr. Lloyd George's Tribute', *The Times*, 30 Oct. 1917.

[32] Clearly, Temperley meant President Warren G. Harding not Viviani here.

[33] *Recte* Berlin.

[34] The Anglo-French military conference at Doullens, 24–25 Mar. 1918.

Foch broke in and demanded a single front and said the full attack was already in swing. Milner took Clemenceau aside and proposed supreme command for Foch. Can you guarantee Haig? Im five minutes, said M[ilner]. Can you guarantee Pétain? In twenty minutes, said Clemenceau. They both went aside, and Haig gave no trouble but Clemenceau emerged after some quarter of an hour with a considerably bedraggled Pétain.

Milner drafted the formula in his rather bad French <A little different from Milner's a[c]c[ount] published later> and gave it to Clemenceau who made a few verbal alterations. It was then read out and accepted by all parties, Foch making some demurrers.

The reserves were in motion before the meeting broke up.

Milner retained the scrap of paper and has it still. When sent out he was given no special instructions.

Sir M[aurice] Hankey has said that he had witnessed some important decisions, but none like that at Doullens where he was not present.

19 April [1921]

Saw Strutt's[35] Diary (Feb[ruary]–March 1919) explaining how he got the Emperor Charles ouf of Austria to Switzerland.[36] There are two memorable dicta of Charles.

Re Franz Ferdinand's murder at Sarajevo 'I don't believe the Serbs were guilty'.

'I made two errors – that of beginning by governing autocratically, then of trying to govern democratically. Of these the latter error was by far the greatest – and he regarded as his most mistaken single act the manifesto amnestying the Czechs'.

20 April [1921]

Birthday, 42, wonder if I'm any better.

By way of celebrating attended H[ouse] of C[ommons] Report stage on Hungarian Treaty. Balfour & Harmsworth both sent for me in the morning and I went round with statistics, chapters from the history papers etc., of which some at least were useful.

---

[35] See entry 21 Oct. 1916.

[36] The Emperor Charles abdicated on 11 Nov. 1918 and retired to his hunting lodge at Eckartsau, outside Vienna; Lieutenant-Colonel Strutt smuggled him across the Swiss border on 23–24 Mar. 1919.

We sat in the litte gallery behind the Speaker's Chair, an admirable place to see and sense the House as you are directly on a level with Ministers. Harmsworth was heavy, kindly, tedious, slow and sincere. Kenworthy,[37] the chief opposition leader, was a force – the eyes and hair of a Red Indian, and the frame of a heavyweight boxer, both of which I understand him, at least, partically to be or to have been.

He declaimed furiously with a kind of strident scream ag[ain]st having so many little Alsace-Lorraines in Central Europe. Few of the MPs had a map and fewer still understood it. That, I suppose, does not matter. Balfour, incidentally, at the last moment forgot, or had not time for consulting me, and therefore went down unprepared. This did not prevent him speaking with his usual dialectic ability on subjects on which he was (at least to the trained observer) noticeably ignorant. He screamed and got pink in the face at one point, when challenged by Wedgwood.[38] 'The hon[ourable] member thinks he can improve things by a perpetual system of lecturing of foreign powers'. Col[onel] Wedgwood then suggested that the miners of Pecs did not want to go back to Hungary because the gov[ernmen]t was bad. A[rthur] J[ames] B[alfour]: 'So I gather the hon[ourable] member wishes to violate the ethnic principles because Hungary has a bad gov[ernmen]t'. The Colonel for once was voiceless.[39]

27 April [1921]

Am now in possession of nearly all the details of the Carl attempt on Hungary.[40] Our old friend Strutt partly in it. On the 23rd Feb[ruary] he went to Prangins,[41] and saw the ex-Emp[ero]r who told him that he was going. S[trutt] advised him not to, but went at his suggestion to Paris to see Prince Sixte[42] and subsequently brought back answer to Carl to the effect that Briand <w[oul]d> approve <if it were> a fait accompli. Subsequently it appears that Poincaré called on Briand and forced a disclaimer from him about the whole thing. But it is not generally

---

[37] Lieutenant-Commander Joseph Montague Kenworthy (1886–1953), 10th Baron Strabolgi, succ. 1934, sailor and politician; entered Royal Navy, 1902; Admiralty war staff, 1917–18; retired, 1920; MP (Asquithian Lib.) Hull Central, 1919–26, (Lab.) 1926–31; Chief Whip, 1938–42. Kenworthy was known as parliamentary 'bruiser'.

[38] Josiah Wedgwood (1872–1943), 1st Baron Wedgwood of Burlaston, cr. 1942, politician; MP (Lib) for Newcastle-under-Lyme, 1906–18, (Independent Radical), 1918–19, (Labour) 1919–42; Chancellor of the duchy of Lancaster, 1924; military service, 1914–18, injured at Dardanelles (DSO), 1915, assistant director of trench warfare, 1917, mission to Siberia, 1918.

[39] *Hansard* (5) cxl (20 Apr. 1921), cols. 1907–71; for Balfour see cols. 1930–39.

[40] Ex-Emperor Charles sought to restore Habsburg rule in Hungary, 27 Mar.–5 Apr. 1921; a second attempt failed, 20–23 Oct. 1921.

[41] Near Nyons, on Lake Geneva (Switzerland).

[42] See entry 16 Apr. 1918.

believed. Briand seems to have been committed and pretty deeply.[43] The Pope was also favourable, and a number of conservative Frenchmen like Lyautey[44] and perhaps Franchet d'Esperey.[45] Strutt, by way of exemplifying his disapproval of Carl's project, carried out an experimental crossing of the frontier on foot & proved it to be possible. Carl told very few people of his design, which makes it more extraordinary. One theory is that he thought Archduke Joseph's son[46] was going to supplant him.

He appears to have walked over the frontier, got a Spanish passport and boarded the Strassburg-Basle train. On the 26 March in the evening he arrived at Steinamanger (Szombathely[47]) and called on the Bishop[48] at his palace. The latter was just sitting down to his evening meal with Vass[49] the Hungarian Minister of Religion. 'Don't you know me?' said Carl. His Eminence only did with difficulty. Teleki,[50] the prime minister, was hunting in the neighbourhood, and summoned posthaste, arrived in the small hours of the morning. He was afraid of telephoning so great a secret and started off to Budapest by motor, but lost his way in the darkness. Carl, who had borrowed his motor from a Jew, whom he made a baron on the spot, got to Budapest before him, dressed in Field Marshal's uniform. The sentry at Horthy's[51] palace thought him an impostor but he at length obtained access to Horthy, and stayed to lunch with him. Horthy behaved with great correctness and implored him to go. He did finally.

---

[43] Charles had been in contact with Briand, but the principal supporter of the scheme was the journalist and historian Jacques Bainville (1879–1936), a prominent advocate of right-wing causes.

[44] See entry 2 Jan. 1917.

[45] See entry 30 Oct. 1918.

[46] Field Marshal Archduke Joseph August Viktor Klemens Maria of Austria, Prince of Hungary and Bohemia (1872–1962), son of Archduke Joseph Karl of Austria (1833–1905); Regent of Hungary, 27–31 Oct. 1918 and 7–23 Aug. 1919; member of the Hungarian Upper Chamber, 1927–44; in German exile since 1946.

[47] In western Hungary, near the Austrian border.

[48] Bishop Count János Mikes (1876–1945), Hungarian Roman Catholic clergyman; Bishop of Szombathely, 1911–36.

[49] Jószef Vass (1877–1930), Hungarian clergyman and politician with strong legitimist connections; Member of the Hungarian diet, 1920–30; Minister of Food, 1920; of Education and Religion, 1920–22; of Welfare, 1922–30.

[50] Pál Count Teleki de Szék (1879–1941), Hungarian academic and politician; Professor of Geography, Budapest University, 1910–14 and 1921–38; delegate at Paris Peace Conference, 1919; Minister of Education and Religion, 1919 and 1938–39; Prime Minister, 1920–21 and 1939–41; Foreign Minister, 1920–21 and 1940–41; committed suicide, Apr. 1941.

[51] Vice-Admiral Miklós Horthy de Nagybánya (1868–1957), Hungarian sailor and politician; aide-de-camp to Emperor Franz Joseph, 1911–14; commander-in-chief, Austro-Hungarian fleet, Mar.–Oct. 1918; commander of Hungarian national army, 1919–20; Regent of the Kingdom of Hungary, 1920–44.

On the 1st April the Ambassadors' Conference met at Paris, and Cambon,[52] the French Amb[assado]r, after vehemently denying all complicity, proposed to issue a decision not permitting the Hapsburg to return to Hungary, and republishing their declaration of 2 Feb[ruary] 1920. This was conveyed by the 3 High Commissioners at Budapest to Horthy.

The 'Little Entente' took a bolder line – concerted measures – and on the 2nd [April 1921] notified the Hungarian Government that they would take strong measures unless carl departed before the 7th.

Carl hung about Szombathely, declaring he w[oul]d not go without direct instruction from France that she w[oul]d not support him. This he apparently got. The game was up. A few sightseers, Count Andrássy[53] and Colonel Lehár,[54] commanding in West Hungary, had rallied to him. No troops to speak of, there were barely enough to protect him against crowds of peasants who thronged around him. There appeared to be no popular movement outside this area. At Brück[55] [sic] in Austria on his way back, however, a number of straying, and possibly pro-Bolshevik workmen, showed a desire to mob him, amd assembled there at 6.30 in the evening for the purpose. In fact, however, owing to delays on the Hungarian frontier (of a rather suspicious kind) the train did not reach Brück [sic] till about 3 a.m. It came on to rain, and the thirst for Karl's blood disappeared, and the meeting broke up before the Ex-Emperor arrived. The men on the train were armed but it would not have been easy to deal with a large mob.

29 April [1921]

Went and saw Philip Kerr who told me he had definitely decided to resign from Ll[oyd] G[eorge], having had four years of it which was quite enough for him.

---

[52] See entry 10 Oct. 1917.

[53] Julius (Gyula) Count Andrássy de Csíkszentkirály et Krasznahorka (1860–1929), Hungarian politician; Minister of Education, 1893–94; Minister *ad laterem*, 1894–95; Minister of the Interior, 1906–1909; Austro-Hungarian Foreign Minister, 1918; imprisoned for involvement in attempted Habsburg restoration, 1921; leader of Royalist opposition.

[54] Colonel Anton (Antal) Baron von Lehár (1876–1962), Austro-Hungarian soldier; entered army, 1894; active service, 1914–18; Commander western Hungary, 1919–21; in German exile, 1921–33; in Austria, 1933–62.

[55] That is, Bruck an der Leitha, in Lower Austria near the Hungarian frontier.

4 May [1921]

Real reasons for Anti-Boche démarche seems to be as follows.[56]

French opinion worked up to det[erminatio]n to occupy Ruhr without more parley since Germ[an]y hedging and unless ec[onomic] assets controlling German industrial life seized, France after expiry of two years will never be paid. Beyond control of Briand who is more mod[era]te. We think no German Gov[ernmen]t is strong enough to make ad[e]q[ua]te rep[aratio]n offer exc[ept] under strong external pressure and new scheme only method of preventing occup[atio]n of Ruhr, perhaps indefinitely.

Brit[ish] policy resisted by Fr[ance] but adopted in sub[sequen]ce if form adapted to Fr[ench] susceptibilities.

Basis of scheme (1) conforming strictly at each stage to the prov[isio]ns of the Treaty of Versailles[;] (2) inviting Rep[aratio]n Comm[issio]n to complete duties laid on it by that Treaty[;] (3) bringing long protracted issues to a head so as to avoid contin[ua]l conf[eren]ces[,] ultimatums[,] notes & sanctions[;] (4) giving thus another opp[ortunit]y.

If USA w[oul]d indicate to Huns their gen[era]l approval & advise accept[an]ce, this w[oul]d be of gr[ea]t service.

5 May [1921]

Went to House of Lords. The gilded Chamber. It came fully up to expectation – as an agency for impressing the Lower middle classes, it is really unsurpassed.[57] Bryce[58] spoke admirably, a little academically as where he demanded aut[onom]y for the

---

[56] The Anglo-French schedule of reparations payments was presented to Germany on 4 May, and accepted by her on 11 May 1921, see *DBFP* (1) xv, ch. III.

[57] Cf. 'The Upper Chamber is the haunt of caste and privilege', H.W.V. Temperley, *Senates and Upper Chambers: Their Uses and Functions in the Modern State, with a Chapter on the Reform of the House of Lords* (London, 1910), 18–19.

[58] James Bryce (1838–1922), Viscount Bryce of Dechmont, cr. 1914, jurist, historian and politician; Regius Professor of Civil Law, Oxford, 1870–93; Professor of Jurisprudence, Owens College, Manchester, 1870–75; MP (Lib.) Tower Hamlets, 1880–85, Abderdeen South, 1885–1907; Parliamentary Under-secretary for Foreign Affairs, 1886; Chancellor of the Duchy of Lancaster, 1892–94; President of the Board, of Trade, 1894–5; Chief Secretary for Ireland, 1905–1907; ambassador at Washington, 1907–13.

Szeklers,[59] as well as for Ruthenia[60] but with profound hist[orica]l knowledge and, with his curious mountaineering instinct, with a realization that cutting off mountains from plains, and from one another, is a highly dangerous game. Newton[61] spoke less well – Curzon ore rotundo and with a kind of pompous flamboyance, which dimmed the gilding of the chamber. Very fluent, easy, and rhetorical. He has a great mastery of his subject, and pays very little attention to the notes and summaries Cadogan[62] and I industriously compiled for him. In this he is good for he always reads and does things himself in the large sense, thereby showing and obtaining a general grasp and idea. But the manner is bad for the audience – and the assurances, the light tone etc. do not really convince. They might have done in the days when superiority was not resented. The debate was mixed up partly with the enforcement of sanctions ag[ain]st Germany[;] in all it seemed to me Curzon shone less than in the Hungarian Treaty.[63]

On the whole the debate was good, but without bite and anger. Much sense but little flame on either side. The gilded Chamber does not seem to me one that counts in the practically [sic] sense. It is like putting a courtier to run a race for a contract with a businessman and I think the press and public knows [sic] this. <6 [May 1921] By illustration of this I found that no paper troubled to give Bryce's speech at length and the Times did not give it at all.>

In one respect the Chamber showed enterprise. I left my coat[,] hat & gloves in the vestibule – when I came back I found only the former two, so that the rights of property, and the respect for it are confined to peers and attendants.

---

[59] Székely, an ethnic group descended from Hungarians but transplanted to the eastern Carpathians (*Székely* = frontier guards); by the nineteenth century, they were concentrated in Transylvania.

[60] Carpatho-Ruthenia, part of the Hungarian kingdom as Kárpátalja since the eleventh century; now straddling eastern Slovakia and western Ukraine.

[61] Thomas Wodehouse Legh (1857–1942), 2nd Baron Newton, succ. 1898; entered diplomatic service, 1881; resigned, 1886; MP (Cons.) for Newton, Lancs, 1886–98; Paymaster-General, 1915–16; Assistant Under-secretary for Foreign Affairs, 1916–19.

[62] Sir Alexander George Montagu Cadogan (1884–1968), diplomat; entered diplomatic service; Private Secretary to Cecil Harmsworth, 1919–20; head of League of Nations section, 1923–33; minister at Peking, 1933–36 (ambassador since 1935); Deputy Under-secretary for Foreign Affairs, 1936–38; Permanent Under-secretary for Foreign Affairs, 1938–46; permanent representative at the United Nations, 1946–50; retired, 1950.

[63] *House of Lords Debates* (5) xlv (5 May 1921), cols. 223–50.

6th May [1921]

Op.[eratio]n between new conditions and those agreed upon by the Allies at Paris (Jan[uary] 21) and at Boulogne (July 20).[64]

Chief objections of Huns to earlier cond[itio]ns were

> (1) large fixed ann[uit]ies to be paid in later years, amounting to 6 milliards (Paris) and 7 milliards (Boulogne). Present proposals ann[uall]y is 2 milliards ann[uall]y variable with G[erman]y's ec[onomic] recovery & dev[elopme]nt of her export trade.
> (2) proposed interf[eren]ce with German financial admin[istratio]n – no admin[istrati]ve interf[eren]ce. Sub-Com[mitt]ee of Guarantees is new to controlling funds resulting from assigned revenues and providing that red[uctio]ns of revenues shall not be agreed to without subvention from other sources.
> (3) Product[io]n of state credit op.[eratio]ns without consent of Rep[aratio]n Committee now abandoned.
> (4) Boulogne proposal as to Allied particip[atio]n in German fin[ancia]l & industrial concerns sh[ou]ld be imposed as a cond[itio]n.

9 May [1921]

Following little billet doux went to the Greek Chargé, M. Rangabé[65], today[:]

> Sir,
> It has come to my notice that you are in the habit of addressing notes and communications on the official business of your legation direct to the P[rime] M[inister]
> 2. This practice, which is unusual and is not justified by precedent, since constitutional practice in this country requires that all questions affecting its foreign relations shall be treated by the S[ecretary] of S[tate] for F[oreign] A[ffairs] serves no useful purpose, and tends to create confusion and delay.
> 3. I shall therefore be grateful if you will be good enough in future to conform to the practice, common to all repress[entatives] in the country of foreign gov[ernment]s of addressing to me all comm[unicatio]ns wh[ich] you may desire to make to H[is] M[ajesty's] G[overnment].

---

[64] See entry 4 May 1921.
[65] Alexander Rizo Rangabé (1880–1972), Greek diplomat; chargé d'affaires at London, 1921–22; minister at London, 1922; at Berlin, 1933–41.

4. You will remember that, in my note of Dec[ember] 11 last, I inf[orme]d you that I was unable to receive you in the capacity of Acting Greek Min[iste]r in London. I added however that the F[oreign] O[ffice] w[oul]d be prepared to conduct business with you as Chargé d'Affaires temporarily in charge of Gr[ee]k interests in this country. I sh[oul]d however have to consider whether this concession sh[oul]d not be withdrawn in the event of your being unable to conform to the procedure indicated in the preceding paragraph.

17 May [1921]

Rangabé replied with the longest despatch ever seen, meaning nothing. Grub Street tells us he thinks Philip Kerr most accessible – is sorry he is going, and he thinks he will be in the Cabinet. An intercepted telegram of his refers bitterly to Grub Street routine in the F[oreign] O[ffice] auth[orit]y in Downing Street, but, <u>for the time being</u>, must obey the former.

18 May [1921]

On the 16th [May] L[loyd] G[eorge] indicates H[ardinge] to remind France (in case of serious rumours about Upper Silesia) of def[ini]te understanding at San Remo that no Allied Gov[ernment]s sh[oul]d take coercive action ag[ain]st enemy sep[ara]t[e]ly from other Allies, and state that, if French Gov[ernmen]t does individually take steps (e.g. invasion of German terr[itor]y) it w[oul]d be inconsistent with Entente spirit and endangering All[ian]ce.

21 May [1921]

L[loyd] G[eorge]'s speech still causing great excitement in France.[66] The majority vote in the Supreme Council causes the greatest excitement. L[loyd] G[eorge] knows in this case that he has the support of Japan (because of her engagements)[,] of Italy (because of her wounded & killed in Silesia) and probably of USA.

The point taken in France is that the elec[tio]n must be unanimous, as L[loyd] G[eorge] was fond of insisting when his proposals were viewed with disfavour by France, Italy & USA.

---

[66] In the House of Commons, on 13 May, Lloyd George had affirmed Silesia as German for hundreds of years, 'Poland And Silesia. Mr. Lloyd George's Statement', *The Times*, 14 May 1921.

31 May [1921]

Received a compliment today – was designated as F[oreign] O[ffice] Delegate to settle Albania's boundaries by Conf[eren]ce at Paris <to instruct Hardinge>, and was at the same time asked for by the League of Nations to instruct Fisher at Geneva on the same subject, though rather on status, I suppose, than on frontiers – I shall be torn between the two.

1st June [1921]

Came across some interesting material in studying Greek terr[itoria]l comm[issio]n. Martino[67] asked Crowe (12 M[ar]ch [19]19) whether G[reat] B[ritain] recognized Conf[eren]ce of St Jean de Maurienne of 19 Ap[ril] 1917[68] wherein Italy was assigned a terr[itoria]l zone, including Smyrna, extending along the coast to Adalia.[69] On July 26, 1917, an agreement between Fr[an]ce & Italy est[ablishe]d the river Lamas[70] as the respective limit of the zones of the two countries in the South of Anatolia. On the 18th August 1917 a convention was agreed upon at London between France, G[reat] B[ritain] and Italy. Italy gave her adhesion to the terr[itoria]l settlement agreed upon by the Allies in May 1916, in regard to part of a Armenia, Syria, Mesopotamia and Palestine; and entered in the capacity of a contracting party into the stipulations concerning Albania and the Red Sea. On the other hand France and Great Britain recognized as Italian 'on the same conditions of admin[astratio]n & interests' the zone marked on the map which I have the honour to submit to you. As you may observe practically the whole of the zone claimed by M. Venizelos, incl[u]d[in]g the town of Smyrna, is comprised in the zone attrib[ut]ed to Italy by virtue of the conv[entio]n in question.

    I therefore permit myself to ask a simple question (This question does not concern the Am[erica]n Deleg[atio]n for 2 reasons – firstly the Am[erica]n Deleg[atio]n has stated that the Gr[ee]k pretensions were without suff[icien]t basis and 2ndly the U[nited] S[tates] has not signed any conv[entio]n with Italy). The question which I have the honour to ask is the following 'How is it possible for the contracting Gov[ernmen]ts, to assign to Greece, even as a proposal by delimit[io]ns, marked on geog[raphica]l maps, terr[itor]ies wh[ich] they had recognized as Italian by virtue of preceding ag[reemen]ts [?]' referred to

---

[67] See entry 8 May 1919.
[68] See entry 2 May 1917.
[69] Now Antalya, on the coast of southwestern Turkey.
[70] Now Limonlu Çayı, a river in southern Turkey between Antalya and Adana.

fact Conv[entio]n of 1917 subject consent of Russia but claimed T[reaty] of L[ondon] as still valid. Art[icles] 9 & 8.

M. Westermann[71] (USA): 'I w[oul]d wish to raise an objection to the statement of the It[alia]n Deleg[a]te. He stated that the U[nited] S[tates] were not concerned in the <question of the> Treaties determining the settlement of terr[itor]ies in Asia Minor and the Dodecanese. I am anxious to state that the U[nited] S[tates] take a gr[ea]t interest in these questions, a moral interest and a practical one. The interest of the U[nited] S[tates] lies in refusing to recognise these treaties as a basis of the settlement of territory in the Near East'.

Sir E[yre] Crowe: 'Not only does the Brit[ish] Gov[ernmen]t not recognize the valid[it]y of the Ag[reemen]t of 1917 but it has informed the It[alia]n Gov[ernmen]t officially of this fact (T[reaty] of L[ondon] did not refer to London. Russia did not consent)[']. M. Gout indicated that Fr[an]ce was bound by Dodecanese ag[reemen]t under 1915 T[reaty] of L[ondon] but not re Smyrna.

Westermann: 'I w[oul]d wish not to allow M. Gout's last remark to pass without explaining the views of the Gov[ernmen]t under whose orders I work. These views apply to the T[reaty] of L[ondon] of 1915; and I repeat that the U[nited] S[tates] cannot recognize these conventions as affecting the settlement of the terr[itor]ies in the Near East. I sh[oul]d here desire to read the second part of the decl[aratio]ns of Pres[ident] Wilson of the 8th July so as to shew clearly the principles wh[ich] direct the opinion of the U[nited] S[tates]. I hasten to observe that I do not make this quotation in a spirit of criticism towards the Great Powers, but simply because I wish to express clearly my point of view based as it is on the principles of action set forth by Pres[ident] Wilson. This is what President Wilson said: 'The settlement of all questions, whether of territory, sov[ereign]ty, eco[nomic] arrangements or politic[al] relations on the basis of a free acceptance of this settlement by the pop[ulatio]ns directly interested and not on the basis of any material interest or advantage of any other nation or people whatsoever who may desire a different settlement for the furtherance of their external influence or their domination'. These last words do not apply to the present case. I wish to quote this paragraph from the general point of view. ['] <The pure milk of the Wilsonian word.>

---

[71] William Linn Westermann (1873–1954), US classicist and papyrologist; educated Nebraska and Berlin universitites; Assistant Professor of Ancient History, University of Missouri, 1902–1906; Minnesota, 1906–1908; Professor of Ancient History, Univeristy of Wiscosin, 1908–20; member of the 'Inquiry', 1917–18; delegate at Paris Peace Conference, 1919; Professor of Ancient History, Cornell University, 1920–23; Columbia University, 1923–48.

30th June [1921]

Arising out of the Parl[iamentar]y question addressed to the P[rime] M[inister] by Lord R[obert] C[ecil] the Cabinet were informed that the Council of the L[eague] of N[ations] had recently considered the differences between Albania and her neighbours in regard to frontiers, and that, insomuch as the boundaries of Albania were the legacy of the London Conf[eren]ce[72] and the Peace Conf[eren]ce, the Council had decided that the question was one for the Allied Powers. It has lately been considered by the Conference of Ambassadors in Paris. The Cabinet agreed that the reply to the question sh[oul]d be given by the Lord President of the Council,[73] who deals with questions relating to the L[eague] of N[ations].

6th July [1921]

Left for Paris.

7th July [1921]

After seeing the embassy attended at the Quai d'Orsay at 4.30 – the same heavy red curtains, the tapestries, the same beautiful tea and Brioches. M. La Roche[74] with his moustache cut a little shorter, but an added address and silkiness in his diplomatic manner. Galli,[75] the Italian, a gross materialistic man. As we went into the room, he pushed forward to take the seat on the right of the President. I did nothing but thought I w[oul]d remember. La Roche smiled and, with infinite delicacy intimated that we sat in alphabetical order, so I sat on the right and Galli on the left, the Japanese a pleasant brownfaced boy on my right.

---

[72] The London ambassadorial conference of 1912–13.
[73] Arthur James Balfour (see entry 2 Dec. 1916), who held the post between Oct. 1919 and Oct. 1922.
[74] Jules Laroche (1877–1963), French diplomat; Secretary-General to Conference of Ambassadors of the Principal Allied and Associated Powers (the successor of the Supreme War Council), 1920–24; Director of the Politicial Department, Foreign Ministry, 1924–26; ambassador at Warsaw, 1926–38.
[75] Carlo Galli (1878–1966), Italian lawyer and diplomat; entered Foreign Ministry, 1911; delegate at Paris Peace Conference, 1919; at Conference of Ambassadors (as Near Eastern specialist), 1920–22; counsellor at Paris embassy, 1922–24; minister at Tehran, 1924–26; Lisbon, 1926–28; at Belgrade, 1928–35; ambassador at Ankara, 1935–38; retired, 1938; Minister of Popular Culture, 1943–44.

8th July [1921]

We met the Albanian Delegates – Frashëri[76] voluble and nervous with gestures of a monkey, Tourtoulis,[77] the old Regent whom I saw in Tirana, dignified, slow, brownfaced and venerable, and an insignificant fluttering secretary. Frashëri began by a long written declaration that Albania stood by the international act of 1913, that the frontiers were intangibles and 'dans son ensemble'.

That Albania was now a happy land and unique in the world in that it had no public debt and its budget balanced, that order was maintained and the people were disarmed, that all they wanted was the support of the powers.

In response to questions, they did not, at any rate at present, deny the compet[en]ce of the Council of Amb[assado]rs to deal with the matter. There were only 123,000 Greeks and a few thousand Kutzo Vlachs[78] in Albania.

Frashëri said in answer to my question – Internat[iona]l navigation or transit on the principles of the Convention of Barcelona[79] w[oul]d meet with their approval.

Tourtoulis: Order was being well preserved by gendarmes etc. The population was disarmed (I afterwards found reason to doubt this).

Frashëri said that the votes of the Mirdites etc. [were] in favour of self-det[erminatio]n.

'Do you adhere to the principle of les frontiers intangible?' Yes. 'What is the position then with regard to the isle of Sasseno?' We adhere to that principle without any exception' (sans aucune exception). This caused much sensation to the Italian delegate. (I subsequently found it became an international incident.)

9th [July 1921]

Received advance unofficial instructions that we must try and confine the discussion of status to the form of recognition, and relegate that to the conference, and adhere on the Committee simply to the frontiers. This makes it very difficult for me on the Committee, but I fortunately took a stand on the [issue].

---

[76] Midhat (Bey) Frashëri (1880–1949), Albanian nationalist activist and politician; one of the signatories of Albanian declaration of independence, 1912; minister in provisional government, 1912–14; exile in Switzerland, 1914–18; chairman of Albanian delegation at Paris Peace Conference, Nov. 1920–22; president of National Front, 1942–45.

[77] See entry 5 Sept. 1920.

[78] Kutsovlachs or Aromanians, a Latin people native to the southern Balkans, more especially the Epirus and western Macedonia.

[79] The Barcelona Convention and Statute on the Regime of Navigable Waterways of International Concern, signed 10 Apr. 1921, enshrined the principle of free navigation on Europe's waterways.

29 [July 1921]

The experts, Tufton,[80] Waterlow[81] etc. who had arrived two days ago, continue to grapple.

3rd Aug[ust 1921]

Dined and had interesting talk with Sir Cecil Hurst.[82] He told me that he was present at what he believed to be the final decision with regard to the Pensions. Wilson showed no sign of embarrassment or consciousness that he was not doing the right thing. I quoted to him the saying in House's book.[83] Wilson was pointed out by his experts the legal & logical objections to the inclusion of pensions. He answered as follows[:] 'Logic, I don't care a damn for logic. I'm going to include pensions'. H[urst] laughed a good deal but wondered if it was true. I think it is – it's not the sort of thing which w[oul]d be invented. H[urst] did not agree with the Keynes[84] theory, that Wilson was unpractised in the agilities of the council-room, slow-witted and therefore bamboozled by Clemenceau and Ll[oyd] G[eorge].[85] 'Wilson', said he, 'was not slow-witted

---

[80] Hon. Charles Henry Tufton (1879–1923), entered diplomatic service, 1901; assistant secretary at the Second Hague peace conference, 1907; Private Secretary to Parliamentary Under-secretary for Foreign Affairs, 1908–11; counsellor in attendance of Paris Peace Conference, 1919; assistant secretary, 1920–22; seconded to League of Nations Branch, Jan.–Sept. 1922; resumed duties at Foreign Office, Nov. 1922; died at Geneva, Dec. 1923.

[81] Sir Sydney Philip Perigal Waterlow (1878–1944), diplomat; entered diplomatic service, 1900; member of the British delegation at the Paris Peace Conference, 1919; Director of the Foreign Division, Department of Overseas Trade, 1922–24; minister at Bangkok, 1926–28; minister at Addis Ababa, 1928–29; at Sofia, 1929–33; at Athens, 1933–39; a contemporary of Temperley's at King's.

[82] Sir Cecil James Barrington Hurst (1870–1963), assistant legal adviser to Foreign Office, 1902–18; Legal Adviser, 1918–29; judge of Permanent Court of International Justice, 1929–46 (president, 1934–36); chairman, United Nations War Crimes Commission, 1943–44.

[83] (Colonel) Edward Mandell House (1858–1938), US politician and diplomat; foreign policy adviser to President Wilson, 1912–19; see E.M. House and C. Seymour, *What Really Happened at Paris: The Story of the Peace Conference, 1918–1919* (New York, 1921).

[84] John Maynard Keynes (1883–1946), Baron Keynes, cr. 1942, economist and public servant; clerk at India Office, 1906–1908; lecturer in economics, Cambridge University, 1908–14; editor, *Economic Journal*, 1912–45; secretary to Royal Commission on Indian finance, 1913; Treasury adviser, 1914–19 and 1939–46; bursar, King's College, 1926–46.

[85] J.M. Keynes, *The Economic Consequences of the Peace* (London, repr. 1920), 38–50, esp. 50: 'it was harder to de-bamboozle him [Wilson] than it had been to bamboozle him'.

though he was not as quick as Ll[oyd] G[eorge]'. That w[oul]d be my view. I think Wilson knew what he was doing when he yielded over pensions though whether that makes his case better or worse, I do not know.

<La Roche has said that, whatever happens, the French will not give up more than Gleiwitz[86] and therefore will sever the industrial triangle.[87]>

11 Aug[ust 1921]

Nothing much until 7.30 p.m. when I was suddenly called up by the Marquis [Curzon]. I went round at once to the Embassy. After some preliminary waiting, I was introduced to the presence. C[urzon]: 'Let us begin about frontiers. What have we done?' H[arold Temperley]: 'The French and Italians have practically agreed to cessions to Jugoslavia in the North and East'.

C[urzon]: 'Very well, I don't want to know what we have agreed to but what we have not agreed on'.

H[arold]: 'Well, there is Koritza,[88] but we have now backed down over this'.

C[urzon]: 'How?'

H[arold]: 'Well we began by saying we w[oul]d insist on it'.

C[urzon]: 'Why?'

H[arold]: 'Because that was the decision of the Peace Conference on the Territorial Commission. Everybody agreed to it on Jan[uary] 14, 1920, except Pres[ident] Wilson. As he did not agree ultimately the arrangement lapsed as an offer and as a binding part of the general Adriatic settlement'.

C[urzon]: 'Well anything else?'

H[arold]: 'Agyrocastro'.[89]

C[urzon]: 'Why don't we want to give that to Greece?'

H[arold]: 'We are afraid of irredentism'.

C[urzon]: 'Do Italy and France oppose this?'

H[arold]: 'Yes'.

C[urzon]: 'What else is there?'

H[arold]: 'Sasseno'.[90]

C[urzon]: 'We'll talk about that presently. Now about the legal position. What rights has Italy over Albania?

H[arold]: 'None'.

C[urzon]: 'How is that?'

---

[86] Gliwice in Upper Silesia.
[87] That is, Beuthen (Bytom), Kattowitz (Katowice) and Gleiwitz (Gliwice).
[88] Korcë (Albania).
[89] Now Gjirokastër (Albania).
[90] The island of Sazan (It. *Saseno*) off the Bay of Vlorë.

H[arold]: 'Well the independence of Albania was established in 1913 by the Powers, including Germany, in the Treaty of London'.[91]

C[urzon]: 'That is the first Treaty of London?'

H[arold]: 'Yes'.

C[urzon]: 'What about the second?'

H[arold]: 'That was in 1915,[92] that assigned the protectorate of Central Albania to Italy and Valona[93] in full sovereignty'.

C[urzon]: 'Has that lapsed?'

H[arold]: 'Yes'.

C[urzon]: 'Why?'

H[arold]: 'Because the opinion of our legal advisers is that these articles were dependent on the General Adriatic settlement, and on Italy obtaining Albania. Also Italy has returned the mandate'.

C[urzon]: 'What was the mandate, not an ordinary one surely?'

H[arold]: 'Yes, certainly so-called in our proposals of 14 Jan[uary] 1920'.

C[urzon]: 'How did it terminate then?'

H[arold]: 'When Italy returned the mandate on 28th June 1920'.

C[urzon]: 'Very well, what then is the position now?'

H[arold]: 'Albania was admitted to the League of Nations as a sovereign & independent State'.

C[urzon]: 'Does Italy recognize this?'

H[arold]: 'Yes (showing passage) because in advocating her admission to the L[eague] of N[ations] Italy said she wanted her to be sovereign and independent'.

C[urzon]: 'Ah, that's very important (takes a note in pencil)'.

H[arold]: 'May I say a word?'

C[urzon]: 'Yes'.

H[arold]: 'It is important to note the words 'sovereign and independent state' because that will distinguish the admission of Albania from that of Canada – already admitted – and, say, Newfoundland,[94] which might be admitted, where [the] status is not sovereign and not independent. If we stress the admission of Albania on these other grounds we are alright'.

C[urzon]: 'I see'.

C[urzon]: 'How about this claim of Italy to a reversionary right or interest? Has she any right to this?

H[arold] 'None that I can see'.

C[urzon]: 'I don't see why we sh[oul]d admit this at all. Why sh[oul]d we?'

---

[91] The Treaty of London, 30 May 1913, which concluded the Second Balkan War.
[92] The Anglo-French-Russian-Italian treaty of 26 Apr. 1915.
[93] Now Vlorë.
[94] Newfoundland, a self-governing colony from 1855 onwards, had Dominion status, 1907–49, and was thus separate from the Dominion of Canada.

H[arold]: 'I can see no reason'.

C[urzon]: 'The Italians have behaved very badly everywhere else[;] I don't see why we sh[oul]d let them behave badly here too. What is their object?'

H[arold]: 'Well so far as I can see they wish to sap the foundations of the new state, with a view to inheriting her reversion'.

C[urzon]: 'Tell me, has Albania a chance of success?'

H[arold]: 'Well, I sh[oul]d say she has a sporting chance. The new gov[ernmen]t has done much better than anyone expected – it is keeping a fair sort of order, and, provided it is left alone, may find itself. The one thing that is absolutely fatal is to allow France and Italy, while she is professedly independent, to squeeze economic concessions from her by gov[ernmen]tal influence etc.'.

C[urzon]: 'Yes, I see. I don't see why we sh[oul]d allow anything of the kind. Now about Sasseno [*sic*], what is the position? I gather it is in Italian military occupation, by virtue of a secret Treaty or protocol with the Albanians'.

H[arold]: 'Yes'.

C[urzon]: 'Is there any ground for this?'

H[arold]: 'Well navally, according to the Admiralty it is strategically very important'.

C[urzon]: 'Have the Italians any other argument?'

H[arold]: 'Well, no good one. They will quote the Treaty of London'.

C[urzon]: 'I gather that in 1913 it was included in Albania and that, if it does not belong to her, it belongs to Greece'.

H[arold]: 'Yes'.

C[urzon]: 'Is there any other argument?'

H[arold]: 'No. When the Italians said the frontiers of 1913 sh[oul]d be maintained intact for Albania I asked if this included Sasseno, and they said no'.

C[urzon]: 'Yes, they complained about that and your attitude'.

H[arold]: 'Well, I thought it the only way of countering their argument'.

C[urzon]: 'I suppose they really want Valona'.

H[arold]: 'Yes'.

C[urzon]: 'Have they any other argument?'

H[arold]: 'No, not unless there are considerations of *la haute politique* apart from this'.

C[urzon]: 'Well, I don't see they have any right to it and I don't see why they sh[oul]d have it. Now I must go and meet these Italians at dinner'.

H[arold]: 'I'm afraid you'll find they'll represent me in a bad light'.

C[urzon]: 'Ah I know, but my dear Temperley, have no fears on that score. Don't think what they say makes any impression on me. You will be properly supported. You have done well'. (Exit.)

11 Aug[ust 1921]

<u>Upper Silesia</u>. I gather today L[loyd] G[eorge] was very angry this morning and told the French that they could take it or leave it <, not a good breakfast dish>. He w[oul]d leave in any case at noon tomorrow, the 12th – and the answer must be ready by 10 a.m.[95]

I gather also that the reason the Marquis was in a massacring mood as regards the Italians was that they had shown much weakness as regards Silesia today. They had in fact pract[icall]y intimated that they were prepared only to back the winning horse, and they had now begun to wonder whether it was France or England.

At close quarters, C[urzon] impressed me by his grasp and certainty. He was well-informed in part but not in all, but quick to see new points. In person, he is extraordinarily broad in the shoulder – his brow is fine, but eye and mouth a little disappointing. The manner grandiose and condescending but not wholly genuine or impressive.

12 [August 1921]

The French turned up at 10.15 today and found L[loyd] G[eorge] unyielding. 'Then this is rupture', said L[loyd] G[eorge]. Briand demurred and said the Cabinet had supported him without a dissentient voice. 'Then I appeal to the League of Nations', said L[loyd] G[eorge]. 'I am very glad indeed', said Briand, 'and I will accept its decision'.

Last night I hear at the dinner with the Italians that Ll[oyd] G[eorge] with great dexterity started on questions dealing with the internal state of Italy. This flattered the ice-creamers and held them entranced. The carefully prepared paper of topics and agenda was forgotten, and each time the bewildered Italianos returned to it they were headed off by the wizard in most masterly fashion. L[or]d C[urzon] had little to do, but was firm on Albania. J.T. D[avies][96] told me two days ago he rather though the P[rime] M[inister] did not agree with the independence of Albania. I said that the thing to insist on was the independence of Albania, to which we were pledged by the League, but personally I did not see why the Italians sh[oul]d not be allowed to occupy Sasseno, tho[ugh] L[or]d C[urzon], I knew, did not see why we sh[oul]d buy them off in this way.

---

[95] The 3rd Paris conference, 8–13 Aug. 1921, to decide the future of Upper Silesia, where, in a plebiscite in Mar., a majority had voted for union with Germany rather than Poland, see mins. in CAB 29/93; also *DBFP* (1) xv, ch. VI

[96] See entry 5 June 1919.

I gather the Italians showed signs of the white flag yesterday at the afternoon meeting and that they seemed rather to let us down.

13 [August 1921]

Winding up today. Commissions – sanctions – Russia finance etc. All the lesser lights aglow. Briand's speech said to have been very fine though of the Pussyfoot order.

Very lengthy interview with Frashëri. He held out for the frontiers of 1913 intact, which, he said, were no less important than the principle of independence. I failed entirely to get him to admit that the status of the Argyrocastro area sh[oul]d be determined by the ascertainment of the wishes of the inhabitants by a commission appointed by the League. Col[onel] Harvey[97] appears to have made an appallingly bad and disappointing speech.

H[ardinge] had some very interesting views on L[or]d Grey. He thought that, in some ways, he was one of our greatest men and was adored by the Staff. Sir H[arold] Stuart[98] dissented strongly but not very intelligently, I thought. (This was 12th.)

Tonight [Sir Cecil] Hurst dealt with [Woodrow] Wilson. Doing full justice to his great achievements as President in his first term, he said his failure was due to his attempt to dragoon the American public and Senate when he did not possess a majority at his back. This autocratic tendency ran through everything he did, made him rely on inferior instruments and work through unorthodox channels, frequently overriding or brow-beating his own ministers. He said a friend of his heard Wilson's famous challenge to the Senate in New York before he returned to Paris in March <1919> and left the meeting with the feeling that an appalling mistake had been committed. In his view had Wilson had a few rep[resentati]ve senators with him in Paris the situation might have been saved.

---

[97] Colonel George Brinton McClellan Harvey (1864–1928), US journalist and diplomat; editor, *New York World*, 1891–94; *North American Review*, 1899–1926; *Harper's Weekly*, 1901–13 and 1918–21; switched allegiance from Woodrow Wilson to Republicans in 1916; opponent of League of Nations; ambassador at London, 1921–24.

[98] Sir Harold Arthur Stuart (1860–1923), civil servant; entered Indian civil service, 1881; Inspector-General of Police, Madras, 1898; Director of Central Criminal Intelligence Department, 1904–1908; Home Secretary to Government of India, 1908–11; Member of Exicutive Council, Madras, 1912–16; retired, 1916; employed in Ministry of Food, 1916–18; High Commissioner of the Inter-Allied Rhineland High Commission, 1920–21; British Commissioner in Allied Administration for the Plebiscite in Upper Silesia, 1921–22.

Much interesting talk with Howorth[99] on the practical working of the Cabinet today. It now met 4 or 5 times a week instead of once in the old days. The minutes were, of course, very important and L[loyd] G[eorge] had complete control. They were circulated to the P[rime] M[inister], Foreign Sec[retar]y, [Lord] Privy Seal, Chanc[ello]r of [the] Exchequer.

Otherwise minutes only go to the ministers interested. L[loyd] G[eorge] is everywhere. He controls the agenda, he can prevent note being taken at a certain point, he need not submit matters to the vote (and very seldom does and then only if he thinks it certain to go in his favour). He can also subseq[uentl]y alter the form of a minute. Other minutes can however suggest alterations in decisions. All ministers are summoned to the Cab[ine]t and receive all papers relating to business. Few, except [H.A.L.] Fisher and Austen [Chamberlain], read them.

There is a curious kind of inner Cabinet, known as the Finance Committee, over which L[loyd] G[eorge] presides. This has its own minutes circulated only to its own members and has great powers, e.g. neither Admir[alt]y or War Office Min[iste]rs are members yet this committee can reduce their estimates (and does) without consulting them.

The Home Affairs Committee, which meets frequently, is also a kind of curious body to which a dep[artmen]t can appeal ag[ain]st the Treasury. Consequently the Treasury's control now is neither complete nor absolute (Anti-Wasters please note).[100] It deals with matters in great detail, quarrels betw[een] dep[artmen]t & dep[artmen]t, dep[artmen]ts & Treasury etc. etc.

On the whole Howorth thought the system did not work very well. The Cabinet was too big (a necessity of parl[iamentar]y minds) – it was held together by the inner Cabinet and by the personality of the P[rime] M[inister]. Winston [Churchill] was believed to be opposed to the system, and detested minutes. There were however several testimonies to the fact that under Asquith the system was hopeless, at any rate for war. No notes were allowed and no minutes taken, hence no decision known.

I made some remarks about Gladstone's[101] Cabinets. H[urst] held very strongly the view that no P[rime] M[inister] really ever allowed himself to be overruled in his own Cabinet (cert[ainl]y this one does not). I quoted the

---

[99] Sir Rupert Beswicke Howorth (1880–1964), barrister and civil servant; entered Board of Education, 1908; transferred to Treasury, 1915; seconded to Cabinet Office, 1919; deputy Secretary of Cabinet, 1930–42; clerk to Privy Council, 1938–42.

[100] The 'anti-waste' rostrum was particularly fashionable among Conservative backbenchers in the coalition government.

[101] William Ewart Gladstone (1809–98), politician; MP (Cons.) Newark, 1832–45, (Peelite, since 1857 Liberal) Oxford University, 1847–65, South Lancashire, 1865–68, Greenwich, 1868–80, Midlothian, 1880–95; President of the Board of Trade, 1843–45; Secretary of State for War and the Colonies, 1843–46; Chancellor of the Exchequer, 1852–55, 1859–66, 1873–74 and 1880–82; Prime Minister, 1868–74, 1880–85, Feb.–July 1886, and 1892–94.

instance of Gladstone being overruled over the question of transferring the Iron Duke's statue to Aldershot.[102] H[urst] answered with some point: 'I don't think that is a matter a P[rime] M[inister] w[oul]d care to consider personal or worth resigning about.['] Howorth intervened with an amusing story about past days illustrating Gladstone's authority. When [Sir Henry] C[ampbell]-B[annerman][103] was Sec[retar]y for War Gladstone quoted from Martial[104] in the Cabinet, C[ampbell]-B[annerman] humorously contested the accuracy of the quotation. Not to be outdone Gladstone sent for a copy, perused it carefully and remarked frigidly 'This time the Secretary of State for War is right and I am wrong. But the passage is from a part of Martial that no decent minded man would read twice'. Thus are Cabinets ruled.

28 Aug[ust] 1921

Started on boat, saw of all people Sir W[illiam] Sutherland,[105] fresh from his honeymoon (or rather starting on it) with a wealthy mine-owning wife. Never did I see anyone less embarrassed. 'I don't like young women, my wife is three years older than me'. He then explained at considerable length that the reason there was so much fuss about his wedding was not that it was of any real importance, but that it was the silly season. 'I know how these things go because I've had a good deal to do with the Press' (we all know that). Turning to me, 'Ah, you are going to the League of Nations and going to act there just as you did at the Peace Conference. Very good for us and for you. It'll give you kudos at the University – but, when I was at the Peace Conference, every day I spent there was wasted. I didn't know what I was doing there, or what my constituents were doing, or what Parliament was doing, or what the people were saying about me in my absence. Politics is a job you can't leave, or your press work and propaganda get out of gear'. (I should think very likely).

---

[102] The large-scale equestrian Wellington Statue (1846) by Matthew Cotes Wyatt (1777–1862) was originally situated on the Wellington Arch at Hyde Park Corner; when the arch was moved to its present location in 1882–83, the statue was removed, to be transferred to Aldershot in 1885.

[103] Sir Henry Campbell-Bannerman (1836–1908), politician; MP (Lib.) Stirling Burghs, 1868–1908; Financial Secretary to the War Office, 1871–4 and 1880–82; Parliamentary Secretary to the Admiralty, 1882–84; Chief Secretary for Ireland, 1884–85; Secretary of State for War, Feb.–July 1886 and 1892–95; Prime Minister, 1905–1908.

[104] Marcus Valerius Martialis (c. 40–104), Roman poet and epigrammatist; his *Coena Trimalchionis* has made many a school boy snigger.

[105] See entry, 6 May 1919. Sutherland married Annie Christine Fountain, widow of a Barnsley colliery-owner, on 27 Aug. 1921.

29 [August 1921]

Arrived at 'clear placid Leman, thy contrasted lake'.[106]

Lunch with A.J.B[alfour].

He touched on many things – anthropology, science, dwellers, Germany in E[astern] Prussia, Slavs, music, ciphers, Albania, Serbia, Mary Q[ueen] of Scots,[107] Greek pottery, Etruscan tombs, Hittites – all with a certain gracious lightness. He touched gently on Sir W[illiam] Sutherland. I doubt whether controlling the Press is worth while. He said that he had no doubt that Mary Q[ueen] of Scots was guilty of the murder of Darnley[108] and that she was quite right to blow him up. We should have done the same. I compared Serbia.[109] Ah yes, said he dreamily, that was when I was Prime Minister. It was really too bad. I had to do something. We kept away from them for three years, I think. He then told us of Eng[lish] & Scotch ways at Pinkie.[110] (1) You know what Maitland[111] says 'that decisive defeat of the Scottish host and the Britannic idea?'[112] Ah, and he talked of Maitland and seemed to wish that he (the professor) had claimed kinship with him. 'I can however claim kinship with one Maitland, the brother of Maitland of Lethington[113][']' – and he seemed to think this near enough. I said Maitland of Lethington was the most intellectual of Mary's advisers, and this seemed to please him.

---

[106] Lacus Lemannus, Lake Geneva; see Lord Byron, *Childe Harold's Pilgrimage* (1812–18), canto 3, LXXV: 'Clear, placid Leman! thy contrasted lake'.

[107] Mary Stuart, Queen of Scots (1542–87).

[108] Henry Stuart, Lord Darnley (1545–67), 1st Duke of Albany, cr. 1565, king-consort of Scotland; murdered in Feb. 1567 after his alienation from Mary following her refusal to grant him the Crown Matrimonial, i.e. the right to co-reign.

[109] Murder of King Alexander Obrenović in 1903; diplomatic relations with Belgrade remained severed 1903–1906.

[110] The Battle of Pinkie Cleugh, on the banks of the River Esk near Musselburgh, on 10 September 1547, the first modern battle on British soil, ending in defeat for the Scottish army.

[111] Frederic William Maitland (1850–1906), jurist and legal historian; called to the bar, 1876; Reader in English Law, Cambridge University, 1884–88; Downing Professor of the Laws of England, 1888–1906.

[112] 'No more decisive defeat could have been inflicted on the Scottish host and the Britannic idea', F.W. Maitland, 'The Anglican Settlement and the Scottish Reformation', *Cambridge Modern History*, ii, *The Reformation* (Cambridge, 1907), 557.

[113] Sir William Maitland of Lethington (1525–73); Queen Mary's Secretary of State. His brother was John Maitland, 1st Lord Mailand of Thirlstane (1537–95), whose John became the 1st Earl of Lauderdale (d. 1645); Balfour was descended from him through his grandmother, Lady Eleanor, daughter of the 8th Earl.

31 [August 1921]

Saw Sir Eric Drummond[114] <re Albania>, a mild, agreeable, cautious and tactful man. His views expressed by a minute he wrote, which was eventually shown me 'I have discussed this question with Mr. Temperley. For technical but important reasons I do not think it is proper to announce the frontier line on Friday but only that the experts appointed by the P[rincipal] A[llied] & A[ssociated] P[owers] to consider the frontier have reached an agreement. The announcement as to the definite frontiers could, I hope, be made at the Assembly; but if your fears as to procedure expressed in the first part of your minute are well-founded (Legal section should be consulted) it would be well for Mr. Balfour to move formally that Friday's question be referred to Assembly in connexion with the Albanian request. You can tell Mr. Temperley that this is my view, if the legal section concur.
E[ric] D[rummond], 31.8.21[']

1 Sept[ember 1921]

In consequence of this, after a letter from Nicolson to the effect that Frangulis[115] was suggesting to the Gr[ee]k Gov[ernmen]t à la d'Annunzio to jump the Argyrocastro claim. This served as a good enough excuse to induce me to get Mr. Balfour to send a telegram stating that he w[oul]d be placed in a very embarrassing position at the Assembly of he could not communicate the details of the frontiers agreement arrived at. He therefore asked for communication directly to governments concerned and for joint declaration. All this is exactly what I told the F[oreign] O[ffice] weeks ago, and implored them to make a declaration – how will they show now?

Before all this however we had an interview with the Albanians and a serious talk on mandates procedure.

1st re Albanians. Fan Noli[116] & Frashëri called on A.J. B[alfour] today while I was present. He received them with a sort of benign archness and superior innocence which was, in all senses, extremely disarming. Thus, 'Ah, you say the Serbs have been violating the frontiers?' 'Yes'. 'Are they Serb bands or Serb Government troops?' 'Bands paid by the Serbs'. 'Who are the leaders?' 'There are three'. 'Are they Serbs?' 'Two of them are majors in the Serbian reserves'. 'And the third?' 'He is an Albanian'. 'Is he the chief leader?' 'Yes'.

---

[114] See entry 20 Feb. 1917.
[115] Antoine F. Frangulis, Greek diplomat; delegate at League of Nations, 1920–22.
[116] Theofan Stilian Noli (1882–1965), known as Fan Noli, Albanian scholar, diplomat, and liberal politician; founded the Albanian Orthodox Church in Boston, MA, 1908; bishop for the Church of Albania, 1923; Prime Minister and Regent of Albania, 1924; in exile since 1924.

A.J. B[alfour]: 'You ask me a member of the Council to intervene in your favour?' 'Yes'.

A.J. B[alfour]: 'But you have appealed to the Assembly over the heads of the Council, have you not?' 'Yes'. A.J.B[alfour]: 'Perfectly right and proper (five minutes before <seeing them> he had said <in private> 'a piece of gross impertinence') but how am I to help you?' 'You have great power'. A.J. B[alfour]: 'But I am a member of the Council and you have appealed against me' – silence – finally the Bishop: 'but why not as a Great Power, as Great Britain [?]' A.J.B[alfour]: 'A member of the Council'. Fan Noli: 'But we have appealed to the Council against the actions of the Yugoslavs in violating the frontier'. A.J. B[alfour]: 'What frontier?' 'That of 1913'. A.J. B[alfour]: 'But we don't admit that it exists and you have appealed against our right qua Council to determine it'.

2. A scene of high-class comedy –

A.J. B[alfour] reported – in the sense desired tho[ugh] in an inimitable style on the question. There were 2 points (1) that Albania had appealed to the Ass[embl]y over the Serbo-Albanian dispute[;] (2) that in June they appealed to the Ass[embl]y ag[ain]st the decision (and over the heads) of the Council to leave the Conference of Ambassadors to settle the question of frontiers. No. 2 went to the Assembly anyway and no. 1 went, if the Council so decided. A.J. B[alfour] put it thus: 'I suggest therefore that as the Ass[embl]y has been requested by the Albanians to deal with the determination of the frontiers, they should also be asked to deal with the violation of frontiers'. This was mostly his own – the rest of the report, consisting of hist[orica]l observations, was mine. It contained one sentence which contained the charter of Albania's freedom in the following short sentence [*sic*]. It alluded to Alb[ani]a having been admitted to the League [on] 17 Dec[ember] 1920 'Now whatever may have been the situation in Albanina previous to the decision recorded above – the legal opinion on this point appears to have been divided – there can be no doubt that the decision of the Ass[embl]y admitted Albania as a fully self-gov[ernin]g State, and on this subject I do not conceive there can be any further debate'.

There was, however, but in an interesting and confirmatory sense. After the Report <had been read> the Yugoslav representative jumped up and said that he had two letters <It is suspicious that, as there were two appeals of Albania, he produced two letters> to read – these were both from a certain Marka Donji[117] [*sic*] and were to the effect that he had established a self-determining republic in North Albania in the Mirdite territory. Consequently he did not know what Gov[ernmen]t he was dealing [with] whether with the Gov[ernmen]t of Tirana which was Mussulman, Bolshevist, Kemalist and spent most of its time killing

---

[117] Kapidan Gjon Marka Gjoni (1888–1966), Albanian clan leader; proclaimed the Republic of Mirdita, July 1921, and served as its president until Nov. 1921.

Christian women and children. Therefore the appeal to the Ass[embl]y was out of order as there was no Albanian Gov[ernmen]t or (two too) many of them.

As soon as he had done, Fan Noli jumped up and said 'The Government of the Mirdite Republic consists of one man who is now at Prisrend, a Serbian town'. Yovanović (interrupting): 'No there are 15 because you have forgotten his 14 ministers'. The B[isho]p then proceeded to explain that he was unlikely to favour the massacring of Xtians, and that in point of fact its tol[eran]ce was complete & 4 religions were rep[resente]d in the Gov[ernmen]t (a) Orth[odo]x <'Je fus stupefait', said Yovanovic afterwards to me>, (b) Cath[oli]c, (c) Mahomedan, (d) Bektashi.[118] 'Who are the last?', said A.J. B[alfour]. 'They are', said the Bishop amid much hilarity, 'a Mahomedan sect who do not believe in Mahomet'. Yovanović was ruled out of order as the whole was a matter internal to Albania – Imperiali,[119] of all people, saying that Albania was already recognised as sov[erei]gn and indep[ende]nt.

<A.J. B[alfour]'s report went through without éclat and the Italians and French who had protested throughout the Committee against the indep[enden]ce of Albania now raised no voice. A Yugoslav and an Albanian were called to order, & the former ruled out as irrelev[an]t by the Chairman of the Council, a Chinaman.[120] Thus works the League.> <2nd Sept[ember] My cup of joy was finally full when Spicer[121] handed me a telegram from the F[oreign] O[ffice] in reply to Balfour's of the 1st: 'I quite agree and Italian & French Gov[ernmen]ts will be approached accordingly to make a joint decl[aratio]n re frontiers'. Thus Independence certainly & frontiers prob[abl]y were settled in one day.>

Very interesting talk with A.J. B[alfour] at dinner – he said of L[loyd] G[eorge] – 'the thing that strikes me most is that he falls into no category that I know of. He views every problems anew and from the beginning. So every day we have a fresh discovery. I dislike his set speeches. I admire him most in impromptus. He has the art of putting exactly the right argument to the right person at the moment. Yet he has very little education – though he has

---

[118] Bektaşi, an Islamic mystical sect that fuses many concepts of Sunni, Shia and Sufi Islam, but with distinct doctrine and rituals, particularly prevalent in the Balkans; the seat of the movement is at Tirana.

[119] See entry 26 Apr. 1919.

[120] Ku Wei-chün (Gù Wéijūn) (1887–1985), better known as V.K. Wellington Koo, Republican Chinese politician and diplomat; minister to the United States and Cuba, 1915–19; representative at Paris Peace Conference; foreign minister, 1926–27; ambassador to France, 1936–40; to Great Britain, 1940–46; participated in founding of the League of Nations and the United Nations; judge at the International Court of Justice at The Hague, 1957–67.

[121] Gerald Sidney Spicer (1874–1942), Foreign Office clerk; entered Foreign Office, 1894; attended Paris Peace Conference, 1919; Assistant Under-secretary, 1919–20; seconded to Cabinet Office, League of Nations Branch, 1920–21; resigned 1 Jan. 1922.

read a great many books. I hear that Morley[122] omitted [him] from his memoirs intentionally. If so he was wrong because he has a position not only among the greatest of English but of European statesmen'.

H.A.L. F[isher]: 'Nobody has the same position since Boney'.

A.J. B[alfour]: 'Ah Boney'.

H.A.L. F[isher]: 'I mean Napoleon'.[123]

A.J. B[alfour]: 'No perhaps not. I sh[oul]d say there are 4 gr[ea]t European Statesmen among Englishmen – Pitt,[124] Castlereagh,[125] Palmerston[126] & L[loyd] G[eorge]'.

H.W.V. T[emperley]: 'It pains me you exclude Canning'.

A.J. B[alfour]: 'Well, what did he do? Recognized Sp[anish] Am[eric]a'.

H.W.V. T[emperley]: 'He mobilised public opinion against the despots'.

A.J. B[alfour]: 'Yes, perhaps so'.

H.A.L. F[isher]: 'Castlereagh had begun that in the Cabinet'.

H.W.V. T[emperley]: 'But Canning brought it into the marketplace'.

A.J. B[alfour]: 'Yes, perhaps'.

H.A.L. F[isher]: 'But what about Gladstone? Was he not important in Greece and Italy?'

A.J. B[alfour]: 'Yes, I grant you that he gave up the Ionian Isles and attacked King Bomba.[127] But he was despised in Germany – and rightly from their point of view. So you see I grant it only for Greece and Italy. But to come back to L[loyd] G[eorge] his ascendancy is remarkable'.

---

[122] See entry 9 June 1917.

[123] Napoleon Bonaparte (1769–1821), French soldier and politician; 1st Consul of the French Republic, 1799–1804; Emperor of the French, 1804–15.

[124] William Pitt the Younger (1759–1806), politician; MP, Appleby, 1781–84, Cambridge University, 1784–1806; Prime Minister, 1783–1801 and 1804–1806; Chancellor of the Exchequer, 1804–1806.

[125] Robert Stewart, Viscount Castlreagh (1769–1822), 2nd Marquess of Londonderry, succ. 1821, politician; MP, Tregony, 1794–96, Orford 1796–97 and 1821–22, Down, 1801–1805 and 1812–21, Plympton Erle, 1806–12; Chief Secretary for Ireland, 1798–1801; President of the Board of Control, 1802–1806; Secretary of State for War and the Colonies, 1805–1806 and 1807–1809; Foreign Secretary, 1812–22.

[126] Henry John Temple, Viscount Palmerston (1784–1865), politician; MP, Newport, 1807–11, Cambridge University, 1811–31, Bletchingley, 1831–32, Hampshire South, 1832–35, Tiverton, 1835–65; Secretary at War, 1809–28; Foreign Secretary, 1830–34, 1835–41 and 1846–51; Home Secretary, 1852–55; Prime Minister, 1855–58 and 1859–65.

[127] King Ferdinand II of the Two Sicilies (1810–59, r. 1830–59), nicknamed 'Rè Bomba' ('King Bomb') on account of his brutal suppression of the 1848 revolution in Naples. Gladstone had condemned the conditions in the kingdom in 1850 as 'the negation of God erected to a system of government'.

H.W.V. T[emperley]: 'Is it not because he is the only European statesman now whose Parl[iamen]t will always support him?'

H.A.L. F[isher]: 'Yes, but other British statesmen have been like that'.

A.J. B[alfour]: 'Yet no statesman has been like L[loyd] G[eorge]. He makes many mistakes – especially when he gets on to history in his speeches. Then I tremble for him – but he always gets round it. He made some absurd mistakes in his last speech about Silesia – said it had been German as long as Normandy had been French. That gave France an opportunity'.

C.J.B. H[urst]: 'Yes but what a fine speech that was to hear – and how it impressed the French even when it irritated them'.

A.J. B[alfour]: 'That is it – even when he irritates and is rude he impresses. How remarkable too is his temper. He makes an attack on a man – and forgets about it that day. He forgets that the other man does not forget, he does not even realize that he is likely to remember'.

[Temperley] I asked him what he thought of President Wilson.

[Balfour:] 'President Wilson – Oh Wilson was very impressive'.

H.W.V. T[emperley]: 'You really think so?'

A.J. B[alfour]: 'Yes, I do'.

H.W.V. T[emperley]: 'Philip Kerr told me that Ll[oyd] G[eorge] thinks Wilson was not a politician but was quite the equal of himself or Clemenceau'.

A.J. B[alfour]: 'Oh – but he was! What an awful tragedy it all is. I hardly like to think of it. Here was a man, who really thought he got hold of the greatest idea in the world, and he had the opportunity of achieving the greatest good the world has ever known'.

H.A.L. F[isher]: 'A man who was great enough to think that [he] had something of that greatness'.

A.J. B[alfour]: 'I hardly like to tell this story but it came from Harding[128] himself. It is custom when the President hands over in March for both to drive together to the Capitol. Harding began (as he thought best and as his kindly way is) to talk of commonplaces and gentle nothings. Suddenly he stopped and could not go on – for he saw tears running down Wilson's face.

As for 1917 I hardly like to dogmatize. My republican friends used always to tell me that Wilson could have brought them in earlier – others have said the opposite and I am sure Wilson himself believed he c[oul]d not do otherwise or he w[oul]d have brought them in quicker'.

H.W.V. T[emperley]: 'Do you not think the divisions since the peace suggest there was no united nation in the war?'

---

[128] Warren Gamaliel Harding (1865–1923), US politician; State Senator (R), Ohio, 1900–1904; Lieutenant Governor, Ohio, 1904–1906; Senator, Ohio, 1915–21; President of the United States, 1921–23.

A.J. B[alfour]: 'I hardly think you can argue from that. I was greatly impressed with him when I saw him in 1917, again in 1918, and at the Peace Conference. I did not hear him speak often in public – and I was not always so impressed then'.

H.A.L. F[isher]: 'His speeches will be among the classics of Anglo-Saxon oratory'.

A.J. B[alfour]: 'Yes in phrasing and utterance great. I do not know enough to speak of them as uttered.

His great mistake was in November 1918 in asking the American public to vote Democrat.

But he always was a party man and treated the opposition with the greatest insolence: I am told too that if he had come to terms – even in quite a small way – with his opponents – he could have passed the Treaty (House[129] (Col[onel]) told me that in July last who likes and admires him still). But his arrogance would not permit him.

I am told his speeches on campaign were some of the finest he ever uttered. What a tragedy – and what a great man – though perhaps his greatness was not intellectual.

Clemenceau had greatness too – of a rough brusque kind coming from so sharp a temper and personality.

Kitchener – I knew him – very closely because I was much concerned about munitions even very early – and lived next door to him (2 Carlton Garden) and dined with him very often. In some ways he was mad. Fitzgerald[130] used to tell me not to pay attention to all he said. After the Marne his one obsession was [that] we were making so much ammunition and leaving it behind in the retreat. One could not get him to consider things properly. He did not understand the territorials – and no one could make him understand them. I remember once coming along to him when he was reading a letter on the subject. He showed it to me – what can I do with a letter with an address like that. It was headed MAYOR'S PARLOR (some town I forget what). That was it – how could the Territorials be dealt with in a Mayor's Parlor, and, if they could, how could they be soldiers? A conundrum unanswerable to a soldier, coming in old age from the East. I remember his favourite von Donop,[131] Master General of the Ordnance – a bugbear of Ll[oyd] G[eorge]'s, who said to me once 'I don't like even the sound of his name'. I tried to arrange with him once for a quick turning out of trench mortars on a new pattern. So far as I could see, it was a splendid plan and very sensible. He would not hear of it or even discuss it. He was a perfectly technically

---

[129] See entry 3 Aug. 1921.

[130] See entry 20 Nov. 1916.

[131] Major-General Sir Stanley Brenton von Donop (1860–1941), soldier; entered Royal Artillery, 1880; active service, South Africa 1900–1902; Inspector-General of Artillery, War Office, 1911–13; Master-General of the Ordnance, 1913–16; Commander, Humber Garrison, 1917–20; Colonel Commandant Royal Artillery, 1925–41.

well-educated and highly trained artillery officer but terribly narrow and without the faintest idea of the new conditions. Yet he was idolised by Kitchener.

Kitchener had a mania for economy – it pursued him everywhere – and it was economy based on Egypt and unsuitable to England. That was why he refused Ll[oyd] G[eorge]'s programme of guns – because of economy – and because he had not devised it himself.

He was unused to – nay absolutely ignorant of – Cabinet Government and at sea more totally than you can imagine. He was an Administrator by himself, and used to Oriental ideas, and unable to take in any others – in short a Sultan and nothing else. Yet all the same he was a great man.

One thing I can neither forgive him nor Asquith – the Newcastle speech about shells.[132] That was a mendacious letter <of Kitchener's> – the situation was very serious we all knew. Yet Kitchener's letter covered Asquith – but Asquith knew it to be mendacious. He sh[oul]d not have read it, he sh[oul]d have adjourned his speech, or feigned illness. I cannot quite pardon that.

Harcourt.[133] He had the most terrible manners – and made himself impossible in the Cabinet and I think so from what I saw – yet I have sat with (Hicks) Beach[134] in the Cabinet. I once saw something of Harcourt under such circumstances, in a committee room where we met to discuss joint policy of opposition and gov[ernmen]t respecting one of these tiresome votes to a Royal Duke. His method was as followed. He advanced his argument flinging back his head haughtily – discussion took place – he then reiterated his argument exactly as before in a still more insolent manner and flung his head back still further. Impossible then, I believe in the Cabinet of Rosebery[135] more impossible still.

---

[132] During the so-called 'Shell Crisis' in the spring of 1915, under pressure from the Northcliffe press and following assurances by Kitchener, Asquith stated in a speech to munitions workers on Tyneside on 20 Apr. 1915 that the army had sufficient stocks of ammunition, see 'The Nation At War. Mr. Asquith at Newcastle', *The Times*, 21 Apr. 1915. This was not in fact the case. The crisis played a significant role in the formation of the first wartime coalition government in May 1915, with Lloyd George as Minister for Munitions.

[133] Sir William Vernon Harcourt (1827–1904), politician; MP (Lib.), Oxford, 1868–80, Derby, 1880–95, West Monmouthshire, 1895–1904; Solicitor-General, 1873–74; Home Secretary, 1880–85; Chancellor of the Exchequer, Feb.–July 1886, 1892–95; Liberal leader, 1896–99.

[134] Sir Michael Edward Hicks-Beach (1837–1916), Viscount St. Aldwyn, cr. 1906, 1st Earl of St. Aldwyn, cr. 1915, politician; MP (Cons.) Gloucestershire East, 1868–85, Bristol West, 1885–1906; Chief Secretary for Ireland, 1874–78 and 1886–87; Colonial Secretary, 1878–80; Chancellor of the Exchequer, 1885–86 and 1895–1902; Minister without Portfolio, 1887–88; President of the Board of Trade, 1888–92.

[135] Archibald Philip Primrose, 5th Earl of Rosebery (1847–1929), politician; Undersecretary for Home Affairs, 1881–83; First Commissioner for Works, 1885; Lord Privy Seal, 1885; Foreign Secretary, 1885–86 and 1892–94; Prime Minister, 1894–95; Liberal leader, 1894–96.

As a young man he was intolerable, coasting on intellect and birth – and people pardoned at a later stage what they could not forgive a boy'.

[Temperley:] Napoleon – I said he worked 15 hours a day. A.J. B[alfour] was impressed but thought that, after all, he stopped at 46 and was by then showing some signs of age – as at Waterloo. He then said that he thought Napoleon had always been a gambler, in spite of his colossal intellect. Egypt, Acre, Marengo were really no more than desperate ventures, the first two almost insane.

We spoke of his civil leg[islatio]n.

H.A.L. F[isher] thought him very great there and said he applied common sense and knowledge of mankind to Roman principles of law and thus benefited half Europe.

A.J. B[alfour]: 'How did he know law?'

H.A.L. F[isher]: 'Oh, he was shut up as a sub-lieutenant one night in a detention house for a breach of discipline, and the only book in it was the Corpus of Justinian. He read it all that night and knew it ever afterwards'.

H.W.V. T[emperley]: 'His speech on divorce is the finest thing I ever read on that subject'.

C.J.B. H[urst]: 'Just to think of that after 110 years!'

A.J. B[alfour]: 'Not so marvellous as what we owe to the detention house'.

5 Sept[ember 1921]

The Assembly opened admirably presided over by Wellington Koo[136] with tact, discretion, enthusiasm & a very fair command of English. His speech was quite excellent and admirably phrased. He provided also a good chairman, but unfortunately was not eligible for the Presidency of the Assembly owing for one thing to his lack of knowledge of French.

Karnebeek[137] (Dutch) was proposed by Balfour, the Swiss apparently objecting to Ador[138] and thereby imposing a self-denying ordinance on all Switzers [sic] in order to prevent his nomination. They succeeded in this but did not succeed in preventing the nomination of Motta,[139] though without backing.

---

[136] See entry 1 Sept. 1921.

[137] Jonkheer Herman Adriaan van Karnebeek (1874–1942), Dutch diplomat and politician; clerk in Colonial Office, 1901–11; delegate at 2nd Hague peace conference, 1907; mayor, The Hague, 1911–18; Foreign Minister, 1918–27; President of the League of Nations Assembly, 1921–22; Minister of State, 1927–28; member of the Court of Arbitration, The Hague, 1935–36.

[138] Gustave Ador (1845–1928), Swiss politician; member of National Council, 1889–1917; Federal Counsellor, 1917–19; Foreign Minister, 1917–19; Minister of the Interior, 1918–19; President of the Helvetic Confederation, 1919–20.

[139] See entry 12 Jan. 1921.

The other candidate, who was 'serious', was da Cunha[140] of Brazil, backed by Latin Americans for himself and by France because Holland harbours the Kaiser under conditions they think too favourable which Carnebeek [sic] has endorsed. After a second ballot Karnebeek was elected, 15 alone at last voting ag[ain]st him. C[arnebeek] is a poor speaker and a balancing judge, a man of learning not of dec[isio]n, a weigher not a decider.

A.J. B[alfour] in great form tonight. He spoke of Disraeli[141] and Gladstone, contrasting them in society. 'D[israeli] sometimes sat silent as a mummy for two or three courses and then let out a very brilliant epigram. Good or bad there was always abundance with Mr. Gladstone. I was standing for Hertford when Disraeli was at Hatfield [House], opposed by a Schoolmaster & scraped home with diff[iculty].[142] Disraeli took gr[ea]t interest in my election as at first he thought he w[oul]d be successful & my poll was declared early. It was a real defeat for him for he was too old to hope for a return to power in the future and and not in the present. Yet what I saw of him raised him higher in my opinion of him'. In response to a question: 'Yes he always had complete courage. He was not a hater. He had large shares of contempt for [an] opponent, less of hatred. Even Peel whom he brutally attacked he attacked on a political account, it was brutal but business and in later years he showed no hositility to Peel. Also in 'Endymion' he satirises everybody but genially.[143]

Cairns[144] was a singular man, of great intellectual powers, but I sh[oul]d not say of brilliancy. He was by training a narrow-minded Ulsterman and he retained the marks of it. He had no breadth but great intellectual power. He was D[israeli]'s most useful adjutant in debate for he had the faculty which, as no lawyer is present (Sir C[ecil] Hurst was), lawyers have not, of taking in and answering all the points of an opponent's case.

---

[140] Gastão da Cunha (1863–1927), Brazilian lawyer, diplomat and politician; Member of Congress, 1900–1908; minister at Asunçion, 1907–11; at the Scandinavian Courts, 1911–13; at the Holy See, 1913–14; at Madrid, 1914–15; Under-secretary for Foreign Affairs, 1915–19; ambassador at Rome, 1919; at Paris, 1919–21; delegate at League of Nations Assembly, 1921–22.

[141] Benjamin Disraeli (1804–1881), 1st Earl of Beaconsfield, cr. 1876, politician; MP (Cons.) Maidstone, 1837–41, Shrewsbury, 1841–47, Buckinghamshire, 1847–76; Chancellor of the Exchequer, 1852, 1858–59 and 1866–68; Prime Minister, 1868 and 1874–80.

[142] At the general election of 1880, Balfour won Hatfield with a majority of 164 votes against E.E. Bowen (Lib.).

[143] *Endymion* (London, 1880) was Disraeli's last novel, a romance centred on the career of the fictional Whig politician, Endymion Ferrars.

[144] Hugh McCalmont Cairns (1819–1885), 1st Baron Cairns, cr. 1868, 1st Earl Cairns, cr. 1878, Ulster lawyer-politician; MP (Cons.) Belfast, 1852–66; Solicitor-General, 1858–59; Attorney-General, 1866; Lord Chancellor, 1868, 1874–80.

As for Gladstone I always liked him and so, I believe, did Salisbury[145] but I think he hated Disraeli. Gilbert Murray[146] then intervened – 'On the Midlothian campaign he was frequently interrupted in one speech by a drunkard. Finally he said majestically "I hope my friend over there realizes that were he in my place, and I in his, I should extent a larger share of indulgence to him than he does to me"'. (Pause and exit of 'my friend').

[H.A.L.] Fisher: 'I remember Mr. G[ladstone] at Oxford in his last years[147] on one occasion in reply to this "Do you see any change in Oxford since your day?" "Yes indeed I do, the other day at the Union when I addressed it[,] in all that vast assemblage there was not one young man that I could not have dressed for five pounds"'. (A vision of Norfolk jackets and flannel trousers flits thro[ugh] the mind.)

A.J. B[alfour] said only that what struck him most of Gladstone was his command of the period. 'He used but often abused it. I often remember him getting up to answer a speech of [blank] when he did not well know what to say at first. So for about as long as w[oul]d fill two columns of Hansard he w[oul]d pour forth a stream of sonorous rotund speech, at the end of which his thought was clear and he w[oul]d really begin.[']

8 [September 1921]

I add here a pendant of A.J. B[alfour]'s about Randolph Churchill[148] though it belongs to a later date. He said the most insolent thing he ever heard in the Commons was Randolph – got up as Harcourt sat down and said '"We" as the Right Hon. Gentleman says doubtless reminiscent of his royal lineage'.[149] He

---

[145] Lord Robert Arthur Gascoyne-Talbot-Cecil (1830–1903), 3rd Marquis of Salisbury, succ. 1868, politician; MP (Con.) Stamford, 1853–68; Secretary of State for India, 1866–67 and 1874–78; Foreign Secretary, 1878–80, 1885–86, 1887–92, and 1895–1900; Prime Minister, 1885–86, 1886–92, 1895–1902; Lord Privy Seal, 1900–1902.

[146] George Gilbert Aimé Murray (1866–1957), classicist and activist; Professor of Greek, Glasgow University, 1889–99; Regius Professor of Greek, Oxford, 1908–36; Vice-president of the League of Nations Society, 1916; South African League of Nations delegate, 1921–22; co-founder, Oxford Committee for Famine Relief (Oxfam), 1942.

[147] In 1890.

[148] Lord Randolph Henry Spencer-Churchill (1849–95), politician; MP (Cons.) Woodstock, 1874–85, Paddington South, 1885–95; Secretary of State for India, 1885–86; Chancellor of the Exchequer and Leader of the House of Commons, 1886.

[149] Harcourt was descended from the Plantagenet dynasty.

said King Edward[150] once asked the Duc d'Harcourt[151] in France for permission to Harcourt to adopt his arms. The Duc said 'Certainly, I have no objection but (genially) you know he is no relative of mine'.

(A.J. B[alfour] told me another story of Randolph. He said on coming to Cambridge at the opening of Newnham in 1885 (?)[152] 'I remember their drive past Newnham Terrace, Randolph was in the carriage with him and Rosebery. Both Rosebery and Randolph began to talk to – and at – one another, I sat silent as tertius gaudens – a fine display of wit and epigram, but I really thought Randolph had the best of it, a great thing to say with Rosebery in his prime'.[)]

I asked him one day on the stairs whether he thought Gladstone the greatest parliamentarian he had ever known. 'Yes', he said, 'but that does not mean he was perfect as a parliamentarian. There are so many things to constitute the great parliamentarian, that there has never been a complete one, at least in my time. But taking the Assemblage of qualities, Gladstone had the most complete armoury I have known'. He said of the old Duke of Devonshire,[153] against whom he retained some animus in the political sense, 'I have heard him put many objections in the Cabinet, but suggestions never'.

8 [September 1921]

Talk with Hurst about Article X of the Covenant. I said that I thought L[or]d R[obert] C[ecil] had interpreted the article in a looser rather than a tighter sense. H[urst] said he thought that, if a dec[isio]n of the Council was taken, the League was bound to fight in so far as the members of the Council were concerned. He doubted whether the <small states> were bound who were only rep[resented] in the Ass[embl]y.

He & L[or]d R[obert] C[ecil] & later the latter talked to me today on the same subject. L[or]d R[obert] C[ecil] said he thought Wilson had not a very precise mind, and was not always acquainted with the details of the Cov[enan]t in Comm[it]tee. He struck him at first as a bit of a bully, who tried to get hold

---

[150] (Albert) Edward VII of Saxe-Coburg-Gotha (1841–1910), King of Great Britain and Ireland, 1901–10; Emperor of India, 1901–10.

[151] Presumably Henri Eugène François Marie, 10th duc d'Harcourt (1864–1908).

[152] Founded in 1871, Newnham College in fact opened its doors in 1875.

[153] Spencer Compton Cavendish (1833–1908), Lord Cavendish, 1934–58, Marquess of Hartington, 1858–91, 8th Duke of Devonshire, succ. 1891, politician; MP (Lib.), Lancashire North, 1857–68, Radnor, 1869–80, Lancashire North East, 1880–85, Rossendale, 1885–91 (Lib. U., since 1886); Under-secretary of State for War, 1863–66; Secretary of State for War, 1866 and 1882–85; Postmaster-General, 1868–71; Chief Secretary of Ireland, 1871–74; Secretary of State for India, 1880–82; Lord President of the Council, 1895–1903; President of the Board of Education, 1900–1902; was thrice asked to form a government, and declined each time.

of men separately, but was prepared to collapse when stood up to. Afterwards he changed his view somewhat and liked him very much.

I said that, when once Wilson became convinced that force was necessary to establish the League and the covenanted peace, it seemed to follow that big powers became <more> important than usual but L[or]d R[obert] C[ecil] doubted if Wilson drew that conclusion.

He said that he personally had advocated a League with a Council simply of big Powers, as he thought that w[oul]d do the trick. He recognized since that he had been quite wrong, and there was suffic[ien]t resistance of small powers, even on the Comm[issio]n[,] to show that.

The dist[inctio]n between small & big Powers was really drawn by Smuts and subsequ[entl]y adopted by Wilson.

Re Article X he said that the idea was Wilson's own, though he original definition was much more clumsy. At one stage he (R[obert] C[ecil]) wished to weaken the language, but Wilson said 'if you do that, France will jump up to the ceiling'.

Sir C[ecil] H[urst] remarked that this was borne out by the language of Tardieu,[154] who regarded the guarantee Treaties signed by the U.S.A. & G[reat] B[ritain] re unprovoked aggression of Germany merely as special cases, and slight extensions, of Art[icle] X. He said that personally he favoured the looser interpretation.

He thought Wilson had behaved with extr[aordinar]y folly in America on his return Feb[ruar]y 1919. He hated both Taft[155] and Root[156] and wanted to refuse to accept their suggested amendments simply because they had been suggested by the Senate. At the famous dinner when he met the Senate during his brief stay in America he was asked a number of questions all of which he refused to anwer – probably he was not sure of the details. Later on, I pointed out, when again examined by the Senate [in] July 1919, he had worked up the subject and did better.

At dinner I happened to remark to A.J. B[alfour] that since I had heard of the fact that Wordsworth[157] had had a natural daughter I despaired of the morals

---

[154] See entry 8 May 1919.

[155] William Howard Taft (1857–1930), US lawyer and politician; called to the Ohio bar, 1882; US Solicitor-General, 1890–92; Judge of Court of Appeal, 1892–1900; Governor-General of the Philippines, 1900–1903; Secretary of War, 1904–1908; 27th US President, 1909–13; Chief Justice, 1921–30.

[156] Elihu Root (1845–1937), US lawyer and politician; US Attorney for Southern New York, 1881–85; Secretary of War, 1899–1904; Secretary of State, 1905–1909; Senator (Rep.) for New York, 1909–15; President of the Carnegie Endowment for International Peace, 1910–25; Nobel Peace Prize Laureate, 1912; co-founder of Permanent Court of International Justice, 1922.

[157] William Wordsworth (1770–1850), poet; his illegitimate daughter, Ann Caroline, was the result of an affair with a French lady, Annette Vallon, in 1793; her existence was first revealed

of anyone at any rate in revolutionary times. He hung a story on this, he said he told this to Grey at dinner one day at Asquith's. 'Grey you know is an admirer of Wordsworth – the only book he knows or, some say, has ever read. I asked Edward Grey "do you think this fact makes any difference to his poetry?" After profound thought Grey replied "No! I don't believe it does".'[158] Sir Rennell Rodd[159] capped the story by saying that all the men he knew who had natural daughters were highly respectable members of society.

B[alfour] spoke of Chauncey Depew[160] who, he said, excelled as an afterdinner speaker, & though a most careful preparer of speeches, seemed to be entirely free from the file in uttering his words.

A remark by [H.A.L.] Fisher interested him greatly. Early in Bismarck's career Germans said of him 'This man, after all, what is he? Merely an episode!' A.J. B[alfour] 'How extraordinarily interesting – and exactly the truth'.

Drifting to parliamentary topics, he spoke of Birrell[161] as one of the most masterly of wits in his own line. He gave one complete parliamentary aside. Birrell had been called upon to defend the appointment of one of his stepsons to a government office. He did so – with some difficulty and, as he sank back on the Treasury Bench, was heard to murmur 'I'll never marry a widow again'.

He said that, when he took over 10 Downing Street from Lord Rosebery in 1895,[162] he walked in the garden with him and the only thing trending on matters of political importance that his lordship said was 'Mind you this is No. 10's garden. Don't you let No. 11 walk in it'. I reminded him of Rosebery's words 'There are two moments of happiness in life, the first imaginary and the second real, when a man receives the ministerial seals and when he returns them'. 'True', said A.J. B[alfour].

---

by G.M. Harper, *Life of Wordsworth* (London, 1916), and É. Legouis, *La jeunesse de Wordsworth* (Paris, 2nd edn, 1921) and É. Legouis, *William Wordsworth and Annette Vallon* (London, 1922).

[158] Grey himself had an illegitimate daughter.

[159] See entry 11 June 1917.

[160] Chauncey Depew (1834–1928), US railway entrepreneur and politician; Senator (Rep.) for New York, 1899–1911.

[161] Augustine Birrell (1850–1933), academic lawyer, politician and man-of-letters; called to the bar, 1875; Professor of Law, University College London, 1896–99; MP (Lib.), West Fife, 1889–1900, Bristol North, 1906–18; President of the Board of Education, 1905–1907; Chief Secretary for Ireland, 1907–16; through his second marriage to Eleanor Bertha Mary Locker-Lampson (1854–1915), widow of Lionel Tennyson, he acquired two step-sons, Tony and Frankie.

[162] Balfour took residence at No. 10 as First Lord of the Treasury and Leader of the House of Commons; the Prime Minister, the Marquis of Salisbury, continued to live at his town house, 20 Arlington Street.

9 Sept[ember 1921]

Nansen[163] made a speech, intensely long but showing the fineness and greatness of the man. He said that, if the League went on at its present rate, it would take it 50,000 years to spend as much as the war had cost. He advocated carrying out relief work with the present Russian Gov[ernmen]t, and thereby provoked dissent in certain quarters. I had had a conversation with him two days before, in which he said that the Soviet idea was in full force politically but quite abandoned economically. His main point was that, unless some relief was undertaken or attempted at once, several millions would die during the winter and, for the future, the loss of animals was almost as serious as the loss of men. For that w[oul]d mean the destruction of all materials of agriculture.

B[alfour] told me in private conversation once, just I was leaving, that Lloyd George was 'all morals and no principles'.

17 Sept[ember] 1921 B[ritish] E[mpire] D[elegation]

Highly interesting discussion chiefly on Art[icle] 26 of the Covenant.[164] What was its meaning?

It is badly drafted and, as it stands, appears to mean that all amendments must be unanimous.

Doherty[165] with strong American accent and Canadian logic argued that the case was an absurdity. For, while amendments take effect when ratified by 51 per cent, they are not passed if 1 per cent opposes. That could not really have been meant.

He said that deeply and sincerely as Canada believed in the League, he could not say, for himself, that she c[oul]d continue in it if the power of amendment was so restricted. As all knew Canada had put up a great opposition to Art[icle] X but had finally refrained from pressing their point when they received a letter from the Big Three to the effect that all provisions to [*sic*] the Covenant would be continued 'largely and liberally'. L[or]d Robert Cecil argued with great

---

[163] Fridtjof Nansen (1861–1930), Norwegian polar explorer, diplomat, humanitarian campaigner; minister at London, 1906–1907; League of Nations High Commissioner for Refugees, 1921–26; Nobel Peace Prize Laureate, 1922.

[164] Article XXVI of the Covenant of the League of Nations stipulated that amendments to the covenant required ratification by its Council members and a majority of the members of the League Assembly.

[165] Charles Joseph Doherty (1855–1931), Canadian jurist and politician; judge on Quebec Superior Court, 1891–1906; Member of the Canadian House of Commons (Cons) St. Ann Riding, Quebec, 1908–21; Minister of Justice and Attorney-General, 1911–21; delegate to the Paris Peace Conference, 1919; delegate to the League of Nations, 1920–22.

dialectical skill as to the meaning and said that he was mainly responsible for the blunder. They had meant to carry amendments by majority but had failed to insert the provision. [H.A.L.] Fisher said that France was the difficulty. Last year she had wanted to amend everything, this year nothing. She was without the Franco-American Alliance – the Guarantee Treaty – and attempts were being made to whittle down Art[icle] X.

He advocated the bold course of getting the Assembly to pass a motion in favour of amendments being made by majority. There was only one danger that one state w[oul]d object. But we must gamble on that.

Finally A.J. B[alfour] backed by Hurst proposed a solution. Each power could sign a protocol or convention, after a vote or resolution of the Assembly. This could then be ratified by the States concerned. The States refusing to ratify would cease to be members.

Art[icle] XVIII. Registration of Treaties. Hurst said the League had had 90 registered but found 120 more ought to be while Italy had not registered a single one. Also the term 'international engagement' was too wide to expect anyone to adhere to it. It might mean an agreement between State A and State B re the lease of a house.

A.J. B[alfour] finally dismissed us with 'If we don't get past this, we shall be broke. This will be the end of the League'. Another time he said – 'corruption & money – that is what the League will break down over'.

18 Sept[ember 1921]

First thing on getting up in the morning I read the Covenant and the official Commentary (under date of June 1919) and find an explanation of Art[icle] XXVI to the effect that amendments are made easy (!) by this method. I show it to A.J. B[alfour] who remarks 'Either the commentator is very insolent or the original article has been altered'. At this point enter L[or]d R[obert] Cecil.

H.W.V. T[emperley]: 'I suppose you're responsible for this'.
L[or]d R[obert] C[ecil]: 'It was done under my authority'.
H.W.V. T[emperley]: 'Then your commentator is better than your draftsman'.
L[or]d R[obert] C[ecil]: 'Well Jim Butler[166] was the commentator and Hurst the draftsman, so it's Hurst's fault'.
H.W.V. T[emperley]: 'I suppose you'll find he'll say it was altered at the last moment'.
L[or]d R[obert] C[ecil]: 'It certainly was'.

---

[166] See entry 22 Mar. 1917.

Later in the day I saw Jim Butler. He said the motion was one made by Venizelos, and ratification was not intended. Amendments were to take place on a bare majority <(according to Wilson's speech)>, while the State refusing to accept them could get out.

He went on to say that the minutes of the Commission on the League of Nations had been suppressed at Wilson's earnest desire. I asked why. He said for two reasons: (i) Wilson said somewhere on the Commission that in case of a conflict between Covenant and Monroe Doctrine, the former would prevail as later in time and more comprehensive in scope; (ii) that the moral compulsion to send troops to Europe etc. is quite clearly indicated in the discussion and that Wilson's denial of this in the heat of the Presidential Election is not in accordance with the facts.

That is the second time Wilson has made an official denial of a previous utterance which we know him to have made – Oh, politics!

19 [September] 1921

9.15 or rather 9.35 a.m. meeting in Fisher's room. Held forth on Albania.

Saw A.J. B[alfour] at 11 a.m. 2 new important Albanian telegrams, one from Rome in which Buchanan[167] is thoroughly frightened: the Italians threaten to leave the League if the Albanian matter comes before the Assembly, and bringing forward the argument that the isle of Sasseno[168] [sic] belongs to them by virtue of a secret agreement with Albania in Tirana, 2nd Aug[ust] 1920.[169] Incidentally the Albanian gov[ernmen]t had not been recognized. The agreement has never been published and, as such, it cannot be binding on Italy according to Article 18 of the Covenant while it c[oul]d not in any case bind either England or France – anything to save face. The F[oreign] O[ffice] telegram offers a formula – tho[ugh] a much worse one – than that we suggested from here.

A.J. B[alfour] read thro[ugh] these telegrams – and, while doing so, L[or]d R[obert] C[ecil] appeared: 'Hallo, Bob, I'm just reading Italian telegrams. These are the most impossible people. They really are. Thank heaven there are not so many like this'.

L[or]d R[obert] C[ecil]: 'Well, [from] what happened about the Lithuanians today, I understand they are worse'.

---

[167] See entry 9 Dec. 1916.
[168] See entry 22 Sept. 1920.
[169] The treaty concluded the so-called War of 1920 between the Italian troops occupying Vlorë (It. Valona) and its hinterland and irregular Albanian forces; in it, Italy renounced its claim on the Vlorë protectorate, occupied since 1917, but retained the Island of Saseno (Alb. Sazan). It was independent Albania's first treaty with a foreign power.

A.J.B[alfour]: 'Yes, both they and the Poles are just like the Irish. I think Slavs and Irish must be of the same blood. Well, the Lithuanian and the Pole both got up – and made speeches about an hour each and Hymans[170] assures me that they are exactly the same speeches as were made about six times before. Nothing – absolutely nothing – new. The Lithuanian's speech spoke all the time of Zeliogowski[171] – the Pole answered and never mentioned a word of him. Yet, I understand Zeligowski made a wholly unauthorized raid and is still actually in occupation'. <(N.B. he made a magnificent speech on the subject the next day).>

20 [September 1921]

At the political commission here on Lithuania and she was well avenged on Poland. The question of admission came up, and Askenazy,[172] the Polish Jew professor, moved the adjournment to save the vote. A lively discussion began. Motta, with violent gestures and earnest voice, pleaded the cause of Lithuania to Askenazy – 'It is a little state, a young state. Can you refuse? You, a nation, now raised from the dead, noble and chivalrous[,] a knight among nations (Askenazy looked a knight indeed) you cannot refuse'.

[H.A.L.] Fisher, serene, cold and clear, but a little academic, supported the same cause, saying with icy directness 'if the frontier of Lithuania was uncertain, so too was that of Poland' and that in the dispute he c[oul]d not think Poland in the right.

Branting[173] and Nansen with ponderous goodwill lent the suffrages of Scandinavia. Then a Columbian, Restrepo,[174] a vast man with a deep humorous growl in his voice, intervened. He had supported Lithuania's admission along with Latvia & Esthonia last year. He had with him Lord Robert Cecil, the Achilles of the fight, but against him the wisdom and power of the British

---

[170] Paul Louis Adrien Henri Hymans (1865–1941), Belgian lawyer and politician; Foreign Minister, 1918–20 and 1927–35; Minister of Justice, 1926–27; Minister without Portfolio, 1935–36; President of the League of Nations Assembly, 1920–21 and 1932–33.

[171] General Lucjan Żeligowski (1865–1947), Polish military commander; led 'Żeligowski's Mutiny' in October 1920, i.e. the seizure of Vilnius, followed by the proclamation of the Republic of Central Lithuania (with Zelikowski as *de facto* military dictator) and its subsequent annexation to Poland; Minister for Military Affairs, 1925–26; Member of the *Sejm*, 1935–39; member of Polish government in exile, 1939–47.

[172] Szymon Askenazy (1866–1935), Polish historian, diplomat and politician; Polish representative at the League of Nations, 1920–23; resigned because of an anti-Semitic campaign against him.

[173] See entry 18 July 1917.

[174] Carlos Eugenio Restrepo (1867–1937), Colombian lawyer and politician; President of Colombia, 1910–14; minister-plenipotentiary at the Holy See, 1930–37.

Empire embodied in Mr. Fisher. Now that he and Achilles had that wisdom and power with him 'I am assured of victory. I do not know what religion Lithuania has – the Greek "Ah" (someone says the Catholic, also a good religion) but that should not influence the question. I vote on general principles. Think of Russia as it now is – so anarchic and so dangerous. Do we not need a strong, a united front of all nations, especially small ones against her. I hope the professor, who knows history well, <u>will not forget this and will not press</u> his adjournment. And thus I leave the professor to his meditations'. The Professor with an angry look in his cold brown eye, said he saw everyone was against him but he must carry out his government's instructions and it was not hatred of Lithuania but love of the quarter of a million Poles in Lithuania, which made him defend them.

The Belgian and French representatives testified that Lithuania had promised to fulfil the Minorities' necessities and then came a strange, wild and impressive speech. Spalaiković, with a wild poetic look in his eye declared 'I shall abstain from voting, not because I have no sympathy with Lithuania but because Serbia, herself a small state, at the moment of peril in 1914, was about to be crushed by Central Europe, and who was it [who] drew the sword in her defence? That great Slav nation of Russia.['] Never could he do ought or anything to make Serbia fail in gratitude to her, though she was in shame and anarchy. Therefore, though he sympathised much with Lithuania, he could not vote. Imperiali,[175] added Italy's vote in words of the lowest bathos but China (Tsai Fou) ended appropriately. She was the largest of nations and was now prepared to vote for one of the smallest, but there should be no great or small nations in the League.

Askenazy then rose and said he w[oul]d not press the adjournment if a civil commission were sent to Kovno[176] to protect the Polish minorities. Fisher pointed out that in the League, the minorities were more likely and able to be protected than out of it. Then came the voting. Askenazy found one supporter only in Rumania, and Lithuania entered into history.

22 [September 1921]

[H.A.L.] Fisher at dinner told anecdotes of L[loyd] G[eorge]. <As an instance of his readiness he gave this. During the railway strike he came and saw Henderson and a number of railwaymen at Downing Street gathered in the front-hall: 'Hullo, Henderson, why are you on the doormat? Take your friends upstairs to the drawing room'. Roars of laughter, for all remembered Henderson's complaint

---

[175] See entry 26 Apr. 1919.
[176] Now Kaunas (Lithuania).

that he had been left an hour outside the Cabinet room on the door-mat, at the time he left the Cabinet.>[177]

He said that the first weekend at Chequers consisted of Hamar Greenwood,[178] Riddell,[179] Lee of Fareham,[180] Milner, Horne,[181] Reading.[182]

They began by talking of their early careers. Ll[oyd] G[eorge]'s education finished at 14. Hamar's at 17, Riddell was a solicitor's clerk, Horne the son of a Dissenting Minister, Milner a doctor's son at Stuttgart[183] who subsequently was at the City of London School, Lee's origins I have forgotten but it was not very exalted and Reading started life as a cabin boy.[184] Certainly the whole was a striking combination.

Said Ll[oyd] G[eorge] was very simple in some ways. One reason of his long hair was, he said, that he always had it cut when a boy with the garden scissors and so always put it off as long as he could. He went nutting like a boy with a party of girls one day, and climbed trees like a squirrel. Said his courage was superb when he faced the Cabinet after the defeat of March 1918. Just after that he sent for F[isher] just before a Welsh educational deputation came to see him and walked with him for five minutes in the garden. Ll[oyd] G[eorge] said he had not wanted to see the deputation, but hardly knew how to drive it away. F[isher] said they came about grants to secondary & higher educ[atio]n, each County Council putting on a 1d rate for it and getting the Exchequer to put down pound for pound for it. The Chancellor of the Exchequer had already consented. The only point was that the money ought to be freely applied where

---

[177] See entry 9 Oct. 1917.

[178] Sir Hamar Greenwood, Bt (1870–1948), Baron Greenwood, 1929, 1st Viscount Greenwood, 1937, Canadian-born lawyer and politician; MP (Liberal) York, 1906–10, Sunderland, 1910–22, (Cons.) Walthamstow East, 1924–29; Parliamentary Under-secretary for Home Affairs, 1919; Additional Under-secretary for Foreign Affairs, 1919–20; Chief Secretary for Ireland, 1920–22.

[179] Sir George Allardice Riddell (1865–1934), Bt, 1909, 1st Baron Riddell of Walton Heath, cr. 1920, solicitor, newspaper proprietor, and Lloyd George confidant; represented British newspaper proprietors at Paris and later peace conferences.

[180] Arthur Hamilton Lee (1868–1947), Baron Lee of Fareham, cr. 1918, 1st Viscount Lee of Fareham, cr. 1922, officer and politician; MP (Cons.) Fareham, 1900–18; Civil Lord of the Admiralty, 1903–1905; Minister of Agriculture, 1919–21; First Lord of the Admiralty, 1921–22; donated Chequers estate to the nation in 1917.

[181] Sir Robert Stevenson Horne (1871–1940), 1st Viscount Horne of Slamannan, cr. 1937; Scottish lawyer, businessman and politician; Director of Railways on Western Front, 1915–17; Assistant Inspector-General of Transportation at Admiralty, 1917–18; Director of Materials, 1918; MP (Cons.), Glasgow Hillhead, 1918–37; Minister of Labour, 1919–20; President of the Board of Trade, 1920–21; Chancellor of the Exchequer, 1921–22.

[182] See entry 15 Nov. 1917.

[183] Milner was in fact born in the Hessian town of Giessen and grew up in Tübingen.

[184] Reading was a ship's boy, in effect a deckhand, on the sailing ship *Blair Athole*, 1876–77.

necessary, and that the two richest coiunties, Monmouth and Glamorgan, should not spend their money within their borders. The deputation was introduced. Ll[oyd] G[eorge] made some inquiries, and then said suddenly 'Are there any conditions attached?' 'Oh yes'. Ll[oyd] G[eorge] (quickly) 'What are they? Let me see them'. They were shown and disclosed that Monmouth and Glamorgan attached stipulations to their grants as indicated. Ll[oyd] G[eorge]'s veins suddenly swelled on his forehead and he burst out 'Gentlemen, we are in a war. When the Great Nations are fighting for the small, when the young man is fighting for the old, and the rich man for the poor man, I know Cardiff and Swansea, and every accent from every part of Wales is known to me, and, as I walk those streets, I hear the accent of the mountaineer from the North as well as every other accent. Now what do you say? That the men whose labour, drawn from every county in Wales to enter those great cities, that that man in unable to enjoy the benefits of education, unless he is born in those two counties which his labour enriches. Gentlemen, I am ashamed of you!'

The scene was tremendous like one, I suppose, when Napoleon met his financiers and onlookers thought that 'thunder fell from the sky'.

Neither financiers nor educators gave further trouble.

He said Ll[oyd] G[eorge] came to the Cab[ine]t one Monday, looked so wretched and washed out that he asked him what was the matter. He told him it was 3 Irish criminals whom T.P. O'Connor[185] had been trying to save who were executed that morning and he had spent all Sunday telephoning Dublin, inquiring into the circumstances. Finally he had decided that he c[oul]d not interfere and the men were to die, but the matter had worried him more than any great decision in the war. 'He is', added F[isher], 'a very humane man'.

I thought of another anecdote F[isher] is fond of telling – an authentic story in Lewes' Robespierre[186] – from a man, who had had an adventure with the great man. A friend of his was condemned to die at 8.30 a.m. the next day, and so he sought Robespierre everywhere, and finally found him at an evening party at 11 p.m. Robespierre, with his curious kind of bourgeois prig politeness, listened to his case with attention, admitted the urgency of the case, and the apparent circumstances justifying reprieve. But, he said, I have to stay here till 3. If I wake up in time I shall do my best to save him. Robespierre did not awake and the condemned man died at the proper time. I added, 'I understand now Acton's story. Sieyes when dying was delirious and told his friends "If Robespierre calls say I am not at home"'.

---

[185] Thomas Power O'Connor (1848–1929), Irish journalist and politician; MP (Irish Nat.) Galway Borough, 1880–85, Liverpool Scotland Div, 1885–1929.
[186] George Henry Lewes (1817–78), philosopher and literary critic; his *Robespierre* (1849) sought to rehabilitate the revolutionary leader.

23 [September 1921]

Listened to a great dialectic display by A.J. B[alfour] on the subject of Article 26 of the Covenant. His case was specially difficult (v[ide] 17–18 Sept[embe]r) but he masterd it very well. His argument was – Is the Covenant as it stands with, in Art[icle] 26, at any rate, some dubious drafting [?]. Yet this was to be immortal, permanent & unchangeable. For the rule that unanimity was necessary meant that one state could always stop everything. This rule was unknown in any legislative Assembly in any part of the world. Hedge about amendment with all precautions such as a ¾ majority etc. but whatever you do, do not deny to it the growth that all living organisms must have, if they are to continue to exist. My point is very simple. If everyone denies it, all is finished. All our labours on the amendments committee, all hope of expansion and elasticity. The French, who had previously opposed, promptly collapsed.

24 [September 1921]

In the morning there was a superb oration by Hymans endeavouring to reconcile Poles and Lithuanians.

Apponyi.[187]

Aix les Bains

Was ordered to go to Aix to see Baldwin[188] in order to obtain his approval of a joint cabinet letter to De Valera[189] after Fisher & A.J. B[alfour] had approved. I passed over fine country via Annécy, a fine town with a chateau, finally down to Aix. There I saw Baldwin drinking iced coffee in a café with his wife and son. I descended, got his aid, despatched a telegram with him, remounted the car and returned just in time for dinner. Text of letter as amusement subjoined. Curiously enough on the way to Annecy I passed three lakes, Geneva, Annecy & Bouget [sic],[190] but for one reason or another saw more.

---

[187] See entry 17 Nov. 1917.

[188] Stanley Baldwin (1867–1947), 1st Earl Baldwin of Bewdley, cr. 1937, politician; MP (Cons.) Worcestershire West, 1908–37; Financial Secretary to the Treasury, 1917–21; President of the Board of Trade, 1921–22; Chancellor of the Exchequer, 1922–23; Prime Minister, 1923–24, 1924–29 and 1935–37; Lord President of the Council, 1931–35; Lord Privy Seal, 1932–33.

[189] Éamon de Valera (1882–1975), Irish politician; President of the *Dáil*, 1919–21; President of the Irish Republic, 1921–22, 1959–73; President of the Executive Council, 1932–37; *Taoiseach*, 1937–48, 1951–54, 1957–59.

[190] *Recte* Lac du Bourges.

25 [September 1921]

Charming drive to Thonton[191] via Taning[e]s – a wonderful panorama of Haute Savoie, much more beautiful than the road to Annécy.

> Sept[ember] 23
> Draft reply begins:–
> 'I am glad that you agree that this correspondence cannot effect the end we have in mind and should be brought to a close.
> I have made it quite clear that H[is] M[ajesty's] Government cannot recognize formally or informally, directly or by implication, an Irish Republic and I note with satisfaction that you do not claim that we should. I therefore invite you to send your delegates to London on October 4th as spokesmen of those whom you represent for the purpose of a conference to ascertain "how the association of Ireland with the community of nations known as the Empire can best be reconciled with the Irish national aspirations"'. (Ends)
>
> CURZON

Published on the 1st.

26 [September 1921]

A.J. B[alfour] remained in bed yesterday but was at dinner today alright. He talked of parliamentary things. On a previous occasion he had spoken of set orators, whom he evidently did not care for much. Bright[192] he had, he thought, never heard at his best – his square stout figure and leonine head were remarkable, as also his phrasing and his command of pure English but he seemed to him not wholly satisfactory. Sexton,[193] of the Irish set orators, was good, but was intolerably long, though finished and almost perfect in phrasing. He thought what he did not like about the set orator was the perfect finish, and careful art.

'A parliamentary style of oratory is very difficult to understand. It must be unpretentious and simple, yet full of meat. It was hard to say what constituted success, but a man must be able to speak on all subjects. On the whole I think Gladstone was the greatest parliamentarian I have met. It takes so many things

---

[191] Presumably Thorens.
[192] John 'Orator' Bright (1811–89), Radical politician; MP (Lib.) Durham, 1843–47, Manchester, 1847–59, Birmingham, 1859–85, Birmingham Central, 1885–89; President of the Board of Trade, 1868–71; Chancellor of the Duchy of Lancaster, 1873–74, 1880–82.
[193] Thomas Sexton (1848–1932), Irish journalist and politician; MP (Irish Nat.), County Sligo, 1880–85, Sligo South, 1885–86, Belfast West, 1886–92, North Kerry, 1892–96; Lord Mayor of Belfast, 1888–89.

to constitute the perfect parliamentarian that no man can have them all, but Gladstone probably had most of them. His sentence was immense in length yet always ended by being properly balanced and grammatically exact. Both what he said and wrote has since become unreadable, but that is, so far as speaking goes, almost a condition of parliamentary success. Look at the speeches of Fox[194] and Pitt the Younger. But what made these speeches was the gestures and appearance of the man, his wonderful eye, his manner, his gestures, some extraordinary as when, <in> reflection, he put his hand behind his head and appeared to scratch it – but all the gestures whatsoever were natural'.

Disraeli he thought was inferior to Gladstone qua parliamentarian – his speeches read better for they were literary, but were hardly so effective in debate.

Palmerston, he had heard, was extraordinarily effective in the House – he c[oul]d never understand why. He was not naturally a speaker and certainly not an orator. But he was always lively and often amusing with an immense fund of practical experience and official knowledge.

He spoke of Randolph, and Winston's biography.[195] He gave a sketch of Randolph's life and said a biography was not really difficult for he was only about 10 months of his life in office. That was not enough to try a man. If you are in very high positions, you can have no conception of the weariness of it and the labour. The difficulties of framing a policy for the future that will go down with the Cabinet, of defending the past and carrying on with the present. Randolph had only a very little time of all that.

H.W.V. T[emperley]: 'I suppose however Randolph stood up to Gladstone'.

A.J. B[alfour]: 'Yes, that is true – at that time Northcote[196] was leader, a man, intelligent, judicious, and prudent, safe. Disraeli chose him because he thought he c[oul]d never by any chance be a rival. It was true but unfortunate as a choice. He might have had Cranbrook,[197] who had fire, but he preferred to be an Earl.

---

[194] See entry 19 June 1916.

[195] W.L. Churchill, *Lord Randolph Churchill* (2 vols, London, 1906).

[196] Sir Stafford Henry Northcote (1818–87), 1st Earl of Iddesleigh, cr. 1885, civil servant and politician; clerk at Board of Trade, 1843–55; co-author of Northcote-Trevelyan Report on civil service reform, 1854; MP (Con.) Dudley, 1855–57, Stamford, 1858–66, Devonshire North, 1866–85; President of the Board of Trade, 1866–67; Chancellor of the Exchequer, 1874–80; Foreign Secretary, 1886–87.

[197] Gathorne Gathorne-Hardy (1814–1906), Viscount Cranbrook, cr. 1878, 1st Earl of Cranbrook, cr. 1892, politician; MP (Con.) Leominster, 1856–65, Oxford University, 1865–78; Under-secretary for Home Affairs, 1858–59; President of the Poor Law Board, 1866–67; Home Secretary, 1867–68; Secretary of State for War, 1874–78 and 1886; for India, 1878–80; Lord President of the Council, 1885–86 and 1886–92; Chancellor of the Duchy of Lancaster, 1886.

1921–1939 549

What was quite wrongly called the "fourth party"[198] was not really a party at all, but only an attempt on the part of some younger Members to supply the defects in opposition by attacking the Government, which the front opposition bench had failed to do.

The story of "I forgot Goschen"[199] was true. Randolph resigned and tried to call Salisbury's[200] bluff [in December 1886]. Salisbury was not the man to try that on. It might be true that Randolph "forgot Goschen". I hardly think that would have made any difference. If Salisbury had only been able to get a bi-armistice as a substitute, from what I knew of him, he would not have given way. Randolph began definitely to fail in health in 1888, so Winston can hardly have known him in reality at all in the prime of his powers.

Winston interests me enormously. He has unlimited ambitions but I don't know where he'll get to. His conversation is excellent – a rush of vivid images – and he is speaking better in the House of Commons. He was extremely hurt that he was absent in Palestine when Bonar Law took it into his head that he was overworked and resigned.[201] Winston was very pained – he wanted to be Chancellor of the Exchequer. That is a point against him. Who can gain now by being Chancellor of the Exchequer? That showed his weak side – he wanted the place not because of its real possibilities but because he wishes to be the second man in the government.

I say that I made him an artist because when he resigned from the Admiralty, I took his place and he had nothing to do – so he sought that artist with a pretty wife. Ah, yes, who was that? Lavery[202] who put paints before him, and gave him a few lessons and he started to paint. He does it in a modern style, but I confess very well.

Randolph was, I think, a better talker even than Winston. I remember driving once in a carriage with Randolph & Rosebery'.[203]

---

[198] A loose grouping of Conservative backbenchers, consisting of Lord Randolph Churchill, A.J. Balfour, Sir Henry Drummond-Wolff and Sir John Gorst.

[199] George Joachiam Goschen (1831–1907), 1st Viscount Goschen of Seacox Heath, cr. 1900, financier and politician; partner in Frühling & Goschen, 1853; director, Bank of England, 1856–63; MP (Lib.), City of London, 1863–80, Ripon, 1880–85, (Lib. U.) Edinburgh East, 1885–86, St. George's, Hanover Square, 1887–1900 (since 1893, Con.); Paymaster-General, 1865–66; Chancellor of the Duchy of Lancaster, 1866; First Lord of the Admiralty, 1871–74 and 1895–1900; Chancellor of the Exchequer, 1887–92.

[200] See entry 5 Sept. 1921.

[201] In Jan. 1919.

[202] Sir John Lavery (1856–1941), Belfast-born portrait-painter; official war-artist, 1914–18; close friend of the Asquith family; he married, in 1909, his second wife Hazel Martyn (1886–1935).

[203] See entry 1 Sept. 1921.

27 Sept[embe]r [1921]

He [Balfour] spoke of Devonshire,[204] a man of extraordinary character and slowness in some respects. 'There was, in 1874, when I was first in Parliament, a great struggle between him and W.E. Forster[205] for the Leadership.[206] But Forster was defeated – his Education Bill had alienated the extreme non-conformists. Forster was a great rough-bearded creature, not a good, still less a great speaker, but always impressive.[']

H.W.V. T[emperley]: 'How could Hartington[207] lead the House. I thought a man must be ready?'

A.J. B[alfour]: 'Yes, that is true, but he had Harcourt at his elbow, and always got up the facts beforehand.[']

H.W.V. T[emperley]: 'I suppose character leads the House as with Castlereagh[208] & Althorp'.[209]

A.J. B[alfour]: 'Yes, in that respect the House has not changed much, I believe. Anyway, Hartington led it well enough in opposition. He spoke slowly, the great pendulous lower lip hanging down – always uttering commonplaces or platitudes but with great energy of conviction, as if they had [been] (and some of them no doubt [were]) as a new revelation of truth to him. In the Cabinet I never heard him make a suggestion and that is what Cabinets are for to make suggestions. He made many objections – that was sometimes good. His questions were to the point and he was not ashamed, when occasion arose, to confess complete ignorance. It was justified sometimes. When I was Prime Minister and the fiscal controversy came on he confessed that, in all such matters, he had surrendered himself body and soul to Gladstone. It implied a colossal effort to him at his age to reconsider the matter. As P[rime] M[inister] I drew up a statement, which I subsequently circulated as a pamphlet (of course 'Economic Notes on Insular Free Trade'[210][)] which may have been right or wrong but which, I thought, was at least a clear indication of the points I wished to urge. The Duke confessed to me that he had read it without understanding it at all. Very strange, for in some

---

[204] See entry 8 Sept. 1921.

[205] William Edward Forster (1818–86), industrialist and politician; MP (Lib.) Bradford, 1861–85; Under-secretary of State for the Colonies, 1865–66; Vice-president of the Committee on Education, 1868–74; Chief Secretary for Ireland, 1880–82.

[206] Of the Liberal Party after Gladstone's first retirement.

[207] From 1858, until he succeeded to the dukedom in 1891, Devonshire was known by the courtesy title of Marquess of Hartington ('Harty-Tarty').

[208] See entry 1 Sept. 1921.

[209] John Charles Spencer (1782–1845), Viscount Althorp, 1783, 3rd Earl Spencer, succ. 1834, politician; MP (Whig) Northamptonshire, 1806–32, Northamptonshire South, 1832–34; Chancellor of the Exchequer, 1830–34; Leader of the House of Commons, 1830–34.

[210] A.J. Balfour, *Economic Notes on Insular Free Trade* (London, 1903).

ways it was a powerful brain'. I quote the story that Hartington yawned in the middle of his first speech and that an old parliamentary hand said 'this young man will go far'. A.J. B[alfour]: 'Well, I don't know if that is true but it ought to be, both of the Duke and the old parliamentary hand'.

(I remember a furious correspondence between A.J.B[alfour] & the Duke on his resignation in 1903, which A.J.B[alfour] had forgotten or touched on very gently.)

He then spoke of the old Parliament at the end of the XVIIIth century – a collection of distinguished advocates, one on each side and between them a common jury of rather stupid, commonplace and independent men. Conditions are no longer like this.

H.A.L. F[isher]: 'No, when I got into the House it was thought by me that I could do what I liked qua Minister with a bill. Quite the contrary[,] one is subject to attack both in public and private by large and small bodies of members, sometimes only 10, sometimes 1, all of whom leave their marks on the bill'.

A.J. B[alfour]: 'Yes, I remember when I had a bill, the Health Consolid[atio]n Bill,[211] which was opposed by a certain troublesome Scotchman, and I got through by dropping 300 of the clauses out of 420.[']

H.W.V. T[emperley]: 'Aren't you paying the price of having abolished private legislations in the last 10 or 15 years? <Before the cranks occupied themselves with their own bills[;] now they occupy themselves with yours.>'

A.J. B[alfour]: 'Yes I suppose so but it was growing long before that I fancy. I think there was practically none in my time[,] certainly none like the bills of Shaftesbury[212] and Romilly[213]'.

H.A.L. F[isher]: 'I think the Parl[iamentar]y Counsels' Office was established in 1870[214] – that is significant'.

A.J. B[alfour]: 'Yes that was, I think, the beginning'.

---

[211] Public Health Bill, 1905, withdrawn in May 1905, see *Hansard* (4) cxlvi (24 May 1905), col. 1347.

[212] Anthony Ashley Cooper (1801–85), 7th Earl of Shaftesbury, 1851, politician and philanthropist; MP (Cons.), Woodstock, 1826–30, Dorchester, 1830–31, Dorset, 1831–46, Bath, 1846–51.

[213] Sir John Romilly (1802–74), 1st Baron Romilly, cr. 1866, politician and judge; MP (Lib.), Bridport, 1832–35, 1846–47, Devonport (1847–52); Solicior-General, 1848–50; Attorney-General, 1850–51; Master of the Rolls, 1851–73.

[214] The Office of Parliamentary Counsel, responsible for drafting all government legislation to be introduced to Parliament, was, in fact, established in 1869.

27 [September 1921]

I have set down my impressions of the Apponyi[215] lunch.

Apponyi began on the frontiers, especially Arad Szatmar.[216] A.J. B[alfour] who had been carefully coached beforehand tried ecc. [?] shut up.

28 [September 1921]

Suddenly summoned to Paris re Albania. Long interview with A.J. B[alfour]. He thought I had to go and that the Italians might yield over the frontiers. I doubted it but thought I had no option except to go, with which he agreed. He then went off into general conversation, highly flattering to myself – he seemed to think I was destined to high office in the State etc. I wonder.[217]

29 [September 1921]

Arrived at Paris after great wakefulness in train. No sort of arrangements made.

3rd March 1922

Saw Balfour. He was greatly impressed with the integrity and ability of Hughes.[218]

He [Balfour] is to receive the garter tomorrow. He told me he considered the political situation very uncertain.

---

[215] See entry 24 Sept. 1921.

[216] Arad and Szatmár counties in southern central and northwestern Transylvania, now western Romania (Arad) and northwestern Romania and northeastern Hungary (Szatmár).

[217] Thus ended Temperley's official career, though he retained hope of some future government work: 'If at any time I get another chance of attending the [League of Nations] Assembly in any capacity I shall take it. There seemed to me more play of international forces there, and consequences more of the current of general life than I have ever seen anywhere else. For the historian it was most instructive', Temperley to Balfour, 28 Oct. 1921, Temperley MSS.

[218] Charles Evans Hughes, Sr. (1862–1948), US lawyer-politician; Governor (Rep.) of New York, 1907–10; Associate Justice of the US Supreme Court, 1910–16; Republican presidential candidate, 1916; Secretary of State, 1921–25; judge of Court of International Justice, 1928–30; Chief Justice, 1930–41.

Ap[ril] 10, <1923>

Brussels. Received by the King.[219] H[arold] 'Do you remember me?['] recalling certain details when he was Prince Albert. 'Oh yes!' H[arold] 'I saw you at the <u>Joyeuse Entrée</u> and taking the coronation oath.['] A[lbert] 'Ah that was a long time ago. Did you fight in the war?' H[arold] 'Yes but for another country, like yours, invaded, martyred, ultimately glorious and victorious'. A[lbert] 'Ah, you mean Serbia'. H[arold] 'Yes'. A[lbert] 'Have you written upon it?' H[arold] 'Oh yes, a history of Serbia'. A[lbert] 'You must send it me'.

Ap[ril] 12, 1922 [recte 1923]

Lunch with Hymans.

We got onto Page.[220] H[ymans] thought that he was a little too pro-Entente, though certainly a great force for us. From the point of his country he seemed to agree with Wilson's dictum 'Page is an Englishman'.

This was hotly contested by Sir C[harles] Walston[221] & Lady Walston[222] from knowledge of America.

We spoke of Keynes.[223] He said he had been 'un peu furios [sic]'. I said 'il est toujours'. Afterwards he said he had several very powerful interviews with Keynes, not personally but over his country. Keynes maintained the Belgium had actually been improved by the German occupation and refuted facts and figures, always with passion, sometimes with inexactness.

Doubtless the Belgian demands had been too high – Keynes put them too low and added des mots blessants.

He did not know why Keynes finally resigned. I said I thought it was because his plans for cancelling debts finally failed.

He thought the two evils of the Conference were the League and Reparations. H[arold] 'Why you were president of an evil then!'

Hy[mans] 'That demands explanation. Well I will tell you. If we had had preliminaries first with a few nations, then we c[oul]d have got the League later.

---

[219] Albert I (Léopold Clément Marie Meinrad) of Saxe-Coburg-Gotha (1875–1934), King of the Belgians, 1909–34.

[220] Walter Hines Page (1855–1918), US journalist and diplomat; editor *The Forum*, 1890–95, *Atlantic Monthly*, 1896–99; vice-president Doubleday, Page and Co., 1900–13; US ambassador at London, 1913–18.

[221] Sir Charles Walston (née Waldstein, Anglicized in 1918) (1856–1927), American-born archaeologist; director Fitzwilliam Museum, 1883–89; director, American School of Classical Studies, Athens, 1889–93; Slade Professor of Fine Art, University of Cambridge, 1895–1901.

[222] Florence Seligman (née Einstein) (d. 1955), married to Sir C. Walston in 1909.

[223] See entry 3 Aug. 1921.

But when, because of Presid[en]t Wilson, we got 27 nations to begin with, prelim[inar]ies were hopeless.[']

Webster 'But you c[oul]d not then have got the League.[']

Hy[mans] 'I daresay. Mine is a jeu d'ésprit intellectuel.[']

At this juncture the band was heard, and we saw troops marching. 'Ah' said Hy[mans] 'it is troops coming back from the Ruhr (smiling). They march as if it was for a victory'.

Of the armistice he said, that at first everyone was very moderate in the prel[iminar]y discussions in order to induce Germany to sign. As soon as Ll[oyd] G[eorge] heard of the Austrian offer, he raised the terms. House was hard pressed by Ll[oyd] G[eorge] supported by Clemenceau over the point on 'Freedom of the Seas'. Finally he gave way and thought he c[oul]d arrange it with the President.

He found House always gentle, moderate, sympathetic, delightful. To his personal sympathy and support he attributed the fact that Belgium got priority of reparations. I said that Baker[224] says that Wilson thought House had sold the pass while he was away in America. Hy[mans] thought this might be true.

About the personalities, he said, Balfour had told him in each of the Big Three 'Wilson, Clemenceau and Ll[oyd] G[eorge] there was a spark of genius'.

Hy[mans] 'In the presence of Clemenceau and Ll[oyd] G[eorge] I felt conscious of personal magnetism, great talents, great abilities, but never absolute and overwheleming power. Once or twice in the presence of Wilson I felt powerless. Wilson was a man'.

About the reasons of the Commission of the League, he did not remember that Wilson's speech on the Monroe doctrine had made the great impression attributed to it. The speech that impressed him most was one in wh[ich] he was personally interested, in the plea that Belgium should be the capital of the League. Wilson spoke for a few minutes and magnificently of the atmosphere of tranquillity and serenity that would be there and the difficulties of Brussels. After he had spoken everyone was crushed.

About the terms of the peace he thought the commission for the responsibilities of the war an absurd body, with still more absurd proposals! All for dealing with war-criminals. It was not true that Belgium had pressed for this – it was Ll[oyd] G[eorge]. Webster collaborated. At one of the first sessions when the French prepared a programme Wilson and Ll[oyd] G[eorge] scrapped it. 'I want the L[eague] of Nations to come first' said Wilson, and 'I the trial of war-criminals' said Ll[oyd] G[eorge].

---

[224] Ray Stannard Baker (pseudo. 'David Grayson') (1870–1942), US journalist and writer; founder-editor, *The American Magazine*, 1906; press secretary to Woodrow Wilson at Paris Peace Conference, 1919; author of *Woodrow Wilson and World Settlement* (3 vols, New York, 1922) and *Woodrow Wilson: Life and Letters* (8 vols, New York, 1927–39).

He thought in ten years there w[oul]d be a monument to Wilson in Brussels and that he had raised his country to a greater height than it had ever reached.

Paderewski[225] – 'a magnificent dramatist'. Poles were not Europeans, nor were Hung[aria]ns. At one stage of the Polish-Lithuanian dispute, he made a speech of the two brother states, clasped the Lithuanian by the hand, and wept real tears. When he got back to Poland he made no impression.

19 May <1923>

On the 17th I heard some curious stories from the Dowager Lady Granville.[226] À propos of Strachey[227] she remarked, when I told her that Stamford[228] [*sic*] had denied that Prince Albert's[229] evening clothes and hot water were put out very night after his death, that it was true and that she had seen them.

She said also that once, when at Balmoral, she was shown the Queen's[230] bedroom and that a portrait of Albert lay on the right hand pillow. Afterwards she thought that she must have been mistaken, and so asked the Queen's old dresser who assured her that it was so.

---

[225] See entry 27 May 1919.
[226] Castalia Rosaline Campbell (1847–1938), married 2nd Earl Granville in 1865.
[227] (Giles) Lytton Strachey (1880–1932), critic and writer; author of *Queen Victoria* (1921).
[228] Lieutenant-Colonel Sir Arthur John Bigge (1849–1931), 1st Baron Stamfordham, cr. 1911, officer and courtier; Private Secretary to Queen Victoria, 1895–1901, and King George V, 1910–31.
[229] Prince (Francis) Albert (Augustus Charles Emmanuel) of Saxe-Coburg-Gotha (1819–61), Prince Consort of the United Kingdom, 1840–61.
[230] (Alexandrina) Victoria of Kent (1819–1901), Queen of Great Britain and Ireland, 1837–1901; Empress of India, 1876–1901.

She told me also a story about her. When the Empress of Germany[231] visited Eng[lan]d, I think, in 1878, she directed Prince Münster,[232] then ambassador, to ask Lord Granville[233] and the Duke of Bedford[234] to a private dinner on Monday.

On Saturday night Prince Münster had unbuttoned his uniform and was yawning in a chair when the butler said a lady wished urgently to see him. Enter Lady Ely,[235] one of Queen Victoria's ladies-in-waiting, in a distraught state. THE LADY: "The Queen has heard that you have invited L[or]d Granville and the Duke of Bedford to meet the Empress. She does not desire them to be so honoured and wishes you to cancel the invitation".

THE PRINCE: "But I have issued the invitations and one has accepted already. I cannot put such an affront to them".

THE LADY: "But the Queen wishes it".

THE PRINCE: "But the Queen is not my sovereign, and I cannot put this affront to them at her desire".

THE LADY: "I cannot take that answer. You must come to the Queen and repeat it".

So they went to Buckingham Palace. After a time, the Lady returned[:] "The Queen has gone to bed. She wishes to speak to you, however, as the thing must be done tonight. You will come and sit in the room next to her bedroom, the door being ajar". He came. After a time a voice came out of the darkness: "I wish L[or]d Granville and the Duke of Bedford not to go to dinner with Empress".

THE PRINCE: "But Madam, I have already issued the invitations".

THE VOICE: "But I wish you to cancel them".

THE PRINCE: "Madam, as a foreign diplomat I cannot put such an affront to them".

THE VOICE: "But if it is my desire".

---

[231] Augusta Marie Luise Katharina of Prussia (née Saxe-Weimar) (1811–90), consort of William I, German Emperor; married Prince Wilhelm of Prussia, 1829; Queen of Prussia, 1861; German Empress, 1871–88.

[232] Georg, Prince zu Münster-Derneburg (1822–1900), Hanoverian then German diplomat; Hanoverian minister at St. Petersburg, 1858–64; German ambassador at London, 1873–85; at Paris, 1885–1900.

[233] George Leveson Gower (1815–91), 2nd Earl Granville, succ. 1846, politician; MP (Lib.) Morpeth, 1837–40, Lichfield, 1841–46; Parliamentary Under-secretary for Foreign Affairs, 1840–41; Postmaster-General, 1848–52; Foreign Secretary, 1851–52, 1870–74 and 1880–85; Lord President of the Council, 1852–54 and 1855–58; Chancellor of the Duchy of Lancaster, 1854–55; Colonial Secretary, 1868–70 and 1886.

[234] Francis Charles Hastings Russell (1819–91), 9th Duke of Bedford, succ. 1872, politician and agriculturalist; MP (Lib.) Bedfordshire, 1847–72; President of the Royal Agricultural Society, 1880–91.

[235] Jane Loftus (née Hope-Vere) (1821–90), Marchioness of Ely; married John Loftus, 3rd Marquess of Ely, 1844; Lady of the Bedchamber, 1851–89.

THE PRINCE: "Very well, Madam, I will cancel the invitations, if you permit me to say to these gentlemen that it is by your desire".

A sigh came out of the darkness: "I suppose I cannot say that. Goodnight Prince, I am not pleased".

"As I stumbled out through the dark rooms", said the Prince, "I wondered what would happen if I met anyone".

Lady Granville said the explanation [was] that Lord Granville had proposed no such title or crown in 1858 when in office, as Victoria had received from Disraeli when she became Empress <of India> as well as Queen of England. He memory was a long one, it seems.

[23 October 1923]

Tel. Curzon (no. 238), 21 Oct. 1923.[236]

Your telegram no. 323.

Major Temperley may return at once for a week as proposed. Will his services be available later.

CURZON

Received 10 am Oct. 23.

---

[236] Inserted in diary for Oct.–Dec. 1918.

17 [December 1924]

[New York] Reunion of Paris Conference men. 4 contributors to my History[237][:] Coolidge,[238] Young,[239] Lord,[240] Hornbeck,[241] Hudson,[242] Haskins,[243] Taussig.[244]

Some interesting reminiscences – Taussig said Wilson told him on his return voyage that he much regretted having given away over the Southern Tyrol question which he did not properly understand at the time. Very strange, for I remember him coming away very cheerfully just after the decision was made, puring over the map lying on the floor, and cheerfully and ably explaining it to us all.

Taussig said beforehand he had seen him in connection with Congress over currency questions and that he confessed the same thing. He showed a diffidence,

---

[237] H.W.V. Temperley (ed.), *A History of the Peace Conference of Paris* (6 vols, London, 1920).

[238] See entry 11 July 1919.

[239] Allyn Abbott Young (1876–1929), US economist; ed. University of Wisconsin; Instructor in Economics, University of Wisconsin, 1901–1902 and 1905–1906; Western Reserve University, 1902–1904; Dartmouth, 1904–1905; Head of Economics, Stanford, 1906–10; Visiting Professor, Harvard, 1910–11; Washington University, St. Louis, 1911–13; Professor of Economics, Cornell, 1913–20; President of the American Statistical Society, 1917; Director of Bureau of Statistical Research, War Trade Board, 1917–18; Head of Economics Division, 'The Enquiry', 1918; Professor of Economics, Harvard, 1920–25; London School of Economics, 1925–29.

[240] See entry 23 Apr. 1919.

[241] Stanley Kuhl Hornbeck (1883–1966), US scholar and diplomat; Instructor in Political Science, University of Wisconsin, 1907–1909; Instructor in Chinese government colleges, 1909–13; Assistant Professor, Wisconsin, 1914–17; enlisted, 1918 (Captain in Ordnance Department); member of President Wilson's Inquiry, 1918; delegate at Paris Peace Conference, 1919; member of US military mission to Near East, Sept. 1919; private secretary to US minister at Peking, 1921–22; drafting officer, State Department, Office of Economic Advisers, 1921–24; Lecturer in Far Eastern History, Harvard, 1924–28; Chief of State Department, Far Eastern Division, 1928–37; special adviser to Secretary of State Cordell Hull, 1937–44; delegate, Dumbarton Oaks conference, 1944; ambassador at The Hague, 1944–47.

[242] Manley Ottmer Hudson (1883–1960), US legal scholar; law lecturer, University of Missouri, 1910–18; member of international law division, US delegation, Paris Peace Conference, 1919; assistant professor, Harvard, 1919–23; Bemis Professor of International Law, Harvard, 1923–53; judge on Permanent Court of International Justice, 1936–46; Chairman, United Nations International Law Commission, 1948–53.

[243] See entry 23 Apr. 1919.

[244] Frank William Taussig (1883–1966), US economist; Assistant Professor, Harvard, 1886–92; Professor of Economics, Harvard, 1892–1930; editor, *Quarterly Journal of Economics*, 1889–90 and 1896–1935; Chairman, US Tariff Commission, 1917–19; adviser on commercial treaties at Paris Peace Conference, 1919.

partly due to natural reserve, partly to consciousness that he did not thoroughly understand a question.

I think of Lansing's anecdote of a chuckle, which Wilson developed at Paris, a sign as he thought of failing, or failed, power.

Taussig gave another instance. He said that Wilson saw him on the question of the priority of the debt while the Italians were absent from the Conference. Taussig used the Italians as an illustration of people. Wilson completely misunderstood him and gave a decision which he thought would conciliate Italy and was, in reality, much to her disadvantage.

Some said Wilson was fond of self-analysis, others the contrary.

I said I thought that Wilson mistakes were becoming revealed – most agreed with this. David Lawrence[245] – D.P. Jones

Taussig said Wilson was not deceived by the Smuts memo[randum] on Reparations. (I heard this from other sources later and that he gave orders 'Don't mention pensions to me again'.) <Taussig said that he had definite knowledge, from his experience on the George Washington beforehand, that the Enemy Property clauses were drawn up by lawyers in [the] USA and imposed on the others.

I said that these were the only articles not altered by the Big Four.>

Heard a story accounting for N.M. Butler's[246] hatred of Wilson. N[icholas Murray] B[utler] is President of Columbia Un[iversit]y which has many Jews. Wilson said to him on day 'Your position is like mine. He that holdeth Israel shall neither slumber, nor sleep'.

3 Jan[uary 1925]

[Washington] Received by the President. A man with pale face, ginger hair, compressed lips and weary eyes is Calvin Coolidge.[247] When he met Lord

---

[245] David Lawrence (1888–1973), US journalist; Associated Press correspondent in Washington after 1912; close to Woodrow Wilson and often derided as his 'spokesman'; founder of *United States News*, 1933 (since 1948, *US News and World Report*).

[246] Nicholas Murray Butler (1862–1947), US philosopher and scholar; President of Columbia University, 1902–45; Republican Vice-presidential candidate, 1912; President, Carnegie Endowment for International Peace, 1925–45; Nobel Peace Laureate, 1931; President, Pilgrims Society, 1928–46.

[247] (John) Calvin Coolidge (1872–1933), US lawyer and politician; admitted to the Massachusetts bar, 1897; Member of Massachusetts House of Representatives (Rep.), 1906–10; State Senator, 1912–16; Lieutenant-Governor, 1916–19; Governor, 1919–21; US Vice-President, 1921–23; 30th US President, 1923–29.

[Robert] Cecil the day before, as the British Ambassador[248] told me, both were very silent after the first exchange. Finally Coolidge turned to him, and said 'I expected to have someone to talk to'.

Today he was more communicative. Lodge[249] did most of the talking among the British delegates. He <Coolidge> spoke of knowing us all by name first. Then of Mount Vernon and of New England.

I mentioned to him the extraordinary concentration of names in the history of the Federation, as seen in the church at Williamsburg. He assented. Finally he said there was much resemblance between England and America. Knowledge exemplified and supplemented this, and both nations were alike in the most important feature – character.

He rose and dismissed us, standing by his table, overshadowed by the American flag, with the gilded eagle atop of it.

Adjourned afterwards to Sir Esmé [sic] Howard. I put to him the point of opening mechanically the records year by year after 1878. This he grasped and said he would write privately about [it] to Crowe.[250] He did not grasp the second point, the records between 1878 and 1903, and the third between 1903 and 1914. He seemed to think Americans might have access to all of these, under same restrictions, at once.

I differed somewhat from this and said I would give him a memorandum.

I then spoke of Malvina Hoffman's[251] proposed group symbolising Anglo-American friendship. He suggested that Lord Balfour, as president of the English-speaking Union, should be asked to inaugurate it with a speech and that I could say that he approved of this suggestion entirely.

He also knew Malvina personally and spoke warmly of her.

Lunch with Ray Stannard Baker.[252] He said that Wilson's mind was primarily political and that he was not concerned chiefly with economics, though interested in them. On the George Washington going out to Paris [in March 1919] he said that he talked to him of Reparations etc., that he thought that that would

---

[248] Sir Esme William Howard (1863–1939), 1st Baron Howard of Penrith, cr. 1930, diplomat; entered diplomatic service, 1885; minister at Berne, 1911–13; at Stockholm, 1913–19; member of the British delegation at the Paris Peace Conference, 1919; ambassador at Madrid, 1919–24; at Washington, 1924–30.

[249] Sir Richard Lodge (1855–1938), diplomatic historian; Professor of History at Glasgow University, 1894–99; at Edinburgh University, 1899–1925; President of the Royal Historical Society, 1929–33.

[250] See entry 26 Jan. 1918.

[251] Malvina Hoffman (1885–1966), American sculptor, best known for her life-size bronze works; Temperley met her in Serbia in August 1919 where she was working for the American Yugoslav Relief Mission – see entry 21 Aug. 1919; see also J.D. Fair, *Harold Temperley: A Scholar and Romantic in the Public Realm* (Newark, 1992), 136.

[252] See entry 12 Apr. 1923.

not play a great portion in the actual Peace Conference. He expected peace to be signed and the territorial boundaries fixed, but that economic and financial questions might be referred to a Commission or be straightened out later by the League [of Nations].

He did not know very much of the territorial details when going to Paris, and trusted his experts to supply him with the facts. This they did not always do. Sometimes the professors[253] were idealists, sometimes looked at things with too narrow a point of view, sometimes they differed with one another, and there was generally a feud with the State Department.

Generally, the experts had no instructions, nor a governmental point of view, [and] did not know what was practicable nor applicable at the moment.

He agreed that President had not a wholly precise mind. He relied on his experts for information, he did not get [it], and abandoned the lawyers.

He thought, however, from a general point of view, Wilson knew what he wanted but that his information failed him at the critical moment more than once.

One instance of this was House. He regarded the Colonel as having a 'cloudy' mind. He always wanted to agree with persons, when he sat at a table, and refused to acknowledge the existence of difficulties. In the case of Fiume he made representations to Wilson, along with Mezes,[254] to which the rest of the Commission was opposed and against which they protested. When they did, Wilson found out, was angry and the breach with House began.

As regards the Tyrol, southern part, Baker confirmed what Taussig said of the attitude of Wilson. He told him, as he told Taussig <v[ide] 17th December [1924]>, on the return voyage of the George Washington, that he had been ignorant of the question and made the decision without proper knowledge. (I remember him waving [?] with the map and explaining it, and he did so very cheerfully that I think this was true.) Wilson added to Baker: [']But they (the Tirolese Germans) are pretty tough fighters and will get their own way in the end.[']

Baker said that Wilson's dinner of the 27th February <1919> with the Senators was a complete failure. (I have heard that Wilson did not understand, or would not explain, the covenant.) Much courtesy, and covert hostility, was shown on both sides.

---

[253] A reference to 'The Inquiry', a study group established by Woodrow Wilson in Sept. 1917, which, under the guidance of Col. House (see entry 3 Aug. 1921) and the philosopher Sidney Mezes (see below), was to prepare the United States for an eventual peace conference.

[254] Sidney Edward Mezes (1863–1931), US philosopher; Professor of Philosophy, University of Texas, 1894–1914; President, University of Texas, 1908–14; President, College of the City of New York, 1914–27; Director of The Inquiry, 1917–8; delegate, Paris Peace Conference, 1919.

On the return to Paris Wilson said to Baker: 'The Senators are making a political matter of this. I see that if I make concessions now, it will not satisfy them – they will only demand more. But I don't want break on the Covenant issue. If I make the concessions, it means I must fight the French, instead of the Senate'. (I heard from Lord Robert [Cecil] confirmation of this at the time.) He did ultimately fight the French and won – in the great Monroe Doctrine speech.

Learned[255] said that the Grey letter was dictated by Knox,[256] on the authority of Charles Warren;[257] that once the six votes to one point was in it, Knox, behind whom were Root[258] and Lodge,[259] recognized that the victory was won. It was published on 2nd February 1920.[260]

Between the end of January and March 1920, Learned pointed out that Wilson hesitated as to reservations, v[ide] his letter of January and of March. Baker knew nothing of this, though he said Wilson saw Hitchcock[261] and various others in the interval.

In reference to the correspondence of Wilson and Mrs Peck,[262] Baker said that it was a platonic friendship and that no one really believed it otherwise. He had not seen the letter but knew someone who had. He knew also that they had been hawked about several press-offices, which did not them worth buying or printing.

---

[255] Billings Learned Hand (1872–1961), US lawyer; ed. Harvard; judge, US District Court for Southern District, New York, 1909–24; US Appeal Court judge, Second Circuit, 1924–61.

[256] Philander Knox (1853–1921), US lawyer and politician; admitted to the Pennsylvania bar, 1875; US Attorney-General, 1901–1904; Secretary of State, 1909–13; Senator (Rep.) for Pennsylvania, 1904–1909 and 1917–21.

[257] Charles Warren (1868–1954), US lawyer; founded Immigration Restriction League, 1894; Assistant US Attorney-General, 1914–18.

[258] See entry 8 Sept. 1921.

[259] Henry Cabot Lodge (1850–1924), US politician and historian; Member of the US House of Representatives (Rep.), Massachusetts, 6th District, 1887–93; Senator, 1893–1924; Chairman of Senate Foreign Relations Committee and Senate Majority Leader, 1919–24.

[260] It was in fact published on 31 January, see 'America and the League: Lord Grey on the Issue', *The Times*, 31 Jan. 1920.

[261] Gilbert Monnell Hitchcock (1859–1934), US lawyer and politician; admitted to the Nebraska bar, 1882; Member of the US House of Representatives (Dem.), Nebraska, 2nd District, 1903–1905 and 1907–11; Senator, 1911–23; Chairman of Senate Foreign Relations Committee, 1917–19.

[262] Wilson was rumoured to have had an affair with the New England widow and socialite, Mary Allen Hulbert Peck (b. 1866).

8 Jan[uar]y 1925

Dinner Armstrong,[263] Bowman,[264] Nicholas Roosevelt.[265]

Colonel House. The latter I had seen at Paris – a very sincere, delightful, simple, unassuming man. He drank no wine, ate little and I wish he had not been so abstemious in talk. On the origins of the war he related his conversation with the Kaiser (told in Page[266]) at the review. He said this was done due to the fact that the entourage knew his impudence and wished to prevent House seeing him. Moi: 'Certainly they staged the matter unfavourably for a discussion on limitation of armaments'.

House resumed. He saw the Kaiser privately. He was very reasonable. But he said that he could not prevent Germany from having a fleet commensurate with that of Great Britain, as a measure of security. He however treated Bryan's[267] celebrated 'cooling-off' treaties with mild ridicule. 'How can I with an army in the last state of finish and ready to the last button, afford to wait a year to settle a dispute with another power?' 'It was just that', said House, 'which destroyed him'. Had he signed that treaty with the United States, the latter would not have made war till May 1918 (allowing for the year's interval after severing diplomatic relations, 7 May 1917). Preparedness might have gone on, but not commensurate with preparations for war. How extraordinarily dramatic!

[263] Hamilton Fish Armstrong (1893–1973), US diplomat and writer; on staff of *New Republic*, 1916–17; commissioned into army, 1917; military attaché to Serbian military mission to USA, 1917–19; assistant military attaché at Belgrade, Jan.–June 1919; managing editor, *Foreign Affairs*, and Executive Director, Council on Foreign Relations, 1922–28; editor, *Foreign Affairs*, and Council Director, 1928–72.

[264] Isaiah Bowman (1878–1950), Canadian-born US geographer; geography lecturer, Yale, 1905–15; Director, American Geographical Society, 1915–35; senior member of 'The Inquiry', 1917–18; chief territorial adviser to Woodrow Wilson at Paris Peace Conference, 1919, and to State Department, 1941–5; Director of Council on Foreign Relations, 1921–50; President, Johns Hopkins University, 1935–46.

[265] Nicholas Roosevelt (1893–1982), US diplomat and journalist; a cousin of Theodore Roosevelt's; attaché at Paris, 1916; secretary of legation at Madrid, 1916–17; Vice-governor of the Philippines, 1930; minister at Budapest, 1930–33; member of Council on Foreign Relations; foreign affairs correspondent and editorial writer, *New York Times* and *New York Herald Tribune*, 1921–46.

[266] B.J. Hendricks, *The Life and Letters of Walter H. Page* (3 vols, London, 1926), iii, 117.

[267] William Jennings Bryan (1860–1925), US politician; member of US House of Representatives (Dem.), Nebraska, 1st District, 1891–95; Democrat presidential candidate, 1896 and 1900; Secretary of State, 1913–15; negotiated arbitration treaties with 28 countries, but failed to do so with Germany.

He said that Tirpitz,[268] though not the most intellectual, was the most able man near the Kaiser and very anti-English.

The whole atmosphere seemed to him electric early in 1914. He laid the chief blame on the General Staff. They had the machine and would have no distinction unless they moved with it. They would just press on and off. He said his opinion was that France did not want war in 1914 and was even beginning to forget Alsace-Loraine.

He told them in Germany most emphatically that, if they went on building their fleet against England, that must be war. He said he found the opinion in Germany was that England was decadent, suffering from industrial troubles, and also from Ireland. She would not fight, said they: 'She will fight, if you go on with your fleet', said House.

He said that, later in the war, he told a group of Cabinet Ministers, including Lloyd George, that England should have fought Germany alone. 'You have spent billions and billions (sic) of men and millions (sic) of lives for France and Russia. Had you fought Germany alone, you would probably have sunk the German fleet, certainly seized all her commerce, and blockaded her, and conquered all her colonies. Peace must have come then, and on terms favourable to England. Instead of this, you have lost all this blood and treasure. "I wish", said Lloyd George, "you would go over and tell that to France"'.

Peace Conference. He said that Wilson made two mistakes over the Fiume business. He forgot what he had already heard over the Southern Tyrol and assigned it to Italy. He recognized, however, that he had made a blunder and afterwards hardened correspondingly over Fiume. House thought himself (which I do not) that the Fiume question would have been settled. At the time he was negotiating with Trumbić[269] in one room, himself in a middle room, and Orlando & Sonnino in a third. He thought he could have fixed a compromise, but Wilson permitted unlimited pressure on the Italians but none on the Yugoslavs. He used to Trumbić the argument that he would get better terms then than later. This I agreed with from my recollections of Trumbić at the moment I said I thought he had his head. House agreed.

He referred to the question of England stopping supplies from France during the Peace Conference, as asserted by Klotz,[270] which had been referred to him for arbitration.

---

[268] Grand Admiral Alfred Peter Friedrich (von) Tirpitz (1849–1930), German sailor; entered Prussian navy, 1865; Rear-Admiral, 1895; State Secretary for the Navy, 1897–1916; leader of Fatherland Party, 1916–18.

[269] See entry 30 Aug. 1918.

[270] Louis-Lucien Klotz (1868–1930), French journalist and politician; editor, *Français Quotidien*, 1895; Member of Chamber of Deputies (Radical Socialist), 1898–1925; Finance Minister, 1910–11, 1911–13 and 1917–20; Minister of the Interior, 1911–13.

9th March 1925

On Friday, the 6th, lunched with A.J. B[alfour] and talked about Origins of the War. He said two things which seemed to me memorable.

One 'I never tried to control anybody', and – as to the origins of the war – 'Don't fall into the trap so many have fallen into – of thinking King Edward made the Entente. He had nothing to do with it'.

15 [August 1928]

[Oslo] At the reception, King Haakon VII[271] spoke to me – he has a gentle laugh, displaying his teeth, amiable and mild.

He talked of our publication[272] and said that there were indiscretions in Sidney Lee's[273] life of Edward. I did not remind him [Haakon VII] that I had seen his indiscretion. He had tried to make his Cabinet join the with England at the beginning of the war, and this fact we omitted in vol. XI. It was not vital to the understanding of the outbreak of the war.

He said on Edward's death he had asked that the private letters should be destroyed. He did not know whether this was done. I said I thought so, as much had certainly been destroyed.

Koht[274] said he was going leave. I said 'Can you, before the King?' He said 'Yes, if he does not see me'. Just at this point the King came up as he was leaving. He saw us and took Koht by the hand & walked out with him.

The King is said not to speak Norwegian. He has at any rate a Danish accent. He is very democratic and goes up to Holmkoben[275] [*sic*] to ski in a tram.

---

[271] See entry 18 Aug. 1918.

[272] G.P. Gooch and H.W.V. Temperley (eds), *British Documents on the Origins of the War, 1898–1914* (11 vols, London, 1926–38). The final volume appeared first, followed by the first three volumes; the fourth had just been advertised.

[273] Sir Sidney Lee (1859–1926), biographer and writer; editor of *Dictionary of National Biography*, since 1891; Professor of English Literature, East London College, 1913–24; his *King Edward VII: A Biography* (2 vols, London, 1925) caused a minor controversy.

[274] Halvdan Koht (1873–1965), Norwegian historian and politician; lecturer, Oslo University, 1908–10; Professor of History, Oslo University, 1910–35; President, Norwegian Historian Association, 1912–27 and 1932–36; Labour Party activist since 1909; Foreign Minister, 1935–40.

[275] *Recte* Holmenkollen, a ski resort in the Vestre Aker area of Oslo.

? August 1928

À propos of my paper Renouvin[276] told me that in France in 1916 there was a discussion as to keeping procès verbaux of Cabinet meetings. Ministers objected. They said that they could not then safely change their minds.

Schmitt[277] says Berchtold told him he meant the ultimatum to Serbia to be accepted. No one, I think, can believe this.

20 August [1928]

Saw the Bolshevik Pokovsky[278] [*sic*] and his wife – the latter speaks English. Pokovsky said that the Embassy documents formerly in Great Britain were now in Moscow. He said that the whole collection there was well and scientifically organized.

I asked him if I could go there. He said that, personally, I should be welcome, but that my entrance was the affair of his government.

He said all the Tsars had kept Diaries and that these were preserved in Moscow. Nicholas II's Diary[279] was very empty. In that of Alexander III[280] you saw a man. He was limited but not stupid, and had introduced Russian into the despatches.

He said there were 25 Krasnij Archiv volumes.[281]

---

[276] Pierre Renouvin (1893–1974), French diplomatic historian; served in French infantry, 1914–17; severely wounded, 1917; lecturer, Sorbonne, 1922–33; Professor of Diplomatic History, Sorbonne, 1933–64; cf. his *Les Origines immediates de la guerre (28 juin–4 août 1914)* (Paris, 1925).

[277] Bernadotte Schmitt (1886–1969), American historian; educated Oxford and Wisconsin; Professor of Modern European History, University of Chicago, 1924–46; founder-editor, *Journal of Modern History*, 1924–46; his *The Coming of the War, 1914* (London, 1930) won the Pulitzer Prize for History; for his interview with Berchtold see his *Interviewing the Authors of the War* (Chicago, privately printed, 1930), 26–30.

[278] *Recte* Mikhail Nikole'evich Pokrovsky (1868–1932), Soviet historian; Bolshevik activist since 1905; Mayor or Moscow, 1917–18; director of the *Institut Krasnoi Professurya* (Institute of Red Professors), 1921–31.

[279] 'Nikolai Romanov v pervykh dnyakh yoyni', *Krasnyi Arkhiv* lxiv (1934), 133–8.

[280] Aleksandr III Romanov (1845–94), Tsar of All the Russias, 1881–94.

[281] *Krasnyi Arkhiv* (Red Archives), historical journal, which appeared from 1922 until 1941, and published archival materials on the history of the Tsarist foreign policy as well as the Russian revolution. Altogether 106 issues were published.

He explained the treaty of Bjorko[282] by saying Nicholas was terrified of the German fleet. He said his ministers were wiser – that Count Witte[283] was a great man. He was not a Jew, though his second wife was, but of the lower nobility. His family was Germanic in origin but he himself could not speak German.

1 July [1929]

[Cape Town] Hofmeyer[284] told me that the Constitutional Convention of 1910 kept minutes, but no record of the arguments used on both sides. I said that the decision was doubtless politically right, but historically most regrettable.

Historians & politicians must ever be at variance. Curzon is a good example, though something of a historian. He persisted in thinking that intense study by him of an problem would solve it, whereas historians knew that a pol[iticia]n's study is unlikely to be final, and even a historian's is open to doubt. There is no country like South Africa to prove this. For no man can write the history of any age or part of it, without making up his mind on native policy.

6 August [1929]

Lunch with General Smuts. The General was very amiable – he speaks lightly, quickly, gently humorously. Two Professors – Haldane[285] & Wildon-Carr[286] – were present. At one stage, Wildon-Carr said 'The man who invents a new idea is better than the man who makes two grass blades grow where one grew before'.

---

[282] Abortive treaty of alliance foisted on the Tsar by Kaiser Wilhelm off Bjørkø in the Baltic in August 1905, see anon., 'Russko-germanskii dogorov 1905 goda, saklotsennie v Byerka', *Krasnyi Arkhiv* v (1924), 5–49.

[283] Count Sergei Yulevich Witte (1849–1915), Russian politician; Transport Minister, 1892; Finance Minister, 1892–1903; chief negotiator at Portsmouth, NH, peace negotiations, 1905; Chairman of Council of Minister, 1905–1906.

[284] Jan Hendrik Hofmeyer the younger (1894–1948), South African politician; Administrator of Transvaal, 1924–29; MP (South African Party, since 1933, United Party), Johannesburg North, 1929–48; Finance Minister, 1939–48; Deputy Prime Minister, 1943–48.

[285] John Scott Haldane (1860–1936), physiologist and pioneer of the study of suffocative gases occurring in coal mines and wells; Fellow of New College, Oxford, 1901–36; Reader in Physiology at Oxford, 1907–13; Director of Mining Research Laboratory founded at Bentley Colliery near Doncaster, 1912–21; President of the Institution of Mining Engineers, 1924–28; invented a portable oxygen administration apparatus (gas mask) in 1916.

[286] Herbert Wildon Carr (1857–1931), philosopher; President, Aristotelian Society, 1916–18; Professor of Philosophy, King's College, London, 1918–25; Visiting Professor, University of Southern California, 1925–31.

It depends on the idea, I said – what about poison gas? Ah, said Smuts (pointing to Haldane): 'He we have the gentlest of men, who spent four years manufacturing it'.

He said he had just been visiting Zimbabwe[287] and camping on the way. He had heard the discussion about it, and said the new anti-Semitic theory was all negative.

At this stage I brought up my old joke about Rhodes.[288] 'Why does not Bent[289] say the Zimbabwe ruins are semitic?' 'Because he is not sure'. 'Ah', said Rhodes, 'that is not the way great empires are made'. Yet, said I, it was the way great works of thought are made.

'Partly only', said Smuts. 'From negative we must proceed to constructive. My friend here (Wildon-Carr) has assembled all the negatives, and is the first of sceptics and doubt[er]s. When are going to tell us what you think?'

'Well', said I, 'a doubter at least found a place, and was not deposed from it among the Apostles'.

This led to another discussion. Wildon-Carr: 'General, in your book you started at the end, and ended with the beginning'. Smuts: 'Well, I began with personality, the greatest gift of God to man, and the most mysterious'.

What about an army? Smuts: 'Ah, you see personally these most of all'.

We spoke of Curzon. Curzon was not what he was said to be in public – he was in some ways very human, and modest. He was extraordinary as an intellect in expression, in assimilation and in power of work. Yet I have often heard him at the Cabinet – his intellect, his power of presentation, was superb, but I always wondered what w[oul]d follow, and what he meant.

That is what Lord Ronaldshay[290] says, that he was satisfied with presentation alone. Smuts: 'Yes, it is not enough for a statesman to make a great speech – he must follow it up. Expression by itself does not suffice.['] I said, Curzon must have it all his own way or surrender. Smuts: 'Yes, he was not a diplomatist. A diplomatist must be prepared to bargain, and to surrender something'. He

---

[287] Great Zimbabwe, ruined capital city of the Kingdom of Zimbabwe, eleventh to fourteenth centuries. The 'semitic' theory was advanced by Karl Mauch, who argued that the buildings replicated the palace of the Queen of Sheba in Jerusalem. The construction of Great Zimbabwe is claimed too by the Lemba, an ethnic group with a tradition of ancient Jewish or South Arabian descent through their male line, which is supported by recent DNA studies.

[288] Sir Cecil John Rhodes (1853–1902), mining magnate and advocate of imperial expansion in southern Africa.

[289] (James) Theodore Bent (1852–97), archaeologist and explorer; his *The Ruined Cities of Mashonaland* (1892) claimed that Great Zimbabwe was of Phoenician or Arab origin.

[290] Lawrence John Lumley Dundas (1876–1961), Earl of Ronaldshay, 1892–1929, 2nd Marquess of Zetland, succ. 1929, politician and writer; MP (Con.), Hornsey, 1907–16; Secretary of State for India, 1935–40; cf. his *Life of Lord Curzon* (3 vols, London, 1928), i, 3–4, ii, 25 and iii, 384–6.

approved highly of Curzon's care for artistic monuments in India, and said it was in accordance with his character and love of ceremonial. His love of that was shown in his ordering of his own tomb, and portraying his own statue and inscription, so that he was, in fact, his own undertaker – there was nothing but the date, which he did not add.

He looked up at the portrait of Rhodes, and said it was not good. It suggested something sly and intriguing – that was not his nature. He was rough and frank, a good fellow. Of course, there was another side. Yes, he had two souls, one idealistic, one commercial. Oh, if we could only unite our selves, and our souls. Then we should perfect man.

He was most interesting about Louis Trichardt.[291] I said I admired greatly the road and the gap through the mountains, which was through bloodied cliffs like Dolomites. 'Ah, Wykes Point', said he, 'I made that for you. I walked up on foot from Louis Trichardt to survey a railway. I found it impossible to run a line through'.

So you made the scenery for us. I thank you, said I.

I told him that I admired greatly the faces of the burghers at the foot of Kruger's statue. Yes, said he, they are – one or two of them – particularly fine and taken from real types of old burghers. The man with the drawn face reminded him of the seventeenth century, a man as dour as one of Job's comforters.[292]

19 Sep[embe]r [1933]

[Istanbul] EASTERN QUESTION.[293] To understand the Eastern Question you must go to Constantinople and stand on Seraglio Point. Look from the window of Abdul Medjid's Kiosk, or from beneath the column of Claudius where Sultans so often sat. Your back is to the Golden Horn and you gaze over sparkling waters on Europe and Asia at once. To the left, your eye fixes on the bright palace of Dolman Bagtche[294] and beyond it again on a little white cupola, on a mosque which gleams like a pearl on the margin of Europe. Above them are hills and stately woods, moving so near to the Asiatic side as if to link Europe to Asia. It seems even that they do, but a careful eye sees just a hint of a gap in the hills on the horizon. It is here indeed that the Bosphorus parts the land and separates one shore from another. Its blue lane runs northward here, in a

---

[291] Formerly Trichardtsdorp, a town at the foot of the Soutpansberg mountain range in the Limpopo province of South Africa, named after Louis Tregardt, a *Voortrekker* leader.

[292] See *Book of Job*, 16.2: 'You are all miserable comforters'.

[293] Cf. H.W.V. Temperley, *England and the Near East: The Crimea* (London, 1936), 3–4.

[294] The Dolmabahçe Palace on the European shores of the Bosphorus, built between 1843 and 1856 for Sultan Abdülmecid I (1823–61), served as the administrative centre of the Ottoman government, 1856–1922.

curiously curved line till it reaches the Black Sea. Turning from the Bosphorus, which is shaped like a scimitar, the eye looks to the right on the Sea of Marmara, which is round like a shield. It looks like a shield of blue enamel on which Prince's [*sic*] Islands[295] show like dark bosses. The Dardanelles and their Straits to the South are too far to be seen.

Now the shield and the scimitar must be in one hand. He who holds the Dardanelles and Marmara repels all attacks from the south, he who holds the Bosphorus separates Asia from Europe, and menaces all invaders from the North. For over four hundred years the Sultans have held both weapons in their hands. So long as the Ottoman did so, all went well. Europe was disinterested so long as 'the strong man armed'[296] kept his weapons bright and sharp. It was when he failed to do so that the Powers of Europe rose to interfere. As the Sultan's grasp weakened, one Power reached for <the> sword, another <for the> shield. In the struggle, England, France, Russia and Austria all played parts. One Napoleon induced Russia to fight England, another Napoleon induced England to fight Russia ~~over the question~~. Many times during the nineteenth century war hovered near; often fleets approached the Dardanelles or Bosphorus. The pretexts were different – Syria, Egypt, Lebanon, Rumania, Jerusalem were the words of strife – but there was only one utmost cause of strife – Constantinople and the command of its Straits.

No one Power was willing that any other should stand on Seraglio Point, and grasp both the Sword and Shield, which defended Constantinople. Only the Turk was to do that, and the greater the danger if his arm wavered and his hand grew feeble. A city commanding two seas would be incomparably strong, if it was strong at all. If the Sultan was strong in the love of his subjects, progressive in his policy, the equal <in arms> of his neighbours, who could expel him from the finest strategic position in the world? But in the nineteenth century the Sultan never possessed the love of his subjects nor strength not wealth nor arms like those of a great Western Power. He might perhaps have done so, had he wished. Here lay the importance of the Reform Movement, for it was a chance of giving life itself to a renovated Turkey. <It might have acted like a transfusion of blood.> But, if reform failed, the city became incomparably weak, so weak that every Power was interested to help or to destroy Turkey. For she would not remain as she was. No one power must command her two seas. This weakness of Turkey, lasting for a century and increasing with every decade, made the question of the Straits a supreme one to Europe. Here in its simplest form lay the European danger known as the ~~Turkish~~ Eastern problem. It is best seen from a

---

[295] Princes' Islands (Turk. *Prens Adaları*, after the ancient Greek name Πριγκήπων νήσοι), a chain of nine islands in the Sea of Marmara.

[296] See *Gospel of St. Luke*, 11.21: 'When a strong man armed keeps his palace, his goods are in peace'.

window over Seraglio Point, where the sparkling waters of the Bosphorus mingle with the calmer blue of the Sea of Marmara.

13 March [1935]

Interview with Sir Clive Wigram.[297] [...] I [Wigram] was under Curzon myself for five years, and loved him. But he was not suited to be Prime Minister. The King never thought of him.

<26 June [1935]. The results of further investigating were as follows: Standfordham[298] went to see Curzon and told him that the King had decided to have a prime minister in the Commons. He left at 2.30, and got back to the Palace and presented his report to the King. It was only at 3.15 that Baldwin was received.

Curzon's assertion that Baldwin was already being interviewed by the King and that, in consequence, the King could not receive 'the further considerations' he proposed to submit, is bunk.

It is the kind of excuse put forward by a small boy for being unsuccessful in a race. He started on the left foot, not on the right, or he failed in an examination because the master taught him wrong.>

20 Dec[ember 1935]

Saw Gruić,[299] <the new Yugoslav minister, the day before> yesterday (18th), and he gave me his reminiscences, first of the Austro-Hungarian ultimatum. He was present when it was presented. He says that, of course, it was not meant to be accepted. He says it is not true that a Russian telegram caused the Government to be stiffer. On the contrary, the first draft of the Serb reply <before the had heard from Russia> was much stiffer than the second. It was altered in the Cabinet, in a milder sense though he himself, then načelnik or permanent Under-Secretary, was not present.

He told me an anecdote of Lord Morley. On one occasion, during the Balkan war, Grey was away fishing and Morley represented him. He interviewed Gruić about the Djakova question – he thought it at the extreme south of Albania whereas it is really right up in the North. Then he said, 'Let me see, was there not some trouble in 1908? About Bosnia?' 'I was astounded. How could I explain all that in

---

[297] See entry 28 July 1918.
[298] See entry 19 May 1923.
[299] Dr Slavko J. Gruić, Serbian diplomat; Secretary-General, Ministry of Foreign Affairs, 1914–15; SHS minister at Washington, 1919–22; Yugoslav minister at London, 1935–37.

a few minutes, and left still astonished'. Incidentally I thought this threw a strong light of Morley's statements about the origin of the war. He there declares that he never saw Crowe's famous anti-German memo[randum] of Jan[uary] 1907.[300] He forgot the memo[randum] then, just as he forgot about Bosnia.

30 [September 1938]

Peace proclaimed – I hope a lasting one and also incidentally, & greatly to my relief, peace with C.K. W[ebster].[301]

8 Ap[ril 1939]

Good Friday celebrated by Germany, with big Bertha bursting into a church in 1918 – celebrated by Mussolini[302] by an attack on undefended Albania, guns, tanks, ships, defiance. Strange ways of commemorating the Lord's passion indeed!

What disturbs me is the badness of our intelligence. We were deceived over the jump on Austria, and the jump on Prague and now over the jump on Albania.

Lord Stanhope[303] on April 6 said 'we expect no trouble' and revealed the Fleet were away on leave; Halifax[304] learned of the rape of Albania <while> out of town, and Neville Chamberlain[305] while on a fishing holiday!

---

[300] Memo. Crowe, 'Memorandum on the Present State of British Relations with France and Germany', 1 Jan. 1907, *BD* iii, app. A.

[301] Temperley sought to heal their latest rift, see Temperley to Webster, 28 Sept. 1938, and reply 29 Sept. 1938, Webster MSS, 1/16.

[302] Benito Mussolini (1883–1945), Italian journalist and politician; editor, *Avanti!*, 1912–14; active service, 1915–18; founder of *Fasci di Combattimento*, 1919; Prime Minister, 1922–43 (since 1925, *Il Duce*); head of Italian Social Republic (Republic of Salò), 1943–45.

[303] James Richard Stanhope (1880–1967), 7th Earl Stanhope, succ. 1905, 13th Earl of Chesterfield, succ. 1952; Parliamentary Secretary to the War Office, 1918–19; Civil Lord of the Admiralty, 1924–29; Parliamentary and Financial Secretary to the Admiralty, 1931; Parliamentary Under-secretary for War, 1931–34; Parliamentary Under-secretary for Foreign Affairs, 1934–36; First Commissioner of Works, 1937–38; First Lord of the Admiralty, 1938–39; Lord President of the Council, 1939–40.

[304] Edward Frederick Lindley Wood (1881–1959), Baron Irwin, cr. 1925, 3rd Viscount Halifax, succ. 1934, 1st Earl of Halifax, cr. 1944, politician; MP (Cons.), Ripon, 1910–25; Parliamentary Under-secretary for the Colonies, 1921–22; President of the Board of Education, 1922–24 and 1932–35; Minister of Agriculture, 1924–25; Viceroy of India, 1926–31; Secretary of State for War, 1935; Lord Privy Seal, 1935–37; Lord President of the Council, 1937–38; Foreign Secretary, 1938–40; ambassador at Washington, 1941–46.

[305] (Arthur) Neville Chamberlain (1869–1940), politician; MP (Cons.), Birmingham Ladywood, 1918–29, Edgbaston, 1929–40; Minister of National Service, 1916–17;

'The lamb, though not doomed to bleed today
Had he thy season would he skip and play?
Pleased to be the last he crops the flowery food,
And licks the hand just raised to shed his blood'.[306]

14 Ap[ril 1939]

Chamberlain's speech condones the rape of Albania, but, in view of our previous obligations, it is difficult to deny their right to priority there, or even to their (obviously lying) version of the facts.[307]

The guarantees to Greece & Rumania extend our obligations and seem to endanger the nations not guaranteed.

16 Ap[ril 1939]

Worked on my Halifax Memo[randum], which will, I hope, do some good.[308] At least I know more than anyone about some phases of the peace – and perhaps the after-peace.

6.30 suddenly felt a new light and great accession of strength.[309]

Postmaster-General, 1922–23; Minister of Health, 1923, 1924–29 and 1931; Chancellor of the Exchequer, 1923–24 and 1931–37; Prime Minister, 1937–40; Lord President of the Council, May–Oct. 1940.

[306] *Recte*: 'The lamb thy riot dooms to bleed to-day,/Had he thy reason, would he skip and play?/Pleased to the last, he crops the flowery food,/And licks the hand just raised to shed his blood', A. Pope, *An Essay on Man* (1732–4), epistle 1.3.

[307] *Hansard* (5) cccxlvi (13 Apr. 1939), cols. 5–17.

[308] Whether Temperley completed this memorandum is not clear. There is a draft, undated document among his papers, and parts of it were incorporated in a letter to Letter to the editor, 'Public Law Of Europe Obligations On The Axis', *The Times*, 21 Apr. 1939.

[309] This was Temperley's last entry. He suffered a coronary thrombosis on 24 Apr., and, although he rallied in early May, died on 11 July.

Index

Abdülhamid II, Ottoman Sultan, 157, 244
Acton, John Emerich Dalberg, 1st Baron Acton, 4, 8, 19, 114, 306, 545
Adam, George Jeffreys, 411
Adams, John Quincy, 7
Adams, William George Stuart, 84, 110, 152, 197, 237, 253
Addison, Dr. Christopher, 1st Viscount, 2, 320
Ador, Gustave, 533
Aehrenthal, Alois Lexa Baron von, 183
Albania, 18, 19, 27, 30, 45, 64, 77, 92, 108, 111, 122, 151, 157, 158, 162, 198, 207, 208, 235, 289, 304, 323, 357, 362, 367, 404, 405, 450, 451, 457, 458, 459, 461, 464, 466, 475, 476, 477, 479, 481, 482, 483, 484, 486, 491, 493, 495, 500, 502, 503, 513, 515, 516, 518–20, 521, 525, 526, 527–8, 541, 552, 572, 573
Albert I (Léopold Clément Marie Meinrad) of Saxe-Coburg-Gotha, King of the Belgians, 136, 563
Alekse'ev, General Mikhail Vasili'evich, 86, 87, 131, 159, 174
Alexander I (Aleksandar I Karadjordjević), Regent of Serbia, 92, 166, 341, 343, 344, 346, 348, 391, 392, 451–2, 454, 465, 466, 467, 488, 493
Alexander I of Schleswig-Holstein-Sonderburg-Glücksburg, King of the Hellenes, 155, 281
Alfonso (León Fernando María Jaime Isidro Pascual Antonio de Borbón y Austria-Lorena) XIII, King of Spain, 51

Allan, Maude (née Beulah Maude Durrant), 282
Allenby, General Edmund Henry Hynman, 206, 223, 224, 311, 312, 314
Amery, Leopold Charles Maurice Stennett, 27, 50, 71, 78, 130, 135, 136, 137, 147, 248, 268, 286, 298, 301, 306, 307, 309
Andrássy de Csíkszentkirály et Krasznahorka, Count Gyula (the Younger), 212, 508
Andreas II, King of Hungary, 15
Andrews, Vice-Admiral Adolphus, 468, 470
Anson, Sir William, 7
Apponyi de Nagyappony, Count Albert, 13, 212, 546, 552
Armistice, Austro-Italian, Villa Giusti, Padua, 3 Nov. 1918, 337
Armstrong, Hamilton Fish, 563
Arthur, Sir George Compton Archibald, 239
Ashley, William J., 3
Ashmead-Bartlett, Ellis, 433, 434
Askenazy, Szymon, 542, 543
Asquith, Herbert Henry, 1st Earl of Oxford and Asquith, 58, 69, 70, 71, 72, 74, 125, 130, 139, 199, 223, 224, 239, 246, 285, 303, 491, 523, 526, 532, 538, 549
Asquith, Margot (née Emma Alice Margaret Tennant), Countess of Oxford and Asquith, 86, 223
Astor, Nancy Witcher (née Langhorne), Viscountess, 268
Astor, Waldorf, 2nd Viscount, 268

Austria-Hungary, 18, 21, 64, 102, 106, 121, 135, 142, 164, 176, 178, 231, 255, 257, 275, 302, 315, 317, 339, 347, 408, 415, 416, 449
Averescu, Marshal Alexandru, 47, 52, 88, 89, 98, 117, 159
Avezzano, Baron Camillo Romano, 288

Baden, Prince Max(imilian Alexander Friedrich Wilhelm) of, 318
Baerlein, Henry, 474, 475, 498
Bairakdar, Mustapha, 20
Baker, Lieutenant-Colonel (Bernard) Granville, 335
Baker, Ray Stannard (pseud. 'David Grayson'), 554, 560, 561, 562
Baker-Carr, Brigadier-General Christopher D'Arcy Bloomfield Saltern, 256, 298
Baldwin, Stanley, 1st Earl Baldwin of Bewdley, 252, 546, 571
Balfour, Arthur James, 1st Earl, 69, 74, 90, 91, 105, 118, 125, 126, 147, 160, 184, 194, 195, 197, 215, 216, 221, 241–2, 246, 254, 255, 285, 293, 294, 300, 302, 303, 321, 401, 403, 404, 408, 410, 413, 414, 415, 416–17, 418, 419, 422, 423, 424, 425, 429, 434, 435, 436, 438, 439, 441, 442, 443, 444, 445, 447, 448, 449, 450, 492, 495, 505, 506, 515, 525, 526, 527, 528–9, 531, 533–4, 536, 537, 538, 539, 540, 541–2, 546, 547, 548, 550, 552, 554, 560
Ballard, Brigadier-General Colin Robert, 132, 193, 259, 265
Ban, Metropolitan Mitrofan, 357
Bandholtz, Major-General Harry Hill, 454
Barclay, Sir George Head, 48, 86, 122, 174, 223, 245, 273
Barker, Ernest, 35
Barker, Lieutenant-Commander George N., 374, 375, 378, 379
Barnes, George Nicoll, 405, 429

Barnes, W. Emery, 35
Barrère, Camille, 321
    Batistić, Josip ('Kokotić'), 384
battles
  Arras, 11–20 May 1917, 141
  Belgrade, 1739, 26
  Brussilov Offensive, July 1917, 174
  Cambrai, 20 Nov.–7 Dec. 1917, 238, 295
  Caporetto (12th battle of the Isonzo), 24 Oct.–19 Nov. 1917, 203, 208, 486, 491
  Dobro Pole, 14–23 Sept. 1918, 310
  French counter-offensive, July–Aug. 1918, 295, 296, 298
  Jemmappes, 6 Nov. 1792, 304
  Königgrätz, 1866, 26
  Kosovo, 1389, 26, 55, 345
  Lake Dojran, Feb., Apr. 1917, and Sept. 1918, 119
  Lechfeld, 955, 26
  Leuthen, 1757, 10
  Mărăşeşti, 6 Aug.–8 Sept. 1918, 62, 265
  Mohács, 1526, 15, 26, 451
  Mollwitz, 1740, 10, 26.
  Monastir (first), 3. Oct.–27. Nov. 1916, 59, 60, 62, 64, 78, 80
  Piave, June 1918, 309, 375, 394
  Poltava, 1709, 26
  Pruth, Nov.–Dec. 1917, 214
  River Argeş, 1–5 Dec. 1916, 107
  Rossbach, 1757, 10
  Sereth (Siret), 22–25 July 1917, 75, 171
  St. Michael's Offensive, Mar.–May 1918, 259, 260, 266, 268, 270, 273, 279, 280, 281, 290, 295, 297
  Tannenberg (Grunwald), 1410, 26
  Zloczow, 19–28 July 1917, 174
  Zorndorf, 1759, 10
Bauer, Archbishop Anton, 351
Baumann, Brigadier-General Albert, 94
Bax-Ironside, Sir Henry George Outram, 66
Beatty, Admiral David Richard, 1st Earl, 70, 71, 349

Beaverbrook, William Maxwell 'Max' Aitken, 1st Baron, 70, 130, 253, 254, 257
Belić, General Vladimir J., 331
Bell, Dr. Johannes, 442, 443
Bénazet, Paul Louis Théodore, 115
Benedict XV (née Giacomo Paolo Giovanni Battista della Chiesa), Pope, 145, 170, 185, 188, 191, 403, 507
Beneš, Edvard, 126, 203, 274, 302, 307, 308, 315.
Beresford, Admiral the Hon. Charles William de la Poer, 1st Baron, 65
Berthelot, General Henri Mathias, 62, 78, 89, 132, 203, 220, 230, 259, 264, 265, 399
Bethmann Hollweg, Theobald von, 101, 144, 167, 411
Bevan, Edwyn Robert, 253
Bibesco, Elizabeth Charlotte Lucy, Princess (née Asquith), 86
Billing, Noel Pemberton, 282
Birdwood, Field Marshal Lord William, 35
Birrell, Augustine, 538
'Black Hand' (*Crna ruka*), 166
Bland, Brigadier-General William St. Colum, 130
Block, Sir Adam Samuel James, 91
Bojović, Field Marshal Petar, 327, 345
Bonaparte, Princess Marie, 125
Bonnier, General (François Xavier Louis Henry) Gaëtan, 162, 235
Borden, Sir Robert Laird, 29, 299
Bosdari, Conte Alessandro De, 153, 161, 213, 288
Bosnia-Herzegovina, 34, 83, 104, 106, 178, 256, 317, 327, 330, 341, 352, 367, 469, 571
Bosnian annexation crisis, 1908–1909, 21, 571–2
Botha, General Louis, 44, 430
Bottomley, Horatio, 66
Bourbon-Parma, Prince Sixtus Ferdinand Maria Ignazio Alfred Robert of, 266, 272

Bourcart, Jacques, 476
Bourgeois, Léon Victor Auguste, 405
Bowman, Isaiah, 563
Bowerman, Charles William, 198
Brandeis, Louis Dembitz, 156
Branting, Karl-Hjalmar, 167, 542
Brătianu, Dinu (Constantin) I.C., 139
Brătianu, Ion I.C., 78, 98, 123, 131, 139, 148, 150–51, 158, 161, 173, 175, 176, 179, 185, 220, 222, 240, 242, 244, 273, 398, 427, 434, 435, 443, 445
Brătianu, Vintilă, 139
Briand, Aristide, 36, 125, 126, 233, 411, 500, 506–7, 509, 521, 522
Bridges, Lieutenant-General Sir (George) Tom (Molesworth), 325, 326, 327, 329
Brockdorff-Rantzau, Ulrich Count von, 410, 433
Browning, Oscar, 3, 18, 25
Bruce Lockhart, Sir Robert Hamilton, 242
Brusilov, General Aleksei Alekse'evich, 107
Bryce, James, Viscount of Dechmont, 59, 153, 316, 509, 510
Buchan, John, 1st Baron Tweedsmuir, 254
Buchanan, Sir George William, 74, 109, 169, 176, 188, 191, 200, 201, 207, 218, 225, 258, 277, 541
Buckley, Brigadier-General Basil Thorold, 157, 191, 240, 251, 314
Buckmaster, Sir Stanley Owen, 1st Viscount, 318
Budisavljević, Srđan, 335
Bukovac, Vlaho (née Biagio Faggioni), 369
Bulić, Dr. Frane, 369
Bulla Aurea, 1222, xi, 15
Bunsen, Sir Maurice William Ernest de, 242, 498
Buonfiglio, Roberto, 377
Burián von Rajecz, Stephan (István) Count, 269
Burkill, Charles, 35
Burrows, (Ronald) Montagu, 71, 95, 216, 296

Butler, Sir (George) Geoffrey Gilbert, 278
Butler, James Ramsay Montagu, 120, 129, 210, 300, 540, 541
Butler, Nicholas Murray, 559
Butterfield, Sir Herbert, xi, 4, 18, 22, 23, 25, 30, 35
Buxton, Noel Edward Noel-, 1st Baron Noel-Buxton, 142, 143, 172, 217
Byng, Field Marshal Sir Julian Hedworth George, 1st Baron Byng of Vimy, 261

Cadorna, General Luigi Cadorna, 203, 207, 209, 211, 213
Cadogan, Sir Alexander George Montagu, 510
Caillaux, Josephe Marie Auguste, 106, 227
Cambon, (Pierre) Paul, 160, 197, 266, 415, 508
Canada, 9, 97, 199, 235, 379, 480, 495, 519, 539
Canning, George, 5, 6, 7, 8, 31, 32, 33, 85, 223, 291, 303, 481, 529
Carlyle, Thomas, 9, 10, 140
Carp, Petre P., 89
Carr, Lieutenant-Colonel Reginald Blakeney, 241
Carson, Sir Edward Henry, Baron Carson of Duncairn, 189, 219, 230, 238
Casement, Sir Roger David, 273
Castlereagh, Robert Stewart, Viscount, 529, 550
Cecil, Lord Hugh Richard Heathcote Gascoyne-, 1st Baron Quickswood, 246
Cecil, Lord (Edgar Algernon) Robert Gascoyne-, 1st Viscount Cecil of Chelwood, 53, 67, 71, 92, 96, 97, 148, 149, 195, 196, 225, 283, 302, 307, 316, 420, 492, 495, 497, 539, 540, 543, 560, 562
Cemal Pasha, Ahmet, 216
Chamberlain, Sir (Joseph) Austen, 71, 117, 130, 184, 314, 523

Chamberlain, (Arthur) Neville, 32, 33, 572, 573
Charteris, Brigadier-General John, x, 102, 124
Chesterton, Gilbert Keith, 349
Churchill, Arabella, 53
Churchill, Colonel Arthur Gillespie, 273, 316
Churchill, John, 1st Duke of Marlborough, 53
Churchill, Lady Randolph, 56
Churchill, Lord Randolph, 535, 549
Churchill, Sir Winston Leonard Spencer-, x, 24, 65, 116, 154, 170, 171, 296, 303, 423, 430, 523, 548, 549
Clemenceau, Georges, 28, 224, 225, 226, 227, 230, 267, 268, 269, 271, 274, 321, 359, 403, 405, 407, 408, 415, 416, 424–5, 426, 427, 430, 431, 440, 442–3, 445–6, 448–9, 504–5, 517, 530–31, 554
Clerk, Sir George Russell, 109, 241
Cockerill, Brigadier-General Sir George Kynaston, 197, 221, 222, 224, 229, 230, 231, 237
'Committee of Unity and Progress' (*İttihat ve Terakki Cemiyeti*), 19, 20, 217
Connaught, Prince Arthur (William Patrick Albert) of Saxe-Coburg-Gotha, Duke of
Connaught and Strathearn, 97, 268, 273, 281
Constantine I of Greece (née de Schleswig-Holstein-Sonderburg-Glücksburg), King of the Hellenes, 47, 48, 49, 51, 52, 55, 57, 58, 59, 62, 66, 67, 68, 69, 72, 75, 76, 79, 80, 84, 85, 87, 89, 91, 92, 94, 96, 97, 104, 113, 115, 119, 121, 125, 130, 133, 134, 135, 138, 139, 140, 141, 147, 148, 149, 151, 153, 154, 155, 159, 160, 161, 172, 182, 183, 184, 185, 200, 206, 213, 499, 500
Coolidge, Archibald Carey, 446, 558
Coolidge, (John) Calvin, 559, 560

Cordonnier, General Victor Louis Émilien, 50
Corkran, Major-General Sir Charles Edward, 189, 190, 192, 282
Cornwall, General Sir James Handyside Marshall, 316, 317
Cowans, General Sir John Stephen, 44, 56
Cowdray, Sir Weetman Dickinson Pearson, 1st Viscount, 211, 241
Cowling, Maurice, 5, 22, 23
Cox, Brigadier-General Edgar William, 212, 213, 234, 268, 305, 308
Crackanthorpe, Dayrell Montague, 192
Crane, Charles Richard, 192
Creasy, Sir Edward Shepherd, 26
Crowe, Sir Eyre Alexander Wichart Barby, 239, 409, 413, 416, 418, 419, 425, 432, 434, 438, 493, 499, 501, 513, 514, 560, 572
Culcer, General Ioan, 52
Cunha, Gastão da, 534
Cuninghame, Brigadier-General Sir Thomas Andrew Alexander Montgomery, 119
Cunliffe-Owen, Lieutenant-Colonel Frederick, 250
Curtis, Lionel George, 420
Curzon, George Nathaniel, 1st Marquess Curzon of Kedleston, 116, 117, 205, 230, 280, 301, 303, 319, 510, 518, 547, 557, 568–9, 571
Czechoslovakia, 32, 118, 126, 178, 274, 282, 283, 287, 289, 293, 294, 301, 302, 310, 314, 355, 433, 434, 437
Czernin, Ottokar (Theobald Otto Maria) Count Czernin von und zu Chudenitz, 203, 267, 269, 270

Danglis, General Panagiotis, 47
d'Annunzio, Gabriele, 306, 468, 481, 526
Davies, David, 1st Baron, 43, 84, 120, 165, 169, 218, 238, 246
Davies, (Sir) John Thomas, 431
Day, Clive Hart, 403
Delvino, Sulejman Bej, 435

Denikin, Lieutenant-General Anton Ivanovich, 307
Denis, Ernest, 126
Department of Information, 145, 170–71, 253–4, 257
Depew, Chauncey, 538
Derby, Edward George Villiers Stanley, 17th Earl of, 218, 219, 232, 247, 248, 268, 304
d'Espèrey, General Louis Félix Marie François Franchet, 310, 325, 385, 407, 433, 507
Devonshire, Spencer Compton Cavendish, 8th Duke of, 536, 550
Devonshire, Victor Christian William Cavendish, 9th Duke of, 184, 232
De Valera, Éamon, 546
Diamandy, Constantin, 455
Dimitrijević, General Aleksandar, 488
Diomedes, Alexandros, 91, 96, 109, 115
Dmowski, Roman Stanisław, 176, 177, 182, 183, 186, 190
Đorđević, Dr. Vladan, 342
Doherty, Charles Joseph, 539
Dokić, General Đuro, 385
Donop, Major-General Sir Stanley Brenton von, 531
Dousmanis, Admiral Sofoklis, 48, 49
Dožić, Dr. Gavrilo, 460
Drašković, Milorad, 465
Drummond, Sir (James) Eric, 16th Earl of Perth, 104, 239, 526
Du Cane, General Sir John (Philip), 295
Dugdale, Blanche Elizabeth Campbell (née Balfour), 90
Duhand-Viel, Vice-Admiral Georges Edmond Just, 338
Durham, (Mary) Edith, 360, 502
Du Vallon, Hubert Caliste de Jacobi, 108

Egerton, Major-General Granville George Algernon Egerton, 208, 237
Eisenmann, Louis, 126
Elliot, Sir Francis Edmund Hugh, 49, 62, 69, 76, 94, 102, 103, 119, 121,

125, 133, 135, 143, 146, 149, 153, 154–5, 182
Embeirikos, Stamatis, 247
Enver Pasha, Ismail, 217
Erzberger, Matthias, 170
Everson, Major-General William G., 337
Eves, Reginald Grenville, 252

Falkenhayn, General Erich von, 53, 65, 178
Ferdinand (Maximilian Karl Leopold Maria) I of Saxe-Coburg-Gotha, King of Bulgaria, 114, 130, 287, 320, 321, 363, 490
Ferrero, Lieutenant-General Giacinto, 306
Findlay, Sir Mansfield de Cardonnel, 302, 303
Finlayson, General Sir Robert Gordon, 204, 205
Fisher, Herbert Albert Laurens, xi, 1, 2, 73, 74, 112, 208, 431, 495–6, 497–8, 513, 523, 535, 538, 540, 541, 542–3, 546
Fisher, William Hayes, 1st Baron Downham, 256
Fitzgerald, Captain Oswald, 63, 531
Fitzmaurice, Gerald Henry, 66, 109, 129, 130, 156, 205, 227, 281
Flanders, Prince Charles Théodore Henri Antoine Meinrad of Saxe-Coburg-Gotha, Count of, 136
Foch, Marshal Ferdinand, 143, 178, 210, 263, 266, 277, 290, 291, 295, 297, 298, 304, 310, 320, 407, 426, 429, 435, 449, 492, 505
Ford, Ford Madox (née Ford Hermann Hueffer), 127
Foreign Office, x, 2, 3, 87, 97, 110, 290
Foreign Office Political Intelligence Department (PID), xi, 3
Forgách von Ghymes und Gács, Johann Count, 244
Forster, Major Edward Seymour, 338
Forster, William Edward, 550
Fournet, Vice-admiral Louis Dartige du, 63, 68, 73, 91, 96

France, 11, 17, 42, 43, 44, 46, 47, 49, 56, 64, 66, 80, 84, 87, 88, 93, 94, 98, 101, 111, 115, 116, 117, 119, 121, 125, 137, 138, 143, 149, 151, 154, 157, 161, 162, 176, 177, 195, 200, 204, 209, 210, 214, 221, 224, 226, 227, 234, 236, 238, 244, 249, 260, 263, 265, 267, 268, 274, 276, 277, 280, 282, 283, 284, 286, 287, 298, 301, 302, 303, 304, 305, 309, 314, 321, 334, 336, 339, 340, 375, 385, 392, 394, 412, 416, 417, 425, 428, 431, 432, 446, 496, 498, 504, 508, 509, 512, 513, 518, 520, 521, 530, 534, 536, 537, 540, 541, 564, 566, 570
Frangulis, Antoine F., 526
Franz Ferdinand von Habsburg, Archduke of Austria-Este, 66, 83, 144, 181, 361, 505
Franz Joseph I of Habsburg-Lorraine, Emperor of Austria, Apostolic King of Hungary, 59, 106, 183, 333, 363, 387
Frashëri, Midhat (Bey), 516, 522, 526
Frederick II of Hohenzollern, King of Prussia, 9, 10, 11, 16, 17, 18, 26, 225, 269
Frederick William of Hohenzollern, Elector of Brandenburg-Prussia, 9
French, Lieutenant-Colonel Charles Newenham, 241
French, Field Marshal Sir John, Earl French of Ypres, 253
Friedjung, Dr. Heinrich, 183, 244, 335

Galitsyn, Prince Nikolai Dmitri'evich, 118
Galli, Carlo, 515
Galliéni, General Joseph Simon, 80, 87
Gambetta, General François Léon Prosper Jouinot-, 346
Garza, Venustiano Carranza de la, 241
Gasparri, Cardinal Pietro, 170, 241, 272, 275
Gauchet, Admiral Dominique-Marie, 73, 103

Geary, Arthur Bernard, 108
Geddes, Sir Auckland Campbell-, 503
Geddes, Sir Eric Campbell-, 56, 225
Gennadius, Ioannis, 97, 206
Germany, 9, 10, 11, 17, 26, 43, 49, 51, 74, 76, 77, 78, 79, 88, 93, 94, 99, 100, 101, 102, 104, 108, 111, 112, 113, 118, 120, 125, 126, 131, 134, 135, 137, 144, 159, 160, 161, 166, 168, 170, 173, 176, 177, 179, 184, 185, 186, 187, 188, 193, 194, 195, 196, 197, 198, 201, 205, 206, 207, 208, 209, 210, 212, 213, 215, 221, 223, 224, 225, 226, 227, 233, 234, 236, 262, 263, 265, 267, 275, 282, 294, 295, 296, 300, 301, 303, 304, 312, 317, 318, 331, 334, 335, 399, 408, 416, 423, 425, 428, 429, 430, 441, 484, 486, 496, 497, 499, 502, 504, 510, 519, 521, 525, 537, 554, 556, 563, 564, 572
Gërmenji, Themistokli, 453
Gibbons, John, 474, 475
Giolitti, Giovanni, 501, 502
Gladstone, William Ewart, 4, 6, 46, 523, 524, 534, 535, 536, 548, 550
Gleichen, Major-General Count (later Lord) (Albert) Edward (Wilfred), 145, 171, 253, 254, 257
Glyn, Elinor, 483
Goethe, Johann Wolfgang von, 19
Goldfinch, Sir Arthur Horne, 314
Gooch, George Peabody, 3, 21, 33
Gordon, Major-General Lochinvar Alexander Charles, 337, 338
Görgey de Görgő et Toporcz, Artúr, 14, 51
Gorton, Brigadier-General Reginald St. George, 454, 464
Gounaris, Dimitrios, 200, 213
Gouraud, General Henri Joseph Eugène, 298–9
Granville, Castalia Rosaline Campbell, Countess of, 555
Granville, Granville George Leveson-Gower, 2nd Earl of, 556

Granville, Granville George Leveson-Gower, 3rd Earl of, 138, 213, 235, 281, 282, 288, 297
Greece, 27, 39, 40, 41, 46, 47, 48, 49, 53, 54, 57, 59, 64, 67, 71, 74, 75, 76, 79, 85, 87, 89, 90, 92, 94, 95, 96, 100, 102, 103, 104, 105, 109, 111, 113, 115, 116, 120, 121, 124, 125, 133, 134, 135, 136, 138, 141, 143, 144, 146, 149, 153, 155, 156, 159, 161, 162, 170, 172, 183, 185, 192, 201, 206, 211, 212, 216, 217, 235, 247, 255, 265, 281, 288, 289, 290, 297, 321, 417, 495, 497, 500, 513, 518, 520, 529, 573
Greene, Lieutenant-Colonel Sir (Walter) Raymond, 273
Gregory, Captain George, 382
Grey, Sir Edward, 1st Viscount Grey of Fallodon, x, 39, 42, 69, 70, 71, 72, 73, 74, 75, 76, 79, 85, 86, 184, 522, 538, 562, 571
Grigorescu, General Eremia, 62
Gruić, Dr. Slavko J., 571, 572
Guillaumat, General Marie Louis Adolphe, 234
Guillemin, Jean Marie Auguste René, 90, 143
Gulland, John William, 285
Gulli, Captain Tommaso, 468, 469
Gurko, General Vasily Iosifovich, 176
Gustavus Adolphus, King of Sweden, 10
Guthrie, W.K.C., 35
Gwynne, Howell Arthur Keir, 110

Haakon VII (née Christian Frederik Carl Georg Valdemar Axel of Schlesig-Holstein-Sonderburg-Glücksburg), King of Norway, 302, 303, 565
Haig, Field Marshal Sir Douglas (later 1st Earl), 55, 102, 124, 204, 209, 234, 235, 237, 238, 246, 247, 249, 257, 261, 276, 305, 435, 504, 505
Haldane, John Scott, 567, 568

Haldane, Richard Burdon, 1st Viscount Haldane of Cloan, 72
Halifax, Edward Frederick Lindley Wood, 1st Earl of, 572, 573
Halifax, George Savile, Viscount (later 1st Marquess of), 4, 41
Hall, Hubert, 300
Hallwood, Bertrand L., 35
Halstead, Albert, 142
Hankey, Captain Maurice Pascal Alers, 1st Baron Hankey, 205, 286, 405, 406, 427, 438, 440, 491, 501, 505
Happold, Captain Frederick Crossfield, 305
Harding, Warren Gamaliel, 504, 530
Hardinge, Sir Charles Hardinge, 1st Baron Hardinge of Penshurst, 97, 117, 191, 231, 239, 241, 401, 435, 503, 513
Harington, General Sir Charles Harington, 271
Harmsworth, Cecil Bisshopp, 1st Baron, 502, 503, 505, 506
Harvard University, 9
Harvey, Colonel George Brinton McClellan, 522
Haskins, Charles Homer, 402, 558
Headlam(-Morley), Sir James Wycliffe, x, 2, 3, 34, 253
Heard, Captain William Beauchamp, 108
Heard, R.G., 35
Heathcote, Walter John, 109
Heaton-Armstrong, Captain Duncan, 77
Henderson, Arthur, 147, 175, 176, 196, 230, 303, 543
Henniker, Colonel Alan Major, 412
Henrys, General Paul Prosper, 342
Herbert, Hon. Aubrey Nigel Henry Molyneux, 92, 97
Hertling, Georg Friedrich Count von, 269
Heywood, Lieutenant-Colonel Thomas George Gordon, 326
Hindenburg, Field Marshal General Paul Ludwig Hans Anton von Beneckendorff und von, 101, 167, 170, 317

Hintze, Admiral Paul von, 112, 303
Hitchcock, Gilbert Monnell, 562
Hitler, Adolf, 32, 56
Hofmeyer, Jan Hendrik the younger, 567
Hoffman, Malvina, 560
Hope-Vere, Edward James, 463
Hornbeck, Stanley Kuhl, 558
Horne, Sir Robert Stevenson, 1st Viscount Horne of Slamannan, 544
Horthy de Nagybánya, Vice-Admiral Miklós, 507, 508
House, (Colonel) Edward Mandell, 517
Howard, Sir Esme William, 1st Baron Howard of Penrith, 560
Howell, Brigadier-General Philip, 232
Howorth, Sir Rupert Beswicke, 523, 524
Hoyos, (Ludwig) Alexander (Georg) Count von, 121,
Hudson, Manley Ottmer, 558
Hughes, Charles Evans Sr., 552
Hughes, Sir Samuel, 97
Hughes, William 'Billy' Morris, 152, 286, 299, 424, 428, 429
Hungarian Revolution, 1848–49, 23
Hungary, 12, 13, 14, 15, 19, 26, 76, 110, 124, 168, 178, 182, 212, 221, 287, 348, 408, 409, 416, 421, 433, 435, 451, 452, 453, 506, 508
Hurst, Sir Cecil James Barrington, 297, 298, 300, 517, 522, 534, 536, 540
Hymans, Paul Louis Adrien Henri, 542, 546, 553

Iliescu, Brigadier-General Dumitru, 88, 98, 99, 103, 107, 123, 131, 134, 135, 150
Imperiali di Francavilla, Guglielmo, marchese, 404, 407, 528, 543
Ionescu, Take, 98, 122, 123, 131, 139, 175, 240

Jagow, Gottlieb von, 178, 262
Jan Sobieski III, King of Poland, 12
Janin, General Pierre-Thiébaut-Charles-Maurice, 60, 111

Janković, General Radivoje, 488
Jászi, Dr. Oszkár, 231
Jeglič, Prince-Bishop Anton Bonaventura, 340, 351
Jellicoe, Admiral Sir John Rushworth, 1st Earl, 70, 71, 127, 225
Joffre, Marshal Joseph Jacques Césaire, 73, 80, 87, 88, 143
Johnson, Douglas Wilson, 411, 413, 418, 426, 427, 439, 446
Jokai, Mór (Maurus), 11, 12, 52, 331, 449, 461
Jones, Sir Henry, 209
Jones, Dr. Thomas (Tom), 2, 124
Jones, (William) Kennedy, 238, 246
Jonnart, Charles Célestin Auguste, 103, 149, 152, 153, 154, 155, 160, 182
Joseph August Viktor Klemens Maria, Field Marshal Archduke of Austria, Prince of Hungary and Bohemia, 507
Joseph II of Habsburg, Emperor of Austria, King of Hungary, 14, 15, 16
Jovanović, General Branko, 464
Jovanović-Pižon, Jovan M., 83, 91, 152, 172, 202, 268, 317, 363

Kalafatović, General Danilo, 450
Kaledin, Aleksei Maksimovich, 214
Kalogeropoulos, Nikolaos, 58, 115
Karađorđević Princess Jelena (Helen), 488
Karl (Franz Joseph Ludwig Hubert Georg Otto Marie) I of Habsburg-Lorraine, last Habsburg emperor, 53, 118, 213, 266, 271, 272, 274, 287, 350, 404, 505, 506, 507, 508
Karl Stephan Eugen Viktor Felix Maria of Austria, Archduke, 177
Karnebeek, Jonkheer Herman Adriaan van, 533, 534
Kemp-Welch, Maurice, 132
Kenworthy, Lieutenant-Commander Joseph Montague, 506

Kerensky, Alexander Fyodorovich, 122, 163, 171, 173, 174, 188, 189, 190, 191, 202, 207
Kerr, Philip Henry, 11th Marquess of Lothian, 74, 84, 147, 178, 179, 185, 199, 231, 257, 267, 270, 315, 401, 406, 422, 493, 508, 512, 530
Keyes, Admiral of the Fleet Roger John Brownlow, 1st Baron, 306, 318, 319
Keynes, John Maynard, Baron, 517, 553
King, Joseph, 76
King's College, Cambridge, 3
Kirke, Major-General Walter Mervyn St. George, 269
Kisch, Brigadier-General Frederick Hermann, 399
Klaessig, Emil jr., 101
Klotz, Louis-Lucien, 564
Knox, Lieutenant-General Sir Alfred William Fortescue, 277
Knox, Philander, 562
Koht, Halvdan, 565
Kolchak, Aleksandr Vasili'evich, 422
Konstantinović, Natalija, 501
Kornilov, General Lavr Georgi'evich, 174, 188
Korošec, Dr. Anton Korošec, 335
Kountouriotis, Admiral Pavlos, 47, 69, 149
Kryeziu, Ceno Beg, 459
Kühlmann, Richard von, 236, 262
Kun, Béla (née Kuhn), 433, 434, 436
Ku Wei-chün (Gù Wěijūn) (V.K. Wellington Koo), 528, 533
Kvaternik, Marshal Slavko, 393, 394

Laffan, Robert George Dalrymple, 329
Lamb, Sir Harry Harling, 108
Lammasch, Heinrich, 266
Lampros, Spyridon, 47, 82
Lansdowne, Henry Charles Keith Petty-Fitzmaurice, 5th Marquess of, 184, 215, 318
Lansdowne, Lieutenant-Colonel Henry William Edmund Petty-Fitzmaurice, Earl of Kerry, 6th Marquess of, 215

Lansing, Robert, 278, 408, 409, 410, 414, 418, 422, 425, 434, 436, 438–9, 443, 444, 445–6, 559
Laroche, Jules, 515
Lavery, Sir John, 549
Law, Andrew Bonar, 110, 115, 205, 272, 273, 549
Lawrence, David, 559
Lawrence, General Hon. Sir Herbert (Alexander), 276
League of Nations, 28, 30, 31, 221, 224, 227, 228, 229, 230, 405, 406, 407, 427, 430, 436, 488, 495, 513, 519, 521, 524, 541
Learned Hand, Billings, 562
Lee, Arthur Hamilton, Baron Lee of Fareham, 544
Lee, Sir Sidney, 535
Leeper, (Alexander Wigram) Allen, 145, 254, 404, 413, 419, 426, 427
Leeper, Sir Reginald Wilding Allen, 254
Lehár, Colonel Anton (Antal) Baron von, 508
Lenin, Vladimir Ilyich (née Ulyanov), 122, 207, 209, 306, 455, 456
Leopold II of Habsburg, Emperor of Austria, King of Hungary, 14
LeRond, General Edouard Louis Henri, 411, 412, 421
Letić, Bishop Dr. Gheorghe, 346, 357, 469
Liberal party, 5, 285
Lichnowsky, Prince Karl Max, 74, 178, 262
Lindley, Hon. Sir Francis Oswald, 435, 503
Lloyd, Commander Edward William, 292
Lloyd George, David, 1st Earl Lloyd George of Dwyfor, x, 1, 2, 6, 27, 28, 42, 54, 56, 65, 68, 69, 70, 71, 72, 73, 74, 75, 76, 77, 79, 81, 83, 84, 110, 111, 112, 115, 117, 119, 122, 124, 126, 128, 129, 130, 136, 137, 138, 139, 141, 142, 143, 147, 150, 152, 165, 169, 174, 175, 176, 177, 178, 179, 180, 181, 185, 190, 196, 199, 205, 208, 210, 211, 215, 216, 218, 221, 223, 224, 225–6, 230, 231, 239, 240, 246, 247, 248, 249, 250, 251, 253, 256, 257, 258, 263, 264, 267, 268, 269, 270, 273, 275, 276, 277, 280, 286, 287, 289, 292, 298, 299, 300, 301, 304, 307, 308, 315, 319, 359, 399, 400, 402, 404, 407, 410–11, 415, 416, 417, 422, 424, 425, 426, 429, 430, 431, 433, 434, 435, 439, 442, 443, 491, 492, 495, 500, 501, 504, 512, 521, 523, 528, 529, 530, 539, 564
Lloyd-Jones, Brevet Major William 193
Lobit, General Paul Joseph Jean Hector de, 453
Locke, John, 15
Lodge, Henry Cabot, 562
Lodge, Sir Richard, 564
Long, Sir Walter Hume, 1st Viscount Long of Wraxall, 165, 300
Lord, Robert Howard, 402
Loti, Pierre (pseud. Julien Viaud), 483
Louis XIV de Bourbon, King of France, 11, 28, 73, 112, 348.
Loveday, Alexander, 292
Low, Sir Frederick, 56
Lubbock, Roy, 35
Ludendorff, General Erich Friedrich Wilhelm, 101, 167, 173, 177, 212, 213, 283, 290
Luther, Dr. Martin, 10, 236, 244
Lvov, Prince Georgy Yevgenyevich, 204
Lyapchev, Andrey Tasev, 313
Lyautey, General (Louis) Hubert (Gonzalve), 81, 87, 143, 507
Lynch, Arthur Alfred, 125
Lytton, Neville Stephen Bulwer-, 3rd Earl of Lytton, 124

McAdoo, William Gibbs Jr., 279
McCabe, Joseph Martin, 349
Macdonald, (James) Ramsay, 175
Macdonogh, Lieutenant-General Sir George Mark Watson, 77, 156, 166, 193, 235, 240. 267, 293, 308, 314

MacEwen, Brigadier-General Douglas Lilburn, 237
Mackensen, Field Marshal (Anton Ludwig) August von, 53, 65, 203, 205, 242, 347
Magna Carta, 1215, 15
Maister, General Rudolf, 393
Maklakov, Vasili Alekse'evich, 443
Maksimović, Colonel Voja, 214, 337
Malinov, Aleksandar Pavlov, 287
Mance, Brigadier-General Harry Osborne, 412, 414, 418
Manos, Aspasia, Consort of King Alexander of the Hellenes, 281
Mantoux, Paul, 442, 492
Marczali, Henrik, 12, 14, 15, 16, 212
Marie (née Marie Alexandra Victoria, Princess of Edinburgh), Queen of Romania, 245
Markagjon, Kapidan Gjon, 476, 527
Martino, Giacomo de, 409, 420, 423, 432, 513
Massey, William ('Farmer Bill') Ferguson, 428
Masterson, Captain Thomas Samuel, 175, 192, 205, 219
Maurice, Major-General Sir Frederick Barton, 68, 93, 102, 132, 204, 218, 225, 246, 250, 267, 272, 273, 275, 276, 277, 280, 312
Maxse, Leopold James, 66, 184, 230
Maxwell, General Sir John Grenfell, 250
Menini, Captain Giulio, 375
Mercier, Cardinal Désiré-Félicien-François-Joseph, 272, 340
Mercouris, Georgios S., 49
Meštrović, Ivan, 336
Metaxas, General Ioannis, 48, 49
Metternich zur Gracht, Paul Count Wolff, 410, 411
Mezes, Sidney Edward, 561
Michaelis, Dr. Georg, 167, 168, 185
Mihalović, Antun, 336, 349
Mijatović, Čedomilj, 157
Mijuskovic, Mirko M., 356

Mikes, Bishop Count János, 507
Milan I. Obrenović, King of Serbia, 157
Miles, General Sherman, 393
Militza, Queen of Montenegro (née Duchess Jutta Auguste Charlotte Jutta Alexandra Georgina Adophine of Mecklenburg-Strelitz), 106
Millo, Admiral Emilio, 372, 376
Milne, Field Marshal Sir George Francis, 146, 311, 312, 313, 492
Milner, Sir Alfred, 1st Viscount, 78, 86, 92, 104, 116, 120, 130, 137, 182, 196, 205, 214, 225, 249, 268, 272, 276, 280, 284, 286, 291, 293, 299, 301, 306, 307, 309, 319, 322, 428, 429, 430, 491, 504, 505, 544
Milutinović, Generalagutin, 354
Milyukov, Pavel Nikola'evich, 122, 126
Mišić, *Vojvoda* (Field Marshal) Živojin, 50, 148, 313, 329, 344, 450
Mişu, Nicolae, 123, 263
Mitford, Captain the Hon. Bertram Thomas Carlyle Ogilvy Freeman-, 3rd Baron Redesdale, 368
Moltke, Lieutenant-General Hellmuth Johannes Ludiwg von (the younger), 178
Mond, Sir Alfred Moritz, 1st Lord Melchett, 72
Montagu, Edwin Samuel, 169, 195, 205, 217, 421, 429
Morgenthau, Henry Sr., 152, 156
Morley, John, Viscount Morley of Blackburn, 153, 223, 265, 529, 571–2
Moschopoulos, Lieutenant-General Konstantinos, 49
Motta, Giuseppe, 496, 533, 542
Mühlon, Dr. Johann Wilhelm, 262
Müller, Hermann, 442, 443
Mundelein, Cardinal George William, 288
Murat, Joachim, 6th Prince, 342
Murphy, Dominic I., 321

Murray, Alexander William Charles Oliphant, 1st Baron Murray of Elibank, 50
Murray, General Sir Archibald James, 250
Murray, George Gilbert Aimé, 535
Murray, General Sir James (Wolfe), 43
Mustapha IV Osmanli, Ottoman sultan, 20
Myres, Sir John Linton, 265

Namier, Sir Lewis Bernstein (née Ludwik Niemirowski), 3, 254, 287
Nansen, Fridtjof, 539, 542
Napoleon Bonaparte, Emperor of the French, 28, 40, 81, 136, 191, 431, 529, 533, 545, 570
Nedić, General Milan, 469
Neklyudov, Anatoly Vasil'evich, 89
Newcastle, Thomas Pelham-Holles, 1st Duke of, 8, 13
Newton, Thomas Wodehouse Legh, 2nd Baron, 510
Nicholas, Prince of Romania, 265
Nicholas II Romanov, Tsar of All the Russias, 86, 566, 567
Nicolson, Sir Harold George, x, 278, 417, 418, 501, 503, 526
Ninčić, Dr. Momčilo, 464
Ninković, Archimandrite Leontije, 460
Nitti, Francesco Saverio Vincenzo de Paola, 317, 486, 487, 502
Nivelle, General Robert Georges, 73, 81, 87, 102, 142, 143
Noli, Theofan Stilian, 526, 527, 528
Norman, Sir Henry, 129
Norman, Herman Cameron, 425
Northcliffe, Alfred Charles William Harmsworth, Baron (later 1st Viscount), 54, 56, 69, 74, 147, 211, 230, 238, 239, 246, 254, 255, 257, 258, 264, 267, 281, 290, 294, 400, 403, 404, 411, 503, 532
Northumberland, Alan Ian Percy, Earl Percy, 8th Duke of, 128, 149, 213, 230, 236, 247, 254, 268, 269, 271, 286, 291, 295, 300, 301

Norton-Griffiths, Lieutenant-Colonel Sir John 'Empire Jack', 78, 86, 107, 120, 136, 273

O'Connor, Thomas Power, 545
Ogilvie, Alan Grant, 3, 427
Oliphant, Sir Lancelot, 297
Oman, Sir Charles William Chadwick, 118, 126
Orlando, Vittorio Emanuele, 224, 274, 403, 417, 424, 431, 446, 564
Otto I, German Emperor, 26

Pacelli, Cardinal Eugenio Marìa Giuseppe Giovanni (later Pope Pius XII), 185
Paderewski, Ignacy Jan, 425, 428, 443, 496
Page, Walter Hines, 553, 563
Painlevé, Paul, 129, 209, 492
Paléologue, Maurice Georges, 201
Palmerston, Henry John Temple, Viscount, 23, 529, 548
Pankhurst, Dame Christabel Harriette, 233
Pankhurst, Estelle Sylvia, 232, 233
Panouse, Major-General (Artus Henri) Louis Vicomte de La, 87, 94, 99, 213, 249, 258, 259, 266, 270, 288, 290, 308
Pariani, Alberto, 426
Parker, Alwyn, 251, 262
Parry, Sir (Charles) Hubert (Hastings), 42
Pašić, Nikola P., 144, 148, 170, 181, 182, 212, 290, 308, 315, 318, 320, 490
Pavelić, Dr. Ante, 335
Pavičić, Ante Tresić, 333, 334, 335
Peck, Mary Allen Hulbert, 562
Penfield, Frederic Courtland, 142
Percy, Lord Eustace Sutherland Campbell, 1st Baron Percy of Newcastle, 278
Pershing, General John Joseph, 224, 268
Pešić, General Petar T., 200, 201, 324, 347, 467
Pétain, Marshal Henri Philippe Omer, 142, 504, 505
Petar I Karađorđević, King of Serbia, 317

Peterhouse, 4, 24, 25, 35, 305, 411, 461, 483
Petrović-Njegoš, Prince Danilo Aleksandar, 105
Petrović-Njegoš, Prince Michael, 501
Petrović-Njegoš, Prince Mirko Dimitri, 99
Petrović-Njegoš, Nikola I Mirkov, King of Montenegro, 55, 84, 99, 105, 106, 353, 356, 360, 366, 367, 368, 386, 395, 472, 473, 483, 489, 493, 499
Petrovic-Njegoš, Princess Xenia (Ksenija), 106, 460
Phillips, Brigadier-General George Fraser, 79, 182
Phillips, Sir Perceival, 366
Pichon, Stéphen, 225, 413, 419, 443
Pickthorn, Sir Kenneth, 24
Picton-Bagge, Sir John, 156
Pilling, John Robert, 226
Pilsudski, General Jozef Klemens, 173, 177, 186, 187, 243
Pitt, William (the Elder), Earl of Chatham, 5, 8
Pitt, William (the Younger), 529, 548
Pius IX (née Giovanni Maria Mastai-Ferretti), Pope, 275
Plamenac, Jovan Simonov, 365
Plunkett, Lieutenant-Colonel Edward Abadie, 154, 351
Poincaré, Raymond Nicolas Landry, 271, 506
Pokrovsky, Mikhail Nikole'evich, 566, 567
Poland, 13, 14, 18, 27, 43, 44, 46, 59, 61, 66, 101, 102, 114, 122, 124, 168, 173, 176, 177, 178, 183, 185, 186, 190, 194, 200, 201, 208, 209, 223, 236, 240, 243, 259, 283, 399, 428, 429, 436, 496, 521, 542, 555
Politis, Nikolaos, 47, 57, 58, 134, 184, 213
Polivanov, General Alexei Andre'evich, 43, 220
Poljak, Franjo, 461
Popović, General Damjan, 99
Popović, Jovo, 356, 365, 420
Postan, Munia, 35

Prezan, General Constantin, 52, 73, 117, 123, 129
Pribićević, Milan, 335, 389
Prince (Friedrich) Wilhelm (Victor August Ernst) von Hohenzollern, German Crown Prince, 567
Prothero, Sir George Walter, 2, 3, 25, 251, 254
Protić, Stojan M., 344
Prussia, 9, 10, 17, 167, 183, 208, 216, 411, 428, 481, 487, 504, 525
Putnik, Field Marshal Radomir, 144, 148

Quarterly Review, 2, 251

Radcliffe, Brigadier-General Sir Charles Delmé-, 264
Radcliffe, Lieutenant-General Sir Percy Pollexfen de Blaquiere, 267, 268, 269, 284
Radić, Stjepan, 389
Radoslavov, Vasil, 114, 206
Radović, Andrija, 105, 357
Rainer, Admiral Guglielmo, 337, 338
Rakovski, Krastyo (also Christian) (née Krastyo Georgiev Stanchev), 163
Rangabé, Alexander Rizo, 511, 512
Ranke, Leopold von, 8
Rasputin, Grigori Yefimovich, 124
Rawlinson, General Sir Henry Seymour, 1st Baron, 263
Reading, Rufus Daniel Isaacs, 1st Marquess of, 210, 289, 544
Reddaway, William Fiddian, 10, 11, 16
Redlich, Josef, xi, 7, 212
Reiss, Dr. Rodolphe Archibald, 22, 350
Rendel, Sir George William, 82
Renouvin, Pierre, 566
Repington, Lieutenant-Colonel Charles À Court, 130, 237, 246–7
Restrepo, Carlos Eugenio, 542
Ribot, Alexandre-Félix-Joseph, 137, 138, 152, 154
Riddell, Sir George Allardice, 1st Baron Riddell of Walton Heath, 544

Rizov, Dimitar Hristov, 108
Robertson, Field Marshal Sir William, 64, 65, 76, 83, 126, 166, 197, 204, 210, 213, 233, 238, 246, 247, 249–50, 251, 263, 268, 271, 272, 276, 280, 286, 298, 300, 435, 492
Rodd, Sir (James) Rennell, 1st Baron Rennell of Rodd, 153, 293, 538
Romanov, Prince Ivan Konstantinovich, 488
Roosevelt, Nicholas, 563
Roosevelt, Theodore, 9, 198, 212
Roth, Dr. Otto, 347
Rothermere, Harold Sidney Harmsworth, Baron (later 1st Viscount), 56, 404
Rowell, Newton Wesley, 495
Runciman, Walter, 1st Viscount Runciman of Doxford, 32, 303
Rupprecht Maria Luitpold Ferdinand von Wittelsbach, Field Marshal, Crown Prince of Bavaria, 283
Russell, Sir (Odo William) Theo(philus Villiers), 104
Russell, Colonel Richard Tyler, 193
Russia, 3, 17, 42, 43, 44, 46, 47, 55, 60, 64, 66, 67, 77, 81, 83, 85, 86, 87, 88, 90, 97, 99, 101, 108, 109, 114, 115, 118, 120, 121, 124, 125, 129, 130, 131, 134, 142, 143, 149, 154, 156, 157, 160, 168, 174, 175, 176, 177, 182, 183, 185, 186, 190, 191, 192, 198, 200, 202, 205, 207, 209, 214, 218, 220, 221, 226, 227, 228, 229, 232, 233, 236, 237, 240, 259, 260, 262, 304, 306, 309, 315, 319, 435, 444, 455, 486, 487, 490, 491, 497, 503, 514, 522, 543, 564, 570, 571
Russky, General Nikolai Vladimirovich, 174
Rycroft, Major-General Sir William Henry, 115

Sackville-West, Charles, 4th Baron Sackville, 266
St Clair Stobart, Mabel Anne, 79
Sakharov, General Vladimir Viktorovich, 65
Salis, Count Sir John Francis Charles de, 170, 272
Sams, H.S., 35
Sandes, Sergeant-Major Flora, 331, 345
Sarrail, General Maurice-Paul-Emmanuel, 39, 41, 47, 50, 55, 60m 62, 75, 79, 81, 84, 90, 91, 92, 99, 102, 109, 119, 120, 121, 125, 138, 143, 146, 147, 148, 149, 151, 152, 154, 162, 172, 181, 183, 216, 222, 227, 320
Satow, Sir Ernest Mason, 24, 27, 128
Saunders, George, 253
Savinkov, Boris, 307
Saxe-Weimar, Bernard of, 10
Sazonov, Sergei Dimitrievich, 43, 148
Scanlon, Brigadier-General Martin Francis, 353, 354, 368
Schiff, Jacob Henry (nee Jakob Heinrich), 106
Schmitt, Bernadotte, 566
Schwarzenberger, Georg, 31
Scialoja, Vittorio, 486, 487
Scott, Sir Walter, 12
Seely, Major-General John Edward Bernard, 1st Baron Mottistone, 296
Selim III Osmanli, Ottoman sultan, 20
Serbia, x, 18, 21, 22, 26, 27, 66, 67, 71, 74, 79, 92, 101, 105, 106, 109, 114–15, 120, 127, 130, 144, 147, 151, 156, 157, 159, 172, 177, 178, 179, 180, 187, 191, 192, 193, 216, 218, 223, 225, 227, 231, 244, 255, 256, 259, 264, 281, 290, 302, 304, 308, 311, 315, 317, 320, 321, 325, 327, 331, 333, 339, 344, 350, 358, 367, 368, 400, 428, 447, 449, 452, 455, 456, 491, 495, 497, 503, 525, 543, 553, 566
Serreqi, Archbishop Jacob (Jakë), 474
Seton-Watson, Robert William, 3, 13, 20, 22, 23, 65, 145, 253, 254, 258, 264, 308, 404
Sexton, Thomas, 547, 548

Seymour, Charles, 402
Shcherbachev, General Dmitri Gregorevich, 202
Sherborne School, 3
Sidebotham, Herbert, 301
Sienkiewicz, Hendryk (Adam Aleksander Pius), 11, 12, 61
Simović, General Dušan T., 352, 353
Singh, Maharaja Sir Ganga, 443
Skouloudis, Stephanos, 39, 40, 57, 58, 200, 201
Skrzyński, Ladislaus Ritter von Skrzynno-, 257, 270
Slovakia, 12, 13
Smodlaka, Josip, 339, 369, 370
Smuts, General Jan Christiaan, 125, 152, 195, 196–7, 221, 227, 231, 254, 257, 270, 299, 300–301, 308, 316, 319, 404, 428, 429, 537, 559, 567–8
Socec, General Alexandru, 107
Sonnino, Baron Sidney Costantino, 28, 138, 149, 151, 153, 154, 160, 226, 227, 274, 284, 288, 293, 321, 388, 408–9, 414, 415, 416, 419, 424, 432, 436–8, 439–41, 443
Sophie (Dorothea Ulrike Alice), Princess of Prussia, Queen of the Hellenes, 54
Soveral, Luis Maria Augusto Pinto, marquês de, 256
Spalajković, Dr. Miroslav, 455
Spears, Major-General Sir Edward Louis (née Spiers), 315, 504
Spencer, Captain Harold Sherwood, 282, 283
Spender, (John) Alfred, 318
Spicer, Gerald Sidney, 528
Spring Rice, Sir Cecil Arthur, 198, 232
Sproxton, Charles R., 23
Stamboliyski, Aleksandur Stoimonov, 490
Stanhope, James Richard Stanhope, 7th Earl, 572
Steed, Henry Wickham, 152, 231, 254, 255, 258, 264, 294, 317

Steel-Maitland, Sir Arthur Herbert Drummond Ramsay-, 241
Štefánik, General Milan Rastislav, 274
Stepanović, Field Marshal Stepa, 385
Stevenson, Frances, 75
Stojanović, Ljubomir, 478
Strachey, (Giles) Lytton, 555
Strickland, Sir Walter William, 457
Stroessmeyer, Bishop Josip Juraj (Joseph Georg), 340
Strutt, Lieutenant-Colonel Edward Lisle, 50, 325, 505, 506, 507
Stuart, Sir Harold Arthur, 522
Sturdza, Colonel Alexandru Dimitrie, 103, 107, 398
Stürmer, Baron Boris Vladimirovich, 66, 118, 131, 134, 159
Sumner, (Benedict) Humphrey, 3, 168
Sutherland, Sir William 'Bronco Bill', 408, 435, 524, 525
Svinhufvud af Qvalstad, Pehr Evind, 244
Swinburne, Algernon, 23
Sykes, Colonel Sir (Tatton Benvenuto) Mark, 97, 115, 129, 221, 316

Taft, William Howard, 537
Talaat Pasha, Mehmet, 217
Tardieu, André Pierre Gabriel Amédée, 409, 415, 419, 420, 423, 424, 427, 432, 437, 438, 440–41, 443–4, 448, 449, 537
Taussig, Frank William, 558, 559, 561
Teleki de Szék, Pál Count, 507
Temperley, Dorothy, 24
Temperley, (Dorothy Mary) Gladys, née Bradford, 24, 146, 167, 252, 253, 353, 373, 374, 384, 401, 406
Temperley, Harold William Vazeille, ix–xi, 1–35, 42, 72, 81, 109, 121, 132, 158, 167, 212, 248, 316, 330, 341, 348, 407, 450, 455, 463, 475, 483, 491, 503, 518–20, 526, 529–33, 557, 560, 572, 573
Tershchenko, Mikhail Ivanovich, 200, 201

Tharp, Lieutenant-Colonel Gerard Prideaux, 166, 248, 268
Theotokis, Georgios, 206
Thomas, Albert, 129
Thomas, David Alfred, 1st Viscount Rhondda, 198, 292
Thomas, James Henry, 196, 197, 198, 199, 230
Thomson, Major Christopher Birdwood, 1st Baron Thomson of Cardington, 50, 132, 150–51, 159, 193, 194, 250, 273
Thwaites, Major General William, 309, 314, 414
Tirpitz, Grand Admiral Alfred Peter Friedrich (von), 564
Tisza, Count István Tisza de Borosjenő et Szeged, 118
Tittoni, Tommaso, 445, 446, 447, 448
Todorov, General Georgi Stoyanov, 313
Toptani, Essad Pasha (Esat Pashë Toptani), 459
Toqueville, Alexis de, 14–15
Torre, Andre, 254
treaties
    Brest-Litovsk, 9 Feb. 1918, 236, 244, 259, 456
    Bucharest,17 Aug. 1916, 50, 215
    Constantinople Convention, 2 Mar. 1888, 209
    Covenant of the League of Nations, 1919, 497, 536, 539, 540, 541, 546, 561, 562
    London, 30 May 1913, 403, 519, 520
    London (Pact of London), of 26 Apr. 1915, 64, 188, 401, 407, 416, 423, 425, 445, 495
    North and Baltic Sea agreements, 1907, 293
    Paris, 20 Nov. 1815, 293, 300
    Rapallo (Italo–Yugoslav), 12 Nov. 1920, 370, 488, 493, 498, 501
    St.-Jean-de-Maurienne, 26 Apr. 1917, 137, 138, 513

    Versailles, 28 June 1919, 210, 344, 430, 433, 422–3, 487, 504, 509
Trenchard, Air Marshal Hugh Montague, 1st Viscount, 270
Trevelyan, George Macaulay, 34, 229, 309
Trotsky, Leon (née Lev Davidovich Bronstein), 220, 221, 230, 236, 240, 306
Troubridge, Admiral Sir Ernest Charles Thomas, 147, 148, 166, 283, 342, 343, 464
Trumbić, Ante, 254, 308, 316, 428, 487, 564
Tufton, Hon. Charles Henry, 516
Tupper, Sir Charles, 7
Turtulli Bej Korçë, Dr. Mihal, 475, 484, 516
Twiss, Brigadier-General John Henry, 412, 433
Tyrrell, Sir William George, Baron Tyrrell of Avon, 251, 262, 269, 283, 284

United States of America, 7, 8, 9, 30, 57, 93, 101, 103, 112, 130, 135, 137, 142, 147, 156, 167, 177, 198, 199, 226, 237, 242, 256, 278, 279, 281, 288, 290, 292, 293, 294, 296, 299, 301, 302, 321, 322, 354, 356, 368, 374, 375, 382, 387, 407, 413, 417, 419, 423, 432, 485, 487, 497, 504, 509, 512, 514, 537, 553, 554, 559, 560

Vannutelli Rey, Luigi Count, 426, 432
Vasić, General Miloš, 370
Vass, Jószef, 507
Venizelos, Eleftherios Kyriakou, 39, 40, 41, 46, 47, 49, 52, 53, 54, 55, 57, 58–9, 60, 62, 67, 69, 70, 79, 82, 85, 87, 89, 90, 91, 92, 94, 95, 96, 97, 100, 102, 103, 109, 111, 112, 113, 115, 116, 117, 119, 120, 123, 125, 126, 127, 132, 133, 134, 135, 138, 139, 140, 141, 143, 145, 149–50, 155, 158, 159, 161, 172, 182, 183, 184, 185, 200, 207, 210, 211–12, 213,

216, 219, 226, 235, 247, 282, 288, 289, 290, 296, 297, 304, 306, 321, 408, 417, 446, 447, 513, 541
Vesnić, Milenko Radomar, 463, 464, 465
Vešović, General Radomir, 231
Vittorio Emanuele III of Savoy, King of Italy, 166
Viviani (Jean Raphaël Adrien) René, 492, 496, 504
Vlachos, Spyridon, 132
Vladislav II Jagellonský, King of Bohemia, 11
Vučović, Jakov, 472
Vukotić, General Janko, 356
Vukotić, Milena, 460
Vukotić, Stevo, 355
Vukotić, Vasilija, 359

Wales, (Edward Albert Christian George Andrew Patrick) David Windsor, Prince of (King Edward VIII), 81, 87
Wake, Lieutenant-Colonel Edward St. Aubyn, 171
Walker, Major-General Sir George Townshend Forestier-, 437, 439
Walpole, Sir Robert, 4
Walston, Sir Charles (née Waldstein), 553
War Office, ix, 24, 27, 97, 102, 108, 129, 139, 150, 165, 191, 212, 234, 235, 240, 248, 273, 305, 323
Ward, Sir Adolphus William, 4, 25, 411
Ward, Major the Hon. Sir John Hubert, 229
wars
    Anglo-Spanish, 1739 ('War of Jenkins' Ear'), 8, 9, 13
    Austro-Turkish, 1683, 13, 26
    Austro-Turkish, 1716–18, 376
    Austro-Turkish, 1738–39, 26
    Balkan (first), 1912, 20, 571–2
    Bavarian Succession, 1778–89, 16
    Crimean, 1853–56, 33, 496
    Magyar-Turkish, 1526, 15, 26, 451
    Punic (Second), 218–203 BC, 312
    Seven Years', 1756–63, 269, 291
    Silesian (first), 1740–42, 26.
    World (First), 1914–18, ix, xi, 1, 2, 16, 23
Wardle, George James, 175
Warren, Charles, 562
Waterlow, Sir Sydney Philip Perigal, 517
Webster, Charles Kingsley, 3, 9, 19, 33, 168, 212, 259, 269, 399, 544, 554
Wedgwood, Josiah, 1st Baron Wedgwood of Burlaston, 506
Weir, William Douglas, 1st Baron, 314
Weizmann, Dr. Chaim, 156, 217, 230
West, Julius, 319
Westermann, William Linn, 514
Westminster Review, 13
Whiggism, 4, 6, 8, 11
White, Henry, 448
Wied, Prince Wilhelm Friedrich Heinrich zu, 77, 283
Wiegand, Karl Henry von, 167
Wigram, Col. Sir Clive, 1st Baron Wigram, 295, 571
Wilbraham, Sir Philip Wilbraham Baker, 297
Wilde, Oscar Fingall O'Flahertie, 483
Wildon Carr, Herbert, 567, 568.
Wilhelm I of Hohenzollern, King of Prussia, German Emperor, 10
Wilhelm II of Hohenzollern, King of Prussia, German Emperor, 49, 54, 79, 101, 114, 118, 122, 125, 160, 161, 167, 185, 206, 225, 266, 320–21, 331, 341, 442, 448, 534, 563, 564
Wilhelm (Victor August Ernst) von Hohenzollern *see* Prince (Friedrich) Wilhelm (Victor August Ernst) von Hohenzollern
Wilkes, John, 8
William III of Orange, *stadholder*, King of England, 4, 5, 162
Wilson, Eleanor Randolph, 279
Wilson, General Sir Henry, 83, 184, 198, 204, 208, 209, 210, 215, 238, 246, 247, 249, 257, 259, 266, 268, 276,

277, 278, 284, 291, 299, 304, 320, 405, 406, 407, 422, 431, 500, 504
Wilson, (Thomas) Woodrow, 28, 30, 78, 90, 101, 156, 221, 224, 232, 264, 269, 279, 285, 288, 289, 294, 296, 298, 301, 204, 318, 343, 388, 400, 401, 403, 405, 407, 408, 415, 416, 424, 425, 426, 428, 429, 432, 433, 434, 439, 440–42, 443, 446, 470, 487, 493, 497, 514, 517, 518, 522, 530, 536, 537, 541, 554, 555, 558, 559, 561, 562–3, 564
Wintour, Ulrick Fitzgerald, 292
Wise, Edward Frank, 294
Wiseman, Sir William George Eden, 294
Woods, Henry Charles, 489
Wu Tingfang (Ng Choy), 113

Young, Allyn Abbott, 558
Young, Robert Fitzgibbon, 59

Young Turk movement *see* Committee of Unity and Progress
Yugoslavism (pan-Serbism), 21

Zaimis, Alexandros, 120, 133, 140, 146, 149, 153, 155, 160, 172
Zaleski, August, 176, 180
Zalokostas, Evgenios, 103
Zayonchkovski, General Andrei Medardovich, 80
Żeligowski, General Lucjan, 542
Zetland, Lawrence John Lumley Dundas, 2nd Marquess of, 568
Zimmermann, Arthur, 160, 218
Zimmern, Alfred, 3
Zitkovszky von Szemeszova and Szohorad, Heinrich, 122
Zog I, Ahmed Bey Zogu, King of Albania, 459
Žolger, Ivan (Ritter von), 403, 420
Zottu, General Vasile, 88, 89, 98, 107